RACISM: ESSENTIAL READINGS

RACISM: ESSENTIAL READINGS

Edited by
ELLIS CASHMORE and JAMES JENNINGS

SAGE Publications
London • Thousand Oaks • New Delhi

First published 2001

SAGE Publications Ltd
6 Bonhill Street
London EC2A 4PU

SAGE Publications Inc
2455 Teller Road
Thousand Oaks, California 91320

SAGE Publications India Pvt Ltd
32, M-Block Market
Greater Kailash - I
New Delhi 110 048

British Library Cataloguing in Publication data

A catalogue record for this book is available from the British Library

ISBN 0 7619 7196 3
ISBN 0 7619 7197 1 (pbk)

Library of Congress control number available

Typeset by SIVA Math Setters, Chennai, India
Printed in India at Gopsons Papers Ltd., Noida

Contents

Contents

Acknowledgements

Chapter 1:   Reprinted with the permission of University of Chicago Press from Paul S. Reinsch, 'The Negro Races and European Civilization', *The American Journal of Sociology*, Vol. XI, No. 2 (1905).

Chapter 2:   Reprinted from G.W. Ellis, 'The Psychology of America Race Prejudice', *The Journal of Race Development*, Vol. 5, No. 3, 1915, pp. 297–315.

Chapter 3:   Reprinted from S.A. Queen and J.R. Gruener, *Social Pathology: Obstacles to Social Participation* (1925, rev. edn 1948), by Thomas Y. Cromwell Co. New York.

Chapter 4:   Reprinted with the permission of Scribner, a division of Simon and Schuster from *Black Reconstructions in America 1860–1880* by W.E.B. Du Bois.
Copyright © 1935, 1962, W.E. Burghardt Du Bois.

Chapter 5:   Excerpts as specified (pp. 582–93, 658–63) from *An American Dilemma: The Negro Problem and Modern Democracy* by Gunnar Myrdal.
Copyright © 1944, 1962 by Harper & Row, Publishers Inc. Reprinted by permission of Harper Collins Publishers, Inc.

Chapter 6:   Reprinted from Oliver C. Cox (1948), 'Caste, Class and Race: A study in social dynamics', pp. 345–52 and 519–25. Doubleday and Co.

Chapter 7:   Reprinted from *Race and Nationality in American Life*, Doubleday Anchor Press (1950). Used by kind permission of Oscar Handlin.

Chapter 8:   Excerpts as specified (pp. 146–50, 612–22, 653) from *The Authoritarian Personality*, by T.W. Adorno, E. Frenkel-Brunswick.
Copyright © 1950 by the American Jewish Committee. Copyright renewed. Reprinted by permission of Harper Collins Publishers Inc.

Chapter 9:   Reprinted from Louis L. Snyder (1962) *The Idea of Racialism: Its Meaning and History*, published originally by D. Van Nostrand Company Inc. Princeton, New Jersey. Reproduced here by kind permission of International Thompson.

Chapter 10:   Reprinted from *Man's Most Dangerous Myth: The Fallacy of Race*, by Ashley Montagu, published in the *Los Angeles Times* (1965). Reproduced here by kind permission of Los Angeles Times Syndicate, California USA.

Chapter 11:   From *Black Power* by Stokely Carmichael and Charles V. Hamilton.
Copyright © 1967 by Stokely Carmichael and Charles V. Hamilton. Reprinted by permission of Random House Inc.

Chapter 12:   Reprinted from *Ethnic and Racial Studies*, Vol. 1, No. 4, October 1978, Routledge (UK); Pierre van den Berghe, 'Race and Ethnicity: A Sociobiological Perspective'.

Chapter 13:   Reprinted from *Racism and Class Struggle: Further Pages from a Black Worker's Notebook* by J. Boggs.
Copyright © 1970 by Monthly Review Press. Reprinted by permission of Monthly Review Foundation.

Chapter 14:   Reprinted from 'The Psychohistory of Racism in the United States', by Joel Kovel. Chapter 8 of *White Racism: A Psychohistory*, Pantheon Books (1970), pp. 177–230. Used by kind permission of Joel Kovel.

Chapter 15:   Reprinted from T. Pettigrew, *Racially Separate or Together?* (1971), McGraw-Hill Publishers. Used by kind permission of McGraw Hill Companies.

Chapter 16:   Reprinted from *A Rap on Race*, © 1971 by James Baldwin and Margaret Mead. Published by Dell Books and reprinted by arrangement with the estates of James Baldwin and Margaret Mead.

Chapter 17:   Reprinted from D.T. Wellman, *Portraits of White Racism* (1977), pp. 90–107 and 228–234. Reproduced here by kind permission of Cambridge University Press.

Chapter 18:   Reprinted from *Hermathena* No. CXVI; H.M. Bracken (1973), 'Essence, Accident and Race'. Reproduced here by kind permission of *Hermathena*, A Trinity College Journal.

Chapter 19:   Reprinted from *Black Scholar: Journal of Black Studies and Research*; Frances Cress Welsing (1974), 'The Cress Theory of Color-Confrontation', *Black Scholar*, Vol. 5, No. 8.

Chapter 20: Reprinted with the permission of University of Chicago Press from W.J. Wilson (1978) *The Declining Significance of Race*, pp. 20–60.

Chapter 21: Reprinted from M. Karenga (1982) *Introduction to Black Studies*, Los Angeles: Kawaida Productions, pp. 198–212.

Chapter 22: Reprinted from *Journal of Social Issues*, Vol. 42, No. 2, pp. 173–87; Paul Sniderman and P. Tetlock, 'Reflections on American Racism'. Reproduced here by kind permission of Blackwell Publishers Inc.

Chapter 23: Reprinted from *Rethinking Marxism*, Vol. 2, No. 2; E. San Juan, Jr. (1989) 'Problems in the Marxist Project of Theorizing Race'. Reproduced here by kind permission of Guilford Publishers Inc.

Chapter 24: Reprinted with permission from *Urban Geography*, Vol. 10, No. 6, pp. 562–77 © V.H. Winston & Son Inc., 360 South Ocean Boulevard, Palm Beach, FL 33480. All rights reserved.

Chapter 25: Reprinted from *Social Science and Medicine*, Vol. 31, No. 8, 1990, pp. 891–906; C. Leslie et al., 'Scientific Racism: Reflections On Peer Review'.

Chapter 26: Reprinted from *Z Magazine*, November 1990; E. Martinez, 'There's More to Racism than Black and White'.

Chapter 27: Reprinted from *Shadows of Race and Class*, pp. viii–xxvii, by R.S. Franklin © 1991 by the Regents of the University of Minnesota.

Chapter 28: Reprinted from *British Journal of Sociology*, Vol. 42, No. 1, pp. 115–30; M. Banton, 'The Race Relations Problematic'. Reproduced here by kind permission of The London School of Economics, Houghton Street, London, WC2A 2AE and Taylor and Francis Ltd, London.

Chapter 29: J.E. King, 'Dyconscious Racism: Ideology, Identity and the Miseducation of Teachers', *Journal of Negro Education*, Vol. 60, No. 2 (1991), pp. 133–46. Copyright © 1991 by Howard University. All rights reserved.

Chapter 30: Reprinted from D. Jenness, 'Origins of the Myth of Race', *International Socialist Review*, February 1992.

Chapter 31: Beverly Daniel Tatum, 'Talking about Race, Learning about Racism: The Application of Racial Identity Development Theory in the Classroom', *Harvard Educational Review*, Vol. 62, No. 1 (Spring 1992), pp 1–24.

Copyright © 1992 by the President and Fellows of Harvard College. All rights reserved.

Chapter 32:   Reprinted from E. Barkan (1992) *The Retreat of Scientific Racism*, pp. 279–96. Used by kind permission of Professor Elazar Barkan and Cambridge University Press (UK).

Chapter 33:   Reprinted from A. Allahar (1993) 'When Black First Became Worth Less', *International Journal of Comparative Sociology*, Vol. 34, No. 1–2.

                Copyright © Koninklijke Brill N.V., Leiden, The Netherlands.

Chapter 34:   Reprinted from *Sociology*, Vol. 28, No. 1, pp. 143–61; Solomos and Back, 'Conceptualizing Racisms: Social Theory Politics and Research'. Used by kind permission of John Solomos, Les Back and Cambridge University Press (UK).

Chapter 35:   Reprinted from Theodore Allen, *The Invention of the White Race: Racial Oppression and Social Control*, Verso, 1994, pp. 27–51. By kind permission of Verso.

Chapter 36:   Reprinted from *The Science and Politics of Racial Research*. Copyright 1994 by Board of Trustees of the University of Illinois. Used bxy kind permission of University of Illinois.

Chapter 37:   Reprinted from *The Racist Mind: Portraits of American Neo-Nazis and Klansmen*, Viking Penguin, 1995, pp. 245–56, 269–78. Used by kind permission of Kathi J. Paton, Literary Agency, 19 West 55th Street, New York, NY 10019-4907.

Chapter 38:   Reprinted from *The Recovery of Race in America*, pp. 163–82, by A.D. Gresson, © 1995 by the Regents of the University of Minnesota.

The editors wish to acknowledge the support and staff at Sage Publications Ltd, especially Jane Evans. Several anonymous readers also provided important suggestions for improving the text. We extend our deepest appreciation to Ms. Yvonne Gomes-Santos of the William Monrae Trotter Institute at the University of Massachusetts Boston. She spent many, many hours tracking sources, contacting publishers, and assisting in the preparation of this textbook.

Introduction

Racism: Essential Readings is primarily a textbook for students and others interested in understanding how the concept and story of racism has been defined, utilized, and debated, in modern society. One goal of this anthology is to show that the concept of racism has a long and complex intellectual history as an idea but also a long track record in how powerful groups have utilized racism as an ideology to advance social, economic, or cultural interests. This collection seeks to show how racism has been utilized not only to explain racial and ethnic differences in living conditions, but also as justification for maintaining such differences. The book is organized by presenting a chronological overview of selections illustrating how racism has been approached by scholars and others to explain racial and ethnic differences in various historical periods throughout the twentieth century, as well as in the contemporary period.

The selections include historical and contemporary essays. They do not include all selections that might be considered 'classical', or the most widely read or cited, or debated. But this particular selection is essential in understanding contemporary debates, and more importantly, how the idea and story of racism has developed in different periods and within certain political and economic contexts. While a few of the articles are theoretical, the majority focus on concrete situations that students can relate to, and explore further through classroom discussion.

Although most of the selections are still relatively recent, we do include a few from much earlier periods in order to emphasize two points: first, discussions about the nature and definition of racism have a long history and tradition; secondly, the earlier articles provide a base or framework for noting how the dialogue about racism has both changed, and remained the same. Readers will discover, for instance, that a scholarly explanation for racial inequality that may be countered and dismissed in one period, arises anew in another period. This is reflected by noting that the first chapter in the anthology, written in 1905 and full of paternalistic observations and conclusions, and actions, may be the kind of problem in dealing with racism today that is identified in the last chapter of the book, published in 1995. We decided to place this article first because it summarizes some of the thinking about the nature and causes of racism at the turn of the century during the height of imperialism. This article is useful because it shows that while the concept of racism and what it is has changed over various periods, there are nevertheless enduring ideas that are continually being proposed and debated by those interested in defining, challenging, or excusing racism in the contemporary period. By presenting the selections chronologically, and beginning with the turn of the century, students have an opportunity to discuss the antecedents of the idea and application of racism today.

Many other articles could easily have been included in this reader. Our collection is presented as one of essential readings because collectively the student can obtain an understanding of the idea of racism and how it has been applied and utilized in economic and political arenas. Since this anthology is conceived as a textbook, we are also concerned that the selections generate dialogue and further investigation. Therefore, the editors have selected essays that are both informative and provocative, and perhaps even controversial; and as suggested above, concrete in terms of actual political and economic situations.

Collectively, the selections cover the justification of racism as expounded by some writers throughout recent history, including theoretical explanations and even justifications for racism, the psychology of racism, and how racism has been molded by political interests, as well as racism as ideology. Some of the selections, for example, explain how racism has been, and continues to be utilized as a political tool by wealthy or powerful class interests, sometimes in subtle ways, but other times more openly.

The selections reflect a wide range of perspectives, including those who advocated racist views, and those who challenged them in various social and economic settings. These selections also show that some scholars have concluded that racism is no longer significant as a social, economic, or political process. Scholars in this school may believe that today class and culture are far more significant than racism in explaining social and economic differences between racial and ethnic groups. Other writers in this anthology suggest, however, that racism is an enduring idea and ideology. These particular selections provide examples of how racism may be a factor in a range of social situations in the United States, and other societies. They argue, furthermore, that while the ideology and justification of racism may have been different in the early 1900s from the 1960s, or 1990s, certain components of this ideology, particularly the social and cultural, and intellectual ranking of racial and ethnic groups, has remained constant throughout many periods. It is interesting to note, for example, selections offering 'evidence' for justifying the belief that Europeans were intellectually and genetically superior to blacks or other non-European groups at the turn of the century. These presentations can be viewed as ignorant and prejudicial today. Yet, we are still debating and responding to works like that of Charles Murray and Richard Hernstein's *The Bell Curve*, where the belief in the genetic and intellectual superiority of European peoples is, again, proposed, albeit with supposedly contemporary and objective data.

The selections in this anthology show that racism is still a pervasive social and intellectual force, and utilized to justify the social status of powerful interests and groups. The selections show that racism represents a way of thinking that emerges from particular economic and political situations and particular distribution of wealth and privilege by race and ethnicity in many societies. Some writers in this volume believe that it is difficult to recognize racism because it is so imbued within a system of white-skin privileges. The social, cultural, and political order that supports such a system becomes normalized in the world-views of some groups, and therefore, the argument that racism is pervasive is both abhorred and challenged. Racism is abnormal, in other words, while white-skin privileges, while unacknowledged, represents the norm. The latter might be invisible, in a sense, because it represents a way of thinking, a socialization process that is not abrupt but rather constantly at play. Again, this reflects the story of racism which is not simply an event, but rather a way of thinking about racial and ethnic differences in society. Racism, this reader concludes, has been and continues to be pervasive, and is represented in fundamental social processes molding political, economic, and educational decisions in modern societies.

1

The Negro Race
and European Civilization

PAUL S. REINSCH

The editors included this article because it reflects the paternalistic view of some scholars in earlier periods regarding race, and "Negroes". The author portrays European civilizations as superior, and the 'negro race' as inferior, lacking in certain qualities, such as lack of social organization and social action, lack of social fellow-feeling (this explains cannibalism, according to the author), lack of originality of thought, and lack of artistic qualities, especially 'deficient on the side of the mechanical arts ...' and in general, 'show[ing] no tendency toward higher development'. These characteristics actually facilitated slavery and the slave trade according to the author. However, in quite liberal terms, Reinsch claims that the negro race will nevertheless survive due to a certain degree of race mixing and their 'buoyant, vigorous constitution and their fundamental commonsense'. The author believes that the proximity of the negro race to Europeans has allowed the former to survive. And certain kinds of race mixing have been beneficial for those groups with African blood, as he points out in his description of women in Martinique: 'the mixed races produced by Europeans and negroes exhibit some very fine qualities. The rich yet delicate beauty of the mulatto women in Martinique, their sweetness of temper and kindness of heart, so excited the admiration of visitors that they all, lay and clerical, French and British, join in the chorus of admiration and declare the women of Martinique the most charming in the world.' While readers may find this selection biased, it is interesting how some of the themes utilized by the author to explain the inferiority of blacks are repeated in various forms in contemporary scholarly dialogue and debates.

While in the past century populations and racial elements which had formerly been far distant from each other have been brought into intimate contact, the twentieth century will witness the formation of new mixed races and the attempt to adjust the mutual relations of all the various peoples that inhabit the globe. The recent great advance in the safeness and rapidity of communication has made the whole world into a community whose solidarity of interests becomes more apparent day by day.

Closer contact with the more advanced nations of the Orient will have a profound influence upon European civilization, because these nations, though ready to adopt our industrial methods, are determined to maintain their national beliefs and customs. Though from the races that stand on a lower level of civilization no such deep-going influence upon European and American life is to be expected, their relations to the peoples of more advanced culture will nevertheless be a matter of great moment. Some of them, the weakest and lowest in organization, may indeed continue to fade away before the advance of European power; but this is not likely to be the fate of the negro race. The negroes have come in contact with the worst side of European civilization; yet their buoyant, vigorous constitution and their fundamental common-sense carry them safely through dangers which have proved fatal to other races. They are therefore destined to be a permanent element in the composite population of the future, and when we consider the extent and fertility of the regions which they hold, the necessity of their ever-increasing co-operation in the economic life of the world becomes apparent.

The negro race may be studied in four different sets of conditions: in their original state in the forests of central Africa; as a mixed race under the control of the Arab and Hamite races of the northern Sudan; living side by side with a white population in respect to which they occupy a socially inferior position, as in South Africa and North America; and in a few isolated communities which enjoy rights of self-government based upon European models, as in Hayti and in the French Antilles. A correct understanding of any part of the negro question demands a review of the situation of the negro under all these varying conditions, because only through a comparison of the aboriginal characteristics of the negro with the qualities acquired through contact with other races and civilizations can we form a just estimate of his relative capacity for progress.

We need not here enter into the controversy between polygenists and unigenists, since it has a purely ethnological interest, whereas we intend to approach the question from the point of view of the political activities of the present. No matter what may be the origin of the diversity which the human races at present exhibit—whether the result of the amalgamation of an almost infinite number of disparate groups, or the consequence of continued diversification of an original type—the negro race today exhibits such characteristic features and such distinct traits as to induce many observers to consider it as entirely incommensurate with the white race; yet, on the other hand, it is physiologically connected with the Aryans through a long series of mixed races. As we pass from Morocco or from Cairo toward the center of the Sudan, the color of the population gradually grows darker, and their features, from the regular and often beautiful type of the Hamite, merge off into the coarser characteristics of the negro race. From the pure white skin of the Berber to the yellow of the Tuareg, the copper tint of the Somali or the Fulbe, the chocolate of the Mombuttu, and the ebony of the Jolof, the color gradations are imperceptible; and no conception is more utterly mistaken than that which would people all of central Africa with a black-skinned race.

The physiological aspects of race-mixture have lately attracted much attention. Mr. James Bryce, in his recent lecture on "The Relations of the Advanced and Backward Races," carefully reviews the experience of mankind in this matter, and adds his support to the current assumption that mixed breeds are morally and physically weak when the parents belong to widely disparate races and civilizations. However, it would seem that this assumption is true only in cases where the two societies to which the parents respectively belong maintain a repugnant attitude to each other, so that the mestizos form an outcast class and suffer a total loss of *morale*. Where friendly relations exist, the mixed races produced by Europeans and negroes exhibit some very fine qualities. The rich yet delicate beauty of the mulatto women in Martinique, their sweetness of temper and kindness of heart, so excited the admiration of visitors that they all, lay and clerical, French and British, join in the chorus of admiration and declare the women of Martinique the most charming in the world. Intellectually, the mulatto race has produced a number of remarkable men, and the liberality of mind among the leaders of this class in Martinique is certainly most noteworthy. Still it is generally true that the men of a mixed race will exhibit fewer pleasing qualities of character than the women: they must make themselves useful often by activities not conducive to sweetness of temper or honesty of mind; while the women naturally develop more gentle and attractive characteristics.

The question of race-mixture between Europeans and negroes is, however, at present of little practical importance. In the regions where large numbers of Europeans and negroes live side by side the social laws more and more stringently forbid a mixture of the two elements; moreover, the number of Europeans who settle in central Africa will probably always be exceedingly small. But there is another racial element which will in the future have a very prominent part in the physiological modification of the African race. All along the east coast of Africa immigration from India is taking place. Both coast and inland regions are very well adapted to settlement by the Hindus, and no race-antipathy exists between them and the negroes. We may in the near future look for a great inpouring of Indian coolies, tradesmen, and settlers, who, together with the Arab and Hamite elements coming from the north, will leaven the mass of the African population.

While physiologically the transition from the negro to the white race is a gradual one, the distinctive type of negro civilization is yet very different from that which we call European. The last few years have witnessed a great change of mind in matters of humanitarianism; the absolute unity of human life in all parts of the globe, as well as the idea of the practical equality of human individuals wherever they may be found, has been quite generally abandoned. Without going into the question of origins, it is clear that conditions of environment and historical forces have combined in producing certain great types of humanity which are essentially different in their characteristics. To treat these as if they were all alike, to subject them to the same methods of government, to force them into the same institutions, was a mistake of the nineteenth century which has not been carried over into our own. But, after all, it is difficult to say which is the more surprising—whether the remarkable recurrence of similar customs and ideas, similar ways of looking at things, in the remotest parts of the world, and in most distant epochs,[1] or whether it is the existence of clearly marked, almost unchangeable psychological types differing radically from each other. Thus when we study the negro race we encounter many characteristics and customs which bear witness to the common unity of mankind, and which can be accounted for only by assuming the same fundamental instincts, or the transmission of ideas and institutions through tradition; on the other hand, we find many psychological characteristics which distinguish the negro race sharply and clearly from the European, the Hamite, or the oriental world. Whether these differences are irreducible is a question which further development alone can solve.

Low social organization, and consequent lack of efficient social action, form the most striking characteristic of the negro race. Among the Africans of the western Sudan the matriarchal organization of the family, combined with the practice of polygamy, makes the mother the real center of the family-group and renders impossible the upbuilding of strong families through the inheritance of power and property combined from father to son. The father's property goes, not to his children, but to those of his eldest sister. He can, therefore, not supplement, by his accumulated wealth, the physical and mental endowment bestowed upon his son. The redeeming social trait of the African race is the love of sons for their mothers, which is often very deep and touching. But no great families, and therefore no truly great men or leaders to the manor born, exist among Africans.

Among most of the tribes, although there are notable exceptions, the duties of the marriage relation are strictly observed. This is due primarily to the fact that the husband has paid a respectable sum to acquire his spouse, and his strongly developed sense of private property would brook no interference. Her person, her labor, her attentions, belong exclusively to him. In fact, there is but a difference in degree between the position of the wife and that of the slave. The reasons for entering into marriage are almost always prudential: among the poorer people, the working power of the wife; among the wealthier, the influence of her relatives, form the main consideration. The African bush traders have a wife in every important village on their route, not only on account of the business advantage accruing from her connections, but also for the reason that traders are in constant danger of having their food poisoned unless the kitchen is managed by a friendly spirit.

Slavery among the African negroes is an institution which does not at all correspond to what we understand by that term. No special social disgrace attaches to it, nor is a slave a mere chattel; on the contrary, his property rights are scrupulously respected. He is merely a more dependent member of the community. Thus a "trade boy" slave on the west coast is obliged only to pay a fixed amount to his master, and he may in prosperous times acquire a good deal of wealth for himself. He may then purchase other slaves, and when he has become powerful even free men will place themselves under his protection, and he will thus become a "king." Even during the last decade, of the three most powerful chieftains in the Oil River region, two were slaves. The fact that a man may be "king" and slave at the same time is certainly unprecedented in any other civilization, which of itself shows that the African institution of slavery can in no way be classed with that of Rome or of the southern states. We shall revert to this matter later on in our discussion of the slave-trade—the dark and terrible side of the institution in Africa.

A lack of social fellow-feeling, an absence of every vestige of patriotism, is shown by the readiness with which negroes allow themselves to be used to fight against their neighbors. The Arab slave-raiders never lack men to fight their battles; for, though their Hamite troops may refuse to attack the bands of another trader, the negroes are always ready for a savage onset, even upon men of very nearly their own flesh and blood. The terrible custom of cannibalism, too, can be explained only by taking into account this absence of a feeling of common humanity. Cannibalistic feasts are usually accompanied by religious frenzy or the fury of war; but this is not always the case. There are thrifty tribes which, in the words of De Cardi, "tap their older people on the head, smoke-dry them, then break them up into small bits, which are rolled into

---

[1] E.g., the almost universal recurrence among the aboriginal peoples of the ordeal, animistic beliefs, marriage by purchase, etc.

balls and laid away for future use in the family stew." It is remarkable that some tribes, like the Mombuttu, which are distinctly advanced in industrial civilization, are the most voracious among the cannibals; thus the greediness of the Sandeh has earned them, among their neighbors, the suggestive nickname of Niam-niam. In the presence of whites these cannibals are, however, generally anxious to conceal their peculiar practice, and when Schweinfurth visited the realm of King Munza, the monarch had forbidden all open cannibalism in order to keep offense from the eyes of his guest.

The greatest deficiency of the negro race lies on the side of the mechanical arts. While they practice the smelting and forging of iron, and while some of the tribes have advanced considerably in the art of weaving, the negroes nevertheless show little originality, and have acquired most of these arts from the Hamites. They are far more ready to engage in trade; in fact, the trend of the African negro mind is primarily commercial. Living in a country endowed with abundant natural resources, the negro tribes have found it far easier to procure the few things they need, in addition to what nature furnishes them, by trading with Arabs and later with the Europeans, than by developing industries among themselves. This is, of course, especially true of the coast tribes, and in general it may be observed that industrial civilization is higher in the interior regions of Africa than on the coast, the negro race reversing in this particular the historical experience of Europe and America. No shrewder merchants can be imagined than the bush traders of the forest belt and the "trade boys" of the coast. The subtlest tricks for practicing deception are known to these simple-minded forest-dwellers. Women who have learned the art of mixing with the rubber balls sold to merchants the largest amount of dirt that can escape detection, are said to be especially sought after in the marriage-market.

When we pass on to the specific psychological traits of the African race, we enter a field of darkness and uncertainty. "Race psychology" has of late become a fashionable term; but with most writers it stands merely for a more or less interesting description of racial characteristics, without that close study of origins and causal relations which constitute the science of psychology. Even when employed with great care and scientific precision, as in the works of Herbert Spencer, the psychological method does not always produce convincing results; and often the material it deals with becomes so unmanageable as to furnish no clear generalization, as in the painstaking and ponderous *Afrikanische Jurisprudenz* of Post. Yet, from the point of view of political activities and social reform, the psychic phenomena of primitive races are a matter of the greatest importance, deserving the most careful attention of the colonial administrator.

The art-sense of the negro is rudimentary. Unlike the Bushman, he has no pictorial or plastic art. His chief pleasure is the dance and the entrancing sound of the tom-tom. Of the marvelous sense for melody that the negro has developed in the Antilles and the plantation states of America hardly a trace is found in the African. But the sense of rhythm exists, and the rhythmic drumming on the tom-tom has an almost hypnotic effect upon the blacks. They sit as in a trance, listening to the marvelous sound for hours; or, should the tom-tom player move about the village, they will follow him in utter abstraction, so that they will often tumble headlong into ditches. On the occasion of great military displays, given in the honor of European commissioners, the various chieftains will each bring forward a band of musicians, who at the height of the festivities all play their instruments with the greatest vigor and totally regardless of their fellow-artists. The tremendous discord and strident volley of sound thus produced give rise to the greatest popular satisfaction. Toutée, however, reports that if a simple tune, like "Casquette du père Bugeaud," is played to the negroes, they will listen to it with rapt attention, and will gladly abandon for a time their accustomed instruments.

The art of oratory is much cultivated in Africa. As most of the tribes have no written language, their rich folk-lore is handed down by word of mouth, and whenever men come together they listen to the expert story-teller and orator. The capacity of the American negro for oratory, which has again and again placed young negroes and mulattoes in the position of class orators at leading universities, is therefore an inheritance from customs practised in the primitive villages of Africa. The great occasion for the display of oratorical talent is the palaver—a meeting for the discussion of questions of public interest among prominent persons, or for the trial of cases at law. The African negro shows great ability in the development of systems of law and in the enforcement of rights; this is especially true of the rules of private property, which are strictly defined and scrupulously observed. Palaver, however, is costly, so that persons who cause much litigation are looked upon as undesirable citizens. Thus, Miss Kingsley saw on a stake before a village the head of a woman whose offense had been that she had "caused too much palaver." In order to prevent the stringing-out of actions, each party has to present the judge with a calabash of palm wine for every day of the sessions.

The intellectual life of the African negro is taken up chiefly with fetishism; that is, with the construction of a spirit-world by which he feels himself surrounded and which he believes is influencing his every act. Fetishism is not unlike the animism of the Brahmin, but it is without the latter's belief in the duality of spirit and matter, and looks upon visible existence as only a grosser form of spirit. According to the belief of the negro, the world was created by potent divinities, who now hold aloof and allow the brutal forces of nature to fight out their battles among themselves. Man, himself a spirit, is caught in the midst of this struggle of forces superior to his own and entirely regardless of his welfare; his only salvation, therefore, lies in escaping as much as possible the attention of these sinister beings. The Africans have neither hero- nor ancestor-worship, and with them, therefore, the idea of divinity is not a development of ancestor-cult. It is true that the spirits of their ancestors are supposed to continue in a sentient existence; they are consulted, but they are not worshiped. Thus, a man will often turn aside, when in company with other men, to say a few words to the spirit of his departed mother, or to ask her advice on the matter in hand. These spirits are called the "friendly ones;" they need not be worshiped; their good-will is already enlisted on account of their natural regard for their mortal relatives. Some of the most cruel customs of Africa result from this conception. Lest the spirit of the husband suffer from solitude, the wives of a deceased man are killed at the time of his funeral. In order that a powerful chieftain may have the proper service and be able to support his dignity in the other world, scores of slaves are beheaded in order to form his spirit retinue. Often the successor of a dead chieftain will send news to him by a slave, to whom the message is given, and who, after being treated to liberal drafts of palm-wine, is then dispatched as messenger to the other world in the most blissful of moods.

In view of the barbarous customs which continue to exist among the negro population, many investigators have entirely denied the capacity of the negro to advance in the scale of civilization. The physical reason assigned for this inability is the fact that the cranial sutures of the negro close at a very early age. Negro children, it is admitted, are exceedingly bright and quick to learn; remarkable instances of precocious intelligence among them are frequently observed. Thus, the young son of Behanzin, the exiled king of Dahomey, carried off all the honors at the Parisian *lycée* to which he had been sent from Martinique. But after the age of puberty development soon ceases, the expectations raised by the earlier achievements are disappointed, and no further intellectual progress is to be looked for. It is true, many investigators claim that the negro continues his mental growth in adult life, although the sutures of his brain have closed; but the proofs given in support of this favorable view relate rather to increased cunning and craftiness in trade than to the growth of the general intellectual capacities; no one would deny that negroes accumulate experience in later life, but organic development of the faculties seems to cease at an early stage. Even if we accept this unfavorable view, however, it does not necessarily follow that the negro race is permanently uncivilizable. When we look at the low stage of civilization among the African negroes, we can

hardly avoid the conclusion that it is due rather to social, political, and climatic conditions than to the physiological, personal incapacity of the negro. The difference between the average negro and the average European does not explain, nor is it at all commensurate to, the difference between their respective civilizations. The social conditions that have kept the negro from acquiring a higher organization lie in the fact of the constant shifting of the African populations, which are not held in place by the physical conformation of territory such as that of Greece and Italy. The African societies were thus not given time to strike roots and to acquire a national tradition and history—the memory of races—which is one of the chief ingredients of civilization.

We have already seen how utterly all social or national self-consciousness is lacking in the negroes, and how localized their interests are. It is a noteworthy fact, in this connection, that as the negroes have no experience of social or political unity, so their languages can express very few general conceptions. In conversing with negroes, Europeans constantly note that the mind of the individual seems far stronger and more apt than the language which he must use to express his thoughts. Can we not here surmise a subtle connection between the realization of true social and national unity and the existence in the psychology of a race of those general conceptions upon which all higher intellectual civilization is founded? No more striking proof could be found of the truth that we are what we are through society, than the fact that the negro race, powerful in physique, strong and normal in intellect, has not achieved a higher social and intellectual civilization. Should favorable conditions for the existence and development of permanent societies in Africa be brought about, it then would admit of little doubt that the negro race would develop in civilization a civilization proper to it, rather than an imitation of the European type. In view of the fact that the physiological characteristics of the white race have been profoundly modified in the course of its development, it may not seem altogether extravagant to say that even the cranial structure of the negro race may be affected by a change in its social, political, and economic conditions; or, if we should decide that cranial structure lacks all demonstrable importance in this matter, it might at least be asserted that, if certain conditions inimical to intellectual development after puberty are removed, the negro race may, notwithstanding its unpromising characteristics, develop in civilization. Now, perhaps the circumstance most unfavorable to progress is the powerful strain of sensuality in negro nature, which swallows up all the best energies after puberty has been reached. The deadly climate of parts of Africa, and the horrid conditions of internecine warfare and cannibalism, have heretofore rendered a high birth-rate necessary. With more peaceful and settled conditions, a gradual moderation of the powerful sexual impulses could reasonably be expected, and we might then hope for the growth of intellectual capacity even after the age of maturity.

In the past the negro race has shown no tendency toward higher development, except under the tutelage of other races; and, among the alien civilizations that have exerted a profound influence upon the African race, that of the Moslem Hamites and Arabs is the most important. Penetrating into Africa from the north by way of the Sahara, the cavalry hordes of the Hamites of north Africa succeeded in forming reasonably permanent states throughout the northern Sudan, and in influencing the native negro societies both physiologically and intellectually. The great principalities founded by the Fulbe in the Niger country, and by the Tuaregs in the region about Timbuctoo, are the most striking examples of this activity. The states thus founded belong to the feudal type; the agricultural negroes form the subject peasant class; while the Moslem invaders constitute a nobility of armed cavaliers. It admits of no doubt that the civilization of Africa has been improved by this conquest. The conquering tribes brought with them a written literature, and many industrial and domestic arts, which they imparted to the conquered races. Of course, this form of conquest was possible only in the regions where cavalry could penetrate; the dense primeval forests of Africa, where the tzetze fly renders the raising and keeping of horses impossible, set limits to the out-and-out conquest by Berber and Arab tribes.

This great forest region, however, the Arabs entered from the north and east as traders, and in so doing they gave an entirely new and sinister meaning to African slavery. As beasts of burden cannot survive in these parts of Africa, the traders needed human carriers to convey their freight. Starting from some commercial town on the upper Nile, they would purchase a sufficient number of slaves to carry their wares into the interior. But the goods transported back, the rubber and ivory, necessitated a much larger number of carriers, so that a great demand for slaves arose wherever the traders penetrated. The chieftains of the interior were naturally anxious to obtain the goods which added to the not very extreme luxury of their existence. They gave up their slaves in payment, and reimbursed themselves by making slave-raids into neighboring territories. The mutual hostility of the African populations was thus increased a hundred fold. Negroes themselves, converted to Islam, or negro and Arab half-breeds, often became the most cruel slave-hunters. One of the most notorious of these—Tippu Tib—had an escort of ten thousand armed slaves when he made his raids in the neighborhood of Nyangwe on the upper Congo. Whole countries were in this way depopulated, among them the fertile and prosperous region of the upper Congo, whose entire population was driven from its villages, murdered, or carried off into slavery. The entire Makololo tribe, which

Stanley had visited, was in this way annihilated, with the exception of the women and children, who were carried to the slave-markets. The cruelty of this traffic and the suffering inflicted upon the captives pass description and comprehension. It is therefore clear that the Moslems acted as a civilizing influence only in the countries where they settled down permanently, and that they brought only woe and destruction to the regions invaded by their slave-trade.

The religion of Islam has been adopted by most of the negro tribes that are subject to Mohammedan rule. But the conversions are usually superficial; a few ceremonious observances are adopted, but for the rest the old customs and practices of fetish continue. Many observers believe that Islam is destined to conquer all of tropical Africa, and that Christianity will not there make any progress. It seems, however, that in the forest region, where the negro race exists in its original form, the rule of fetish is not as yet seriously threatened by either of the two great Aryan religions. Christianity has one advantage over Islam: it can use images to typify noble qualities and characteristics, and thus can make its teachings more comprehensible to the mind of the African, who is not trained to deal with abstract ideas. This Islam cannot do because of its iconomachy; on the other hand, the latter cult has a great advantage in the fact that it demands only a few concrete observances of prayer and fasting, whereas Africa continues. All these considerations render the labor question in Africa exceedingly intricate and difficult.

In all discussions of African slavery it is very important to distinguish between the slave-trade and domestic serfdom. We have already described the suffering and desolation wrought in large parts of Africa by slave-raids and transportation. Through the efforts of a number of humanitarian spirits, like Cardinal Lavigérie, the public opinion of Europe has been directed toward the extirpation of the slave-trade, and by international agreement the traffic is now forbidden throughout the European dominions in Africa. It has not, however, been possible as yet entirely to suppress it; in fact, such a radical cure could be hoped for only after a total revolution in the methods of African trade has been accomplished. Today the slave-trade is carried on covertly, under the name of "contract labor," even by Europeans in their own colonies, especially in the Congo Free State and in the Portuguese possessions.

When we consider the real nature of the African slave-trade, we shall see how completely its existence is conditioned by the general character of African economic life. As slaves are the only beasts of burden that can be used in the interior, so they are also the most universal and satisfactory currency. At present, when the slave-trade cannot be openly carried on in the coast towns, the trader will start with a consignment of powder and guns, which are comparatively easy to transport. When he reaches the confines of the slave-holding regions, he will begin to purchase slaves, whom he carries with him on his journey, and uses partly to pay for the ivory and rubber which he buys, partly to convey these purchased goods back to the trading-stations. An example of the status of African currency is given by Miss Kingsley, when she describes the fine paid by a local chieftain to a British commissioner for having killed and eaten several converts. It consisted of one hundred balls of rubber, six ivory teeth, four bundles of fiber, three cheeses, a canoe, two china basins, and five "ladies in rather bad repair." The commissioner, being a newcomer, was much astonished, especially at the last item, but Miss Kingsley assured him that they were perfectly "correct" and could be traded off for ivory. This combination of servant, carrier, and currency makes the slave almost indispensable as long as no railways, roads, and metal money exist. In the remoter regions of Africa this abuse will therefore continue to thrive in some more or less veiled form until the industrial conditions of the country have been changed radically. One result of the long-continued slave-trade is that the population of Africa is far below the natural limit, and large districts of fertile land are almost entirely deserted; an opportunity is thus afforded for bringing in large bodies of alien settlers, from India or other regions, without any displacement of native tribes.

When we turn to consider domestic slavery among the Arabs and negroes in Africa, we encounter far fewer abuses. The African slave is not looked down upon, nor is the door of hope forever closed to him. Slaves who have survived the sufferings of transport, when exhibited in the market-places of such towns as Kano in Nigeria, were often apparently in the happiest of moods. Being an object now of considerable value, they were cared for more properly and groomed up so as to present the best appearance to intending purchasers. The slave women know that they may, through gaining the favor of their masters, become powerful and even be the mothers of kings. The male slaves also may rise to importance and wealth, if luck favors them; of course, there is still a good deal of suffering in domestic slavery, and the separation from home and dear ones is most cruel; but it does not mean absolute and abject degradation forever, and often it even opens the door to new opportunities and to a welcome change of experiences.

The slave-trade is throughout European colonies and dependencies made a criminal offense; a man so influential as the cousin of the sultan of Zanzibar was imprisoned for six months and lost all his slaves, by sentence of his sovereign relative, for being mixed up with the slave-trade. Domestic slavery, however, cannot be dealt with so harshly. The experience in Zanzibar and Pemba in this respect is most instructive. By the decree of the sultan of Zanzibar, any slave in the protectorate may demand his freedom by simply applying to the so-called "Court of Slavery." Comparatively few, however, make use of this opportunity; thus, in the year 1899, the total number was only 3,757. As a matter of fact the slaves in Zanzibar have little to gain by seeking emancipation. They are usually bound to work for only three days on the lands of their masters; in return for this they receive a house and a land-allotment. The word *mtumwa*, unlike our "slave," carries no stigma, and is simply a class designation. In fact, the relation is generally a mild kind of serfdom. The slaves often say: "Why should we seek freedom? We have a good home, plenty of food, and no hard work. Our master is kind, and we are fond of the children. What should we gain by being freed?" The serfs live in small communities around the master's house, where they enjoy fellowship and protection; emancipation, therefore, means a loss of caste and home to them. When freed, they find life dull and monotonous, and have to work too hard for a living. They often come before the court, asking to be returned to slavery, and are deeply disappointed because this cannot be done. Among those who are liberated, a large number become vagrants and a public charge. For a time it was attempted to enforce Article VI of the sultan's decree, which provides that "any person who applies for emancipation shall show that he will have a regular domicile and means of subsistence." The usual method of showing this was by bringing in a labor contractor who was ready to hire the emancipated slave and give him shelter. While the two senior missions approved of this method as preventing vagrancy, the junior mission, less experienced in African affairs, objected on the ground that it was merely a way of transferring the slave from one master to another, and its view was adopted in England. Article VI is therefore no longer enforced, and vagrancy has again increased. This example is a typical one, and shows that domestic slavery does not press very heavily upon the serfs, and that those who seek freedom generally become a public charge.

The true and complete abolition of slavery can come only with a structural change in African economic life, and can only gradually be brought about. The economic ruin of the large Arab plantations on the east coast, which is already beginning, as a result of the changed economic conditions, will throw a larger population into the towns, and will lead to a parceling-out of the estates among peasant holders. Among the negroes in central and west Africa the increased opportunity of the slaves for gaining wealth is also tending to break down the system.

With the gradual disappearance of slavery, the question arises what system of labor organization is to take its place. The importation of contract labor from China and India is far too costly in most parts of Africa to become a general system. In western Africa it is made well-nigh impossible on account of the unfavorable climatic conditions. When it was attempted to use coolie labor in the French Congo, the mortality among the laborers ran as high as 70 per cent. In east Africa alone has Hindu contract labor been used successfully. Another method of gaining an adequate labor supply is to sanction labor contracts with the natives, or force them to work by imposing heavy taxes upon them. The high hut-taxes of southern Africa are levied for this purpose, as the only way in which the native can get the currency for paying his taxes is by working for white men in the mines or on the farms. In more direct fashion, the Glen Grey Act levies a tax of ten shillings upon every native who has not worked outside of his district for three months in the year. The extension of this peculiar use of fiscal methods to central and west Africa is often advocated, and a moderate hut-tax has already been introduced in many colonies on the west coast; but, as the conditions in these regions are so utterly different from those which prevail in white man's Africa, the initiation of methods which do not pass without challenge even in the Rhodesian sphere would certainly be unwise, and would probably invite disastrous consequences.

While it is true that the natives of the tropical regions of Africa are at present not much inclined to labor, there are still certain tribes, like the Krumen and the Hausas, and the agricultural populations under Mohammedan rule, that prove the capacity of the African for toil under proper economic conditions. Before all, there is one prominent fact which must not be overlooked in this matter: with the establishment of peace throughout Africa, with the stoppage of the murderous slave-raids and of cannibalism, with the introduction of sanitary measures, such as vaccination, the population of Africa, which has a great natural fecundity, will rise rapidly toward the limits of subsistence. While the natives are now surrounded with an abundance of natural fruits, methods of intensive agriculture and of careful industrial work will soon become necessary in order to support the growing population. Thus far the African has made his life possible by killing his neighbor; this resource being cut off, the only alternative will be to work. No legislation, no contract-labor system, will be necessary to induce the natives to work more steadily. Moreover, it should not be believed that they are without economic wants. As a matter of fact, they already require large amounts of European manufactured goods, and their demands are constantly expanding; a corroding climate and careless habits make them far more frequent purchasers of textiles than are the thrifty Chinese. A policy that would attempt unduly to accelerate the operation of these natural causes, and would not shrink from breaking down native societies and employing force, in order to gain a quick supply of labor for the exploitation of African natural wealth, must be qualified as distinctly opposed to the purposes of civilizing activity in Africa. The general enslavement of the negro race does not offer a proper solution of the problems of African development.

It will be seen that, throughout, the foundation of a civilizing policy in Africa must be an economic one. The prevention of wasteful exploitation, and construction of roads and railways, the introduction of a metallic currency, will do away with the most inhuman abuses in African life. It will change the constitution of African society so as to prevent the exploitation of the dependent classes, while the establishment of universal peace will turn the energies of the people toward economic development. The negro population in Africa has thus far lived in the presence of overwhelming natural phenomena, and in a constant state of fluidity which has allowed but very little of settled civilization and of national self-consciousness to grow up. The negroes have, however, developed a strong sense of individual justice, and it is justice that they require, rather than the rarer gifts of benevolence and the blessings of civilization. Now, if justice has any definite meaning, it implies respect for the sphere of an individual existence. We certainly cannot be just to the African if we demolish all his native institutions, simply because we will not take the trouble to understand them. No cruelty of war, no suffering, will be resented by the African so much as an attack upon his private property; and unless the system of concessions to European companies is to prove a curse to Africa, it must respect scrupulously the native property rights. The European must also have a care not to break up further such tribal and social unity as exists among the African populations. The basest forms of social life exist among the jetsam and flotsam of tribal populations along the African coast and in south Africa, where the original unity has been dissolved by European interference. It is here that the missions have their greatest work to do, by creating a new social unity and morality for those which have been so recklessly destroyed.

We have seen that European interference may succeed in creating a new economic basis for African life. Whether it can do more, whether it can deeply and permanently influence African life in the direction of specifically European civilization in its intellectual and moral aspects, is more doubtful. The most potent civilizing agency at all times has been example, and in this respect the relations of the white to the negro race have been particularly unfortunate. The white men who have come to Africa have either been colonial officials, impatiently waiting for their next leave of absence, with little insight into the true needs of native society; or traders whose sole purpose was to get the wealth of the natives rapidly and for the cheapest possible return. The missionaries, men often of single-hearted devotion, have been too few to act as a leavening force upon the entire mass of the African negroes. Moreover, many of them have found it difficult to put their message into the form of greatest helpfulness to the African. Their example, too, holds up the ideal of an intellectual and spiritual life, rather than that of mechanical and industrial efficiency which the Africans so much need. In these respects the Islamitic races have the advantage. They come in contact with the Africans in large numbers, as merchants, industrials, and rulers; and it is not unlikely that they will continue to exert a far greater personal influence upon the African race than will the Europeans. This is true also of the Hindus, who are settling in large numbers along the east coast. The French seem of all European nations to be most successful in charming the African natives into civilization. Their missionaries work in large communities, and are thus assisted by the experience of many societies operating for a long time. Moreover, the French do not exhibit an excessive sense of race-superiority over the negroes. They have therefore already exercised a distinctive civilizing influence in northern Africa. The classical example of a relation of mutual friendliness between the white race and the black is the life of the unhappy island of Martinique—unhappy not only on account of cruel natural catastrophes, but on account of the terrible force of atavism which, with the gradual departure of the white population, is dragging the charming race of the island back toward the dark superstitions of African life. It is remarkable that in countries like Martinique, Hayti, and the southern states of the Union, the vices of the negro populations assume more repulsive aspects than they bear in the African home. This is due no doubt to the fact that the original social unity has in these cases been destroyed. An African society, although it may have barbarous customs, still has a certain moral character which preserves individual morality and dignity of life. This social check is very much impaired, and often totally absent, among the American negroes.

The two things which the negro race needs most are a feeling of social cohesion and responsibility, and the presence of true models in the person of leaders. The mass of the negroes cannot pattern primarily upon the whites with whom they come in contact, but should have leaders of their own race to look up to. It is only by showing consideration to negroes of high character and intelligence that the whites can assist in setting up the best models for social imitation among the negro race. No more statesman-like and far-seeing principle, both for Africa and for America, can be imagined in this matter than that of President Roosevelt, when he says that " the door of hope must not be closed upon the negro race." This does not mean, even in its most distant implication, political power over the whites, nor does it demand general social equality; it simply means that the men who are natural leaders among the negroes, on account of high qualities of mind and soul, shall not be degraded by being excluded from all chance of preferment on account of their color, and that no better service can be done the negro race than a generous recognition of the worth of its best men. Applied to Africa, it means that any policy which would treat the native negro race as destined to permanent bondage in favor of the whites, that would destroy African social life and degrade its leaders, is taking the straight road away from the salvation of the African race, and from rendering it a truly useful member of the family of nations.

2

The Psychology of American Race Prejudice

GEORGE W. ELLIS

This 1915 essay illustrates that the definition and concept of racism, and works reflecting scientific racism, may not have changed dramatically throughout the century. It claims that racism in the United States may be unique throughout the world. In this society racism is based on two factors: first a belief that blacks (and other 'non-whites') are 'naturally inferior to the white race', and a system of social, economic, and political benefits for whites at the expense of blacks. The author also points out that the US system of racism has been supported by a 'false' science. A major weakness in the scientific racism as reflected in the works of Gobineau, Ammon, Galton, and de Laponge, is the unquestioned assumption that 'the white race' is monolithic culturally and anthropologically. The weaknesses in these authors were repeated in the succeeding works of Darwin, Wallace, Huxley, Spencer, and others. Although Ellis focuses on the United States, he does show that racism is an international problem/dynamic as well.

Civilization is confronted with many sociological problems, among the greatest of which, perhaps, is the worldwide existence of interracial prejudice between 606,000,000 white and 1,099,000,000 colored people, inhabiting the continents of Europe, Asia, Africa, Australia and the islands of the sea.

Its menacing era began with the physical conquest of the Americas in the New World, with the social and baneful institution of slavery, founded upon race and color. Its causes were chiefly economic on the one hand, with the political weakness of the Negro Africans on the other.

MODIFIED FORM OF SLAVERY

Physical slavery was abolished and this era was followed by another more modified form of slavery, in which the white nations took control by force and violence of the colored races and reduced them to political subjection in Asia, Africa and a number of islands. The causes were still at bottom economic, supported by superior military power against political disunity and disintegration; yet, tempered by the development of humane sentiments, the growth of democracy and the progress of civilization.

Awakening of Colored Races

The birth and expansion of the Senussi movement in the African black belt, the dissemination of the propaganda of "Africa for Africans" in South Africa, the efforts for independence in India and Egypt, and the rapid assimilation of western methods and culture by Japan and her sudden entrance into the first rank of the white nations, announce the gradual awakening of the colored races and the ultimate arrest and overthrow of the world sway and extension of white political supremacy over the colored peoples.

Prejudice of World's Colored Belt

The world's colored belt is more and more being marked by frequent expressions of increasing acute race antagonism. In Mexico it is the whites against the Indian; in Australia the whites against the Asiatics and blacks; in South Africa the whites against the Asiatics and blacks; in the West Indies in a very modified form the whites against the blacks; and in the United States the whites against the Asiatics and blacks. One may well pause, therefore, and inquire what is the psychology, the mental significance of all this anti-interracial feeling and hostility?

America as Center of Prejudice

One of the most striking and interesting illustrations of the universal problem of race prejudice exists in the United States, where the supposed two most widely dissimilar and divergent types of the human race are brought together in large numbers and close contact, in the atmosphere of theoretical freedom and democratic equality. A general diagnosis of this situation, therefore, will afford the key to the understanding of the larger question, of which this is but one of the worst and yet most hopeful phases.

The American race situation is the most important because it is the most complex and dynamic. It possesses every element of the other phases and more. Here it challenges the further progress of Christianity and civilization in the foremost democracy of the earth. Here it presents the acid test to the culture of the most modern and progressive branch of the white race. And those who are responsible for the bringing of colored people to the United States in such large numbers as to present so grave a sociological problem, transmitted to this and other generations the high moral responsibility of finding a solution that is not only just to both races, but in harmony with democracy and liberty enlightening the world.

Accepted Meaning of Terms

In what we are now considering, we accept psychology as the science of the phenomena and functions of the mind and soul. Race is used as a mere convenience to designate the different branches of the human family. And prejudice is a prejudgment without facts, a decision or opinion of the mind formed without examination and knowledge; and therefore without any reasonable basis and justification for its existence.

The psychology of race prejudice then involves the erroneous mental attitudes which one race entertains for or against another, formed in advance and without foundation in either reason or fact.

Factors of American Race Prejudice

If we want to understand the race question in the United States, an examination must be made into the historical antecedents of the false opinions the whites have and hold against other race groups and vice versa.

In the United States race prejudice is predicated upon the belief that the colored race is naturally inferior to the white race, physically, intellectually, religiously, socially and morally. As a matter of ultimate fact it is actually based upon the advantages, temporary and imaginary, which the white groups believe they derive from this superior attitude to the colored groups economically, politically and socially. A historical study of these beliefs discloses that two powerful factors have contributed above others to the abnormal American situation, and that in their broadest sense they are ethnological and sociological.

Quality of Natural Prejudice

There is a natural antipathy or prejudice which one entertains toward new things and strange persons about which one knows little or nothing. Anything is liked or disliked as it harmonizes with one's present opinion or is strong enough to win approval and establish its supremacy. When brought into contact with new phenomena, in the human mind there is at once precipitated a struggle of established ideas and thought-forms to preserve themselves against the ascendency of new thoughts and ideas.

There is the same natural antipathy between dissimilar groups and races to maintain their institutions against the substitution of others, as in individuals; and this antipathy continues until the stronger group assimilates the weaker. The degree of natural antipathy, individual or group, toward another is in proportion to the extent of believed or actual dissimilarity. Whether in the individual, group or race, this antipathy disappears with contact, knowledge and understanding. It assumes the more permanent form of prejudice with its dangers and penalties, when the stronger group consciously and wilfully refuses to assimilate and cultivates and encourages this natural antipathy until it forms a part of the mores and exercises the function of a social norm. Then all the political and social power of the stronger group is invoked to maintain an attitude of artificial difference and superiority, and the natural process of assimilation is checked and postponed. Until this artificial attitude is unquestionably and permanently established or overthrown its maintenance is constantly attended with friction and confusion, destroying and undermining the best of the participating groups. India illustrates the national decay and death which attend the permanent triumph of prejudice founded upon class. But in the United States race prejudice is more to be dreaded and feared than the caste of India; for while one may change his class he can never change his race. So that as long as there is hope for democracy in the United States there will be a vital and serious challenge to the final supremacy of race prejudice.

PREJUDICE SUPPORTED BY FALSE SCIENCE

Toward making permanent the prejudice between the white and colored races, ethnologists have played an important part, by placing upon ill-founded and erroneous conclusions concerning the white and colored races the stamp and authority of science.

Ethnological writers like Gobineau of France and Ammon of Germany taught and established the false theories that the races were naturally unequal; and that their intellectual and moral capacities were indicated by craniological differences, shape and size of limbs, color of the skin, texture of the hair, the weight and size of brain, &c. In Gobineau's work, entitled *Essai sur l'Inégalité des Races Humaines*, 1854, he claimed that art, science, and civilization sprang solely and exclusively from the Aryan race in seven civilizations: Indian, Egyptian, Assyrian, Greek, Chinese, Italic and Germanic. Galton, in his *Inquiries into Human Faculty*, and M. Vacher de Laponge, in *L'Anthropologie et la Science Politique*, successors to Gobineau, accordingly contend, that Greece and Rome fell because the dolichocephalic elements in the European population were succeeded and invaded by the brachycephalic types; and that the Germans and English, and all Europe, are threatened by the infusion of the inferior blood of the brachycephalic nations like France, Poland, Turkey, and Italy, and that dolichocephalic and

Aryan elements predominate in Belgium, Holland, Scandinavia, Germany, and England, and thus making them naturally superior to all other national groups. These claims are interesting in view of the present European situation, and especially the intellectual claim, and conflicting views put forth by the leading scholars and scientists in Germany, France and England.

ADOPTION OF FALSE ETHNOLOGICAL STANDARD

The Gobineau and Ammon school adopted the best form of the white race as the standard of measurement and judged all other race varieties as they approximated or diverged from it. As the Negro presented apparently the widest physical divergence, they assigned to this race the lowest intellectual and moral estate in the genus homo. Because of differences in the Negro's color, hair and the weight of the brain; because of differences of the angle of the cephalic index and the general anatomical structure of his organism, as compared to that of the white standard, scientists not only condemned the Negro to the lowest human plane, but they exaggerated these differences, gave to them meanings and interpretations which are not and never were true. In the zest of their cause they overlooked the additional facts that the standard they adopted is not representative of the white races, whose differences among themselves are quite as substantial as from the Negro.

ADOPTION OF THE FALSE NEGRO TYPE

As representative of the Negro they selected the ugliest type, and after exaggerating its deformities, they held it up to the white mind of the reading world, in striking contrast to the white standard, to give permanence and stability to the false doctrine of natural Negro inferiority. In geographies, encyclopedias, ethnological writings and anthropological works, in high schools, colleges and universities, this false Negro type was circulated with this perfect white standard to impress the rising generations of all nations against the black, and to solidify with the sanctity of science that natural antipathy which always attends the initial contact of unassimilated individuals or groups, whether they be human, and of the same race or of different races or of the lower animal forms.

FEATURES OF ABNORMAL NEGRO TYPE

The picture of the Negro as set forth by the ethnological type is the next thing in order to the ape family. Types corresponding to it, however, are to be found in all races. European and American writers in the fields of science and literature, not only asserted Negro inferiority, but denied to this race any capacity for improvement. In word and picture they taught the world that the true Negro was less than human, with

> an oval skull, flat forehead, snout-like jaws, swollen lips, broad, flat nose, short, crimped hair, calfless legs, highly elongated heels, and flat feet.

If an attempt were made to describe one of the higher man-apes it would be difficult to find a more exact and fitting description.

INTERPRETATION OF EVOLUTION

Concomitant with this anti-Negro ethnological propaganda, Darwin, Wallace, Huxley, Spencer, Haeckal, and others, announced the doctrine of evolution and supported it with such force by evidences from all the allied and other sciences, that the leaders of modern philosophy, religion and science, accepted this principle and ultimately embraced it as the most tenable explanation of that grand process in accord with which the universe and all therein came into being and advanced to its present state. In the light of this view, more than other races, the proximity of the Negro to the anthropoid apes—the gorilla, gibbon, chimpanzee, and the orang-outang—was believed to have additional scientific proof and demonstration.

METHODS OF PREJUDICE MANUFACTURE

Writers in history and other departments of literature, designedly excluded the Negro, contrary to fact, from honorable mention and participation in historical progress, and after a time went so far as to assert that the Negro had made no contributions to civilization. For several generations, from the fortified ramparts of school, college, university, literature, and science, the white mind was so assiduously assailed and so constantly besieged, that the white race was thoroughly inoculated and filled with the virus and poison of race prejudice. It is through these potent agencies and powerful channels that the ethnological science has been such an influential factor in creating, diffusing and crystallizing race prejudice in the social mind of the whites, by the use of false data and ill-founded opinions against the Negro, in the educational and social system.

The great newspapers of the country have coöperated in the propaganda of race prejudice by making the crime of every Negro racial, rather than individual, and employing the use of the word, "Negro" in glaring head-lines for no other purpose than to inflame the popular mind against this race, and to teach the false doctrine that the Negro is more criminal and naturally inferior to other race groups. The newspapers have played upon this prejudice until they have created a hostile sentiment against all colored races, and the popular mind has been so contorted and misguided that the announcement of the most wilful falsehood in the papers creates a riot and mob rule, which overrides reason and law, often erroneously and wrongfully destroying property and taking human life before this falsehood can be corrected. At first this sentiment was developed to be directed against the Negro alone, but it has so grown that it is now used against the different elements of the white race itself, in which the foundations of law and democracy are being completely undermined.

Disfranchisement, Jim-crow cars, illegal discrimination, mob violence, and segregation are but abnormal expressions growing out of the distorted condition of the popular mind, which have attended the development and growth of race prejudice.

IMPORTANT SOCIOLOGICAL CONTENTIONS

Dr. Albion W. Small, the noted sociologist of the Chicago University, contends that society is a series of social processes. Dr. Schaffle, of Germany, insists that it is a social body. Herbert Spencer, the distinguished philosopher, and one of the greatest of sociologists, held that society is a social organism, with highly differentiated and integrated parts with specialized functions. And if the book of Professor Ellwood, of the department of sociology of Missouri University, on Social Psychology, is correct, society has a social mind.

THE POISONING OF THE SOCIAL BODY

With all the blighting and baneful effects which race prejudice has wrought by reason of its firm intrenchment in the white social mind, it has not rested there, but extended the domain of its dangers and disasters, by injecting its poison into the life blood of the great social body or organism, with all of its sacred institutional organs, economic, religious, social, political and moral. Long before race prejudice had poisoned the social mind of the white race, it had entered and found permanent lodgment in the white social system, through the institution of African slavery, as it existed in the two Americas.

Historically speaking, as with its beginning in the new world, slavery was economic, and it became racial when the development of humane agitation made its continued existence no longer even temporarily defensible, except upon the new and invented doctrine of natural Negro inferiority.

Writers in history and anthropology began then to write more to justify Negro slavery than to advance the cause of truth and knowledge. It is through the institution of Negro slavery, and the white man's vested and imaginary interests therein, economic, social and political, and the false and unjust propaganda which he set in force and motion against the Negro to perpetuate them, that rank and importance are given to the sociological contributions to American race prejudice.

Economic Loss of Slavery

Whether it includes the members of one race group, or those of many, all slavery at least contributes to class prejudice in many ways. In the South it gave rise to economic prejudice, and divided labor and industry into two departments, free and slave, and after a time the work performed by the slave was considered beneath the dignity of a white person to do. So that both labor factors were confined within artificial limitations, and neither of them were allowed to work freely in accord with their capacities and the natural laws of industry; nor to contribute their full strength to the economic life of the South and the nation. Under this system the whites established the doctrine that because of their superiority they had a right to have the darker races work for them for nothing. The injustice of that doctrine is still everywhere to be seen in the industrial life of the nation, where colored peoples are treated industrially differently from other American citizens, and are not permitted to advance and work in positions according to their capabilities and character. Certain lines of work and certain positions are not open to colored persons no matter how high in character or brilliant in qualifications. In numerous instances colored people are denied the opportunity to work and contribute their highest and best toward the economic life and strength of the country, and the terrible injustice of this economic situation is a survival of the still greater injustice of American slavery. The economic life of the nation, therefore, will not be free until this racial barrier is removed, and all citizens are permitted to contribute their best toward the economic welfare of the country.

Intellectual Prejudice

Aside from an economic prejudice, society through slavery made the white mind feel that it was created naturally superior to the Negro mind, and all the social institutions and machinery were so arranged as to give to the Negro mind the same impression. The whites were educated in all the arts, sciences and literature; the Negro was kept by law and custom in abject ignorance of all the treasures of learning, except that they were intended alone for the service and adornment of white mentality. Much of the white man's time and talents were diverted from constructive efforts for social progress, to repressive and obstructive measures in keeping the Negro mind ignorant, and self-conscious of its own supposed natural inferiority. Neither the whites nor the blacks were permitted to think and develop mentally according to their full capacity; and because of this intellectual prejudice no one can tell what the country and the world has lost through the want of the intellectual coöperation of the white and colored people in the South.

The intellectual attitude between the two races today is the result of the extreme position taken by the South to perpetuate slavery. The slavery doctrine that the Negro could not learn the white man's culture and which at the same time made it a crime to teach him to read and write, has been modernized to the effect that education spoils the Negro. In the South the Southern whites believe in giving the Negro, therefore, as little education as possible, while in the North they give him as much education as he can absorb, but they deny to him any opportunity to earn a living with his education. The great fact is, that the whites have not recovered from the false theory of natural inequality of races on the one side, and the colored peoples have not fully awakened to the truth of their own natural racial equality, on the other. The intellect of the nation will assume its normal condition when these old false ideas have been completely eradicated from the public mind, and all classes and races are given their true intellectual status, in accord with their merits rather than their race. The intellectual strength of the nation will be greatly augmented by the positive and constructive use of its great natural talents, unfettered by racial and class limitations.

Religious Prejudice

The Christian religion is the highest expression of religious development. Conceived in love and established by practice, it is founded upon the broad principles of the fatherhood of God, and the brotherhood of man, of every race and country. From Nazareth the lowly spirit of the Christ, for nineteen centuries, has invaded in triumph every continent and delivered its message of love and salvation to every race, that each might know and feel its duty to its fellow man, and secure peace on earth and redemption in the great beyond. In carrying forward this noble work the white race has been the great missionary to other races. But because of economic and intellectual race prejudice, the white race has shown, with all the aid and assistance of its great religion, an amazing inability or disinclination to practice toward the Negro what it so vehemently preaches to the world. And few things show more truly how injurious race prejudice really is, than the said historical fact that it corrupted the practice of the white race in so sacred a matter as its religion, and that in the white race of Europe and America, it dimmed the glory and lustre of the Cross.

POLITICAL PREJUDICE

The government of the United States represented at its birth the political dream of centuries. By its constitution it substituted for the capricious control of man the government of the people regulated by law. Founded upon the freedom and equality of all men, it invited to its shores the oppressed of every land. Its founders laid the foundations of a democracy that was supposed to be a political light to the nations of the earth. But before this government was established the institution of slavery had manufactured so much class prejudice in industry, education and religion, that at the adoption of the constitution, the white race was unable to make this government in fact what in theory it was announced to the world. American society generated and condoned so much prejudice before the abolition of slavery, that the country since has not been able politically to remove the evil effects of its former bad example. One white man South has always had greater political power than two or three white men North, to say nothing of the practical exclusion of the Negro people from their proportionate representation and participation in the government of which they have long been a contributing and important factor. That the government has been unable in the hands of the white man to do political justice to itself and to the Negro, is in great measure due to the influence of the sociological factor in race prejudice. American injustice to her colored citizens deprives the American people of their just influence in the world movement of freedom and democracy. The practice of the people must be more in harmony with the theory of the government before this nation will be on a safe and sound political basis.

INFLUENCE OF PREJUDICE ON MORALS

To my mind the supreme destiny of man is moral. This is alike true of a nation. Whether we consider morals as intuitive or utilitarian, to be right is the crowning glory of social conduct and achievement. During two and a half centuries, the white race went to Africa, and took the Negro race from its home and country, and compelled it by superior political force to work for the white race for nothing. This was and is a great moral wrong. For it justice demanded in part atonement the awful pains and

penalty of a terrible civil war, with all its prodigious waste of life and treasure.

The class prejudice, which mentally attends any kind of slavery, impaired American and European morals toward the Negro in all the important institutions of society, and seriously threatened the overthrow of the monogamic marriage in the Southern part of the United States. The unbalancing of the morals of the white race was so widespread that European nations still insist upon controlling colored races for the benefit of the whites; and the American people have abandoned the Negro to those who insist on excluding him from the equal opportunities, benefits and protection of democratic institutions, and of governing the blacks in the interest and welfare of the whites alone.

The terrible and devastating war, now raging in Europe, with all its world-wide consequences and effects, is a splendid illustration of the unexpected, yet unerring rewards which follow the acceptance and adoption of false and erroneous doctrines. The practice by European powers of controlling colored races in the interest of themselves and against the governed has impaired and weakened European morals and led to the European struggle among the great nations in an effort to exploit and annex the weaker peoples. It is a strange irony of fate that these great white nations of Europe in their extremity have been compelled to call upon the darker races to save white civilization against itself.

Carefully studied and thoroughly understood the conflict in Europe has important lessons for the American people in their interracial attitudes and relationships.

AMERICAN SOCIAL SITUATION

It is therefore due to the educational influence of science, literature, and Negro slavery, acting upon the social body and mind of the white race against the Negro, supported by an active and increasingly hostile sentiment and emotion, that constitute the historical cause of that abnormal social situation in the United States, which keeps before the country a menacing social question, the nature and genesis of which the future destiny of democracy on this continent and the coöperation of the white and colored races require that we carefully study and understand.

The social situation, with its intellectual error on its psychic side and crystallized sentiment on the sociological, is a threatening social malady; it embraces years of ethnological misrepresentation on the one hand and social customary practice on the other. It is rational to believe that normal conditions will be restored when the intellectual and social poison has been removed from the social mind and body, in the historical way. This situation has more in it than race prejudice. This is disclosed by such anomalous facts as that the Southern whites do not object to Negro servants occupying the same cars and hotels as themselves but they object to educated Negro gentlemen and ladies upon an independent basis. They are opposed strongly to social equality as they interpret it, yet Southern men do not object to the most intimate social relations with colored women. These, and many other contradictory positions in the Southern situation, force the conclusion, that there is something besides race prejudice upon the alleged basis of inferiority. They announce that they are opposed to the Negro because of his lowly condition, and yet they antagonize his efforts to move into better localities, and to occupy better premises. At one time they said that the basis of their opposition was on account of the criminal and the lower classes of the Negro people but the sanction of segregation in the Federal government at Washington is conclusive proof that the opposition is directed toward the upper and most highly selected classes of the colored people.

RACE ORTHODOXY IN THE SOUTH

In a recent book published by Neale Publishing Company and written by Prof. Thomas Pearce Bailey of the University of Mississippi, under the title of *Race Orthodoxy in the South*, the writer leaves no further doubt, if any existed, as to the creed and principles in accord with which the South keeps by its racial conduct a menacing race problem before the country. In numerous passages through the book the author admits that the conduct of the South toward the Negro is in support of a social program, which is out of harmony with the principles of Christianity and democracy; but, that this abnormal and extraordinary Southern attitude is required by the necessities of the Southern situation, the same plea which has been made by the oppressors against the oppressed in every age.

On page 93 Professor Bailey sets forth the principles of what he calls Race Orthodoxy in the South as interpreted by a group of representative Southerners. It is interesting to note what he says are the essentials of Southern racial creed and action. They are:

1. "Blood will tell."
2. The white race must dominate.
3. The Teutonic peoples stand for race purity.
4. The Negro is inferior and will remain so.
5. "This is a white man's country."
6. No social equality.
7. No political equality.
8. In matters of civil rights and legal adjustments give the white man, as opposed to the colored man, the benefit of the doubt; and under no circumstances interfere with the prestige of the white race.
9. In educational policy let the Negro have the crumbs that fall from the white man's table.
10. Let there be such industrial education of the Negro as will best fit him to serve the white man.
11. Only Southerners understand the Negro question.
12. Let the South settle the Negro question.
13. The status of peasantry is all the Negro may hope for, if the races are to live together in peace.
14. Let the lowest white man count for more than the highest Negro.
15. The above statements indicate the leadings of Providence.

This book is remarkable in the fullness and frankness with which the author boldly presents the South's new challenge to the further progress of Christianity and democracy in the United States. No doubt the more advanced views concerning the Southern situation as given by Gardner in *The Basis of Ascendency*, Weatherford in *Negro Life in the South* and *Present Forces in Negro Progress*, and Merriam in *The Negro and the Nation* have contributed toward the necessity which now requires that the position of the South be defended by all the resources of the ripest scholarship and the most skillful argumentation. Already the contest is on not only in the South, but in the nation for justice, freedom, opportunity and equality before the law, for the white and colored races alike. What will the outcome be?

NEW ETHNOLOGY BEING WRITTEN

In the meantime ethnologists like Boas and Chamberlain of the United States and Peschel of Germany are making a new ethnology, in which the truth is being told concerning the Negro as well as the whites. We now know that in nature there is only one race—the human race; that physical features, the cephalic angle, the texture of hair, the shape of the head, the color of the skin, the size and shape, or the size and weight of brain, have little or nothing to do with the capacity of the mind or the moral quality of the soul; that like other race varieties the Negro is a product of the complex and subtle forces of his milieu, whether in this country or elsewhere, acting upon him for centuries past; that there is no naturally superior and inferior race, and that no race has a monopoly on either beauty, intellect or culture.

As Royce of Harvard says in his *Race Questions and Prejudices*:

We are now interested in the minds of men. We want to know what the races of men are socially good for. And not in the study of skulls or of hair, or of skin color, and not in the survey of all these bewildering complications with which physical anthropology deals, shall we easily find answer to our more practical questions, viz., to our questions in which these various races of men are related to the interests of civilization, and regarding the spirit in which we ought to estimate and practically to deal with these racial traits of mankind.

All men, so far as we can yet study them, he continues, appear to us not, of course, the same in mind, but yet surprisingly alike in their minds, in their morals, and in their arts.

Supposed Negro Type Condemned

Winwood Reade says:

The typical Negro is a rare variety even among Negroes.

And speaking of that cruel and accepted Negro type, which still pictures the Negro so unjustly to each rising generation of both races in America and Europe, Peschel virtually announces its ultimate doom in these positive words:

No single tribe, however, possessed all these deformities. The color of the skin passes through every gradation, from ebony black, as in the Jolofs, to the light tint of the mulattoes, as in the Wakilema, and Barth even describes copper-colored Negroes in Margli. As to the skull in many tribes, as in the above Jolofs, the jaws are not prominent, the lips are not swollen. In some tribes the nose is pointed, straight, or hooked; even Grecian profiles are spoken of, travelers say with surprise that they cannot perceive anything of the so-called Negro type even among Negroes.

The Negro in Civilization

Not only is the Negro coming into his own in ethnology, but through white writers and scholars like Winwood Reade, Dr. Bradford, Professor Taylor, Sir Harry H. Johnston, Dr. J. Scott Keltie, Dr. Nasseau, Mary H. Kingsley, E. D. Morel, Count de Cardi and numerous social workers like Madam Woolley; travelers like Bruce, Baker, Felix DuBois, Stanley, Livingstone and Mungo Park, are lifting the veil of misrepresentation which, for so long, has covered the Negro in Africa and elsewhere, and he is coming forth in his notable place with other races in history and in civilization.

Ripley and Sergi have brought together a vast array of facts to show that in prehistoric times, a branch of the African Negro race, on the shores of the Mediterranean, gave to the world the foundations in art, science, astronomy, mathematics and religion.

Volney and Eckler contend with convincing proof, that the Negro in Ethiopian Africa originated those various religious systems to which many branches of the Semitic and Aryan races are today so numerously and reverently attached.

And as to the origin of modern civilization, of which some of the white race never tire of boasting, Hoskins, Heeren, Champollion, Rossellini and other white European investigators and travelers support the claim that the arts and learning of Egypt, and ultimately of Greece and Rome, came from the Ethiopian kingdom and Negroland of Meroe in the upper valley of the Nile.

Example of Noted Negroes

In poetry, music and literature distinguished and scholarly Negroes like Baba and Sadi of Timbuctu; Hayford, Sarbah and Blyden of West Africa; Pushkin, Dumas and Taylor of Europe; Ferris, Dunbar and Braithwaite, Chesnut, Miller and Lynch, Douglass, Williams, Scarborough, Washington and DuBois, and social service workers like Mesdames Barnett of Chicago and Terrell of Washington, are convincing examples of the demonstrated equality of colored people, and of the notable contributions which Negroes can render in behalf of the intellectual and social freedom of all the races of men.

If the Negro and the white people who love justice are determined to know the truth regarding the equality of the races, and through education and literature, assist in giving it to the world, the citadel of race prejudice in the United States will tremble until it falls.

No Negro need be ashamed of his race. In this thought I am reminded of those appropriate lines which the Negro scholar and writer, Dr. Blyden, translated from Homer, written when the Gods were pleased to dine with members of the Negro race:

The sire of Gods and all the ethereal train,
On the warm limits of the farthest main,
Now mix with mortals, nor disdain to grace,
The feasts of Ethiopia's blameless race,
Twelve days the powers indulge the genial rite,
Returning with the twelfth revolving night.

3

Social Pathology: Obstacles to Social Participation

STUART ALFRED QUEEN
AND JENETTE ROW GRUENER

'There are many white people in the United States who are firmly convinced of the inherent inferiority of Negroes, Orientals, Indians, Jews, and other ethnic groups commonly called "races". On the basis of this belief, and the accompanying feelings, they join in denying to these minority peoples various opportunities for social contacts and cultural participation. So sharply has the line been drawn that many members of these ethnic groups have had no real chance to demonstrate what capacities they do possess. Social barriers prevent achievement, and lack of achievement constitutes a new barrier.'

This passage was written by Stuart Alfred Queen and Jenette Row Gruener in the second edition of their *Social Pathology: Obstacles to Social Participation*, first published in 1925 and revised in 1948. The choice of words betrays the statement's age, though its import is as relevant today. 'Race prejudice continues to be an active force in American life', wrote Queen and Gruener.

Over the decades, we have learned to distinguish between 'race prejudice' or racial prejudice and racism, which is an underlying belief system or theory that can lend prejudice its rationale. But the 'force' of which Queen and Gruener wrote remains an active one. They offered three illustrations and follow with an explanation of the 'nature and origins of race prejudice'.

Race Prejudice: American Negroes

There are many white people in the United States who are firmly convinced of the inherent inferiority of Negroes, Orientals, Indians, Jews, and other ethnic groups commonly called "races." On the basis of this belief, and the accompanying feelings, they join in denying to these minority peoples various opportunities for social contacts and cultural participation. So sharply has the line been drawn that many members of these ethnic groups have had no real chance to demonstrate what capacities they do possess. Social barriers prevent achievement, and lack of achievement constitutes a new barrier. The life of Booker T. Washington illustrates some of the obstacles that keep Negroes from sharing fully in American life. It displays also a large measure of white recognition for a black man, a great contribution to the cultural development of Negroes, and the effective promotion of interracial co-operation.

Booker T. Washington[1]

Booker T. Washington was born a slave on a large plantation in Virginia, probably in April, 1856. His father is not known, but is believed to have been a white man who lived in the vicinity. At all events, there is no record of his having shown any interest in the mulatto son. With his mother, brother, and sister, Booker Washington lived in a one-room cabin without wooden floor or glass windows. Furniture was very meager. Mr. Washington later said that he could not remember having slept in a bed until he was seven years old. As to food, "it was a piece of bread here and a scrap of meat there." Regular meals served at a table were unknown. When other breakfast failed, the boy went out where the cows and pigs were fed to share their boiled corn. Dress was also meager, the boy's principal garment being a rough flax shirt. Toward the white master, there was no bitterness, although there was an earnest hope for freedom.

Soon after emancipation, the family moved to West Virginia. Its few belongings were taken in a cart, but the children walked most of the way. The stepfather found work in salt furnaces. The mother got hold of Webster's "blue-back" spelling book, and the boy's education began. He worked by day and studied at night under the guidance of a colored teacher. Later he attended school, working several hours a day before and after classes. While digging coal, he heard about Hampton Normal and Agricultural Institute in Virginia and determined to get there somehow. Meantime he found employment with a white family, which enabled him to save a little money and to do some more studying. Most important of all, his mistress taught him to be clean, orderly, systematic, thorough, and honest.

In the fall of 1872, Booker Washington set out for Hampton, arriving with only fifty cents in his pocket. His entrance examination consisted in sweeping and dusting a classroom. This he did so thoroughly that he was admitted as a student. A Northern friend of the principal paid his tuition. His board and incidental expenses he earned by janitor work and odd jobs. At Hampton, Booker Washington learned the trade of brickmason, came to know cultured people, and acquired the habits associated with regular meals, tablecloth, toothbrush, bathtub, bed linen, and so on. He graduated in 1875.

On leaving Hampton, he worked in a summer hotel, then returned to his home in West Virginia as schoolteacher. Here he worked from early in the morning till late at night. Besides the day school, he taught night classes, established a small reading room, started a debating society, and taught two Sunday schools. After two years of this, followed by one at a seminary in Washington, D.C., he was called back to Hampton as a sort of "house father" for about seventy-five Indian students. He also took charge of the night school and became secretary to the principal.

In 1881, efforts were being made to start a Negro Normal School in Tuskegee, Alabama. A prominent white citizen and an ex-slave joined in addressing General Armstrong, the principal of Hampton Institute, asking him to recommend someone to head the new school. As a result of the correspondence, Booker Washington undertook the venture. The legislature had appropriated $2,000 for instructors' salaries, but there was no provision for land, building, or equipment. Work was begun in a rather dilapidated shanty near the colored Methodist Church, the latter being used as an assembly hall. About three months after the school opened, an abandoned plantation of 100 acres was offered for sale at $500. Mr. Washington borrowed $250 for the initial payment, and soon the school was moved. The "big house" had burned, so the stable and henhouse were used for classrooms. Both teachers and students helped to renovate buildings and clear the land. Thus was started an institution which Booker Washington headed for over thirty years and which, under his leadership, developed into one of the best-known industrial schools in the world.

When he died in 1915, Tuskegee Institute had become a really great institution—2,000 acres of land, 100 buildings, 1,500 students, 200 teachers, an endowment of $2,000,000, training in 38 trades and professions. But more than that, it had won favor in the eyes of both races. In 1881, many white people had looked upon the project with misgiving. They had in their minds, said Mr. Washington, "pictures of what was called an educated Negro, with a high hat, imitation gold eye-glasses, a showy walking-stick, kid gloves, fancy boots, and what not." They feared the loss of agricultural and domestic workers and the rise of a troublesome parasitic class of black men. But with the passing of time, these attitudes changed. At the twenty-fifth anniversary of Tuskegee's founding, addresses were made by the Secretary of War, the Governor of Alabama, the President of Harvard University, and a famous industrialist.

One secret of this success lay in the fact that the educational program was always kept close to the life of the people, the rural Negroes of the black belt. Mr. Washington went about the South eating and sleeping with the humble black folk in their little cabins. He found them desperately poor and ignorant, miserably clad, malnourished, unclean, in debt, limited in social

---

[1] This account is based largely on *Up From Slavery*, Booker T. Washington's autobiography (copyright 1901, 1929, by Doubleday, Doran and Company, Inc.), and Anson Phelps Stokes, *A Brief Biography of Booker Washington* (1936). By permission of Doubleday, Doran and Company, Inc., and Hampton Institute.

contacts, and untouched by many phases of our culture. Schools were often held in miserable frame shacks or log cabins, lacking blackboards, desks, and sometimes books. The teachers were poorly trained. The school term ran from three to five months. Often there was none at all. The churches were quite as crude as the schools. Leisure-time activities consisted in loafing on the streets of the nearest town all day Saturday and attending some "big meeting" on Sunday. To remove these limitations, Booker Washington chose the way of self-help rather than the way of demanding rights. So firmly did he adhere to this philosophy and program that some of his fellow Negroes accused him of playing up to the whites.

Perhaps the best statement of his personal philosophy and the finest recognition Mr. Washington ever received occurred in connection with the Cotton States and International Exposition in Atlanta in 1895. As he put it, "This was the first time in the entire history of the Negro that a member of my race had been asked to speak from the same platform with white Southern men and women on any important National occasion. ... Not a few of the Southern white papers were unfriendly to the idea of my speaking." He advised Negroes to make the most of opportunities about them. "It is important and right that all the privileges of the law be ours, but it is vastly more important that we be prepared for the exercise of these privileges." He urged white people to avail themselves of the potential contribution of Negroes instead of counting on immigration to build up the South. "Draw on the eight millions of Negroes whose habits you know, whose fidelity and love you have tested ... who have tilled your fields, cleared your forests, built your railroads and cities." He held the future of the two races to be bound inextricably together. Prosperity, health, law, and order must come to both or to neither. "In all things that are purely social we can be as separate as the fingers, yet one as the hand in all things essential to mutual progress." Newspapers in all parts of the country published this address in full. The President of the United States wrote Mr. Washington a letter of congratulation.

Despite the efforts of Booker Washington and of many other eminent Negroes, race prejudice continues to be an active force in American life. Three illustrations are offered showing difficulty in securing employment, education, and participation in civic movements.

A Negro Seeks Employment

A young woman, a graduate of the commercial department of the high school in a large New England city, took an additional postgraduate course in shorthand and typewriting. She is a native of the city and a member of one of its most respected colored families. Shortly after her graduation, she applied, in response to an advertisement in a local paper, for office work with a large commercial corporation, and received from one of the department heads a request to call in person as soon as possible. She was directed to a room where scores of young women were engaged in work similar to that for which she had applied. Her appearance in this room created evident surprise and excited a ripple of subdued laughter. The surprise of the young women was exceeded by that of their chief when she learned that this Negro girl was the one whom she had invited for a conference regarding work. But in spite of that invitation, the caller was told that the place had been filled.

Two months later, there appeared in a local paper an advertisement by the same company for a woman to do clerical work, but this time in another department. Again the colored girl wrote her application and mailed it at once to the head of the department. On this occasion, she gave her residence telephone number as well as the street address. On the following day, she had a telephone message from the department head who, after asking a few questions, requested her to call and see him next morning.

At the designated hour, she appeared at his desk. After questioning her as to her fitness, he found himself unable to give a decisive answer, but assured her that he would give her application serious consideration shortly. While the decision was pending, it occurred to the young woman that a good word spoken in her behalf by someone whose influence might have weight would not be amiss at this juncture. She accordingly sought and secured the intercession of two such persons. One of these went so far as to lay her case before the vice-president of the company, who is reputed to be a man of generous impulses and a firm believer in a square deal. Having listened attentively to the facts, this official promised to investigate the matter and see what could be done. He did so, and within a week the intercessor received from him a letter in which he said: "I have talked with Mr. —— in regard to the employment of the young woman you spoke to me about, and find that while his sympathy is in favor of doing so, yet on conferring with his employees, he is convinced that the exigencies of the service will not allow him to act as he really wishes to act. We all regret the circumstances very much." And with this the incident closed.

Her next experience was with a publishing house whose advertisement in a local paper she answered after the manner already described. The manager of the firm replied, asking her to call the following morning. When the applicant went to the house and, following directions, ascended the long stairway to a room above, she again found herself in the presence of scores of young women of the more favored race, and with exactly the same humiliating experience as before. But, on this occasion, her feelings suffered even more, for among the young women who ridiculed her presumption were those who had been her classmates in the high school. In the business manager of this company, who soon faced her, she met with an honesty which had been sadly lacking in all the others to whom she had applied. He frankly told her that he could not consider her application on account of her color.

Not quite hopeless, but thoroughly discouraged, she now abandoned the search for clerical work—the kind for which she had spent four years in special preparation—and rather than accept the alternative of leaving home, decided to see what the chances were in other lines of employment outside of domestic service. She then applied for work in a large department store where her name was filed away for future reference; in a confectionery manufactory, in the office window of which was the conspicuous placard, GIRLS WANTED, but where she was told that only girls experienced in the manufacture of candy could be employed; and then in a dozen other places, where help was "wanted"—in each and every instance to be turned away.

[* * *]

A City Club Excludes a Negro

The city club of a Middle Western city, one of the largest in the country, was afraid it might have to face the color problem when a Negro was recommended for membership. The issue was dodged; the Negro's application was "tactfully withdrawn," "without offense"—so it was alleged. There are hundreds of educated, refined Negroes in that city. The city club has been for many years the most stalwart defender of public rights and public morality; it is a club which people enter, for the most part, to render public service in one way or another and not simply for its social amenities. Yet its members, or some of them, rejoiced in what they looked upon as a "narrow escape" from having to take up the question whether Negroes, qualified by education, professional status, and personal reputation, should be permitted to take part in these efforts.[2]

Ethnic Groups in the United States

In 1930, the Bureau of the Census reported 11,900,000 Negroes, 1,400,000 Mexicans, 330,000 Indians, 140,000 Japanese, 75,000 Chinese, 45,000 Filipinos, and several smaller ethnic groups in the continental United States. In addition to these peoples, distinguished to a certain extent by color and other external features, there were several large groups distinguished by language and other culture traits, but reported in terms of birthplace. Among the largest were Italians 1,800,000, Germans 1,600,000, Scandinavians 1,125,000. In addition, there is one very large group not counted separately by the Bureau of the Census, namely,

Jews, who were estimated to number 4,200,000.[3] Within the space limits of this chapter, it is not possible to consider each of these separately. Some generalizations appear to be valid for all of them, while in other respects their circumstances differ. Hence, we have chosen to present certain general statements, supplemented by a discussion of the largest of these groups, the Negroes.

Nature and Origins of Race Prejudice

In discussing race prejudice, it is important to distinguish the biological and the sociological definitions of race. From the biological standpoint, a race is a large body of people, relatively homogeneous as to heritable, nonadaptive features. But instead of sharp lines, there is a great deal of overlapping. Hence, racial types really represent averages about which variation occurs. The shading off of one race into another may be owing in part to having a common origin; it is complicated by interbreeding. There are various criteria of race—head form, hair, skin color, stature, blood group, and so on. But these do not appear in consistent combinations. Hence, it might be well to substitute for the misleading term "race" the colorless phrase "ethnic group."

But this does not mean that the concept of race has ceased to play an important part in human affairs. Many people still *believe* that there are distinct races, with consistently different combinations of physical characteristics, mental capacities, ancestry, and destiny. It is customary for the members of a given ethnic group to *believe* that they are different from and (usually) better than other such groups, that they are descended from a common ancestor or ancestors, and that they have a mission to the world. They build up a mythology of racial separateness, superiority, and destiny, like the current "Aryan" mythology in Germany. Even though it be unfounded in fact, they behave *as if* it were true. They come to hate, or fear, or despise the members of other ethnic groups. If strong, they oppress, harass, and exploit the weaker groups. How has all this come to be?

Whether the so-called races evolved separately from different subhuman ancestors or all emerged from the same ancestral group, they developed apart from each other. In the isolation of their distinctive environments, variation and natural selection operated to develop somewhat distinctive human types. Close interbreeding, within a local area, produced a homogeneity which might easily be taken as proof of a separate species. Along with this physical differentiation went cultural differentiation. In a given geographic setting, certain topographic features, climatic conditions, and natural resources facilitated the development of certain kinds

---

[2] The foregoing stories have been taken from *And Who Is My Neighbor?* The Inquiry (1924), pp. 77–9, 109–10, 171, by permission of the Publication Department of the National Council of the Young Men's Christian Associations of the United States of America.

---

[3] *American Jewish Year Book*, vol. 30, pp. 101–08.

of food, clothing, and means of transportation, perhaps art and religion, size and quality of groups. When peoples who had thus gone their separate ways for long periods of time came together, they looked upon each other inevitably as strange, often as dangerous. If their contacts were infrequent, if one group was represented by only a few individuals, if they became interested in the exchange of goods or services, they might make a peaceful adjustment to one another. But if they came together in considerable numbers, if one group sought to eliminate or dominate the other, then the differences in physical appearance and in culture became symbols of fear and hatred. The memories of such conflicts live long and are revived by every appearance of these symbols. Even after the immediate threat to security or status is gone, those who bear the hallmark of the other group are treated as enemies. If the struggle has ended in slavery or other form of subjugation, the inferior group may remain bitter, and the victors may fear an uprising. If the two groups have finally become adjusted to the relations of dominance and submission, the superior group probably rationalizes its exploitation of the other as "natural" or "divinely ordered," and thinks little further of the matter unless someone threatens the status quo.

In America, the history of black and white relations is briefly this. Colonial times were marked by the arrival of rather small numbers of Negro slaves directly from Africa. So far as America was concerned, the slave trade rested on no previous racial antipathy; it was purely a business proposition. The presence of slaves was nothing new in the world. These Negroes seemed ugly and uncouth. Their culture was meager. They were not Christian, and they did not speak English. They could do only unskilled labor. They came as slaves. Over a period of 200 years, the races became accommodated to each other. However, even before the Civil War, there was some tension. Poor whites envied Negroes on account of their security and hated them because of economic competition. Not a few masters hired their slaves out in competition with white laborers. With emancipation came an upheaval. To be sure, the personal relations between many former masters and slaves changed slowly, but there was a great deal of mobility and insecurity. The old masters were impoverished and bitter, the freedmen were destitute, and white workers were poor. During the Reconstruction era, feelings ran high. Out of this confusion came a conscious effort to "keep the Negro in his place." Cultural isolation was continued and emphasized. Negroes were segregated as to residence, education, religion, recreation, transportation, and employment. They were politically disfranchised. These were the methods whereby desperate white men of all classes sought to maintain some degree of status and security, creating a permanent sense of differentiation from the emancipated black men. Then came the migration to cities, and increasing participation in industry. These changes demanded of the Negroes new habits of life; they offered new contacts with white people; they left members of both races wondering what to expect. Negroes took over jobs previously held only by white men; they invaded areas previously occupied only by white residents; they met on streetcars and busses. In the North, they went to the same parks and theaters; their children attended the same schools. Everywhere there was uncertainty as to privileges and obligations. Intermittently conflict broke into the open: Negro homes were bombed, men suspected of crime were lynched, large-scale riots occurred.

Thus, the rise of race prejudice in ethnic groups involves contact in large numbers and strange situations, economic competition, and some physical differences which can identify members of the opposite camps. Similar in some respects, different in others, is the development of race prejudice in individuals. On first contact with a strange-looking person, there is likely to be an expression of interest or curiosity. If previous experience with other kinds of strangers has been unfortunate, there may be suspicion or fear. But usually there is accommodation and acceptance of physical differences. Thus, young children play freely with familiar members of other ethnic groups. But as they grow older, they observe marks of social distance. For example, white children note that Negroes usually hold menial positions, use rear entrances, eat in the kitchen, are addressed by first names, kowtow to white people, and are the butts of white people's jokes. So they come gradually to accept the adult attitudes thus displayed. Thus, the young members of the numerically superior group acquire the attitudes of domination and derision, while those of the minority group acquire attitudes of submission, fear, and resentment. Sometimes these ideas and feelings are taught deliberately, but usually they are passed along by innuendo, avoidance, and perhaps abuse. If there comes into the life of an individual some dramatic experience in which he or another member of his group is threatened or injured by a member of the opposite group, the conventional attitudes are strongly reinforced. Furthermore, members of the privileged race discover that status in their own group demands rejection of close social contact with members of the subordinate race. All these notions and feelings are strengthened by rationalizations about innate superiority, and symbolized by stereotypes of the "nigger," "greaser," "Jap," and the like.

Economic Opportunities and Exploitation

The general hypothesis with reference to economic participation by members of minority ethnic groups, especially Negroes, is that they are in the main restricted to the least attractive and most poorly paid occupations, that for the same work they are paid less than white persons, that in hard times they are the first to be laid off and the last to be hired; that they are usually excluded from professional and trade associations and from labor unions. Let us examine the evidence bearing on these and related points.[4]

As to occupations, the largest numbers of Negroes are found in agriculture, domestic and personal service. The percentages of gainfully employed Negroes who are found in trade, clerical occupations, and the professions are much smaller than the corresponding percentages of white workers. The percentage of Negro women who work outside the home is twice as great as the percentage of white women. Two fifths of the colored-women workers are domestic servants, the next largest groups being farm laborers and laundry operatives.

Of the Negro farmers, only one fifth are owners, contrasted with three fifths of white farmers. On the average, they operate smaller farms with cheaper land and buildings. Until recently, nearly half of all Negro farmers have been sharecroppers. This situation is being changed as many landlords are evicting their tenants and hiring them as day laborers. The sharecropping system is one under which the owner furnishes rations, clothing, and other necessities of life in addition to land, buildings, tools, livestock, and seed. The landowner directs the work, keeps the accounts, and disposes of the crop. While a means of providing credit for impecunious Negroes, the system facilitates exploitation. An unscrupulous landlord can keep his sharecroppers constantly in debt, and the laws of some states forbid the tenant's leaving while he owes anything. This, together with the practice of arresting rural Negroes and compelling them to work for white men who pay their fines or assume the role of "voluntary probation officers," helps to perpetuate a status of virtual peonage for many.

In industry, Negroes have been handicapped by limited training in skilled trades, a general belief in their inability to perform technical tasks, a reputation for shiftlessness, and the hostility of trade-unions. As a result, colored workers are restricted chiefly to unskilled trades. In any line of work, they are likely to receive lower wages than those of white employees. Even W.P.A. (work relief) wages have been lower in areas where Negroes predominate than in sections where they are a small minority. While the American Federation of Labor has professed an opposition to racial discrimination, its member organizations have not in general shown themselves friendly

to Negroes. A large number of them specifically exclude Negroes by constitutional provisions. Others discourage rather than forbid the admission of colored workers. Still others admit Negroes, but only to separate locals. A few accept colored members, but bar them from holding office. The United Mine Workers and the garmentworkers' unions are among the few that admit Negroes on terms of equality with white persons. It should be noted that these last-named are industrial unions, two of them affiliated with the C.I.O. (Congress of Industrial Organizations). The older craft unions affiliated with the A.F. of L. have usually refused or restricted membership of Negroes.

Negroes are particularly hampered in entering and carrying on the professions. There are few professional schools especially for them; they are not admitted to white schools in the South; and they find various difficulties in the way of attending professional schools in the North. Often they are not wanted; commonly the cost is beyond their ability to pay; internships are hard to arrange. There are relatively more clergymen among Negroes than among whites, but most of them are men of very limited education. Their teachers make a somewhat better showing, especially in cities. They have some able physicians, dentists, and nurses, but the numbers of these are pitifully small. In most instances, Negroes are excluded from professional associations to which white people belong. Their own organizations are smaller, less ably led, less well financed, and, in general, less able to serve their needs and interests.

Other indications of the low economic status of Negroes are the small number of independent business enterprises of which they are proprietors, the small percentage of home ownership, and the low valuation of their houses. The unemployment-relief census of October, 1933, showed 9.5 per cent of the white population and 17.8 of Negroes to be receiving relief at that time. But, contrary to expectation, an analysis of urban workers on relief in 1934 showed little difference in the duration of unemployment of white and colored.[5] In general, however, statistical data support common observation that Negroes have low incomes and little wealth, work chiefly at menial tasks, and are commonly excluded from organized economic groups.

Educational Opportunities and Neglect[6]

During the early days of American history, there was little formal schooling for either white or black.

[4] Data are drawn principally from *Negroes in the United States, 1920–1932* (U. S. Bureau of the Census [1935]); E. B. Reuter, *The American Race Problem* (1938).

[5] *Urban Workers on Relief* (Works Progress Administration, Research Monograph IV [1936]), pp. 89–90.

[6] Data are drawn principally from the *Biennial Survey of Education, 1932–34* (U. S. Office of Education [1935]); *Negroes in the United States, 1920–1932* (U. S. Bureau of the Census [1935]); and E. B. Reuter, *The American Race Problem* (1938).

Throughout the period of slavery, there continued to be very little for Negroes. But during and following the Civil War, various philanthropic organizations established schools for colored children. The Freedmen's Bureau, under the War Department, started others and assumed general supervision over Negro education. By 1870, it was able to report about 150,000 Negro children in school. Presently there appeared elementary, secondary, and collegiate institutions under the auspices of various denominational boards. They tended to stress the conventional, classical learning. But soon emphasis began to shift to industrial training, as at Hampton and Tuskegee. Between 1890 and 1914, there were established seventeen land-grant schools. Public-school systems in the Southern states arose during the period of Reconstruction. At first, under pressure of the North, schools were "mixed," but, after the withdrawal of troops and readmission of the states, the races were separated. In the beginning, Negro schools were very inferior to white. This condition is still widely prevalent, but there has been much improvement.

At the present time, discrimination against Negroes manifests itself in a number of ways. The relative availability of education to the two races is indicated first in the length of the school term. In 1933–1934, in the seventeen states with separate schools, the average term for Negro schools was 142 days, contrasted with 164 days for white schools. At the same time, there were 44 pupils per teacher in Negro schools as against 33 in white schools. In 1929, the annual expenditure for teachers' salaries per pupil enrolled averaged $11.78 for the colored and $32.57 for the white. The per capita value of school property is much greater for whites than for Negroes, the ratio being sometimes as high as seven to one. Partly because the schools are less adequate and partly for other reasons, pupil status and educational attainments of Negroes are poorer than those of white persons. In 1933–1934, the ratio of school enrollment to the population of school age (7–13) was 0.826 for Negroes and 0.837 for whites, practically the same. But the average number of days attended was 111 for Negroes and 134 for white children. Of the Negro school children, 59.1 per cent were in grades one to three; only 6.6 per cent were in high school. Of the white children, only 38.6 per cent were in grades one to three, while 18.8 per cent were in high school. Hypothetically this might be attributed to differences in mental ability, but there is no good reason to believe intellectual differences are as great as these figures might suggest. Dropping out is to be attributed largely to lack of high-school facilities, distance between home and school, poverty, and other discouraging features of the situation. A final measure of the limited participation of Negroes in our educational system is the percentage of illiteracy. In 1930, this was 16.3 for Negroes, contrasted with 1.5 for native whites. This again might be charged to lower native ability, but the steady decline over the last thirty years indicates that it is more properly attributed to limited opportunity. During this period, Negro illiteracy has dropped from 44.5 per cent to 16.3, while native-white illiteracy has dropped from 4.6 per cent to 1.5.

Other Aspects of Segregation

Other aspects of segregation may be touched upon more briefly. The most obvious is residential segregation. This physical separation of the races limits their social contacts; but might be presumed to promote the development of neighborhood and community organization within each racial group. Whether or not this is really the case, we do not know. The main objections raised by Negroes to the districts within which they are often confined are that these areas are dilapidated, unhealthy, unsightly, and shared by the least acceptable white people. The Jim Crow laws pertaining to transportation are similarly annoying and humiliating.

Separate recreation facilities—parks, playgrounds, theaters, dance halls, young people's associations, and all the rest—might not be so hampering if the quality and adequacy of Negro agencies were on the same level as those open to white people. But this is not often the case. Moreover, opera, symphony concerts, and some other forms of high-class entertainment are almost inaccessible to Negroes. As to churches, 24 of the 213 religious bodies reported in the 1926 census were exclusively for Negroes. The great majority of Negroes who belong to any church are affiliated with one of these denominations. Almost the same percentages of whites and of Negroes are members of some church. But we know that great numbers of the colored churches are ill-equipped, poorly staffed, and limited in their program of religious, educational, and social activities. Hence, segregation actually implies deprivation.

It is notorious that Negroes are restricted in the matter of political activity. As slaves, they were obviously outside the party system and could take no part in government. Before the Civil War, free Negroes were generally forbidden to vote, to testify against white people, to serve on juries, to carry firearms, and to assemble freely. Such laws were adopted in Northern as well as in Southern states. Under the Reconstruction Act of 1867, Negroes voted and held office. After the period of chaos passed, the white leaders of the South felt impelled to restrict political activity to members of their own race, which they did through a number of devices such as "grandfather clauses," poll taxes, and tests of ability to read or interpret the constitution. Gradually, here and there, Negroes were permitted to vote. They always took an important part in the affairs of the Republican Party in the South. But in the late 1920's, the Republican Party sought to win Southern white men, and to accomplish this end pushed Negroes somewhat into the background. The Democratic Party has often assumed the right to restrict its membership to white men. Of course, they alone could vote in the Democratic primaries where public officials were really chosen, since the Republicans rarely had a chance to carry an election in the South. Nevertheless, there has been an increase in the Negroes' participation in political affairs, in the South as well as in the North.

Negroes have, of course, been debarred from holding office in the South since the Reconstruction period. But a small number have been elected to city councils, state legislatures, and to Congress, from Northern and Western states. A few have been made policemen and probation officers. Some have been appointed to Federal positions, but the *Negro Year Book* reports that their number has decreased during the past twenty-five years.

In court, the Negro has less chance for justice than has a white man. If he has a white "angel," he may get off very easily. Otherwise, he is more likely to be found guilty, likely to receive a heavier sentence, and, in general, to be more harshly dealt with. Usually, he may not serve on juries, although this occasionally happens.

Thus, by segregation as to residence, transportation, recreation, religion, politics, and government, Negroes are restricted in the range of social contacts, group memberships, and cultural participation.

Negro Reactions to Prejudice and Segregation

Negroes have displayed a variety of reactions to the social restrictions placed upon them. What is the relative frequency of each attitude, we do not know, but we can identify several distinct lines of thinking, feeling, and behaving. In the first place, many Negroes, especially in the rural South, appear to accept their situation without feeling, or at least without expectation of change. Whether they are really apathetic or merely inarticulate is hard to tell. At all events, they make little if any effort to alter their conditions of life. This general group of reactions seems to involve recognition of white superiority. Sometimes it includes imitation of the white people. The urge to be like white folk manifests itself variously, in the seeking of a mate who is lighter colored than oneself, dreaming of being white, and, in some cases, attempting to pass as white.

A second type of response to the interracial code is that of servility. This manifests itself in a whining, cajoling tone; in numerous forms of deference, such as tipping the hat, saying "Yes, sir, boss," and such; in telling white people what Negroes think they want to hear; in studying how to make white people comfortable in body and mind. Sometimes this "being a good Negro," or behaving in accordance with the conventional code, seems to be defensive, the avoiding of hurts to body or to pride.

Sometimes it seems to be a rather clever means of "working" white people. The external conduct is similar to that of the first type, but the attitudes are not necessarily so. Those of the first group are more passive forms of accommodation.

A third and very general reaction is that of escape through religion. If one is hampered in this world, perhaps he can escape all restrictions in heaven. Meanwhile, in the emotional experiences of the church service or the revival meeting, the oppressed find temporary release. This fact is believed to account for the important role of religion among American Negroes.

A less complete form of withdrawal from the difficult issues of race relations is that of Negro solidarity and ethnic pride. Some members of the group rationalize the advantage that lies in having obstacles to overcome. They glorify the attainments of Negroes in music, literature, painting, athletics, business, or the professions. They promote Negro fraternal orders, civic associations, churches, commercial establishments, and other groups and institutions. These various manifestations of racial pride and attempts at self-sufficiency have sometimes been described as a sort of Negro nationalism.

Superficially like the last type of response, but fundamentally different, is the effort to win the respect of white people for Negroes in new roles. This involves refusal to accept the status quo, and an attempt to demonstrate Negroes' capacity for something different. Such was the program of Booker Washington. He sought to teach his people how to take maximum advantage of the opportunities at their disposal and thereby win approval of the ruling race, not merely for achievements already demonstrated, but also for new ventures about to be undertaken. He advised taking one step at a time, conciliating the white people, but never losing sight of the goal—a maximum participation in American life.

Finally, there is the response of conflict. Under slavery, it took the forms occasionally of crimes against white persons and rarely of insurrection. After the Civil War, and under the leadership of scalawags and carpetbaggers, it involved extreme abuse of the Southern whites. More recently, it has shown itself in the denunciation of lynching, segregation, and peonage, in demands for civil liberties, and sometimes in joining the Communist Party. Those who take the lead in assailing the dominant race, decrying injustice, and insisting on their constitutional rights are frequently Northern mulattoes rather well educated and highly articulate. Some of this group used to accuse Booker Washington of "selling out the race." They press hard on the white conscience, "calling some to repentance," but alienating and antagonizing others.

As stated before, we are unable to report the relative frequency of these various reactions. Neither do we find ourselves in a position to evaluate them, except that to us it seems obvious that apathy, servility, and otherworldliness solve few problems on any but a temporary basis. Between Negro solidarity, interracial co-operation, and the steady pressing of demands, we have personal preferences, but no present ability to predict results.

Agencies and Programs for Increasing Social Participation of Negroes

All through this chapter, we have indicated ways in which the social participation of Negroes is being increased. The public schools are making an especially important contribution at the present time in passing on to colored children the cultural heritage of white America. The demand for Negro labor in Northern industries, especially marked between 1914 and 1929, has opened new worlds to many a black man and his family. Mention might also be made of the city-ward movement, both South and North, and the changing attitudes of white people throughout the country. But at this point, we may call special attention to a number of organizations whose primary or incidental purpose is to expand the social and cultural experience of colored people.

The National Association for the Advancement of Colored People was founded in 1909 to carry forward the struggle for the "civil, legal, economic, and political rights" of Negroes. It carries on investigations, publicizes its facts, conducts lawsuits, and lobbies for desired legislation. It protests against inadequate schools, housing, health conditions, opportunities for employment. It seeks to break down segregation, and aims at equality of opportunity for all.

The National Urban League was established in 1910 with a somewhat more conciliatory program than that of the N.A.A.C.P. However, it too has engaged in fact finding, and publicizing the results of its investigations. It has sought to develop job opportunities; it has helped Negro laborers to organize; it has promoted neighborhood associations; it has initiated and demonstrated the usefulness of various kinds of social service for Negroes. It is perhaps natural that it should seem to have a larger measure of co-operation from white people than the N.A.A.C.P. has. However, both organizations have officers chosen from both races.

In many cities, interracial conferences have been organized. These are somewhat informal bodies holding meetings at various intervals to promote intergroup discussion of common problems. They stress the proposition that sickness, crime, and ignorance in any part of the population are menaces to everyone, being no respecters of race lines. Committees and discussion groups have been set up by the Christian Associations, community chests, and others. Certain fighting organizations have given special attention to the interests of Negroes and have given Negroes membership on terms of equality with whites. Such are the American Civil Liberties Union, Workers' Alliance of America, Southern Tenant Farmers' Union, the Socialist and Communist parties, and, to a certain extent, the C.I.O. We do not know how useful each of these organizations may be in getting a larger place in the sun for colored people, but the very admission of Negroes to their ranks is itself a significant bit of social participation.

SUGGESTED READINGS

Chicago Commission on Race Relations, *The Negro in Chicago*. Chicago: The University of Chicago Press, 1922. A survey of circumstances underlying the Chicago race riot of 1919.

Dollard, John, *Class and Caste in a Southern Town*. New Haven: Yale University Press, 1937. An intensive study of race relations in a single Community, under the auspices of the Yale Institute of Human Relations. Sociological and psychiatric techniques are here combined.

Doyle, Bertram W., *The Etiquette of Race Relations in the South*. Chicago: The University of Chicago Press, 1937. An examination of various ways in which the race line is drawn.

Du Bois, W. E. Burghardt, *The Souls of Black Folk*. Chicago: A. C. McClurg and Company, 1922. A collection of brilliant essays and sketches by a Negro leader.

Johnson, Charles S., *The Negro in American Civilization*. New York: Henry Holt and Company, 1930. A general work by a Negro sociologist.

Johnson, James Weldon, *The Autobiography of an Ex-Coloured Man*. New York: Alfred A. Knopf, Inc., 1927. A striking piece of fiction by a Negro author.

Reuter, Edward B., *The American Race Problem*. New York: Thomas Y. Crowell Company, 1927 and 1938. Probably the most satisfactory textbook in this field.

4

Black Reconstruction in America, 1860-1880

W.E.B. DU BOIS

This is a classic work by W.E.B. Du Bois, originally published in 1935. The work focuses on how blacks attempted to democratize and modernize the South after the Civil War period, and how racism was utilized to stop this social movement. The chapter excerpted here, 'The White Worker', explains the emerging relationship between white workers, industrialization, and race. Du Bois explains that the role of the white working class is a critical one during this period if the black-led movement for social and economic reform is to succeed in the South. But, prescient of the more recent scholarship on white skin privileges in the United States, Du Bois shows how the white working class succumbed to racism during this period. Du Bois discusses how racism is molded fundamentally by economic forces seeking to maintain positions of wealth and power.

The White Worker

How America became the laborer's Promised Land; and flocking here from all the world the white workers competed with black slaves, with new floods of foreigners, and with growing exploitation, until they fought slavery to save democracy and then lost democracy in a new and vaster slavery

The opportunity for real and new democracy in America was broad. Political power was at first as usual confined to property holders and an aristocracy of birth and learning. But it was never securely based on land. Land was free and both land and property were possible to nearly every thrifty worker. Schools began early to multiply and open their doors even to the poor laborer. Birth began to

count for less and less and America became to the world a land of opportunity. So the world came to America, even before the Revolution, and afterward during the nineteenth century, nineteen million immigrants entered the United States.

The new labor that came to the United States, while it was poor, used to oppression and accustomed to a low standard of living, was not willing, after it reached America, to regard itself as a permanent laboring class and it is in the light of this fact that the labor movement among white Americans must be studied. The successful, well-paid American laboring class formed, because of its property and ideals, a petty bourgeoisie ready always to join capital in exploiting common labor, white and black, foreign and native. The more energetic and thrifty among the immigrants caught the prevalent American idea that here labor could become emancipated from the necessity of continuous toil and that an increasing proportion could join the class of exploiters, that is of those who made their income chiefly by profit derived through the hiring of labor.

Abraham Lincoln expressed this idea frankly at Hartford, in March, 1860. He said:

"I am not ashamed to confess that twenty-five years ago I was a hired laborer, mauling rails, at work on a flat boat—just what might happen to any poor man's son." Then followed the characteristic philosophy of the time: "I want every man to have his chance—and I believe a black man is entitled to it— in which he can better his condition—when he may look forward and hope to be a hired laborer this year and the next, work for himself afterward, and finally to hire men to work for him. That is the true system."

He was enunciating the widespread American idea of the son rising to a higher economic level than the father; of the chance for the poor man to accumulate wealth and power, which made the European doctrine of a working class fighting for the elevation of all workers seem not only less desirable but even less possible for average workers than they had formerly considered it.

These workers came to oppose slavery not so much from moral as from the economic fear of being reduced by competition to the level of slaves. They wanted a chance to become capitalists; and they found that chance threatened by the competition of a working class whose status at the bottom of the economic structure seemed permanent and inescapable. At first, black slavery jarred upon them, and as early as the seventeenth century German immigrants to Pennsylvania asked the Quakers innocently if slavery was in accord with the Golden Rule. Then, gradually, as succeeding immigrants were thrown in difficult and exasperating competition with black workers, their attitude changed. These were the very years when the white worker was beginning to understand the early American doctrine of wealth and property; to escape the liability of imprisonment for debt, and even to gain the right of universal suffrage. He found pouring into cities like New York and Philadelphia emancipated Negroes with low standards of living, competing for the jobs which the lower class of unskilled white laborers wanted.

For the immediate available jobs, the Irish particularly competed and the employers because of race antipathy and sympathy with the South did not wish to increase the number of Negro workers, so long as the foreigners worked just as cheaply. The foreigners in turn blamed blacks for the cheap price of labor. The result was race war; riots took place which were at first simply the flaming hostility of groups of laborers fighting for bread and butter; then they turned into race riots. For three days in Cincinnati in 1829, a mob of whites wounded and killed free Negroes and fugitive slaves and destroyed property. Most of the black population, numbering over two thousand, left the city and

trekked to Canada. In Philadelphia, 1828-1840, a series of riots took place which thereafter extended until after the Civil War. The riot of 1834 took the dimensions of a pitched battle and lasted for three days. Thirty-one houses and two churches were destroyed. Other riots took place in 1835 and 1838 and a two days' riot in 1842 caused the calling out of the militia with artillery.

In the forties came quite a different class, the English and German workers, who had tried by organization to fight the machine and in the end had to some degree envisaged the Marxian reorganization of industry through trade unions and class struggle. The attitude of these people toward the Negro was varied and contradictory. At first they blurted out their disapprobation of slavery on principle. It was a phase of all wage slavery. Then they began to see a way out for the worker in America through the free land of the West. Here was a solution such as was impossible in Europe: plenty of land, rich land, land coming daily nearer its own markets, to which the worker could retreat and restore the industrial balance ruined in Europe by the expropriation of the worker from the soil. Or in other words, the worker in America saw a chance to increase his wage and regulate his conditions of employment much greater than in Europe. The trade unions could have a material backing that they could not have in Germany, France or England. This thought, curiously enough, instead of increasing the sympathy for the slave turned it directly into rivalry and enmity.

The wisest of the leaders could not clearly envisage just how slave labor in conjunction and competition with free labor tended to reduce all labor toward slavery. For this reason, the union and labor leaders gravitated toward the political party which opposed tariff bounties and welcomed immigrants, quite forgetting that this same Democratic party had as its backbone the planter oligarchy of the South with its slave labor.

The new immigrants in their competition with this group reflected not simply the general attitude of America toward colored people, but particularly they felt a threat of slave competition which these Negroes foreshadowed. The Negroes worked cheaply, partly from custom, partly as their only defense against competition. The white laborers realized that Negroes were part of a group of millions of workers who were slaves by law, and whose competition kept white labor out of the work of the South and threatened its wages and stability in the North. When now the labor question moved West, and became a part of the land question, the competition of black men became of increased importance. Foreign laborers saw more clearly than most Americans the tremendous significance of free land in abundance, such as America possessed, in open contrast to the land monopoly of Europe. But here on this free land, they met not only a few free

Negro workers, but the threat of a mass of slaves. The attitude of the West toward Negroes, therefore, became sterner than that of the East. Here was the possibility of direct competition with slaves, and the absorption of Western land into the slave system. This must be resisted at all costs, but beyond this, even free Negroes must be discouraged. On this the Southern poor white immigrants insisted.

In the meantime, the problem of the black worker had not ceased to trouble the conscience and the economic philosophy of America. That the worker should be a bond slave was fundamentally at variance with the American doctrine, and the demand for the abolition of slavery had been continuous since the Revolution. In the North, it had resulted in freeing gradually all of the Negroes. But the comparatively small number of those thus freed was being augmented now by fugitive slaves from the South, and manifestly the ultimate plight of the black worker depended upon the course of Southern slavery. There arose, then, in the thirties, and among thinkers and workers, a demand that slavery in the United States be immediately abolished.

This demand became epitomized in the crusade of William Lloyd Garrison, himself a poor printer, but a man of education, thought and indomitable courage. This movement was not primarily a labor movement or a matter of profit and wage. It simply said that under any condition of life, the reduction of a human being to real estate was a crime against humanity of such enormity that its existence must be immediately ended. After emancipation there would come questions of labor, wage and political power. But now, first, must be demanded that ordinary human freedom and recognition of essential manhood which slavery blasphemously denied. This philosophy of freedom was a logical continuation of the freedom philosophy of the eighteenth century which insisted that Freedom was not an End but an indispensable means to the beginning of human progress and that democracy could function only after the dropping of feudal privileges, monopoly and chains.

The propaganda which made the abolition movement terribly real was the Fugitive Slave—the piece of intelligent humanity who could say: I have been owned like an ox. I stole my own body and now I am hunted by law and lash to be made an ox again. By no conception of justice could such logic be answered. Nevertheless, at the same time white labor, while it attempted no denial but even expressed faint sympathy, saw in this fugitive slave and in the millions of slaves behind him, willing and eager to work for less than current wage, competition for their own jobs. What they failed to comprehend was that the black man enslaved was an even more formidable and fatal competitor than the black man free.

Here, then, were two labor movements: the movement to give the black worker a minimum legal status which would enable him to sell his own labor, and another movement which proposed to increase the wage and better the condition of the working class in America, now largely composed of foreign immigrants, and dispute with the new American capitalism the basis upon which the new wealth was to be divided. Broad philanthropy and a wide knowledge of the elements of human progress would have led these two movements to unite and in their union to become irresistible. It was difficult, almost impossible, for this to be clear to the white labor leaders of the thirties. They had their particularistic grievances and one of these was the competition of free Negro labor. Beyond this they could easily vision a new and tremendous competition of black workers after all the slaves became free. What they did not see nor understand was that this competition was present and would continue and would be emphasized if the Negro continued as a slave worker. On the other hand, the Abolitionists did not realize the plight of the white laborer, especially the semi-skilled and unskilled worker.

While the Evans brothers, who came as labor agitators in 1825, had among their twelve demands "the abolition of chattel slavery," nevertheless, George was soon convinced that freedom without land was of no importance. He wrote to Gerrit Smith, who was giving land to Negroes, and said:

"I was formerly, like yourself, sir, a very warm advocate of the abolition of slavery. This was before I saw that there was *white* slavery. Since I saw this, I have materially changed my views as to the means of abolishing Negro slavery. I now see, clearly, I think, that to give the landless black the privilege of changing masters now possessed by the landless *white* would hardly be a benefit to him in exchange for his surety of support in sickness and old age, although he is in a favorable climate. If the Southern form of slavery existed at the North, I should say the black would be a great loser by such a change."[1]

At the convention of the New England anti-slavery society in 1845, Robert Owen, the great champion of coöperation, said he was opposed to Negro slavery, but that he had seen worse slavery in England than among the Negroes. Horace Greeley said the same year: "If I am less troubled concerning the slavery prevalent in Charleston or New Orleans, it is because I see so much slavery in New York which appears to claim my first efforts."

Thus despite all influences, reform and social uplift veered away from the Negro. Brisbane, Channing, Owen and other leaders called a National Reform Association to meet in New York in May, 1845. In October, Owen's "World Conference" met. But they hardly mentioned slavery. The Abolitionists did join a National Industrial Congress which met around 1845-1846. Other labor leaders were openly hostile toward the abolitionist movement, while the movement for free land increased.

Thus two movements—Labor-Free Soil, and Abolition, exhibited fundamental divergence instead of becoming one great party of free labor and free land. The Free Soilers stressed the difficulties of even the free laborer getting hold of the land and getting work in the great congestion which immigration had brought; and the abolitionists stressed the moral wrong of slavery. These two movements might easily have coöperated and differed only in matters of emphasis; but the trouble was that black and white laborers were competing for the same jobs just of course as all laborers always are. The immediate competition became open and visible because of racial lines and racial philosophy and particularly in Northern states where free Negroes and fugitive slaves had established themselves as workers, while the ultimate and overshadowing competition of free and slave labor was obscured and pushed into the background. This situation, too, made extraordinary reaction, led by the ignorant mob and fomented by authority and privilege; abolitionists were attacked and their meeting places burned; women suffragists were hooted; laws were proposed making the kidnaping of Negroes easier and disfranchising Negro voters in conventions called for purposes of "reform."

The humanitarian reform movement reached its height in 1847-1849 amid falling prices, and trade unionism was at a low ebb. The strikes from 1849-1852 won the support of Horace Greeley, and increased the labor organizations. Labor in eastern cities refused to touch the slavery controversy, and the control which the Democrats had over the labor vote in New York and elsewhere increased this tendency to ignore the Negro, and increased the division between white and colored labor. In 1850, a Congress of Trade Unions was held with 110 delegates. They stressed land reform but said nothing about slavery and the organization eventually was captured by Tammany Hall. After 1850 unions composed of skilled laborers began to separate from common laborers and adopt a policy of closed shops and a minimum wage and excluded farmers and Negroes. Although this movement was killed by the panic of 1857, it eventually became triumphant in the eighties and culminated in the American Federation of Labor which today allows any local or national union to exclude Negroes on any pretext.

Other labor leaders became more explicit and emphasized race rather than class. John Campbell said in 1851: "Will the white race ever agree that blacks shall stand beside us on election day, upon the rostrum, in the ranks of the army, in our places of amusement, in places of public worship, ride in the same coaches, railway cars, or steamships? Never! Never! or is it natural, or just, that this kind of equality should exist? God never intended it; had he so willed it, he would have made all one color."[2]

New labor leaders arrived in the fifties. Hermann Kriege and Wilhelm Weitling left their work in Germany, and their friends Marx and Engels, and came to America, and at the same time came tens of thousands of revolutionary Germans. The Socialist and Communist papers increased. Trade unions increased in power and numbers and held public meetings. Immediately, the question of slavery injected itself, the question of abolition.

Kriege began to preach land reform and free soil in 1846, and by 1850 six hundred American papers were supporting his program. But Kriege went beyond Evans and former leaders and openly repudiated abolition. He declared in 1846:

"That we see in the slavery question a property question which cannot be settled by itself alone. That we should declare ourselves in favor of the abolitionist movement if it were our intention to throw the Republic into a state of anarchy, to extend the competition of 'free workingmen' beyond all measure, and to depress labor itself to the last extremity. That we could not improve the lot of our 'black brothers' by abolition under the conditions prevailing in modern society, but make infinitely worse the lot of our 'white brothers.' That we believe in the peaceable development of society in the United States and do not, therefore, here at least see our only hope in condition of the extremest degradation. That we feel constrained, therefore, to oppose Abolition with all our might, despite all the importunities of sentimental philistines and despite all the poetical effusions of liberty-intoxicated ladies."[3]

Wilhelm Weitling, who came to America the following year, 1847, started much agitation but gave little attention to slavery. He did not openly side with the slaveholder, as Kriege did; nevertheless, there was no condemnation of slavery in his paper. In the first German labor conference in Philadelphia, under Weitling in 1850, a series of resolutions were passed which did not mention slavery. Both Kriege and Weitling joined the Democratic party and numbers of other immigrant Germans did the same thing, and these workers, therefore, became practical defenders of slavery. Doubtless, the "Know-Nothing" movement against the foreign-born forced many workers into the Democratic party, despite slavery.

The year 1853 saw the formation of the Arbeiterbund, under Joseph Weydemeyer, a friend of Karl Marx. This organization advocated Marxian socialism but never got a clear attitude toward slavery. In 1854, it opposed the Kansas-Nebraska bill because "Capitalism and land speculation have again been favored at the expense of the mass of the people," and "This bill withdraws from or makes unavailable in a future homestead bill vast tracts of territory," and "authorizes the further extension of slavery; but we have, do now, and shall continue to protest most emphatically against both white and black slavery."

Nevertheless, when the Arbeiterbund was reorganized in December, 1857, slavery was not mentioned. When its new organ appeared in April, 1858, it said that the question of the present moment was not the abolition of slavery, but the prevention of its further extension and that Negro slavery was firmly rooted in America. One small division of this organization in 1857 called for abolition of the slave trade and colonization of Negroes, but defended the Southern slaveholders.

In 1859, however, a conference of the Arbeiter-bund condemned all slavery in whatever form it might appear, and demanded the repeal of the Fugitive Slave Law. The Democratic and pro-slavery New York *Staats-Zeitung* counseled the people to abstain from agitation against the extension of slavery, but all of the German population did not agree.

As the Chartist movement increased in England, the press was filled with attacks against the United States and its institutions, and the Chartists were clear on the matter of slavery. Their chief organ in 1844 said: "That damning stain upon the American escutcheon is one that has caused the Republicans of Europe to weep for very shame and mortification; and the people of the United States have much to answer for at the bar of humanity for this indecent, cruel, revolting and fiendish violation of their boasted principle—that 'All men are born free and equal.'"

The labor movement in England continued to emphasize the importance of attacking slavery; and the agitation, started by the work of Frederick Douglass and others, increased in importance and activity. In 1857, George I. Holyoake sent an anti-slavery address to America, signed by 1,800 English workingmen, whom Karl Marx himself was guiding in England, and this made the black American worker a central text. They pointed out the fact that the black worker was furnishing the raw material which the English capitalist was exploiting together with the English worker. This same year, the United States Supreme Court sent down the Dred Scott decision that Negroes were not citizens.

This English initiative had at first but limited influence in America. The trade unions were willing to admit that the Negroes ought to be free sometime; but at the present, self-preservation called for their slavery; and after all, whites were a different grade of workers from blacks. Even when the Marxian ideas arrived, there was a split; the earlier representatives of the Marxian philosophy in America agreed with the older Union movement in deprecating any entanglement with the abolition controversy. After all, abolition represented capital. The whole movement was based on mawkish sentimentality, and not on the demands of the workers, at least of the white workers. And so the early American Marxists simply gave up the idea of intruding the black worker into the socialist commonwealth at that time.

To this logic the abolitionists were increasingly opposed. It seemed to them that the crucial point was the matter of freedom; that a free laborer in America had an even chance to make his fortune as a worker or a farmer; but, on the other hand, if the laborer was not free, as in the case of the Negro, he had no opportunity, and he inevitably degraded white labor. The abolitionist did not sense the new subordination into which the worker was being forced by organized capital, while the laborers did not realize that the exclusion of four million workers from the labor program was a fatal omission. Wendell Phillips alone suggested a boycott on Southern goods, and said that the great cause of labor was paramount and included mill operatives in New England, peasants in Ireland, and laborers in South America who ought not to be lost sight of in sympathy for the Southern slave.

In the United States shortly before the outbreak of the Civil War there were twenty-six trades with national organizations, including the iron and steel workers, machinists, blacksmiths, etc. The employers formed a national league and planned to import more workmen from foreign countries. The iron molders started a national strike July 5, 1859, and said: "Wealth is power, and practical experience teaches us that it is a power but too often used to oppress and degrade the daily laborer. Year after year the capital of the country becomes more and more concentrated in the hands of a few, and, in proportion as the wealth of the country becomes centralized, its power increases, and the laboring classes are impoverished. It therefore becomes us, as men who have to battle with the stern realities of life, to look this matter fair in the face; there is no dodging the question; let every man give it a fair, full and candid consideration, and then act according to his honest convictions. *What position are we, the mechanics of America, to hold in Society?"*

There was not a word in this address about slavery and one would not dream that the United States was on the verge of the greatest labor revolution it had seen. Other conferences of the molders, machinists and blacksmiths and others were held in the sixties, and a labor mass meeting at Faneuil Hall in Boston in 1861 said: "The truth is that the workingmen care little for the strife of political parties and the intrigues of office-seekers. We regard them with the contempt they deserve. We are weary of this question of slavery; it is a matter which does not concern us; and we wish only to attend to our business, and leave the South to attend to their own affairs, without any interference from the North."[4]

In all this consideration, we have so far ignored the white workers of the South and we have done this because the labor movement ignored them and the abolitionists ignored them; and above all, they were ignored by Northern capitalists and Southern planters. They were in many respects almost a forgotten mass of men. Cairnes describes the slave South, the period just before the war:

"It resolves itself into three classes, broadly distinguished from each other, and connected by no common interest—the slaves on whom devolves all the regular industry, the slaveholders who reap all its fruits, and an idle and lawless rabble who live dispersed over vast plains in a condition little removed from absolute barbarism."

From all that has been written and said about the ante-bellum South, one almost loses sight of about 5,000,000 white people in 1860 who lived in the South and held no slaves. Even among the two million slaveholders, an oligarchy of 8,000 really ruled the South, while as an observer said: "For twenty years, I do not recollect ever to have seen or heard these non-slaveholding whites referred to by the Southern gentleman as constituting any part of what they called the South."[5] They were largely ignorant and degraded; only 25% could read and write.

The condition of the poor whites has been many times described:

"A wretched log hut or two are the only habitations in sight. Here reside, or rather take shelter, the miserable cultivators of the ground, or a still more destitute class who make a precarious living by peddling 'lightwood' in the city....

"These cabins ... are dens of filth. The bed if there be a bed is a layer of something in the corner that defies scenting. If the bed is nasty, what of the floor? What of the whole enclosed space? What of the creatures themselves? Pough! Water in use as a purifier is unknown. Their faces are bedaubed with the muddy accumulation of weeks. They just give them a wipe when they see a stranger to take off the blackest dirt. ... The poor wretches seem startled when you address them, and answer your questions cowering like culprits."[6]

Olmsted said: "I saw as much close packing, filth and squalor, in certain blocks inhabited by laboring whites in Charleston, as I have witnessed in any Northern town of its size; and greater evidences of brutality and ruffianly character, than I have ever happened to see, among an equal population of this class, before."[7]

Two classes of poor whites have been differentiated: the mountain whites and the poor whites of the lowlands. "Below a dirty and ill-favored house, down under the bank on the shingle near the river, sits a family of five people, all ill-clothed and unclean; a blear-eyed old woman, a younger woman with a mass of tangled red hair hanging about her shoulders, indubitably suckling a baby; a little girl with the same auburn evidence of Scotch ancestry; a boy, and a younger child all gathered about a fire made among some bricks, surrounding a couple of iron saucepans, in which is a dirty mixture looking like mud, but probably warmed-up sorghum syrup, which with a few pieces of corn pone, makes their breakfast.

"Most of them are illiterate and more than correspondingly ignorant. Some of them had Indian ancestors and a few bear evidences of Negro blood. The so-called 'mountain boomer,' says an observer, 'has little self-respect and no self-reliance.... So long as his corn pile lasts the "cracker" lives in contentment, feasting on a sort of hoe cake made of grated corn meal mixed with salt and water and baked before the hot coals, with addition of what game the forest furnishes him when he can get up the energy to go out and shoot or trap it.... The irregularities of their moral lives cause them no sense of shame. ... But, notwithstanding these low moral conceptions, they are of an intense religious excitability.'"[8]

Above this lowest mass rose a middle class of poor whites in the making. There were some small farmers who had more than a mere sustenance and yet were not large planters. There were overseers. There was a growing class of merchants who traded with the slaves and free Negroes and became in many cases larger traders, dealing with the planters for the staple crops. Some poor whites rose to the professional class, so that the rift between the planters and the mass of the whites was partially bridged by this smaller intermediate class.

While revolt against the domination of the planters over the poor whites was voiced by men like Helper, who called for a class struggle to destroy the planters, this was nullified by deep-rooted antagonism to the Negro, whether slave or free. If black labor could be expelled from the United States or eventually exterminated, then the fight against the planter could take place. But the poor whites and their leaders could not for a moment contemplate a fight of united white and black labor against the exploiters. Indeed, the natural leaders of the poor whites, the small farmer, the merchant, the professional man, the white mechanic and slave overseer, were bound to the planters and repelled from the slaves and even from the mass of the white laborers in two ways: first, they constituted the police patrol who could ride with planters and now and then exercise unlimited force upon recalcitrant or runaway slaves; and then, too, there was always a chance that they themselves might also become planters by saving money, by investment, by the power of good luck; and the only heaven that attracted them was the life of the great Southern planter.

There were a few weak associations of white mechanics, such as printers and shipwrights and iron molders, in 1850-1860, but practically no labor movement in the South.

Charles Nordhoff states that he was told by a wealthy Alabaman, in 1860, that the planters in his region were determined to discontinue altogether the employment of free mechanics. "On my own place," he said, "I have slave carpenters, slave blacksmiths, and slave wheelwrights, and thus I am independent of free mechanics." And a certain Alfred E. Mathews remarks: "I have seen free white mechanics obliged to stand aside while their families were suffering for the necessaries of life, when the slave mechanics, owned by rich and influential men, could get plenty of work; and I have heard these same white mechanics breathe the most bitter curses against the institution of slavery and the slave aristocracy."

The resultant revolt of the poor whites, just as the revolt of the slaves, came through migration. And their migration, instead of being restricted, was freely encouraged. As a result, the poor whites left the South in large numbers. In 1860, 399,700 Virginians were living out of their native state. From Tennessee, 344,765 emigrated; from North Carolina, 272,606, and from South Carolina, 256,868. The majority of these had come to the Middle West and it is quite possible that the Southern states sent as many settlers to the West as the Northeastern states, and while the Northeast demanded free soil, the Southerners demanded not only free soil but the exclusion of Negroes from work and the franchise. They had a very vivid fear of the Negro as a competitor in labor, whether slave or free.

It was thus the presence of the poor white Southerner in the West that complicated the whole Free Soil movement in its relation to the labor movement. While the Western pioneer was an advocate of extreme democracy and equalitarianism in his political and economic philosophy, his vote and influence did not go to strengthen the abolition-democracy, before, during, or even after the war. On the contrary, it was stopped and inhibited by the doctrine of race, and the West, therefore, long stood against that democracy in industry which might have emancipated labor in the United States, because it did not admit to that democracy the American citizen of Negro descent.

Thus Northern workers were organizing and fighting industrial integration in order to gain higher wage and shorter hours, and more and more they saw economic salvation in the rich land of the West. A Western movement of white workers and pioneers began and was paralleled by a Western movement of planters and black workers in the South. Land and more land became the cry of the Southern political leader, with finally a growing demand for reopening of the African slave trade. Land, more land, became the cry of the peasant farmer in the North. The two forces met in Kansas, and in Kansas civil war began.

The South was fighting for the protection and expansion of its agrarian feudalism. For the sheer existence of slavery, there must be a continual supply of fertile land, cheaper slaves, and such political power as would give the slave status full legal recognition and protection, and annihilate the free Negro. The Louisiana Purchase had furnished slaves and land, but most of the land was in the Northwest. The foray into Mexico had opened an empire, but the availability of this land was partly spoiled by the loss of California to free labor. This suggested a proposed expansion of slavery toward Kansas, where it involved the South in competition with white labor: a competition which endangered the slave status, encouraged slave revolt, and increased the possibility of fugitive slaves.

It was a war to determine how far industry in the United States should be carried on under a system where the capitalist owns not only the nation's raw material, not only the land, but also the laborer himself; or whether the laborer was going to maintain his personal freedom, and enforce it by growing political and economic independence based on widespread ownership of land.

This brings us down to the period of the Civil War. Up to the time that the war actually broke out, American labor simply refused, in the main, to envisage black labor as a part of its problem. Right up to the edge of the war, it was talking about the emancipation of white labor and the organization of stronger unions without saying a word, or apparently giving a thought, to four million black slaves. During the war, labor was resentful. Workers were forced to fight in a strife between capitalists in which they had no interest and they showed their resentment in the peculiarly human way of beating and murdering the innocent victims of it all, the black free Negroes of New York and other Northern cities; while in the South, five million non-slaveholding poor white farmers and laborers sent their manhood by the thousands to fight and die for a system that had degraded them equally with the black slave. Could one imagine anything more paradoxical than this whole situation?

America thus stepped forward in the first blossoming of the modern age and added to the Art of Beauty, gift of the Renaissance, and to Freedom of Belief, gift of Martin Luther and Leo X, a vision of democratic self-government: the domination of political life by the intelligent decision of free and self-sustaining men. What an idea and what an area for its realization—endless land of richest fertility, natural resources such as Earth seldom exhibited before, a population infinite in variety, of universal gift, burned in the fires of poverty and caste, yearning toward the Unknown God; and self-reliant pioneers, unafraid of man or devil. It was the Supreme Adventure, in the last Great Battle of the West, for that human freedom which would release the human spirit from lower lust for mere meat, and set it free to dream and sing.

And then some unjust God leaned, laughing, over the ramparts of heaven and dropped a black man in the midst.

It transformed the world. It turned democracy back to Roman Imperialism and Fascism; it restored caste and oligarchy; it replaced freedom with slavery and withdrew the name of humanity from the vast majority of human beings.

But not without struggle. Not without writhing and rending of spirit and pitiable wail of lost souls.

They said: Slavery was wrong but not all wrong; slavery must perish and not simply move; God made black men; God made slavery; the will of God be done; slavery to the glory of God and black men as his servants and ours; slavery as a way to freedom—the freedom of blacks, the freedom of whites; white freedom as the goal of the world and black slavery as the path thereto. Up with the white world, down with the black!

Then came this battle called Civil War, beginning in Kansas in 1854, and ending in the presidential election of 1876—twenty awful years. The slave went free; stood a brief moment in the sun; then moved back again toward slavery. The whole weight of America was thrown to color caste. The colored world went down before England, France, Germany, Russia, Italy and America. A new slavery arose. The upward moving of white labor was betrayed into wars for profit based on color caste. Democracy died save in the hearts of black folk.

Indeed, the plight of the white working class throughout the world today is directly traceable to Negro slavery in America, on which modern commerce and industry was founded, and which persisted to threaten free labor until it was partially overthrown in 1863. The resulting color caste founded and retained by capitalism was adopted, forwarded and approved by white labor, and resulted in subordination of colored labor to white profits the world over. Thus the majority of the world's laborers, by the insistence of white labor, became the basis of a system of industry which ruined democracy and showed its perfect fruit in World War and Depression. And this book seeks to tell that story.

> Have ye leisure, comfort, calm,
> Shelter, food, love's gentle balm?
> Or what is it ye buy so dear
> With your pain and with your fear?
>
> The seed ye sow, another reaps;
> The wealth ye find, another keeps;
> The robes ye weave, another wears;
> The arms ye forge, another bears.
>
> PERCY BYSSHE SHELLEY

NOTES

1 Schlüter, *Lincoln, Labor and Slavery*, p. 66.

2 Campbell, *Negromania*, p. 545.

3 Schlüter, *Lincoln, Labor and Slavery*, pp. 72. 73.

4 Schlüter, *Lincoln, Labor and Slavery*, p. 135.

5 Schlüter, *Lincoln, Labor and Slavery*, p. 86.

6 Simkins and Woody, *South Carolina During Reconstruction*, p. 326.

7 Olmsted, *Seaboard Slave States*, p. 404.

8 Hart, *The Southern South*, pp. 34, 35.

5

An American Dilemma: The Negro Problem and Modern Democracy

GUNNAR MYRDAL

First published in 1944, *An American Dilemma* brought together the work of a multi-disciplinary team of scholars under the leadership of Swedish scholar Gunnar Myrdal. While many of its conclusions now seem limited and outdated, the report presented a radical challenge to existing thought on the 'Negro Problem', which Myrdal effectively redefined in his title.

The book takes issue with existing theories on racism, most of which were informed by what Myrdal called a 'fatalistic philosophy'. Racism should not be conceived as the product of historical inevitability or unchangeable mental attitudes. Even earlier sociological theories, in particular that of Robert E. Park, viewed racism as the product of a 'natural' causation and ignored the possibilities of change 'by conscious effort'. Myrdal offered a conception of racism that was dynamic: it changed in accordance with social and economic conditions; and, as such, it needs to be theorized in historical context. This context was produced by a combination of conscious design and social forces, choice and necessity. To understand it otherwise surrenders to a policy of 'do-nothing'.

In the extracts presented here, Myrdal explores the social bases of beliefs in 'the racial inferiority of Negroes' and the Negroes' functions the beliefs serve. They make clear that racism is not restricted to parochial values or region-specific attitudes: rather, it is a complex of beliefs and values, equal in magnitude and efficacy to the more palatable 'American Creed'.

BELIEFS SUPPORTING SOCIAL INEQUALITY

In attempting to understand the motivation of segregation and discrimination, one basic fact to be taken into account is, of course, that many Negroes, particularly in the South, are poor, uneducated, and deficient in health, morals, and manners; and thus not very agreeable as social companions. In the South the importance of this factor is enhanced by the great proportion of Negroes in the total population. It is enhanced also by the democratic structure of public institutions in America.[1] William Archer, who, among the English observers of the Negro problem in America, probably better than anyone else was able to withstand the influence of race prejudice, declares himself for separation in railroad traveling for this reason:

> It is the crowding, the swamping, the submerging of the white race by the black, that the South cannot reasonably be expected to endure.[2]

This point is, however, much more complicated. For one thing, there is a great class of Southern whites who are also poor, uneducated, coarse and dirty. They are traditionally given various epithets, all with the connotation of social inferiority: "crackers," "hill-billies," "clay-eaters," "rednecks," "peckerwoods," "wool hats," "trash," "low-downers," "no 'counts." White farm laborers, sharecroppers, the permanently unemployed, and a great proportion of textile workers and other unskilled laborers are considered to be in this submerged group of lower class whites. Their presence in the South does not help the Negroes, however. It is, rather, the very thing which raises the need for a sky-high color bar. This class of whites knows that upper class whites are disposed to regard them as "just as bad as niggers," and they know, too, that they have always been despised by the Negroes, who have called them "poor white trash," "mean whites," or "po' buckra." It is in their interest, on the one hand, to stress the fundamental equality among all white people, which was the explicit assumption of the slavery doctrine, and, on the other hand, the gulf between whites and Negroes. The rising Negroes became an assault on the status of these poor whites.

The very existence of whites in economic and cultural conditions comparable to those of the masses of Negroes thus becomes a force holding Negroes down. Most middle and upper class whites also get, as we shall find, a satisfaction out of the subserviency and humbleness of the lower class Negroes. As Embree points out: "The attitudes of the aristocrat and of the poor white, starting from opposite motives, often result in the same discrimination."[3] The ordinary vicious circle—that the actual inferiority of the Negro masses gives reason for discrimination against them, while at the same time discrimination forms a great encumbrance when they attempt to improve themselves—is, in the social sphere, loaded with the desire on the part of lower class whites, and also perhaps the majority of middle and upper class whites, that Negroes remain inferior.

This fact that a large class of whites is not much better off than the masses of Negroes, economically and culturally, while whole groups of Negroes are decidedly on a higher level—in this situation when a general segregation policy protecting *all* whites against *all* Negroes has to be justified—makes the beliefs in the racial inferiority of Negroes a much needed rationalization. We have studied the racial stereotypes from this very viewpoint earlier. We pointed out that the racial inferiority doctrine is beginning to come into disrepute with people of higher education and is no longer supported by the press or by leading public figures. As a result, racial beliefs supporting segregation are undoubtedly losing some of their axiomatic solidity even among the masses of white people, although they still play a dominant role in popular thinking.

A tendency to exaggerate the lower class traits of Negroes also is apparent. This would seem to meet the need for justification of the caste order. We are being told constantly that all Negroes are dirty, immoral and unreliable. Exceptions are mentioned, but in an opportunistic fashion those exceptions are not allowed to upset the absolutistic theses. The fact that the average white man seldom or never sees an educated Negro facilitates the adherence to the stereotypes. Even people who are modern enough not to regard these traits as biological and permanent find in them reasons to keep Negroes at a social distance. The feeling may be that Negroes have capacity but that it needs to be developed, and that takes a long time—"several centuries," it is usually said. Often it is argued that the low morals and the ignorance of Negroes are so prevalent that Negroes must be quarantined. It is said that at the present time any measure of social equality would endanger the standards of decency and culture in white society. It is also pointed out that Negroes are different in physical appearance even if they have the same basic mental capacity and moral propensities. These differences are claimed to be repugnant to the white man. Occasionally this repugnance is admitted to be an irrational reaction, as in the following comment by a young, middle class man of Savannah:

> You can't get a white man in the South to call them "Mr." I don't say "Mr." because it makes me feel uncomfortable. I know that's prejudice, but it's instinctive and not reasoning.[4]

Besides these beliefs centering around Negro inferiority, there are a great number of other popular thoughts arranged to justify social segregation. One such belief was mentioned in the opening section of this chapter—namely, that Negroes like to be separated, that they are happy in their humble status and would not like to be treated as equals. Another idea with the same function is that separation is necessary in order to prevent friction between the two groups. This thought is usually supported by the reflection that the whites "would not stand for"—or "would not *yet* stand for"—another social order. Segregation thus becomes motivated directly by the whites' will to segregate and by certain untested assumptions regarding the state of public opinion. Segregation and subordination of Negroes are also commonly supported by the consideration that they have "always been" subordinate and that it is part of the mores and social structure that they remain subordinate for a long time. A remark by a machine shop manager in Newport News will illustrate this point of view:

I explain it in this way. A mule is made to work; a horse is made for beauty. The Negro is the working man of the South. Plenty of Negroes here are much better than the whites. But as a class that is not as true for white people about being the workers.[5]

Earlier, and to some extent even today, this direct application of the conservative principle was bolstered with a religious sanction. Race prejudice is presented as "a deep-rooted, God-implanted instinct."[6] It is often said in the South that God did not create two distinct races without having some intention in so doing. This theological sanction may be illustrated by a remark by a state official in Arkansas:

> The Negro in his place is really an assistant in the South. He's what the Lord Almighty intended him to be, a servant of the people. We couldn't get along without them.[7]

This thought that Negro subordination is part of God's plan for the world has, however, never been uncontested. The Bible, especially the New Testament, is filled with passages supporting equality, and the heart of Christian teaching is to "love thy neighbor as thyself."

Two points need to be made about the beliefs mentioned thus far: First—with the exception of the racial and theological beliefs both of which are gradually losing out—they support segregation but not discrimination, not even that discrimination which arises out of segregation. Second, they do not support a wholesale segregation, for *some* Negroes are not educationally, morally, or occupationally inferior; *some* Negroes do not want to be segregated; and *some* whites feel no repugnance to the physical appearance of the Negro. If one held these beliefs alone, therefore, and were willing to act upon them, and if he were provided with relevant facts, he would not advocate complete segregation and would permit immediate social equality to some Negroes in their relations to some whites (at the same time he would want to restrict equality for some whites). Further, he would look forward to a time when segregation would be wiped out, and full equality permitted.[a] As this is not the attitude of most whites, we have an indication that those beliefs fundamentally are rationalizations of valuations.

It would, indeed, be possible to defend the caste order simply by arguing that it is in the white people's interests to keep the Negroes subordinate. Such a defense would be logically tight. It could not be challenged as an unscientific belief. Unlike the rationalizations mentioned in previous paragraphs, it need not look forward to an ultimate social equality as ideal. It differs from the other beliefs we have been considering also in that it demands discrimination primarily and segregation only incidentally.[8]

The remarkable thing, however, is that, *in America, social segregation and discrimination will practically never be motivated in this straightforward way as being in white people's interests.* Indeed, to judge from the discussion in all social classes of whites, and this is particularly true of the South, one is led to believe that such base and materialistic considerations never enter into their thoughts. The nearest approach one hears is oblique statements of the type: "This is a white man's country," or: "We've got to make these niggers work for us." Otherwise the matter is only touched by some liberal reformers who, interestingly enough, always try to prove to the whites that it is "in white people's own interest" to do away with this or that injustice against Negroes. I have become convinced that actually the interest motivation seldom explicitly and consciously enters the ordinary white man's mind. It is suppressed, as being in flagrant conflict with the American Creed and the Christian religion. But it is equally clear that most white people actually take good care of their interests and practice discrimination even when it is not required for segregation, and that segregation most often has the "function" of allowing a discrimination held advantageous to the whites.

Again a partial allegiance to the American Creed must be noted. Thomas P. Bailey talked about "the dissociation of a sectional personality."[9] The conflict between moral principles and actual conduct has its locus *within* persons; for this reason it will not be represented clearly in public discussion. The interests will have a part in setting the patterns of behavior and will give the emotional energy for the search for all the rationalizing beliefs we have mentioned. The Creed not only will prevent the interests from being explicitly mentioned and, indeed, from being consciously thought of, but will often qualify those rationalizing beliefs by hopes for improvement in Negro status toward greater equality and will actually also bend the behavior patterns considerably away from the crudest forms of outright exploitation.

But as yet we have not discussed the most powerful rationalization for segregation, which is the fear of amalgamation. It is this fear which gives a unique character to the American theory of "no social equality."

THE THEORY OF "NO SOCIAL EQUALITY"

In his first encounter with the American Negro problem, perhaps nothing perplexes the outside observer more than the popular term and the popular theory of "no social equality." He will be made to feel from the start that it has concrete implications and a central importance for the Negro problem in America. But, nevertheless, the term is kept vague and elusive, and the theory loose and ambiguous. One moment it will be stretched to cover and justify every form of social segregation and discrimination,

---

[a] Even if one felt that the Negro was repugnant in his physical appearance to some white men, scientific knowledge could reveal to him that antipathies of this sort could be removed, and new ones avoided.

and, in addition, all the inequalities in justice, politics and breadwinning. The next moment it will be narrowed to express only the denial of close personal intimacies and intermarriage. The very lack of precision allows the notion of "no social equality" to rationalize the rather illogical and wavering system of color caste in America.

The kernel of the popular theory of "no social equality" will, when pursued, be presented as a firm determination on the part of the whites to block amalgamation and preserve "the purity of the white race."[10] The white man identifies himself with "the white race" and feels that he has a stake in resisting the dissipation of its racial identity. Important in this identification is the notion of "the absolute and unchangeable superiority of the white race."[11] From this racial dogma will often be drawn the *direct* inference that the white man shall dominate in all spheres.[12] But when the logic of this inference is inquired about, the inference will be made *indirect* and will be made to lead over to the danger of amalgamation, or, as it is popularly expressed, "intermarriage."

It is further found that the ban on intermarriage is focused on white women. For them it covers both formal marriage and illicit intercourse. In regard to white men it is taken more or less for granted that they would not stoop to marry Negro women, and that illicit intercourse does not fall under the same intense taboo.[13] Their offspring, under the popular doctrine that maternity is more certain than paternity, become Negroes anyway, and the white race easily avoids pollution with Negro blood. To prevent "intermarriage" in this specific sense of sex relations between white women and Negro men, it is not enough to apply legal and social sanctions against it—so the popular theory runs. In using the danger of intermarriage as a defense for the whole caste system, it is assumed both that Negro men have a strong desire for "intermarriage,"[14] and that white women would be open to proposals from Negro men, *if* they are not guarded from even meeting them on an equal plane. The latter assumption, of course, is never openly expressed, but is logically implicit in the popular theory. The conclusion follows that the whole system of segregation and discrimination is justified. Every single measure is defended as necessary to block "social equality" which in its turn is held necessary to prevent "intermarriage."[15]

The basic role of the fear of amalgamation in white attitudes to the race problem is indicated by the popular magical concept of "blood." Educated white Southerners, who know everything about modern genetic and biological research, confess readily that they actually feel an irrational or "instinctive" repugnance in thinking of "intermarriage." These measures of segregation and discrimination are often of the type found in the true taboos and in the notion "not to be touched" of primitive religion. The specific taboos are characterized, further, by a different degree of

excitement which attends their violation and a different degree of punishment to the violator: the closer the act to sexual association, the more furious is the public reaction. Sexual association itself is punished by death and is accompanied by tremendous public excitement; the other social relations meet decreasing degrees of public fury. Sex becomes in this popular theory the principle around which the whole structure of segregation of the Negroes—down to disfranchisement and denial of equal opportunities on the labor market—is organized. The reasoning is this: "For, say what we will, may not all the equalities be ultimately based on potential social equality, and that in turn on intermarriage? Here we reach the real *crux* of the question."[16] In cruder language, but with the same logic, the Southern man on the street responds to any plea for social equality: "Would you like to have your daughter marry a Negro?"

This theory of color caste centering around the aversion to amalgamation determines, as we have just observed, the white man's rather definite rank order of the various measures of segergation and discrimination against Negroes. The relative significance attached to each of those measures is dependent upon their degree of expediency or necessity—in the view of white people —as means of upholding the ban on "intermarriage." In this rank order, (1) the ban on intermarriage and other sex relations involving white women and colored men takes precedence before everything else. It is the end for which the other restrictions are arranged as means. Thereafter follow: (2) all sorts of taboos and etiquettes in personal contacts; (3) segregation in schools and churches; (4) segregation in hotels, restaurants, and theaters, and other public places where people meet socially; (5) segregation in public conveyances; (6) discrimination in public services; and, finally, inequality in (7) politics, (8) justice and (9) breadwinning and relief.[17]

The degree of liberalism on racial matters in the white South can be designated mainly by the point on this rank order where a man stops because he believes further segregation and discrimination are not necessary to prevent "intermarriage." We have seen that white liberals in the South of the present day, as a matter of principle, rather unanimously stand up against inequality in breadwinning, relief, justice and politics. These fields of discrimination form the chief battleground and considerable changes in them are, as we have seen, on the way. When we ascend to the higher ranks which concern social relations in the narrow sense, we find the Southern liberals less prepared to split off from the majority opinion of the region. Hardly anybody in the South is prepared to go the whole way and argue that even the ban on intermarriage should be lifted. Practically all agree, not only upon the high desirability of preventing "intermarriage," but also that a certain amount of separation between the two groups is expedient and necessary to prevent it.

Even the one who has his philosophical doubts on the point must, if he is reasonable, abstain from ever voicing them. The social pressure is so strong that it would be foolish not to conform. Conformity is a political necessity for having any hope of influence; it is, in addition, a personal necessity for not meeting social ostracism.

T. J. Woofter, Jr., who again may be quoted as a representative of Southern liberalism, observes that "... unless those forms of separation which are meant to safeguard the purity of the races are present, the majority of the white people flatly refuse to coöperate with Negroes" and finds no alternative to "constant discontent and friction or amalgamation ..., except the systematic minimization of social contacts."[18] But when Woofter has made this concession in principle to the segregation system of the South, he comes out with demands which, in practice, would change it entirely. He insists that all other forms of segregation than "those ... which are meant to safeguard the purity of the races" be abolished, and that the administration of the system be just and considerate and, indeed, founded upon the consent of the ruled.[19]

> ... all that most Negroes see in separation is that it is a means to degrade, an opportunity to exploit them. So long as it presents this aspect to them, it will be galling and insulting, and they will oppose it. Stated positively, this means that, in the final analysis, if segregation is to be successfully maintained, it must not be confused with discrimination and must finally be approved by the colored people themselves as beneficial to race relations.[20]

Virginius Dabney, to quote another prominent Southern liberal, actually goes so far as to assert that "there is ... a growing conviction on the part of a substantial body of Southerners that the Jim Crow laws should be abolished,"[21] and argues that even if and in so far as the two population groups in the South should be kept apart, "the accommodations provided for Negroes should be identical with those provided for whites."[22]

It should be noted that neither Woofter nor Dabney takes up for discussion any segregation measure higher up on the white man's rank order than those imposed by the Jim Crow legislation. There they take their stand on the time-honored formula "separate, but equal," and insist only that separation should be rationally motivated, and that the constitutional precept of equality should be enforced.

CRITICAL EVALUATION OF THE "NO SOCIAL EQUALITY" THEORY

The sincerity of the average white person's psychological identification with the "white race" and his aversion to amalgamation should not be doubted; neither should his attitude that the upholding of the caste system, implied in the various segregation and discrimination measures, is necessary to prevent amalgamation. But the manner in which he constantly interchanges the concepts "amalgamation" and "intermarriage"—in the meaning of a white woman's marriage to, or sex relations with, a Negro man—is bewildering. Amalgamation both in the South and in the North is, and has always been, mainly a result, not of marriage, but of illicit sexual relations. And these illicit sex relations have in the main been confined to white men and colored women. It is further well known that Negro women who have status and security are less likely to succumb to sexual advances from white men.[23] Deprivations inflicted upon Negroes in the South must therefore be a factor tending to increase amalgamation rather than to reduce it. Together these facts make the whole anti-amalgamation theory seem inconsistent.

But here we have to recall the very particular definition of the Negro and white "races" in America. Since all mixed bloods are classified as Negroes, sex relations between white men and colored women affect only the Negro race and not the white race. From the white point of view it is not "amalgamation" in a crucial sense. From the same point of view the race of the father does not matter for the racial classification of a Negro child. The child is a Negro anyhow. Sex relations between Negro men and white women, on the other hand, would be like an *attempt* to pour Negro blood into the white race. It cannot succeed, of course, as the child would be considered a Negro. But the white woman would be absolutely degraded—which the white man in the parallel situation is not. She must be protected and this type of amalgamation prevented by all available means. This is, of course, only an extreme case of the morality of "double standards" between the sexes. It is slowly withering away, and white men are gradually also coming to be censured for relations with women of the other group. Still, there is in popular sentiment an abysmal difference between the two types of sexual relations.

The statement frequently made by whites in the South that there is an instinctive and ineradicable sexual repulsion between the two groups is doubtful, in view of the present genetic composition of the Negro people. Besides, if it were true, the insistence upon the whole equipage of measures for racial separation for preventing "intermarriage" would be unnecessary, even to the white Southerner.[24] Even the more general allegation that there is an inherent repulsion to personal intimacies and physical contact between the two groups is unfounded. The friendly behavior of Negro and white children untrained in prejudice and also the acceptability of physical contact with favorite servants are cases in point. There are no reasons brought forward to make it likely that there are sex differentials in this respect, so that white men should react differently from white women. This brings us to a consideration of the extent to which the anti-amalgamation doctrine is merely a rationalization of purely social demands, particularly those concerning social status.

We have already observed that the relative license of white men to have illicit intercourse with Negro women does not extend to formal marriage. The relevant difference between these two types of relations is that the latter, but not the former, does give social status to the Negro woman and does take status away from the white man. For a white woman both legal marriage and illicit relations with Negroes cause her to lose caste. These status concerns are obvious and they are serious enough both in the North and in the South to prevent intermarriage. But as they are functions of the caste apparatus which, in this popular theory, is itself explained as a means of preventing intermarriage, the whole theory becomes largely a logical circle.

The circular character of this reasoning is enhanced when we realize that the great majority of non-liberal white Southerners utilize the dread of "intermarriage" and the theory of "no social equality" to justify discriminations which have quite other and wider goals than the purity of the white race. Things are defended in the South as means of preserving racial purity which cannot possibly be defended in this way. To this extent we cannot avoid observing that *what white people really want is to keep the Negroes in a lower status.* "Intermarriage" itself is resented because it would be a supreme indication of "social equality," while the rationalization is that "social equality" is opposed because it would bring "intermarriage."

Not denying the partial reality of the white person's psychological identification with the "white race" and his serious concern about "racial purity," our tentative conclusion is, therefore, that more fundamentally the theory of "no social equality" is a rationalization, and that the demand for "no social equality" is psychologically dominant to the aversion for "intermarriage." The persistent preoccupation with sex and marriage in the rationalization of social segregation and discrimination against Negroes is, to this extent, an irrational escape on the part of the whites from voicing an open demand for difference in social status between the two groups for its own sake. Like the irrational racial beliefs, the fortification in the unapproachable regions of sex of the unequal treatment of the Negro, which this popular theory provides, has been particularly needed in this nation because of the strength of the American Creed. A people with a less emphatic democratic *ethos* would be more able to uphold a caste system without this tense belief in sex and race dangers.

The fixation on the purity of white womanhood, and also part of the intensity of emotion surrounding the whole sphere of segregation and discrimination, are to be understood as the backwashes of the sore conscience on the part of white men for their own or their compeers' relations with, or desires for, Negro women.[25] These psychological effects are greatly magnified because of the puritan *milieu* of America

and especially of the South. The upper class men in a less puritanical people could probably have indulged in sex relations with, and sexual day-dreams of, lower caste women in a more matter-of-course way and without generating so much pathos about white womanhood.[26] The Negro people have to carry the burden not only of the white men's sins but also of their virtues. The virtues of the honest, democratic, puritan white Americans in the South are great, and the burden upon the Negroes becomes ponderous.[27]

Our practical conclusion is that it would have cleansing effects on race relations in America, and particularly in the South, to have an open and sober discussion in rational terms of this ever present popular theory of "intermarriage" and "social equality," giving matters their factual ground, true proportions and logical relations. Because it is, to a great extent, an opportunistic rationalization, and because it refers directly and indirectly to the most touchy spots in American life and American morals, tremendous inhibitions have been built up against a detached and critical discussion of this theory. But such inhibitions are gradually overcome when, in the course of secularized education, people become rational about their life problems. It must never be forgotten that in our increasingly intellectualized civilization even the plain citizen feels an urge for truth and objectivity, and that this rationalistic urge is increasingly competing with the opportunistic demands for rationalization and escape.

There are reasons to believe that a slow but steady cleansing of the American mind is proceeding as the cultural level is raised. The basic racial inferiority doctrine is being undermined by research and education. For a white man to have illicit relations with Negro women is increasingly meeting disapproval. Negroes themselves are more and more frowning upon such relations. This all must tend to dampen the emotional fires around "social equality." Sex and race fears are, however, even today the main defense for segregation and, in fact, for the whole caste order. The question shot at the interviewer touching any point of this order is still: "Would you like to have your daughter (sister) marry a Negro?"

ATTITUDES AMONG DIFFERENT CLASSES OF WHITES IN THE SOUTH

Certain attitudes, common in the South, become more understandable when we have recognized that, behind all rationalizing stereotyped beliefs and popular theories, a main concern of the white man is to preserve social inequality for its own sake. One such attitude is the great sympathy so often displayed in the upper classes of Southern whites toward the "old time darky" who adheres to the patterns of slavery. The "unreconstructed aristocrat" after the Civil War believed with Carlyle that "[the Negro] is useful in God's creation only as a servant";[28] he remained paternalistic; he wanted to keep the Negroes dependent and resented their attempts to rise through education; he mistrusted the younger generation of Negroes; he had a gloomy outlook on the future of race relations. But he liked the individual Negro whom he knew personally and who conformed to the old relation of master-servant—who "stayed in his place."[29]

Even today this attitude helps to determine the relations between the two groups in rural districts.[30] It particularly forms the pattern of the relationship between employer and employee on the plantation and in household service. It is also the basis for the quasi-feudal use of white character witnesses for Negro offenders, and for the great leniency in punishing Negro offenders as long as they have not intruded upon white society. One is amazed to see how often, even today, white people go out of their way to help individual Negroes and how many of them still take it for granted that Negro cooks shall be allowed to pilfer food for their own families from the white man's kitchen. The other side of this paternalistic relation is, of course, that servants are grossly underpaid. But it is not to be denied that on this point there is—in the individual case—a break in the bitterness of caste relations. Negro beggars who make their appeal to this old relationship will often be amply and generously rewarded by white people who are most stingy in paying ordinary wages and who deprive Negro children of their share of the state appropriations for schools in order to provide for white children.[31]

This is a survival of slavery society, where friendliness is restricted to the individual and not extended to the group, and is based on a clear and unchallenged recognition from both sides of an insurmountable social inequality. There are obvious short-term gains in such relations for the Negroes involved.[32] The whites in the South always stress that they, and not the Northerners, like and love the Negro and that they provide for him. The conservative Negro leaders in the Booker T. Washington line—and occasionally the others also—have endorsed this claim by pronouncing that the "best people of the South" always could be counted among "the friends of the race."[33] "No reputable Southerner is half as bad as Senator Tillman talks," exclaimed Kelly Miller,[34] and even the most violent Negro-baiting politicians occasionally show great kindness toward the individual Negroes who are under their personal control.[35]

The paternalistic pattern becomes particularly cherished by the white men as it so openly denotes an aristocratic origin. This gives it its strength to survive. It is a sign of social distinction to a white man to stand in this paternalistic relation to Negroes. This explains why so much of the conversation in the Southern white upper and middle classes turns around the follies of Negro servants. *Their Negro dependents and their own relations to them play a significant role for white people's status in society.*

To receive this traditional friendliness on the part of Southern white upper class persons, a Negro has to be a lower class Negro and to behave as an humble servant. James Weldon Johnson observed:

> ... in fact, I concluded that if a coloured man wanted to separate himself from his white neighbours, he had but to acquire some money, education, and culture ... the proudest and fairest lady in the South could with propriety—and it is what she would most likely do—go to the cabin of Aunt Mary, her cook, if Aunt Mary was sick, and minister to her comfort with her own hands; but if Mary's daughter, Eliza, a girl who used to run around my lady's kitchen, but who has received an education and married a prosperous young coloured man, were at death's door, my lady would no more think of crossing the threshold of Eliza's cottage than she would think of going into a bar-room for a drink.[36]

When the Negro rises socially and is no longer a servant, he becomes a stranger to the white upper class. His ambition is suspected. He is disliked.

...

> It is easy for men to discount and misunderstand the suffering of harm done others. Once accustomed to poverty, to the sight of toil and degradation, it easily seems normal and natural; once it is hidden beneath a different color of skin, a different stature or a different habit of action and speech, and all consciousness of inflicting ill disappears.[37]

Under the old master-servant relationship, the white man's "understanding" of the Negro was not great, but with the disappearance of this relationship even this small amount of sympathetic knowledge declined. What remains is a technique of how to work Negroes and how to keep them "in their place," which is not a difficult task for a majority group which can dispose of all the social power instruments—economic, legal, political, and physical—and has made up its mind to use them for this purpose.[38] But insight into the thoughts and feelings of Negroes, their social organization and modes of living, their frustrations and ambitions is vanishing. Some white Southerners are aware of this fact. Baker reported that they were already so thirty years ago:

> I don't know how many Southern people have told me in different ways of how extremely difficult it is to get at the real feeling of a Negro, to make him tell what goes on in his clubs and churches or in his innumerable societies.[39]

The present author has often met the same revealing curiosity on the part of white Southerners. In spite of human curiosity, however, Southerners do not really seek to know the Negro or to have intimate contacts with him, and consequently their feelings toward Negroes remain hard.

On their side, Negroes in the South instantaneously become reserved and secretive when they are in company with "their own whites." I have also witnessed how submissiveness, laughter, and fluent talking—which are sometimes displayed by Negroes in accordance with the rural tradition of interracial formality—most of the time, in reality, are nothing but a mask behind which they conceal their true selves.[40] Robert R. Moton, when writing a book on *What the Negro Thinks*, for white people, confirms the growing seclusiveness of his group. The Negro "seldom tells all the truth about such matters," he point out, and adds: "a great deal of it may not find its way into this volume."[41] Baker drew the conclusion, after observing the Negro's deliberate secretiveness, that this was a major source of deteriorating race relations.

> The Negro has long been defensively secretive. Slavery made him that. In the past, the instinct was passive and defensive; but with growing education and intelligent leadership it is rapidly becoming conscious, self-directive and offensive. And right there, it seems to me, lies the great cause of the increased strain in the South.[42]

The Northerner also is ignorant about the Negro, but his ignorance is less systematic and, therefore, often less deep. As he is ordinarily less inhibited from looking upon the Negro as a normal human being, and as his observation of the Negro is not blinded by the etiquette, he is usually more cognizant of Negro attitudes and capacities and is more willing to lend a sympathetic ear to the Negro's plight. But he is much more ignorant of the conditions which the Negro faces. If the Southerner's whole race philosophy and even his kindliest thoughts are insulting to the new type of Negro emerging out of the cultural assimilation process, the Northerner is likely to insult him out of sheer ignorance. The average Northerner does not realize that to call a Negro woman a "Negress" is taken as an insult, and he does not understand in what high esteem the Negro holds the title "Mr." He does not see the discrimination under which the Negroes labor. Not knowing the patterns of violence and of laxness of law in the South, the Northerner does not comprehend the full reason for the Negroes' pathological bitterness and fear.

On his side, the Negro is inclined to be suspicious of the Northerner's good intentions and to retain in the North the cynical attitude and secretive manners that he has developed as a camouflage in the Southern race warfare. As a servant the Negro goes into middle and upper class homes even in the North and acquires a sort of knowledge about white people. But this knowledge is distorted, since it covers only the private life of the whites and not the public life. Seldom does a Negro know how white people on his own level live and think. In part, the Negro's ignorance is an effect of exclusion from white society. In part, it is the result of the Negro's having different interests and worries. He is preoccupied with Negro life and problems, and this makes him a little blind to the general American ones.

Mutual ignorance and the paucity of common interests is a barrier to, and a modifier of, social contact between even educated and liberal whites and Negroes in the North, even in the extraordinary circles where segregation and discrimination play no role. I have seen Negro and white social scientists together as friends and colleagues. But I know that when their minds meet it usually concerns some aspect of the Negro problem. The Negro is ordinarily not present—and if he is present, he is a stranger—when the whites meet to discuss more general problems. If this is true among liberal social scientists, it is still more true among prejudiced people in all classes. The Negro is an alien in America, and in a sense this becomes the more evident when he steps out of his old role of the servant who lives entirely for the comfort of his white superiors. Ignorance and disparity of interests, arising out of segregation and discrimination on the part of whites, increased by voluntary withdrawal and race pride on the part of Negroes, becomes itself an important element increasing and perpetuating isolation between the groups.

PRESENT DYNAMICS

Negroes adjust and have to adjust to this situation. They become conditioned to patterns of behavior which not only permit but call for discriminatory observance on the part of the whites. The people who live in the system of existing relations have to give it a meaning. The Negroes have the escape, however, that they can consider the system unjust and irrational and can explain it in terms of white people's prejudices, material interest, moral wrongness and social power. They can avoid contacts and in the unavoidable ones have a mental reservation to their servility. It becomes to them a sign of education and class to do so and thereby preserve their intellectual integrity. Many Negroes succeed in doing this, and their number is growing. *But the unfortunate whites have to believe in the system of segregation and discrimination and to justify it to themselves.* It cannot be made intelligible and defensible except by false assumptions, in which the whites force themselves to believe.

So the social order perpetuates itself and with it the sentiments and beliefs by which it must be expressed. The lower caste may with some exertion release themselves intellectually. The higher caste, on the contrary, is enslaved in its prejudices by its short-range interests. Without their prejudices, white people would have to choose between either giving up the caste system and taking the resultant social, political, and economic losses, or becoming thoroughly cynical and losing their self-respect. The whites feel the Negroes' resentment and suspect new attitudes. Formerly, the whites got some support for their false prejudices from the Negroes. This is becoming less and less true. Now they can hardly claim to "know their Negroes" and are forced to admit their ignorance. The social separation they asked for is becoming a reality. Thus the tragedy is not only on the Negro side.

But the system *is* changing, though slowly. Modern knowledge and modern industrial conditions make it cumbersome. The South is becoming "normalized" and integrated into the national culture. Like every other "normal" province, it is beginning to dislike being provincial. The world publicity around the Dayton trial, for instance, did much to censor fundamentalism in Southern religion. A great part of the region's peculiarities in its racial relations is becoming, even to the Southerner, associated with backwardness. The Southerner is beginning to take on an apologetic tone when he speaks of his attitude toward the Negro. To insist upon the full racial etiquette is beginning to be regarded as affectation.

The South has long eagerly seized upon every act of prejudice practiced against the Negro in the North and, indeed, all other social ills of the other region. The visitor finds even the average run of white Southerners intensely aware of the bad slum conditions in Northern metropolises and of the North's labor troubles. Even the Southern liberal has the habit of never mentioning a fault of the South without mentioning a corresponding condition in the North. Many a Northern visitor to the South gets the feeling that the South is "still fighting the Civil War." But, as Kelly Miller observed, the "you also" argument is never resorted to except in palliation of conduct that is felt to be intrinsically indefensible.[43]

Southerners travel and migrate and are visited by Northerners and Europeans. They listen to the radio[44] and read papers, magazines and books directed to the wider national audience. Southern writers—in social science, politics, and *belles-lettres* aspire to national recognition and not only provincial applause. The thesis that the region is poor and culturally backward, and that this is largely due to the presence of the Negroes and to the Southern Negro policy, has been for a long time developed by Southern authors. The average Southerner is beginning to feel the need for fundamental reforms. Many Southern newspapers have become liberal. Inter-racial work is beginning to be recognized as socially respectable.

The diffusion of scientific knowledge regarding race cannot be regionalized any more effectively than it can be segregated along a color line. Racial beliefs are becoming undermined, at least for the younger generation in the middle and upper classes. Most of them never reach the printing press or the microphone any more, as they are no longer intellectually respectable. The educated classes of whites are gradually coming to regard those who believe in the Negro's biological inferiority as narrow-minded and backward. When a person arrives at the point where he says that he knows his views are irrational but that "they are just instinctive" with him, he is beginning to retreat from these views.

The capital N in "Negro" is finding its way into the Southern newspapers as it earlier did into books. It is becoming a mark of education in the white South to speak of Negroes as "niggras" and not as "niggers"—a compromise pronunciation which still offends the Yankee Negro but is a great step from the Southern white man's traditional point of view. In Southern newspapers Negro problems and Negro activity even outside crime are beginning to be commented upon, not only to draw Negro subscribers, but also because these matters are actually found to be of some general community interest. Letters from Negroes are not infrequently printed and sometimes the content discussed with respect. It would be no great revolution, at least not in the Upper South, if a newspaper one morning carried a portrait of a distinguished Negro on the front page. In liberal newspapers in the Upper South, Negro pictures have already occasionally been printed in the back pages.

The educated, respectable, self-possessed Negro is to the average white Southerner not so often as earlier just the "smart nigger" or the "uppity nigger." As the South becomes urbanized and some Negroes rise in status, it is becoming increasingly impracticable and, in some relations, actually impossible to bracket all Negroes together and treat them alike. Social classes among Negroes are becoming recognized. Titles of respect, the offer to shake hands, permission to use the front door and other symbols of politeness are more and more presented to certain Negroes who have attained social success.

We must not exaggerate these signs of wear and tear on the Southern color bar. *"Social equality" is still a terribly important matter in the region. But it is not as important as it was a generation ago.* One needs only to compare the tremendous upheaval in the South when President Theodore Roosevelt in the first decade of the twentieth century had Booker T. Washington to a luncheon at the White House[45] with the relatively calm irritation the white South manifested in the 'thirties when President Franklin Roosevelt and his gallant lady did much more radical things. It even continued to vote for him. The South is surely changing.

But the changes themselves elicit race prejudice. From one point of view, Robert E. Park is right, of course, in explaining race prejudice as "merely an elementary expression of conservatism," as "the resistance of the social order to change." When the Negro moves around and improves his status, he is bound to stimulate animosity.[46] The white South was—and is—annoyed whenever the Negro showed signs of moving out of his "place." And the white North definitely became more prejudiced when hundreds of thousands of crude Southern Negroes moved in. But conditions for Negroes are improving, Southerners are being jolted out of their racial beliefs, and the group of white people interested in doing something positive for the Negro has grown. The increase in prejudice due to the rise of the Negro is a local and temporary phenomenon in both the North and South.

The Second World War is bound to influence the trends of prejudice and discrimination. At the time of revising this book (August, 1942) it is still too early to make a more definite prediction. It would seem though, that the War would tend to decrease social discrimination in the North. The equalitarian Creed has been made more conscious to the Northerners. Radio speeches and newspaper editorials keep on pointing to the inequalities inflicted upon the Negroes as a contradiction to the democratic cause for which America is fighting. There have been some incidents of racial friction in Detroit and other places but, generally speaking, race relations have rather improved. In New Jersey and other states the police and the courts have become more active in stamping out illegal discrimination in restaurants and other public places.

In the South, however, reports in the press as well as what we hear related by competent Negro and white observers point to a rising tension between the two groups. There seems to be an increased determination on the part of white Southerners to defend unchanged the patterns of segregation and discrimination. Even some Southern liberals fall in with the tendency toward a hardened white opinion. Mark Ethridge, former chairman of the President's Committee on Fair Employment Practice and editor of a liberal Southern newspaper, the Louisville Courier-Journal, declared at the Birmingham hearings of the F.E.P.C. in July, 1942, that:

> There is no power in the world—not even in all the mechanized armies of the earth, Allied and Axis— which could now force the Southern white people to the abandonment of the principle of social segregation. It is a cruel disillusionment, bearing the germs of strife and perhaps tragedy, for any of their [the Negroes'] leaders to tell them that they can expect it, or that they can exact it as the price of their participation in the war.[47]

There has been some friction between Negro soldiers and Southerners, and the South's old fear of the armed Negro is rising.

Much the same thing happened during the First World War. But this time the isolation between the two groups is more complete. White people in the South know less about Negroes and care less about them. This time the Negroes, on their side, are firmer in their protest, even in the South. And this time the North is likely to be more interested in what happens to race relations in the South.

NOTES

1 Referring to the Jim Crow arrangement in the railway system, William Archer remarks:

"Remember that the question is complicated by the American's resolute adherence to the constitutional fiction

of equality. As there are no 'classes' in the great American people, so there must be no first, second, or third class on the American railways. Of course, the theory remains a fiction on the railroad no less than in life. Everyone travels first class; but those who can pay for it may travel in classes higher than first, called parlour-cars, drawing-room cars, and so forth. The only real validity of the fiction, it seems to me, lies in the unfortunate situation it creates with regard to the negro. If our three classes (or even two) were provided on every train, the mass of the negro population would, from sheer economic necessity, travel third. It might or might not be necessary to provide separate cars on that level; but if it were, the discrimination would not be greatly felt by the grade of black folks it would affect. In the higher-class cars there would be no reasonable need for discrimination, for the number of negroes using them would be few in comparison, and personally unobjectionable. The essential elbow-room would seldom be lacking; conditions in the first and second class would be very much the same as they are at present in the North." (*Through Afro-America* [1910], pp. 72-73.)

2 *Idem.* "But elbow-room is just what the conditions of railway traveling preclude; wherefore I hold the system of separate cars a legitimate measure of defense against constant discomfort. Had it not been adopted, the South would have been a nation of saints, not of men. It is in the methods of its enforcement that they sometimes show themselves not only human but inhuman." (*Ibid.*, p. 72.)

3 Edwin R. Embree, *Brown America* (1933; first edition, 1931), p. 205.

4 Cited in Charles S. Johnson, *Patterns of Negro Segregation*, p. 207.

5 Quoted from *ibid.*, pp. 195-196. Similar remarks are: "We have always had caste in the world"; "I imagine the average [Negro] is probably happiest when he is waiting on white folks and wearing their old clothes." (See *idem.*)

6 William M. Brown, *The Crucial Race Question* (1907), p. 118.

7 Charles S. Johnson, *Patterns of Negro Segregation*, p. 195.

8 The full gamut of interest motives is suggested by John Dollard (*Caste and Class in a Southern Town* [1937], pp. 98-187) in his theory of gains. It should be noted that Dollard considers these gains—which he classifies as economic, sexual, and prestige—as a means of interpreting and ordering the facts of Negro-white relations in the South. He does not mean that the gains theory is held consciously and unqualifiedly by the majority of Southern whites who receive these gains from Negro subordination.

9 *Race Orthodoxy in the South* (1914), p. 48.

10 The popular theory usually does not reach the level of articles and books any more; even the recent scientific literature on the Negro problem is likely to avoid this central notion. Thomas P. Bailey, a Mississippi professor writing just before the First World War, gives perhaps the clearest pronouncement in print of the prevalent view:

"Some representatives of the humanitarian group feel it difficult to understand why an illiterate and even vicious white man should object to dining with a highly cultured negro gentleman. To them the attitude of the 'low' white man seems essentially illogical and absurd; but it is not so to the men who know the 'low-grade' white man from the *inside*. The whole picture changes when one knows 'what it is about.' *Social attitudes at bottom are concerned with marriage*, and all it stands for. Now, race conscience may prevent the enlightened humanitarian from encouraging in any way the interbreeding of the two races. Race-pride will deter the average man who is willing to acknowledge the excellence of certain individual negroes. *But may it not require race enmity to prevent the amalgamation* of the 'lower' grades of the higher race with the higher grades of the lower race?" (*Op. cit.*, pp. 11-12; second and third italics ours.)

11 Thomas N. Page, *The Negro: The Southerner's Problem* (1904), p. 292. See also Chapter 3, Section 3, and Chapter 4. Under the influence of modern research this doctrine is in process of disappearing from the literature but it lives on in the conviction of white people. It has even today the gist exemplified by the quotation in the text.

12 Again the prevalent sentiment is best exemplified by a citation of old literature. The rhetorical intensity of the following paragraphs from Henry W. Grady gives something of the emotional tone of even present-day popular views:

"But the supremacy of the white race of the South must be maintained forever, and the domination of the negro race resisted at all points and at all hazards, because the white race is the superior race. This is the declaration of no new truth; it has abided forever in the marrow of our bones and shall run forever with the blood that feeds Anglo-Saxon hearts." (*Op. cit.*, p. 104.)

"Standing in the presence of this multitude, sobered with the responsibility of the message I deliver to the young men of the South, I declare that the truth above all others to be worn unsullied and sacred in your hearts, to be surrendered to no force, sold for no price, compromised in no necessity, but cherished and defended as the convenant of your prosperity, and the pledge of peace to your children, is, that the white race must dominate forever in the South, because it is the white race, and superior to that race with which its supremacy is threatened." (*Ibid.*, pp. 107-108.)

13 See Chapter 3, Section 2. James Weldon Johnson observes that in the South "... a white gentleman may not eat with a colored person without the danger of serious loss of social prestige; yet he may sleep with a colored person without incurring the risk or any appreciable damage to his reputation," and concludes, "Social equality signifies a series of far-flung barriers against amalgamation of the two races; except so far as it may come about by white men with colored women." (*Along This Way*, pp. 312-313.)

14 "The intelligent Negro may understand what social equality truly means, but to the ignorant and brutal young Negro, it signifies but one thing: the opportunity to enjoy, equally with white men, the privilege of cohabiting with white women. This the whites of the South understand; and if it were understood abroad, it would serve to explain some things which have not been understood hitherto. It

will explain, in part, the universal and furious hostility of the South to even the least suggestion of social equality." (Page, *op. cit.*, pp. 112-113.)

15 "Even the most liberal Whites in the community claim that the equality for which the Negroes ask is not possible without the 'social equality'—the intermingling and intermarriage—they so deeply fear. They also hint that the Negroes 'unconsciously' do desire this sort of social equality." (Hortense Powdermaker, *After Freedom* [1939], p. 350.)

16 Bailey, *op. cit.*, p. 42.

17 It so happens that Negroes have an interest in being released from segregation and discrimination in a rank order just the opposite of the whites' expressed rank order of having them retained. This is a principal fact in all attempts to change and reform race relations.

18 *The Basis of Racial Adjustment* (1925), pp. 240-241. Woofter distinguishes between contacts which are "helpful" and those which are "harmful." In the latter category he places "social intermingling" along with "vice" and "crime," "violence, economic exploitation, unfair competition, and demagogic or exploitative political contacts." (*Ibid.*, p. 215.)

19 *Ibid.*, pp. 235 ff.

20 *Ibid.*, p. 239.

21 *Liberalism in the South* (1932), p. 254. Dabney continues:

"The argument runs that such laws were desirable twenty or thirty years ago when the great majority of blacks were unclean in person and slovenly in attire, and when the ubiquitous saloon and its readily purchased fire water were conducive to clashes between the lower orders of both races. It is contended that these reasons for separating the races in public gatherings and on public conveyances do not now obtain to anything like the same extent, and that the Negroes should no longer be humiliated in this manner."

22 *Ibid.*, p. 255.

23 "Here, as elsewhere, however, it has been rather the social inequality of the races, than any approach to equality, which has been responsible for the mixture, in so far as such has occurred. It was the social inequality of the plantation days that began the process of mixture.... If race-amalgamation is indeed to be viewed as always an evil, the best way to counteract the growth of that evil must everywhere be the cultivation of racial self-respect and not of racial degradation." (Josiah Royce, *Race Questions, Provincialism and Other American Problems* [1908], pp. 21-22.)

24 Race prejudice has, therefore, a "function" to perform in lieu of the absence of sex repulsion.

"It is just because primary race feeling is *not* deeply based in human instinct, whereas the mating instinct *is* so based, that a secondary racial feeling, race-pride, comes in from a more developed reflective consciousness to minimize the natural instinct for amalgamation ..." (Thomas P. Bailey, *Race Orthodoxy in the South* [1914], p. 43.)

25 See Chapter 27, Section 3. W. F. Cash, in his *The Mind of the South* (1941), gives with much insight and

understanding, the story of how in the Old South the sex relations of white men with Negro women tended to inflate white womanhood (pp. 84 ff). The Negro woman, torn from her tribal restraints and taught an easy complaisance, was to be had for the taking:

"Boys on and about the plantation inevitably learned to use her, and having acquired the habit, often continued it into manhood and even after marriage. For she was natural, and could give herself up to passion in a way impossible to wives inhibited by Puritanical training. And efforts to build up a taboo against miscegenation made little real progress." (*Ibid.*, p. 84.)

The white women were naturally disturbed by what they could not help knowing about. The Yankees were not slow to discover the opening in the Southern armor:

"And the only really satisfactory escape here, as in so many other instances, would be fiction. On the one hand, the convention must be set up that the thing simply did not exist, and enforced under penalty of being shot; and on the other, the woman must be compensated, the revolting suspicion in the male that he might be slipping into bestiality got rid of, by glorifying her; the Yankee must be answered by proclaiming from the housetops that Southern Virtue, so far from being inferior, was superior, not alone to the North's but to any on earth, and adducing Southern Womanhood in proof." (*Ibid.*, p. 86.)

After the War this led to "the Southern rape complex." (*Ibid.*, pp. 116 ff.) Every attempt to rise socially on the part of the Negro became an insult to the white woman:

"What Southerners felt, therefore, was that any assertion of any kind on the part of the Negro constituted in a perfectly real manner an attack on the Southern woman. What they saw, more or less consciously, in the conditions of Reconstruction was a passage toward a condition for her as degrading, in their view, as rape itself. And a condition, moreover, which, logic or no logic, they infallibly thought of as being as absolutely forced upon her as rape, and hence a condition for which the term 'rape' stood as truly as for the *de facto* deed." (*Ibid.*, p. 116.)

"... the increased centrality of woman, added up with the fact that miscegenation, though more terrifying than it had been even in the Old South, showed little tendency to fall off despite efforts to build up standards against it, served to intensify the old interest in gyneolatry, and to produce yet more florid notions about Southern Womanhood and Southern Virtue, and so to foster yet more precious notions of modesty and decorous behavior for the Southern female to live up to." (*Ibid.*, p. 128.)

26 The "woman on the pedestal" pattern is found outside the American South, of course. It is a general trait in Western civilization and had extreme expression among the feudal nobility of the Middle Ages and the court nobility of France after Louis XIV. It was given added impetus by the loss of the economic function of middle class women at the end of the 18th century. But nowhere did it appear in such extreme, sentimental, and humorless form and so far down in the social status scale as in the American South. (For a general description of the Romantic "pure women" ideology, see Ernest W. Burgess, "The Romantic

Impulse and Family Disorganization," *The Survey* [December 1, 1926], pp. 290-294.)

27 All the moral conflicts involved in preserving the institution of color caste in a democracy, but quite particularly the association of the caste theory with sex and social status, explain the fear complex upon which most investigators of the race problem in the South have commented. Thomas P. Bailey was early outspoken on this point:

"But the worst has not been told. The veriest slavery of the spirit is to be found in the deep-seated anxiety of the South. Southerners are afraid for the safety of their wives and daughters and sisters; Southern parents are afraid for the purity of their boys, Southern publicists are afraid that a time will come when large numbers of negroes will try to vote, and thus precipitate race war. Southern religionists are afraid that our youth will grow up to despise large numbers of their fellow-men. Southern business men are afraid that agitation of the negro question will interfere with business or demoralize the labor market. Southern officials are afraid of race riots, lynchings, savage atrocities, paying not only for negro fiendishness but also for the anxiety caused by fear of what might be." (*Op. cit.*, pp. 346-347.)

28 Thomas Carlyle, *Occasional Discourse on the Nigger Question* (1853; first printed in *Fraser's Magazine* [December, 1849]), p. 28.

29 Quite ordinarily this attitude is directly associated with cherished memories from slavery. The pattern was set early after the Civil War. Again Henry W. Grady can be used to illustrate the consolidation of white thinking on race relations after Reconstruction. He talked touchingly of the relations that "did exist in the days of slavery":

"...how the negro stood in slavery days, open-hearted and sympathetic, full of gossip and comradeship, the companion of the hunt, frolic, furrow and home, contented in the kindly dependence that has been a habit of his blood, and never lifting his eyes beyond the narrow horizon that shut him in with his neighbors and friends. But this relation did exist in the days of slavery. It was the rule of that *regime*. It has survived war, and strife, and political campaigns in which the drum-beat inspired and Federal bayonets fortified. It will never die until the last slaveholder and slave have been gathered to rest. It is the glory of our past in the South. It is the answer to abuse and slander. It is the hope of our future." (*Op. cit.*, pp. 152-153; compare Page, *op. cit.*, pp. 80, 164 *passim*.)

30 "For those still living in the country there is, it would appear, one unfailing rule of life. If they would get along with least difficulty, they should get for themselves a protecting white family. 'We have mighty good white folks friends, and ef you have white folks for your friends, dey can't do you no harm.'" (Charles S. Johnson, *Shadow of the Plantation* [1934], p. 27.)

31 Woofter remarks:

"The liberality with which these colored beggars are treated is often more of a liability than an asset to racial adjustment, because such emotional but unscientific giving often leaves the givers with a paternalistic feeling toward the whole race and a belief that by giving small alms they have discharged their full civic duty toward their colored neighbors." (*Op. cit.*, p. 199.)

32 Dollard, *op. cit.*, pp. 389-432.

33 It was part of Washington's tactics to exaggerate this point. An interesting comparison can be made between his first book, published in 1899, and his later writings. In the former, *The Future of the American Negro*, he painted the cruelties of slavery in glaring terms; in the latter he rather elaborated on the lighter sides of the institution. This was part of his attempt to gain the assistance or at least the tolerance of the Southern whites, and he had found out that this appealed to the Northern philanthropist also. In his last book, *The Story of the Negro* (1909), he wrote, for instance, in explaining why "a mob in the South ... does not seek to visit its punishment upon the innocent as well as upon the guilty":

"In the South every Negro, no matter how worthless he may be as an individual, knows one white man in the town whose friendship and protection he can always count upon; perhaps he has gained the friendship of this white man by reason of the fact that some member of the white man's family owned him or some of his relatives, or it may be that he has lived upon this white man's plantation, or that some member of his family works for him, or that he has performed some act of kindness for this white man which has brought them into sympathetic relations with each other. It is generally true, as I have said before, that in the South every white man, no matter how bitter he may seem to be toward the Negro as a race, knows some one Negro in whom he has complete confidence, whom he will trust with all that he has. It is the individual touch which holds the two races together in the South, and it is this individual touch between the races which is lacking, in a large degree, in the North." (Vol. 1, p. 189.)

This was a gross overstatement even when Washington wrote, and is still less accurate today. (See Chapter 27, Section 2.)

34 Kelly Miller, *Race Adjustment—Essays on the Negro in America* (1908), p. 92.

35 "Vardaman, declaiming violently against Negro colleges, has actually, in specific instances, given them help and encouragement. I was told how he had cut off an $8,000 appropriation from Alcorn College because he did not believe in Negro education; but he turned around and gave Alcorn College $14,000 for a new lighting system, because *he had come in personal contact with the Negro president of Alcorn College, and liked him.*" (Ray Stannard Baker, *Following the Color Line* [1908], p. 250.)

36 *Autobiography of an Ex-Coloured Man* (1927; first edition, 1912), p. 79.

37 W. E. B. Du Bois, *Black Reconstruction* (1935), p. 52.

38 Concerning the Southerner who says he knows the Negro, Moton observes:

"When one of these says he 'knows the Negro' it means that he has had them under his control for very practical purposes and has come to a pretty wide and thorough knowledge of the habits, mannerisms, foibles, weaknesses, defects, deficiencies, virtues, and excellencies of this particular type of the race. It means, too, that he is thoroughly familiar with the ethical, social, and moral code that obtains among white men of his class in dealing with Negroes of this class and under the conditions obtaining in these fields. In such a declaration he means to say that he knows how to get the required amount of work from any given group of such Negroes, that he knows the conditions under which they will work best, the amount of pressure they will stand, what abuse they will submit to, what they will resent, under what conditions they will remain cheerful, when they will become sullen, what and when to pay them, what food to provide, what housing to furnish, what holidays to recognize, and what indulgences to grant. Such a man knows, too, to what extent public opinion in his own race will support him in his relations with his men. He is familiar with all the local prejudices and practices involved in race adjustments; he is adept according to these in 'keeping the Negro in his place'; and above all else he can be counted on to be firm and resolute in all his dealings with black folk of every type and class....

"Thus a great part of 'knowing the Negro' is a thorough understanding of the operations of this type of interracial sentiment and of how to employ it in managing the Negro and 'keeping him in his place.' Where firmness is required rather than sympathy, where ruthlessness is the order of the day rather than consideration, a white man who 'knows the Negro' is the most effective agent procurable. What he *doesn't* know about the Negro is the factor that produces the race problem." (*Op. cit.*, pp. 6-7 and 8.)

"Perhaps no single phrase has been more frequently used in discussing the race problem in America than the familiar declaration, 'I know the Negro ...'

"Negroes have always met this remark with a certain faint, knowing smile. Their common experience has taught them that as a matter of fact there are vast reaches of Negro life and thought of which white people know nothing whatever, even after long contact with them, sometimes on the most intimate terms." (*Ibid.*, p. 1.)

39 Baker, *op. cit.*, pp. 38-39. As early as 1899, ex-Governor Northen of Georgia, in a speech at Boston, noted that the two races were drifting apart in the South. ("The Negro at the South," p. 7, quoted by Walter F. Willcox, "Negro Criminality," *Journal of Social Science* [*December*, 1899], pp. 87-88.)

40 For an example of how laughter is a part of the interracial etiquette, see Jonathan Daniels, *A Southerner Discovers the South* (1938), pp. 255-259.

41 P. 67.

42 Baker, *op. cit.*, p. 39.

43 Kelly Miller, *Race Adjustment, Essays on the Negro in America* (1908), p. 92.

44 I have the impression that Southern radio stations make less use of national networks than do Northern radio stations. If this were found to be a fact, an analysis of the reasons for it would be suggestive.

45 Scott and Stowe, *op. cit.*, pp. 115 ff., and Alfred Hold Stone, *Studies in the American Race Problem* (1908), pp. 242 ff.

46 "The Bases of Race Prejudice," *The Annals of the American Academy of Political and Social Science* (November, 1928), p. 13.

47 Quoted from John Temple Graves, "The Southern Negro and the War Crisis," *The Virginia Quarterly Review* (Autumn, 1942), pp. 504-505. This article, too, is an example of the recent tendency toward increased unfriendliness toward the Negro on the part of Southern liberals.

6

Caste, Class, and Race: A Study in Social Dynamics

OLIVER CROMWELL COX

Cox's bold attempt to construct a political economy of racism was a work of magisterial quality. In many ways a response to Myrdal's theory, Cox advanced a Marxian analysis of racism as an inevitable product of capitalism. There is no 'natural' cause of racism: its sources must be sought in the economic matrix of society. It is part of the stabilizing strategies of the ruling class; a way of dividing the proletariat and keeping them fighting among themselves rather than united on the basis of a shared class position. On this view, it is in the capitalists' interests to perpetuate and deepen divisions among the working class: any other development may result in challenge.

Cox presented a historically detailed and comparatively balanced analysis and the fact that contemporary theorists (including Marxists) have criticized his reductionism should not diminish the enormity of Cox's feat. His was the first scholarly thesis to marshall Marxism to the study of racism. As such, we should understand his work as that of a pioneer rather than a finished study: it inspired a generation of scholars to locate the origins of racism in economic spheres.

The first selection from his classic *Caste, Class and Race*, published in 1948, situates his general theory, while the second hints at what later developed into a fully fledged critique of Myrdal's work.

The Modern Caste School of Race Relations

During the last decade a prolific school of writers on race relations in the United States, led mainly by social anthropologists, has relied religiously upon an ingenious, if not original, caste hypothesis. Professor W. Lloyd Warner is the admitted leader of the movement, and his followers include scholars of considerable distinction.[1] We propose here to examine critically the position of this school.

_____

[1] See the leading hypothesis by W. Lloyd Warner, "American Caste and Class," *American Journal of Sociology*, Vol. XLII, September 1936, pp. 234–37. See also, by the same author, "Social Anthropology and the

The Hypothesis

If we think of a hypothesis as a tentative statement of a theory which some researcher sets out to demonstrate or to prove, then the school has no hypothesis. But we shall quote liberally so that the authors might have an opportunity to speak for themselves about the things which they believe. These we shall call loosely the hypothesis. The school is particularly interested in race relations in the Southern states of the United States, and its members believe that they have struck upon an

_____

Continued

Modern Community," ibid., Vol. XLVI, May 1941, pp. 785–96; W. Lloyd Warner and W. Allison Davis, "A Comparative Study of American Caste," in *Race Relations and the Race Problem*, pp. 219–40; W. Allison Davis and John Dollard, *Children of Bondage*; W. Lloyd Warner, Buford H. Junker, and Walter A. Adams, *Color and Human Nature*; W. Allison Davis, Burleigh B. Gardner, Mary R. Gardner, and W. Lloyd Warner, *Deep South*; John Dollard, *Caste and Class in a Southern Town*; Buell G. Gallagher, *American Caste and the Negro College*; Robert Austin Warren, *New Haven Negroes*; Kingsley Davis, "Intermarriage in Caste Societies," *American Anthropologist*, Vol. 43, September 1941, pp. 376–95; Robert L. Sutherland, *Color, Class and Personality*; Edward A. Ross, *New-Age Sociology*; William F. Ogburn and Meyer F. Nimkoff, *Sociology*; Kimball Young, *Sociology*; Robert L. Sutherland and Julian L. Woodward, *Introductory Sociology*; Stuart A. Queen and Jeanette R. Gruener, *Social Pathology*; Alain Locke and Bernhard J. Stern, *When Peoples Meet*; Wilbert E. Moore and Robin M. Williams, "Stratification in the Ante-Bellum South," *American Sociological Review*, Vol. 7, June 1942, pp. 343–51; Allison Davis, "Caste, Economy, and Violence," *American Journal of Sociology*, Vol. LI, July 1945, pp. 7–15; James Melvin Reinhardt, *Social Psychology*; Guy B. Johnson, "Negro Racial Movements and Leadership in the United States," *American Journal of Sociology*, Vol. 43, July 1937, pp. 57–71; M. F. Ashley Montagu, *Man's Most Dangerous Myth*; "The Nature of Race Relations," *Social Forces*, Vol. 25, March 1947, pp. 336–42; Paul H. Landis, *Social Control*; Ina Corinne Brown, *National Survey of the Higher Education of Negroes*, U.S. Office of Education, Misc. No. 6, Vol. 1; Verne Wright and Manuel C. Elmer, *General Sociology*; W. Lloyd Warner, Robert J. Havighurst, and Martin B. Loeb, *Who Shall Be Educated*; St. Clair Drake and Horace R. Cayton, *Black Metropolis*; Mozell C. Hill, "A Comparative Analysis of the Social Organization of the All-Negro Society in Oklahoma," *Social Forces*, Vol. 25, 1946, pp. 70–77; and others.

The counterpart of this group of thinkers is another school which has with equal enthusiasm attempted to explain caste relationship in terms of racial antagonism. See chapter on the origin of caste

unusually revealing explanation of the situation. In the South, they maintain, Negroes form one caste and whites another, with an imaginary rotating caste line between them. "The white caste is in a super-ordinate position and the Negro caste in a subordinate social position." The following definition of caste has been most widely accepted.

> Caste ... describes a theoretical arrangement of the people of a given group in an order in which the privileges, duties, obligations, opportunities, etc., are unequally distributed between the groups which are considered to be higher and lower.... Such a definition also describes class. A caste or organization ... can be further defined as one where marriage between two or more groups is not sanctioned and where there is no opportunity for members of the lower groups to rise into the upper groups or of members of the upper to fall into the lower ones.[2]

A class system and a caste system "are antithetical to each other.... Nevertheless they have accommodated themselves in the southern community...." The caste line is represented as running asymmetrically diagonally between the two class systems of Negroes and whites as in the following diagram.[3]

It is assumed that during slavery the caste line, AB in diagram, was practically horizontal but that since then, with the cultural progress of Negroes, it has rotated upward. It may become perpendicular so as to coincide with the line DE; indeed, though unlikely, it may swing over toward the whites. The point here is that it would be possible for the line to take a vertical position while the caste system remains intact.

It is thought further that the social disparity between Negro classes and white classes is particularly disconcerting to upper-class Negroes. The "emotional instability of many of the individuals in this group" may be readily explained since:

> In his own personality he feels the conflict of the two opposing structures, and in the thinking and feeling of the members of both groups there is to be found this same conflict about his position. ... Although he is at the top of the Negro class hierarchy, he is constantly butting his head against the caste line.[4]

It is believed that in many countries of the world besides India there are developed caste systems, but the school has never found it convenient to demonstrate this proposition. "Caste," Warner and Davis assert without proof, "is found in most of the major areas of the world; this is particularly true of Africa, Asia, and America. The Indians of the southeastern United States and those of British Columbia

_____

[2] W. Lloyd Warner, "American Caste and Class," *American Journal of Sociology*, Vol. XLII, p. 234. 1936.

[3] Ibid., p. 235.

[4] Ibid., p. 236. See also *Deep South* by Davis, Gardner, Gardner, and Warner, p. 13.

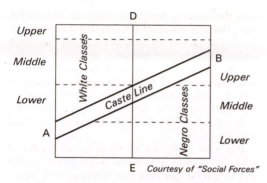

Position of "Caste Line" between Whites and Negroes in the United States

have well-developed, if not castes, then caste-like structures. We cannot take time to examine those American systems, but we shall briefly summarize the material on East Indian caste....”[5] Thus the caste system in India has been taken as the criterion; nowhere has the school relied upon any other system.

On the crucial question of marriage among castes Warner and Davis give Emile Senart credit for the belief that castes "isolate themselves to prevent intermarriage"; while they regard hypergamy as an example of "variations from the caste ideal."[6] Kingsley Davis, however, thinks that hypergamy distinguishes two major types of caste systems. In India hypergamy is possible because the Indian caste system is a "non-racial caste system"; in the United States and South Africa, on the other hand, hypergamy is impossible because there are in these situations "racial caste systems."[7] Warner and Davis depend further upon Senart and Bouglé for their significant conclusion that *"no one occupation has but one caste assigned to it."*[8]

Considerable emphasis is put upon the fact that a Negro or a white person, who is born Negro or white, could never hope to become anything other than Negro or white. "Children and grandchildren of Negroes will continue to be born into, live in, and only die out of the Negro 'caste.'"[9] Further, this biological fact of inheriting racial marks strikes Kingsley Davis as providing an ideal foundation for a caste system:

> The reason that race serves as an excellent basis of caste is that one gets one's racial traits by birth from parents

having those traits, and one cannot change these traits during the rest of one's life.[10]

These, then, are some of the leading postulates of the caste school of race relations. Without continuing to introduce fragmentary statements at this point, we shall attempt an evaluation.[11]

ESTIMATE OF BASIC PRINCIPLES

Although the school has relied completely upon references to the caste system in India for its authority, it has nowhere made anything approaching a careful study of the caste system. Yet, even so, it has been difficult to determine which of their selected "essences" of the caste system will be controlling in given situations; and one is seldom certain about the degree of concentration of these extracts. For example, after their most elaborate discussion of caste in India, the following conclusion is reached:

> There has been no attempt in these last few paragraphs to demonstrate that our caste structure and Indian caste structure are exactly the same, but rather we have attempted to show that they are the same kind of social phenomena.[12]

At this point the question may easily devolve upon the meaning of the expression "same kind." At least the reader might have expected that the authors would now attempt to show that the phenomena are indeed commensurable. But they do not. From this point on they proceed to discuss race relations in the United States, totally oblivious of a theory of caste or of whether caste ever existed in India. Apparently their thin discussion of Indian caste is merely intended to provide subject atmosphere.

We have had considerable difficulty also in finding clear-cut statements of principle. Usually some such phrase as "for our purpose," "as here used," "in so far as," or "generally" limits conclusions that are forthwith given universal applicability. To be sure, one could hardly question such a contrivance, yet it may be likened to the researcher who says: "This animal before us is not a horse, but *for our purpose* it is convenient to call it a horse. If you examine it closely, you will discover that it is a water buffalo. That does not matter, however, for we are not going to use it in the water-buffalo sense. Obviously, you cannot say the animal is not a horse; it is, in so far as it has four legs; and four legs are

---

[5] "A Comparative Study of American Caste," in *Race Relations and the Race Problem*, Edgar T. Thompson, ed. Observe, incidentally, this editor's own involvement with the ideas of the school: *Ibid.*, p. xiii.

[6] *Ibid.*, pp. 229, 230.

[7] "Intermarriage in Caste Societies," *American Anthropologist*, Vol. 43, July–September 1941, pp. 376–95.

[8] In *Race Relations and the Race Problem*, p. 231.

[9] W. Lloyd Warner, Buford H. Junker, Walter A. Adams, *Color and Human Nature*, pp. 11–12.

[10] *Op. cit.*, note, p. 387. See also *Deep South*, p. 15.

[11] We should add that sometimes members of the school speak of "the American system of color-caste" with probable implication that the Indian system is not based upon color.

[12] Warner and Davis, in *Race Relations and the Race Problem*, p. 232.

generally understood to be the essence of all horses and water buffaloes."

At points where clarity is most needed the school invariably becomes obscure, impressionistic, or circuitous. It has been accepted that the form of social organization in Brahmanic India constitutes a caste system. This system has certain distinguishing characteristics; hence we shall consider these the norm.

Definitions of a society are difficult to formulate; they are usually insufficient. For example, A. L. Kroeber wrote an article on caste[13] and came to the conclusion that a caste system is not possible in Western society; notwithstanding this, Warner, without even so much as a reference to Kroeber's negative conclusion, adopted his definition of "a caste" and reached the opposite position: "The social system of Old City [in the South] fits this definition of Kroeber's and of most of the ethnologists and social anthropologists."[14] A play with definitions usually results in debate rather than constructive interest in the social problem. At any rate, Warner's own definition of caste considers two factors as determining: (a) that intermarriage between groups is not sanctioned, and (b) that there is no opportunity for members of lower groups to rise into upper groups, nor for those of the upper groups to fall into the lower groups.

It should be emphasized that a definition of *a caste* does not describe the *caste system*. We have shown elsewhere that upper-caste men in India have always been able to marry women of lower castes without disturbing the caste system, a procedure which could not be sanctioned in the South. Then, too, endogamy may be an isolator of social classes, castes, tribes, sects, millets, or any other social groups which think they have something to protect; hence, the final test of caste is not endogamy but the social values which endogamy secures. Indeed, A. C. Mace sees marrying out of one's class as an offense second only to the commission of crime, while Bouglé speaks of the horror of misalliances and the belief in impurity of contact between upper and lower classes in Europe.[15] Endogamy is not the essence of caste; if there is an essence of caste, endogamy merely bottles it up.

Probably the most insidious analogy between race and caste relations resides in the idea of life membership in each group. The identity of these phenomena, however, is only apparent. It must be obvious that a man born in a certain race cannot

have the choice of leaving it and going into another race. But it is not at all obvious that a person born in one caste could not become a member of another caste. The biological affiliation of persons belonging to a given race has not been the position of one caste-man with respect to another in India. In fact, this very distinction should raise the suspicion that different social forces are operating in the caste system from those in situations of racial adjustment.

But what really do we mean by saying that a white man cannot fall into the Negro group? To the extent that he can have sex relations with Negro women he can "fall" biologically. The mixed-blood children that are born are, in the long run, the most potent equilibrator of the races; and the lawmakers of the South are by no means unmindful of this fact. The Negro may "rise" biologically if he is able to pass.

From too much preoccupation with the unchangeableness of physical inheritance, the conclusion is reached that the social status of Negroes and whites in the South may become identical, yet they will continue to constitute two castes. In explaining his diagram, Warner holds that there is a theoretical possibility of Negroes advancing to the point where they may become the dominant caste. And this makes his theory particularly illogical and sterile.

So far as its logic is concerned, it asserts that Negroes may become equal to whites, evidently in wealth, in learning, in opportunity to control the government of the state; in short, culturally equal. Yet Negroes and whites will still be unequal; unequal, obviously, in color. For a person born white could never have the privilege of becoming black. Clearly, it must be on the grounds of the latter disability that his caste system will still be maintained. And since, so far as we know, time will not alter the possibility of a man's changing his racial marks, we must expect the white caste and the black caste to remain indefinitely intact—an ideal leopard-and-spots theory of race relations.

The race-caste assumption is sterile because it has no way of confronting the real dynamics of race relations. It goes happily past the meaning of the racial dichotomy in the South. Engrossed with ideas of "social structure," the school remains oblivious of the physiology of the society. It presumes that the white man is protecting his color and that the Negro is equally interested in protecting his, so that with the ballot in the hands of Negroes and with the opportunity for cultural participation open to them as normal citizens, the black code which keeps the races segregated will still be the law of the South. Elsewhere we have attempted to show, however, that the greater the relative cultural advancement of Negroes, the less will be the need of the white man's protecting his color. The theory sees a caste system set up in the South in the interest of the white man's color and, for that matter, the Negro's

---

[13] "Caste," *Encyclopedia of the Social Sciences*.

[14] *Deep South*, p. 9.

[15] A. C. Mace, "Beliefs and Attitudes in Class Relations," in *Class Conflict and Social Stratification*, T. H. Marshall, ed., p. 159; C. Bouglé, *Essais sur le régime des castes*, 3d ed., p. 6.

also.[16] Nonetheless, it may be shown that the white man has no such obsession about his color. He will protect it only so long as it helps him to reserve a calculable cultural advantage.

The caste interpretation of race relations in the South cannot see that the intermarriage restriction laws are a social affront to Negroes; it cannot perceive that Negroes are smarting under the Jim Crow laws; it may not recognize the overwhelming aspiration among Negroes for equality of social opportunity; it could never realize that the superiority of the white race is due principally to the fact that it has developed the necessary devices for maintaining incontestable control over the shooting iron; and it will not know that "race hatred" may be reckoned in terms of the interests of the white ruling class. Hence, it is possible for the school to imagine the anomaly of Negroes fully assimilated culturally and yet living symbiotically apart from whites on the basis of some unexplained understanding that their colors should never be mixed. In other words, the races will, as Warner and Davis believe "isolate themselves to prevent intermarriage"! When this static approach is given up, the caste belief must also be given up.

In order that the authors might come to terms with the disturbing question of the relationship of occupation and caste, it is concluded that even in India there is no identification of every occupation with a caste. It is argued, in other words, that since many castes have the same occupation, occupation is no significant factor in the system.[17] The point to remember here, however, is that every caste has a traditional occupation or a limited number of cognate occupations, and not that every occupation has a caste.

Considerable importance is ascribed to interracial etiquette in the South as a social device supporting the supposed caste system there. Thus, according to Davis, Gardner, and Gardner:

> The most striking form of what may be called caste behavior is deference, the respectful yielding exhibited by the Negroes in their contacts with whites.... The

behavior of both Negroes and white people must be such that the two are socially distinct and that the Negro is subordinate. Thus the Negro when addressing a white person, is expected to use a title such as "Sah," "Mistah," or "Boss," etc., while the white must never use such titles of respect to the Negro, but should address him by his first name or as "Boy."[18]

However, in the South there is also an etiquette intended to keep poor whites at a proper distance from the upper-class whites, and it is probably more severely non-reciprocating there than in other parts of the country. To upper-class Negroes, also, lower-class Negroes are very respectful. The titles "Boss," and so on, of themselves, may indicate only a recognition of superior rank. Indeed, a system of social etiquette which distinguishes superior persons or classes is no exclusive trait of the caste system. It is found in schools, in churches, among social classes, as well as among peoples and races who live in relationship of subordination and superordination.

The method of selecting and identifying isolatedly certain aspects of intercaste relationship, such as endogamy, non-commensality, or other marks of social distinction with their apparent counterparts in race relations, may at first seem convincing. In almost every case, however, the comparison is not between caste and race but merely a recognition of apparently common characteristics of all situations of superior-inferior or superordination-subordination relationships.[19] In conversation with the writer, one advocate of the caste school said: "No better illustration of the existence of caste in the South can be found than the practice of the races refusing to eat at the same table." But ordinarily only social equals eat, sleep, or play together. Army officers may not eat with privates, and medical doctors may resent sharing the same table with orderlies of the hospital; and so, too, a race bent upon maintaining a position of dominance can seldom engage in so socially leveling an act as that of eating together with members of the subordinate race.

The social-essence method of making comparisons between the caste system and other forms of social relationship makes it possible for different members of the caste school to choose different essences as their criterion of caste and yet not

---

[16] Guided by the idea of Warner's caste line, Guy B. Johnson goes into the following monstrosity: "The great question in the coming era of race relations in the South will be, how far and how fast can the horizontal line of caste shift toward the vertical line of a biracial society? That is, how much equality can Negroes secure in the separate order? In so far as the gradual revision of racial attitudes makes caste distinctions obsolete, there will be change with a minimum of conflict." In *Race Relations and the Race Problem*, p. 150. In other words, this writer reasons that changing social attitudes are making caste distinctions obsolete, and that when all caste distinctions become obsolete, the caste line will be vertical!

[17] See Warner and Davis in *Race Relations and the Race Problem*, p. 231.

[18] Op. cit., p. 22. Incidentally, we may observe that the authors present this passage concerning interracial etiquette with the implicit freshness of a discovery. No one reading it would ever suspect that *The Etiquette of Race Relations in the South*, by Bertram W. Doyle, had been on the bookshelves some years before.

[19] It is this same kind of eclecticism which leads Gunnar Myrdal to conclude that the "status" and "problems in society" of women and children reveal, "striking similarities to those of Negroes." *An American Dilemma*, pp. 1073ff.

disturb the equanimity of the school. For example, according to John Dollard, the essence of caste is "a barrier to legitimate descent"; to W. Lloyd Warner, it is endogamy; to Guy B. Johnson, it is the achievement of "accommodation"; to Robert E. Park, "etiquette is the very essence of caste"; and to some, like Buell G. Gallagher, the criterion of analogy is not mentioned at all, the assumption evidently being that the identity of the phenomena should be taken for granted. Thus, it is possible for these writers to take hold of any one of a number of apparent analogues and proceed with it to identify caste and race relations.[20] If we study the caste system as the proverbial blind men studied the elephant, who will trust our conclusions?

PERSONALITY OF UPPER CLASS NEGROES

It is a common belief, not peculiar to the caste school, that upper-class Negroes are especially maladjusted. The biracial system in the United States, it must be admitted, is a pathological situation; and to the extent that this is so, it affects adversely the personalities of both whites and blacks.[21] But sensitivity to social wrongs need not imply

derangement or an "off-balance" personality. We may mention at this point, however, that although this assertion calls for explanation, the caste theorists evidently do not realize that it is most damaging to their hypothesis. A person belonging to a lower caste is not "constantly butting his head against the caste line." In fact, the absence of such a phenomenon is so vital to the persistence of a caste order that it would hardly be inaccurate to maintain that it is definitely incompatible with a caste system. Caste barriers in the caste system are never challenged; they are sacred to caste and caste alike.[22] The personalities developed in the caste system are normal for that society.

Negroes are moving away from a condition of extreme white domination and subjection to one of normal citizenship. The determinant of unrest or social dysphoria among a people is not so much their *state* of subjugation or seeming oppression; rather it is either the process of their changing from some accommodated stage of well-being to one of subservience, or some political-class movement itself determined by some fundamental economic change. At any rate, since the Civil War the situation among Negroes in the South has been culturally progressive. Hortense Powdermaker makes the significant observation that it is not difference in class so much as difference in age which determines the attitude of Negroes toward whites. "Among the younger [Negro] generation, those in their teens, twenties, and thirties, resentment is keen and outspoken."[23] Older Negroes were reared in an earlier school of racial beliefs; and, indeed, the younger are not infrequently very impatient with their elders' compromising attitudes toward whites. Among Negroes in the South the "Uncle Toms" are distributed all through the social classes.

Of course militance in the interest of racial progress should not be mistaken for personality imbalance. In fact, dissatisfaction with the status

---

[20] As an illustration of this possibility, consider the following remarks by Jawaharlal Nehru concerning the Indian-European relations. "It was a notorious fact," he says, "that whenever an Englishman killed an Indian, he was acquitted by a jury of his own countrymen. In railway trains, compartments were reserved for Europeans; and, however crowded the train might be—and they used to be terribly crowded—no Indian was allowed to travel in them even though they were empty.... Benches and chairs were also reserved for Europeans in the public parks and other places. I was filled with resentment against the alien rulers of my country who misbehaved in this manner; and, whenever an Indian hit back, I was glad." *Toward Freedom*, pp. 20–21.

It would seem possible by some ingenious eclecticism, to use even this limited information to identify Indian-European relations with caste relations, but we should expect the dullest of Hindus to remain unimpressed with the suggestion that in India there are two castes: the one East Indian and the other European. And this even though another statement by the same writer is cited in apparent support of this caste theory: "What a great gulf divides the two races, and how they distrusted and disliked each other! ... each side was a little afraid of the other and was constantly on its guard in the other's presence. To each the other appeared as a sour-looking, unamiable creature, and neither realized that there was decency and kindliness behind the mask." Ibid., p. 3.

[21] On this point Gunnar Myrdal observes: "The conservative Southerner is not so certain as he sometimes sounds. He is a split personality.... The Southern

Continued

conservative white man's faith in American democracy, which he is certainly not living up to, and the Constitution, which he is circumventing, are living forces of decisive dynamic significance. Op. cit., pp. 461–62.

Another member of the school sees the inner strife as a personality difficulty of the whites. "With peculiar poignancy," says Buell G. Gallagher, "the individual white man feels within himself the warfare between profession and practice which he shares with his institutions. Two general streams of experience interweave in this shifting pattern of uneasiness." *Color and Conscience*, p. 24.

[22] Under the impact of Western culture the caste structure in India is being shaken, but it should be remembered that Western civilization is not attacking another civilization in the South, for this is itself Western civilization.

[23] *After Freedom*, pp. 325, 331.

quo must necessarily be the common preoccupation of all Negro leaders. There is, furthermore, some compensation to upper-class Negroes. Frequently they meet whites in flattering situations, mostly in business relations. They have considerable prestige among their own people, sometimes even more than that which whites of similar attainments can hope for within their own group. This windfall may not only compensate for loss of respect from low-class whites, but it may even result in a sort of grandiose importance inconsistent with reality. The "big Negro," a recognized personality type, is usually indelicate and grossly lacking in humility; yet he is not pathological.[24]

Upper-class Negroes do not envy poor whites in the South because the latter are beyond the purview of the black code. One might as well argue that some human beings suffer severe personality traumas because they recognize that the dogs and cats of the rich have certain advantages that they cannot have. The resentment of upper-class Negroes is rather against the ruling class, the guardians of the status quo. Enlightened Negroes recognize clearly the cultural inferiority of the poor whites. As a youth, W. E. B. Du Bois says of himself: "I cordially despised the poor Irish and South Germans, who slaved in the mills, and annexed the rich and well-to-do as my natural companions."[25] The power of sublimation and conceit to rescue persons from isolation and frustration must be reckoned with. Bitter as it is, therefore, the real conflict is usually between Negroes and their cultural equals or superiors. Sometimes it may seem to end in despair, as when Countee Cullen exclaimed:

> Yet do I marvel at this curious thing:
> To make a poet black, and bid him sing![25a]

Ordinarily, however, it is a persistent challenge to Negroes, an integrating force in a cause which must be served. Claude McKay, in his *America*, symbolizes this situation.

> Although she feeds me bread of bitterness,
> And sinks into my throat her tiger's tooth
> Stealing my breath of life, I will confess
> I love this cultured hell that tests my youth
> Her vigor flows like tides into my blood,
> Giving me strength erect against her hate.
> Her bigness sweeps my being like a flood.

> Yet as a rebel fronts a king in state,
> I stand within her walls with not a shred
> Of terror, malice, not a word of jeer.[25b]

At this point we should mention another crucial misconception of Warner's. He believes that Dr. Du Bois has achieved leadership of a movement for "parallelism" among American Negroes.[26] However, the fact that Du Bois as an assimilationist had a secure following, yet on his advocating a compromise with segregation was speedily wound up in his position and left to the thankless and interminable business of explaining his policy,[27] should have led Warner to give a different significance to the place of "parellelism" in the social aspirations of Negroes. He might have been on safer ground had he referred to the open plan of white South Africans ostensibly to develop a nation of whites and one of blacks within the same economically competitive area.

At any rate, segregation is a white man's principal anti-color weapon of oppression; therefore, Negroes can have but one quite obvious attitude toward it. Du Bois's leadership was doomed—and is still so—when, as he says of himself, he "proposed that in economic lines, just as in lines of literature and religion, segregation should be planned and organized and carefully thought through."[28] We may assert, as a sort of social axiom, that, with population ratios approximately as they are, the Southern aristocracy could never yield to the Negro political equality—the right to vote and to campaign for votes without intimidation—and still maintain public segregation barriers. Therefore, it is nonsense to speak of political and economic equality of opportunity with segregation.

THE SOCIAL ORGANIZATION OF NEGROES

Symptomatic of the potentialities of the caste hypothesis of race relations is the classification of societies of the world by Warner and Davis.[29] From simple "theoretical" classless societies to "our own

---

[24] Perhaps there should be no objection to a transient assertion of personality disorganization such as the following by Gunnar Myrdal. It makes no point as a basis for significant conclusions. "This national *ethos* [the American Creed] undoubtedly has a greater force in the North than in the South.... But ... even the [white] Northerner has a split personality." Op. cit., p. 439.

[25] *Darkwater*, p. 10.

[25a] From "Yet Do I Marvel" in *Caroling Dusk*, an anthology by Countee Cullen, p. 182.

[25b] From Claude McKay, *Harlem Shadows*, 1922.

[26] "American Caste and Class," *American Journal of Sociology*, Vol. XLII, No. 2, September 1936, pp. 235–36.

[27] See W. E. Du Bois, *Dusk of Dawn*, pp. 301ff, for a recent defense.

[28] Ibid., p. 305. Many years ago, when Alexis de Tocqueville said, "The Negroes and the whites must either wholly part or wholly mingle," he saw clearly the only possibilities of a stable racial adjustment; and it is doubtful whether today anyone will seriously question the inevitability of the latter alternative. See *Democracy in America*, Vol. II, p. 238.

[29] In *Race Relations and the Race Problem*, pp. 225–27.

society [which] possesses ranked internal structures, class and caste orders, groups with diverse cultural [ethnic] traditions, as well as sex and age evaluations," all the types of societies in the world are included. Thus the dichotomized racial system in the South becomes a natural type of social ranking. "The ranking changes from a status situation in which there is little or no ranking to one in which almost all behavior is given an evaluation of rank."[30]

Unless clearly limited, the term "society" is very ambiguous. It is properly used with reference to Western society or to a consumers' co-operative society; however, the authors did not limit the concept. It becomes necessary, then, to settle upon some meaning of the term before discussing it. According to John Dewey:

> Persons do not become a society by living in physical proximity any more than a man ceases to be socially influenced by being so many feet or miles removed from others.... Individuals do not even compose a social group because they all work for a common end.... What they must have in common in order to form a community or society are aims, beliefs, aspirations, knowledge—a common understanding.[31]

Assimilation and consensus seem to be necessary. John S. Mackenzie emphasizes this:

> When a people is conquered and subject to another, it ceases to be a society, except in so far as it retains a spiritual life of its own apart from that of its conquerors.... So long as the citizens of the conquered state are merely in the condition of atoms externally fitted into a system to which they do not naturally belong, they cannot be regarded as parts of the society at all.[32]

Another way of looking at a society is in terms of its capacity to perpetuate itself. Hinduism, or the caste society of India, is a powerful form of social organization which may go on self-satisfiedly, so to speak, forever. It carries within itself no basic antagonisms. But the social aims and purposes of whites and Negroes in the South are irreconcilably opposed. If such a situation could be termed a society at all, it must be a society divided against itself. Sapir has used this idea in his analysis of culture. Thus he writes:

The genuine culture is not of necessity either *high or low*, it is merely inherently harmonious, balanced, self-satisfactory.... If the culture necessitates slavery, it frankly admits it; if it abhors slavery, it feels its way to an economic adjustment that obviates the necessity of its employment.[33]

In like manner we may think of the larger American society as fundamentally antipathetic to the non-Christian, non-democratic, biracial system in the South; hence it is continuously "feeling its way" to something else. To put such a situation easily into a typology of societies which includes the caste system in India, indeed to identify it with the caste system, must be misleading to say the least. The caste system of India is a minutely segmented, assimilated social structure; it is highly stable and capable of perpetuating itself indefinitely. Castes in India constitute a natural status system in one society, while Negroes and whites in the South tend to constitute two status systems, i.e., two social-class systems in two societies that are in opposition.

When two racial or nationality groups become more or less isolated from each other because of some continuing conflict situation or basic repugnance, we do not refer to them as forming a social-status hierarchy even though their relationship is one of superordination and subordination or of conqueror and conquered. As an illustration, Adolf Hitler says in his *My Battle*: "It must be held in greater honour to be a citizen of this Reich, even if only a crossing-sweeper, than to be a king in a foreign state."[34] Suppose now that this philosophy be made a reality in future German-Polish relationships; all Poles will then be considered inferior to the least of Germans, and an etiquette will be developed to implement the attitude. But there will be here no social-status hierarchy; neither would Hitler there and then have enacted a caste system. The Poles will seek a *modus vivendi* in some sort of society of their own; and the intergroup relationship will most likely be one of antagonism, a latent power-group relationship.[35]

So, too, Negroes and whites in the Deep South do not constitute an assimilated society. There are rather two societies. Thus, we may conceive of Negroes as constituting a quasi or tentative society

---

[30] Ibid., p. 227. See also Emile Durkheim, *The Rules of Sociological Method*, trans. by Sarah A. Solovay and John H. Mueller, pp. 81–83, for a discussion of the misleading possibilities of such a typology of societies.

[31] *Democracy and Education*, p. 5.

[32] Quoted by J. S. McKenzie, "The Assimilation of the American Indian," *Proceedings of the American Sociological Society*, Vol. III, p. 45; see also Emile Durkheim, op. cit., pp. 85–86. "By a society," says Robert Redfield, "is meant a recognizable system of human relations characterizing a group, the members of which are aware of their unity and of their difference from others." *The Folk Culture of Yucatan*, p. 80.

[33] "Culture, Genuine and Spurious," *American Journal of Sociology*, Vol. XXIX, January 1924, p. 410. See also Albert Bushnell Hart, *Slavery and Abolition*, 1831–1841, p. 32.

[34] E. T. S. Dugdale, trans., p. 182.

[35] Consider the following circular reasoning by Guy B. Johnson, a member of the caste school: "Caste may be thought of as an accommodation, since its very existence is evidence that two or more unlike groups have worked out some sort of *modus vivendi*." In *Race Relations and the Race Problem*, p. 126.

developed to meet certain needs resulting from their retarded assimilation. Unlike the permanence of a caste, it is a temporary society intended to continue only so long as whites are able to maintain the barriers against their assimilation.[36] It provides the matrix for a universe of discourse in which members of the group give expression to their common sympathies, opinions, and sentiments, and in which their primary social institutions function. The political and economic structure is controlled by another and larger society to which the whites are assimilated and toward which all Negroes are oriented.

The "public" of the white society includes Negroes only in the broadest sense; and when Negroes in their institutional functions declare that "everybody is invited," white people who turn up must assume the role of strangers. The "we feeling" of the white and of the Negro society tends to be mutually exclusive. Says Robert E. Park: "Gradually, imperceptibly, within the larger world of the white man, a smaller world, the world of the black man, is silently taking form and shape."[37] Ray Stannard Baker reports an interview with a Negro store owner in Atlanta:

"What do you mean by protection?" I asked.

"Well, justice between the races. That doesn't mean social equality. We have a society of our own."[38]

---

[36] Professor Robert Redfield described the evolution of a racial dichotomy into a social class system. It is significant to note that no such process could be suggested as a means of liquidating the caste system. "It requires little special knowledge to assert that the contact of the Spanish with the Maya, as is generally the case with long-continuing interaction between diverse ethnic groups, began with the existence of two separate societies, each with its own racial and cultural characteristics, and moved toward the formation of a single society in which the original racial and cultural differences disappear. At the time of the Conquest there were two groups that looked across at each other, both aware of the marked ethnic differences that attended their sense of distinctness one from the other. As the two groups came to participate in a common life and to interbreed, the ethnic differences became blurred, so that other criteria of difference, such as occupation, costume, or place of residence, came to be relatively more significant signs of social distinctness than was race or general culture.... At first there were two societies, ethnically distinct. At last there is a single society with classes ethnically indistinct." Op. cit., p. 58.

[37] "Racial Assimilation of Secondary Groups," *Proceedings of the American Sociological Society*, Vol. VIII, p. 77.

[38] *Following the Color Line*, p. 40. Cf. Carl C. Zimmerman, "The Evolution of the American Community," *American Journal of Sociology*, Vol. XLVI, May 1941, p. 812; Hortense Powdermaker, op. cit., p. 71.

One device for retarding Negro assimilation, which does not have to be resorted to in the caste system, is the policy of guarding against any development of an overt expression of indispensability of Negroes within the social organization. Whatever their *de facto* importance, they must never appear as an integral part of the society. Instead, they pay little taxes; hence little or none of certain public expenditures should be diverted to their benefit. The theory of taxation according to ability to pay and expenditure according to need does not include them. Crime, sickness, high mortality rates, and poverty almost characterize Negroes, hence they are a drag on "society" and may be ostensibly sloughed off to advantage. Whites are generally protected from contact with cultured Negroes. The successful practice of this contrivance tends to give the Negro a sense of worthlessness and unwantedness, which contributes finally to the retardation of his assimilation. In Brahmanic India, however, where the population is assimilated to the caste culture, it is openly admitted that low-caste men are indispensable to the system, and this admission does not conduce to any advancement in the latter's social status.

By using the caste hypothesis, then, the school seeks to explain a "normal society" in the South. In short, it has made peace for the hybrid society that has not secured harmony for itself; and in so far as this is true, its work is fictitious.

CONTRIBUTION OF THE SCHOOL

An astonishing characteristic of this caste school of race relations is its tendency to conceive of itself as being original. It believes not only that it has made a discovery, but also that it has "created" something.[39] It is difficult, however, to determine wherein rests its originality. We do not know who first made the analogy between race relations and the caste system of India, but it is certain that the idea was quite popular during the middle of the last

---

[39] "The view that the relationships of whites and Negroes in the South are systematically ordered and maintained by a caste structure, and that the status of individuals within each of these groups is further determined by a system of social classes existing within each color-caste, was the creation of Warner." Davis and Dollard, *Children of Bondage*, p. xvi. "The presence of caste and class structures in the society of the deep South was reported upon first by a member of our research group...." Davis, Gardner, Gardner, and Warner, *Deep South*, p. 5. "An original interpretation of class and caste distinctions in the United States, providing a useful frame of reference for an appreciation of caste phenomena in this country." Ogburn and Nimkoff, *Sociology*, p. 343.

century. One of the most detailed and extended discussions of this hypothesis is that of the Hon. Charles Sumner published in 1869; and in 1904 William I. Thomas brought his full genius into play upon the subject.[40] Since then many textbooks have accepted the idea.[41] Some students, like Sir Herbert Risley, have used the hypothesis as the basis of extensive research.[42] Many writers, such as E. B. Reuter and Charles S. Johnson, have applied the term casually to the racial situation in the United States.[43] Donald Young has discussed the concept rather elaborately.[44] Among these we take somewhat at random from the writings of a journalist who in 1908 published in book form the findings of his study of race relations in the South.

In explaining the "class strata" among Negroes Ray Stannard Baker says:

I have now described two of the three great classes of Negroes: First, the worthless and idle Negro, often a criminal, comparatively small in numbers but perniciously evident. Second, the great middle class of Negroes who do the manual work of the South. Above these, a third class, few in number, but most influential in their race, are the progressive, property owning Negroes, who have wholly severed their old intimate ties with the white people—and who have been getting further and further away from them.[45]

With respect to the color line, called a caste line by the modern school, Baker states:

When the line began to be drawn, it was drawn not alone against the unworthy Negro, but against the Negro. It was not so much drawn by the highly-intelligent white man as by the white man. And the white man alone has not drawn it, but the Negroes themselves are drawing it—and more and more every day. So we draw the line in this country against the Chinese, the Japanese, and

in some measure against the Jews; and they help to draw it[46]

Baker then proceeds to clinch the full idea of the caste hypothesis:

More and more they [Negroes] are becoming a people wholly apart—separate in their churches, separate in their schools, separate in cars, conveyances, hotels, restaurants, with separate professional men. In short, we discover tendencies in this country toward the development of a caste system.[47]

It is difficult to see what the modern caste school has added to this, unless it is perhaps publicity and "scientific" prestige.[48] Certainly anyone who has a taste for art might use the information given above to draw a caste line between the white and the black class structures. But Baker, like most other former advocates of the caste hypothesis of race relations in the United States, thinks almost fancifully of the idea and does not stipulate that his work should stand or fall with the belief. He realizes that the consideration of primary significance is not the "caste line" but the way in which that line holds. Thus he concludes:

This very absence of a clear demarcation is significant of many relationships in the South. The color line is drawn, but neither race knows just where it is. Indeed, it can hardly be definitely drawn in many relationships, because it is constantly changing. This uncertainty is a fertile source of friction and bitterness.[49]

With respect to the scientific precision of the word "caste" the school insists: "By all the physical tests the anthropologists might apply, some social Negroes are *biologically* white," hence the term "race" cannot have meaning when applied to Negroes.[50] We should remember here, however, that the racial situation in the South never depended upon "physical tests of anthropologists." It developed long before anthropometry became of age. Furthermore, the sociologist is interested not in what the anthropometrists set up as their criteria of race, but in what peoples in interaction come to accept as a race. It is the latter belief which controls their behavior and not what the anthropometrist thinks.

[40] Charles Sumner, *The Question of Caste.* William I. Thomas, "The Psychology of Race Prejudice," *American Journal of Sociology*, Vol. XI, March 1904, pp. 593–611. As early as 1828 Governor William B. Giles of Virginia referred repeatedly to the free Negroes as a "caste of colored populations." See John H. Russell, *The Free Negro in Virginia*, p. 165.

[41] Among the best of them are C. H. Cooley, *Social Process*, p. 279, and *Social Organization*, pp, 209–28; Park and Burgess, *Introduction to the Science of Sociology*, pp. 205–06, 722.

[42] See, for example, *The Peoples of India*, p. 263, and *Census of India, 1901.*

[43] Reuter, *The Mulatto in the United States*, p. 360; Johnson, "Caste and Class in an American Industry," *American Journal of Sociology*, Vol. XLII, July 1936, pp. 55–65.

[44] *American Minority Peoples*, pp. 580–85. See also R. E. Park, "Racial Assimilation in Secondary Groups," op. cit., p. 73.

[45] *Following the Color Line*, p. 65.

[46] Ibid., p. 218.

[47] Ibid., p. 300.

[48] It is true that sometimes members of the modern caste school have referred to race relations as "*color*-caste." But, so far as we know, they have never shown in what way "*color*-caste" is different from caste. In fact, some of the early theories on the origin of caste have sought to identify caste with racial antagonism. Therefore, the substitution of the term "color-caste" for caste does not seem to have relieved the fundamental confusion.

[49] Ibid., p. 31.

[50] Davis, Gardner, Gardner and Warner, op. cit., pp. 7–8.

But in reality the term "caste" does not economize thinking on this subject; it is a neology totally unjustified. Before we can know what the Negro caste means it is always necessary first to say what kind of people belong to the Negro caste. Therefore, in the course of defining "Negro caste" we have defined "Negro race," and the final achievement is a substitution of words only. One may test this fact by substituting in the writings of this school the words "Negroes" or "white people" where-ever the words "Negro caste" or "white caste" appear and observe that the sense of the statement does not change.

For this reason the burden of the productions of this school is merely old wine in new bottles, and not infrequently the old ideas have suffered from rehandling. In other words, much that has come to us by earlier studies has taken on the glamour of caste, while the school seldom refers to the contributions of out-group students.[51]

One could hardly help recalling as an analogous situation the popularity which William McDougall gave to the instinct hypothesis. Without making any reference to William James, Lloyd Morgan, and

others, who had handled the concept with great care, McDougall set out with pioneering zeal to bend all social behavior into his instinct theory. It was not long, however, before reaction came. And so, too, until quite recently, the race-caste idea had a desultory career. This idea has now been made fashionable, yet already students who had once used the term "caste" are beginning to shrink from it.[52] However, we should hasten to add that this school has none of the anti-color complexes of the instinct school; its leadership merely relies a little too much upon sophistry and lacks a sociological tradition.

In the following chapter we shall consider the major contribution of the Carnegie Studies, which also relies upon a "caste hypothesis" but which seems important enough to justify separate discussion.

An American Dilemma: A Mystical Approach to the Study of Race Relations

If the theoretical structure of our most elaborate study of race relations in America, *An American Dilemma* by Gunnar Myrdal,[1] is correct, then the hypotheses developed in the preceeding three chapters cannot be valid, for the two views are antithetical. It thus becomes incumbent upon us to examine carefully Myrdal's approach. In this examination some repetition is unavoidable, and it seems advisable to quote rather than to paraphrase the author. This critical examination, to be sure, is not intended to be a review of *An American Dilemma*. As a source of information and brilliant interpretation of information on race relations in the United States, it is probably unsurpassed.[2] We are interested here only in the validity of the meanings which Dr. Myrdal derives from the broad movements of his data. The data are continually changing and becoming obsolescent; but if we understand their social determinants we can not only predict change but also influence it. In fact, Myrdal himself directs attention to his social logic in saying: "This book is an analysis, not a description. It presents facts only for the sake of their meaning in the interpretation."[3]

In his attempt to explain race relations in the United States the author seems to have been

---

[51] As a typical example of this, see Davis and others, op. cit., pp. 15–136 and 228–39. Consider, in illustration, the weighty significance and originality with which the following commonplace is introduced: "The critical fact is that a much larger proportion of all *Negroes* are lower class than is the case with *whites. This is where caste comes to bear. It* puts the overwhelming majority of Negroes in the lowest class group, and keeps them there." (Italics added.) Davis and Dollard, op. cit., p. 65. This quotation also illustrates the mystical way in which real problems have been explained away.

[52] See R. E. Park in the introduction to Bertram W. Doyle, *The Etiquette of Race Relations*, and Charles S. Johnson, *Growing Up in the Black Belt*. But observe Johnson's relapse. In speaking of Negro-white relationship in the United States he says: "A racial or caste division of labor is one type of adjustment growing out of economic conflict between racial groups." In *Sociological Foundations of Education*, Joseph S. Roucek, ed., p. 423; also in *Patterns of Negro Segregation*, pp. xvi *passim*. Professor Park has been toying with the idea. For instance, Dr. Donald Pierson gives him credit approvingly for the following simple and somewhat inadequate scheme. "In a caste system," Pierson writes, "the racial lines may run thus:

	White
	───────────
Race Lines	Mixed-blood
	───────────
	Black

."

Negroes in Brazil, p. 337. For a similar diagram by Park, see "The Basis of Race Prejudice," *The Annals*, Vol. CXXXX, November 1928, p. 20. See also the preceding chapter.

[1] Gunnar Myrdal, *An American Dilemma*. Although this is a work of considerable scholarly collaboration, we shall, in this discussion of it, assume that it is entirely by Dr. Myrdal.

[2] Herbert Aptheker would disagree heartily with this, for he has published a small book devoted entirely to a criticism of Myrdal's factual data and of their interpretation. See *The Negro People in America*.

[3] Op. cit., p. li.

confronted with two principal problems: (a) the problem of avoiding a political-class interpretation, and (b) the problem of finding an acceptable moral or ethical interpretation.[4] In the first part of this discussion we shall attempt to show how his "value premise" and the caste theory are employed and, in the second part, how a shying away from the obvious implications of his data is contrived as solution for these problems. We shall not discuss the concept from which the book derives its title, for it seems quite obvious that none of the great imperialist democracies either can or intends to practice its democratic ideals among its subject peoples.[5] Myrdal does not bring to light the social determinants of this well-known dilemma; he merely recognizes it and rails against its existence. It is a long time indeed since Negro newspapers have observed: "The treatment of the Negro is America's greatest and most conspicuous scandal."[6] The dilemma is not peculiarly American; it is worldwide, confronting even the white masses of every capitalist nation.[7] At any rate, what seems to be of immediate significance is Myrdal's explanation of the basis of race relations.

---

[4] Myrdal conceives of his problem—that is to say of race relations in the United States—as "primarily a moral issue of conflicting valuations" and of his "investigation" as "an analysis of morals." Ibid., p. xlvi. Cf. Leo P. Crispi, "Is Gunnar Myrdal on the Right Track?" *The Public Opinion Quarterly*, Summer, 1945.

[5] In a debate at an imperial conference in 1923 on the status of South African Indians, General Smuts faced the dilemma in this way: "I do not think our Indian fellow-subjects in South Africa can complain of injustice. ... They have prospered exceedingly in South Africa. People who have come there as coolies, people who have come there as members of the depressed classes in India, have prospered. ... They have been educated, and their children and grandchildren today are many of them men of great wealth. They have all the rights, barring the rights of voting for parliament and the provincial councils, that any white citizen in South Africa has. ... It is only political rights that are in question. There we are up against a stone wall and we cannot get over it." Quoted in P. S. Joshi, op. cit., p. 107.

[6] Myrdal, op. cit., p. 1020. Dr. Myrdal understands clearly that expressions such as this have now achieved respectability; in fact, they are desirable, since "it is becoming difficult for even popular writers to express other views than the ones of racial equalitarianism and still retain intellectual respect." Op. cit., p. 96.

[7] Years ago Nathaniel Peffer entitled his book *The White Man's Dilemma* and sought to make it clear that "at bottom" the problem is economic—the problem of worldwide economic exploitation by "white capital," of which the American race problem is but one variation.

"The Value Premise"

At the beginning of his study, in a chapter on "American ideals," Dr. Myrdal lays the atmosphere for his conclusions on race relations. The way in which the author handles this subject, as he himself recognizes with some contradiction, has been long ago in dispute among American historians. He considers certain national ideals as if they were phenomena *sui generis*, having an existence apart from and indeed determinative of the economic life of the people. Although he concedes that "the economic determinants and the force of the ideals can be shown to be interrelated,"[8] he is mainly concerned not with showing this interrelationship but rather with elaborating an implicit hypothesis that the "American Creed" is *the* vital force in American life.

> The unanimity around, and the explicitness of, this Creed is the great wonder of America.... The reflecting observer comes to feel that this *spiritual convergence*, more than America's strategic position behind the oceans and its immense material resources, is what makes the nation great and what promises it a still greater future.[9]

We need not be detained here with the question as to whether either of the foregoing alternatives is the sufficient explanation of the "nation's greatness"; our immediate purpose is to observe the author's abstract orientation. He seems never to recognize the determining role of class interest but rather sets his study against a backdrop of an apparently common American ideology which he says "is older than America itself." Thus:

> Americans of all national origins, classes, regions, creeds, and colors, have something in common: a social *ethos*, a political creed. ... When the American Creed is once detected, the cacophony becomes a melody ... as principles which *ought* to rule, the Creed has been made conscious to everyone in American society.... America is continuously struggling for its soul.[10]

---

[8] Op. cit., p. 6.

[9] Ibid., p. 13. (Italics added.) Myrdal describes "the American Creed" as follows: "These principles of social ethics have been hammered into easily remembered formulas. In the clarity and intellectual boldness of the Enlightenment period these tenets were written into the Declaration of Independence, the Preamble of the Constitution, the Bill of Rights, and the constitutions of the several states. ... But this Creed is ... no American monopoly. With minor variations ... the American Creed is the common democratic creed. 'American ideals' are just humane ideals as they have matured in our common Western civilization upon the foundation of Christianity and pre-Christian legalism and under the influence of the economic, scientific, and political development over a number of centuries. The American Creed is older and wider than America itself." Ibid., pp. 4, 25.

[10] Ibid., pp. 3–4.

The cultural unity of the nation is this common sharing of both the consciousness of sin and the devotion to high ideals.[11]

Contrary to Myrdal's rhapsodic description of class and group unity, James Madison, one of the Founding Fathers of the United States, had this to say about the "sentiments" and beliefs of some of the interest groups:

The most common and durable source of factions has been the various and unequal distribution of property. Those who have and those who are without property have ever formed distinct interests in society. Those who are creditors and those who are debtors fall under a like discrimination. A landed interest, a manufacturing interest, a mercantile interest, a moneyed interest, with many lesser interests, grow up of necessity in civilized nations and divide them into different classes, actuated by different sentiments and views. The regulation of these various and interfering interests forms the principal task of modern legislation, and involves the spirit of party and faction in the necessary and ordinary operations of government.[12]

The views of Myrdal and Madison are significantly different. Myrdal is seeking to detect the harmony and "melody" in American life, which he assumes are produced by unquestioned acceptance of certain generalized national symbols by all the people. Madison, on the other hand, is trying to see what fundamentally sets group against group within the nation—what it is that produces the "spirit of party faction." We think that Myrdal is abstract and unreal because he implicitly homogeneates the material interests of the American people and then declares animistically, "America is continually struggling for its soul." Madison recognizes the importance of group sentiments, but he does not say they are determined essentially by a creed. Probably if Myrdal had approached his problem from the point of view of group interests he might have recognized the irreconcilable inconsistency even in "these ideals ... of the fundamental equality of all men, and of certain inalienable rights to freedom." It should be recalled here that the author's assignment was that of discovering the pertinent social factors entering into a situation of continuing social conflict and antagonism.

The following is an intimation of the significance of Myrdal's creedal analysis for his main problem: "From the point of view of the American Creed the status accorded the Negro in America presents *nothing more and nothing less* than a century-long *lag of public morals*. In principle the Negro problem was settled long ago...."[13] Had this statement been a mere figure of speech, it should, of course, be of no consequence. It is, however, in this area of elated abstraction that our author intends to keep the subject. Probably it may be said rather conclusively that the Negro problem cannot be solved "in principle" because it is not basically an ideological problem. Indeed, speaking abstractly, we may conclude similarly that all the major social problems of the Christian world were solved "in principle" by the opening words of the Lord's Prayer—to say nothing of the whole Sermon on the Mount.

Many years ago Professor Charles A. Beard effectively criticized this romantic approach to the study of American society. He said: "In the great transformations in society, such as was brought about by the formation and adoption of the Constitution, economic 'forces' are primordial or fundamental and come nearer 'explaining' events than any other 'forces.'" And further: "Whoever leaves economic pressures out of history or out of the discussion of public questions is in mortal peril of substituting mythology for reality and confusing issues instead of clarifying them."[14] To be sure, social ideologies are always significant, but they are, on the whole, dependent social phenomena.

It is just such a relationship with which Abraham Lincoln was confronted when he declared: "... our fathers brought forth on this continent a new nation, conceived in liberty, and dedicated to the proposition that all men are created equal. Now we are engaged in a great civil war, testing whether that nation, or any nation so conceived and so dedicated, can long endure." Neither side in this civil war questioned the ideals, yet they were—and to this very day are—not fully agreed on the interpretation of the ideals.[15] The crucial circumstances, then, are

---

[11] Ibid., p. 22.

[12] *The Federalist*, No. 10. See, for a similar observation, Woodrow Wilson, *Constitutional Government of the United States*, pp. 217–18.

[13] Op. cit., p. 24. (Italics added.)

[14] *An Economic Interpretation of the Constitution of the United States*, 1st ed., pp. xii, xvii.

[15] In the Federal Constitutional Convention of 1787 General Pinckney of South Carolina intimated realistically the interests behind the contemporary Negro problem. Said he: "An attempt to take away the right [to import slaves] as proposed would produce serious objections to the Constitution." And he "declared it to be his firm opinion that if he himself and all his colleagues were to sign the Constitution and use their personal influence, it would be of no avail towards obtaining the assent of their constituents. South Carolina and Georgia cannot do without slaves. As to Virginia she will gain by stopping the importation. Her slaves will rise in value, and she has more than she wants. It would be unequal to require South Carolina and Georgia to confederate on such unequal terms. ... He contended that the importation of slaves would be for the interest of the whole Union. The more slaves, the more produce to employ the carrying trade; the more consumption also, and the more of this, the more of revenues for the common treasury." See Max Farrand, ed., *The Records of the Federal Convention of 1787*, Vol. II, p. 371.

not the presumed universal acceptance of the "Creed," but rather the interests which make its peculiar and divergent interpretations inevitable. In other words, each side had different material interests and, as is ordinarily the case, the ideals of each were made subservient to the material interests. To put it otherwise, the Creed, in its formative stage, was seriously debated and contested, but since it had become stereotyped, neither side questioned it. Each side, however, insisted upon a self-interested interpretation of it.

The Declaration of Independence and the Constitution have become national symbols, like the flag. It is quite another thing, however, to say that the content of these documents is accepted even as a creed by the whole people. As E. E. Schattschneider points out: "The truth of the matter is that the American public has never understood the Constitution, nor has it ever really believed in it, in spite of the verbal tradition of Constitutionalism."[15a] One pertinent illustration is the non-acceptance of the Thirteenth, Fourteenth, and Fifteenth amendments either in spirit or in practice by the ruling class of the South. Again we cite a statement on this point by James Madison: "Neither moral nor religious motives can be relied on as an adequate control"; and, in another context: "Wherever there is an interest and power to do wrong, wrong will be done."[16]

The Constitution did not settle or remove the vitally conflicting interests of the infant capitalist system; it simply compromised or ignored them. In other words, it postponed for a later date the real solution of latent antagonisms—postponed it until such time as one side or the other developed sufficient power to force a solution in its favor. And yet the Constitution is so ample in its scope that with certain amendments and abrogations it may become the fundamental law of a consummate democracy.[17]

Moreover, Myrdal's "value premise" appears to be demonstrably weakened in consequence of its being built principally upon certain fictitious attributes of ideal types, such as "the citizen," "American popular thought," "the American soul," "the common good American." For instance, the foregoing concept is employed in this way: "Today it is necessary in everyday living for the common good American citizen to decide for himself which laws should be observed and which not."[18]

THE CASTE HYPOTHESIS

The whole theoretical frame of reference of *An American Dilemma* is supposedly couched in a caste hypothesis. As Myrdal himself puts it: "Practically the entire factual content of ... this book may be considered to define caste in the case of the American Negro."[19] However, it is evident that Myrdal—in spite of the lamentable use of such phrases as "in our view," "as we have defined it," and so on—does not intend to coin a new concept. In criticizing Charles S. Johnson's idea of caste he declares, "We do not believe that such a caste system as he has defined ever existed."[20] Therefore, in his explanation of race relations in the United States, our author means to accept the known concept as a norm. Of some significance is the way in which the term is selected. This is the reasoning:

> The term "race" is ... inappropriate in a scientific inquiry since it has biological and genetic connotations which ... run parallel to widely spread false racial beliefs. The ... term, "class," is impractical and confusing ... since it is generally used to refer to a non-rigid status group from which an individual member can rise or fall. ... We need a term to distinguish the large and systematic type of social differentiation from the small and spotty type and have ... used the term "caste."[21]

Obviously, in arriving at this decision to use the term "caste" in explaining race relations in the United States, Dr. Myrdal employs the method of successive elimination. Without attempting to be facetious, it may be compared with that of the scientist who comes upon a strange animal and, having the necessity to classify it, says to himself: "This is not a cat, I am sure; neither is it a dog, I am positive of that; therefore, since I do not think of anything else, I am going to call it a duck."

There is no new theory of race relations in this study, but it develops the most elaborate defense of the caste belief. Dr. Myrdal has adopted not only the whole theory of the caste school of race relations in the United States but also its procedure. Like the leadership of this school, he appears to have taken some pride in regarding as worthless a study

---

[15a] *Party Government,* p. 53.

[16] *Documentary History of the Constitution,* Vol. V, p. 88.

[17] "The federal Constitution was a reactionary document from the point of view of the doctrines of the Revolution. Its bill of rights was a series of amendments added by dissatisfied elements after the instrument had been drawn up and submitted to the people. The rule of the few ... soon began, and government lent its hand to the few who could invest in its financial paper and who gave their efforts to the building of cities and commerce and industry. ... A new order of bourgeois acquisitiveness ... was in the saddle. Democracy, like the rest of the hindmost, was left for the devil." Avery Craven, *Democracy in American Life,* p. 13. See also Woodrow Wilson, op. cit., p. 192.

[18] Myrdal, op. cit., p. 17.

[19] Ibid., p. 669.

[20] Ibid., p. 1375.

[21] Ibid., p. 667.

of Hindu society as a basis for making comparisons with Western society. Yet, as we should expect, he depends entirely upon the Hindu system for his orientation.

Thus the reader is asked to accept generalizations about the caste system in America when no other reference is made to the cultural norm than the following:

> It should be pointed out ... that those societies to which the term "caste" is applied without controversy—notably the ante-bellum slavery society of the South and the Hindu society of India—do not have the "stable equilibrium" which American sociologists from their distance are often inclined to attribute to them.... A Hindu acquaintance once told me that the situation in the United States is as much or more describable by the term "caste" as is the situation in India.[22]

From this, one thing is clear: Myrdal is very much in error in believing that it is recognized without controversy that slavery in the South constituted a caste system.[23] Moreover, it is difficult to see how one could avoid the conclusion that the author has descended to some vulgar means in referring to the hearsay of "a Hindu acquaintance" as authority for the sociology of caste.

THE BIOLOGICAL PROBLEM

Probably the crucial circumstance in attempts to use some term other than race in describing race relations is a desire to get around the biological implications in the term. Yet it has never been shown that there is a real necessity for this. In fact, those who verbally eschew the biological connotation of the term proceed, nonetheless, to make physical differences the crux of their discussion. This is particularly true of Myrdal. Says he, "Negro features are so distinct that only in the Negro problem does [belief in the desirability of a light skin and "good" features] become of great social importance."[24] And he proceeds, evidently without realizing it, to point out the relationship of skin color to caste:

> ... the average Negro cannot effectively change his color and other physical features. If the dark Negro accepts the white man's valuation of skin color, he must stamp himself an inferior. If the light Negro accepts this valuation, he places himself above the darker Negroes but below the whites, and he reduces his loyalty to his caste.[25]

Myrdal continues his biological interpretation of race relations with great clarity. "When we say that Negroes form a lower caste in America," he asserts, "we mean that they are subject to certain disabilities solely because they are 'Negroes,'"[26] manifestly; that is to say, solely because they are colored or black. Moreover, although the writer did not elaborate this point, he refers to Asiatics, Indians, and Negroes as "the several subordinate castes."[27] It should be interesting to see how he fits these peoples into an American caste hierarchy. At any rate, with this conception of race relations, the author inevitably comes to the end of the blind alley: that the caste system remains intact so long as the Negro remains colored.

> The change and variations which occur in the American caste system relate only to caste relations, not to the dividing line between castes. The latter stays rigid and unblurred. It will remain fixed until it becomes possible for a person to pass legitimately from the lower caste to the higher without misrepresentation of his origin. The American definition of "Negro" as a person who has the slightest amount of Negro ancestry has the significance in making the caste line absolutely rigid.[28]

Myrdal is so thoroughly preoccupied with the great significance of skin color that, although he realizes that in America Negroes of lighter complexion have greater social opportunities, he believes that they may as well be unmixed blacks so far as the "caste line" is concerned. Accordingly he asserts: "Without any doubt a Negro with light skin and other European features has in the North an advantage with white people when competing for jobs available for Negroes.... Perhaps of even greater importance is the fact that the Negro community itself has accepted this color preference."[29] This, however, has nothing to do with the rigidity of the caste line.

When Dr. Myrdal strays from his physical emphasis he becomes confused. For instance, he concludes that "being a Negro means being subject to considerable disabilities in practically all spheres of life."[30] Evidently it must follow logically from this that to the extent to which these "disabilities" are removed, to that extent also a person ceases to remain a Negro. The confusion is further deepened by the combination of a cultural and biological view of caste.

> Caste ... consists of such drastic restrictions to free competition in various spheres of life that the individual in

---

[22] Ibid., p. 668. See also note c.

[23] We cannot be certain, however, that Myrdal has a settled view on this point, for he says elsewhere: "After the [Civil] War and Emancipation, the race dogma was retained in the South as necessary to justify the caste system which succeeded slavery. ..." Ibid., p. 88. See also pp. 221–24.

[24] Ibid., p. 669.

[25] Ibid., p. 669.

[26] Ibid., p. 669.

[27] Ibid., p. 670.

[28] Ibid., pp. 668–69.

[29] Ibid., p. 697.

[30] Ibid., p. 668.

a lower caste cannot, by any means, change his status except by a secret and illegitimate "passing" which is possible only to the few who have the physical appearance of members of the upper caste.[31]

In other words, caste consists in restrictions to free competitions, but restrictions to free competition are entirely limited by a man's physical appearance. Now, we may ask, what is the nexus between physical appearance and caste?

RIGIDITY OF THE CASTE SYSTEM

We may reiterate that the caste school of race relations is laboring under the illusion of a simple but vicious truism. One man is white, another is black; the cultural opportunities of these two men may be the same, but since the black man cannot become white, there will always be a white caste and a black caste: "The actual import of caste is gradually changing as the Negro class structure develops— except in the fundamental restrictions that no Negro is allowed to ascend into the white caste."[32] Yet, if this is so, what possible meaning could the following observation have? "We have been brought to view the caste order as fundamentally a system of disabilities forced by the whites upon the Negroes."[33]

Closely related to this amorphous concept of the rigidity of caste is the meaning given to interracial endogamy. Myrdal uses it to identify the races in the United States as castes.

> The scientifically important difference between the terms "caste" and "class" is … a relatively large difference in freedom of movement between groups. This difference is foremost in marriage relations…. The ban on intermarriage is one expression of the still broader principle … that a man born a Negro or a white is not allowed to pass from the one status to the other as he can pass from one class to another.[34]

Now it could hardly be too much emphasized that endogamy of itself is no final criterion of caste. Endogamy is an isolator of social values deemed sacrosanct by social groups, and there are many kinds of social groups besides castes that are endogamous. The final test of caste is an identification of the social values and organization isolated by endogamy. To say that intercaste endogamy in India means the same thing as interracial endogamy in the United States is like saying that a lemon and a potato are the same things because they both have skins.

An illustration of Myrdal's complete disregard of the nature of caste organization is his discussion of "caste struggle." This concept of "caste struggle," to be sure, is totally foreign to our norm, the Indian caste system. Moreover, this must be so because castes in Brahmanic India do not want to be anything other than castes. There is no effort or logical need to homogeneate themselves. A caste is a status entity in an assimilated, self-satisfied society. Regardless of his position in the society, a man's caste is sacred to him; and one caste does not dominate the other. The following description of caste has absolutely no application to caste in India.

> The caste distinctions are actually gulfs which divide the population into antagonistic camps. The caste line … is not only an expression of caste differences and caste conflicts, but it has come itself to be a catalyst to widen differences and engender conflicts.[35]

MYSTICISM

If the scientist has no clear conception of the norm which he is using to interpret social phenomena, the norm itself is likely to become lost in the data. When this happens he will ordinarily have recourse to mystical flights. In our case Myrdal seems to attribute magical powers to caste. Speaking of the cause of the economic position of Negroes in the United States he says: "Their caste position keeps them poor and ill-educated."[36] And, "Caste consigns the overwhelming majority of Negroes to the lower class."[37] Indeed, the whole meaning of racial exploitation in the United States is laid at the altar of caste. Thus it is observed: "The measures to keep the Negroes disfranchised and deprived of full civil rights and the whole structure of social and economic discrimination are to be viewed as attempts to enforce *the caste principle*."[38]

More immediately, this mysticism is due primarily to a misapprehension of the whole basis of race relations. Caste is vaguely conceived of as something, the preservation of which is valuable per se. "The caste system is upheld by its own inertia and by the superior caste's interests in upholding it."[39] It is no wonder, then, that Myrdal falls into the egregious error of thinking that the subordination of Negroes in the South is particularly the business of poor whites. In this light he reasons: "That 'all Negroes are alike' and should be treated in the same way is still insisted upon by many whites, especially in the lower classes, who actually feel, or

---

[31] Ibid., p. 675.

[32] Ibid., p. 693.

[33] Ibid., p. 669.

[34] Ibid., p. 668.

[35] Ibid., pp. 676–77.

[36] Ibid., p. 669.

[37] Ibid., p. 71.

[38] Ibid., p. 690. (Italics added.)

[39] Ibid., p. 669.

fear, competition from the Negroes and who are inclined to sense a challenge to their status in the fact that some Negroes rise from the bottom."[40] This, obviously, is a conception of race relations in terms of personal invidiousness. Surely, to say that "Southern whites, *especially in the lower brackets* ... have succeeded in retaining [the] legal and political system" is to miss the point entirely. We shall return to this question in the following section.

One primary objection to the use of the caste belief in the study of race relations rests not so much upon its scientific untenability as upon its insidious potentialities. It lumps all white people and all Negroes into two antagonistic groups struggling in the interest of a mysterious god called caste. This is very much to the liking of the exploiters of labor, since it tends to confuse them in an emotional matrix with all the people. Observe in illustration how Myrdal directs our view: "All of these thousand and one precepts, etiquettes, taboos, and disabilities inflicted upon the Negro have a common purpose: to express the subordinate status of the Negro people and the exalted position of the whites. They have their meaning and chief function as symbols."[41]

It thus appears that if *white people* were not so wicked, if they would only cease wanting to "exalt" themselves and accept the "American Creed," race prejudice would vanish from America. "Why," asks Myrdal, "is race prejudice ... not increasing but decreasing?" And he answers sanctimoniously: "This question is ... only a special variant of the enigma of philosophers for several thousands of years: the problem of Good and Evil in the world."[42] Clearly, this is an escape from the realities of the social system, inexcusable in the modern social scientist.[43] At any rate, the philosophers'

enigma apparently leads him directly into a mystical play with imponderables. As he sees it, "white prejudice" is a primary determinant in race relations. "White prejudice and discrimination keep the Negro low in standards of living. ... This, in turn, gives support to prejudice. White prejudice and Negro standards thus mutually 'cause' each other."[44] Moreover, "the chief hindrance to improving the Negro is *the white man's firm belief in his inferiority*."[45] We shall discuss this controlling idea in a later section.

Poor Whites

It should be pointed out again that Myrdal not only closes his eyes to the material interests which support and maintain race prejudice but also labors the point that there is basic antagonism between poor whites and Negroes. Says he: "... what a bitter, spiteful, and relentless feeling often prevails against the Negroes among lower class white people in America. ... The Marxian solidarity between the toilers ... will ... have a long way to go as far as concerns solidarity of the poor white American with the toiling Negro."[46] In fact, the author goes

---

Continued

refers only to legal marriage and to relations between Negro men and white women, but not to extra-marital sex relations between white men and Negro women." Ibid., p. 59.

This excerpt is not exceptional; it characterizes the writing. Its meaning is probably this: "This theory of color caste is a rationalization. Besides the economic interests upon which this rationalization is based, we should take into account certain appetites and instinctual drives common to all human beings." The conclusion in the last sentence is incorrect. It is contrary to both the logic of race relations and the data as recorded in the literature including some of the earliest court records on white-man, Negro-woman sex relations. The deplorable fact about this writing is not so much that it is obscure as that it seeks to maneuver the reader into accepting the rationalization as the real reason for racial antagonism. We could hardly emphasize too much that "sexual urges, inhibitions," and so on, traits common to Negroes as well as whites, cannot explain why certain whites dominate Negroes. Moreover, the author does not show that anyone has ever argued that the mere fact that a rationalization is recognized for what it is destroys it. This, obviously, is a straw man set up to cover the author's obsession with abstractions.

---

[40] Ibid., p. 689.

[41] Ibid., p. 66.

[42] Ibid., p. 79. See W. Cunningham, *The Growth of English Industry and Commerce*, Vol. I, pp. 556–57, for a review of this tendency among sixteenth-century English moralists to explain social problems by attributing them to human sinfulness.

[43] Probably we should mention here another deplorable achievement of Myrdal's—his developed capacity for obscuring the basis of racial antagonism. Consider in illustration the following paragraph:

"Though the popular theory of color caste turns out to be a rationalization, this does not destroy it. For among the forces in the minds of the white people are certainly not only economic interests (if these were the only ones, the popular theory would be utterly demolished), but also sexual urges, inhibitions, and jealousies, and social fears and cravings for prestige and security. When they come under the scrutiny of scientific research, both the sexual and the social complexes take on unexpected designs. We shall then also get a clue to understanding the remarkable tendency of this presumably biological doctrine, that it

[44] Ibid., p. 75.

[45] Ibid., p. 101. (Italics added.)

[46] Ibid., p. 69. In almost identical terms André Siegfried interprets the racial situation: "In the wealthy families some of the old-time sentimentality still survives from the slave days, but the 'poor white' sees in the Negro nothing

further to intimate that the poor whites may assume a dominant role in the oppression of Negroes in the South, because the interest of the poor whites is economic, while that of the ruling class is a feeling for superiority:

> Lower class whites in the South have no Negro servants in whose humble demeanors they can reflect their own superiority. Instead, they feel actual economic competition or fear of potential competition from the Negroes. They need the caste demarcations for much more substantial reasons than do the middle and upper classes.[47]

The author hesitates to come to that obvious conclusion so much dreaded by the capitalist ruling class: that the observed overt competitive antagonism is a condition produced and carefully maintained by the exploiters of both the poor whites and the

Negroes. Yet he almost says this in so many words: "Plantation owners and employers, who use Negro labor as cheaper and more docile, have at times been observed to tolerate, or co-operate in, the periodic aggression of poor whites against Negroes. It is a plausible thesis that they do so in the interest of upholding the caste system which is so effective in keeping the Negro docile."[48] And even more strikingly he shows by what means white workers are exploited through the perpetuation of racial antagonism. Says he: "If those white workers were paid low wages and held in great dependence, they could at least be offered a consolation of being protected from Negro competition."[49]

At any rate, Myrdal refuses to be consistent. Accordingly, he asserts, attitudes against interracial marriage "seems generally to be inversely related to the economic and social status of the informant and his educational level.... To the poor and socially insecure, but struggling, white individual, a fixed opinion on this point seems an important matter of prestige and distinction."[50] It would not do, of course, to explain the situation realistically by concluding that if the revised black codes written by the white exploiting class against intermarriage were abrogated an increasing number of marriages between

---

Continued

but a brutal competitor who is trying to rob him of his job. His hatred is unrelenting, merciless, and mingled with fear. To understand the South, we must realize that the lower we descend in the social scale, the more violent the hatred of the Negro." *America Comes of Age*, p. 97. See also Edwin R. Embree, *Brown America*, p. 201.

[47] Op. cit., p. 597. This social illusion concerning the naturalness of racial antagonism between Negroes and poor whites, a mirage ordinarily perpetuated by the white ruling class, is deeply embedded in the literature. For instance, Professor Louis Wirth declares with finality: "It has been repeatedly found by students of Negro-white relations in the South that the so-called white aristocracy shows less racial prejudice than do the 'poor whites' whose own position is relatively insecure and who must compete with Negroes for jobs, for property, for social position, and for power. Only those who themselves are insecure feel impelled to press their claims for superiority over others." See "Race and Public Policy," *The Scientific Monthly*, April 1944, p. 304.

Now, we may ask, why should competition be more natural than consolidation in the struggle for wealth and position? Why should insecurity lead more naturally to division than to a closing of ranks? Suppose the Negro and the white proletariat of the South decide to come together and unite for increasing power in their struggle for economic position, what are the sources of opposing power—disorganizing power—that will be immediately brought into action? Wirth might just as well argue that the antagonism and open conflicts which ordinarily develop between union strikers and scabs are caused by a feeling of insecurity among the scabs. In the end this argument must be put into that category of vacuus universals which explain nothing, for who in this world does not feel insecure? And if it is a matter of the degree of insecurity, then we should expect Negroes to take the initiative in interracial aggression since they are the most insecure. In the theoretical discussion of race relations "human nature" or the behavior of human beings as such should be taken for granted.

Continued

Sometimes thought is effectively canalized by such apparently objective statements by social scientists as the following: "A standard saying among the southern common folks is that we ought to treat the Negro as we did the Indian: kill him if he doesn't behave and, if not, isolate him and give him what we want to." Howard W. Odum, "Problem and Methodology in an American Dilemma," *Social Forces*, Vol. 23, October 1944, p. 98. Clearly the implication here is that the Southern aristocrats and their university professors are the protectors of the Negroes against the pent-up viciousness of the "southern common folks"—a complete perversion of reality.

[48] Ibid., p. 598. In another context he recognizes that "there had been plenty of racial competition before the Civil War. White artisans had often vociferously protested against the use of Negroes for skilled work in the crafts. But as long as the politically most powerful group of whites had a vested interest in Negro mechanics, the protesting was of little avail." Ibid., p. 281.

[49] Ibid., p. 286. In the South African situation Lord Olivier makes a similar observation: "When the capitalist employer comes on the scene, making discriminations as to the labor forces he must employ for particular work in order to make his profits, which is the law of this activity to do, then, and not till then, antagonism is introduced between the newly-created wage-working proletarian white and the native—who, in regard to the qualifications which properly determine wage contracts, are on exactly the same footing." *The Anatomy of African Misery*, p. 135.

[50] Op. cit., p. 57.

the white and the black proletariat would take place, the consequence of which would be a considerably reduced opportunity for labor exploitation by this class.[51]

THE RULING CLASS

Myrdal does not like to talk about the ruling class in the South; the term carries for him an odious "Marxist" connotation. Yet inevitably he describes this class as well as anyone:

> The one-party system in the South ... and the low political participation of even the white people favor a *de facto* oligarchic regime.... The oligarchy consists of the big landowners, the industrialists, the bankers, and the merchants. Northern corporate business with big investments in the region has been sharing in the political control by this oligarchy.[52]

And he stresses the ineffectiveness of the exploited masses. "The Southern masses do not generally organize either for advancing their ideals or for protecting their group interests. The immediate reason most often given by Southern liberals is the resistance from the political oligarchy which wants to keep the masses inarticulate."[53] Furthermore, he indicates the desperate pressure endured by Southern workers when he says: "The poorest farmer in the Scandinavian countries or in England ... would not take benevolent orders so meekly as Negroes and white sharecroppers do in the South."[54]

Sometimes Myrdal shakes off the whole burden of obfuscation spun about caste, creeds,[55] and poor-white control to show, perhaps without intending to do so, the real interest of the ruling class and how it sets race against race to accomplish its exploitative purpose:

> The conservative opponents of reform proposals [that is to say the ruling class in the South] can usually discredit them by pointing out that they will improve the status of the Negroes, and that they prepare for "social equality." This argument has been raised in the South against labor unions, child labor legislation and practically every other proposal for reform.
>
> It has been argued to the white workers that the Wages and Hours Law was an attempt to legislate equality between the races by raising the wage level of Negro workers to that of whites. The South has never been seriously interested in instituting tenancy legislation to protect the tenants' rights ... and the argument has again been that the Negro sharecropper should not be helped against the white man.[56]

It seems clear that in developing a theory of race relations in the South one must look to the economic policies of the ruling class and not to mere abstract depravity among poor whites. Opposition to social equality has no meaning unless we can see its function in the service of the exploitative purpose of this class. "When the Negro rises socially," says Myrdal, "and is no longer a servant, he becomes a stranger to the white upper class. His ambition is suspected and he is disliked."[57] Again: "The ordinary white upper class people will 'have no use' for such Negroes. They need cheap labor—faithful, obedient, unambitious labor."[58] And the author observes further: "In most Southern communities the ruling classes of whites want to keep Negroes from joining labor unions. Some are quite frank in wanting to keep Negroes from reading the Constitution or studying social subjects."[59]

In the South the ruling class stands effectively between the Negroes and the white proletariat. Every

---

[51] Hinton R. Helper, the renegade Southerner who never bit his tongue in his criticism of the white ruling class of the South and who, however, never concealed his prejudices against the Negroes, spoke more than a grain of truth when he described the position of the poor whites. It is essentially applicable to present-day conditions. "Notwithstanding the fact that the white non-slaveholders of the South are in the majority as five to one, they have never yet had any part or lot in framing the laws under which they live.... The lords of the lash are not only absolute masters of the blacks ... but they are also the oracles and arbiters of all the non-slaveholding whites, whose freedom is merely nominal and whose unparalleled illiteracy and degradation is purposely and fiendishly perpetuated. How little the 'poor white trash,' the great majority of the Southern people, know of the real conditions of the country is indeed sadly astonishing.... It is expected that the stupid and sequacious masses, the white victims of slavery, will believe and, as a general thing, they do believe, whatever the slaveholders tell them; and thus it is that they are cajoled into the notion that they are the freest, happiest, and most intelligent people in the world, and are taught to look with prejudice and disapprobation upon every new principle or progressive movement." *The Impending Crisis*, pp. 42–44 *passim*.

[52] Op. cit., p. 453.

[53] Ibid., p. 455.

[54] Ibid., p. 466.

[55] This statement is made advisedly. The following unreal conflict between status and ideals may indicate further the nebulous level at which the theoretical part of this study is sometimes pitched: "The American Creed represents the national conscience. The Negro is a 'problem' to the average American partly because of a palpable conflict between the status actually awarded him and those ideals." Ibid., p. 23.

[56] Ibid., p. 456.

[57] Ibid., p. 593.

[58] Ibid., p. 596.

[59] Ibid., p. 721.

segregation barrier is a barrier put up between white and black people by their exploiters. Myrdal puts it in this way: "On the local scene the accommodation motive by itself does not usually encourage Negro leaders to such adventures as trying to reach behind the white leaders to the white people."[60] Moreover, it is not the poor whites but the ruling class which uses its intelligence and its money to guard against any movement among Negroes to throw off their yoke of exploitation. "In many communities leading white citizens make no secret of the fact that they are carefully following ... all signs of 'subversive propaganda' and unrest among the Negroes in the community, and that they interfere to stop even innocent beginnings of Negro group activity."[61]

The reasoning which we are now following, it may be well to state, is not Myrdal's; we are merely culling those conclusions which the data seem to compel the author to make but which he ordinarily surrounds with some mysterious argument about caste.

From one point of view the masters did not have so great a need for racial antagonism during slavery. Black workers could be exploited in comparative peace; the formal law was on the side of the slave owner. As Myrdal observes: "Exploitation of Negro labor was, perhaps, a less embarrassing *moral conflict* to the ante-bellum planter than to his peer today.... Today the exploitation is, to a considerable degree, dependent upon the availability of extralegal devices of various kinds."[62] Obviously, among these extralegal devices are race prejudice, discrimination, and violence—especially lynching and the threat of lynching. "Discrimination against Negroes is ... rooted in this tradition of economic exploitation."[63]

Emphasis upon Sex

In spite of this, however, Myrdal refuses to accept a realistic interpretation of race relations. Throughout these volumes he warns his readers not to put too much reliance upon a socioeconomic explanation. Thus he declares: "The eager intent to explain away race prejudice and caste in the simple terms of economic competition ... is an attempt to *escape from caste to class*."[64] The reasoning here, of course, is unrelieved nonsense. Incidentally, it illustrates the hiatus in understanding which an inappropriate use of the concepts "caste" and "class" might entail. At any rate, our author thinks it is more revealing to take sex as our point of reference. In fact, Myrdal

presents a scheme of social situations in which he ranks intermarriage and sexual intercourse involving white women as the highest in motives for discrimination, while he ranks economic conditions sixth and last.

(1) Highest in this order [of discrimination] stands the bar against intermarriage and sexual intercourse involving white women (2) ... several etiquettes and discriminations ... (3) ... segregations and discriminations in use of public facilities such as schools ... (4) political disfranchisement ... (5) discrimination in the law courts ... (6) ... discriminations in securing land, credit, jobs ...[65]

This rank order evidences the degree of importance which "white people" attach to certain social facts calculated to keep the Negro in his place, and it is "apparently determined by the factors of sex and social status."[66] The Negroes' estimate, however, is just the reverse of this: "The Negro's own rank order is just about parallel, but inverse, to that of the white man."[67] Here, then, is a perfect example of social illusion, an illusion that must inevitably come to all those who attempt to see race relations in the South as involving two castes.

In reality, both the Negroes and their white exploiters know that economic opportunity comes first and that the white woman comes second; indeed, she is merely a significant instrument in limiting the first. Moreover, these selected elements of social discrimination should not be thought of as discrete social phenomena; they are rather intermeshed in a definite pattern supporting a dominant purpose. If the white ruling class intends to keep the colored people in their place—that is to say, freely exploitable—this class cannot permit them to marry white women; neither can it let white men marry Negro women. If this were allowed to happen Negroes would soon become so whitened that the

---

[60] Ibid., p. 727.

[61] Ibid., p. 459.

[62] Ibid., p. 220. (Italics added.)

[63] Ibid., p. 208.

[64] Ibid., p. 792. (Italics added.)

[65] Ibid., p. 61. In similar vein he asserts: "It is surely significant that the white Southerner is much less willing to permit intermarriage or to grant 'social equality' than he is to allow equality in the political, judicial and economic spheres. The violence of the Southerner's reaction to equality in each of these spheres rises with the degree of its relation to the sexual and personal, whcih suggests that *his prejudice is based upon fundamental attitudes toward sex and personality.*" (Italics added.) Ibid., p. 61.

[66] Ibid., p. 61. It is further emphasized: "The concern for 'race purity' is *basic* in the whole issue; the primary and essential command is to prevent amalgamation.... Rejection of 'social equality' is to be understood as a precaution to hinder miscegenation and particularly intermarriage. The danger of miscegenation is so tremendous that segregation and discrimination inherent in the refusal of 'social equality' must be extended to all spheres of life." Ibid., p. 58.

[67] Ibid., p. 61.

profit makers would be unable to direct mass hatred against them[68] and would thus lose their principal weapon in facilitating their primary business of exploiting the white and the black workers of the South.[69] If a Negro could become governor of Georgia it would be of no particular social significance whether his wife is white or colored; or, at any rate, there would be no political power presuming to limit the color of his wife. But if, in a "democracy," you could insist that his wife must be black, you could not only prevent his becoming governor of Georgia, but you could also make him do most of your dirty and menial work at your wages.[70] Sexual obsession, then, functions in the fundamental interest of economic exploitation.

As a matter of fact, Myrdal is apparently so concerned with his sexual emphasis that he is here led to compare incommensurable arrays: the "white man's" system of rationalization with the real basis of race relations, as the Negroes react to it. If he had been consistent in dealing with economic reality, he would probably have been able to extricate its superstructure of rationalization with sex as its emotional fundament. Indeed, this very approach might have led him to discover the pith of the problem, for Negroes "resist" least that which is of comparatively little moment and most that which is of crucial significance. Sex is not "basic" in race relations, but it is basic in the system of rationalization which supports racial antagonism.

Again our author sees the problem in this light: "It is inherent in our type of modern Western civilization that sex and social status are for most individuals the danger points, the directions whence he fears the sinister onslaughts on his personal security."[71] This passage is intended as an explanation of the "white man's theory of color caste," determined by sexual fears. However, it seems inadequate for two reasons: (a) it is not significantly characteristic of "Western civilization" and (b) it tends to conceive of race prejudice as a personal matter. In all societies "sex and social status" are "danger points" to the individual. In apparently most of them they are much more so than in Western society; in Brahmanic India, for instance, they are infinitely more so, but there has been no race prejudice in Brahmanic India. Then, too, we could hardly overemphasize the fact that race prejudice is not a personal attitude. The individual in the South is not allowed to exercise personal discretion in this matter. Indeed, it is obviously the very fear of sexual attraction between individual members of the races which caused the ruling class to make laws supported by propaganda for its control.

THE VICIOUS CIRCLE

Capitalist rationalizations of race relations have recently come face to face with a powerful theory of society and, in order to meet this, the orthodox theorists have become mystics. This evidently had to be so because it is exceedingly terrifying for these scientists to follow to its logical conclusion a realistic explanation of race relations; and yet they must either do this or stultify themselves. Here the social scientist is "on the spot"; he must avoid "the truth" because it is dangerous, regardless of how gracefully he eases up to it. In illustration, Myrdal advises Negroes not to become too radical and to think of many causes as of equal significance with the material factor: "Negro strategy would build on an illusion if it set all its hope on a blitzkrieg directed toward a basic [economic] factor. In the nature of things it must work on the broadest possible front. There is a place for both the radical and the conservative Negro leaders."[72] This, obviously,

---

[68] It should be made crystal-clear that the design of the ruling white people is not primarily to keep the blood of the white race "pure," but rather to prevent race mixture; it is therefore definitely as frustrating to their fundamental purpose of economic exploitation to infuse white blood into the Negro group. Their purpose can be accomplished only if the Negroes remain identifiably colored.

[69] Decades ago George W. Cable observed: "The essence of the offence, any and everywhere the race line is insisted upon, is the apparition of the colored man or woman as his or her own master; that masterhood is all that all this tyranny is intended to preserve.... The moment the relation of master and servant is visably established between race and race there is a hush of peace.... The surrender of this one point by the colored man or woman buys more than peace—it buys amity." *The Negro Question*, pp. 22–23.

And, as if it were in confirmation of this, C. R. Goodlatte writes, "It may be said of us that we welcome the native as a servant: as a rule we treat him individually in a fairly humane fashion; we often win his esteem and trust; but in any other capacity than that of a docile servant we consider him intolerable." "South Africa: Glimpses and Comments," *Contemporary Review*, CXXXIII, 1928, p. 347.

[70] In order to support his specious argument Myrdal relies pivotally upon such sour-grape expressions as the following by R. R. Moton: "As for amalgamation, very few expect it; still fewer want it; no one advocates it; and only a constantly diminishing minority practise it, and that surreptitiously. It is generally accepted on both sides of the color line that it is best for the two races to remain ethnologically distinct." Op. cit., p. 62. This, from a Negro, is assumed to be evidence that Negroes do not want intermarriage. On its face, Myrdal might have asked: Why should something that is not wanted be practiced "surreptitiously"? Moreover, would the white ruling class be obsessed with the prevention of intermarriage if the natural likelihood of its occurring were exceedingly remote?

[71] Ibid., p. 59.
[72] Ibid., p. 794.

will lead to a situation in which the ideas of one group of leaders will tend to offset those of another.

Although Myrdal overlays his discussion of race relations with a particularly alien caste belief, his controlling hypothesis has nothing whatever to do with caste. His "theory of the vicious circle"[73] is his controlling idea. This theory is essentially an abstract formulation, inspired by a largely inverted observation of "a vicious circle in caste" by Edwin R. Embree,[74] and rendered "scientific" by the application of certain concepts which Myrdal seems to have used to his satisfaction in his study, *Monetary Equilibrium*.

As we have seen in a previous section, the vicious circle runs as follows: "White prejudice ... keeps the Negro low in standards of living.... This, in turn, gives support to white prejudice. White prejudice and Negro standards thus mutually 'cause' each other." These two variables are interdependent, but neither is consistently dependent; a change in either will affect the other inversely. If we initiate a change in Negro standards, say, by "giving the Negro youth more education," white prejudice will go down; if we change white prejudice, say, by "an increased general knowledge about biology, eradicating false beliefs concerning Negro racial inferiority," then Negro standards will go up.

It is this kind of mystical dance of imponderables which is at the basis of the system of social illusions marbled into Myrdal's discussion. In the first place, Myrdal does not develop a careful definition of race prejudice. He does say, however: "For our purpose [race prejudice] is defined as discrimination by whites against Negroes."[75] But he does not use this definition, in fact we do not see how he can, for race prejudice is a social attitude, an acquired tendency to act; it is not some act or action which is the meaning of discrimination.[76] Myrdal's studied analysis would lead us rather to deduce the following definition of race prejudice: a feeling of bitterness, especially among poor whites, aroused particularly by a standing sexual threat of Negro men to white women. As he sees it, the white man's "prejudice is based upon fundamental attitudes toward sex and personality."

If, according to Myrdal's "rank order of discrimination," the whites are most concerned with sex and the Negroes with economic advancement, his

fundamental equilibrium of social forces should be a direct correlation between white prejudice and Negro sexual aggression—not Negro standards, which are clearly basically economic. In this way white prejudice will tend to vanish as Negro men give up their interest in white women; Negro standards will also go up, but only incidentally. If, for instance, Negro men would relinquish their desire to marry white women, "white people" would no longer be prejudiced against Negroes; the latter would be encouraged, say, to vote and campaign for political office and to demand their share of jobs and public funds in the Deep South.[77] To be sure, Myrdal does not demonstrate any such proposition. We may put it in still another way: If Negro standards go up and at the same time Negroes increase their interest in white women, then, to be consistent with Myrdal's sexual emphasis, white prejudice must increase. From this it follows that Negro standards are a non-significant variable.

The point which the author seems to have avoided is this: that both race prejudice and Negro standards are consistently dependent variables. They are both produced by the calculated economic interests of the Southern oligarchy. Both prejudice and the Negro's status are dependent functions of the latter interests. In one variation of his theory of the "vicious circle" Myrdal reasons:

> Assuming ... that we want to reduce the bias in white people's racial beliefs concerning Negroes, our first practical conclusion is that we can effect this result to a degree by *actually improving Negro status*.... The impediment in the way of this strategy is ... that white beliefs ... are active forces in keeping the Negroes low.[78]

Here beliefs are assumed to be prime movers; they "keep the Negroes low." This is mysticism. If we can "improve Negro status" the reason for the existence of derogatory beliefs about Negroes is, to the extent of the improvement, liquidated. With a rise in the standard of living of Negroes there tends to be merely a concomitant vitiation of the rationalizations for the depressed conditions of Negroes. The belief is an empty, harmless illusion, like beliefs in werewolves or fairies, without the exploitative interest with which it is impregnated. If the economic

---

[73] Ibid., pp. 75–78, 207–09, and Appendix 3.

[74] Ibid., p. 1069, note.

[75] Ibid., p. 78.

[76] In another connection Myrdal seems to give a different meaning to the concept: "If for some reason ... white workers actually came to work with Negroes as fellow workers, it has been experienced that *prejudice* will often adjust to the changed amount of *discrimination*." Ibid., p. 1067. (Italics added.) See also pp. 1141ff.

[77] "Negroes are in desperate need of jobs and bread.... The marriage matter [to them] is of rather distant and doubtful interest." Ibid., p. 6. The Negroes, thus goes the logic, want jobs and the white men want to protect their women from Negro men. But white men are rather willing to let Negroes have jobs, while Negro men are not particularly interested in white women. If this is so, if these two admittedly antagonistic groups are vitally interested in different things, why is there antagonism at all? It would seem that men fight only when they are possessed of conflicting interests in the same object.

[78] Ibid., p. 109. (Italics added.)

force could be bridled, the belief would collapse from inanition. There is a vested interest in anti-racial beliefs.

The effective interest is a need for slaves, or peons, or unorganized common laborers—a need for "cheap, docile labor." The latter interest, of course, is involved in a complicated web of feeling established by both immemorial and recent rationalizations. If beliefs, per se, could subjugate a people, the beliefs which Negroes hold about whites should be as effective as those which whites hold about Negroes.

This assumption of Myrdal's, that racial beliefs are primary social forces, leads him to conclude almost pathetically that the "white man's" beliefs are only a "mistake," which he would gladly correct if only he had truthful information. Accordingly our author suggests the following attack upon the beliefs themselves:

> A second line of strategy must be to rectify the ordinary white man's observations of Negro characteristics and inform him of the specific mistakes he is making in ascribing them wholesale to inborn racial traits.... People want to be rational, to be honest and well informed.[79]

Evidently the misapprehension in this presentation inheres in Myrdal's moral approach. He does not recognize consistently that the propagators of the ruling ideas, those whose interest it is to replace debunked beliefs with new ones, are not mistaken at all, and that they should not be thought of merely as people or white people. They are, in fact, a special class of people who fiercely oppose interference with the established set of antagonistic racial beliefs. The racial beliefs have been intentionally built up through propaganda. They are mass psychological instruments facilitating a definite purpose; therefore, they can best be opposed by realistic aggressive propaganda methods.[80] It is, to repeat, consummate naïveté to assume that the ruling class in the South will permit a free, objective discussion of race relations in its schools or public places.[81] Today such a practice can succeed only as a hazardous underground movement.

Furthermore, the author's unstable equilibrium between race prejudice and Negro standards is evidently too simple. For instance, if Negro standards go up because of interference from some outside force, say the Federal Government, the cultivated race prejudice among the poor whites may tend to diminish, but at the same time the hostility of the ruling-class whites may increase. The reason for this is that, because of the interference, the status and problems of Negroes and those of the poor whites may be made more nearly to coincide and thus enhance the possibility of an establishment of a community of interest between these two groups, a process diametrically opposed to the purpose and interests of the white ruling class. Therefore, it becomes incumbent upon the latter class to re-establish its position by bringing into play those very well-known means of reaffirming racial antipathy.

Although Myrdal never permits himself to accept a consistently realistic approach to the study of race relations, he recites as historical fact that which his theory confutes. For instance, the following historical passage says quite clearly that race prejudice is an attitude deliberately built up among the masses by an exploiting class, using acceptable rationalizations derogatory to the Negro race, so that the exploitation of the latter's labor power might be justified.

> The historical literature of this early period ... records that the imported Negroes—and the captured Indians—originally were kept in much the same status as the white indentured servants. *When later the Negroes gradually were pushed down into chattel slavery* while the white servants were allowed to work off their board, *the need was felt ... for some kind of justification above mere economic expediency and the might of the strong.* The arguments called forth by this need ... were broadly these: that the Negro was a heathen and a barbarian, an outcast among the peoples of the earth, a descendant of Noah's son Ham, cursed by God himself and doomed to be *a servant* forever on account of an ancient sin.[82]

Now there is no mysticism here—nothing about "sexual drives," "fears," "inhibitions," "labile balance," and so on—the historical process is clear. The exploitative act comes first; the prejudice follows. It explains unequivocally that a powerful white exploiting class, by "the might of the strong" and for "economic expediency," pushed the Negroes down into chattel slavery and then, as a justification and facilitation of this, utilized the means of propaganda, which are ordinarily in its control, to develop racial antagonism and hate in the white public for the Negroes.[83]

Attacking beliefs by negation is obviously a negative procedure—sometimes even a futile one.

---

[79] Ibid., p. 109.

[80] This view also holds against certain popular conceptions of race prejudice as "superstition" or "myth."

[81] On this point, see Stetson Kennedy, *Southern Exposure*, p. 349.

---

[82] Op. cit., p. 85. (Italics added.)

[83] It is interesting to observe with what anonymity Myrdal uses such key concepts as "imported," "captured," "kept," "pushed down," and so on. One would think that the subject referred to by these terms of action would be of primary concern in the investigation. It is, however, highly impersonalized, and the whole social situation tends to remain as if it were an act of Nature.

In an essay of epoch-making significance, written in about the year 1800, Henri Grégoire[84] demonstrated, probably as clearly as ever, that the white man is "making a mistake in ascribing Negro characteristics to inborn racial traits"; yet this assignment is still freshly advocated. As a matter of fact, Count Arthur de Gobineau almost put men like Grégoire out of existence.[85] In like manner, Dr. W. T. Couch, formerly editor in chief of probably the most influential Southern press, proceeds to "gobinize" Myrdal.

Couch, in a caustic criticism of Myrdal, referring to him as "silly" and "ignorant," says the white man cannot make concessions to Negroes because these will ultimately lead to Negro men's marrying white men's daughters. "One concession will lead to another, and ultimately to intermarriage."[86] Here both the thinking of both authors is bogged down in the slough of sexual passion from which we may not hope for light on race relations. Moreover, in this unrealistic world of beliefs Couch has Myrdal where he wants him; he seems to triumph with such intuitive declarations as: "The assertion of equality is an assertion of values."[87] And, in a characteristically pre-Civil War, slaveholders' contention about the meaning of the Declaration of Independence, he becomes involved with Myrdal's moral orientation. "I believe," says Couch, "*An American Dilemma* was written under gross misapprehensions of what such ideas as equality, freedom, democracy, human rights, have meant, and what they can be made to mean."[88] Thus, without restraint and without enlightenment, the mystics, steeped in metaphysical truck, set upon each other.

A positive program, on the other hand, calls for an attack upon the source of the beliefs, so that it might be divested of its prestige and power to produce and to substitute anti-racial beliefs among the masses. In other words, the problem is that of converting the white masses to an appreciation and realization of the ruling-class function of the beliefs and their effect as instruments in the exploitation of the white as well as of the black masses. Then, not only will the old beliefs lose their efficacy, but also the new ones will die aborning.

A positive program calls for the winning of the white masses over to a different system of thinking—not merely a campaign of scholarly denials of spectacular myths about creation, stages of biological progress, cultural capacity, and so on. Indeed, such negation may even play into the hands of the "racists," for they may not only divert attention from the realities of race relations but also help to spread and implant the myths among the public. However, the effectuation of such a program, the intent of which must be to alienate public support of the aristocracy, will undoubtedly evoke terrific opposition from this class. To be sure, this fact merely demonstrates further the basis of racial antagonism in the South and the correctness of the suggested positive program. At the same time, of course, Negroes must learn that their interest is primarily bound up with that of the white common people in a struggle for power and not essentially in a climb for social status.

At any rate, it is precisely this realization which Dr. Myrdal constantly seeks to circumvent. Accordingly he argues inconsistently that the ruling class in the South is the Negroes' best friend.

> Our hypothesis is similar to the view taken by an older group of Negro writers and by most white writers who have touched this crucial question: that the Negroes' friend—or the one who is least unfriendly—is still rather the upper class of white people, the people with economic and social security who are *truly a "non-competing group."*[89]

---

[84] *An Inquiry Concerning the Intellectual and Moral Faculties, and Literature of Negroes*, trans. by D. B. Warden, Brooklyn, 1810.

[85] After Professor Donald Young had completed his examination of the conditions of American minority peoples he made the following conclusionary statement: "Action, not cautious and laborious research, is demanded of those who would lead the populace. Thus a Chamberlain, a Gobineau, or a Stoddard attracts myriads of followers by a pseudo-scientific program based on a doctrine of God-given white supremacy … while the very names of Franz Boas, Eugene Pittard, Herbert A. Miller, E. B. Reuter, Friedrich Hertz, and other scholarly students of the peoples of the world are unknown outside of a small intellectual circle. 'Give us the solution and let sterile scholars while away their time with obscure facts which lead but to quibbling books!' is the cry of the masses." Yet the reason that Gobineau *et al.* have been widely accepted by the white ruling classes of the world is not that they presented a course of "action" but that they had the timely ingenuity to contrive a system of plausible logic which justified an accomplished act: the white racial mastery of the world. Explanations and justifications were desperately needed. For the most part the scholars mentioned have the been able only to point out flaws in the anti-racial arguments; that had already lost their conviction when they innocently accepted the spurious grounds of discussion which the apologists of racial exploitation had chosen. They apparently did not recognize that both the racial antagonism and its pseudo-scientific rationalizations are products of a peculiar social system.

[86] *What the Negro Wants*, Rayford W. Logan, ed., p. xvi.

[87] Ibid., p. xvii.

[88] Ibid., p. xv.

[89] Op. cit., p. 69. (Italics added.) It is interesting to observe how Dr. Myrdal has finally become almost reactionary in the sense of the incorrigible segregationist, W. T. Couch, who also says: "Nothing is more needed in the South today than rebirth of [Booker Washington's] ideas, restoration of the great leadership that he was giving." Op. cit., p. xxiii.

The author, by one symptom or another, cannot help showing of what he is really apprehensive: the bringing into consciousness of the masses the identity of the interests of the white and the black workers. In accordance with this attitude he takes a superficial view of the economic order and asks Negroes to go to the labor market and see who is their real enemy. Thus he asserts:

> The aim of [the theory of labor solidarity] is to unify the whole Negro people, not with the white upper class, but with the white working class.... The theory of labor solidarity has been taken up as a last solution of the Negro problem, and as such is escapist in nature; its escape character becomes painfully obvious to every member of the school as soon as he leaves abstract reasoning and goes down to the labor market, because there he meets *caste* and has to talk race, even racial solidarity.[90]

As a justificatory illustration of the validity of his principle of "cumulative causation," the summary interaction of the elements of Negro standards and other social factors, Myrdal says: "The philanthropist, the Negro educator, the Negro trade unionist ... and, indeed, the average well-meaning citizen of both colors, pragmatically applies the same hypothesis."[91] In reality, however, this is not a confirmation of a sound theory of race relations; it is rather an apology for reformism. Within the existing system of power relationship this is the most that is respectably allowed. Reformism never goes so far as to envisage the real involvement of the exploitative system with racial antagonism. Its extreme aspiration does not go beyond the attainment of freedom for certain black men to participate in the exploitation of the commonalty regardless of the color of the latter. This aspiration is the prospect which the Southern oligarchy with some degree of justification ordinarily refers to as "Negro domination."

Then, too, with reformation as an end, the logical "friend" of the Negro leader must necessarily be this same white aristocracy; for he must ultimately become, like the aristocracy, the inevitable economic adversary of the exploited masses; he must become, in other words, a "black Anglo-Saxon." Indeed, assuming bourgeois proclivities, his very appeal to the masses for support in his struggle for "equality" is an unavoidable deception. The reformer seeks to eliminate only the racial aspects of the exploitative system; he compromises with the system which produces the racial antagonism. But the white ruling class cannot willingly accept even this compromise, for it knows that the whole system is doomed if Negroes are permitted to achieve unlimited status as participating exploiters. In such an event there would be no racial scapegoat or red herring to brandish

before the confused white commonalty as a means of keeping them and the Negro masses from recognizing the full impact of political-class oppression.

Today "conservative" theories of race relations are not merely denied; they are confronted with a countertheory, the theory that racial antagonism is in fact *political-class* antagonism and that race prejudice is initiated and maintained by labor exploiters. It is not, it would seem clear, that the aristocracy is less antagonistic to the Negroes but that this class uses more respectable weapons against them, which are also infinitely more powerful and effective. As a matter of fact, the poor whites themselves may be thought of as the primary instrument of the ruling class in subjugating the Negroes. The statement attributed to a great financier, "I can pay one half of the working class to kill off the other half," is again in point.

As we have seen, Myrdal does not favor this explanation. He declares that all the Negro's troubles are due to the simple fact that "white people" want to be superior to colored people; or, indeed, merely to the fact that the Negro is colored. His argument follows:

> We hear it said ... that there is no "race problem" but only a "class problem." The Negro sharecropper is alleged to be destitute not because of his color but because of his class position—and it is pointed out that there are white people who are equally poor. From a practical angle there is a point in this reasoning. But from a theoretical angle it contains escapism in a new form. It also draws too heavily on the idealistic Marxian doctrine of the "class struggle." And it tends to conceal the whole system of special deprivations visited upon the Negro *only because he is not white.*[92]

Throughout the study the author has frequently found it sufficient simply to mention the name of Karl Marx in order to counter views based upon the determining role of the "material conditions of production" and distribution.[93] After a studied argument

---

[90] Myrdal, op. cit., p. 793. (Italics added.)
[91] Ibid., p. 1069.

[92] Ibid., p. 75. (Italics added.)

[93] And yet Myrdal has shown himself to be vitally wanting in an understanding of the difference between status rivalry and class struggle. Observe, for instance, the following typical confusion: "Our hypothesis is that in a society where there are broad social classes and, in addition, more minute distinctions and splits in the lower strata, the lower class groups will, to a great extent, take care of keeping each other subdued, thus relieving, to that extent, the higher classes of this otherwise painful task necessary to the monopolization of the power and the advantages.

"It will be observed that this hypothesis is contrary to the Marxian theory of class society.... The Marxian scheme assumes that there is an actual solidarity between the *several lower class groups* against the *higher classes*, or, in any case, a potential solidarity.... The inevitable result is

in favor of the futility of Negroes adopting a Marxian view of society, he concludes: "'Even after a revolution the country will be full of crackers' is a reflection I have often met when discussing communism in the Negro community."[94] The least we could say about this is that it is very crude. On this kind of thinking John Stuart Mill is emphatic: "Of all the vulgar modes of escaping from the consideration of the effect of social and moral influences on the human mind, the most vulgar is that of attributing the diversities of conduct and character to inherent natural differences."[95] More especially it expresses the fatalism upon which the whole orthodox school of race relations inevitably rests.

Myrdal, as a confirmed moralist, is not concerned with problems of power but rather with problems of "regenerating the individual" by idealistic preachments. If only the individual could be taught to accept the morality of the Creed, then society would lose its fever of racial pathologies and settle down to a happy existence. However, the point we are trying to make is that, in a feudal system, serfdom is natural and the serf will be treated like a serf regardless of whether the lord is a bishop or a secular noble; in the slavocracy of the South the slave was treated like a slave, whether his master was white or black; in modern capitalism black workers are exploited naturally and race hatred is a natural support of this exploitation. In other words, morality is a function of the social system, and a better system can change both morality and human nature for the better.

There will be no more "crackers" or "niggers" after a socialist revolution because the social necessity for these types will have been removed. But the vision which the capitalist theorist dreads most is this: that there will be no more capitalists and capitalist exploitation. If we attempt to see race relations realistically, the meaning of the capitalist function is inescapable. At any rate, although Myrdal criticizes Sumner and Park for their inert and fatalistic views of social change, he himself contends that any revolutionary change in the interest of democracy will be futile:

> ... a national policy will never work by changing only one factor, least of all if attempted suddenly and with great force. In most cases that would either throw the system entirely out of gear or else prove to be a wasteful expenditure of effort which could be reached much further by being spread strategically over various factors in the system and over a period of time.[96]

This is not the place to discuss the theory of revolution, but it must be obvious that the purpose of revolution is not to "throw the system out of gear." It is to overthrow the entire system, to overthrow a ruling class; and the cost of revolution did not frighten the capitalists when it became their lot to overthrow the feudalists.

An American Dilemma, the most exhaustive *survey* of race relations ever undertaken in the United States, is, for the most part, a useful source of data. In detail it presents many ingenious analyses of the materials. But it develops no hypothesis or consistent theory of race relations; and, to the extent that it employs the caste belief in interpretations, it is misleading. Clearly, the use of "the American Creed" as the "value premise" for his study severely limits and narrows Dr. Myrdal's perspective. Even though we should grant some right of the author to limit the discussion of his subject to its moral aspects, he still develops it without insight. He never brings into focus the two great systems of morality currently striving in our civilization for ascendancy, but merely assumes a teleological abstraction of social justice toward which all good men will ultimately gravitate. Moreover, since we can hardly accuse him of being naïve, and since he clearly goes out of his way to avoid the obvious implications of labor exploitation in the South, we cannot help concluding that the work in many respects may have the effect of a powerful piece of propaganda in favor of the status quo. If the "race problem" in the United States is pre-eminently a moral question, it must naturally be resolved by moral means, and this conclusion is precisely the social illusion which the ruling political class has constantly sought to produce. In this connection we are conscious of the author's recognition that "social science is essentially a 'political' science." One thing is certain, at any rate: the work contributes virtually nothing to a clarification of the many existing spurious social theories of race relations—indeed, on the latter score, Myrdal's contribution is decidedly negative. And for this reason evidently he has been able to suggest no solution for the dilemma, but, like the fatalists whom he criticizes, the author relies finally upon time as the great corrector of all evil.

Continued

a 'class struggle' where all poor and disadvantaged groups are united behind the barricades." Ibid., p. 68. (Italics added.) Myrdal thinks that Marx thinks the *upper class* and the *lower class*, mere social illusions, are in conflict. No wonder he seems to conclude that Marx is rather foolish. And he does not trouble himself at all to explain how the "higher classes" exercise the "necessary painful task" of keeping the lower classes subdued when, perchance, the latter stop fighting among themselves and turn their attention to their common enemy. This is, to use the term so frequently employed by Myrdal, "escapism."

[94] Ibid., p. 509.

[95] *Principles of Political Economy*, Vol. 1, p. 390. Long before this John Locke had said quite as much; see *Essay Concerning Human Understanding*.

[96] Op. cit., p. 77.

7

Race and Nationality in American Life

OSCAR HANDLIN

Historian Oscar Handlin had written widely on the subjects of immigration, settlement and government policy. His *The Uprooted* won the Pulitzer Prize for literature in 1952. He was uneasy with theoretical developments such as those initiated by Cox.

The conception of racism as an epiphenomenon – a secondary phenomonenon accompanying though not necessarily connected to underlying economic conditions – grew in currency following the Second World War. Cox's was the boldest and most challenging of several theories, all based on the conception of racism as a product of capitalism.

Handlin took issue with Cox's work and that of Carey McWilliams and Abram Léon, all of which he found reductive and insensitive to the characteristics of racism, particularly antisemitism. For Handlin, racism needed to be analysed as a form of ideology in itself and not just as a reflection of economic conditions. The 'degradation' of black people is 'clearly connected' to economic exploitation, wrote Handlin in the introduction to his *Race and Nationality in American Life*, but it "did not altogether explain [that] degradation'. "The idea of race rested on a body of knowledge ... and a full understanding of it demands an assessment of the intellectual and emotional context within which it took hold."

To view it as a by-product of capitalist exploitation was not only inadequate but misleading, argued Handlin. The extract selected contains Handlin's evaluation and critique of the then (1950) emerging school of thought that was to gain in currency over succeeding decades.

Prejudice and Capitalist Exploitation

The appeal to prejudice to justify the exploitation of a dependent group was not peculiar to the United States. Illustrations of the same deceptive use of racism are abundant in other parts of the world.

Yet to proceed from that fact to the conclusion that exploitation causes prejudice is a misleading oversimplification. In the years just after the Second World War, when the defeat of nazism seemed to have opened the way to solution of all these problems, there was a superficial plausibility to that conclusion. The prestige of the Marxist view of the class struggle and the delusion that all race conflicts had disappeared in the Soviet Union seemed to confirm the analysis that economic disorders were at the roots of prejudice. It will be necessary to examine critically certain ideas derived from that oversimplified belief.

Three significant books published between 1946 and 1948 present striking statements of the conception of group prejudice as a social disease produced by capitalism. Two of the volumes deal with the Jews, the third with the Negroes, the two racial groups who were the victims of social hatred in our times. These books offer an opportunity for the comparison of the phenomenon in the United States and elsewhere. Finally, the three works have in common an identical conception of the nature of the disease; all found it the product of exploitation in Western capitalist society.

Perhaps more than any other writer of his time, Carey McWilliams made popular the cause of America's "minorities" and exposed the dangers that lie in all the manifestations of prejudice. He possessed a quick and easy pen; he had a knack for assimilating scholarly opinions and making them readable; and he had strong opinions–on the whole, good ones.

A Mask for Privilege (1948) was, however, one of his weaker efforts. It labored under the burden of an untenable thesis and was all too often careless in matters of detail.

The key to the book was its title. For Mr. McWilliams, anti-Semitism in the United States was always a "mask for privilege." The development of industrialism between 1860 and 1877 left patent injustices in the structure of American society. By the latter year "the industrial bourgeoisie had triumphed." Once triumphant, "the industrial tycoons discovered that they could not function within the framework of the social and political ideals of the early Republic. To insure their triumph, a new social order had to be established." That new order involved the creation of a status system to protect the position of the privileged classes. "To trick a freedom-loving people into accepting industrial regimentation in the name of democracy, the tycoons of the period needed a diversionary issue." They therefore devised a counter-tradition to oppose the democratic tradition, and they based that countertradition on the myth of anti-Semitism, first applying it in the social, then in the economic, and finally, in recent times, in the political sphere. A pattern of exclusion, established first in resorts, clubs, and colleges, restricted the opportunities open to Jews and drove them into marginal occupations. As capitalism approached its crisis, concentration in undesirable trades left the Jews in an exposed position, increasingly open to attack by

fascist groups like the anti-Semitic Columbians, who were making trouble in Georgia in 1947.

To prove his position McWilliams had to argue that a single line of development generated anti-Semitism in the United States. He therefore assumed throughout that all anti-Semitic forces grew up indigenously within the country. On the level of ideology he failed to treat the influence from abroad of the works of Gobineau, Lapouge, Drumont, and Chamberlain. On the practical level he did not mention the impact of German government propaganda in the 1930's through such agencies as the Friends of New Germany, the German-American Bund, and George Sylvester Viereck.

Again, since he felt compelled to attribute the whole to the activities of the "tycoons," he consistently slurred over the influence of liberal thinkers tainted with anti-Semitic ideas. Yet in the total development Edward A. Ross and John R. Commons, who were well-intentioned reformers, but who popularized racist conceptions, probably had a wider effect than did outright champions of "Aryanism" like Madison Grant and Lothrop Stoddard. Bolstered by the prestige of academic reputation, of affiliation with worthy causes, and of good intentions, the books of the liberals were doubly dangerous because they did not carry the poison labels of the openly biased.

Similarly McWilliams disregarded the part played by organized farmers and laborers in the anti-Semitic movements. There it not a reference to the fact that populist hatred of Wall Street sometimes fell into the anti-Semitic pattern. There is no recognition of the fact that trade unions also adopted exclusionist practices. No more vicious racist ideas were ever expressed than those spewed out by Samuel Gompers in the A F. of L. campaign against the Chinese. If these same ideas were ultimately used against the Jews, that only illustrated further the complexity of the subject and the dangers of oversimplification.

The necessities of its thesis led *A Mask for Privilege* to the erroneous proposition that the position of the Jews as objects of prejudice was unique in American society. McWilliams could not make clear, for example, that the prejudiced comments he quoted were often directed against all new immigrants and not only against Jews. One would never learn from his book that Americans of Irish descent experienced the same difficulties as Jews in penetrating the elite social clubs, that the sons of Italian parents also faced quota barriers when they sought admission to medical and dental schools, and that the Ku Klux Klan between 1920 and 1928 was decidedly more hostile to Catholics than to Jews. Until the 1930's, indeed, there was no anti-Semitic movement in the United States that was not also anti-Catholic.

To support the contention that the Jews occupied a unique position in America, McWilliams argued that they had been crowded, by prejudice, into a marginal and insecure role in the nation's economy: they were excessively concentrated in the professional and white-collar occupations; they engaged in consumption and in distribution rather than in basic production, in light rather than in heavy industry. He viewed the anomalous position of the Jews as basically due to their forced adjustment to exclusion from the more desirable places in the economy. Anti-Semitic bias, he pointed out, "more than any other single factor … has brought about the peculiar distribution of Jews on the checkerboard of our economic system."

This line of reasoning rested upon two fallacious suppositions: first, that Jews could have gotten the most desirable places had they not been thus handicapped; and second, that the conception of what were the most desirable places was the same among all people. To McWilliams the facts that only thirty-three of the four hundred and twenty directors of New York banks were Jews, that only three of the mass-circulation magazines were owned by them, and that in "not a single sector of the heavy industry front" did their influence "amount to dominance or control" were evidences of discrimination. But it could just as well–or just as badly–be argued, in view of the recency of Jewish settlement and in view of the poverty of the Jews when they arrived, that to produce almost ten per cent of the bank directors in the financial capital of the nation was evidence of a *lack* of discrimination. Certainly the representation in banking and in heavy industry of other groups descended from recent immigrants was no larger.

Conclusive evidence on this point could be drawn from the situation in agriculture. The American farm was individually owned. Prejudice could bar from this occupation no one who had the capital, and for more than half a century a melancholy succession of unsuccessful organizations stood ready to provide Jews with the capital. If Jews did not become tillers of the soil in America, it was not because the could not, but because they would not. That indicated that such groups had their own occupational preferences.

Finally, McWilliams depended entirely upon the power of coincidence to explain the beginnings of anti-Semitism, and he endowed the American capitalists with amazing foresight in relating social to economic discrimination. Joseph Seligman, a prominent Jewish banker, was excluded from a Saratoga hotel in 1877, the year of the triumph of the industrial bourgeoisie. That this "first overt manifestation of anti-Semitism in the United States took place in 1877 is to be explained," McWilliams held, "in terms of the corrosion which the industrial revolution had brought about in the American scheme of values." That American values were so instantly and automatically corroded was itself rather farfetched. More important, this explanation implied

that those who excluded Seligman envisaged and consciously planned the subsequent development of the status system and of the pattern of economic discrimination that emerged thirty years later. This rational conspiracy, simple and all-embracing, was dubious on the face of it and did not square with the character of American capitalists at the turn of the century. But without such a conspiracy there was a fatal gap in McWilliams's argument.

The idea of economic marginality, applied in *A Mask for Privilege* to the American scene, was earlier applied by some thinkers to the role of the Jews in the European economy. Dov Ber Borochov, for one, believed that a normal distribution of occupations took the form of a pyramid, with the great mass of the population concentrated in agriculture and in the heavy industries and tapering off in numbers through distribution, light industry, trade, and the professions. In the case of the Jews the pyramid was reversed, and their difficulties were ascribed to the fact that they lacked the security of a proper base in the productive system. This theory accounted for the effort by progressive Jewish leadership to "productivize" the Jews of eastern Europe, and was also at the root of certain elements of Zionist ideology.

The questions of how and why this situation came to exist were usually skirted. McWilliams, too, passed the questions by with the comment that they were interesting but irrelevant. But the importance of the problem did not escape the attention of a young Polish Jew who spent most of his short life in Belgium. As a member of Hashomer Hatzair–a left-wing Zionist group–Abram Léon absorbed Borochov's interpretation of the Jewish situation, and his awareness of the problem was certainly sharpened during the war, when he became a member of the section of the anti-German underground allied with the Fourth International. Actively engaged in the resistance movement, he nevertheless found time to compose a shrewd analysis of the historical sources of the Jewish economic position, and had just about finished this book when he was arrested. In Auschwitz, at the age of twenty-six, he met the fate of millions of his fellows.

Léon's approach was that of the orthodox Marxist. His analysis, despite errors of detail, was a solid statement of the materialistic interpretation of the Jewish question. Its bias was evident. But its thoughtfulness and originality were nonetheless stimulating.

Running through two and a half millenniums of the Jewish past, Léon found two points of crisis in the secular history of that people. The first crisis occurred when the economy of the Roman Empire broke down and gave way to the kind of natural economy associated in western Europe with feudalism, a mode of production characterized by self-sufficient agriculture and the absence of commerce.

This transformation coincided with the emergence, as state religions, first of Christianity and then of Islam. Léon believed that these developments set in motion a selective process that froze the Jews in commerce: that is, the settled Jewish farmers tended to be absorbed by the dominant creeds, and only those continued to adhere to Judaism who had the relative independence of the trader's status.

At this stage, Léon continued, a rigid and exceptional occupational pattern was fixed upon the Jews. In the long period until the thirteenth century, while the whole of Europe lived by agriculture, the Jews engaged in itinerant trade. And since all those with whom the Jews dealt were self-sufficient, that commerce of necessity centered largely on the importation of luxuries and catered to the tastes of the nobility, who alone had the surpluses to pay for them. Of necessity also the Jews engaged in usury to finance the feudal lords in the frequent intervals when the manors failed to produce sufficient surplus. Naturally the status of the Jews was high and they enjoyed the protection of the highly placed.

This relatively pleasant situation began to change in the era of the Crusades. The natural economy disintegrated as exchange developed. But now commerce and mercantile capital were directly connected with production; the objects of trade were no longer exotic luxuries, but the products of industry. (The famous Italian banking houses, for instance, established themselves in the woolen business.)

The Jewish merchants, unable to enter the new commerce, were gradually excluded from all trade. Consequently they were compelled to live by usury and by its ancillary occupations, pawnbrokering and dealing in secondhand goods. In this role they battened off the nobility and off the townspeople, who ultimately became their bitter enemies. For a time the sovereign, who profited by extorting the wealth of his subjects through the Jews, offered some protection. But in the end the hostility of the new middle class and the gentry led to harsh measures, to the growth of the ghetto, and finally to exclusion. A remnant of Jews saved themselves only by migrating eastward to Poland and Bohemia, less developed regions still in the natural-economy stage.

Thereafter the Jews hung on in the west on a very marginal basis until the end of the eighteenth century, when emancipation loosed the old restrictions and assimilative forces began steadily to absorb the new citizens into the sprouting national states. But at that very moment the position of the eastern Jews, which had been quite favorable until then, began to deteriorate through the workings of the same forces which had operated in the west several centuries earlier. In Poland and in Russia a new middle class rising from the disintegration of the old economy was jealous of the place of the Jews in commerce and in the professions. Competition for status led to political restrictions upon the Jews and to emigration to France, Germany, and England, which only worsened the position of their co-religionists in the west.

At this point the internal contradictions of capitalism deprived the Jews, a marginal group at best, of the last vestiges of security. Excluded from the cartels of the great capitalists, the Jews were driven into speculation, a development which offered the monopolists an opportunity to divert the discontent of the masses to the Jews alone. Theorists began to distinguish between "bad" (speculative) capital and "useful" (productive) capital, terms which Nazi economists eventually translated into parasitic-Jewish and productive-national. Ultimately the masses fell subject to a new ideology which identified speculative capitalism with Judaism and contrasted it with a planned national socialist economy, which was really war capitalism. Under the successive blows of persecution in the name of this ideology the Jews were helpless and took refuge in a nationalism of their own.

By this survey Léon attempted to demonstrate that the Jewish question was the outcome of an identification of the Jewish group, through definite historical circumstances, with certain limited occupations which the rest of the society found inferior or degrading or hostile. Anti-Semitism then could readily be understood as a device consciously contrived by the capitalists for their own end.

The questions raised in specific form by Léon with reference to the Jews were essentially the same as those treated a few years later by Oliver Cromwell Cox (*Race, Class and Caste*) in a more general way; basically both men were concerned with the phenomena of caste, class, and race, and of the relationships among them. Unfortunately Mr. Cox's enormously prolix volume, winner of the George Washington Carver award, fell far short of its goal of definitive analysis.

The book was cluttered with the deceptive paraphernalia of scholarship. But through it ran a very simple thesis, a product of the confused years in which it was written; and that thesis must be understood before the mazes of argument can be unraveled. The following quotations will make clear the author's point of view and will also throw light upon his methods. In a discussion of the modern state Cox wrote, "From the standpoint of degrees of development of democracy in the three great nations of the world … the United States is probably most backward and Russia farthest advanced." Of the New Deal he wrote, "Most of what [Franklin Roosevelt] said and did was really democratic and consequently socialistic or communistic." In other words, Cox was then taken in by the pervasive identification of all social ills with capitalism, of all social advances with socialism.

These sentences also illustrate this author's peculiar use of language; words were divorced from their usual meanings and endowed with esoteric connotations appropriate to a closed system of thought. In the fantastic sequences of seeming inaccuracies it was hard to differentiate between what was only double talk and what was really error of fact. The reader could decide for himself. Thus the Hindus "never attained a conception of nationality." There is only one political party in the United States, "with two factions: Republicans and Democrats." Mercantilism is state capitalism. A ruling class is always intolerant. "Businessmen constitute our ruling class." Democracy "is in fact communism." De Tocqueville was an advocate of democracy. "The bourgeosie is unalterably opposed to democracy." Russia is the only foe of fascism; most respectable Americans are facists; Southern poor whites are not hostile to the Negro; the late Senator Bilbo was a spokesman of capitalism. And no previous scholars revealed these truths because their "bread and butter" depended upon "avoiding the study of contemporary class conflict."

Beyond these semantic diversions lay the central thesis: Cox viewed racial antagonism as one of the fundamental traits of the class struggle within the capitalist system. Prejudice was, to his mind, an attitude built up by the capitalists to keep control over the proletariat, whom they exploited.

The point was made in a long, tortuous argument complicated by Mr. Cox's difficulty in defining race in such a way as to take in the Negroes in the United States and not much more. What finally emerged, however, was somewhat broader than that. For if a race was "any group of people that is generally believed to be, and generally accepted as, a race in any given area of ethnic competition," then the Chinese in California, the Jews in Nazi Germany, the Italians in Australia, the Mexicans in Texas, and the French Canadians in Maine were also races.

But many of the groups just named found their most prejudiced persecutors not among the capitalists. Cox therefore had to reason that any antagonisms not inspired by the capitalists, despite his definition, were not really race conflicts. He disposed thus of the anti-Oriental movement on the Pacific coast, which–inconveniently–was led by workingmen, indeed by the trade unions. Likewise, the Jews who faced hostility even before the rise of capitalism were, he said, never victims of race prejudice, only of intolerance.

Similarly, to demonstrate that racial antagonism could not exist without capitalism, a long section of the book was devoted to demolishing the thesis that the caste system of India was a product of precapitalist color prejudices. Cox's refutation is convincing, although his own explanation of the causes is open to question. At the same time he seized the occasion to lay a basis for comparison between the idyllic Hindus and the horrid capitalists. He managed, for example, to overlook the terrible punishments meted out to violators of the caste laws and thus found no violence in the caste system; in his view the depressed portions of society, there, by persuasion, happily granted privileges to their superiors.

Having tied race prejudice to Western capitalism, Cox proceeded to show, by another ingenious exercise in terminology, that prejudice was an aspect of the class struggle inherent in capitalism. He created an entity, the "political class," which, by definition, was a "power group" struggling for control of the state. In his own day, then, there were two political classes, the challengers of the *status quo* and its defenders, the proletariat and the bourgeoisie, the communists and the non-communists.

Cox did not trouble to relate his "political class" to any social or economic groupings that could be shown actually to exist in the real world and which he variously denominated "estate," "social class," and "functional class." Consequently he found no difficulty in emerging with the conclusion that there could be no solution to prejudice short of the violent overthrow of the capitalist system by revolution, which, in view of the premises and of the methods employed, was not altogether suprising.

What was surprising was how close this position brought the author to the racist's own picture of race relations. Like the most reactionary white Southerner, although for different reasons, Mr. Cox argued that laws against lynching must necessarily be ineffective, that there could be no contact between races without either conflict or amalgamation, and that whites acted as a unit in opposition to blacks.

For all the differences among them these three books had a basic element in common: all regarded prejudice as an instrument used by capitalists to justify or to increase exploitation.

Such a theory must pass the test of one crucial question: why should one group rather than another have been selected as the object of prejudice? And, indeed, each of the three books, in its own fashion and to some degree, attempts to demonstrate that an occupational peculiarity in the group singled out rendered it particularly appropriate for its role as object of the exploiter's prejudice. For Cox the problem was simple. The Negro had been a slave; he remained an oppressed worker. Hence the odium attached to him as an inferior human being.

But the case of the Jew was more difficult. Insofar as McWilliams confronted this problem, his solution was essentially the same as that of Abram Léon: that concentration in certain marginal employments left the Jews vulnerable. But the mere fact that Jews clustered in certain callings could not explain the appearance of racist anti-Semitism. Faith in such an explanation rested on the questionable assumption that some occupations were, of their nature, undesirable. The distinction between productive and

unproductive trades sometimes made by economists–
Marxist as well as orthodox–has not been one that
greatly influenced popular values; witness the attitudes toward movie stars and athletes. In modern
times, at least, people have measured the agreeable-
ness and the utility of any employment by the yard-
sticks of income and status, and if Jewish callings
seemed less desirable than others, it is because they
somehow fell short in terms of those criteria.

So far as income was concerned, there seem to
have been no disabilities connected with Jewish
occupations; no one ever charged that Jews
made too little money. But inferiority of status was
undoubtedly attached to trades that were distinctively Jewish. That inferiority was not, however,
inherent in the occupations involved. On the contrary, it arose from the fact that Jews pre-empted
certain trades; these were "Jewish businesses." The
Jews were not held in low repute because they
engaged in callings intrinsically disreputable.
Rather those callings lost esteem because the Jews
were identified with them.

Most important of all, concentration in a limited
number of occupations was characteristic of all ethnic groups and not simply of those, like the Jews
and the Negroes, who suffered from prejudice.
Some, like the Quakers in the United States and
the Scots in England, to name only two, displayed
a markedly eccentric occupational pattern and
still attained an exceptionally high social status.
In European and American society there always
remained a kind of hereditary element in occupation
as in every other aspect of culture; skill, training,
values, and opportunities were, to some extent,
handed down from father to son even in the most
fluid economies. No ethnic group was normal,
because normality in this sense could only be an
average of many ethnic groups.

But if Western society comprehended a multitude
of ethnic groups, all differentiated to some degree in
economic structure, then prejudice could not be explained simply in terms of exploitation. Why should
the exploiter have directed his prejudice against one
group rather than another? Neither McWilliams nor
Léon could, in these terms, explain why the Jews
should have been the "chosen people." And
Mr. Cox could not explain why seventeenth-century

Americans bore the same prejudice against both
white and black servants.

Nor was there any accounting for the difference
in tastes of the capitalists of other countries. Why
should the Brazilians and Frenchmen not have
picked on the Negroes? Why should color have
been a bar to a Hindu in India but not in England?
Why should capitalist prejudice anywhere not have
taken a quite different form?

These are important questions. They cannot be
answered simply by reference to the fact that race
prejudice has often been used to justify the exploitation of men by their masters. Economic exploitation
was somehow involved; in the experience of the
American Negro in slavery the link certainly existed.
And in other societies, too, race hatred has been a
device of oppression, of political rivalry, and of
national aggression. There is evidence enough that, in
some way, exploitation, an expression of economic
or political maladjustment, meshed in with race prejudice. The difficulty is to define the relationship.

A clue to the solution is the fact that exploitation
created a sense of social uneasiness in which there
was room for, and psychological and political unity
in, prejudiced behavior. A society weighed down by
such uneasiness found relief by dividing against
itself: in other words, by sanctioning the hatreds of
some of its members against others. Those individuals most disturbed in personality or situation
yielded most readily. But as attacks from without or
depression or political crisis exacerbated uneasiness, the impulse to seek such relief became more
universal and more compelling and the cathartic
hatreds more intense. Not the fringes alone, but
society as a whole was affected.

Such hatreds were, of course, not always oriented
along ethnic lines. Sometimes people held prejudices against "Reds" and "unions," against "capitalists" and "Wall Street." But when that bias took an
ethnic direction, it acquired a special depth and an
entirely different quality. To comprehend that depth
and quality it is necessary to recognize the fact that
race prejudice rested upon a system of beliefs and
drew into play the innermost emotions of man. An
understanding of those beliefs and emotions will
reveal the characteristics that made race an instrument of exploitation in Western society.

8

The Authoritarian Personality

T.W. ADORNO, E. FRENKEL-BRUNSWICK, D. LEVINSON AND R. NEVITT SANDFORD

In 1944, the year in which *An American Dilemma* was published, the American Jewish Committee invited scholars of various backgrounds to a conference on 'religious and racial prejudice'. At the conference, a research program was outlined; its objective was to seek a solution to antisemitism. Six years later, the research bore fruit in the form of *The Authoritarian Personality.* As in Myrdal's work, 'social organization' was emphasized over 'racial heredity'; though Adorno *et al.* were specifically interested in how membership of a cultural group affected psychological characteristics.

The first extract reproduced here was authored by Daniel J. Levinson and outlines the theoretical approach of the study. Its conclusions may look unexceptional today, but the research was conducted while the atrocities of the Second World War were still fresh in the mind and the question of whether antisemitism and racism were natural or inevitable was in urgent need of an answer.

The second extract was written by Theodor Adorno and addressed the "functional" character of antisemitism. *Mutatus mutandis*, all the points made of antisemitism may also be made about other forms of racism. Adorno presented a powerful and, in some ways, fearful account of the ways in which racism fulfils what he called an "economic" function in a person's psychology. His utilization of Freudian concepts to shed light on the workings of racism produced an original series of insights into the formal structures of the racist personality. [The code numbers refer to interviewees.]

We may now return to a consideration of the preliminary definition of ethnocentrism as an ideology concerning ingroups and outgroups and their interaction.

The term "group" is used in the widest sense to mean any set of people who constitute a psychological entity for any individual. If we regard the individual's conception of the social world as a sort of map containing various differentiated regions, then each region can be considered a group. This sociopsychological definition includes sociological groups such as nations, classes, ethnic groups, political parties, and so on. But it also includes numbers-of-people who have one or more common characteristics but who are not formal groups in the sense of showing organization and regulation of ways. Thus, it is legitimate in a sociopsychological sense to consider as groups such sets of people as criminals, intellectuals, artists, politicians, eccentrics, and so on. Psychologically, they are groups in so far as they are social categories or regions in an individual's social outlook–objects of opinions, attitudes, affect, and striving.

"Ingroup" and "outgroup" are sociopsychological rather than purely sociological concepts, since they refer to identification and, so to speak, contraidentification, rather than to formal membership in the group. A person may be identified with groups to which he does not formally belong. This is exemplified by the type of socially upward mobile person who is identified with groups of higher status and power (class, profession, political faction) than those to which he now belongs; also by the person with motivated downward mobility[1] who identifies with lower status and power groups such as Negroes, Jews, "the proletariat," "the weak and suffering."

An individual may, of course, be concerned with many groups which are neither ingroups nor outgroups for him. One may feel sympathetic towards Negroes or the Catholic Church without actually identifying with them. Conversely, one may be opposed to many groups in the sense of feeling a difference in interest or values, or merely of feeling that their aims and existence are irrelevant to him; but these are not outgroups if there is not the sense of contraidentification, of basic conflict, of mutual exclusiveness, of violation of primary values.

A primary characteristic of ethnocentric ideology is the *generality* of outgroup rejection. It is as if the ethnocentric individual feels threatened by most of the groups to which he does not have a sense of belonging; if he cannot identify, he must oppose; if a group is not "acceptable," it is "alien." The ingroup-outgroup distinction thus becomes the basis for most of his social thinking, and people are categorized primarily according to the groups to which they belong. The outgroups are usually entirely subordinate (Negroes, Mexicans), or groups with relatively low status and power who are struggling to better their position in society. The major outgroups in America today appear to be Jews, Negroes, the lower socioeconomic class, labor unions, and political radicals, especially Communists. Other groups whose outgroup status varies somewhat are Catholics, artists, intellectuals; Oklahomans and Japanese (in the West); pacifists, Filipinos, Mexicans, homosexuals. Most other nations, especially the industrially backward, the socialistic, and those most different from the "Anglo-Saxon," tend to be considered outgroups. While there are probably considerable sectional, class, and individual differences regarding which groups are regarded as outgroups, it would appear that an individual who regards a few of these groups as outgroups will tend to reject most of them. An ethnocentric individual may have a particular dislike for one group, but he is likely nonetheless to have ethnocentric opinions and attitudes regarding many other groups.

Another general characteristic of ethnocentric ideology is the *shifting* of the outgroup among various levels of social organization. Once the social context for discussion has been set, ethnocentrists are likely to find an outgroup-ingroup distinction. Thus, in a context of international relations ethnocentrism takes the form of pseudopatriotism; "we" are the best people and the best country in the world, and we should either keep out of world affairs altogether (isolationism) or we should participate–but without losing our full sovereignty, power, and economic advantage (imperialism). And in either case we should have the biggest army and navy in the world, and atom bomb monopoly.

However, the superior American "we" breaks down when the context shifts to intranational affairs. In a religious context the ingroup-outgroup distinction may shift in various ways: religious-nonreligious, Christian-Jewish, Protestant-Catholic, among Protestant sects. Similar outgroup-ingroup distinctions can be found in various other phases of American life. It seems, then, that the individual who has a pseudopatriotic conception of America in relation to other nations actually regards most of America as an outgroup: various religions, nonwhites, "the masses," too-educated people and too-uneducated people, criminals, radicals, and so on, tend largely to fall in the outgroup category. This is not to say that nonethnocentrists regard all these groups as ingroups; rather, the nonethnocentrist can take a supportive attitude without necessarily identifying, and he can be critical without a sense of alien-ness and of categorical difference.

The social world as most ethnocentrists see it is arranged like a series of concentric circles around a bull's-eye. Each circle represents an ingroup-outgroup distinction; each line serves as a barrier to exclude all outside groups from the center, and each group is in turn excluded by a slightly narrower one. A sample "map" illustrating the ever-narrowing ingroup would be the following: Whites, Americans, native-born Americans. Christians, Protestants, Californians, my family, and finally–I.

---

[1] The word "motivated" is used to distinguish this type of downward mobility–which is psychologically desired and sought–from a loss of status which is externally imposed by depression or economic failure (and in which the individual usually remains identified with the higher status group). Similarly, a person may want to rise in economic status primarily because of the desire for comfort, leisure, and so on; this is psychologically different from that upward mobility in which the desire for status and power, and identification with powerful groups, are primary motivating forces.

The ethnocentric "need for an outgroup" prevents that identification with humanity as a whole which is found in anti-ethnocentrism. (This lack in identification is related to the ethnocentrists' inability to approach individuals *as* individuals, and to their tendency to see and "prejudge" each individual only as a sample specimen of the reified group. Their experience of interpersonal relations involves, so to speak, the same stereotypy as their opinions regarding groups generally.) The inability to identify with humanity takes the political form of nationalism and cynicism about world government and permanent peace. It takes other forms, all based on ideas concerning the intrinsic evil (aggressiveness, laziness, power-seeking, etc.) of human nature; the idea that this evil is unchangeable is rationalized by pseudo-scientific hereditarian theories of human nature. The evil, since it is unchangeable, must be attacked, stamped out, or segregated wherever it is found, lest it contaminate the good. The democratic alternative–humanitarianism–is not a vague and abstract "love for everybody" but the ability to like and dislike, to value and oppose, *individuals* on the basis of *concrete specific experience*; it necessarily involves the elimination of the stereotypical ingroup-outgroup distinction and all that goes with it.

What is the *content* of ethnocentric ideology regarding outgroups? There are, of course, individual differences here, and the same individual has different conceptions of, and attitudes toward, different outgroups. Nevertheless, certain common trends seem to exist, and these are generally the same as those found in anti-Semitic ideology. Most essentially, outgroups are seen as *threatening* and *power-seeking*. Accusations against them tend to be moralistic and, often, mutually contradictory. One of the main characteristics of most outgroups is that they are objectively *weaker* than the groups whom they supposedly threaten. Sometimes this weakness is perceived by the ethnocentrist, but this does not seem to lessen his sense of being threatened. The conflict as he sees it is between an ingroup trying to maintain or recapture its justly superior position, and an outgroup, resentful of past hurts, trying to do to others what they have done to it. But the conflict is seen as permanent and unresolvable; the only alternatives are dominance and submission; justice requires dominance by the superior ingroup, and the subordinate group will always remain resentful and rebellious. Because he considers hierarchy and power conflict "natural" he has difficulty in grasping a conception of group relations in which power considerations are largely dominated and in which no group can control the lives of other groups.

The moralistic accusations against outgroups are similar to those that were seen in the case of anti-Semitism; again we find stereotypy, an absence of theories–save simple hereditarian ones–to explain why groups are as they are, and a readiness to place all the blame for group conflict upon outgroups.

The general outlook just described must, it would seem, have to do primarily with psychological trends within the ethnocentrist rather than with the actual characteristics of the outgroups. For one thing, many people who have had bad experiences with members of minority groups–and most of us have had unhappy experiences with members of most groups including ingroups–or who have heard derogatory remarks about these groups, do not have ethnocentric imagery and attitudes. It is not the experience as such that counts, but the way in which it is assimilated psychologically. Also, the prejudiced individual is prepared to reject groups with which he has never had contact; his approach to a new and strange person or culture is not one of curiosity, interest, and receptivity but rather one of doubt and rejection. The feeling of difference is transformed into a sense of threat and an attitude of hostility. The new group easily becomes an outgroup. The stereotypy, the illogicality, the large number of outgroups, the consistency of outgroup imagery–all these point to things in the psychological functioning of ethnocentrists which differentiate them from anti-ethnocentrists.

Ethnocentric ideology regarding ingroups shows similar trends, though often in an opposite direction, to that regarding outgroups. The ingroups are conceived of as superior in morality, ability, and general development; they ought also to be superior in power and status, and when their status is lowered or threatened the ethnocentrist tends to feel persecuted and victimized. Attempts by subordinate groups to improve their status are regarded as threats; he cannot imagine that they are struggling for equality and mutual interaction because he does not think in these terms. The ingroup is idealized and blindly submitted to. Obedience and loyalty are the first requirements of the ingroup member. What is called power-seeking and clannishness in the outgroup is transformed into moral righteousness, self-defense, and loyalty in the ingroup. In all other respects the ingroup is regarded as the opposite of the outgroup: clean, unaggressive, hard-working and ambitious, honest, disciplined, well-mannered. The same values, then, are applied to both ingroups and outgroups, and in the same stereotyped way.

The interaction of ingroups and outgroups, and indeed all social interaction, is conceived in hierarchical and authoritarian terms. Groups as well as individuals must "find their level," and the greatest danger is that certain groups will attempt to rise above their natural position. The same conceptions are applied to ingroup structure and functioning. As in the army, there should be a series of levels, and individuals on a given level should submit to those above and dominate those below. The conception of the ideal family situation for the child is similar: uncritical obedience to the father and elders, pressures directed unilaterally from above to below, inhibition of spontaneity and emphasis on conformity to externally imposed values.

We can now consider the ethnocentric solution to problems of group conflict. The ingroup must be kept pure and strong. The only methods of doing this are to *liquidate* the outgroups altogether, to keep them entirely *subordinate,* or to *segregate* them in such a way as to minimize contact with the ingroups. The first method represents politicized ethnocentrism–fascism and the dissolution of democratic values. This method so obviously violates traditional American values of nonviolence, fairness, and equal opportunity that it has found relatively little support in this country. The second and third methods are supported, however, by large numbers of ordinary citizens.

Attitudes that the main outgroups should be subordinated and segregated are characteristic of American ethnocentrism because, it would seem, they combine so well ethnocentric imagery and sense of threat on the one hand, and certain democratic values which still prevail even in ethnocentrists, on the other. The democratic values often prevent more drastic action, but they may also serve to permit discrimination and oppression behind a pseudo-democratic front.

From these considerations the following general statement emerges. *Ethnocentrism is based on a pervasive and rigid ingroup-outgroup distinction; it involves stereotyped negative imagery and hostile attitudes regarding outgroups, stereotyped positive imagery and submissive attitudes regarding ingroups, and a hierarchical, authoritarian view of group interaction in which ingroups are rightly dominant, outgroups subordinate.*

THE IMAGINARY FOE

Our examples of the "functional" character of anti-Semitism, and of the relative ease by which prejudice can be switched from one object to another, point in one direction: the hypothesis that prejudice, according to its intrinsic content, is but superficially, if at all, related to the specific nature of its object. We shall now give more direct support for this hypothesis, the relation of which to clinical categories such as stereotypy, incapacity to have "experience," projectivity, and power fantasies is not far to seek. This support is supplied by statements which are either plainly self-contradictory or incompatible with facts and of a manifestly imaginary character. Since the usual "self-contradictions" of the anti-Semite can, however, frequently be explained on the basis that they involve different layers of reality and different psychological urges which are still reconcilable in the over-all *"Weltanschauung"* of the anti-Semite, we concern ourselves here mainly with evidence of imaginary

constructs. The fantasies with which we shall deal are so well known from everyday life that their significance for the structure of anti-Semitism can be taken for granted. They are merely highlighted by our research. One might say that these fantasies occur whenever stereotypes "run wild," that is to say, make themselves completely independent from interaction with reality. When these "emancipated" stereotypes are forcibly brought back into relation with reality, blatant distortions appear. The content of the examples of stereotyped fantasy which we collected has to do predominantly with ideas of excessive power attributed to the chosen foe. The disproportion between the relative social weakness of the object and its supposed sinister omnipotence is by itself evidence that the projective mechanism is at work.

We shall first give some examples of omnipotence fantasies projected upon a whole outgroup abstractly, as it were, and then show how the application of such ideas to factual experience comes close to paranoid delusion.

5054, a middle-aged woman with fairly high scores on all the scales, who is greatly concerned with herself and characterized by a "domineering" manner, claims that she has always tried "to see the other side" and even to "fight prejudice on every side." She derives her feelings of tolerance from the contrast with her husband whom she characterized as extremely anti-Jewish (he hates all Jews and makes no exceptions) whereas she is willing to make exceptions. Her actual attitude is described as follows:

> She would not subscribe to a "racist theory," but does not think that the Jews will change much, but rather that they will tend to become "more aggressive." She also believes that "they will eventually run the country, whether we like it or not."

The usual stereotype of undue Jewish influence in politics and economy is inflated to the assertion of threatening over-all domination. It is easy to guess that the countermeasures which such subjects have in mind are no less totalitarian than their persecution ideas, even if they do not dare to say so in so many words.

Similar is case *5061a*, chosen as a mixed case (she is high-middle on E, but low on F and PEC), but actually, as proved by the interview, markedly ethnocentric. In her statement, the vividness of the fantasies about the almighty now seems to be equalled by the intensity of her vindictiveness.

> "My relations with the Jews have been anything but pleasant." When asked to be more specific it was impossible for her to name individual incidents. She described them, however, as "pushing everybody about, aggressive, clannish, money-minded. ... The Jews are practically taking over the country. They are getting into everything. It is not that they are smarter, but they work so hard to get control. They are all alike." When

asked if she did not feel that there were variations in the Jewish temperament as in any other, she said, "No, I don't think so. I think there is something that makes them all stick together and try to hold on to everything. I have Jewish friends and I have tried not to treat them antagonistically, but sooner or later they have also turned out to be aggressive and obnoxious.... I think the percentage of very bad Jews is very much greater than the percentage of bad Gentiles.... My husband feels exactly the same way on this whole problem. As a matter of fact, I don't go as far as he does. He didn't like many things about Hitler, but he did feel that Hitler did a good job on the Jews. He feels that we will come in this country to a place where we have to do something about it."

Sometimes the projective aspect of the fantasies of Jewish domination comes into the open. Those whose half-conscious wishes culminate in the idea of the abolition of democracy and the rule of the strong, call those antidemocratic whose only hope lies in the maintenance of democratic rights. *5018* is a 32-year-old ex-marine gunnery sergeant who scores high on all the scales. He is suspected by the interviewer of being "somewhat paranoid." He knows "one cannot consider Jews a race, but they are all alike. They have too much power but I guess it's really our fault." This is followed up by the statement:

He would handle the Jews by outlawing them from business domination. He thinks that all others who feel the same could get into business and compete with them and perhaps overcome them, but adds, "it would be better to ship them to Palestine and let them gyp one another. I have had some experiences with them and a few were good soldiers but not very many." The respondent went on to imply that lax democratic methods cannot solve the problem because "they won't cooperate in a democracy."

The implicitly antidemocratic feelings of this subject are evidenced by his speaking derogatorily about lax democratic methods: his blaming the Jews for lack of democratic cooperation is manifestly a rationalization.

One more aspect of unrealistic imagery of the Jew should at least be mentioned. It is the contention that the Jews "are everywhere." Omnipresence sometimes displaces omnipotence, perhaps because no actual "Jewish rule" can be pretended to exist, so that the image-ridden subject has to seek a different outlet for his power fantasy in ideas of dangerous, mysterious ubiquity. This is fused with another psychological element. To the highly prejudiced subject the idea of the total right of the ingroup, and of its tolerating nothing which does not strictly "belong," is all-pervasive. This is projected upon the Jews. Whereas the high scorer apparently cannot stand any "intruder"—ultimately nothing that is not strictly like himself—he sees this totality of presence in those whom he hates and whom he feels

justified in exterminating because one otherwise "could not get rid of them." The following example shows the idea of Jewish omnipresence applied to personal experience, thus revealing its proximity to delusion.

6070, a 40-year-old woman, is high-middle on the E scale and particularly vehement about the Jews:

"I don't like Jews. The Jew is always crying. They are taking our country over from us. They are aggressive. They suffer from every lust. Last summer I met the famous musician X, and before I really knew him he wanted me to sign an affidavit to help bring his family into this country. Finally I had to flatly refuse and told him I want no more Jews here. Roosevelt started bringing the Jews into the government, and that is the chief cause of our difficulties today. The Jews arranged it so they were discriminated for in the draft. I favor a legislative discrimination against the Jews along American, not Hitler lines. Everybody knows that the Jews are back of the Communists. This X person almost drove me nuts. I had made the mistake of inviting him to be my guest at my beach club. He arrived with ten other Jews who were uninvited. They always cause trouble. If one gets in a place, he brings two more and those two bring two more."

This quotation is remarkable for more reasons than that it exemplifies the "Jews are everywhere" complex. It is the expression of Jewish *weakness*–that they are "always crying"–which is perverted into ubiquity. The refugee, forced to leave his country, appears as he who *wants* to intrude and to expand over the whole earth, and it is hardly too far-fetched to assume that this imagery is at least partly derived from the fact of persecution itself. Moreover, the quotation gives evidence of a certain ambivalence of the extreme anti-Semite which points in the direction of "negatively falling in love." This woman had *invited* the celebrity to her club, doubtless attracted by his fame, but used the contact, once it had been established, merely in order to personalize her aggressiveness.

Another example of the merging of semi-psychotic idiosyncrasies and wild anti-Jewish imagery is the 26-year-old woman, *5004*. She scores high on the F scale and high-middle on E and PEC. Asked about Jewish religion, she produces an answer which partakes of the age-old image of "uncanniness." "I know very little, but I would be afraid to go into a synagogue." This has to be evaluated in relation to her statement about Nazi atrocities:

"I am not particularly sorry because of what the Germans did to the Jews. I feel Jews would do the same type of thing to me."

The persecution fantasy of what the Jews *might* do to her, is used, in authentic paranoid style, as a justification of the genocide committed by the Nazis.

Our last two examples refer to the distortions that occur when experience is viewed through the lens of congealed stereotypy. *M732c* of the Veterans Group, who scores generally high on the scales, shows this pattern of distorted experience with regard to both Negroes and Jews. As to the former:

"You never see a Negro driving (an ordinary car of which subject mentions a number of examples) but only a Cadillac or a Packard.... They always dress gaudy. They have that tendency to show off.... Since the Negro has that feeling that he isn't up to par, he's always trying to show off.... Even though he can't afford it, he will buy an expensive car just to make a show...." Subject mentions that the brightest girl in a class at subject's school happens to be a Negro and he explains her outstandingness in the class in terms of Negro overcompensation for what he seems to be implying is her inherent inferiority.

The assertion about the Negro's Cadillac speaks for itself. As to the story about the student, it indicates in personalized terms the aspect of inescapability inherent in hostile stereotypy. To the prejudiced, the Negro is "dull"; if he meets, however, one of outstanding achievement, it is supposed to be mere overcompensation, the exception that proves the rule. No matter what the Negro is or does, he is condemned.

As to the "Jewish problem":

"As far as being good and shrewd businessmen, that's about all I have to say about *them*. They're *white* people, that's one thing.... Of course, they have the Jewish instinct, whatever that is.... I've heard they have a business nose.... I imagine the Jewish people are more *obsequious*.... For example, *somehow* a Jewish barber will entice you to come to *his* chair." Subject elaborates here a definite fantasy of some mysterious influence by Jews.... "They're mighty shrewd businessmen, and you don't have much chance" (competing with Jews).

The story about the barber seems to be a retrogression towards early infantile, magical patterns of thinking.

F359, a 48-year-old accountant in a government department, is, according to the interviewer, a cultured and educated woman. This, however, does not keep her from paranoid story-telling as soon as the critical area of race relations, which serves as a kind of free-for-all, in entered. (She is in the high quartile on E, though low on both F and PEC.) Her distortions refer both to Negroes and to Jews:

Subject considers this a very serious problem and she thinks that it is going to get worse. The Negroes are going to get worse. She experienced a riot in Washington; there was shooting; street-car windows were broken, and when a white would get into the Negro section of the car, the shooting would start. The white man would have to lie on the floor. She did not dare to go out at night. One day the Negroes were

having a procession and some of them stared pushing her off the sidewalk. When she asked them not to push, they looked so insolent that she thought they would start a riot, and her companion said, "Let's get out of here or we will start a riot." A friend of hers told her that she had asked her maid to work on a Thursday, but the maid had refused because she said it was "push and shove" day–the day they shoved the whites off the sidewalk. Another friend of hers in Los Angeles told her not to let her maid use her vacuum cleaner because they tamper with it in such a way as to cause it to tear your rugs. One day she caught the maid using a file on her vacuum cleaner and asked her what she was doing. The maid replied, "Oh, I'm just trying to fix this thing." They just want to get revenge on whites. One cannot give them equal rights yet, they are not ready for it; we will have to educate them first. Subject would not want to sit next to a Negro in a theatre or restaurant. She cited the case of a drugstore man who addressed a Negro janitor, a cleaner, as "Mr." You just can't do that to them or they will say, "Ah'm as good as white folks." (Outcome?) "I think there will be trouble." She expects riots and bloodshed.

(Jews?) "Well, they are to blame too, I think. They just cannot do business straight, they have to be underhanded–truth has no meaning for them in business." (What has been your personal experience?) She cited the case of a friend who is interested in photography and brought some second-hand cameras from pawn shops. One day when he was in one, a woman came in with a set of false teeth. She was told that they were not worth anything (there was some gold in them). Finally, the Jew gave her a few dollars for them. As soon as she had gone out, he turned to the man and said, "She didn't know it, but see that platinum under here?" In other words the teeth were worth many times what he gave for them. Subject's friend did not get gypped because he knew them and called their bluff.

It is often advocated as the best means of improving intercultural relations that as many personal contacts as possible be established between the different groups. While the value of such contacts in some cases of anti-Semitism is to be acknowledged, the material presented in this section argues for certain qualifications, at least in the case of the more extreme patterns of prejudice. There is no simple gap between experience and stereotypy. Stereotypy is a device for looking at things comfortably; since, however, it feeds on deep-lying unconscious sources, the distortions which occur are not to be corrected merely by taking a *real* look. Rather, experience itself it predetermined by stereotypy. The persons whose interviews on minority issues have just been discussed share one decisive trait. Even if brought together with minority group members as different from the stereotype as possible, they will perceive them through the glasses of stereotypy, and will hold against them whatever they are and do. Since this tendency is by no means confined to people who are actually "cranky" (rather, the whole complex of the Jew is a kind of recognized red-light district of legitimatized psychotic distortions), this inaccessibility to experience may not be limited to people of the kind discussed here, but may well operate in much milder cases. This should be taken into account by any well-planned policy of defense. Optimism with regard to the hygienic effects of personal contacts should be discarded. One cannot "correct" stereotypy by experience; he has to reconstitute the capacity for *having* experiences in order to prevent the growth of ideas which are malignant in the most literal, clinical sense.

Anti-Semitism for what?

It is a basic hypothesis of psychoanalysis that symptoms "make sense" in so far as they fulfill a specific function within the individual's psychological economy–that they are to be regarded, as a rule, as vicarious wishfulfillments of, or as defenses against, repressed urges. Our previous discussion has shown the irrational aspect of anti-Semitic attitudes and opinions. Since their content is irreconcilable with reality, we are certainly entitled to call them symptoms. But they are symptoms which can hardly be explained by the mechanisms of neurosis; and at the same time, the anti-Semitic individual as such, the potentially fascist character, is certainly not a psychotic. The ultimate theoretical explanation of an entirely irrational symptom which nevertheless does not appear to affect the "normality" of those who show the symptom is beyond the scope of the present research. However, we feel justified in asking the question: *cui bono?* What purposes within the lives of our subjects are served by anti-Semitic ways of thinking? A final answer could be provided only by going back to the primary causes for the establishment and freezing of stereotypes. An approach to such an answer has been set forth in earlier chapters. Here, we limit ourselves to a level closer to the surface of the ego and ask: what does anti-Semitism "give" to the subject within the concrete configurations of his adult experience?

Some of the functions of prejudice may doubtless be called rational. One does not need to conjure up deeper motivations in order to understand the attitude of the farmer who wants to get hold of the property of his Japanese neighbor. One may also call rational the attitude of those who aim at a fascist dictatorship and accept prejudice as part of an over-all platform, though in this case the question of rationality becomes complicated, since neither the goal of such a dictatorship seems to be rational in terms of the individual's interest, nor can the wholesale automatized acceptance of a ready-made formula be called rational either. What we are interested in, for the moment, however, is a problem of a somewhat different order. What good does accrue to the actual adjustment of otherwise "sensible" persons when they subscribe to ideas which have no basis in reality and which we ordinarily associate with maladjustment?

In order to provide a provisional answer to this question, we may anticipate one of the conclusions from our consideration of the political and economic sections of the interview (Chapter XVII): the all-pervasive ignorance and confusion of our subjects when it comes to social matters beyond the range of their most immediate experience. The objectification of social processes, their obedience to intrinsic supra-individual laws, seems to result in an intellectual alienation of the individual from society. This alienation is experienced by the individual as disorientation, with concomitant fear and uncertainty. As will be seen, political stereotypy and personalization can be understood as devices for overcoming this uncomfortable state of affairs. Images of the politician and of the bureaucrat can be understood as signposts of orientation and as projections of the fears created by disorientation. Similar functions seem to be performed by the "irrational" imagery of the Jew. He is, for the highly prejudiced subject, extremely stereotyped; at the same time, he is more personalized than any other bogey in so far as he is not defined by a profession or by his role in social life, but by his human existence as such. For these reasons, as well as for historical ones, he is much better qualified for the psychological function of the "bad man" than the bureaucrats or politicians, who, incidentally, are often but handy substitutes for the real object of hatred, the Jew. The latter's alienness seems to provide the handiest formula for dealing with the alienation of society. Charging the Jews with all existing evils seems to penetrate the darkness of reality like a searchlight and to allow for quick and all-comprising orientation. The less anti-Jewish imagery is related to actual experience and the more it is kept "pure," as it were, from contamination by reality, the less it seems to be exposed to disturbance by the dialectics of experience, which it keeps away through its own rigidity. It is the Great Panacea, providing at once intellectual equilibrium, counter-cathexis, and a canalization of wishes for a "change."

Anti-Semitic writers and agitators from Chamberlain to Rosenberg and Hitler have always maintained that the existence of the Jews is the *key* to everything. But talking with individuals of fascist leanings, one can learn the psychological implications of this "key" idea. Their more-or-less cryptic hints frequently reveal a kind of sinister pride; they speak as if they were in the know and had solved a riddle otherwise unsolved by mankind (no matter how often their solution has been already expressed). They raise literally or figuratively their forefinger, sometimes with a smile of superior indulgence; they know the answer for everything and present to their partners in discussion the absolute security of those who have cut off the contacts by which any modification of their formula may occur. Probably it is this delusion-like security which casts its spell over those who feel insecure. By his very ignorance or confusion or semi-erudition the anti-Semite can often conquer the position of a profound wizard. The more primitive his drastic formulae are, due to their stereotypy, the more appealing they are at the same time, since they reduce the complicated to the elementary, no matter how the logic of this reduction may work. The superiority thus gained does not remain on the intellectual level. Since the cliché regularly makes the outgroup bad and the ingroup good, the anti-Semitic pattern of orientation offers emotional narcissistic gratifications which tend to break down the barriers of rational self-criticism.

It is these psychological instruments upon which fascist agitators play incessantly. They would hardly do so if there were no susceptibility for spurious orientation among their listeners and readers. Here we are concerned only with the evidence for such susceptibility among people who are by no means overt fascist followers. We limit ourselves to three nerve points of the pseudocognitive lure of anti-Semitism: the idea that the Jews are a "problem," the assertion that they are all alike, and the claim that Jews can be recognized as such without exception.

The contention that the Jews, or the Negroes, are a "problem" is regularly found in our interviews with prejudiced subjects. We may quote one example picked at random and then briefly discuss the theoretical implications of the "problem" idea.

The prelaw student, 105, when asked, "What about other groups?" states:

"Well, the Jews are a ticklish problem–not the whole race; there are both good and bad. But there are more bad than good."

The term "problem" is taken over from the sphere of science and is used to give the impression of searching, responsible deliberation. By referring to a problem, one implicitly claims personal aloofness from the matter in question–a kind of detachment and higher objectivity. This, of course, is an excellent rationalization for prejudice. It serves to give the impression that one's attitudes are not motivated subjectively but have resulted from hard thinking and mature experience. The subject who makes use of this device maintains a discursive attitude in the interview; he qualifies, quasi-empirically, what he has to say, and is ready to admit exceptions. Yet these qualifications and exceptions only scratch the surface. As soon as the existence of a "Jewish problem" is admitted, anti-Semitism has won its first surreptitious victory. This is made possible by the equivocal nature of the term itself; it can be both a neutral issue of analysis and, as indicated by the everyday use of the term "problematic" for a dubious

character, a negative entity. There is no doubt that the relations between Jews and non-Jews do present a problem in the objective sense of the term, but when "the Jewish problem" is referred to, the emphasis is subtly shifted. While the veneer of objectivity is maintained, the implication is that the *Jews* are the problem, a problem, that is, to the rest of society. It is but one step from this position to the implicit notion that this problem has to be dealt with according to its own special requirements, i.e., the problematic nature of the Jews, and that this will naturally lead outside the bounds of democratic procedure. Moreover, the "problem" calls for a *solution*. As soon as the Jews themselves are stamped as this problem, they are transformed into objects, not only to "judges" of superior insight but also to the perpetrators of *an action*; far from being regarded as subjects, they are treated as terms of a mathematical equation. To call for a "solution of the Jewish problem" results in their being reduced to "material" for manipulation.

It should be added that the "problem" idea, which made deep inroads into public opinion through Nazi propaganda and the Nazi example, is also to be found in the interviews of low-scoring subjects. Here, however, it assumes regularly the aspect of a *protest*. Unprejudiced subjects try to restore the objective, "sociological" meaning of the term, generally insisting on the fact that the so-called "Jewish problem" is actually the problem of the non-Jews. However, the very use of the term may be partially indicative, even with unprejudiced persons, of a certain ambivalence or at least indifference, as in the case of *5047*, who scored low on the E scale but high on F and PEC.

"Yes, I think there is a so-called Jewish problem and a Negro problem, but essentially I believe that it is really a majority problem." He felt that there was a need for more education of the ignorant masses and for improving economic conditions so that there would not be a necessity for seeking a scapegoat. Generally, his understanding of the problems seemed to be quite sound, and he expressed disagreement with anti-Semitism and discrimination against Negroes. However, the manner in which he approached the matter and his tendency to treat it as a purely academic problem seemed to indicate that he was not thoroughly convinced of his statements and was merely using verbal clichés.

The term "problem" itself seems to suggest a too naive idea of common sense justice, following the pattern of democratic compromise in areas where decision should be made only according to the merits of the case. The man who speaks about the "problem' is easily tempted to say that there are two sides to every problem, with the comfortable consequence that the Jews *must* have done something wrong, if they were exterminated. This pattern of conformist "sensibleness" lends itself very easily to the defense of various kinds of irrationality.

The statement that the Jews are all alike not only dispenses with all disturbing factors but also, by its sweep, gives to the judge the grandiose air of a person who sees the whole without allowing himself to be deflected by petty details—an intellectual leader. At the same time, the "all alike" idea rationalizes the glance at the individual case as a mere specimen of some generality which can be taken care of by general measures which are the more radical, since they call for no exceptions. We give but one example of a case where traces of "knowing better" still survive although the "all alike" idea leads up to the wildest fantasies. *F116* is middle on the E scale, but when the question of the Jews is raised:

(Jews?) "Now this is where I really do have strong feeling. I am not very proud of it. I don't think it is good to be so prejudiced but I can't help it. (What do you dislike about Jews?) Everthing. I can't say one good thing for them. (Are there any exceptions?) No, I have never met one single one that was an exception. I used to hope I would. It isn't pleasant to feel the way I do. I would be just as nice and civil as I could, but it would end the same way. They cheat, take advantage. (Is it possible that you know some Jewish people and like them without knowing they are Jews?) Oh no, I don't think any Jew can hide it. I always know them. (How do they look?) Attractive. Very well dressed. And as though they knew exactly what they wanted. (How well have you known Jews?) Well, I never knew any in childhood. In fact, I never knew one until we moved to San Francisco, 10 years ago. He was our landlord. It was terrible. I had a lovely home in Denver and I hated to leave. And here I was stuck in an ugly apartment and he did everything to make it worse. If the rent was due on Sunday, he was there bright and early. After that I knew lots of them. I had Jewish bosses. There are Jews in the bank. They are everywhere—always in the money. My next-door neighbor is a Jew. I decided to be civil. After all, I can't move now and I might as well be neighborly. They borrow our lawn mower. They *say* it is because you can't buy one during the war. But of course lawn mowers cost money. We had a party last week and they called the Police. I called her the next day because I suspected them. She said she did it so I asked if she didn't think she should have called me first. She said a man was singing in the yard and woke her baby and she got so upset she called the police. I asked her if she realized that her baby screamed for 3 months after she brought him home from the hospital. Ever since then she has been just grovelling and I hate that even worse."

"Knowing better" is mentioned not infrequently by high scorers: they realize they "should" not think that way, but stick to their prejudice under a kind of compulson which is apparently stronger than the moral and rational counteragencies available to them. In addition to this phenomenon, there is hardly any aspect of the anti-Semitic syndrome discussed in this chapter which could not be illustrated by this quotation from a truly "all-out," totalitarian anti-Semite. She omits nothing. Her insatiability is indicative of the tremendous libidinous energy she has invested in her Jewish complex. Acting out her anti-Semitism obviously works with her as a wish-fulfillment, both with regard to aggressiveness and with regard to the desire for intellectual superiority as indicated by her cooperation in the present study "in the interests of science." Her personal attitude partakes of that sinister contempt shown by those who feel themselves to be "in the know" with respect to all kinds of dark secrets.

Her most characteristic attitude is one of pessimism—she dismisses many matters with a downward glance, a shrug of the shoulders, and a sigh.

The idea of the "Jew spotter" was introduced in the Labor Study, where it proved to be the most discriminating item. We used it only in a supplementary way, in work with the Los Angeles sample, but there can be no doubt that people who are extreme on A-S will regularly allege that they can recognize Jews at once. This is the most drastic expression of the "orientation" mechanism which we have seen to be so essential a feature of the prejudiced outlook. At the same time, it can frequently be observed that the actual variety of Jews, which could hardly escape notice, leads to a high amount of vagueness with regard to the criteria according to which Jews might be spotted; this vagueness does not, however, interfere with the definiteness of the spotter's claim. One example for this configuration will suffice. It is interesting because of the strange mixture of fantasy and real observation.

5039, a 27-year-old student at the University of Southern California and a war veteran, who scores high on E:

"Yes, I think I can ... of course, you can't always, I know, But usually they have different features: larger nose, and I think differently shaped faces, more narrow, and different mannerisms.... But mainly they talk too much and they have different attitudes. Almost always they will counter a question with another question (gives examples from school); they are freer with criticism; tend to talk in big terms and generally more aggressive—at least I notice that immediately...."

CONCLUSION

It has often been said that anti-Semitism works as the spearhead of antidemocratic forces. The phrase sounds a bit hackneyed and apologetic: the minority most immediately threatened seems to make an all-too-eager attempt to enlist the support of the majority by claiming that it is the latter's interest and not their own which really finds itself in jeopardy today. Looking back, however, at the material surveyed in this, and other, chapters, it has to be recognized that a link between anti-Semitism and antidemocratic feeling exists. True, those who wish to exterminate the Jews do not, as is sometimes claimed, wish to exterminate afterwards the Irish or the Protestants. But the limitation of human rights which is consummated in their idea of a special treatment of the Jews, not only logically implies the ultimate abolition of the democratic form of goverment and, hence, of the legal protection of the individual, but it is frequently associated quite consciously, by high-scoring interviewees, with overt antidemocratic ideas. We conclude this chapter with two examples of what appear to be the inescapable antidemocratic consequences of anti-Semitism. *M106*, a man high on the E, F, and PEC scales, still pretends to be democratic; but it is not difficult to infer what is in the back of his mind:

> "Hitler's plan—well, Hitler carried things just a little too far. There was some justification—some are bad, but not all. But Hitler went on the idea that a rotten apple in the barrel will spoil all the rest of them." He doesn't approve of ruthless persecution. "If Hitler had handled the Jews as a minority group, had segregated them and set certain standards for them to live by, there would be less

trouble for Hitler now. (Same problem in this country now?) Same problem, but it's handled much better because we're a democratic country."

While the suggestion that a minority be segregated is incompatible with the basic concepts of the same "democratic country" of which the subject professes to be proud, the metaphor of the rotten apple in the barrel conjures up the imagery of "evil germs" which is associated with appalling regularity with the dream of an effective germicide.

Perversion of a so-called democrat is manifested in *5019*, another man whose scale scores are all high. He is a 20-year-old laborer, characterized above all, by his blind, authoritarian acceptance of his humble position in life. At the same time, he "dislikes timid people" and has "great admiration for real leaders":

> Respondent believes that the "laws of democracy should favor white, Gentile people," yet he "would not openly persecute Jews in the way the Hitler program treated them."

The reservation of the second sentence is disavowed by the momentum of the convictions expressed in the first one.

9

The Idea of Racialism:
Its Meaning and History

LOUIS L. SNYDER

What is the meaning of the term 'race' and its corollaries 'racism' and 'racialism'? asked Snyder in the preface to his short but pithy volume which was published in 1962. The first half of the book was a clear-headed, almost surgical account of the concept and its manifestations; the second contained short extracts from some of the classical texts on racism, including those by Buffon, Blumenbach and Müller. The volume remains one of the most illuminating books on the subject.

Snyder refers to an 'unending search for classification' as the dynamic behind early research on demarcation lines between sections of human populations, but, with most other scholars, he agrees that the quality that sets contemporary racism apart from its earlier counterparts is domination, political and economic. Snyder's chapter 'Race and History' provides a neat guide to the changing character of racism in recent times. The main change was the use of scientific theories to complement, justify or simply rationalize the exploitation of subjugated populations. In this respect the notion of a permanent and distinguishable white superiority was of great utility.

While Snyder does not present a coherent theory of racism, he closes his overview with a summary of possible causes, being careful to avoid any reductionist reasoning.

Race and History

HISTORICAL DEVELOPMENT
OF MODERN RACIALISM

Racialism, a relatively recent phenomenon, is historically a concomitant movement with modern nationalism and imperialism. There was little consciousness of race before the sixteenth century. The ancient world was a small world in which physical differences of peoples were not noticeable. For example, the Graeco-Roman peoples and the Germanic barbarians were not very different in physical character. Until the rise of national states in the late medieval and early modern eras, antagonisms between peoples were motivated chiefly by cultural, religious, and linguistic differences. Little was understood about intermarriage and racial intermixture.

According to the British statesman and historian Lord Bryce, self-conscious racial feeling hardly existed in any country until the French Revolution. "However much men of different races may have striven with one another, it was seldom any sense of racial opposition that caused their strife. They fought for land. They plundered one another. They sought glory by conquest.... But strong as patriotism and national feeling might be, they did not think of themselves in terms of ethnology, and in making war for every sort of reason they never made it for the sake of imposing their type of civilization.... In none of such cases did the thought of racial distinction come to the front."

From the sixteenth century onward, Europeans ranged the earth conquering native peoples and establishing themselves as conquering and ruling aristocracies. Especially during the era of colonization in the sixteenth and seventeenth centuries and again in the era of neo-mercantilist revival called imperialism in the nineteenth century, ruling white men and subjugated black, brown, and red men became increasingly conscious of their racial differences.

Until the late eighteenth century, thinking on race was distinguished chiefly by its verbosity. In theory, Christianity argued that all men were spiritually alike in the sight of God, but in practice, all sorts of arguments could be found to prove the inferiority of the black man. By the late eighteenth century, the Enlightenment was in full swing, and efforts were made for the first time to assure a scientific understanding of race. Biologists, building upon the pioneer studies of Linnaeus and Buffon, turned to the classification of races. Animals, as well as human beings, were arranged in systematic hierarchies. Distinctions were made between "higher" and "lower" races. European whites were placed at the summit in the hierarchy of races.

In the late eighteenth and early nineteenth centuries, the discussion on race turned into a heated argument between monogenists and polygenists. The monogenists believed that all races resulted from a single creation. Varieties have arisen naturally from a once homogeneous stem. This concept was strengthened by two powerful allies: the Biblical story of creation from a single original human pair, and the doctrine of the brotherhood of man. The monogenistic view advocated an essential identity in kind of racial and specific differences; they originated in hereditary deviations. Monogenism was advocated by a long string of scholars including Hunter, Blumenbach, Camper, Zimmermann, Lawrence, Omalius, d'Halloy, Latham, Godwin, and others.

The polygenists, on the other hand, held that God created each race separately. Mankind, they said, is composed not of one but of several species. Adam and Eve were only the stem ancestors of the Jews, while other human species were descended from other pairs of stem ancestors. Advocates of this view included Virey, Desmoulins, C. H. Smith; Robert Knox, Nott, Gliddon, and Morton.

The advent of Darwinism and evolutionary thought strengthened the idea of the superiority and inferiority of races. In the first half of the nineteenth century, linguistic paleontologists began to confuse language with race, with the result that racialism began more and more to assume a pseudo-scientific character. The idea was once more projected on a rising note of racial arrogance that physical appearance was an outward mark of an innate and permanent inferiority of non-European peoples.

Thus, we see the development of the race concept from verbosity, to rationalism, to pseudo-scientific racialism.

With the onset of imperialism in the late nineteenth century it became necessary to show that weaker races should die out to make room for the stronger. To substantiate this view, any argument became acceptable. Racialism became more and more irrational. The only important thing was to prove the inferior races as "outsiders," a kind of racial proletariat meant to be kept in subjugation. False, pseudo-scientific myths were used to justify the control of one people by another. "Race relations" became essentially social and economic, and race as such had little to do with the real situation. Yet, race differences were widely held to account for important cultural or economic differences and were used to excuse politically repressive actions.

Today, racialism, while scientifically outmoded and fallen from intellectual respectability, retains considerable historical importance. Systematic racial thought had strong influence on the growth and conduct of peoples in the Age of Imperialism. Our contemporary world took its political shape when racialism was at its height.

RACE AND LANGUAGE

The identification of race and language is one of the more obvious fallacies in the lexicon of racialism. The two terms are used interchangeably without the slightest justification. There is a persistent notion that the race of peoples can be identified by the language they speak. There are these additional assertions:

(1) All people who speak one language are united by identical physical characteristics of one race.
(2) The superior qualities of the mother tongue indicate superior mental and physical qualities of the race.
(3) A language which is widely distributed throughout the world reveals the civilizing capacity of all those who have the good fortune to speak that tongue.

All these assumptions are invalid.

Historically, race, in its only intelligible (that is, *biological*) sense, is altogether indifferent to the development of language. The French historian, Julien Havet (1853-1893), made this clear in a letter written to Salomon Reinach (1858-1932), the French archaeologist: "The truth is that language and race are two entirely distinct notions between which one must not for a single instant admit even the shadow of a likeness; no anthropological argument, under the smallest pretext, should contain a single word of linguistics, nor should any linguistic argument contain a single word of anthropology. When this essential separation has been resolved upon, both sciences may be made to progress. Till then we shall be only wasting paper and ink."

The structure of language is determined by factors quite apart from racial considerations. A nation may include people who speak the same language yet are of varied ethnic strains. A good example is to be found in the United States, where conglomerate ethnic groups speak an Americanized form of English.

Europe provides many arguments for the fallacy of linking race and language. The Scandinavian Northmen adopted the French language when they settled in France and the English tongue when they appeared in England. In northern Italy there is a percentage of Germanic blood, a vestigial remain of the barbarian migrations, but no survivals of Teutonic tongues. The Franks in Gaul and the Goths in Italy adopted vulgate Latin as their language. The Slavic peoples of the Balkan countries who came under the influence of Islam still speak Turkish dialects. Bulgarians have given up their original Finnish speech in favor of Slavic. Similarly, the Rumanian language, originally Latin in form, is becoming more and more Slavic.

Another example of the lack of correspondence between race and language may be found in the South Pacific. There are three ethnic groups in this area: Papuans in New Guinea and Melanesia; Malays in Indonesia; and Polynesians in the outer islands. Polynesians and Malays speak languages of their own group, while the Papuans' speech belongs partly to the Melanesians and partly to the unrelated language group of New Guinea. The racial division is Papuan-Polynesian, but the linguistic division is Malayan-Melanesian-Polynesian.

Often the term "Latin race" is used instead of the more precise "Latin civilization." Yet, there never has been a Latin race. There were people who spoke Latin and spread their civilization over the major portion of Western Europe, including England and Germany. But neither the British nor Germans regard themselves as part of the Latin world. The relationship with Latin language and culture is close, while the measure of so-called Latin blood is minute.

Language, by its very nature, never has been, and cannot be, a test of race. Languages reflect socio-political developments, particularly migrations of peoples sweeping over countries regardless of ethnic boundaries. The use of a common language does not mean that all the individuals speaking it are of a common race. The fact that a person speaks English, Hebrew, Arabic, or Japanese is determined, not by biological heredity, but simply by what tongue he has learned in his environment.

RACE AND CULTURE

Race differs from culture. Race is essentially a question of *heredity*, while culture is one of *tradition*. Race is concerned with the inheritance of bodily characteristics, while culture is concerned with that which is transmitted through society. Thus, in a broad sense, culture includes the transmittal of customs or attitudes from previous generations, the continuation of legends by word of mouth, and the continuity of beliefs, knowledge, and literature. A whole structure of concepts, sentiments, institutions, and ideas is carried from one generation to another mainly through the vehicle of language.

In the popular mind it is fashionable to attribute gestures, bodily attitudes, even facial expressions to certain races. Yet, these are by no means racial attitudes, but, instead, cultural attributes acquired by a group through imitation or education. It is sometimes said that orthodox Jews, with their rigid rites and traditions, can be recognized by their outward similarity. This is, of course, true, but such outward similarity arises from traditional, linguistic, and religious attributes, in a word from Jewish culture, and certainly not from any distinct ethnic, morphological differences. While such cultural characteristics enable us to recognize some Jews, we fail to identify a much larger number of Jews who take on the traits of those people among whom they live. Here, again, we see the danger of identifying race with culture.

Still another fallacy is the attempt to find in the biology of race an explanation for differences between the cultural achievements of peoples. Cultural diversity is almost always found in historical, not racial, factors. "The history of mankind," wrote Franz Boas, "proves that advances of culture depend upon the opportunities presented to a social group to learn from the experience of their neighbors." Peoples with high cultures owe their status to frequent contact with contrasting groups, certainly not to any inherent racial characteristics.

In the problem of heredity versus environment, racialists advocate the preeminence of heredity. Anti-racialists hold the opposite point of view—that environment is of greater importance for the human species. The powerful way in which society can mold the individual temperament was revealed by Ruth Benedict in her *Patterns of Culture* (Boston, 1934).

The Kwakiutl Indians of the northwestern coast and the Pueblo Indians of the south-western desert belong to the same major divisions of the Mongoloid peoples and have a similarity of biological inheritance. The Kwakiutl Indians led a life of frenzied competitiveness, always seeking to dominate others, always seeking to demonstrate their prestige, always loud and combative. The Pueblos, on the other hand, disapproved excesses of every kind, avoided competitiveness as useless and ill-advised, and were sober, kindly, quiet, and inoffensive. Thus, two groups of Amerindians, biologically very similar, developed behavior patterns, temperaments, and institutions that could scarcely have been less similar.

RACE AND PSYCHOLOGY

A central theme in the idea of racialism is that racial characteristics, physical or mental, are inherited. It is assumed that such characteristics remain unchanged. Heredity, it is said, sets an unvarying and unchanging pattern. Human reactions are automatic and instinctive. The influence of home, school, church, public opinion, and general cultural environment is dismissed as negligible, inasmuch as the character of the individual from birth is predestined by membership in a particular racial group.

In thus lauding heredity, racialists reject the idea that environmental conditions, as manifested in education, public opinion, and cultural development, can change the physical and mental characteristics of a race within one or two generations. It is claimed that the Aryan, or the Celtic, or the Anglo-Saxon race is superior to others simply because it possesses superior inborn traits.

There is little satisfactory evidence for this point of view. Admittedly, it is incorrect to assume that heredity plays no part whatever in the existence of psychological differences. It is clear that *individuals* and *families* may not be equally endowed in either physical character or mental capacity. But this does not mean that entire races differ in their psychological inheritance. Each race, whether white, black, or yellow, contains individuals of superior, median, and inferior capacity. No one race contains all superior or all inferior individuals.

A great amount of research has been conducted among Negro, white, Indian, and Eskimo groups to determine the effects of environment on the races. Such testing is continuing. As yet there are no perfect answers. Thus far the evidence is overwhelming in favor of this conclusion: While it is likely that there are differences in the distribution of genetic elements determining personality in different ethnic groups, the study of cultural forms shows that such differences are insignificant when compared with the influence of the environment in which the group lives. There are no innate racial differences in intelligence. Descent of the individual plays a comparatively insignificant role in his behavior. The human organism is so plastic that it follows closely the pattern of cultural environment. Racial differences that have been established thus far are so much dependent on outer circumstances that no proofs can be stated for the existence of innate or inborn racial differences.

For this research, scholars devised the psychological test. The first scale of intelligence tests was introduced in 1905 by the French experimental psychologist Alfred Binet (1857-1911). Binet understood the faults of his system: he believed that his tests could be used to measure innate differences, *but only if the individuals or groups tested had substantially the same opportunities*. He was aware that the interpretation of test results depended upon many more factors than merely the innate capacity of the person tested, such as education, familiarity with subject matter, motivations, emotions, knowledge of language, attitude toward the test itself, etc.

The intelligence test, then, is far from perfect as a measuring rod for differences between individuals and groups. It is not a completely objective method nor an unassailable technique. Psychologists are still searching for the culture-free test. Results obtained thus far indicate that: (1) Innate racial differences do not exist; and (2) as environmental opportunities for various social groups become more alike, the differences in test results tend to disappear.

RACE AND NATION

Loose usage of the terms race and nation as synonyms is responsible for much of the confusion surrounding both words. In popular thinking, race and nation are often identified as one and the same thing. "The reason is," according to Frederick Hertz (1878-), "that most people find it difficult to conceive a close social unity without a physical bond, and that they cannot think of common mentality without common blood. An intimate solidarity of fraternity between members of a nation seems to them to imply a real relationship between members of a family."

The average man may be forgiven for confusing the terms when even distinguished scholars speak again and again of the "British race." Many who consciously reject racialism unconsciously use its catchwords. Even Lord Bryce (1838-1922), in his *Race Sentiment as a Factor in History*, made the surprising comment that in the thought and imagination of every civilized people there is "an unquestionable racial strain," that "race sentiment is one of the elements that goes to make up national sentiment and national pride and helps to make a people cohesive." The psychologist, W. B. Pillsbury (1872-) called descent, *i.e.* race, a criterion of nationality and implied that a common physical descent is essential if a nation is to be made a unit in the best and fullest sense. The French philologist, Maximilien Paul Émile Littré (1801-1881), defined a nation as "a union of men inhabiting the same territory, whether or not subject to the same government, and possessing such common interests of long standing that they may be regarded as belonging to the same race."

Such invalid concepts as these contribute much to the disorder, nebulosity, and lack of precision surrounding the entire idea of race. The term *nation* belongs properly within the sphere of the social sciences, while *race* is used in natural science. The nation designates historical and social characteristics that can be altered by society; race refers to hereditary, biological traits not easily changeable by education or assimilation. There never has been a British, a German, nor an American race, but there are British, German, and American nations.

"A nation," in the words of the British historian, Ernest Barker (1874-1960), "is not the physical fact of one blood, but the mental fact of one tradition. A gulf is fixed between the race and nation. The one is a common physical type; the other is a common mental content. The one is a natural fact which is already given at the dawn of history; the other is an artificial structure acquired by the thinking, feeling, and willing of human minds in the course of history."

Sir Arthur Keith (1879-1944), British anthropologist, saw the problem in a slightly different light. In his estimation, when a land is peopled with a mixture of old races, a new effort at race-building is initiated sooner or later just as a wren's nesting instincts are re-awakened as soon as the first nest is destroyed. "A nation always represents an attempt to become a race; nation and race are but different degrees of the same evolutionary movement."

The fact is that parallels do exist between race and nation. It is, indeed, possible that a nation may acquire a number of similar traits by isolation and inbreeding, and, when it mixes with another group of different acquired traits, a population may result that possesses some of the characteristics of one group, of the second parent group, and of an intermediate, intermingled group. But this is rare, and it is difficult if not impossible to measure these variable factors.

RACE AND NATIONALISM

Nationalism, too, admits of no simple definition. Like other historical innovations of the modern period, it is a complex phenomenon, with vague and mysterious overtones. It may usefully be defined as a condition of mind, feeling, or sentiment of a group of people living in a well-defined geographical area, speaking a common language, possessing a literature in which the aspirations of the nation have been expressed, attached to common traditions, and, in some cases, possessing a common religion. There are, of course, exceptions to every part of this definition.

In its integral form ("our country, right or wrong!"), nationalism is the twin and alter ego of racialism. Both movements emerged as dynamic factors of almost immeasurable cultural and politico-economic significance in our times. With the sharpening of rivalries among national states, nationalism assumed a form decidedly hostile to liberalism and humanitarianism. Integral nationalists rejected sympathy for and coöperation with other nations, promoted jingoism and militarism, and opposed all personal liberties when they interfered with the aims of the state. They were attracted by the idea of racialism, with its emphasis upon racial purity and racial superiority, with its exclusiveness and distrust for the outsider. They identified nation with race and used the terms interchangeably. A nation was superior, they claimed, because it was composed of a people of superior race.

RACE AND IMPERIALISM

In the decade after 1870 there was a revival of neo-mercantilism, called the New Imperialism, a new era of overseas expansion by which European nations engaged in a scramble for rich territories in Africa, Asia, and the Near and Middle East. The basic motive for such expansion was economic, but together with it was a strong psychological pattern. Exaggerated national self-consciousness entered an acute stage. Poets and historians began to speak about the historic mission of expansion. Nationalism merged into imperialism; both were saturated with the same romanticism and mysticism. There was talk about "a place in the sun," "manifest destiny," "the lamp of life," and, particularly, "the white man's burden."

Racialism, with nationalism and imperialism, formed the third branch of this historically significant trident. Although there was no justification for asserting that one race was intellectually superior to another, imperialists assumed that special aptitudes were inherent in the mental make-up of the white European. This was the teleological view of race differences: God had created unequal races. This inequality had a purpose. European whites were more intelligent than the African blacks, hence the former had the right and duty to direct the labor of the latter. The imperialist-minded were certain that the blacks, who had strong backs but weak minds and a lazy disposition, would work better under European direction.

There was no more justification for this attitude than for the custom in the ancient world of placing all non-Greek (later non-Graeco-Roman) peoples in the category of "barbarians." In the imperialist view, Europeans were civilized champions of social progress, while black Africans and yellow Chinese were "savages." This argument was combined with a high-flown cultural arrogance to excuse expansionism. Imperialists conveniently forgot that there were many more human cultures than human races. For the racialists Rudyard Kipling was merely stating a fact of life when he wrote of

> Your new-caught sullen peoples,
> Half devil and half child.

Granted that the white man brought great vitality and energy as well as industrialization to Africa and Asia, it should also be added that he brought with him such badges of civilization as gin, the acquisitive urge, syphilis, and other diseases. Moreover, the basic arts of civilization, discovered in Neolithic times—agriculture, stockrearing, pottery, and weaving—were introduced long before the era of the Western white man. The fact that the white man improved these discoveries in a period of 10,000 years by no means gave him the right to claim racial superiority.

The image of racial superiority has continued into the twentieth century and into recent years at a time when Western imperialism is losing its impetus and drive. Into the vacuum has come the Soviet Union, which has constructed its own tremendous empire based on white colonialism or the subjugation of contiguous peoples who happen to be white. Meanwhile, in the areas of Africa and Asia once subjected to Western imperialism, Africans and Asians respond to emotional racial appeals with curt disregard for logic and fact. Here we witness a kind of reverse racialism. Congolese soldiers slaughter a dozen Italian troops serving with the United Nations because the white Italians are mistaken for hated Belgians. In Ceylon, the Singhalese majority keep the Tamil minority in subjection on racial grounds. Efforts in India to wipe out the caste system make painfully slow progress. In Japan, thousands of lower-class Eta are forced into ghettos and denied a normal social life. Apparently, there is no limit to human self-deception. As racialism recedes in the Western world, it rises now in Africa and Asia, where new nations seek to emulate the West's older form of nationalism and racialism.

RACE CONFLICT

One of the most potent elements of contemporary socio-political unrest, race conflict is also one of the most dangerous, surrounded as it is by emotion, passion, and fear. Once started, it progresses like a brush fire.

Historically, race conflicts had their origin in the migration of races and in the conquest of one people by another. In North America, the invading white man, who considered himself on a level above the native red Indian, drove the latter into small confined areas or exterminated him altogether. We have seen the nature of race conflict in nineteenth-century imperialism. Always the process followed the attempt of a stronger or more advanced race to invade the territory of a weaker race. The oppressed race, finding its social and cultural structure radically changed by the invasion, responded with a new or heightened racial consciousness.

The major contemporary areas of race conflict are Africa, Asia, and the United States. Only a few years ago Africa was regarded as a Dark Continent inhabited by backward races. There was little discontent, little dynamism. But today the entire continent is seething with unrest, tension, and change. New and critical problems have arisen as the old colonial rule is being liquidated. Ghana, the Congo, South Africa—these and other states have become new laboratories of race relations.

There are similar problems in Asia, where two thousand years of racial movement and mixture have produced a population of infinite diversity. There are no pure races left in Asia, but there is a residue of racial conflict. Asians passionately hate Western imperialism. The prestige of the white man has evaporated in Asia. After World War II, the peoples of Asia, usually typed as phlegmatic, fatalistic, and conditioned to lack of change, called loudly for independence. For the white man, whom they condemned as the source of all Asia's troubles, they expressed resentment and seething anger.

In the United States, race conflict took the form of a continuing struggle of the Negro American for equal political and socio-economic rights. There are about 15,000,000 Negroes in the United States, most of them descended from slaves brought from Africa after 1619 and until the Civil War, 1861-1865. In recent years, pointing to the doctrine of human equality and of the natural or divine rights of man (the American Declaration of Independence and the American Constitution), such organizations as the National Association for the Advancement of Colored Peoples (N.A.A.C.P.), the Committee on Racial Equality (C.O.R.E.), and the Urban League called for a speed-up in Negro rights. If these rights were not granted on a citizenship basis, then they would be fought for on a racial basis. "Freedom Riders" ranged through the South demanding desegregation and the implementation of the U.S. Supreme Court decision on educational desegregation.

These conflicts were primarily concerned with color. On a different level, the Jewish "race" was attacked as destructive, imitative, and culturally unfit. With the accession of Hitler to power in 1933, the theory of the Aryan-Jewish clash was accepted as an official doctrine of the German state. Some 6,000,000 Jews were slaughtered by Hitler's Nazis in a horrible, inhuman climax of racial conflict.

RACIAL PREJUDICE

Racial prejudice, the main prop of racialism, has deep historical roots. Prejudice of one people against another has existed throughout the course of history. There are many examples. In the *Rigveda* (X.22.8), the oldest sacred book of the Hindus, is an expression of the usual pre-condition of racial prejudice: "We are surrounded on all sides by Dasyu tribes. They do not perform sacrifices; destroyer of foes! Kill them. Destroy the Dasa race." No age has been free of group prejudice and no society has existed without it. By the nineteenth century, racial prejudice was accompanying political movements and had become a virulent historical force. Conditions conferred upon this distorted and emotional sentiment a pragmatic reality. In the words of A. L. Kroeber (1876-): "The apparently theoretical beliefs held as to race capacity by people who are actually confronted by a race conflict or problem are by no means the outcome of impartial examination and verifications but are the result of the decisions taken and emotions experienced in the course of acts performed toward the other race."

There are many causes for racial prejudice, some fickle and emotional, others derived from and excused by national feeling:

Economic

Deep chasms arise between men because of economic needs or rivalries. The prejudiced seek material advantages and benefits. Prejudice can always provide an excuse or rationalization for economic exploitation as, for example, in imperialism. Similar techniques can be used locally by manipulating wages and rent in such a way that certain groups are obliged to live in segregated areas.

Political

Modern dictators cater to feelings of racial superiority to obtain, retain, and extend their personal power. In democracies, too, politicians sometimes base their campaigns on appeals to racial prejudice. German anti-Semitism after 1871, the Tsarist pogroms after 1880 and the Dreyfus case in France beginning in 1894 all had political undertones of racial prejudice.

Socio-cultural

Racial prejudice may grow as a result of cultural differences between peoples. Orientals resisted the influx of Western customs and traditions because they dreaded change in their long-established institutions. Each culture despised the other as a barbarian or backward race. Barriers of language accentuated the cultural differences.

Psychological

There is also an irrational element, the belief in the physical and mental superiority of chosen races, which cannot be explained in political or cultural terms. For example, in South Africa, all differences of nationality or class among the whites disappeared quickly once the native problem became critical.

Religious

Religious differences, too, are apt to create racial antagonisms. Though the doctrine of most major religions abhors violence and injustice, it still remains true that there have been periods of violence between Christians and Muslims, between Catholics and Protestants, between Western and Eastern religions. Nonbelievers, especially those of another race, are condemned as agents of evil, as advocates of heresy and corruption.

Biological

Still another cause of racial prejudice is exaggeration of physical traits of other peoples. Individuals with different physical features are regarded as obnoxious.

All these causes may exist in part or in combination. Racial prejudice is neither instinctive nor inborn. If it were, then all children would show unreasoning prejudice in their early contacts with other ethnic types, which is obviously not the case. Prejudice is learned, in the home, in the school, in textbooks, even in imaginative child's play.

10

Man's Most Dangerous Myth: The Fallacy of Race

ASHLEY MONTAGU

'The point I wish to bring out here is that "race" prejudice is merely a special case of class prejudice,' wrote Montagu in his authoritative exercise on the 'fallacy' of race. First published in 1962 and subsequently revised, the text is a formidable thesis that explains racism as a 'convenience' to distinguish groups which were to be treated as inferior. He wrote: 'In socially stratified class societies, the shift from class prejudice to "race" prejudice is easily achieved and, in fact amounts to little more than a change of names, for the "race" against which prejudice is now especially directed is but another class or case, even though it may be regarded as something substantially different.' It is an appealing explanation, though one that has been brought into question.

While Montagu subscribed to the view that racism was part of a more generic human propensity, his was no crudely reductive account. He explored several dimensions in his exposition, one of the more interesting being the psychological. Typical of much of the theorizing of the early 1960s, Montagu saw racism as, in some measure, a psychological 'vent' for other emotions, many aggressive. In a way, the racist hostility of the period served as a kind of purgatory for whites. Montagu examines racism as a method of what he called 'easing tensions'.

Psychological Factors

At this stage of our discussion I wish to focus attention upon the general factor which is too frequently overlooked in discussions of the "race" problem. This is the factor of the normal psychological and psychophysical traits of the person—traits which are utilized in the generation of "racial" enmities and which have already been touched upon in the preceding chapter.

The one thing clear concerning "racial" hostility and prejudice is the ease with which persons are led to exhibit it. There are few persons in our society who have not, at one time or another, exhibited "race" prejudice. It would seem clear that most persons are capable of being brought to a state of mind in which they are glad of the opportunity of freely releasing their feelings against some group or person representing such a group. When society as a whole sanctions such provocations against any group, the free exercise of "racial" intolerance is enjoyed as a happy release for feelings which are ever ready to find expression. It is in the nature of such feelings—the character of which we shall presently discuss—that they can be suitably directed against some person or particular group of persons, and it is for this reason that they can be so easily directed to the support and maintenance of "race" prejudices. The person exhibits "race" prejudice because it affords him a means of easing certain tensions within himself; because his tensions are reduced when he is most freely able to discharge those tensions. As far as the person is concerned, the prejudice itself is unimportant, it merely provides the channel through which his feelings are allowed necessary expression. Such feelings should, and for the sake of the health of the person must, find expression. As I have already said, feelings will attach themselves to the most suitable object offered—whatever it may be. Such feelings are *not* feelings of "race" prejudice or any other kind of prejudice; and they are not inborn. On the contrary, such feelings are to a large extent generated during the early childhood development of almost every person. There can, however, be little doubt that the elementary forms of these affective states in their undifferentiated condition are physiologically determined.[1] The manner in which such feelings are generated has been discussed in great detail by the psychoanalysts and others. I shall here briefly review the process involved in these dynamisms.

The aggressiveness which adults exhibit in the form of "race" hatred would appear to have universally the same origin. That is to say, the aggressiveness, not the "race" hatred, has the same origin universally and that aggressiveness is merely arbitrarily directed, in some societies, against certain groups. Under other conditions, this same aggressiveness could be directed against numerous different objects, either real or imagined. The object against which aggressiveness is directed is determined by particular conditions, and these we shall later briefly consider. If in "racial" intolerance and prejudice a certain amount of aggressiveness is always displayed, we must ask and answer two questions: (1) where does this aggressiveness originate and (2) why is it exhibited?

Briefly, a considerable amount of the aggressiveness which adults exhibit is originally produced during childhood by parents, nurses, teachers, or whoever else participates in the process of socializing the child. By depriving the infant, and later the child, of many of the means of satisfaction which it seeks—the nipple, the mother's body, uncontrolled freedom to excrete and to suck, the freedom to cry at will, to stay up as late as one wishes, to do the thousand and one things that are forbidden—expected satisfactions are thwarted and frustration upon frustration is piled up within the child. Such frustrations lead to resentment, to fear, to hatred, and to aggressiveness. In childhood this aggressiveness or resentment is displayed in "bad temper" and in general "naughtiness." Such conduct almost invariably results in further frustration—in punishment. At this stage of his development the child finds himself in a state of severe conflict. He must either control the expression of his aggressiveness or else suffer the punishment and the loss of love which his aggressiveness provokes. Such conflicts are usually resolved by excluding the painful situation from consciousness and direct motor expression—in short, by the repression of one's aggressive energies. These are rarely completely repressed, but only in so far as they permit a resolution of the original conflict situation, and the further the original derivatives of what was primarily repressed become removed from the latter, the more freely do these energies gain access to consciousness and the more available for use do they become.[2] The evidence renders it overwhelmingly clear that these energies are never to any extent destroyed or exhausted. As a part of the total organism, they must, in one way or another, find expression, and the ways in which they can find expression are innumerable. "Race" hatred and prejudice merely represent familiar patterns of the manner in which aggressiveness may express itself.[3]

Fear of those who have frustrated one in childhood and anxiety concerning the outcome of the situation thus produced lead to the repression of aggression against the original frustraters and thereby to the *conditioning* of an emotional association between certain kinds of frustrative or fear situations and aggressive feelings. As a result of such conditioning, any object even remotely suggesting such fear or frustrative situations provokes the aggressive behavior with which such fears and frustrations have become associated.

---

[1] Fremont-Smith, "The Physiological Basis of Aggression," *Child Study*, XV (1938), 1–8, and "The Influence of Emotional Factors upon Physiological and Pathological Processes," *Bulletin of the New York Academy of Medicine*, XV (1939), 560–69; Jost, "Some Physiological Changes during Frustration," *Child Development*, XII (1941), 9–15; De Fleur and Westie, "The Interpretation of Interracial Situations," *Social Forces*, XXXVIII (1959), 17–23, who found that autonomic physiological responses below the threshold of awareness indicated the degree of involvement.

---

[2] Adorno *et al.*, *The Authoritarian Personality*.

[3] For interesting treatments of this view see Dollard *et al.*, *Frustrations and Aggression*, and Durbin and Bowlby, *Personal Aggressiveness and War*; Bender, *Aggression, Hostility, and Anxiety in Children*; Jackson, *Aggression and Its Interpretation*; Lewin, *Resolving Social Conflicts*; Maier, *Frustration*; Scott, *Aggression*; Buss, *The Psychology of Aggression*.

The aggressiveness, more or less common to all human beings, is not a cause of "race" prejudice, but merely represents a motive force or affective energy which can be attached, among other things, to the notion that other groups or "races" are hateful and may thus serve to keep such ideas supplied with the emotional force necessary to keep them going. Under such conditions "race" becomes important, not as a biological description or ethnic classification but as a means of expressing an unconscious conflict.

Since the infliction of mental, and even physical, pain, as well as the frustration and depreciation of others, is involved in the process of "race" prejudice, and since much of the aggressiveness of the individual owes its existence to early experiences of a similar sort, it is perhaps not difficult to understand why it is that most persons are so ready to participate in the exercise of "race" prejudice. By so doing they are able to find an object for their aggressiveness which most satisfactorily permits the free expression of aggressiveness by means almost identically resembling those which in childhood were indulged in against them. In this way is the individual enabled, as an adult, to pay off—quite unconsciously—an old score of childhood frustration. The later appreciable frustrations suffered in adolescence and adult life naturally add to the store and complexity of aggressiveness, and require no discussion here. At this point reference should be made to such important psychological mechanisms as "displacement," which defines the process whereby aggression is displaced from one object to another, and "projection," the process of attributing to others feelings and impulses originating in ourselves which have been refused conscious recognition.

When the release of aggression toward certain objects or agents is socially interdicted or otherwise made difficult, as in the case of parents, teachers, or employers, aggressiveness may then be displaced toward some more accessible target. The government, Negroes, Jews, Catholics, bankers, et cetera, will conveniently serve as such targets, and where such displacement of aggression occurs the object of it becomes the scapegoat. Collective displacement of this sort is a well-known phenomenon. Both on the individual and on the group level forbidden thoughts and aggressions are by its means turned into socially acceptable activities. Man in search of a target readily utilizes social tension for the displacement of individual tension.[4] Since the displacement occurs from that which is forbidden to that which is not, it would be a psychologically sound procedure to make the socially acceptable in this case socially unacceptable in demonstrable form such as by legal fiat. For the displacers

displace because they are, among other things, great respecters of authority, and will displace their aggression only where it is socially permissible.

This analysis is fully supported by several recent clinical studies which were instituted in order to discover what kind of persons adopt and become active carriers of anti-Semitic ideas, why they so readily become "scapegoat-addicts," and what function, if any, anti-Semitism serves in their personality structure.[5]

A group of approximately 100 state university students, 76 of them women, provided the material for this study. Subjects giving evidence of a high degree of anti-Semitism were classified as "high extremes," those showing the contrary tendency were classified as "low extremes," and those with in-between attitudes, as "intermediate."

The high extremes were conservative in their attitudes, automatically tending to support the status quo; they were generally Republicans, although they showed few signs of having developed an organized social-political outlook; and there was a tendency to hold their own ethnic or social group in high esteem, to keep it unmixed and pure, and to reject everything that differed from it. The fathers' income was higher than that of the fathers of the average intermediate or low-extreme subjects, and the appearance of the high-extreme girls was in the best middle-class tradition of good grooming (almost all subjects were members of the middle class), very different from that of the low-extreme girls. On the surface these anti-Semitic girls appeared composed and untroubled. They seemed to have little familiarity with their inner lives, but were characterized rather by a generally externalized orientation. They were sensitive to any encroachment from the outside. On the surface they showed an uncritical devotion and obedience to their parents, and to authority in general. They were mostly interested in social standing, and in making an appropriate marriage.

The low extremes, on all these points, contrasted strongly with the high extremes, being nondescript in appearance, less at ease socially, possessed of varied interests, quite willing to talk about themselves and their situations, and able to make critical appraisals of their parents.

Examination of the results of tests and interviews revealed the fact that the high extremes were markedly characterized by unconscious aggressive drives of a destructive nature, the repression of basic impulses, ambivalent attitudes of love and hate toward their parents, basic insecurity. Both sexes in the high-extreme group tended to be intellectually underproductive, somewhat lower in intelligence,

[4] Hartmann, Kris, and Lowenstein, "Notes on the Theory of Aggression," *The Psychoanalytic Study of the Child*, III/IV (1949), 9–36.

[5] Frenkel-Brunswik and Sanford, "Some Personality Factors in Anti-Semitism," *Journal of Psychology*, XX (1945), 271–91.

and lacking in creative imagination. They were less interested in human beings as individuals, and tended to be more hypochondriacal. "The analysis of the content of their responses suggests that the adoption of an aggressive attitude towards out-groups may stem from frustrations received (mainly at the hands of the mother-figure) in childhood"—frustrations which appeared to have produced definite inferiority feelings.

The rigidity with which the high-extreme girl adhered to her conventional values or stereotypes of behavior and the anxiety which she exhibited in the presence of opposite tendencies afforded the clue to the sources of her behavior. Insecurity was the condition with which such girls were struggling. "The fear of losing status is associated with the fear that they will be tempted to release their inhibited tendencies in the way they believe Jews and proletarians do." Anti-Semitism thus helps them to maintain their identification with the middle class and to ward off anxiety.

"Thus," the authors of this valuable study go on to say, "it is not so much middle class values themselves that we would call into question, but rather the rigidity with which they are adhered to. And in the individual case this appears to be the result of the manner in which they have been put across. The mischief is done when those trends which are taboo according to the class standards become repressed, and hence, no longer susceptible to modification or control. This is most likely to happen when parents are too concerned and too insistent with respect to their positive aims for the child and too threatening and coercive with respect to the 'bad' things. The child is thus taught to view behavior in terms of black and white, 'good' and 'evil'; and the 'evil' is made to appear so terrible that he cannot think of it as something in himself which needs to be modified or controlled, but as something that exists in other 'bad' people and needs to be stamped out completely."[6]

Parent-child relationships clearly need to undergo a substantial change in the direction of greater understanding and sympathy on the part of parents, in the dropping of "either-or" attitudes, for disjunctive commands give rise to disjunctive personalities. As Frenkel-Brunswik and Sanford say, if the kind of repression which they have uncovered in their high-extreme girls, and its consequences, is to be prevented, "there must be less fear of impulses on the part of parents. The parental attitude toward children must be more tolerant and permissive. Parents must learn that 'bad' impulses can be modified and controlled and that it is of crucial importance to invite the child's participation in these processes."[7] Parents must learn how to give their children the maximum degree of security consonant with the ideal of a socially fully integrated personality. Parents must develop a greater interest in the significance of the whole socialization process. In this task teachers must play almost as large a part as parents.[8]

Ackerman and Jahoda have made available the results of a study calculated to reveal the dynamic basis of anti-Semitic attitudes in a number of persons who have experienced psychoanalytic therapy. The material was collected from some 30 accredited psychoanalysts, and the conclusions both enlarge and confirm those of Frenkel-Brunswik and Sanford as well as those of other investigators.

Two extreme categories of anti-Semitic types were theoretically set up by the authors. The one is the anti-Semite whose attitude seems to be one of superficial conformity to the values, in this respect, of the dominant group; the other is the anti-Semite whose hostility derives from some definite disorder in his own personality structure to which his anti-Semitism has a specific relation. All the cases encountered fell between the two extremes, presenting both elements in varying proportions.

All the patients suffered from anxiety. They were insecure in their group membership. They had a basic feeling of rejection by the world, a feeling of not belonging. They failed to form safe and secure personal attachments. They felt a continuous apprehension of injury to their integrity as individuals. They frequently suffered from an exaggerated sense of vulnerability. They did not seem able to derive support from their own identity as persons. Because of their insecurity, their confused and unstable image of themselves, they lacked direction and made erratic shifts in their group associations. Fundamentally they were weak, immature, passive, dependent, with the desire to control unrealized in the normal channels of constructive action. They endeavored to deny to consciousness the image of themselves as inferior and crippled. "Overtly they have the urge to conform but unconsciously they resent the compulsory submission and react with destructive rebellion. At the unconscious level they have no hope of being able to repair their damaged identity as persons; basically they accept it as irreversible. However, this basic despair is concealed from consciousness, where they behave in exactly the opposite manner. The core of these character traits is the weak identity, the immaturity, the unconscious passivity, the intense sense of vulnerability to social injury—all of which are denied in consciousness where they are replaced by aggression."[9]

---

[6] *Ibid.*, p. 289.

[7] *Ibid.*, p. 290. See also Bettelheim and Janowitz, *Dynamics of Prejudice*, p. 170.

[8] See Adorno *et al.*, *The Authoritarian Personality*.

[9] Ackerman and Jahoda, "Toward a Dynamic Interpretation of Anti-Semitic Attitudes," *American Journal of Orthopsychiatry*, XVIII (1948), 168.

In relation to such a syndrome anti-Semitism plays a functionally well-defined role. It is a defense against self-hate, a displacement of the self-destroying trends of the character structure described. At the psychic level anti-Semitism assumes the function of a profound though irrational effort to restore the crippled self, and at the social level it constitutes a pattern producing secondary emotional gain. Were the anti-Semite to permit his internal conflict, between what he *is* unconsciously and what he thinks of himself as being consciously, to proceed to its logical conclusion, he would find the consequences unbearable. And so he escapes the dilemma by preoccupation with external events, thus achieving a spurious relief from tensions and the bogus satisfaction of being a member of a powerful, united group, an ingroup in whose program of action he can join. Nevertheless, the central conflict continues with unabated intensity.

To summarize: the prejudice pattern is created through the mobilization of the following series of mechanisms: (*a*) by denial of anxiety and substitution of aggression, (*b*) by an effort to reinforce affiliation with dominant social groups, (*c*) by the elaboration of a variety of reaction formations and compensatory emotional drives, and (*d*) by renunciation of parts of the person's image of self and the concomitant substitution of a borrowed identity. Associated with this there is a suppression and repression of anxiety-ridden impulses. "Having submissively renounced parts of their own individuality they feel deep resentment against any one who does not do likewise. They demand that other people should conform to the same restrictions. The demand for conformity is thus a result of partial self-renunciation. The person who is forced to renounce his real self as the price of social acceptance is doubly sensitive to others who do not conform. Here lies the root of the excessive reaction to difference which characterizes our anti-Semitic patients. Every sign of non-conformity in another person is, as it were, an unwelcome reminder of the painful sacrifice that the prejudiced person has made by renouncing part of his self in the vain hope of achieving group identification. The fear of the 'different' is hence not in proportion to the extent of objective, measurable differences; rather it grows in proportion to the implied ego threat, in other words, to the degree to which the difference symbolizes the fruitless suppression of the self. All prejudiced people insist on conformity to the extent of trying to destroy the non-conformist. Since conformity denotes surrender of the individuality, a person who is 'different' symbolizes non-surrender, and therefore, an individual who is strong, mature, independent, superior, able to stand up against others with his differences. The prejudiced person cannot bear the implied comparison. Because of the inherent weakness of his own self-image, the 'different'

person represents a potential menace to his own integrity as an individual or whatever there is left of it. The inevitable response is to attack the menace, the person who symbolizes the difference."[10]

The elaborated and inconsistent picture of the stereotype Jew forms a perfect projective screen for the anti-Semite's irreconcilable impulses. The Jew is at once successful and low class; capitalist and communist; clannish and an intruder into other people's society; highly moral and spiritual and given to low forms of behavior such as greed, sharp business practices, and dirt; magically omnipotent and omniscient, and incredibly helpless and defenseless and therefore readily destroyed.

What any individual projects upon the Jew invariably represents unacceptable components of the self or components envied in others, at least unacceptable on the conscious level though unconsciously such attributes form an active part of the person's psychic drives.[11] Hence, the object which is consciously rejected, the Jew, may, at the unconscious level, be represented by a strong identification with him. This identification, because of the symbolic aspect of the Jew's weakness, his crippled, defenseless position, cannot be admitted, because to do so would be to endanger the person's ego and social position. It is therefore denied and in its place there is substituted an identification with the attacker, in order to avoid being victimized and also to draw strength through identification. "Thus the Jew at one and the same time stands for the weakness or strength of the self; for conscience, for those parts of the person which blame and accuse the weakness of the self, and also for those primitive appetites and aggressions which must be denied as the price of social acceptance."[12]

It may be objected that inferences based on data obtained from patients who have been psychoanalytically treated cannot be justly applied to the analysis of the behavior of normal persons. To this objection several replies may be made. First, it is doubtful whether normal persons are ever anti-Semitic in the disordered sense here described, and since a large proportion of persons give evidence of disordered character structure it is likely that the observations made and the conclusions drawn from them are valid for a great segment of the population of anti-Semites. Second, the inability to pay the fees of a psychoanalyst is no mark of normality; and, third, in any event the study of the pathological is still one of the best ways of learning

---

[10] *Ibid.,* p. 171.

[11] Ackerman, "Anti-Semitic Motivation in a Psychopathic Personality," *Psychoanalytic Review,* XXXIV (1947), 76–101.

[12] Ackerman and Jahoda, "Toward a Dynamic Interpretation of Anti-Semitic Attitudes," *American Journal of Orthopsychiatry,* XVIII (1948), 173.

to understand the nature of the pathological, and anti-Semitism is a pathological disorder of persons and of societies.

Anti-Semitism is, of course, only one form of group prejudice, as is "race" prejudice in general.[13] Other kinds of group prejudice, such as religious prejudices, national prejudices, sex prejudices, class prejudices, and the like, as has already been pointed out, are merely special forms of the same general phenomenon of group prejudice. As soon as one becomes aware of group membership and identifies oneself with that group the ground is laid for the development of group prejudice in some particular form. The prejudice may be of the most benign kind and socially not make for the least disharmony. On the other hand, it may develop under certain conditions in so disoperatively strong a manner as to threaten the very existence of the society in which it appears. This happens to be the case in the United States as well as in some other lands. Awareness of this fact, together with our understanding of the psychodynamics of the development of such forms of behavior, suggests the immediate necessity of reconsidering our processes of socializing children in relation to the health of the social structure as a whole. "Race" prejudice is at its strongest where social maturity is at its weakest.

The teaching of the facts about "race" or "race" prejudice will not be adequate to solve the problem. The roots of prejudice are woven into the very psychic structure of the person, and unless we attend to the soil from which they draw nourishment it will not help either the resulting plant or ourselves if we attempt to cure its sickness by lopping off the ailing leaves. The soil in which "race" prejudice grows is the social experience to which the developing person is exposed, and it is to this that we must attend if we are ever to be delivered from the sickness which is "race." As Bettelheim and Janowitz put it, "It seems reasonable to assume that as long as anxiety and insecurity persist as a root of intolerance, the effort to dispel stereotyped thinking or feelings of ethnic hostility by rational propaganda is at best a half-measure. On an individual level only greater personal integration combined with social and economic security seems to offer hope for better inter-ethnic relations."[14] These authors point out that on the social level a change of climate is necessary. Their subjects who accepted social controls and were more tolerant of other minorities were also less tolerant of the Negro, because discrimination against Negroes is more commonly condoned, both publicly and privately. They suggest, therefore, that this should lead, among other things, to additional efforts to change social practices in ways that will tangibly demonstrate that ethnic discrimination is contrary to the mores of society.

MacCrone, in a valuable study of the psychology and psychopathology of "race" prejudice in South Africa, has written that "the extra-individual conflicts between the two racial groups are but the intra-individual conflicts within the mind writ large, and until the latter are removed, reduced, or modified, they must continue to exercise their baleful influence upon the race relations and the race contacts of white and black."[15]

It is these intra-individual conflicts, the psychological factor, the deep, early conditioned motive forces represented by the aggressiveness which is produced in so many human beings and is continually being augmented by the frustrations of adolescent and adult life, that must receive more attention than they have in the past. It is this aggressiveness which renders so easily possible the usual emotional and irrational development of "race" prejudice. A rational society must reckon with this factor, for since a certain amount of frustration is inevitable, and even desirable, in the development of the person and a certain amount of aggressiveness is inevitably produced by some social controls, and by some even considered a necessary part of the equipment of most human beings,[16] the task of an intelligent society is clear. Society must provide outlets for the aggressiveness of the person which will result in benefits both to him, and through him, to society. Outlets for aggression which result in social friction and in the destruction of good relations between human beings must be avoided. Frustrations in the early and subsequent development of the person must be reduced to a minimum, and

---

[13] For the material on anti-Semitism see Ackerman and Jahoda, "The Dynamic Basis of Anti-Semitic Attitudes," *Psychoanalytic Quarterly*, XVII (1948), 240–60; Ackerman and Jahoda, *Anti-Semitism and Emotional Disorder*; Massing, *Rehearsal for Destruction*; Adorno et al., *The Authoritarian Personality*; Bettelheim and Janowitz, *Dynamics of Prejudice*; Lowenthal and Guterman, *Prophets of Deceit*; Graeber and Britt (eds.), *Jews in a Gentile World*; Sachar, *Sufferance Is the Badge*; Samuel, *The Great Hatred*; Livingston, *Must Men Hate?*; McWilliams, *A Mask for Privilege*; Tenenbaum, *Why Men Hate*; Simmel (ed.), *Anti-Semitism: A Social Disease*; McDonagh, "Status Levels of American Jews," *Sociology and Social Research*, XXXII (1948), 944–53; Parkes, *The Jewish Problem in the Modern World*; Parkes, *An Enemy of the People: Antisemitism*; Finkelstein (ed.), *The Jews*; Sartre, "Portrait of the Anti-Semite," *Partisan Review*, XIII (1946), 163–78; Epstein and Forster, *Some of My Best Friends ...* ; Hay, *Europe and the Jews*; Trachtenberg, *The Devil and the Jews*.

[14] Bettelhiem and Janowitz, "Prejudice," *Scientific American*, CLXXXIII (1950), 13.

[15] MacCrone, *Race Attitudes in South Africa*, p. 310.

[16] See Freud on this subject, Appendix I.

aggressiveness always directed toward ends of constructive value. Indeed, as the writers of *The Authoritarian Personality* conclude, all that is really necessary is that children be genuinely loved and treated as human beings.[17]

The findings revealed in the studies of *The Authoritarian Personality* have been challenged as probably not applying to all classes of society. The subjects of that study were largely middle class. The findings and conclusions as a whole, however, have been supported by the independent studies of other investigators.[18] A study by McCord, McCord, and Howard, based on interviews, in 1948, with 48 males aged 20 years of lower class origin revealed that the apparently tolerant did not differ from the bigoted members of this small sample.[19] As Allport[20] and others have pointed out, not all prejudice is necessarily related to the personality as a whole, some prejudices are conformative or mildly ethnocentric. And as McDill has shown, in a study of 146 female and 120 male white non-Jewish adults in Nashville, Tennessee, anomie and authoritarian influences are equally important in accounting for intolerant attitudes toward minority groups.[21] The McCords and Howard incline to the belief that prejudice in the lower classes is based on a generally stereotyped culture, which is not related to specific personality needs or to unique familial environments. Prejudice in the lower classes appears to be the result of adult rather than childhood experiences, according to these investigators.

If this hypothesis is correct, and it would certainly appear to be so in many cases, then improvement in economic and educational opportunities and other social conditions would offer some hope of reducing the quantum of bigotry.

Koenig and King, in a study of students on a coeducational campus in the Southwest, found that "Cognitively simple persons tend to overlook nuances and to classify experience into a few, inclusive categories. Unable to perceive the behaviors of others accurately, they project their own characteristics (including attitudes) onto others. This tendency is related to stereotyping and to intolerance or prejudice."[22] Such findings have been many times independently made by other investigators.

Martin, in a study designed to determine whether some of the findings of *The Authoritarian Personality* would also obtain in a randomly selected adult sample drawn from a balanced urban community, Indianapolis, secured results which confirmed the California studies strikingly. The study involved visits to 668 households and preliminary interviews with 429 persons. The final study was reduced to 41 tolerant and 49 prejudiced individuals. Martin has described his findings in the strongly prejudiced and strongly tolerant syndromes so well, they will be given here at some length.

In general, the strongly prejudiced person presents the following pattern or syndrome of traits and characteristics: he tends to be quite ethnocentric; he makes sharp distinctions between his in-groups and out-groups; he is a "social reductionist," in that his reference groups reflect an *exclusive* rather than an *inclusive* emphasis; he is unlikely to identify with "humanity," but prefers more exclusive levels of identification; he thrives on selective membership with himself on the "inside." Such an attitude provides a sustaining and compensating mechanism for psychological and social insecurity. Although typically obscure himself, he borrows prestige from his "race," nation, etc.

The prejudiced person tends to be suspicious, distrustful and extrapunitive. He attributes ulterior motives to Negroes and other out-group members. The "Negro problem" is due to Negroes, and if their lot is not to their liking then it is because they are at fault. He is afraid of contact with minority group members, and foresees dire consequences of intergroup interaction. Segregation is the political-social policy he urges and defends because he "knows" that Negroes and whites cannot live peacefully together.

He views the world as an arena of conflict, involving power struggles and competition among individuals and groups. Other people are not to be trusted in general, because everyone is seeking to maximize his own advantage at the expense of others. He prides himself on his "realism" and tends to regard "idealistic" people as naive and even dangerous, and he favors the "practical" over the "theoretical."

The strongly prejudiced person seeks certainty through the use of dichotomized absolutes. He does not think in relative terms; he keeps his fear of doubt repressed by the dogmatism he substitutes for it. He therefore views Negroes and whites as being essentially and markedly different; a person is either good or evil, and a statement is either true or false.

---

[17] Adorno *et al., The Authoritarian Personality*, p. 975.

[18] Harris, Gough, and Martin, "Children's Ethnic Attitudes: II, Relationships to Parental Beliefs Concerning Child Training," *Child Development*, XXI (1950), 169–81; Frenkel-Brunswik, "Patterns of Social and Cognitive Outlook in Children and Parents," *American Journal of Orthopsychiatry*, XXI (1951), 543–58; Ackerman and Jahoda, *Anti-Semitism and Emotional Disorder*.

[19] McCord, McCord, and Howard, "Early Familial Experiences and Bigotry," *American Sociological Review*, XXV (1960), 717–22.

[20] Allport, *The Nature of Prejudice*, pp. 395, 408.

[21] McDill, "Anomie, Authoritarianism, Prejudice, and Socio-Economic Status: An Attempt at Clarification," *Social Forces*, XXXIX (1961), 239–45.

[22] Koenig and King, "Cognitive Simplicity and Prejudice," *Social Forces*, XL (1962), 220–22.

The strongly prejudiced person favors obedience and submission to authority. This trait is congruent with his zeal for definiteness and his basic distrust of the impulses and motives of other people. He prefers order, discipline, and conformity in the social environment. He is likely to be conservative in his social attitudes and interests, and is often a vigorous supporter, at the verbal level, of conventional morality. He is moralistic, but distinctly unsentimental. Such a person evidently represses much and engages in considerable projection, particularly in connection with the matter of conventional moral norms and their violation.

The strongly prejudiced person also tends to be poorly endowed with imagination, humanitarianism, creativeness, and compassion. He tends to be fatalistic; he is pessimistic about the scientific study of human behavior. Superstition has a considerable appeal to him, as do the magical, the mystical, and the mysterious.

Compared to the tolerant type he tends to be more emotional and less rational, and he is more moralistic rather than ethical (in terms of the connotations of these two words). The strongly prejudiced individual is typically non-intellectual and frequently anti-intellectual; he is very often dogmatic in expression and angers easily when he meets with disagreement. He is likely to interpret intellectual disagreement as a personal affront.

In religion the bigot subscribes to the more fundamentalistic, dogmatic, irrational, and authoritarian doctrines and beliefs. He is less likely to concur with ideals and values relating to brotherhood, basic humanity, and unselfish deeds. He is opposed to "modernism," and would appear to resent having to donate money to his religious group.

In terms of social characteristics, the prejudiced person has less formal education, a lower occupational level, and perhaps a smaller circle of friends than the tolerant type, even though the latter may often have a lower income.

In general the very tolerant, or relatively unprejudiced person presents the following pattern or syndrome of traits and characteristics: His tolerance tends to be general with respect to people; perhaps the only exception is his intolerance of persons who are bigoted. A conspicuous trait is his trust of other people. The tolerant person is inclined to look for the best in people; he gives them the "benefit of the doubt." He tends to judge individuals *as individuals*, and rejects the practice of group stereotyping. He expects other people to be friendly, fair, and cooperative, and he is likely to suspend his judgment of others beyond the first impression.

The tolerant person apparently feels reasonably secure, or at least he is not prone to exaggerate actual threats from other people. He may be neurotic but he is rarely paranoid. He is inclined to be rational, humanitarian, liberal in social attitudes, and intropunitive.

The tolerant person is also characterized by a high degree of empathic ability, and is much more likely to be sympathetic and compassionate than the strongly prejudiced person. He is "sensitive" as distinct from being "tough"; he is opposed to cruelty, violence, and harsh discipline where the strongly prejudiced person would be likely to condone it. Whereas the bigoted male is often ultra-masculine (to the point of having almost no compassion), the tolerant male seemingly has no obsessive need to "prove" his masculinity, at least he is seldom "swaggering and arrogant" in his maleness.

The tolerant type is able to perceive variation accurately and realistically; thus he is less impelled to resort to stereotyping and dogmatism. He apparently realizes and recognizes that each individual is unique (though not radically different from other persons), and that good and evil, shortness and tallness, darkness and lightness, stupidity and intelligence, are all relative concepts. He has no obsessive fear of being mistaken or wrong, he is willing to admit his own shortcomings and weaknesses.

The tolerant personality is not a highly rigid one. He is more likely to be witty and have a highly developed sense of humour than the bigot. For example, the tolerant person is capable of engaging in self-ridicule, whereas the image of a grim and rigidly serious expression is more plausibly associated with the bigot.

The tolerant person is typically interested in and optimistic about the improvement of human society. He is likely to stress cooperation as against competition in achieving human progress. He is often idealistic and utopian, and interested in intellectual matters. Likewise, the tolerant person values creative activities and is not so prone to stress the "practical" over the "theoretical." The tolerant type is much less of a "social reductionist." It is "humanity" that interests him. Being a member of an "exclusive" group has a weak appeal for him.

The unprejudiced person tends to be "kind-hearted," if not "softhearted"; he is typically in sympathy with the underdog, and is not characterized by the "threat-competition orientation" so evident in highly intolerant people. This is readily observable in the religious values and beliefs of tolerants; there is an emphasis upon brotherhood, humanitarianism, charity, reason, and tolerance of personal deviation. Similarly, he is likely to be altruistic and somewhat sentimental, and be more appreciative of the aesthetic, as compared to the strongly prejudiced person.

Such a personality is more concerned with *serving* than *leading*; is likely to be relatively autonomous; does not have a strong need for dominance; is rarely ever obsessively conformist; and dislikes both subordination and superordination of any appreciable degree. He tends to view his social interaction and social relationships as possibilities for expression, mutual assistance, affective response, etc., rather than as opportunities for exploitation and manipulation.

Socially speaking, the relatively unprejudiced person is almost certain to have more formal education than the highly intolerant person, and his occupational status is usually higher. Although it is not borne out by the reports of the subjects in this study, the investigators are of the opinion that the tolerant type usually experiences a childhood family environment characterized by an absence of harsh discipline and authoritarian parental control.

The child-rearing attitudes of the strongly prejudiced subjects certainly suggest that authoritarian discipline is actually applied by such parents, and one would assume that their offspring would show the effects of this conditioning in their intergroup attitudes. It is surmised that the tolerant person would usually come from a more relaxed, secure, and lenient home environment, and would experience more affection and less rejection and hostility from parents than the highly intolerant person.[23]

Thus, it will be seen that the Indianapolis study in every way supports the findings of the California authoritarian-personality study.

"RACE" PREJUDICE
AND CLASSIFIED HOSTILITIES

"Race" prejudice in many cases may be regarded as one of a number of *classified hostilities* that are not a result of an immediate inter-personal relationship, but which arise out of the person's need to fit his hostility into the dynamic framework of his personality structure, altogether apart from the presence of a direct and immediate stimulus situation.

In one very significant sense "race" prejudice arises from the individual's failure to make use of his own potentialities, particularly his powers to relate himself to other beings, to establish human ties. The failure to establish human ties on the basis of the integrity of the individuality of the self allows only one alternative—the adoption of attitudes which seek to justify to himself this failure. "Race" prejudice or the adoption of classified hostilities is one of the methods of trying to satisfy or complete the constellation of needs springing from this failure.

If the constellation of needs in itself arises from a failure to make use of one's powers to love, then there can be no satisfactory solution of the problem in any real sense. For the solution, as offered by rationalizing that there is no basis in reality to love, only succeeds in further stifling this potentiality.

Man is born a social being who can reach his fullest development only through interaction with his fellows. The denial at any point of this social bond between man and man brings with it disintegration. A major symptom of this denial is "race" prejudice. What is observed in this connection is not the failure to develop into that which the individual, the person, in the utmost sense, potentially is, but rather the failure to carry on the process of development. "Race" prejudice functions primarily as a barrier to the further development of the person.

What is the alternative to holding these prejudices or rationalizations? What does it mean to the person to give up these rationalizations? In brief, what is the danger which the person must face if he were to give up these prejudices? That there is a danger is apparent, otherwise men would not cling to ideas, however early formed and strongly held, that can be demonstrated to be factually false.

All the evidence of research and inquiry indicates that the danger seems to lie in the fact that if rationalizations are perceived for what they are and abandoned, the individual faces the necessity of taking his own life seriously, and the necessity of forming meaningful human relations on the basis of his personal integrity is challenged. He must give up the primary dependent ties. He is forced to see himself as an individual entity, and not as a part of another person either in the capacity of master or subject, ruler or ruled. He must be willing to bear the pain of isolation that is concomitant with mature independence.[24] He must recognize his actual position in the universe, feel his aloneness, and at the same time his power to overcome this through love on the basis of his own integrity.

The inability to give up the primary ties is crucial—the ties to the nurturing authority. Often men rationalize that they have given up what could be called their incestuous ties, when a closer examination will reveal that what they have done has been to transfer these ties to a more acceptable object. An interesting fact here is that when group affiliations are of this nature, i.e., a source of power for the person ("I am a member of this strong group"), we find that accompanying this group attachment is a complementary feeling of out-group hostility. That is to say, the stronger and more permanent the person's attachment to the particular group the stronger does his out-group hostility tend to be.

This particular consequence of group allegiances is one of the services the group performs for the person. If the group functions primarily as a *transferred source* of strength for the person, a place of worship of power, this consequence will almost

---

[23] Martin, "Tolerant and Prejudiced Personality Syndromes," *Journal of Intergroup Relations*, II (1961), 171–75.

[24] For a penetrating discussion of this, see Dostoevski, *The Brothers Karamazov*, Chapter V, Book V.

always follow. If, on the other hand, the group serves a cooperative function, if the individual on the basis of his integrity can lend support to efforts that cannot be accomplished on a personal basis, then the consequence of out-group hostility is not a necessary result of such group relationships.

It is evident that this problem can be manipulated in part by manipulation of the groups. In working with boys' clubs and children's groups, some of the hostility which is the side effect of in-group allegiance can be eliminated by reducing the strength of the in-group allegiance. This can be done by making the groups less permanent and the membership more flexible.[25] However, it is further clear that it is not the group as such which generates the out-group hostility, but rather the private and personal use to which the group is put by the persons constituting it.

In a sense what develops is a vicious circle. If the group in some (usually disguised) way serves the person as a primary source of strength, a place where he can transplant his umbilical cord, where he can deny his individuality, then it becomes progressively necessary for him to develop the power of the group, but not his own strength. Since the group is a direct source of security, and since he cannot bear to have his security threatened, then progressively more and more effort must be supplied to this source of strength. But what happens is that the person only more firmly binds himself to the nourishing mother. More and more it becomes clear to him that it is his position in the group that is of importance, and not his position in terms of his responsibility to himself. The greater the crippling of his own individualization, the greater the need to cripple it until at last we find men ready blindly to negate their own lives or even life in general in their efforts to protect and revere this source of strength.

The in-group has certain characteristics, too; it must be just that, an in-group. Its membership must be restricted and of relative permanency. For if its membership should be accessible to all mankind (in actuality, not pretense), and if that goal were reached, this group could no longer serve as a source of strength. This kind of strength involves "power over" and there would no longer be any scapegoat to exercise this "power over."

In contrast to this vicious circle is the kind of group relationship where the effort is supplied to achieving "power of"—power of thought, power of understanding, power of growth. The person's relation to the group is one where his individuality is affirmed by his particular contribution to the group effort. Though the group here is also a source of power for the individual, it is a power that affirms life and his own identity. It is an affirmative strength that does not seek the negation of life itself, but rather the enhancement and growth of those conditions which lead to the fullest development of the person's unique identity.[26]

The satisfactions yielded by and the epidemiology of hostility are interconnected phenomena. Thorne has investigated the epidemiology of hostility through family studies. He has drawn attention to the contagious quality of hostility, its tendency toward chain reactions, and its extreme potency when the recipient is in an inescapable position. A further result of such hostilities is the building up of mutually suspicious and paranoid attitudes.[27]

ATTITUDES OF MIND

The problem of "race" in our society is social, and not biological in any but a vague technical sense.[28] Fairness toward other groups of persons or a person is a matter of simple human decency; and decency is an attitude of mind, for the most part culturally conditioned. Whether ethnic groups or castes are biologically equal is an utterly irrelevant consideration where fair-mindedness is concerned. Whatever differences exist between peoples and however they may have been determined, the willingness to understand those differences and to act upon them sympathetically ought to increase in proportion to

---

[26] I have a feeling that I am not altogether the author of the words or ideas in this section on classified hostilities. My notes, made long ago, indicate no outside source. If I have used someone else's ideas or words without individual acknowledgement, I hope this brief note will serve both as explanation and apology.

[27] Thorne, "The Attitudinal Pathoses," *Journal of Clinical Psychology*, V (1949), 1–21; *Idem*, "The Frustration-Anger-Hostility States: A New Diagnostic Classification," *Journal of Clinical Psychology*, IX (1953), 334–39. See also Buss, *The Psychology of Aggression*; Siegal, "The Relationship of Hostility to Authoritarianism," *Journal of Abnormal and Social Psychology*, LII (1956), 368–72; Hokanson, "The Effects of Guilt Arousal and Severity of Discipline on Adult Aggressive Behavior," *Journal of Clinical Psychology*, XVII (1961), 29–32.

[28] This statement has been interpreted to mean that race in the biological sense in man has no existence. Much more is meant here than that, namely that, in so far as social action is concerned, the *biological facts about population differences* do not constitute the social *problem* of "race." It is the *social attitude* toward "race" that constitutes the problem.

---

[25] Lewin, *Resolving Conflicts*; Sherif and Sherif, *Groups in Harmony and Tension*; Spicer (ed.), *Human Problems in Technological Change*; Argyris, *Personality and Organization*; Maier, *Principles of Human Relations*.

the magnitude of the differences which are believed to exist between ourselves and others. As Professor E. G. Conklin has so well put it: "To the naturalist the differences between human races, subraces, and individuals are small indeed as compared with their manifold resemblances. Biology and the Bible agree that 'God hath made of one blood all nations of men.' Our common traits and origin and fate, our common hopes and fears, joys and sorrows, would call forth our common sympathy with all mankind, if it were not for the lessons of hate which have been cultivated and instilled by selfish and unscrupulous persons and social groups. These racial antagonisms are not the results of inexorable nature, nor of inherited instincts, but of deliberate education and cultivation." [29]

The plea for fairness in dealing with ethnic groups not our own is usually phrased in terms of "tolerance." But if we are to make progress in ethnic relations, it is desirable to recognize that tolerance is not good enough, for tolerance defines an attitude which constitutes a somewhat reluctant admission of the necessity of enduring that which we must bear, the presence of those whom we do not like. A New York high-school girl put the whole matter in a nutshell. "Tolerance," she said, "is when you put up with certain people but you don't like to have them around anyhow." That, it is to be feared, is the general nature of tolerance, the hand-washing indifference of the "superior" person who patronizingly condescends to endure the co-existence of "inferior" beings on condition that they keep their "proper" distance. Tolerance is the attitude of mind of those who consider themselves not only different but superior. It implies an attitude toward different ethnic or minority groups, not of understanding, not of acceptance, not of recognition of human equality, but of recognition of differences which one must suffer—generally, not too gladly. We must be more than tolerant; we must be fair.

Tolerance is the best one can hope from bigots; fairness is the attitude of mind we look for in decent, humane people. By fairness, where ethnic relations are concerned, is meant the attitude of mind which takes it for granted, there being no actual evidence to the contrary, that for all their individual differences no human being is really superior to another by virtue of his group affiliation, and that, given the necessary opportunities, it is probable that the average person of any one group is capable of doing at least as well as the average individual of the culturally most advanced group. It is more than merely being willing to concede that the *others* are not inferior to *us*; it is readiness to accept the verdict that *we* are not superior to the *others*. One is not called upon to be magnanimous, still less is one called upon to condemn or condone, but one is called upon to attempt to be fair—to understand and then to act upon that understanding.[30] Until such an attitude of mind becomes part of the equipment of every person, no amount of instruction in the facts concerning the biology of "race" will ever succeed in eliminating "race" prejudices.

"Race" prejudice is ultimately merely the effect of an incompletely developed personality—a personality, that is, which has not learned any of the simple fundamental facts concerning its nature or of the nature of other human beings, for to understand others it is first necessary to understand oneself. Such a personality is still utilizing the infantile method of beating the object which it imagines has in some way been the cause of its frustration; it is a personality which is still shifting the blame onto someone else for its errors and boasting that "my father is bigger than yours." It is a personality that contrasts sharply with the mature personality which tries to understand and does not seek to wash its hands of its fellows by condemning or condoning their conduct and thus dismissing them from its mind. The mature personality does not automatically resort to the infliction of punishment because he has been frustrated, but he attempts to understand the cause of his frustration and then, in the light of that understanding, so to act that such frustrations will not again be produced. He does not try to escape the exercise of understanding by emotionally letting off steam. He accepts responsibility for his own acts and is moved by the injustice of the acts of others to attempt to remedy the conditions which give rise to them. He understands that no one's father is really bigger than anyone else's father, and that to act in a superior manner is merely a childish way of asserting one's desire to feel important, to feel that one amounts to something. He realizes that, on the other hand, the desire to feel that one belongs with all mankind and not above or below any group, to feel that one is of them and belongs with them, is the most satisfying and efficient way of living and thinking. He not only insists upon the right of everyone to be different, but rejoices in most of those differences and is not unsympathetically indifferent to those which he may dislike. He understands that if people are characterized by likenesses and differences, it is no argument against the likenesses to dwell on the differences, or that difference in any way implies inequality. He realizes that diversity is

---

[29] Conklin, "What Is Man?" Rice Institute Pamphlet, XXVIII (1941), 163.

[30] This is what Oscar Wilde meant when he stated that "it is only by the cultivation of the habit of intellectual criticism that we shall be able to rise superior to race prejudices." "The True Function and Value of Criticism," *Nineteenth Century*, XXVIII (1890), 123–47.

not only the salt of life but also the true basis of collective achievement, and he does everything in his power to further the purposes of that collective achievement.[31]

True culture has been defined as the ability to appreciate the other fellow. While this particular ability has many sources, it is generally derived from varied, sympathetic, and understanding contacts between people who differ from each other in several respects. [32]

If "race" prejudice is ever to be eliminated, society must assume the task of educating the individual—not so much in the facts of "race" as in the processes which lead to the development of a completely integrated human being. The solution here, as in so much else, lies in education; education for humanity first and with regard to the facts afterward. For of what use are facts unless they are intelligently understood and humanely used?

Suppose for a moment that significant differences did exist between different peoples which rendered one, in general, superior to the other; a reasonably developed human being would hardly consider such differences sufficient reason for withholding opportunities for social and cultural development from such groups. On the contrary, he would be the more anxious to provide them with such opportunities. Undeveloped personalities operate in the opposite manner and, creating most of the differences they condemn, proceed to intensify those differences by making it more and more difficult for the groups thus treated to avoid or overcome them.

Fromm writes: "The implicit assumption underlying much reactionary thinking is that equality presupposes absence of difference between persons or social groups. Since obviously such differences exist with regard to practically everything that matters in life, their conclusion is that there can be no equality. When the liberals conversely are moved to deny the fact of great differences in mental and physical gifts and favorable or unfavorable accidental personality conditions, they only help their adversaries to appear right in the eyes of the common man. The concept of equality as it has developed in Judaeo-Christian and in modern progressive tradition means that all men are equal in such basic human capacities as those making for the enjoyment of freedom and happiness. It means, furthermore, that as a political consequence of this basic equality no man shall be made the means to the ends of another group. Each man is a universe for himself and is only his own purpose. His goal is the realization of his being, including those very peculiarities which are characteristic of him and which make him different from others. Thus, equality is the basis for the full development of difference, and it results in the development of individuality." [33]

It is or should be axiomatic that the natural inequality of endowment which exists between all human beings does not render equality of opportunity a contemptible principle.

There exist no really separative or divisive biological differences between the major, or ethnic, groups of mankind; there are differences only between persons. In every group there will be found a large range of differences in the native endowment of its members, some individuals are naturally inferior to others in the realizable potentials of intelligence, in vigor, or in beauty. Such differences may, by some, be made the pretext for heaping contumely and humiliation upon those who are less fortunately endowed than their fellows; but it would be scarcely human to do so, and less than decent.

The form of the mind and body are so dependent upon social conditions that when the latter are unequal for different groups, little or no inference can be made as to the mental and physical potentialities of these groups. As the great American anthropologist Alfred Louis Kroeber wrote many years ago, "Most ethnologists, at any rate, are convinced that the overwhelming mass of historical and miscalled racial facts that are now attributed to obscure organic causes or at most are in dispute, will ultimately be viewed by everyone as social and as best intelligible in their social relations." [34]

"Race" prejudice is a pigment of the imagination. It begins in the minds of men, but it doesn't end there. Until we have succeeded in producing emotionally secure, mature human beings, instead of emotionally insecure, immature human beings, until we have succeeded, by means of the proper educational methods,[35] in producing that cultivation of

---

[31] For a valuable discussion of this aspect of the subject see Davidson, "The Anatomy of Prejudice," *Common Ground*, I (1941), 3–12; and Huxley, *Man Stands Alone*; see also, Myers, *Are Men Equal?*; Abernethy (ed.), *The Idea of Equality*; Tawney, *Equality*; Thompson, *Equality*; Bryson *et al.* (eds.), *Aspects of Human Equality*.

[32] Taft, "Cultural Opportunities through Race Contacts," *Journal of Negro History*, XIV (1929), 19; Williams, Jr., *The Reduction of Intergroup Tensions*, pp. 69–73; Lewin, *Resolving Social Conflicts*; Bryson *et al.* (eds.), *Approaches to Group Understanding*; Stegner, *One Nation*; Marrow, *Living Without Hate*; MacIver (ed.), *Unity and Difference in American Life*; Johnson (ed.), *Foundations of Democracy*; Handlin, *Race and Nationality in American Life*.

[33] Fromm, "Sex and Character," *Psychiatry*, VI (1943), 23.

[34] Kroeber, "The Superorganic," *American Anthropologist*, XIX (1917), 163–213.

[35] See Montagu, *On Being Human*; Montagu, *The Direction of Human Development*; Miller, *The Community*

mind which renders nothing that is human alien to it, the "race" problem will never be completely solved. The means by which that problem may to some extent be ameliorated have already been indicated, and will be further discussed in the last chapter.

There is one more aspect of the psychology of "race" prejudice to which I should like to draw attention, that is, the process of rationalization, the process of finding reasons to justify emotionally held, essentially irrational beliefs, and the construction of one's "logic" to fit one's rationalizations.

We saw in Chapter 1 by what means "race" prejudice originally came into existence in the United States, that is, in large part as the stratagem by means of which the proslavery party attempted to meet the arguments of the abolitionists that the slaves were men and brothers and should be free. The upholders of slavery avidly sought for reasons with which to justify their interest in maintaining that institution, and they brought those reasons forward in force and from all sorts of sources, including the Bible. But no matter from what source they drew their reasons, they were nothing but the most patent rationalizations.

Since "race" prejudice invariably rests on false premises, for the most part of emotional origin, it is not surprising to find that it is practically always rationalized. As Professor W. O. Brown points out: "The rationalization is a moral defense. And the rationalizer is a moralist. The rationalization, in the nature of the case, secures the believer in his illusion of moral integrity. The morality of the rationalization is perhaps intensified by the fact that it represents an effort to make that which is frequently vicious, sorbid, and inhumane rational, idealistic, and humane. The semi-awareness of the real nature of the attitude being rationalized intensifies the solemnity with which the rationalization is formulated. Securing moral values the rationalization naturally partakes of a moral quality. This fact explains, in part, perhaps, the deadly seriousness of the devotee of the rationalization. Its value lies in the fact that it removes the moral stigma attached to race prejudice, elevating this prejudice into a justified reaction." [36]

Practically every one of the arguments used by the racists to prove the inferiority of this or that "race" was not so long ago used by the antifeminists to prove the inferiority of that "lower race," the female of the species. In the case of these sexual prejudices one generation has sufficed to show how completely unfounded they were. [37] It need not take longer to do the same for "race" prejudice. Since this subject provides an instructive and pertinently parallel case history, we shall devote the next chapter to its discussion.

The rationalization is not, of course, regarded as the expression of prejudice, but rather as an explanation of one's behavior—the reason for it. Few rationalizers are aware of the fact that their reasons are simply devices for concealing the real sources of their antipathies, many of which may be quite unconscious. [38] They fail to understand that thought is a means both of concealing and of revealing feelings and that a conviction in the rationality of one's conduct may signify little more than a supreme ability at self-deception. As Professor Brown remarks, "the rationalization is not regarded as cloaking antagonism, but is regarded as a serious interpretation of conduct. No good rationalizer believes that he is prejudiced." Hence, the stronger the reasons we hold for any belief the more advisable it is to inquire into the soundness of the supports upon which such beliefs rest. This is especially true when the beliefs are as strongly held as they are in connection with "race" prejudice.

The prejudiced individual, constellating ahead of experience, is usually a conformist who worships institution. He fashions an island of security for himself and clings to it. Any exceptions to his views or beliefs are regarded by him as nonrepresentative and dismissible, for they do not conform to his encrusted system of expectations. What is more, they make him uncomfortable and anxious. They must therefore be suppressed. As Oliver Wendell Holmes remarked, "The mind of a bigot may be compared to the pupil of the eye; the more light you pour on it the more it contracts."

When men have no moral justification for their beliefs or their conduct, they will invent one. Intelligence and humanity call for a tentative attitude, "for an attitude subject to change, 'good for this day only': prejudice is lack of plasticity. A tentative attitude decreases prejudice, for it replaces absolute with relative values ... breadth of understanding decreases prejudice." [39]

> Through the distorting glass of Prejudice
> All nature seems awry, and but its own
> Wide-warped creations straight; but
>   Reason's eye
> Beholds in every line of nature—truth,
> Immortal truth, and sees a God in all.

Continued

of Man; Frank, *Nature and Human Nature*; Ulich, *The Human Career*; Waddington, *The Ethical Animal*; Eiseley, *The Firmament of Time*; Highet, *Man's Unconquerable Mind*.

[36] Brown, "Rationalization of Race Prejudice," *International Journal of Ethics*, LXIII (1933), 305.

[37] Montagu, *The Natural Superiority of Women*.

[38] Alexander, "Antipathy and Social Behavior," *American Journal of Sociology*, LI (1946), 288–92.

[39] Wallis, "Some Phases of the Psychology of Prejudice," *Journal of Abnormal and Social Psychology*, XXIV (1930), 426.

11

Black Power: The Politics of Liberation in America

STOKELY CARMICHAEL
AND CHARLES V. HAMILTON

The term *institutional racism* has become part of our vocabulary. It was first used in a systematic manner by Stokely Carmichael and Charles V. Hamilton in their *Black Power: The Politics of Liberation in America*, which was as much a prospectus as an argument. First published in 1967, it gave theoretical substance to what was in danger of becoming a mere slogan. 'Black Power' was an exhortation for black people to exercise control over their lives. 'If we fail to do this, we face continued subjection to a white society that has no intention of giving up willingly or easily its position of priority and authority,' wrote Carmichael and Hamilton in their opening statement. Later, they elaborated on this, at the same time presenting an explanation of *why* only a seizure of power would alter this: 'Racist assumptions of white superiority have been so deeply engrained into the fiber of the society that they infuse the entire functioning of the national subconscious' (p. 31).

The book's impact was enhanced by the repudiation of the concept of integration. This was both an ideal and an organizing framework for the future, but it was based on the premise that black people were inferior. As the authors wrote: ' Implicit is the idea that the closer you get to whiteness, the better you are' (p. 157). Racism, on this account, is ubiquitous and informs every level of discourse in American society.

White Power: The Colonial Situation

The dark ghettos are social, political, educational and—above all—economic colonies. Their inhabitants are subject peoples, victims of the greed, cruelty, insensitivity, guilt, and fear of their masters.

DR. KENNETH B. CLARK,
Dark Ghetto, p. 11.[*]

---

[*] In order to avoid excessive bibliographical footnoting, the authors have provided such footnotes only where

*In an age of decolonization, it may be fruit-
ful to regard the problem of the American
Negro as a unique case of colonialism, an
instance of internal imperialism, an underdeveloped people in our very midst.*

I. F. STONE,
The New York Review of Books
(August 18, 1966), p. 10.

What is racism? The word has represented daily
reality to millions of black people for centuries, yet
it is rarely defined—perhaps just because that reality
has been such a commonplace. By "racism" we
mean the predication of decisions and policies on
considerations of race for the purpose of *subordinating* a racial group and maintaining control over that
group. That has been the practice of this country
toward the black man; we shall see why and how.

Racism is both overt and covert. It takes two,
closely related forms: individual whites acting
against individual blacks, and acts by the total white
community against the black community. We call
these individual racism and institutional racism.
The first consists of overt acts by individuals, which
cause death, injury or the violent destruction of
property. This type can be recorded by television
cameras; it can frequently be observed in the
process of commission. The second type is less
overt, far more subtle, less identifiable in terms of
specific individuals committing the acts. But it is no
less destructive of human life. The second type
originates in the operation of established and
respected forces in the society, and thus receives far
less public condemnation than the first type.

When white terrorists bomb a black church and
kill five black children, that is an act of individual
racism, widely deplored by most segments of the
society. But when in that same city—Birmingham,
Alabama—five hundred black babies die each year
because of the lack of proper food, shelter and medical facilities, and thousands more are destroyed and
maimed physically, emotionally and intellectually
because of conditions of poverty and discrimination
in the black community, that is a function of institutional racism. When a black family moves into a
home in a white neighborhood and is stoned, burned
or routed out, they are victims of an overt act of individual racism which many people will condemn—at
least in words. But it is institutional racism that keeps
black people locked in dilapidated slum tenements,
subject to the daily prey of exploitative slumlords,

merchants, loan sharks and discriminatory real
estate agents. The society either pretends it does not
know of this latter situation, or is in fact incapable of
doing anything meaningful about it. We shall examine the reasons for this in a moment.

Institutional racism relies on the active and pervasive operation of anti-black attitudes and practices.
A sense of superior group position prevails: whites
are "better" than blacks; therefore blacks should be
subordinated to whites. This is a racist attitude and it
permeates the society, on both the individual and
institutional level, covertly and overtly.

"Respectable" individuals can absolve themselves from individual blame: *they* would never
plant a bomb in a church; *they* would never stone a
black family. But they continue to support political
officials and institutions that would and do perpetuate institutionally racist policies. Thus *acts* of overt,
individual racism may not typify the society, but
institutional racism does—with the support of covert,
individual *attitudes* of racism. As Charles Silberman
wrote, in *Crisis in Black and White*,

> What we are discovering, in short, is that the United
> States—all of it, North as well as South, West as well as
> East—is a racist society in a sense and to a degree that
> we have refused so far to admit, much less face.... The
> tragedy of race relations in the United States is that
> there is no American Dilemma. White Americans are
> not torn and tortured by the conflict between their devo-
> tion to the American creed and their actual behavior.
> They are upset by the current state of race relations, to
> be sure. But what troubles them is not that justice is
> being denied but that their peace is being shattered and
> their business interrupted [pp. 9–10].

To put it another way, there is no "American
dilemma" because black people in this country form
a colony, and it is not in the interest of the colonial
power to liberate them. Black people are legal citizens of the United States with, for the most part,
the same *legal* rights as other citizens. Yet they
stand as colonial subjects in relation to the white
society. Thus institutional racism has another name:
colonialism.

Obviously, the analogy is not perfect. One normally associates a colony with a land and people
subjected to, and physically separated from, the
"Mother Country." This is not always the case,
however; in South Africa and Rhodesia, black and
white inhabit the same land—with blacks subordinated to whites just as in the English, French,
Italian, Portuguese and Spanish colonies. It is the
objective relationship which counts, not rhetoric
(such as constitutions *articulating* equal rights) or
geography.

The analogy is not perfect in another respect.
Under classic colonialism, the colony is a source of
cheaply produced raw materials (usually agricultural or mineral) which the "Mother Country" then
processes into finished goods and sells at high

Continued

the source is a monograph, periodical, newspaper, etc. In
the case of book sources, the title, author and page reference will be found together with the quoted material, in
the body of the text. A bibliography at the back of this
book will provide the reader with publisher, place and data
of publication.

profit—sometimes back to the colony itself. The black communities of the United States do not export anything except human labor. But is the differentiation more than a technicality? Essentially, the African colony is selling its labor; the product itself does not belong to the "subjects" because the land is not theirs. At the same time, let us look at the black people of the South: cultivating cotton at $3.00 for a ten-hour day and from that buying cotton dresses (and food and other goods) from white manufacturers. Economists might wish to argue this point endlessly; the objective relationship stands. Black people in the United States have a colonial relationship to the larger society, a relationship characterized by institutional racism. That colonial status operates in three areas—political, economic, social—which we shall discuss one by one.

Colonial subjects have their political decisions made for them by the colonial masters, and those decisions are handed down directly or through a process of "indirect rule." Politically, decisions which affect black lives have always been made by white people—the "white power structure." There is some dislike for this phrase because it tends to ignore or oversimplify the fact that there are many centers of power, many different forces making decisions. Those who raise that objection point to the pluralistic character of the body politic. They frequently overlook the fact that American pluralism quickly becomes a monolithic structure on issues of race. When faced with demands from black people, the multi-faction whites unite and present a common front. This is especially true when the black group increases in number: "... a large Negro population is politically both an asset and a liability. A large Negro populace may not only expect to influence the commitments and behavior of a governor, but it also may expect to arouse the fears of many whites. The larger the Negro population, the greater the perceived threat (in the eyes of whites) and thus greater the resistance to broad civil rights laws."[1]

Again, the white groups tend to view their interests in a particularly united, solidified way when confronted with blacks making demands which are seen as threatening to vested interests. The whites react in a united group to protect interests they perceive to be theirs—interests possessed to the exclusion of those who, for varying reasons, are outside the group. Professor Robin M. Williams, Jr. has summed up the situation:

In a very basic sense, "race relations" are the direct outgrowth of the long wave of European expansion, beginning with the discovery of America. Because of their more highly developed technology and economic and political organization, the Europeans were able by military force or by economic and political penetration to secure control over colonies, territories, protectorates and other possessions and spheres of influence around the world. In a way, the resulting so-called race relations had very little to do with "race"—initially it was an historical accident that the peoples encountered in the European expansion differed in shared physical characteristics of an obvious kind. *But once the racial ideologies had been formed and widely disseminated, they constituted a powerful means of justifying political hegemony and economic control.*

In much the same way, present-day vested political, economic and social privileges and rights tend to be rationalized and defended by persons and groups who hold such prerogatives.

… Whenever a number of persons within a society have enjoyed for a considerable period of time certain opportunities for getting wealth, for exercising power and authority, and for successfully claiming prestige and social deference, there is a strong tendency for these people to feel that these benefits are theirs "by right." The advantages come to be thought of as normal, proper, customary, as sanctioned by time, precedent and social consensus. Proposals to change the existing situation arouse reactions of "moral indignation." Elaborate doctrines are developed to show the inevitability and rightness of the existing scheme of things.

An established system of vested interests is a powerful thing, perhaps especially when differences in power, wealth and prestige coincide with relatively indelible symbols of collective membership, such as shared hereditary physical traits, a distinctive religion, or a persistently held culture. *The holders of an advantaged position see themselves as a group and reinforce one another in their attitudes; any qualms about the justice of the status quo seem to be diminished by the group character of the arrangements.*[2]

But what about the official "separation of powers"—the system of "checks and balances"? We are well aware that political power is supposedly divided at the national level between the President, the Congress and the courts. But somehow, the war in Vietnam has proceeded without Congressional approval. We are aware that Constitutional niceties (really, they quickly become irrelevancies) divide power between the Federal Government and the states. But somehow the Supreme Court has found no difficulty in expanding the powers of Congress over interstate commerce. At the same time, we are

[1] James Q. Wilson, "The Negro in American Politics: The Present," *The American Negro Reference Book* (ed. by John P. Davis), Englewood Cliffs, New Jersey: Prentice-Hall, 1966, p. 453.

[2] Robin M. Williams, Jr., "Prejudice and Society," *The American Negro Reference Book* (ed. by John P. Davis), Englewood Cliffs, New Jersey: Prentice-Hall, 1966, pp. 727–29.

told that the Federal Government is very limited in what it can do to stop whites from attacking and murdering civil rights workers. A group interest does exist and it crosses all the supposed lines when necessary, thereby rendering them irrelevant. Furthermore, whites frequently see *themselves* as a monolithic group on racial issues and act accordingly.

The black community perceives the "white power structure" in very concrete terms. The man in the ghetto sees his white landlord come only to collect exorbitant rents and fail to make necessary repairs, while both know that the white-dominated city building inspection department will wink at violations or impose only slight fines. The man in the ghetto sees the white policeman on the corner brutally manhandle a black drunkard in a doorway, and at the same time accept a pay-off from one of the agents of the white-controlled rackets. He sees the streets in the ghetto lined with uncollected garbage, and he knows that the powers which could send trucks in to collect that garbage are white. When they don't, he knows the reason: the low political esteem in which the black community is held. He looks at the absence of a meaningful curriculum in the ghetto schools—for example, the history books that woefully overlook the historical achievements of black people—and he knows that the school board is controlled by whites.[3] He is not about to listen to intellectual discourses on the pluralistic and fragmented nature of political power. He is faced with a "white power structure" as monolithic as Europe's colonial offices have been to African and Asian colonies.

There is another aspect of colonial politics frequently found in colonial Africa and in the United States: the process of indirect rule. Martin Kilson describes it in *Political Change in a West African State, A Study of the Modernization Process in Sierra Leone*: "Indirect rule is the method of local colonial administration through the agency of Chiefs who exercise executive authority. It was applied in one form or other throughout British colonial Africa and was, from the standpoint of the metropolitan power's budget, a form of colonialism-on-the-cheap" (p. 24). In other words, the white power structure rules the black community through local blacks who are responsive to the white leaders, the downtown, white machine, not to the black populace. These black politicians do not exercise

effective power. They cannot be relied upon to make forceful demands in behalf of their black constituents, and they become no more than puppets. They put loyalty to a political party before loyalty to their constituents and thus nullify any bargaining power the black community might develop. Colonial politics causes the subject to muffle his voice while participating in the councils of the white power structure. The black man forfeits his opportunity to speak forcefully and clearly for his race, and he justifies this in terms of expediency. Thus, when one talks of a "Negro Establishment" in most places in this country, one is talking of an Establishment resting on a white power base; of hand-picked blacks whom that base projects as showpieces out front. These black "leaders" are, then, only as powerful as their white kingmakers will permit them to be. This is no less true of the North than the South.

Describing the political situation in Chicago, Wilson wrote in *Negro Politics*:

> Particularly annoying to the Negro politicians has been the partial loss of their ability to influence the appointment of Negroes to important or prestigious jobs on public boards and agencies. Negroes selected for membership on such bodies as the Board of Education, the Land Clearance Commission, the Community Conservation Board, the Chicago Plan Commission, and other groups are the "token leaders" … and control over their appointment has in part passed out of the Negro machine [p. 84].

Before Congressman William O. Dawson (black Congressman from the predominantly black First Congressional District of Southside Chicago) was co-opted by the white machine, he was an outspoken champion of the race. Afterward, he became a tool of the downtown white Democratic power structure; the black community no longer had an effective representative who would articulate and fight to relieve their grievances. Mr. Dawson became assimiliated. The white political bosses could rule the black community in the same fashion that Britain ruled the African colonies—by indirect rule. Note the result, as described in Silberman's *Crisis in Black and White:*

> Chicago provides an excellent example of how Negroes can be co-opted into inactivity…. Dawson surrendered far more than he has obtained for the Negro community. What Dawson obtained were the traditional benefits of the big-city political machine: low-paying jobs for a lot of followers; political intervention with the police and with bail bondsmen, social workers, housing officials, and other bureaucrats whose decisions can affect a poor constituent's life; and a slice of the "melon" in the form of public housing projects, welfare payments, and the like.
>
> What Dawson surrendered was the pride and dignity of his community; he threw away the opportunity to force Chicago's political and civic leaders to identify

---

[3] Studies have shown the heavy preponderance of business and professional men on school boards throughout the country. One survey showed that such people, although only fifteen percent of the population, constituted seventy-six percent of school board members in a national sample. The percentage of laborers on the boards was only three percent. William C. Mitchell, *The American Polity: A Social and Cultural Interpretation*, Glencoe, Illinois: Free Press, 1962.

and deal with the fundamental problems of segregation and oppression [p. 206].

Dawson, and countless others like him, have an answer to this criticism: this is the proper way to operate; you must "play ball" with the party in order to exact maximum benefits. We reject this notion. It may well result in particular benefits—in terms of status or material gains—for individuals, but it does not speak to the alleviation of a multitude of social problems shared by the masses. They may also say: if I spoke up, I would no longer be permitted to take part in the party councils. I would be ousted, and then the black people would have neither voice nor access. Ultimately, this is, at best, a spurious argument, which does more to enhance the security of the individual person than it does to gain substantial benefits for the group.

In time, one notes that a gap develops between the leadership and the followers. The masses, correctly, no longer view the leaders as their legitimate representatives. They come to see them more for what they are, emissaries sent by the white society. Identity between the two is lost. This frequently occurred in Africa, and the analogy, again, is relevant. Former President of Ghana, Kwame Nkrumah, described the colonial situation in pre-independent Africa in his book *Africa Must Unite*:

The principle of indirect rule adopted in West Africa, and also in other parts of the continent, allowed a certain amount of local self-government in that chiefs could rule their districts provided they did nothing contrary to the laws of the colonial power, and on condition they accepted certain orders from the colonial government. The system of indirect rule was notably successful for a time in Northern Nigeria, where the Emirs governed much as they had done before the colonial period. But the system had obvious dangers. In some cases, autocratic chiefs, propped up by the colonial government, became inefficient and unpopular, as the riots against the chiefs in Eastern Nigeria in 1929, and in Sierra Leone in 1936, showed.

In wide areas of East Africa, where there was no developed system of local government which could be used, headmen or "warrant" chiefs were appointed, usually from noble families. They were so closely tied up with the colonial power that many Africans thought chiefs were an invention of the British [p. 18].

This process of co-optation and a subsequent widening of the gap between the black elites and the masses is common under colonial rule. There has developed in this country an entire class of "captive leaders" in the black communities. These are black people with certain technical and administrative skills who could provide useful leadership roles in the black communities but do not because they have become beholden to the white power structure. These are black school teachers, county agents, junior executives in management positions with companies, etc. In a study of New Orleans contained in Professor Daniel C. Thompson's *The Negro Leadership Class*, public school teachers emerge as the largest professional group in the black community of that city: there were 1,600 of them in 1961. These people are college-trained, articulate, and in daily contact with the young minds of the black South. For the most part (fortunately there are a few exceptions), they are not sources of positive or aggressive community leadership. Thompson concluded:

Depending as they do upon white officials, public school teachers have been greatly restricted in their leadership role ... several laws passed by the Louisiana State Legislature, as well as rules and regulations adopted by the state and local school boards in recent years, have made it almost impossible for Negro teachers to identify with racial uplift organizations, or even to participate actively in the civil rights movement. This is definitely an important reason why some teachers have remained inactive and silent during heated controversies over civil rights [p. 46].

It is crystal clear that most of these people have accommodated themselves to the racist system. They have capitulated to colonial subjugation in exchange for the security of a few dollars and dubious status. They are effectively lost to the struggle for an improved black position which would fundamentally challenge that racist system. John A. Williams tells in *This is My Country Too* of how he went to Alabama State College (the state college for black people) in 1963 to interview a black professor, who brusquely told him: "Governor Wallace pays my salary; I have nothing to say to you. Excuse me, I have a class to get to" (p. 62).

When black people play colonial politics, they also mislead the white community into thinking that it has the sanction of the blacks. A professor of political science who made a study of black people in Detroit politics from 1956–1960 has concluded:

The fact that the Negro participates in the system by voting and participating in the party politics in the North should not lead us to conclude that he has accepted the popular consensus of the society about the polity. His support and work for the Democratic party is more a strategic compromise in most cases than a wholehearted endorsement of the party. My own work in Detroit led me to conclude that Negro party officers are not "loyal" to the Democratic party in the way that the ethnic groups or other organized groups such as labor have been. Although the Democratic Party-UAW coalition in Detroit has given the Negro a number of positions in the party hierarchy, it has not included him in the decision-making process.

... As in the colonial situation, the Negro has developed a submission-aggression syndrome. When he attends campaign strategy meetings he appears to be submissive, willingly accepting the strategies suggested by the white leaders. Despite their seeming acceptance of this condescending treatment, after these meetings the Negro precinct workers will tell you that they had to "go along with all that talk" in order to make sure that they were represented. They openly express their resentment of the party hierarchy and reveal themselves as much more militant about the Negro cause than was apparent during the meeting.[4]

This stance is not an uncommon one. More than a handful of black people will admit privately their contempt for insincere whites will whom they must work and deal. (In all likelihood, the contempt is mutual.) They feel secure in articulating their true feelings only when out of hearing range of "the man."

Those who would assume the responsibility of representing black people in this country must be able to throw off the notion that they can effectively do so and still maintain a maximum amount of security. Jobs will have to be sacrificed, positions of prestige and status given up, favors forfeited. It may well be—and we think it is—that leadership and security are basically incompatible. When one forcefully challenges the racist system, one cannot, at the same time, expect that system to reward him or even treat him comfortably. Political leadership which pacifies and stifles its voice and then rationalizes this on grounds of gaining "something for my people" is, at bottom, gaining only meaningless, token rewards that an affluent society is perfectly willing to give.

A final aspect of political colonialism is the manipulation of political boundaries and the devising of restrictive electoral systems. The point is frequently made that black people are only ten percent of the population—no less a personage than President Johnson has seen fit to remind us of this ratio. It is seldom pointed out that this minority is geographically located so as to create potential majority blocs—that strategic location being an ironic side-effect of segregation. But black people have never been able to utilize fully their numerical voting strength. Where we could vote, the white political machines have gerrymandered black neighborhoods so that the true voting strength is not reflected in political representation. Would anyone looking at the distribution of political power and representation in Manhattan ever think that black people represent sixty percent of the population? On the local level, election to City Councils by the at-large system, rather than by district, reduces the number of representatives coming out of the black community. In Detroit, which uses the at-large system, there was not a black man on the City Council until 1957 despite a vast black population, especially during World War II. Also, the larger the

electoral district, the greater the likelihood of there not being a Negro elected because he has to appeal to whites for their votes too. Los Angeles, with very large City Council electoral districts, saw the first black Councilman only in 1963.

The decision-makers are most adept at devising ways or utilizing existing factors to maintain their monopoly of political power.

The economic relationship of America's black communities to the larger society also reflects their colonial status. The political power exercised over those communities goes hand in glove with the economic deprivation experienced by the black citizens.

Historically, colonies have existed for the sole purpose of enriching, in one form or another, the "colonizer"; the consequence is to maintain the economic dependency of the "colonized." All too frequently we hear of the missionary motive behind colonization: to "civilize," to "Christianize" the underdeveloped, backward peoples. But read these words of a French Colonial Secretary of State in 1923:

> What is the use of painting the truth? At the start, colonization was not an act of civilization, nor was it a desire to civilize. It was an act of force motivated by interests. An episode in the vital competition which, from man to man, from group to group, has gone on ever increasing; the people who set out to seize colonies in the distant lands were thinking primarily of themselves, and were working for their own profits, and conquering for their own power.[5]

One is immediately reminded of the bitter maxim voiced by many black Africans today: the missionaries came for our goods, not for our good. Indeed, the missionaries turned the Africans' eyes toward heaven, and then robbed them blind in the process. The colonies were sources from which raw materials were taken and markets to which finished products were sold. Manufacture and production were prohibited if this meant—as it usually did—competition with the "mother country." Rich in natural resources, Africa did not reap the benefit of these resources herself. In the Gold Coast (now Ghana), where the cocoa crop was the largest in the world, there was not one chocolate factory.

This same economic status has been perpetrated on the black community in this country. Exploiters come into the ghetto from outside, bleed it dry, and leave it economically dependent on the larger society. As with the missionaries, these exploiters frequently come as the "friend of the Negro," pretending to offer worthwhile goods and services, when their basic motivation is personal profit and their basic impact is the maintenance of racism.

---

[4] A. W. Singham, "The Political Socialization of Marginal Groups." Paper presented at the 1966 annual meeting of the American Political Science Association, New York City.

[5] Albert Sarraut, French Colonial Secretary of State, speaking at the Ecole Coloniale in Paris. As quoted in Kwame Nkrumah's *Africa Must Unite*. London: Heinemann Educational Books, Ltd., 1963, p. 40.

Many of the social welfare agencies—public and private—frequently pretend to offer "uplift" services; in reality, they end up creating a system which dehumanizes the individual and perpetuates his dependency. Conscious or unconscious, the paternalistic attitude of many of these agencies is no different from that of many missionaries going into Africa.

Professor Kenneth Clark described the economic colonization of the *Dark Ghetto* as follows:

> The ghetto feeds upon itself; it does not produce goods or contribute to the prosperity of the city. It has few large businesses.... Even though the white community has tried to keep the Negro confined in ghetto pockets, the white businessman has not stayed out of the ghetto. A ghetto, too, offers opportunities for profit, and in a competitive society profit is to be made where it can.
>
> In Harlem there is only one large department store and that is owned by whites. Negroes own a savings and loan association; and one Negro-owned bank has recently been organized. The other banks are branches of white-owned downtown banks. Property—apartment houses, stores; businesses, bars, concessions, and theaters—are for the most part owned by persons who live outside the community and take their profits home....
>
> When tumult arose in ghetto streets in the summer of 1964, most of the stores broken into and looted belonged to white men. Many of these owners responded to the destruction with bewilderment and anger, for they felt that they had been serving a community that needed them. *They did not realize* that the residents were not grateful for this service but bitter, as natives often feel toward the functionaries of a colonial power who in the very act of service, keep the hated *structure of oppression intact* [pp. 27–28].

It is a stark reality that the black communities are becoming more and more economically depressed. In June, 1966, the Bureau of Labor Statistics reported on the deteriorating condition of black people in this country. In 1948, the jobless rate of non-white[6] males between the ages of fourteen and nineteen was 7.6 percent. In 1965, the percentage of unemployment in this age group was 22.6 percent. The corresponding figures for unemployed white male teen-agers were 8.3 percent in 1948, and 11.8 percent in 1965.

In the ten-year period from 1955 to 1965, total employment for youth between the ages of fourteen and nineteen increased from 2,642,000 to 3,612,000. Non-white youth got only 36,000 of those 970,000 new jobs. As for adults, the ratio of non-white to white adult unemployment has remained double: in June, 1966, 4.1 percent for whites and 8.3 percent for non-whites.[7]

Lest someone talk about educational preparation, let it quickly be added here that *unemployment rates in 1965 were higher for non-white high school graduates than for white high school drop-outs.* Furthermore, the median income of a non white male college graduate in 1960 was $5,020—actually $110 less than the earnings of white males with only one to three years of high school. Dr. Andrew F. Brimmer, the Negro former Assistant Secretary for Economic Affairs in the Department of Commerce, further highlights this situation in speaking of expected lifetime earnings:

> Perhaps the most striking feature ... is the fact that a non-white man must have between one and three years of college before he can expect to earn as much as a white man with less than eight years of schooling, over the course of their respective working lives. *Moreover, even after completing college and spending at least one year in graduate school, a non-white man can expect to do about as well as a white person who only completed high school.*[8]

A white man with four years of high school education can expect to earn about $253,000 in his lifetime. A black man with five years or more of college can expect to earn $246,000 in his lifetime. Dr. Brimmer is presently a member of the Federal Reserve Board, and many people will point to his new position as an indication of "the progress of Negroes." In Chapter II, we shall discuss the absurdity of such conclusions.

Again, as in the African colonies, the black community is sapped senseless of what economic resources it does have. Through the exploitative system of credit, people pay "a dollar down, a dollar a week" literally for years. Interest rates are astronomical, and the merchandise—of relatively poor quality in the first place—is long since worn out before the final payment. Professor David Caplovitz of Columbia University has commented in his book, *The Poor Pay More*, "The high markup on low-quality goods is thus a major device used by merchants to protect themselves against the risks of their credit business" (p. 18). Many of the ghetto citizens, because of unsteady employment and low incomes, cannot obtain credit from more legitimate businesses; thus they must do without important items or end up being exploited. They are lured into the stores by attractive advertising displays hawking, for example, three rooms of furniture for "only $199." Once inside, the unsuspecting customer is persuaded to buy lesser furniture at a more expensive price, or he is told that the advertised items are temporarily out of stock and is shown other goods. More frequently than not, of course, all the items are over-priced.

---

[6] Non-white in this and subsequent statistics includes Puerto Ricans, but the vast majority of non-whites are black people.

[7] William A. Price, "Economics of the Negro Ghetto," *The National Guardian* (September 3, 1966), p. 4.

[8] Andrew F. Brimmer, "The Negro in the National Economy," *The American Negro Reference Book* (ed. by John P. Davis), Englewood Cliffs, New Jersey: Prentice-Hall, 1966, p. 260.

The exploitative merchant relies as much on threats as he does on legal action to guarantee payment. Garnishment of wages is not particularly beneficial to the merchant—although certainly used—because the employer will frequently fire an employee rather than bc subjected to the bother of extra bookkeeping. And once the buyer is fired, all payments stop. But the merchant can hold the threat of garnishment over the customer's head. Repossession is another threat; again, not particularly beneficial to the merchant. He knows the poor quality of his goods in the first place, and there is little resale value in such goods which have probably already received substantial use. In addition, both the methods of garnishment and repossession give the merchant a bad business image in the community. It is better business practice to raise the prices two to three hundred percent, get what he can—dogging the customer for that weekly payment—and still realize a sizeable profit. At the same time the merchant can protect his image as a "considerate, understanding fellow."

The merchant has special ways of victimizing public welfare recipients. They are not supposed to buy on credit; installment payments are not provided for in the budget. Thus a merchant can threaten to tell the caseworker if a recipient who isn't meeting his payments does not "come in and put down something, if only a couple of dollars." Another example: in November, 1966, M.E.N.D. (Massive Economic Neighborhood Development), a community action, anti-poverty agency in New York City, documented the fact that some merchants raise their prices on the days that welfare recipients receive their checks. Canned goods and other items were priced as much as ten cents more on those specific days.

Out of a substandard income, the black man pays exorbitant prices for cheap goods; he must then pay more for his housing than whites. Whitney Young, Jr. of the Urban League writes in his book, *To Be Equal*: "most of Chicago's 838,000 Negroes live in a ghetto and pay about $20 more per month for housing than their white counterparts in the city" (pp. 144–45). Black people also have a much more difficult time securing a mortgage. They must resort to real estate speculators who charge interest rates up to ten percent, whereas a FHA loan would carry only a six percent interest rate. As for loans to go into business, we find the same pattern as among Africans, who were prohibited or discouraged from starting commercial enterprises. "The white power structure," says Dr. Clark in *Dark Ghetto*, "has collaborated in the economic serfdom of Negroes by its reluctance to give loans and insurance to Negro business" (pp. 27–28). The Small Business Administration, for example, in the ten-year period prior to 1964, made only *seven* loans to black people.

This is why the society does nothing meaningful about institutional racism: because the black community has been the creation of, and dominated by, a combination of oppressive forces and special interests in the white community. The groups which have access to the necessary resources and the ability to effect change benefit politically and economically from the continued subordinate status of the black community. This is not to say that every single white American consciously oppresses black people. He does not need to. Institutional racism has been maintained deliberately by the power structure and through indifference, inertia and lack of courage on the part of white masses as well as petty officials. Whenever black demands for change become loud and strong, indifference is replaced by active opposition based on fear and self-interest. The line between purposeful suppression and indifference blurs. One way or another, most whites participate in economic colonialism.

Indeed, the colonial white power structure has been a most formidable foe. It has perpetuated a vicious circle—the poverty cycle—in which the black communities are denied good jobs, and therefore stuck with a low income and therefore unable to obtain a good education with which to obtain good jobs. (We shall discuss this in detail in Chapter VII.) They cannot qualify for credit at most reputable places; they then resort to unethical merchants who take advantage of them by charging higher prices for interior goods. They end up having less funds to buy in bulk, thus unable to reduce overall costs. They remain trapped.

In the face of such realities, it becomes ludicrous to condemn black people for "not showing more initiative." Black people are not in a depressed condition because of some defect in their character. The colonial power structure clamped a boot of oppression on the neck of the black people and then, ironically, said "they are not ready for freedom." Left solely to the good will of the oppressor, the oppressed would never be ready.

And no one accepts blame. And there is no "white power structure" doing it to them. And they are in that condition "because they are lazy and don't want to work." And this is not colonialism. And this is the land of opportunity, and the home of the free. And people should not become alienated.

But people *do* become alienated.

The operation of political and economic colonialism in this country has had social repercussions which date back to slavery but did not by any means end with the Emancipation Proclamation. Perhaps the most vicious result of colonialism—in Africa and this country—was that it purposefully, maliciously and with reckless abandon relegated the black man to a subordinated, inferior status in the society. The individual was considered and treated as a lowly animal, not to be housed properly, or given adequate medical services, and by no means a decent education. In Chapter VII we will discuss the specific effects of colonialism on the education, housing and health of black people; here, we shall concentrate on the human and psychological results of social colonialism, first as it affected white attitudes toward blacks and then the attitude of black people toward themselves.

As we have already noted, slaves were brought to this land for the good of white masters, not for the purpose of saving or "civilizing" the blacks. In *From Slavery to Freedom*, Professor John Hope Franklin writes:

> When the countries of Europe undertook to develop the New World, they were interested primarily in the exploitation of America's natural resources. Labor was, obviously, necessary, and the cheaper the better [p. 47].

Indians would have been a natural solution, but they were too susceptible to diseases carried by Europeans, and they would not conform to the rigid discipline of the plantation system. Poor whites of Europe were tried but proved unsatisfactory. They were only indentured servants, brought over to serve for a limited time; many refused to complete their contract and ran away. With their white skins, they assimilated easily enough into the society. But black Africans were different. They proved to be the white man's economic salvation. Franklin concludes:

> Because of their color, Negroes could be easily apprehended. Negroes could be purchased outright and a master's labor supply would not be in a state of constant fluctuation. Negroes, from a pagan land and without exposure to the ethical ideals of Christianity, could be handled with more rigid methods of discipline and could be morally and spiritually degraded for the sake of stability on the plantation. In the long run, Negro slaves were actually cheaper. In a period when economic considerations were so vital, this was especially important. Negro slavery, then, became a fixed institution, a solution to one of the most difficult problems that arose in the New World. With the supply of Negroes apparently inexhaustible, there would be no more worries about labor. European countries could look back with gratitude to the first of their nationals who explored the coasts of Africa, and brought back gold to Europe. It was the key to the solution of one of America's most pressing problems [p. 49].

The fact of slavery had to have profound impact on the subsequent attitudes of the larger society toward the black man. The fact of slavery helped to fix the sense of superior group position. Chief Justice Taney, in the Dred Scott decision of 1857, stated "... that they (black people) had no rights which the white man was bound to respect; and that the negro might justly and lawfully be reduced to slavery for his benefit." The emancipation of the slaves by legal act could certainly not erase such notions from the minds of racists. They believed in their superior status, not in paper documents. And that belief has persisted. When some people compare the black American to "other immigrant" groups in this country, they overlook the fact that slavery was peculiar to the blacks. No other minority group in this country was ever treated as legal property.

Even when the black man has participated in wars to defend this country, even when the black man has repeatedly demonstrated loyalty to this country, the embedded colonial mentality has continued to deny him equal status in the social order. Participation of black men in the white man's wars is a characteristic of colonialism. The colonial ruler readily calls upon and expects the subjects to fight and die in defense of the colonial empire, without the ruler feeling any particular compulsion to grant the subjects equal status. In fact, the war is frequently one to defend the socio-political status quo established between the ruler and subject. Whatever else may be changed by wars, the fundamental relation between colonial master and subordinates remains substantially unaltered.

Woodrow Wilson proclaimed that this country entered World War I "to make the world safe for democracy." This was the very same President who issued executive orders segregating most of the eating and rest-room facilities for federal employees. This was the same man who had written in 1901:

> An extraordinary and very perilous state of affairs had been created in the South by the sudden and absolute emancipation of the Negroes, and it was not strange that the Southern legislatures should deem it necessary to take extraordinary steps to guard against the manifest and pressing dangers which it entailed. Here was a vast "laboring, landless, homeless class," once slaves; now free; unpracticed in liberty, unschooled in self-control; never sobered by the discipline of self-support; never established in any habit of prudence; excited by a freedom they did not understand, exalted by false hopes, bewildered and without leaders, and yet insolent and aggressive; sick of work, covetous of pleasure—a host of dusky children untimely put out of school.[9]

"... dusky children untimely put out of school," freed too soon—it is absolutely inconceivable that a man who spoke in such a manner could have black people in mind when he talked of saving the world (i.e., the United States) for democracy. Obviously, black people were not included in Woodrow Wilson's defense perimeter. Whatever the life of blacks might have been under German rule, this country clearly did not fight Germany for the improvement of the status of black people—under the saved democracy—in *this* land.

Even during the war, while black soldiers were dying in Europe, Representative Frank Park of Georgia introduced a bill to make it unlawful to

---

9 Woodrow Wilson, "Reconstruction in the Southern States," *Atlantic Monthly* (January, 1901).

appoint blacks to the rank of either noncommissioned or commissioned officers. Following the war, black veterans returned to face a struggle no less fierce than the one overseas. More than seventy black people were lynched during the first year after armistice. Ten black soldiers, some still in uniform, were lynched. And few who are knowledgeable of twentieth-century American history will fail to remember "the Red summer" of 1919. Twenty-five race riots were recorded between June and December of that year. The Ku Klux Klan flourished during this period, making more than two hundred public appearances in twenty-seven states. The Klan cells were not all located in the South; units were organized in New York, Indiana, Illinois, Michigan and other northern cities.

World War II was basically little different. The increased need for manpower in defense industries slowly opened up more jobs for black people as a result of the war effort, but as Professor Garfinkel has pointed out in *When Negroes March*, "When defense jobs were finally opened up to Negroes, they tended to be on the lowest rungs of the success ladder." Garfinkel also tells of how the President of the North American Aviation Company, for example, issued this statement on May 7, 1941:

> While we are in complete sympathy with the Negroes, it is against company policy to employ them as aircraft workers or mechanics ... regardless of their training....
> There will be some jobs as janitors for Negroes [p. 17].

This country also saw fit to treat German prisoners of war more humanely than it treated its own black soldiers. On one occasion, a group of black soldiers was transporting German prisoners by train through the South to a prisoner-of-war camp. The railroad diner required the black American soldiers to eat in segregated facilities on the train—only four at a time and with considerable delay—while the German prisoners (white, of course) ate without delay and with other passengers in the main section of the diner!

Thus does white man regard the black, an attitude rooted in slavery. Clearly it would be and has been very difficult for subsequent generations of whites to overcome—even if they wanted to—the concept of a subordinate caste assigned to blacks, of black inferiority. They had to continue thinking this way and developing elaborate doctrines to justify what Professor Williams has called "the inevitability and rightness of the existing scheme of things." Herbert Blumer draws the following conclusion:

> ... The sense of group position is a norm and imperative—indeed, a very powerful one. It guides, incites, cows, and coerces ... this kind of sense of group position stands for and involves a fundamental kind of group affiliation for the members of the dominant racial group. To the extent that they recognize themselves as belonging to that group they will automatically come under the influence of the sense of position held by that group.[10]

Blumer allows for the exception: those who do not recognize themselves as belonging to the group. Inside and outside the civil rights movement, there have been whites who rejected their own whiteness as a group symbol and who even tried sometimes "to be black." These dissidents have endured ostracism, poverty, physical pain and death itself in demonstrating their non-recognition of belonging to the group because of its racism. But how fully can white people free themselves from the tug of the group position—free themselves not so much from overt racist attitudes in themselves as from a more subtle paternalism bred into them by the society and, perhaps more important, from the conditioned reaction of black people to their whiteness? For most whites, that freedom is unattainable. White civil rights workers themselves have often noted this:

> Too often we have found our relationships with the local community leaders disturbingly like the traditional white-black relationship of the deep South: the white organizer finds the decision-making left up to him, while the local leader finds himself instinctively assuming a subservient role.... Since the organizer's purpose is not to lead but to get the people to lead themselves, being white is an unsurmountable handicap.[11]

The social and psychological effects on black people of all their degrading experiences are also very clear. From the time black people were introduced into this country, their condition has fostered human indignity and the denial of respect. Born into this society today, black people begin to doubt themselves, their worth as human beings. Self-respect becomes almost impossible. Kenneth Clark describes the process in *Dark Ghetto*:

> Human beings who are forced to live under ghetto conditions and whose daily experience tells them that almost nowhere in society are they respected and granted the ordinary dignity and courtesy accorded to others will, as a matter of course, begin to doubt their own worth. Since every human being depends upon his cumulative experiences with others for clues as to how he should view and value himself, children who are consistently rejected understandably begin to question and doubt whether they, their family, and their group really deserve no more respect from the larger society than they receive. These doubts become the seeds of a pernicious self- and group-hatred, the Negro's complex and debilitating prejudice against himself.

The preoccupation of many Negroes with hair straighteners, skin bleachers, and the like illustrates this

---

[10] Herbert Blumer, "Race Prejudice as a Sense of Group Positions," *Pacific Sociological Review* (Spring, 1958).

[11] Bruce Detwiler, "A Time to be Black," *The New Republic* (September 17, 1966).

tragic aspect of American racial prejudice—Negroes have come to believe in their own inferiority [pp. 63–64].

There was the same result in Africa. And some European colonial powers—notably France and Portugal—provided the black man "a way out" of the degrading status: to become "white," or assimilated. France pursued a colonial policy aimed at producing a black French elite class, a group exposed and acculturated to French "civilization." In its African colonies of Mozambique and Angola, Portugal has attempted a colonial policy of assimilation which goes even further. There is no pretense—as in the British colonies and in American rhetoric—of black people moving toward self-government and freedom. All Independence groups have been suppressed. There prevails in these Portuguese colonies a legal process whereby an African may become, in effect, a "white" man if he measures up to certain Western standards. The *assimilado* is one who has adopted Portuguese customs, dress, language, and has achieved at least a high school education. He is, of course, favored with special jobs and better housing. This status likewise qualifies him to receive a passport to travel abroad, mainly to Portugal and Brazil. Otherwise, such freedom of movement is denied. The *assimilado* is accepted socially by the whites in the restaurants and night clubs. In fact, the Portuguese officials will even import a white Portuguese woman to Mozambique to marry an *assimilado* man. (American colonialism has not gone this far.) But to submit to all of this, the *assimilado* must reject as intrinsically inferior his entire African heritage and association.

In a manner similar to that of the colonial powers in Africa, American society indicates avenues of escape from the ghetto for those individuals who adapt to the "mainstream." This adaptation means to disassociate oneself from the black race, its culture, community and heritage, and become immersed (dispersed is another term) in the white world. What actually happens, as Professor E. Franklin Frazier pointed out in his book, *Black Bourgeoisie*, is that the black person ceases to identify himself with black people yet is obviously unable to assimilate with whites. He becomes a "marginal man," living on the fringes of both societies in a world largely of "make believe." This black person is urged to adopt American middle-class standards and values. As with the black African who had to become a "Frenchman" in order to be accepted, so to be an American, the black man must strive to become "white." To the extent that he does, he is considered "well adjusted"—one who has "risen above the race

question." These people are frequently held up by the white Establishment as living examples of the progress being made by the society in solving the race problem. Suffice it to say that precisely because they are required to denounce—overtly or covertly—their black race, *they are reinforcing racism in this country*.

In the United States, as in Africa, their "adaptation" operated to deprive the black community of its potential skills and brain power. All too frequently, these "integrated" people are used to blunt the true feelings and goals of the black masses. They are picked as "Negro leaders," and the white power structure proceeds to talk to and deal only with them. Needless to say, no fruitful, meaningful dialogue can take place under such circumstances. Those hand-picked "leaders" have no viable constituency for which they can speak and act. All this is a classic formula of colonial co-optation.

At all times, then, the social effects of colonialism are to degrade and to dehumanize the subjected black man. White America's School of Slavery and Segregation, like the School of Colonialism, has taught the subject to hate himself and to deny his own humanity. The white society maintains an attitude of superiority and the black community has too often succumbed to it, thereby permitting the whites to believe in the correctness of their position. Racist assumptions of white superiority have been so deeply engrained into the fiber of the society that they infuse the entire functioning of the national subconscious. They are taken for granted and frequently not even recognized. As Professors Lewis Killian and Charles Grigg express it in their book, *Racial Crisis in America*:

> At the present time, integration as a solution to the race problem demands that the Negro foreswear his identity as a Negro. But for a lasting solution, the meaning of "American" must lose its implicit racial modifier, "white." Even without biological amalgamation, integration requires a sincere acceptance by all Americans that it is just as good to be a black American as to be a white American. Here is the crux of the problem of race relations—the redefinition of the sense of group position so that the status advantage of the white man is no longer an advantage, so that an American may acknowledge his Negro ancestry without apologizing for it…. They [black people] live in a society in which to be unconditionally "American" is to be white, and to be black is a misfortune [pp. 108–9].

The time is long overdue for the black community to redefine itself, set forth new values and goals, and organize around them.

12

Race and Ethnicity: A Sociobiological Perspective

PIERRE L. VAN DEN BERGHE

When Edward O. Wilson's tome *Sociobiology: The New Synthesis* (Harvard University Press) was published in 1975, many scholars believed that genetic analysis had turned full circle. Intellectuals had emphasized the necessity of analyzing cultural process and social forces as the influences that shape how we think, feel and act. Yet, in Wilson's work, there was a reminder that, without biology, phenomena such as culture and society are not possible: we should, argued Wilson, apply Darwinian evolutionary theory to the social behavior of animals, including *Homo sapiens.*

In one such application, van den Berghe explained racism as an extension of nepotism, itself a genetically based mechanism of animal sociality. It followed that racism, far from being only a convenient rationalization for capitalism, or a legitimization of some form of exploitive arrangements, was deeply rooted in our biology. The contention drew a predictable reaction: that sociobiology was an apology for racism and might even excuse it.

Closer inspection of van den Berghe's work reveals that this was far too simplistic an interpretation. Van den Berghe wished to offer an explanation of the causes of racism that were biologically based; he did not, as the following extract shows, believe that racism was biologically determined. In fact, the logic of his argument suggests that cultural phenomena can overcome or subordinate nature. It offers a way of confronting racism, as well as understanding it. Van den Berghe wrote several books on the subject; the extract chosen here is a journal article that preceded his larger *The Ethnic Phenomenon* (Elsevier) by three years. Published in 1978, it is perhaps the clearest and most accessible account of sociobiology and its utility in explaining the character of racism.

Two contrasting positions on the nature of race and ethnicity have been taken or at least, have been implicit, in the literature. Some scholars have viewed ethnic and racial group affiliation as an ascribed 'primordial identity,' deeply rooted, given at birth, and largely unchangeable. Such was the dominant view until the 1920s when ethnically and racially defined collectivities were taken for granted and generally assumed to have an unquestionable objective reality of their own, beyond their constituent members. Both racist and nationalist ideologies were popular expressions of this early version of the 'primordialist' view. During the next half-century the dominant social science view became culturally determinist, and increasingly argued that ethnic and racial identities, far from being primordial, were, in fact, culturally defined, changeable, manipulable to political ends, situationally sensitive, and often ecologically determined (Barth, 1969). What we may term the 'subjectivist' view of ethnicity probably became the dominant position in the 1960s and early 1970s. Only recently is the primordialist view being once more cautiously advanced (Francis, 1976; Keyes, 1976; Stein and Hill, 1977).

Such crudely dichotomous ways of characterizing intellectual positions and periodizing intellectual history serve little purpose beyond clarifying basic issues, and they do violence to many scholars' thinking. In my own writings, I repeatedly stressed the need to consider both the objective and the subjective aspects of race and ethnicity (van den Berghe, 1970, 1974, 1978a), and I was far from alone in doing so (Hoetink, 1967; Kuper and Smith, 1969; Schermerhorn, 1970). I was also in good company in emphasizing the irreducibility of ethnic and/or racial membership to class affiliation, and vice versa. Class, ethnicity and race, I asserted, are fundamentally different principles of social affiliation, although each of them must be looked at in both subjective and objective terms. I now believe that what we in my prior works I left at the level of analytical concepts and categorical assertions can be subsumed under a more comprehensive theoretical umbrella derived from sociobiology. This is what I propose to do here.

Unfortunately, there is room here only for the sketchiest presentation of sociobiological concepts. The reader will find early theoretical formulations in Hamilton (1964), and Maynard Smith (1964), more recent and extensive treatments in Wilson (1975), Barash (1977), and Dawkins (1976), and human applications in Alexander (1971), Parker (1976), van den Berghe and Barash (1977), Hartung (1976), Greene (1978), Fox (1975), Chagnon and Irons (1978), Barkow (1978), and Dyson-Hudson and Smith (1978), among others. Although the label 'sociobiology' has only recently gained currency, thanks largely to Wilson's book (1975), the emerging new discipline is nothing but a systematic application of Darwinian evolutionary theory to animal behavior, especially to social behavior. Sociobiology is, in fact, little else than a more theoretically grounded, and less descriptive brand of ethology informed by behavior genetics.

The most basic question asked by sociobiology as well as sociology is: why are animals social, that is, why do they cooperate? Why are some species more social than others? The answer was long intuitively known: animals are social to the extent that cooperation is mutually beneficial. What sociobiology does is supply the main genetic mechanism for animal sociality, namely *kin selection* to maximize *inclusive fitness*. Natural selection operates through differential reproduction. Different alleles of the same gene compete with each other, and the ones that are carried by the more reproductively successful individuals have a greater probability of being replicated in the population's next generation. The successful alleles are the ones which, in a given environment, favor the reproductive success or 'fitness' of their carriers.

The great theoretical contribution of sociobiology has been to extend the concept of fitness to that of 'inclusive fitness' (Hamilton, 1964). Indeed, an animal can duplicate its genes directly through its own reproduction, or indirectly through the reproduction of relatives with which it shares specific proportions of genes. Animals, therefore, can be expected to behave cooperatively, and thereby enhance each other's fitness to the extent that they are genetically related. This is what is meant by kin selection (Maynard Smith, 1964). Animals, in short, are nepotistic, i.e. they prefer kin over non-kin, and close kin over distant kin. This may happen consciously, as in humans, or, more commonly, unconsciously. Kin selection does not presuppose consciousness in order to be operative.

The propensity to be 'altruistic,' i.e. to contribute to alter's fitness at the expense of ego's fitness, is directly proportional not only to the coefficient of relatedness between ego and alter, but also to the benefit/cost ratio of the altruistic act. To use a human example, a post-menopausal mother could be expected to sacrifice her life more readily for a young adult child about to reproduce than a young mother to forego her life for the benefit of her first foetus. The genetic relationship is the same in both cases (namely, one half), but the fitness cost is low in the first case, high in the second. Altruism then, is directed mostly at kin, especially close kin, and is, in fact, a misnomer. It represents the ultimate form of genetic selfishness. It is but the blind expression of inclusive fitness maximization. In fact, a simple formula leads one to predict that 'altruism' can be expected if the cost/benefit ratio of the transaction is smaller than the coefficient of relatedness between alter and ego.

There is no reason to doubt that kin selection is a powerful cement of sociality in humans as it is in other animals. Yet, it is also clear that kin selection does not explain all of human sociality. There are, in my view, two additional bases of human sociality: reciprocity and coercion. Rudimentary forms of these are also present in many animals, but human forms of reciprocity and coercion greatly overshadow in complexity and importance anything we know in other species. Not surprisingly, therefore, even the simplest and smallest human societies, though far less 'perfect' than those of the social insects (termites, ants, bees, wasps), are much more complex than those of any other known species. Reciprocity is cooperation for mutual benefit, and with expectation of return, and it can operate between kin or between non-kin. Coercion is the use of force for one-sided benefit, that is, for purposes of intra-specific parasitism or predation. All human societies continue to be organized on the basis of all three principles of sociality: kin selection, reciprocity, and coercion. However, the larger and the more complex a society becomes, the greater the importance of reciprocity, and, with the emergence of the state, coercion becomes in relation to kin selection.

This is the barest sketch of an argument which I develop elsewhere (van den Berghe, 1978b). In the last analysis, this view of human sociality seeks to reduce individual behavior, social structure and cultural superstructure to the competition for scarce resources between individual organisms, each one acting, consciously or unconsciously, to maximize its gains or minimize its losses. This view of human affairs is sufficiently at variance with much of contemporary social science to arouse passionate rejection as a return to simplistic instinct theory, biological reductionism, speculative evolutionism, social Darwinism, racism, hereditarianism, and so on. Lacking the space to present the full theory here, I can even less examine the objections and refute them. Suffice it to say that sociobiology is indeed reductionist (as all modern science), evolutionist (as all modern biology), and materialist (as much good social science), but that it is emphatically not a return to social Darwinism, instinct theories or racism, and that it does not belittle the importance of environmental factors, the unique characteristics of *Homo sapiens*, and the significance of human culture. It merely asserts in the most undogmatic fashion that human behavior is the product of a long process of adaptive evolution that involved the complex interplay of genotypical, ecological and cultural factors.

How do these prolegomena relate to race and ethnicity? My central thesis is that both ethnicity and 'race' (in the social sense) are, in fact, extensions of the idiom of kinship, and that, therefore, ethnic and race sentiments are to be understood as an extended and attenuated form of kin selection. Class relations, on the other hand, are in the realm of reciprocity, and are therefore of a fundamentally different nature. In more general form, I am suggesting that there are two broad types of human collectivities: the ones that I shall call Type I tend to be ascriptive, defined by common descent, generally hereditary, and often endogamous, and those of Type II that are joined in the defense of common interests. Type I includes racial, caste and ethnic groups, while Type II encompasses such varied

associations as trade unions, political parties, professional bodies, sports clubs, neighborhood groups, parent-teacher associations, and so on. Empirically, of course, a group may have mixed characteristics, as an ethnically-based political party, or a hereditary occupational guild. Nevertheless, in their ideal-typical form, each kind of group has a clearly distinct basis of solidarity: kinship and interest respectively.

Type I groups are generally preferentially or prescriptively endogamous but internally subdivided into exogamous kin groups: nuclear families, lineages, clans, kindreds. Indeed, until the last few thousand years of human history, Type I groups were synonymous with human societies. They were small in-bred populations of a few hundred individuals, prototypical 'tribes' that regarded themselves as 'the people', sharing common descent, real or putative, and as children of the mythical founder couple or creator god. Members of the tribe, though subdivided into smaller kin groups, saw themselves as a single people, solidary against the outside world, and interlinked by a web of kinship and marriage making the tribe in fact a superfamily. A high rate of inbreeding insured that most spouses were also kinsmen. The cultural inventions of unilineal descent and lineage exogamy permitted the extension of that primordial model of social organization to much larger societies running into the tens of thousands of people, and yet where Type II organizations were almost totally absent (with the exception of age sets).

Ethnic groups, for nearly all of human history, were what geneticists call breeding populations, inbreeding superfamilies, in fact, which not only were much more closely related to each other than to even their closest neighbors but which, almost without exception, explicitly recognized that fact, and maintained clear territorial and social boundaries with other such ethnic groups. This is, of course, not to deny that migration, conquest, and interbreeding took place with some regularity, and thus that the common ancestry of 'the people' was always partially fictive. But this was also true of smaller kin groups: the *pater* is not necessarily the *progenitor*. That the extended kinship of the ethnic group was sometimes putative rather than real was not the important point. Just as in the smaller kin units, the kinship was real often enough to become the basis of these powerful sentiments we call nationalism, tribalism, racism, and ethnocentrism. The ease and speed with which these sentiments can be mobilized even in modern industrial societies where they have to compete with many Type II groups, the blind ferocity of the conflicts to which these sentiments can lead, the imperviousness of such sentiments to rational arguments are but a few indications of their continued vitality and their primordiality.

What I am suggesting is that ethnocentrism evolved during millions, or at least hundreds, of thousands of years as an extension of kin selection. Reciprocity was also involved, especially in the exchange of women in marriage, but as spouses were typically also kinsmen there was no sharp distinction between kin selection and reciprocity. As hominids became increasingly formidable competitors and predators to their own and closely related species, there was a strong selective pressure for the formation of larger and more powerful groups. Group size in hunting and gathering societies was, of course, severely constrained by ecological factors, but, still, there was an obvious selective advantage for kin groups to form those solidary superfamilies we call tribes; this, in turn, as Bigelow (1969) so clearly argues, necessarily meant organizing *against* other competing groups, and therefore maintaining and defending ethnic boundaries.

Of Type II groups, little needs to be said here. With the exception of age sets, they tend to be characteristic of larger, more complex, state-organized societies, and therefore to have arisen much later in human evolution, and to be more exclusively cultural. They are, of course, also important, especially in industrial societies, but they are not primordial, they can be more readily formed and disbanded, they are more amenable to cool, rational calculations of interest, and they do not as readily unleash orgies of passion. Nor, of course, have they stamped out Type I groups. Another fundamental difference between Type I and Type II groups is that the former tend to be mutually exclusive in membership and thus to form the basis of most primary relationships, while the latter are segmental, and non-mutually exclusive. Millions of people in individual societies belong to a multiplicity of Type II groups, few of which involves them very deeply or permanently. Some people are ethnically alienated, marginal or mobile or they are the product of mixed marriages, but most people belong to a single ethnic group or sub-group, and remain there for life. Even allowing for all the complications of the real world, and the existence of mixed-type groups, the categorical distinction remains nevertheless quite striking.

Let us return to Type I groups, our special concern here. I have suggested that they evolved as an extension of kin selection, and thus probably have a partial biological basis, in the same sense as human kinship systems are rooted in biology. This contention is, of course, hotly contested by anthropologists such as Sahlins (1976), who counter that human kinship is cultural, not biological. Almost every aspect of human behavior takes a cultural form, from sneezing and defecating to writing poetry and riding a motorcycle. But this is not to say that some of these things do not *also* have a biological basis. I am definitely not arguing that we have a gene for ethnocentrism, or for recognizing kin; rather I am arguing that those societies that institutionalized norms of nepotism and ethnocentrism had a strong selective advantage over those that did not (assuming that any such ever existed), because kin selection has been the basic blueprint for animal sociality. To explain the universality of ethnocentrism and kinship organization in human societies by invoking culture is completely question begging. Culture is merely a *proximate* explanation of why people behave ethnocentrically and nepotistically. As every ethnographer knows, when natives are asked why they behave a certain way, they answer: because it is the custom. The anthropologist then translates: because of his culture; the sociologist says: because he has been socialized into the norms of his society; and the psychologist counters: because of his learning experiences. All of them are right as far as they go, but none of them has explained why all human societies practice kin selection and are ethnocentric.

So far, I have stressed ethnicity rather than race or caste in my treatment of Type I groups. Caste is a very special case, limited, even if one adopts a wide definition of the term, to highly differentiated, stratified societies, and may be considered an extreme case of the grafting of the principle of occupational specialization into what is basically a Type I group. Castes are not unique in being occupationally specialized Type I groups. Ethnic and racial groups also tend to become so (Hechter, 1976). Castes are merely extreme cases of occupational specialization linked with rigid endogamy and hierarchization.

Race is a different matter. First, I should make it clear that, even though I have presented a partially biological argument, I am most emphatically *not* using the word 'race' in the sense of a sub-species of *Homo sapiens*. Instead, I mean by 'race' the social definition which it is variously ascribed in different societies. Social race typically seizes on biologically trivial phenotypes, and, equally typically, corresponds only very imperfectly with genetically isolated populations. It thus has no intrinsic biological significance, as indicated by the fact that only a few of the world's societies use primarily morphological phenotypes to define themselves, and to differentiate outsiders.

At first blush, this would seem to invalidate my argument that ethnic and racial sentiments represent an extension of kin selection. If that is the case, why should most human societies seize primarily on such obviously culturally transmitted traits such as language and dialect, religious beliefs, dress, hair styles, manners, scarifications, and the like as badges of group recognition and membership? If the name of the game is to identify kinsmen in order to enhance one's inclusive fitness, then why are not inherited physical characteristics chosen as recognition signals, rather than acquired cultural traits? Sometimes, of course, morphological phenotypes such as skin color, facial features, stature, hair texture, eye color, and so on are used, not only to define group membership, but also, within the group, as tests of ever questionable paternity. Generally, however, cultural criteria of membership are far more salient than physical ones, if the latter are used at all. Societies that stress physical phenotypes more than cultural traits are exceptional. Why?

The answer must again be sought in our evolutionary history. Until the last few millenia, that is, until the rise of conquest states, sudden, large-scale, human migration was rare, and human breeding populations were small. There was migration and interbreeding, but on an individual scale, and mostly between neighboring groups. The result was that neighboring populations were typically not sharply discontinuous in their genetic composition. The relative proportions of alleles of the same gene often constituted a gradient as one travelled through several breeding populations. Eye color in Europe would be a good example. The further north one goes from, say, Sicily to Sweden, the higher the proportion of lightly pigmented eyes. Yet at no point in the journey is there a noticeable discontinuity. Eye color, therefore, is a poor criterion of national membership in Europe. Indeed, it varies much more *within* national groups, and indeed even within families, than *between* groups.

Now, Europeans do use some morphological phenotypes to distinguish various ethnic groups. They speak loosely of 'Nordic', 'Mediterranean', 'Jewish', and so on, types. In the absence of any other clue, probabilistic guesses are often made on the basis of physical appearance as to a stranger's ethnic origin. Most groups probably have what Hoetink (1967) termed a 'somatic norm image,' that is, a mental picture of what a model group member looks like. The point, however, is that morphological phenotypes tend to be used either in the absence of more reliable cultural clues (such as language), or when physical appearance is widely discrepant from the somatic norm image (as, for instance, in Europe with Asians or Africans).

A good test of group membership for the purpose of assessing kin relatedness must meet the basic requirement of discriminating more reliably *between* groups than *within* groups. That is, the criterion chosen must show more *inter*group than *intra*-group variance. Until recently, cultural criteria met that condition far more reliably than physical ones. The problem was for small groups to distinguish themselves from their immediate neighbors, not with unknown populations thousands of kilometers away. Even the most trivial differences of accent, dialect, vocabulary, body adornment, and so on, could be used far more reliably to assess *biological* relatedness or unrelatedness than any physical phenotype.[1] Therefore, whatever test was easiest to apply and correlated best with kin relatedness was used. That the correlation was spurious did

not matter. What mattered was that it discriminated accurately.

This theory accounts not only for the general prevalence of cultural diacritica in assessing group membership. It also accounts for the appearance of racism when and where it does occur better than any competing theory. The kin selection argument predicts that physical criteria *will* be salient to the extent that they do a good and easy job of discriminating kin and non-kin. This obviously occurs in the aftermath of large-scale, long-distance migration, whether through conquest, incursions, slavery, indenture, or voluntary immigration. The colonial expansion of Europe beginning some five centuries ago, and all of the massive population transfers it brought in its wake are, of course, the overwhelmingly important genetic event of our species. Predictably, it brought about a great surge in racism, because all of a sudden, it became possible to make a fairly accurate kin selection judgment from a distance of several hundred meters. The Dutchman at the Cape, the Portuguese in Brazil, the Englishman in Kenya did not have to ask questions and pick up subtle clues of accent to detect kin relatedness. By using a simple test of skin pigmentation he could literally shoot and ask questions later at little risk of killing a kinsman.

Competing theories of racism based on arguments about the nature of capitalism, or normative differences between Catholicism and Protestantism, explain little by comparison with the simple kin selection argument. Humans, like other animals are selected to favor kin, and whatever does a quick, easy and accurate job of differentiating kin and non-kin will be used. In most cases, and until recently, cultural criteria have been predominantly used. Physical criteria became salient only after large, strikingly different-looking populations found themselves in sudden and sustained contact.

The story of Western racism did not stop with the sudden contact of large numbers of different-looking people. As soon as strangers met, they started mating, as indeed any members of the same species can be expected to do. Interbreeding, in turn, began to blur physical differences between human groups, and obviously had the consequence of reducing the validity of physical traits as a predictor of kin relatedness. It has sometimes been argued that 'miscegenation' is evidence of the relative absence of racial prejudice. This is nonsense. Racism has never stopped dominant group men from mating with subordinate group women. But the reverse is probably true. Racism requires a special effort to sustain when most of your closest relatives belong to the despised race, that is, when phenotypes become poor predictors of genetic relatedness. Not only do the physical markers between races become blurred but they cut across kin ties. Fully institutionalized racism can only be maintained, in short, in societies like South Africa and the United States that retain a high degree of racial endogamy, or that have reestablished racial endogamy after a phase of miscegenation under slavery.

Slavery was euphemistically referred to in the nineteenth-century United States as the 'peculiar institution.' There was, in fact, nothing very peculiar about slavery as such, for it had existed in the vast majority of stratified preindustrial societies. What was indeed peculiar was the special brand of Western Hemisphere, *racial* slavery. All slavery systems involved extensive interbreeding between male masters and female slaves. Sexual exploitation is the inevitable concomitant of the situation of domination which characterizes slavery. The peculiarity of racially defined slavery, however, was the internal contradiction inherent in attempting to keep a racial boundary between kinsmen. In Brazil, much of the Caribbean and Spanish America, racial lines were so extensively blurred that, even though several of these societies remain race-conscious, no distinct, corporate racial groups can now be said to exist. In the United States, slavery was abolished in time to preserve a rigid racial dichotomy by establishing a segregated system of endogamous racial groups after the Civil War.

The American slave plantation was a big family of sorts, albeit an extraordinarily perverse one. Masters, overseers and slaves inhabited a little world which maximized inequality while at the same time fostering all kinds of intimacy. Slaves cooked their master's food, wetnursed their legitimate children, and bore their illegitimate ones. The legitimizing ideology of plantation slavery, not surprisingly was paternalistic. Paternalism was not new to slavery; indeed it is one of the commonest rationalizations for tyranny and exploitation. What better way of making the oppressed accept their lot than to disguise parasitism as kin selection? Exploitation is said to be in the best interest of the oppressed because the despot is a surrogate father who loves them. But whereas the paternalism of traditional despotic states was a fiction often maintained by an elaborate origin myth and an all-encompassing familistic ideology such as Confucianism, paternalism under chattel slavery often described actual kinship. Slave children of owners often did receive better treatment, and were more likely to be freed. Nevertheless, there was a fundamental incompatibility between the institution of slavery, the essence of which was parasitism, and kin selection.

Paternalism was simply not a workable ideology for slavery. Either the owner was not the father of his slaves, and it was little use pretending he was, as his exploitative behavior fooled no one, or else, he was his slaves' father, grandfather, or half-brother, in which case the master–slave relationship and the color line were difficult to maintain.

We suggested at the outset that there were three main mechanisms of human sociality: kin selection, reciprocity and coercion. Ethnic and racial groups command our unreasoned loyalty because they are in fact, or at least in theory, superfamilies. But ethnic and race relations are not only relations of cooperation and amity with the in-group; they are equally importantly relations of competition and conflict between groups. While intra-group relations are primarily dictated by kin selection, real or putative, intergroup relations are typically antagonistic. Occasionally, ethnic groups may enter a symbiotic, mutually beneficial relationship based, for instance, on the exploitation of two specialized and noncompetitive niches in the same habitat. Relations between some pastoralist and sedentary groups are of this type. More commonly, there is open competition for, and conflict over scarce resources, and not infrequently the establishment of multi-ethnic states dominated by one ethnic group at the expense of others. Coercion then becomes the basis of inter-ethnic (or inter-racial) relations.

Unlike kin selection and reciprocity which require no justification because they contribute to the fitness of all actors in the system, coercion, which leads to asymmetrical parasitism, often does attempt to legitimate itself. Interestingly, there are but two basic ideologies in support of coercion. One seeks to disguise coercion as kin selection, and here we have the many brands of paternalism and familism that have been used to justify nearly all preindustrial forms of despotism. The other attempts to present coercion as reciprocity and exchange, it is characteristic of the various 'democratic' ideologies of industrial societies in the last two centuries, from liberalism to socialism. Why this ideological shift from paternalism to *liberté, égalité, fraternité* in justifying tyranny during the last two centuries?

Perhaps this ideological shift reflects in part the increasing incorporation of small nation-states into multi-national states. Paternalism is a peculiarly well suited ideology for the small, ethnically homogeneous nation-state. Not surprisingly, it was independently reinvented in societies as far distant as China, Japan, Inca Peru, Tzarist Russia, Ancient Egypt, Ottoman Turkey, Renaissance Europe and countless African kingdoms. Paternalism works in monoethnic states because the very concept of the nation is an extension of kin selection. For the same reason, it breaks down in multi-ethnic states. It was one thing for the Japanese peasant to look on his emperor as a divine super-father, the living incarnation of Nippon, quite another for the Hindu peasant to regard that polluted beef eater, Queen Victoria, as the living symbol of Mother India. An ideology based on reciprocity, on the other hand, can transcend ethnic boundaries. It is therefore a suitable one for the 90 per cent of the world's states which are multi-ethnic conglomerates, and, furthermore, being ethnically neutral, it exports remarkably well as revolutionary ideology. It is no accident that France launched into the most imperialistic phase of its history immediately after the Revolution.

The ideas sketched here are still tentative. They do not so much supplant other theories of ethnicity and race as supplement them by putting them in the broader context of evolutionary thinking. They do not purport to explain everything about these phenomena; they do not predict detailed historical occurrences, nor account for subtle cultural differences. They do, however, suggest parsimonious hypotheses to account for features of race and ethnicity which had hitherto remained elusive and problematic. Their plausibility to the reader hinges on whether he accepts the most fundamental paradigm for the evolution of different life forms and societal organization on our planet, Darwinian evolutionary theory, and on whether he is willing to apply that enormously successful model to our own species, or prefers to invoke an act of special creation for mankind.

NOTES

1. The classical historical anecdote is that the massacre of French occupation forces by Flemings in 1302, in Bruges. The insurgent Flemings massacred their enemies at night in their beds. To make sure that no Flemings would be accidentally killed, the person was made to repeat a sentence 'schilde ende vriend' containing Dutch phonemes which are virtually unpronounceable for a native speaker of French. I daresay this kin selection test was well over 99 per cent effective, and no physical trait could have come closer to it for reliability.

REFERENCES

Alexander, R. D. 1971 'The Search for an Evolutionary Philosophy of Man,' *Proceedings of the Royal Society of Victoria*, 84, pp. 99–120.

Barash, D. P. 1977 *Sociobiology and Behavior*. New York: Elsevier.

Barkow, J. H. 1978 'Culture and Sociobiology,' *American Anthropologist*, 80, No. 1, pp. 5–20.

Barth, F., ed. 1969 *Ethnic Groups and Boundaries*. Boston: Little Brown.

Bigelow, R. 1969 *The Dawn Warriors*. Boston: Little Brown.

Chagnon, N. A. and Irons, W., eds. 1978 *Evolutionary Biology and Human Social Behavior*. North Scituate, Mass: Duxbury Press (in press).

Dawkins, R. 1976 *The Selfish Gene*. London: Oxford University Press.

Dyson-Hudson, R. and Smith E. A. 1978 'Human Territoriality, An Ecological Reassessment,' *American Anthropologist*, 80, No. 1, pp. 21–41.

Fox, R., ed. 1975 *Biosocial Anthropology*. New York: Wiley.

Francis, E. K. 1976 *Interethnic Relations*. New York: Elsevier.

Greene, P. 1978 'Promiscuity, Paternity and Culture,' *American Ethnologist*, 5, No. 1, pp. 151–159.

Hamilton, W. D. 1964 'The Genetical Evolution of Social Behaviour,' *Journal of Theoretical Biology*, 7, pp. 1–52.

Hartung, J. 1976 'On Natural Selection and the Inheritance of Wealth,' *Current Anthropology*, 17, No. 4, pp. 607–622.

Hechter, M. 1976 'Ethnicity and Industrialization,' *Ethnicity*, 3, No. 3, pp. 214–224.

Hoetink, H. 1967 *Caribbean Race Relations*. London: Oxford University Press.

Keyes, C. F. 1976 'Toward a New Formulation of the Concept of Ethnic Group,' *Ethnicity*, 3, No. 3, pp. 202–213.

Kuper, L. and Smith, M. G., eds. 1969 *Pluralism in Africa*. Berkeley: University of California Press.

Maynard Smith, J. 1964 'Group Selection and Kin Selection,' *Nature*, 201, No. 4924, pp. 1145–1147.

Parker, S. 1976 'The Precultural Basis of the Incest Taboo,' *American Anthropologist*, 73, No. 2, pp. 285–305.

Sahlins, M. 1976 *The Use and Abuse of Biology*. Ann Arbor: University of Michigan Press.

Schermerhorn, R. A. 1970 *Comparative Ethnic Relations*. New York: Random House.

Stein, H. F. and Hill R. F. 1977 *The Ethnic Imperative*. University Park: Pennsylvania State University Press.

Van Den Berghe, P. L. 1970 *Race and Ethnicity*. New York: Basic Books.

Van Den Berghe, P. L. ed. 1974 *Class and Ethnicity in Peru*. Leiden: Brill.

Van Den Berghe, P. L. 1978a *Race and Racism*. New York: Wiley.

Van Den Berghe, P. L. 1978b *Man in Society*. New York: Elsevier.

Van Den Berghe P. L. and Barash, D. P. 1977 'Inclusive Fitness and Human Family Structure,' *American Anthropologist*, 79, No. 4, pp. 809–823.

Wilson, E. O. 1975 *Sociobiology, The New Synthesis*. Cambridge, Mass: Belknap.

13

Racism and the Class Struggle: Further Pages from a Black Worker's Notebook

JAMES BOGGS AND GRACE
LEE BOGGS

The chapter included here is written by James Boggs and Grace Lee Boggs. The authors challenge the findings and manner in which the U.S. Kerner Commission report approach the problem of racism. They argue that a root cause of racism, capitalism, was side-stepped by this report in its discussion of white racism. James and Grace Lee Boggs propose that racism is actually functional in terms of protecting the economic interests of the rich and upper class in the United States. This claim should remind the reader of the selection by Du Bois, 'White Workers' written in 1935. Interestingly, this is a different approach than that reflected in the selection by Carmichael and Hamilton, where the focus is on the black experience within the context of groups in society, rather than classes.

Uprooting Racism and Racists in the United States

In March 1968, one month before the racist murder of Dr. Martin Luther King Jr., the President's Commission on Civil Disorders, headed by Illinois Governor Otto Kerner, issued its monumental report charging white racism with responsibility for the degraded conditions of blacks in this country. In the year and a half since the report appeared, white racist hostility toward blacks, particularly among white workers, has increased, not decreased. Polls indicate that today fewer whites believe that blacks are the victims of discrimination, and that, in fact, a growing number of whites believe that blacks are the villains rather than the victims.

The obvious contradiction of the Kerner report is that after diagnosing whites as responsible for racist oppression of blacks, the report goes on to make recommendations for the treatment not of *whites* but of blacks. As we pointed out at the time, "It is like saying that the way to keep white sheriffs, policemen, Ku Klux Klansmen, White Citizens' Councilmen, Minutemen, Birchites, and other American fascists from lynching any more blacks is to put the blacks to work, send them to school, and build some new housing developments in the ghetto." The victims are the ones who need rehabilitation, the villains are not even acknowledged to exist.

It is, of course, no accident that the Kerner Commission did not tackle the question of white racists. First of all, the "white, moderate, responsible, Establishment" Americans (in Tom Wicker's words[1]) who made up the Commission are not in the habit of using their power to expose or confront the crimes and barbarism of white racists any more than the white, moderate, responsible Germans of Hitler's days were in the habit of exposing or confronting the crimes and barbarism of German racists. Note, for example, how little appears in the "white, moderate, responsible" American press today about Minutemen, KKKsmen, and Birchites, contrasted to the constant scare headlines about Black Panthers and other black militants.

Moreover, the Kerner Commission, including as it did such pillars of capitalism as the senior officials of North American Rockwell Corp., Litton Industries, General Mills Corp., Bank of America, etc., could hardly have been expected to undertake the kind of probe of white racism which might have led to its roots in capitalist economics and ideology. So from the outset the Commission made it clear that its aim was to attack "the root causes of racial disorder," not the root causes of racism.

It seems a minor difference, but those planning a career in journalism should pay it special attention. The one line of attack–against the root causes of racism–leads ultimately, as we shall show, to a revolution against the system. The other–against the root causes of racial disorder–leaves the door wide open for a counter-revolution against those making a revolution against the system. For it should be obvious to anyone not blinded by racism that the root cause of racial disorders in Northern cities over the last five years is the revolt against racism. If blacks were ready to submit to racism, there would be no racial disorders.

The first thing we have to understand is that racism is not a "mental quirk" or a "psychological flaw" on an individual's part.[2] Racism is the systematized oppression by one race of another. In other words, the various forms of oppression within every sphere of social relations–economic exploitation, military subjugation, political subordination, cultural devaluation, psychological violation, sexual degradation, verbal abuse, etc.–together make up a whole of interacting and developing processes which operate so normally and naturally and are so much a part of the existing institutions of the society that the individuals involved are barely conscious of their operation. As Fanon says, "The racist in a culture with racism is therefore normal."

This kind of systematic oppression of one race by another was unknown to mankind in the thousands of years of recorded history before the emergence of capitalism four hundred years ago–although racial prejudice was not unknown. For example, some Chinese in the third century B.C. considered yellow-haired, green-eyed people in a distant province barbarians. In Ancient Egypt the ruling group, which at different times was red or yellow or black or white, usually regarded the others as inferior.

Slave oppression had also existed in earlier times, but this was usually on the basis of military conquest and the conquerors–the ancient Greeks and Romans–did not develop a theory of racial superiority to rationalize their right to exploit their slaves.

Just as mankind, prior to the rise of capitalism, had not previously experienced an economic system which naturally and normally pursues tbe expansion of material productive forces at the expense of human forces, so it had never known a society which naturally and normally pursues the systematic exploitation and dehumanization of one race of people by another. An organic link between capitalism and racism is therefore certainly suggested.

The parallel between the rise of capitalism and the rise of racism has been traced by a number of scholars. The Portuguese, who were the first Europeans to come into contact with Africans at the end of the fifteenth and beginning of the sixteenth centuries, treated them as natural friends and allies. They found African customs strange and exotic but also found much to admire in their social and political organization, craftsmanship, architecture, and so on. At this point the chief technological advantages enjoyed by the Europeans were their navigation skills and firepower (both, by the way, originally learned from the Chinese). In the next four centuries these two advantages would be used to plunder four continents of their wealth in minerals and people and thereby to increase the technological superiority of Europeans by leaps and bounds.

Africa was turned into a hunting ground for slaves to work the land of the West Indies and the Southern colonies that had been stolen from the Indians. As the slave trade expanded, its enormous profits concentrated capital in Europe and America for the expansion of commerce, industry, and invention, while in Africa the social fabric was torn apart. In the Americas the blood and sweat of African slaves produced the sugar, tobacco, and later cotton to feed the refineries, distilleries, and textile mills, first of Western Europe and then of the Northern United States.

The more instrumental the slave trade in destroying African culture, the more those involved directly and indirectly in the slave traffic tried to

---

[1] Special *Introduction* to the Kerner report.

[2] See Frantz Fanon, "Racism and Culture," in *Toward the African Revolution* (New York and London: Monthly Review Press, 1967).

convince themselves and others that there had never been any African culture in the first place. The more brutal the methods needed to enforce slavery against rebellious blacks, the more the brutalizers insisted that the submissiveness of slavery was the natural state of black people. The more valuable the labor of blacks to Southern agriculture, precisely because of the relatively advanced stage of agriculture in their African homeland, the more white Americans began to insist that they had done the African savage a favor by bringing him to a land where he could be civilized by agricultural labor. Thus, step by step, in order to justify their mutually reinforcing economic exploitation and forceful subjugation of blacks, living, breathing white Americans created a scientifically cloaked theory of white superiority and black inferiority.

In order to understand the ease with which racism entrenched itself in Europe and North America, it is important to emphasize that not only the big merchants, manufacturers, and shipowners benefited from the slave trade and slavery. All kinds of little people on both sides of the Atlantic drew blood money directly from the slave traffic. Thus, "though a large part of the Liverpool slave traffic was monopolized by about ten large firms, many of the small vessels in the trade were fitted out by attorneys, drapers, grocers, barbers, and tailors. The shares in the ventures were subdivided, one having one-eighth, another one-fifteenth, a third one-thirty-second part of a share and so on.... 'almost every order of people is interested in a Guinea cargo.'"[3]

The middle classes benefited indirectly from the general economic prosperity created by the slave trade. "Every port to which the slave ships returned saw the rise of manufactures in the eighteenth century–refineries, cottons, dyeworks, sweetmaking– in increasing numbers which testified to the advance of business and industry."[4] In the expanding economy the shopkeeper found a growing number of customers for his goods, the farmer for his produce, the doctor and lawyer for their skills.

To white workers at the very bottom of white society, African slavery also brought substantial benefits. First, the expanding industry made possible by the profits of slave trafficking created jobs at an expanding rate. Second, in the Americas particularly, white indentured servants were able to escape from the dehumanization of plantation servitude only because of the seemingly inexhaustible supply of constantly imported African slaves to take their place.

Contrary to racist mythology, blacks did not thrive any better in the rice swamps and on the sugar and cotton plantations than whites. Nor had blacks been treated significantly worse than white indentured servants in the early days of colonial settlement when convicts and poor whites, kidnapped off the wharfs of Liverpool and London, had been crowded onto dirty transatlantic ships en route to Southern plantations to work as white indentured servants. These whites had been bracketed with blacks and treated as "white trash." But they had one advantage denied the blacks: they were of the same color as their masters. Therefore, when their contracts expired or they were able to escape, they could not be easily detected, and, *because there were blacks to take their place*, the slave masters did not put out the great effort which would have been needed to capture them. Thus the ex-indentured servant climbed into the free society as farmer or worker on the backs of black slaves.

It is only when we understand this immediate economic and social stake which not only the slave owners and the capitalist entrepreneurs but the entire white population–including doctors, lawyers, bakers, and candlestickmakers (but not, of course, the Indian chiefs whose lands were taken for the plantations and farms)–had in the enslavement of blacks that we can understand the realities of racism in this country. Racism was real because there were real people with a stake in racism–racists–and these real people were ready to resort to force to protect their stake. As Eugene Genovese has pointed out, blacks were often safer on the slave plantation than off it because of the hostile, armed non-slaveholding whites.[5]

Radical historians have tended to underplay these realities, pointing out how, in the final analysis, slavery impoverished the soil, drove the free farmers farther West, kept down the wages of white workers, etc. This is because these historians, usually white, have begun their analysis with the plight of white workers in the process of capitalist production and then have tried to fit the grievances and revolt of blacks into this theoretical framework. Hence, like the Kerner commissioners, they have failed to prepare us for the surfacing of white racist workers. Also, addressing themselves chiefly to white workers and trying to convince these workers of the need to destroy capitalism, they have insisted that black and white workers are "really" (i.e., according to their theory) allies, kept apart only by a vertical color line which the evil slave owners and capitalists have conspired to draw down the middle between them.

[3] Eric Williams, *Capitalism and Slavery* (New York: G. P. Putnam, 1966).

[4] Ernest Mandel, *Marxist Economic Theory* (New York: Monthly Review Press, 1969), p. 444.

[5] Eugene Genovese, *The Legacy of Slavery and the Roots of Black Nationalism*, a speech delivered at the 1966 Socialist Scholars Conference and reprinted by the New England Free Press.

The historical fact is that without African slavery the class struggle between capitalists and workers could not even have been joined in the first place. For the capitalist, it served the functions of primitive accumulation. That is, it provided both the initial capital *and* the labor force freed from the means of production which is a prerequisite for the process of capitalist accumulation inside the factory.[6]

For the individual white indentured servant or laborer, African slavery meant the opportunity to rise above the status of slave and become farmer or free laborer. Thus, early in the history of this country a pattern was created which persists to this day: physical and social mobility for white workers into and within increasingly modernized industries, possible only because there is a reserve army of black labor to scavenge the dirty, unskilled jobs in the fields and sweatshops.

Instead of the vertical color line dreamed up by white radicals, there has actually existed a horizontal platform resting on the backs of blacks and holding them down, while on top white workers have been free to move up the social and economic ladder of advancing capitalism. This horizontal platform, a ceiling for blacks and a floor for whites, has created and maintained a black labor force serving the economic needs of advancing capitalism, as it has developed, stage by stage, from manufacturing capitalism to industrial capitalism to monopoly capitalism to its present stage of military-industrial capitalism, or what is more popularly known as the "military-industrial complex."

Capitalist production is unlike all previous exploitative economic systems. In previous exploitative societies the ruling classes consumed the proceeds of exploitation in lavish personal living, including an ever expanding personal retinue, or in the purchase of more land and slaves. Under capitalism, on the other hand, the major part of the profits derived from the exploitation of labor is reinvested in new and more advanced means of production. This, the essential law of motion of capitalism, is known as capitalist accumulation. Constant expansion and modernization of the means of production, made possible by the exploitation of labor, have now become the driving force of the system.

The results of capitalist accumulation are all around us. Constant revolutionizing of production, ceaselessly advancing technology, mammoth factories and, controlling this gigantic accumulation of industrial plant and fluid (finance) capital, an ever diminishing number of interlocking corporations and individuals.

With increasing investment in modern equipment has come the increasing productivity of labor and therefore a constantly decreasing proportion of capital invested in labor compared to that invested in machinery. This value composition of capital, changing along with changing technology, is called the organic composition of capital.

A hundred years ago Karl Marx pointed out the internal contradictions inherent in the changing organic composition of capital. One of the chief contradictions, he pointed out, is the fall in the rate of profit as less and less capital is invested in labor (variable capital) compared to that invested in machinery (constant capital). This is because only the capital invested in human labor can produce varying quantities of surplus value, depending on how long or how hard you work the workers. That is why Marx called it variable capital, in contrast to the constant capital invested in machinery whose value is simply transferred into the finished product on a *pro rata* basis.

Closer to common experience, this contradiction expresses itself as the difficulty in maintaining the value of existing capital–i.e., that already invested in means of production–when newer and more modern means of production are constantly being created. How can the relatively obsolete machines and factories be kept in production, producing profit, so that the total social capital available for modernization will not be reduced because of the building of new plants? This is what Marx called the *general* contradiction of capitalism.[7]

Advancing capitalism has been able to counteract these contradictions only by using the colonized people in Latin America, Africa, Asia, and inside the United States itself.

In the late nineteenth century, in order to counteract the decline in the rate of profit, monopoly capitalism began to export "surplus capital" to what we today call the Third World. This exported

---

[6] "In themselves, money and commodities are not more capital than are the means of production and of subsistence. They want transforming into capital. But this transformation can only take place under certain circumstances that centre in this, viz., that two very different kinds of commodity-possessors must come face to face and into contact; on the one hand, the owners of money, means of production, means of subsistence, who are eager to increase the sum of values they possess, by buying other people's labor power; on the other hand, free laborers, the sellers of their own labor-power and therefore the sellers of labor. Free laborers, in the double sense that neither they themselves form part and parcel of the means of production, as in the case of slaves, bondsmen, etc., nor do the means of production belong to them, as in the case of peasant-proprietors; they are, therefore, free from, unencumbered by, any means of production of their own. With this polarization of the market for commodities, the fundamental conditions of capitalist production are given." ("The Secret of Primitive Accumulation," *Capital*, Vol. 1, p. 785.)

[7] *Capital*, Vol. III, p. 292.

capital was surplus in the sense that in the colonies it did not have to be invested in the same growing ratio between constant and variable capital as it had in the imperialist fatherland. The capital invested in the colonies could be used to extract surplus value from a work force prevented by the military power of a colonial administration from organizing for better working conditions, shorter hours, higher wages. Finally, the surplus profits thus extracted from the colonial work force were not reinvested in the colonies but were sent home to add to the total social capital available for modernization in the oppressing country. In this way the colonial countries were systematically kept in a state of undevelopment in order to accelerate economic development at home.

An analogous process has taken place within the borders of the United States, where the black work force has been used as a colonial work force to preserve the value of existing capital.

The role which blacks were to play in this process was fixed after Reconstruction when blacks were kept on the cotton plantations not only by the brute force of Southern planters and sheriffs but by the violent hostility of white workers to their entry into the advancing industries of the North and South. Between 1880 and 1890 alone there were fifty strikes in the North against the employment of black workers in industry. The result was that in 1910 the number of blacks in industries other than cotton production was less than 0.5 percent, while as late as 1930, 68.75 percent of gainfully employed blacks were still in agriculture and domestic service.

As blacks began to move into the cities in this country, white workers acted as the principal human agent assisting American capitalism to counteract the fundamental contradiction between constantly advancing technology and the need to maintain the value of existing plant. They have done so by collectively and often forcibly restricting blacks to technologically less advanced industries or to what is known as "common labor" inside the modern plant or in construction. A perfect example of the system in operation on the job has been in the building industry. "The black man digs a ditch. Then the white man steps in and lays the pipes and the black man covers the ditch. The black man cleans the tank and then the white boilermaker comes on and makes the repairs."[8]

This is the scavenger role in production which white workers, acting *consciously* on behalf of their own social mobility and *unconsciously* on behalf of constantly advancing capitalism, have assigned to blacks and other colored peoples, such as the Chinese and Japanese on the West Coast, and the Mexicans and Puerto Ricans.

But the scavenger role has not been restricted to jobs. In the same way that blacks have been forced to take on the old substandard jobs, disdained and discarded by socially mobile whites, they have been confined to used homes, used schools, used churches, and used stores. (Only in the matter of the most ephemeral consumer goods–cars, deodorants, hair spray, clothing, etc.–are they able and in fact encouraged to buy the latest models.) For the used homes and churches they make excessive payments which add to the total capital available to the entire economy for new buildings, new plants, new churches, new homes. As in the days of primitive accumulation, the entire white community benefits, not only from the direct receipt of interest and principal on these homes and churches but in terms of new industries with their streamlined buildings and their increasingly skilled jobs.

The situation has reached its climax in the role assigned by the military-industrial state to young blacks on the frontlines of Vietnam. The disproportionate number of black youth fighting and dying to preserve the system in Asia makes it possible for an increasing number of white youth to attend college and be prepared for the new industries of the future. The systematic undevelopment of the black community is thus the foundation for the systematic development of the white community.

The economic advantages to the United States of having a colony inside its own borders have been tremendous. By using the colonial force of blacks, U.S. capitalism has been able to moderate the general contradiction of capitalist accumulation. That is to say, it has been able to accelerate technological expansion and at the same time keep profits coming in from continuing exploitation of its obsolescent, "used" factories, homes, schools, stores, etc. As a result, the United States has developed into the technologically most advanced country in the world.

But the human costs of this counteracting of internal economic contradictions have been equally tremendous. On the one hand, for the sake of American economic development, 20 to 30 million blacks and thousands of black communities across the country have paid the high cost of economic backwardness. As I noted earlier, "Their present stage of decay, decline, and dilapidation–their present stage of undevelopment–is a product of capitalist exploitation. They have been used and re-used to produce profit by every form of capitalist: landlords, construction industries, merchants, insurance brokers, bankers, finance companies, racketeers, and manufacturers of cars, appliances, steel, and every kind of industrial commodity."

Less obvious but increasingly dangerous has been the human price paid by the entire country for advancing capitalism by all means necessary. In the course of making America a unique land of opportunity in which whites climb up the social and

---

[8] Sterling D. Spero and Abram L. Harris, *The Black Worker* (New York: Atheneum, 1968).

economic ladder on the backs of blacks, the American people have become the most materialistic, the most opportunistic, the most individualistic–in sum, the most politically and socially irresponsible people in the world. Step by step, choice by choice, year after year, decade after decade, they have become the political victims of the system they themselves created, unable to make political decisions on the basis of principle no matter how crucial the issue. So long have they evaded the question of right and wrong that the question of what is right and what is wrong now evades them. Thus, while counteracting the economic contradictions of capitalism, the American people have come up against an even more dangerous, even graver contradiction in capitalism, the contradiction between being the technologically most advanced and the politically most backward people in the world.

The American political system, based upon two barely distinguishable political parties, is a structural manifestation of this backwardness. In other advanced countries the workers formed political parties of labor early in this century. These parties, despite their obvious shortcomings (especially their failure to create a revolutionary alternative to fascism), nevertheless served not only to represent the economic and social interests of labor but also to educate the entire country in some sense of social and political consciousness. In the United States, however, all efforts to create a political party of the working classes, particularly in the late nineteenth century and in the 1930's, have come to naught because white workers have focused on the individual's opportunity to climb into the middle class. The result is that the political process has been reduced to a meaningless ritual whose mechanics and outcome are decided by Madison Avenue hucksters.

The manifestations of this contradiction between economic overdevelopment and political underdevelopment are everywhere. The chickens have really come home to roost. Unable to subordinate material values to human values, the United States is consistently unable to put politics in command over economics or to choose men over weapons. Twenty-five years ago it could not resist dropping atom bombs on the Japanese people. Today it cannot resist dropping napalm in Vietnam or manufacturing it for use against other peoples struggling for liberation, particularly in Africa. Its universities, professed centers for the Humanities, are being turned into arsenals of research into the most advanced means for destroying humanity. Its cities are being transformed into parking spaces, its highways into poison gas chambers by a ceaselessly expanding auto industry, its lakes and rivers into catch-basins for industrial waste. Successive administrations, Republican and Democrat alike, know that the United States cannot win the genocidal war in Vietnam and that virtually the whole world and its own youth see no distinction between its behavior and that of Hitler. At home the country is coming apart at the seams. Yet white, moderate, responsible America cannot mobilize the political will to get out of Vietnam.

Inside the United States this contradiction is equally devastating. Faced with the civil war conditions created by the black revolt, "white moderate responsible America" continues to try to meet the crisis with the same methods and the same philosophy which created the crisis in the first place. Thus the Kerner Commission, far from suggesting any fundamental change in the system of white labor mobility on the backs of blacks, proposes its continuation. In outlining its crash program for the black hard-core, the Commission explicitly states:

> We do not intend with our program for the hard-core disadvantaged to stimulate the "leap-frogging" by the hard-core unemployed of the other two groups. Certainly the already employed must not lose their jobs in order to make room for the hard-core unemployed. Only a program which both *upgrades* the already employed and *thereby* creates openings for the hard-core, can satisfy this need. (*Emphasis added.*)

In other words, blacks are to remain scavengers.

At the same time the Kerner Commission predictably proposes bringing a few blacks into the system at a higher level, as black capitalists, black project directors, black administrators, etc. These black collaborators, like the African rulers who recruited their own people for the slave traders, or the "house niggers" and drivers who identified with "old Massa" on the plantation, or the black elite today governing the neo-colonies in Africa, are then supposed to have enough of a stake in the operation of the system to cooperate in pacification programs against their black brothers and sisters. Ultimately these black collaborators are being programmed for the same role in suppressing black revolt which the South Vietnamese government has been set up to play in relation to the Vietnamese people.

Unfortunately for these "white moderate responsible Americans," but fortunately for the future of humanity, this program for perpetuating the system of scavengers and collaborators is doomed to failure. This is not only because the black revolt has already advanced too far for blacks to accept being put back into their place at the bottom of the ladder. It is also because of the counter-revolt which is now growing by leaps and bounds among white workers and white administrators who feel themselves threatened by the black upheaval beneath them and by the concessions which the white power structure seems inclined to make to those "uppity niggers." The real living breathing racists whose existence was ignored by the Kerner Commission refuse to be ignored. Conscious of increasing automation and cybernation and imbued with the conviction that labor mobility should be the basis of increasing status and increasing income, regardless of what happens to anybody else, white workers regard the upgrading of every black man or woman as an immediate danger to their jobs and to their most sacrosanct principles. Likewise, the white middle classes–especially the school principals, teachers, policemen, social workers, and other white collar workers who have been receiving high salaries for the "dirty work" of administering the black colony–feel increasingly threatened by the demand for black control of the black community. Together these white workers and middle-class administrators, calling themselves the "forgotten Americans," constitute a growing counter-revolutionary force, threatening not only the black community but also all those "white moderate responsible Americans" who are so high on the social and economic ladder that they do not feel threatened by minor concessions to black America.

The chief value of the Kerner report is that it has exposed, to all those willing to look, the counter-revolutionary dangers inherent in trying to end racism and at the same time maintain the economic and social system inseparable from it.

As long as the economic system of expansion by all means necessary (i.e., capitalism) and the philosophy corresponding to this system (i.e., materialism, individualism, and opportunism) continue to exist, this country will continue to produce a working class which is racist, i.e., determined to maintain its economic and social mobility at the expense of blacks.

To succeed in destroying racism in this country, the revolutionary movement must overthrow the practice of putting economics in command of politics, which has been the governing principle of American development, and replace it with the practice of putting politics in command of economics, which is the essence of *today's* social revolutions the world over.

Before politics can be put in command of economics, power must be taken away from those living, breathing Americans who have governed and continue to govern this country according to the system of economic expansion by all means necessary.

Black people in the United States are the ones who have been most economically undeveloped by the American economic system, but at the same time they have been forced by the racism inseparable from the system to become more concerned with human values than with material values. Racism and capitalism have also concentrated them into a social force, situated at the heart of the major cities of this country and conscious of their common oppression as black people. Hence blacks are the ones best suited to lead the struggle for the revolutionary power necessary to put politics in command of economics.

Not only is this the only way to destroy racism in the United States. It is also the only way to solve what has become the essential contradiction in this country, the contradiction between economic overdevelopment and political underdevelopment.

14

White Racism: A Psychohistory

JOEL KOVEL

Joel Kovel's unusual book brought a novel approach to a subject that was exercising the minds of a great many commentators and analysts as the 1960s passed into the 1970s: 'The irrational power racism holds over us.' It was, as Kovel put it, 'part of the larger unreason in which we live.'

Kovel's starting point was "that racism, far from being the simple delusion of a bigoted and ignorant minority, is a set of beliefs whose structure arises from the deepest levels of our lives — from the baric of assumption we make about the world, ourselves, and others, and from the patterns of our fundamental social activities." In other words, racism is not the pathological condition identified by earlier theorists, but a phenomenon germane to American culture; something, in fact, that provides culture with its stability. Racism, in this outlook, is a system of shared meanings, symbols created by humans to regulate, order and tie together otherwise disparate elements of experience.

Kovel's task was to uncover racism the entity embedded within an unconscious matrix of meanings. Today, the conception of racism as culturally embedded and infused with new meaning as culture changes, is not fresh. But, Kovel brought a psychoanalytic calculus to his study and argues for an unconscious unity between racism and the ideals of American culture.

The Psychohistory of Racism in the United States

The flaw in the psychohistory of American slave society arose from a radically uneven development of its elements. An exceptional degree of abstractification was applied to one group within culture—the blacks—while the dominant group of whites used them to ensure a degree of seigneurial pleasure unheard of in the West since feudal times. One group was pushed ruthlessly into the total dehumanization that is the ultimate threat of the modern Western order, while the other group literally capitalized upon this—but used their power to move, not forward, but back into a mythic dream. Only a new, open continent could afford this kind of opportunity.

But the slaveholders were parasites upon their human commodities, and needed them for every facet of their lives. While enjoying the prerogatives of barons, they were, in one critical but profound sense, participating more deeply in the capitalist order than the Yankee money-grubbers they despised. The only real difference was that the Southerner missed the turnoff into the generalized abstractification of the whole world that bore its fruit in a money-centered economy. Not money, but human bodies were their goal. The Southerner would live in close proximity, in intimacy, with his black bodies: only thereby could he have his baronial splendor. Total power and the lack of restraints gave him liberty to go as far as he pleased in this direction.

The only check on the development of slave-holding culture could have been from inner control—conscience balanced by morality, or cultural superego. But superego cannot grow unless instinctual gratifications are relinquished. This the Southerner was doubly loath to do: first, because his life was so immediately enjoyable, so gallant, so virile; and second, because of the ever-present threat of slave revolts. This menace, the offspring of projected guilt as much as of a real potential for black violence, always hung just beyond the horizon of the bright Southern sky. Any relaxation of the Southerner's headlong course would awaken the threat as much as the slightest degree of actual Negro insubordination. To each of these sources of danger, the Southerner became inordinately sensitive, even paranoid; and well he might have, for as time passed, the entire inner structure of his culture, composed as it was of a bizarre mixture of the primitive and the hyperabstract, became more brittle and thus more fragile.

The system of American slavery was perfected, then, at the price of its petrification. The black man, denied personage, was split symbolically into a thinglike commodity and a warm, amoral body. Both aspects were drawn helplessly into the white man's self-system, and within its less conscious layers an incorporation occurred: the "good nigger," in the world of the dominative racist, is part of the white self; his presence swells that self into a spectacle of phallic pride. This self-aggrandizement, or narcissism, is one of the central issues in the psychology of dominative racism. The dominative racist of today, let us recall, is he whose sense of failure and exclusion from modern life produces a chronically diminished narcissism. Through his desperate identification with the authoritarian, past or present, he hopes to regain that necessary pride. Such a pride was the Southerner's most characteristic trait, and when granted by a whole culture, it became the prize which he would defend at all cost. Any critical comments, even any attempts to rationalize and make his productive system more efficient, were all spurned as unworthy of white pride, gained by the illusion of holding within the self the possessed bodies of black people. The white Southerner would not hear of any guilt, and so guilt was twisted and exteriorized, to return from

without, impinging now in the harsh, sin-ridden revivalist religion, now in the dialectical criticism from the North, and, most of all, in the fatalistic ruin, the sloth, inefficiency, wastefulness and torpor of his slave economy. When slaves sat down on the job, "clumsily" destroyed farm implements, or otherwise behaved in the shiftless way their stereotype demanded, they were engaging in an act of passive revenge; but they were also giving their masters what unconscious guilt demanded—punishment and destruction. A crime that had begun in the transformation of a man into an economic commodity was punished by economic failure. Small wonder that the Southerners despised commercial activity. They projected onto the North a worship of commercial abstraction that was in fact the rock upon which their whole society rested; they attacked the North for pushing wider what they had already pushed deeper; and, when demise came, it came from the very rock that had served them so well. If ever a society rushed headlong for ruin, it was the classical South; the very élan with which it entered the war must have been the fruit of the release of unbearable inner tensions, and, more deeply, of a wish for self-destruction. And yet, even at the end, amid smoking ruins, the Southerner retained his fatal pride.

AVERSIVE RACISM AND THE RISE OF THE NORTH

No matter how hateful partisans of each region found those of the other, there can be no doubt that the ties which united North and South were deeper and stronger than the differences which separated them. Brothers may destroy one another, yet still remain brothers, and, in the final analysis, North and South were brothers, of common background, in the same cultural stream and equally engaged in the heroic undertaking of establishing a new civilization. And the hate between them, though it was to assume greatly complex forms, ultimately derived from one central point of distinction: the differing roles of black people within the two subcultures.

At this point, the unfolding of the symbolic matrix takes on a different aspect in the two regions. Many factors were at work to channel each region into its own path. Varying geography and climate, individual religious and subcultural styles, different institutional patterns, etc.—all worked in concert to select two distinct patterns from among the endless possibilities of Western growth. As time passed, each regional style would further act upon the other to drive the sections further apart. The essence of their differences lay in the pattern of abstraction that each applied to the world. In the South, as we have noted, a few extreme schismatic abstractions were made—black person into thing, and white woman into ideal—not as ends in themselves, but as means to the provision of a directly gratifying, narcissistic feudalism. In the North, on the other hand, abstraction was diffuse and comprehensive: it extended outwardly to the whole world of nature and man and, most decisively, inwardly to the self: it was an end in itself. The Northern system brought fluidity and adaptability to the matrix of culture; it allowed for indirect domination, and, within the loosened, fluid boundaries of its terms, provided the possibility for democracy and political liberty. These could arise, after all, only within a matrix which ensured the individuality of the self while making possible a kind of equivalency between selves. And through its general abstraction, the Northern matrix offered to history for the first time the possibility of realizing the ageless dream of freedom. Unfortunately—and most unfortunately for black people—that possibility would become seriously compromised by certain other terms of the matrix, to be discussed below; nonetheless, it was there, and it presented the most indubitable and precious contribution of the West to civilization.

In evolutionary terms, then, there could be no doubt that the North was more "advanced" than the South; and, since history, like biological evolution, is the survival of the fittest, the success of the North over the South—which had become economically evident long before the Civil War—certified this advancement. And the historical weakness of Southern culture lay exactly where the white masters took their extreme pleasure–in the oppressed bodies of black people.

This powerless yet alive body, with its enduring and seemingly foolproof tag of black skin for identification, was the cardinal creation of the Southern order. It was this body that the Southerner enjoyed and presented to his Northern brother. And although the black body fascinated the Northerner as much as it did the Southerner, the terms of his culture left him unable to obtain the same kind of gratification from it.

There it was—and one puts the matter harshly but accurately, for slavery stamped an "it-ness" upon the black person which became his enduring curse wherever he went within America–there the body was, enticing, alive, helpless, and yet forbidden. The Northerner had made his pact with history; Faustian, he had achieved the potential for freedom and power by renouncing his own body and deadening the world. The temptation was there, and was powerful; but the prohibition was a little bit more powerful, and made of what was desired a taboo, to be obeyed henceforth by aversion. And now we are in a position to begin understanding *aversive racism*, that form most typical of American, and, indeed, of wherever the bourgeois-capitalist style of life prevails.

Consider first the range of temptations offered. Here, in one living apersonal body, all of the objects of the partial sexual impulses were combined and concentrated: here was phallus, vagina, anus, mouth, breast all available and ordained to be without inhibition because they were without guiding self. And more, here was the magical excremental body itself, the body-as-a-whole: black, warm, odorous, undifferentiated—the very incarnation of that fecal substance with which the whole world had been smeared by the repressed coprophilia of the bourgeois order. Here was the central forbidden pleasure that had become generalized into the pursuit of world mastery: the playing with, the reincorporation of lost, bodily contents, the restoration of the narcissistic body of infancy, the denial of separation and the selfhood that had been painfully wrung from history. Here was the excremental body that had been hated, repressed, spread over the universe, but which was still loved with the infant's wish to fuse with the maternal image. In its own direct pursuit of narcissism, the South had created this body; in its own convoluted, tortuous search for the same goal, the North was confronted with it.

The best that the North could do within the terms of its symbolic matrix was to express hatred and rage against the black body. Buried beneath the rage rested the layers of affinity, repressed incestuous wishes, love of the body lost in childhood, love of body contents—even more deeply buried—held back by the historical search for power. All that surfaced of this iceberg of submerged feeling was the disgust that came last in the series of instinctual developments, and which sealed off all the rest. An obscure yet violent hatred for Negroes arose, puzzling indeed, yet scarcely examined because of its intensity, a violent passion contrary to the external moral principles of the culture, yet congruent with the deeper symbolic sources of that morality. The conflict between ideals and disgust has been a very potent one in our history; in its many forms, it has spread from this core to become the central American dilemma of race relations. Thus the underlying instinctual conflict between love and hatred of the body becomes transmuted with the advance of civilization to higher ground. In its "higher" form, the conflict is between id and superego, or between the disgust, which is the only one of the many layers of instinctual feeling to remain exposed, and the pure ideality of moral principle. Within the terms of the higher-order conflict, aversion becomes the paradigmatic resolution. And the reason for this is that aversion has rich symbolic content of its own.

In itself, aversion is an ego activity, effected as a compromise between the diverse forces pressing in upon the ego. But it is also—for such is the multiple functioning by which we carry out important tasks—a form of gratification, attenuated perhaps, but the best that can be managed under the circumstances.

The prototype of aversion is the physical turning away from what is bodily disgusting, and the prototype of the latter is filth. Filth must not touch the body, or, to the magical infantile thinking that persists alongside of the most mature mental function, it will contaminate it, despoil its purity, perhaps get back inside. Needless to add, such an intense repulsion corresponds to, and is the negation of, its contrary desire—to take back in what is lost and hated. Negations affirm their repressed positive contradictions: hatred affirms love, disgust affirms the lost desire for incorporation, aversion affirms lost body narcissism.

Just as the dominative Southerner needed to keep "his" black body powerless, so does the aversive Northerner need a powerless object with which to play out the symbolic game. And not only must this object be powerless; it must be suitable to represent what has to be projected upon it. Thus for the black to fit into the aversive equation, he must be made into the affirmation of the excremental body. He must become the double negative of anality, the fantasy of a fantasy—not cold, pure, clean, efficient, industrious, frugal, rational (that is, not the pantheon of anal-negative ego traits which are the *summum bonum* of the bourgeois order) but rather warm, dirty, sloppy, feckless, lazy, improvident and irrational, all those traits that are associated with blackness, odor, and sensuality to make their bearer worthy of aversion. And so, throughout our history, whites have created the institutions by which black people are forced to live, and which force them to live in a certain way, almost invariably so as to foster just that constellation of unworthy traits. From slavery itself to modern welfare systems, this has been the enduring pattern, reinforced in popular culture and education by a panoply of stereotypes along the same lines.

The result of these cultural manipulations has been to ensure to the black person a preassigned degraded role, no matter where he turned. This has been true, to some extent, of every group subjected to prejudice, but the quantitative differences have been enormous. For here was a people recognizably distinct from others, easily manipulated because of this and because of their initially abysmal state of slavery, and most of all, dragged down by the profundity of the symbolic equations into which they were drawn. The accumulation of negative images forced upon blacks in America amounted to presenting them with one massive and destructive choice: either to hate one's self, as culture so systematically demanded, or to have no self at all, to be nothing. With the passage of time and abstraction, these alternatives amounted to the same thing: the only self available for black people within the increasingly remote and cold cultural matrix of industrial America and its sewer-cities would be nothingness, the final attenuation of abstracted filth.

Thus black people have been the last to be included into the democratic equation. Such participation requires full and equal selfhood; and while American culture provided selfhood to most, it needed some left-over people to degrade so that the majority could rise. Consequently, the nation that pushed the idea of freedom and equality to the highest point yet attained was also the nation that pulled the idea of degradation and dehumanization to the lowest level ever sounded, to pure nothingness.

In Northern culture, the one activity which permitted unlimited gratification was the making of money. The pursuit of money, the purified and abstract residue of the excremental body, paralleled the repulsion felt toward black people. The incorporation of money into a refined self could be allowed, even as aversion from blacks allowed that self to repudiate its body. Again the two processes mutually fed upon each other, driving an increasing wedge into culture and generating power. Thus it was that throughout the era of slavery, Yankee capitalists, by exploiting the remote operations of finance and commerce, extracted more wealth out of black bodies than the Southerners, with all their direct control, could manage to do. And when machine technology entered the culture of the West at the close of the eighteenth century, it was the North that quickly seized upon these remote means of bodily magnification, and employed them for the infinite multiplication of wealth. Machines, especially the cotton gin, rescued slavery from the doldrums and breathed new vitality into an institution that was beginning to sag under mounting moral opprobrium. The same machines now became the executors of the Northern will. Combined with the mystique of property that had become institutionalized in the Constitution, and directed by that abstract impersonal spirit which was steadily in the process of creation, a machine civilization began to arise, generating endless quantities of money and pushing blacks, by the dialectical process we have been describing, into new depths of degradation. This occurred both within the increasingly ruthless, large scale operations of cotton plantations, and, more productively, in the industrial centers of the non-slave North. For the industrial North, the primary object of degradation was labor itself; wherever this degradation occurred, and no matter how bad matters became for white labor, blacks fared worse, and have done so in industrial work until the present day: last to be hired, first to be fired, lowest wages, most onerous work, tool of management to break strikes, scapegoat of the frustrations of labor. Nor was the process one-directional: just as the creation of white wealth pushed blacks down, so must the presence of degraded black bodies have exerted a continual stimulation to the further pursuit of abstracted money. And the more these simultaneous processes advanced, the more would aversion have to be practiced.

Thus we have reached at least a partial explanation to account for de Tocqueville's observation that the prejudice of race was greatest in areas which had never known slavery. An equivalent rephrasing would be that the (aversive) prejudice of race was forced precisely in fleeing from the temptations of slavery, and out of the resulting creation of higher, more abstract, things. Either aversion, or direct bodily possession: such was the choice for Americans. Those who chose the former, abstracted course would have to contend with the fact that aversion dialectically degrades what it excludes; and that the more pure and refined they were to become, the less tolerable would be the concrete presence of blacks.

15

Racially Separate or Together?

THOMAS F. PETTIGREW

Thomas Pettigrew's work is often cited as among the most illuminating social psychological work on racism. A student of Gordon Allport, he extended Allport's research, addressing questions of changes in what they both called 'racial attitudes'. In the introduction to *Racially Separate or Together?*, a volume that collects many of his articles and chapters from the previous decade, Pettigrew wrote: '"White racism", if it is to have any practical usefulness beyond supplying the epithet "white racist", must be thought of as operating at two levels: the individual and the institutional' (pp. xvii-xviii).

Pettigrew's research in the 1960s confirmed his agreement with the Kerner Commission of Civil Disorders, which concluded that: 'Our nation is moving toward two societies, one black, one white – separate and unequal.' The following extract illustrates how his work gave empirical validity to this development.

Parallel and Distinctive Changes in Anti-Semitic and Anti-Negro Attitudes

A revealing incident occurred in Little Rock, Arkansas, during the city's hectic days in the late 1950s. The vociferous local chapter of the segregationist White Citizens' Council suddenly and summarily expelled one of its principal leaders on the grounds that he was an anti-Semite. "You see," a Council official explained candidly, "we had to throw him out, because we can't afford to be seen as an anti-Jewish organization. Why, we are having trouble enough just being anti-Negro!"

Even for the White Citizens' Council in Little Rock, then, it has become inadvisable to be too explicitly bigoted. Indeed, "prejudice" is now a derogatory term in the United States. Obviously, this is not to say that the nation is free from prejudice; many bigoted groups and individuals are still extremely active. But these generally take pains to maintain that they are not prejudiced.[1] Thus, the White Citizens' Councils stoutly insist that they work, not to keep the Negro down, but only to prevent racial strife. Similarly, in Northern cities, segregationist groups of white parents claim that they are not resisting desegregation but only supporting neighborhood schools.

This phenomenon signals a significant change in relation with American minority groups. The new situation has, perhaps, been captured best in Peter Viereck's concept of "transtolerance":

> Transtolerance is ready to give all minorities their glorious democratic freedom—provided they accept McCarthyism or some other mob conformism of Right or Left.... Transtolerance is also a sublimated Jim Crow, against "wrong" thinkers, not "wrong" races.... It is ... a strictly kosher anti-Semitism.[2]

There is considerable evidence that transtolerance has its uses. For example, Robert Welch, the leader of the far-right John Birch Society, boasts of his group's Jewish and Roman Catholic members. According to Alan Westin, the Society even has two segregated Negro chapters in the South.[3] Though well-known anti-Semitic and anti-Negro figures are prominent in the organization, Welch insists that it is a "communist tactic to stir up distrust and hatred between Jews and Gentiles, Catholics and Protestants, Negroes and Whites."[4] In the same vein, the Reverend Billy James Hargis, a far-right fundamentalist minister who leads what he calls a crusade against Communism, tells his followers: "We cannot tolerate anti-Semitic statements [or] anti-Negro statements."[5]

Transtolerance was widely apparent in the campaigns of the Republican Presidential and Vice-Presidential candidates in 1964—the candidates overwhelmingly supported by far-right organizations. The triple religious nature of the team of Barry M. Goldwater and William E. Miller had a special appeal. "Barry's a Protestant and a Jew, and I'm a Catholic," Miller was quoted as remarking during the campaign. "Anybody who's against that ticket is a damn bigot."[6] Miller's lyrics are different, but the tune is somehow the same.

From data such as these, Seymour Martin Lipset concludes:

> ... The object of intolerance in America has never been as important as the style, the emotion, the antagonism and envy toward some specified other who is seen as wealthier, more powerful, or particularly, as a corrupter of basic values. ... Anti-elitism oriented toward groups that cannot be regarded as oppressed minorities or victims of bigotry, or anti-Communism directed against the agents or dupes of an evil foreign power, can serve as much more palatable outlets for those who require a scapegoat than "un-American" attacks on minorities.... The current crop of radical rightists seems to understand this difference.[7]

Obviously, this shift on the part of the far right reflects a sharp change in public norms concerning minorities in the United States during recent years. Charles Stember's useful compilation of data derived from opinion polls demonstrates conclusively that this change is reflected in reduced prejudice toward Jews.[8] It is the purpose of this chapter to explore further aspects of this critical change in norms. Have the attitudes of white Americans toward Negro Americans also undergone a major change? How do anti-Semitic and anti-Negro attitudes today resemble each other, and how do they differ?

RESEMBLANCES BETWEEN ANTI-SEMITIC AND ANTI-NEGRO ATTITUDES: RESPONSES TO POLLS

In many ways, attitudes toward Negroes provide the acid test of American tolerance of minorities. From the first landing of Africans at Jamestown in 1619 to the racial crisis of the 1970s, the relations between blacks and whites have been inseparable from the nation's roots and development. Anti-Semitism is not nearly as deeply embedded in American life as anti-Negro sentiment; explicit discrimination against Jews did not begin here until late in the nineteenth century, two centuries after slavery had received legal sanction. Therefore, if we want to learn whether the striking reduction in anti-Semitism between 1937 and 1962 represents a more general trend in intergroup relations, we must see if responses to polls manifesting a hostility to Negroes show a similar reduction over the same years.

Herbert H. Hyman and Paul B. Sheatsley present the relevant data in an analysis of replies to certain questions concerning blacks, which were asked periodically from 1942 to 1963 by the National Opinion Research Center.[9] A look at their results reveals marked parallels with Stember's, both where stereotypes and where discriminatory practices were concerned. Thus, while the percentage of Americans who did not think Jews less honest than others rose from 56 to 82 between 1938 and 1962, the percentage who believed Negroes to be as intelligent as whites rose from 42 to 74 between 1942 and 1963. While the percentage who did not think colleges should limit enrollment of Jews increased from 74 to 96, the percentage favoring racially desegregated schools increased from 30 to 63. Analogous shifts also occurred in attitudes toward heterogeneous neighborhoods: over the same years, the percentage voicing no objections to a Jewish neighbor went up from 75 to 97, and those with no objections to a Negro neighbor rose from 35 to 63 percent.[10]

A further parallel may be found in the high points of animosity against the two groups. Stember shows that during the closing years of the Second World War American anti-Semitism reached its highest point within the last generation; Hyman and Sheatsley note a peak in anti-Negro opinions about the same time. Stember presents evidence of this parallel intensity as of 1944: four groups—Protestants, Catholics, Jews, and Negroes—were named, and respondents were asked: "Against which *one* of these groups, *if any*, do you think prejudice or feeling has increased the most?" Thirty-seven percent named Jews; 31 percent chose Negroes.[11] Anti-Semitic and anti-Negro attitudes, then, have both declined over the past generation from peaks of intensity reached simultaneously during the tense war years.

Such striking parallels raise two questions. Do the changes in responses reflect actual reductions in prejudice? And, if so, are these reductions endangered by the so-called "white backlash"—the widely reported reaction of threatened whites in Northern cities against the blacks' demands for change? Each of these issues deserves discussion, for each might well limit severely the conclusions which can be safely drawn from the data so carefully compiled by Stember and by Hyman and Sheatsley.

With some justification, certain observers doubt whether polling can fathom the full depth of most respondents' anti-Semitic or anti-Negro prejudices. What has decreased from the late 1930s to today, they argue, is not prejudice, but the respectability of prejudice—in this case, readiness to admit bigotry to a poll taker. Yet, even if only this standard of respectability had changed, that would itself be noteworthy. For what is "real" prejudice? A change in verbal behavior is certainly "real" in a most important sense.

In any case, need we be so limiting? No doubt the open espousal of anti-Jewish and anti-Negro attitudes became markedly less respectable during the past generation. But this change would seem to be only one among many symptoms of a deeper, more meaningful lessening of prejudice. Indeed, there are a number of reasons for accepting the major shifts reported by the opinion polls as genuine, at least in large part.

First, rapport in the polling situation is generally far closer than those unfamiliar with the technique realize. A pleasant, attentive stranger who has gone to some trouble to record your opinion on vital issues, and who does not provide any cues of disagreement, is often a much safer confidant than acquaintances.

Second, the remarkable consistency of the trends in attitudes toward Jews and Negroes extends to a wide variety of questions, asked by different polling agencies. Presumably, the questions vary considerably in "respectability bias" (or, to use the parlance of modern testing theory, in "social desirability"); thus, if the results were largely a reflection of "respectability bias," we would not expect the consistency noted both by Stember and by Hyman and Sheatsley.

Third, certain questions concerning Jews and Negroes which appear to involve a built-in "respectability bias" as great as any of Stember's items have *not* changed over the past few decades. For example, the National Opinion Research Center has repeatedly asked representative nationwide samples if they "think most Negroes in the United States are being treated fairly or unfairly." The responses have remained quite stable over the years; in both 1946 and 1956, 63 percent answered, "Fairly."[12]

Fourth, election results have borne out the evidence from polls on intergroup attitudes. Ithiel de Sola Pool and his associates attempted to simulate the 1960 Presidential election using only data from polls gathered before 1959.[13] To predict the crucial anti-Catholic vote against John F. Kennedy, Pool used the simple and straightforward question, "Would you be willing to vote for a qualified Catholic for President?"—surely as frontal a measure of prejudice as any employed to explore attitudes toward Jews and Negroes. Yet, for all its obviousness, the question produced a response that proved remarkably accurate and useful in simulating the actual 1960 election. As the authors state in their intriguing volume:

> Millions of Protestants and other non-Catholics who would otherwise have voted Democratic could not bring themselves to vote for a Catholic. In total—so our model says—roughly one out of five Protestant Democrats or Protestant Independents who would otherwise have voted Democratic bolted because of the religious issue. The actual number of bolters varied with the voter-type and was determined in the model by the proportion of that voter-type who had replied on surveys that they would not want to vote for a Catholic for President. What our model tends to show is that the poll question was a good one. The model suggests that the number of people who overcame the social inhibitions to admitting prejudice to a polltaker was about the same as the number who overcame the political inhibitions to bolting their party for reasons of bias.[14]

The final reason for accepting data from polls as an adequate measure of prejudice is the most compelling of all. The sharp diminution of anti-minority responses in the polls is completely consistent with the changes in the treatment of minorities over the same years. Discrimination in a wide range of American institutions has lessened at least as much as verbalized prejudice. This process is a two-way street: on the one hand, reductions of prejudice speed the erosion of discrimination; on the other hand—what is probably more important—the decline of discrimination permits increasing contact between groups on a basis of equality, and thus tends to decrease prejudice.[15]

Of course, none of these arguments implies that discriminatory practices against minorities have ceased in the United States. Roughly two-thirds of the nation's private clubs retain religious restrictions; housing patterns based on religious discrimination continue; and some major law firms, as well as the executive corps of the automotive and utility industries, still discriminate against Jews in their recruitment.[16] Moreover, the most elaborate and debilitating barriers of all—those maintained for three centuries against the Negro—are only now slowly beginning to be dismantled. The polls clearly reflect these remaining barriers, indicating that prejudice is still intense in certain sectors of the society. The actual treatment of Jews and Negroes, then, substantiates findings concerning attitudes toward these groups in two separate respects: it confirms that hostility has markedly diminished during recent years, but it also confirms that hostility remains concentrated in particular sectors.

What about the "white backlash"? Does this much-publicized phenomenon indicate a rise in anti-Negro prejudice? Relevant data strongly suggest that it does not. The concept of a backlash was fashioned by journalists for its sensational flavor, not by social scientists for its heuristic value; the evidence that purports to demonstrate its existence lacks the most rudimentary research controls and safeguards. A more detached view, relying upon controlled data, and free from the pressure of deadlines that characterizes the mass media, leads one to doubt that a significant anti-Negro reaction has swept the nation.

The term "backlash" implies that many whites in the North, once mildly sympathetic to Negro aspirations, have suddenly changed their minds and hardened their resistance to racial change. The term first gained favor in the mass media during 1964, when George C. Wallace, the segregationist Governor of Alabama, made a number of relatively successful political sorties into the North. He entered the Democratic Presidential primaries in Wisconsin, Indiana, and Maryland and, to the surprise of many, polled sizable minorities—from roughly 30 percent in Indiana to 43 percent in Maryland. Many observers inferred from these results that an anti-Negro "backlash" was in full swing. Soon every reasonably large vote for a reactionary candidate anywhere in the North and West was cited as a symptom of the supposed "backlash," and even Lyndon Johnson, who was then President, freely used the term in his conversations with reporters.

But throughout this period, national public-opinion polls conducted by Louis Harris revealed a steadily mounting majority in favor of pending civil rights legislation, though these polls were largely overlooked. In November, 1963, an estimated 63 percent of adult Americans favored the Federal Civil Rights Bill; by February, 1964, the figure had risen to 68 percent, and by May it stood at 70 percent—a steady gain of 7 percent in six months, and a strange phenomenon to be occurring in the midst of an alleged anti-black reaction.

Why, then, did Wallace do so well in the primaries in three Northern and border states? An array of well-established principles of social science suggests a number of answers. For one thing, the mass media emphasized the percentage of the votes won by Wallace without thoroughly considering the size of the total vote. The number of votes cast in

the three state elections was considerably above the usual turnouts for Democratic Presidential primaries. The apparent "backlash," then, was evidently caused by large numbers of people who do not normally vote in these primaries, people attracted to the polls by the protest implied in Wallace's candidacy but not necessarily by his position on racial matters. Furthermore, Wallace's candidacy did not have to be regarded seriously, and this is a factor of major importance in protest voting. Hadley Cantril has shown, for instance, that many French and Italian voters find their support of the Communist ticket a satisfying expression of protest, though they are not members of the Communist Party and would not want the Communists to gain control of their governments.[17] "Voting Communist can't hurt me," reasons one Frenchman. "it may help me. Nothing like putting a big scare into the *patron*."[18] By the same token, Wallace made an ideal magnet for protest voters of all varieties, precisely because there was so little chance of his actually becoming President. His relative success in the primaries, then, did not necessarily require or reflect any large-scale changing of minds. The many journalists who reasoned that it did were guilty of a blatant form of the ecological fallacy.[19] We shall return to the "Wallace phenomenon" in Chapter 10, where the basis of Wallace's support in 1968 will be considered in detail.

The analyses by the mass media also assumed, without the benefit of before-and-after comparisons, that the racial attitudes of many white Americans were changing, notably in Northern industrial areas. To be certain that people were generally more anti-Negro in July of 1964 than they had been in 1963, we obviously need to know their attitudes in both years. Yet the media did not provide such necessary evidence.

The nearest attempt to obtain before-and-after data was a city-wide poll administered by reporters for *The New York Times* in September, 1964.[20] This survey employed the risky procedure of asking the respondent in retrospect whether he had changed his mind. In addition, the wording of the questions asked was strongly biased: "Have you been affected in any way by a 'white backlash'? Have you changed your thinking during the last couple of months? Which category [of those detailed below] describes your feelings?" To mention the supposed phenomenon by its familiar name and then to suggest the "backlash" alternative the respondent is expected to select is, of course, contrary to all standards of competent polling. Indeed, it is virtually equivalent to asking a sample of ladies: "Do you like the chic new Parisian fashions which simply everyone is raving about?"

As it happens, New Yorkers are a relatively hardy, independent lot. Only 27 percent of a roughly random selection of the city's whites agreed they were now "more opposed to what

Negroes want"; 62 percent insisted they still felt "pretty much the same"; and 6 percent maintained that they actually were "more strongly in favor of what Negroes want" than they had been earlier. Abandoning its usual caution, the *Times* captioned the story, "Results Indicate 'Backlash' Exists"; but, once again, the evidence is hardly conclusive. Many of the persons included in the critical 27 percent may actually have been as hostile to Negroes in 1963 as in 1964, and an undetermined number were undoubtedly swayed by the "loaded" questions.

Fortunately, before-and-after data derived from both elections and polls do exist. In Boston's School Committee elections, for example, a ticket of candidates ran for five positions in 1961, before the issue of *de facto* school segregation had erupted in the city, and a similar group ran again in 1963, after the issue had become important. One of the candidates on both occasions was a militant black; another was a white woman, Mrs. Hicks, who between the two elections had become prominent as an outspoken defender of school segregation. (We shall discuss Mrs. Hicks, her campaigns, and her voters in Chapter 9.) In both contests the Negro candidate ran a strong, though losing, seventh; the segregationist won a seat each time. The mass media emphasized that the segregationist had received a sharply higher percentage of the vote in 1963 than in 1961, presenting this fact as evidence of a powerful "white backlash." Actually, in this case, as in the primaries where Wallace ran strongly, great numbers of voters seem to have come out from under the rocks. About twice as many voters went to the polls in 1963 as in 1961, an increase large enough to account for much of Mrs. Hicks's improved showing. it should be noted that the Negro candidate, too, held or bettered his record in total votes in virtually every precinct.

Relevant data from public-opinion polls have been compiled by the National Opinion Research Center.[21] An intensive study of racial attitudes throughout the United States was conducted in December, 1963. In a follow-up the next summer, re-interviews using the same unbiased questions were held with those white members of the original sample who lived in large Northern industrial areas, where the "backlash" was allegedly occurring. Analyses of the results are instructive. Basic attitudes toward the goals of racial change had not shifted: those whites who had previously favored the desegregation of schools, public facilities, and neighborhoods still predominantly favored it; those who had previously opposed it still opposed it.[22] Nor had voting intentions for the Presidency shifted because of the race issue, except among a minute fraction,[23] as was amply borne out in the November election, when the heralded "white backlash" for Goldwater failed to materialize.

What *was* apparent was opposition to the current form and pace of the civil rights movement.[24] "The Negroes are pushing too hard too fast," went the familiar phrase. But this attitude was not new; polls had consistently revealed it throughout the 1960s, with each new militant technique initially provoking a comparable degree of resistance from whites.[25] Thus, in 1961 a nationwide Gallup poll found that 64 percent of the public disapproved of "freedom rides" and 57 percent believed the rides would "hurt the Negroes' chance of being integrated in the South."[26] In 1963, 65 percent of white Northerners and 73 percent of white Southerners thought mass demonstrations by Negroes were "likely to hurt the Negro's cause for racial equality."[27] It is noteworthy that in each case the resistance of white Americans focused upon means, not ends; throughout all the racial turbulence—in part perhaps because of it—attitudes toward the Negroes' ultimate aspirations have continued to improve.

Finally, a comparison of nationwide Gallup polls taken in 1963 and 1965 affords significant evidence. During these years, when the "backlash" was presumed to be raging, increasing percentages of white parents in the South and North said they would not object to sending their children to a school with Negro children. The most dramatic shifts occurred in the South; the proportion of white parents there who stated that they would not object to having their children attend classes with "a few" Negro children rose from only 38 percent in 1963 to 62 percent by 1965. Consistently favorable shifts also characterized opinions of whites in the North: a school with "a few" Negro children was declared unobjectionable by 87 percent of white parents in 1963, by 91 percent in 1965; a school where the student body was half Negro was acceptable to 56 percent in 1963, to 65 percent in 1965; and a school with a majority of Negro students was unobjectionable to 31 percent in 1963, to 37 percent in 1965. Once again, specific data directly refute the notion of a widespread growth in anti-Negro sentiment among white Americans during the period from 1963 to 1965. But, it may be asked, what happened to these attitudes after 1965? Gallup asked the same questions of white parents in 1966 and 1969, and the same trend continued. For example, by 1969 78 percent of white parents in the South had no objection to token integration of schools, 47 percent had no objection to half-Negro schools (compared with only 17 percent in 1963), and 26 percent no objection to predominantly Negro schools compared with 6 percent in 1963). Opinions of white parents in the North did not show such dramatic change, but the percentages continued to increase for all three questions by from 2 to 4 percent over 1965, a result which is obviously at odds with the "backlash" theory.[28]

The developments popularly described as a "white backlash," then, turn out, when placed in full scientific perspective, to have been something quite different. Anti-black candidates for political office in the North, conspicuous under the glare of television klieg lights, siezed on the race issue and made it more salient; they drew upon preexisting bigotry and alienation, and they often succeeded, at least for a time, in attracting to the polls many apathetic, alienated, authoritarian, or uninformed citizens who usually do not vote.[29] What followed was the familiar phenomenon of activation in a crisis: persons who favored racial change in the first place became more active, and so did persons who opposed it.

The mass media, interpreting this process as a "backlash," went wrong in ignoring the size of the total vote in elections involving anti-Negro candidates; in disregarding the rising support for the Civil Rights Act of 1964 among whites; in misunderstanding the "out-from-under-the rocks" quality of protest voting; in neglecting to seek before-and-after evidence of change; in relying upon questions with highly biased wording; in failing to differentiate clearly between attitudes toward the means and attitudes toward the goals of the civil-rights movement; and, because of all these errors, in mistaking activation for a change in opinion. What really happened in the course of the so-called "white backlash" does not contradict the steady and dramatic reduction in anti-Negro prejudice throughout the nation over the past generation.

Basically, the expectation of a simple negative reaction among whites toward Negroes' recent demands failed because the attitudes of white Americans toward Negro Americans are anything but simple. And here we come to a final parallel between attitudes toward Jews and attitudes toward Negroes in the United States: in both cases, a fundamental ambivalence is at work. Halpern traces the ambivalent feelings of gentiles toward Jews through the years, and Stember presents data from polls that document it for the past generation.[30] A similar ambivalence is to be found in the white American's feelings toward the Negro. But here the parallel ends, for the ambivalence stems from markedly contrasting images, and this is only one among many distinctions between hostility toward Jews and toward blacks.

DISTINCTIONS BETWEEN ANTI-SEMITIC AND ANTI-NEGRO ATTITUDES

Bettelheim and Janowitz, among others, have observed that Americans' attitudes toward the Jew are rooted in concerns having to do with the superego, and their attitudes toward the Negro in concerns having to do with the id.[31] Consider, for example, the adjectives typically applied to Jews by anti-Semites: ambitious, striving, crafty, clannish, shrewd, hyperintelligent, sly, dishonest. And compare these with the adjectives typically applied to Negroes by Negrophobes: unambitious, lazy, happy-go-lucky, irresponsible, stupid, dirty, smelly, uninhibited, oversexed. The psychoanalytic interpretation of these distinctive, though strangely reciprocal, stereotypes is straightforward: animosity toward outgroups is explained as a projection of unacceptable inner impulses. Jews and Negroes serve in part as *alter egos* for the bigot. The bigot's own sins of the superego, such as ambition, deceit, and egotism, are personified in the Jew; his sins of the id—sins of the flesh—are seen in the Negro.[32]

The psychoanalytic distinction between superego and id stereotypes is useful in a wide range of cross-cultural situations, because many groups besides Jews and Negroes have evoked these contrasting images. Outgroups that are assigned a superego image are typically alien merchants or middlemen caught between the landed and laboring classes. This, of course, was the typical position of European Jews during the Middle Ages, and the similarity is not lost on people who project superego stereotypes upon other groups: the Chinese merchants of Malaysia and Indonesia are often called the "Jews of Asia," and the Muslim Indian merchants of East and South Africa the "Jews of Africa." The id image is attributed, in many parts of the world, to groups that rank at the bottom of the social structure; in Europe, gypsies and Southern Italians often play this role.[33] Occasionally, the two types of images are fused into a single, contradictory stereotype; in Germany before the Second World War, for instance, the lack of a significant id-type outgroup made it necessary for the anti-Semitic image of the Jew to do double duty as the personification of both id and superego concerns, with the result that Jews were seen as both lazy and overambitious, both oversexed and anemic. In America, however, bigots enjoy the luxury of having a variety of outgroups to choose from, and more specific, differentiated stereotypes have evolved.

These cross-cultural examples suggest some further reasons why the images of Jews and Negroes in the United States are so distinctively different. The two stereotypes are, of course, more than just projections of the bigot's impulses; they also reflect, if only in distorted ways, the contrasting social positions and values of the two groups, and particularly their radically different histories both in and outside America. Anti-Semitism in the United States is derived in large part from the image of the Jew as middleman or "economic man," a stigma originally developed in Europe. Anti-Negro prejudice stems from the far more serious stigma left upon Negroes by the uniquely destructive form of slavery sanctioned in the South, and by the subsequent century of segregation and poverty.[34]

A crucial element in these historically implanted stigmata, in addition to position and values, is the concept of "race." In its distorted popular meaning, the term "race" often carries connotations of innate inferiority, of unalterable distinctiveness, of a biological threat. It is thus not surprising that, as Stember shows, persons who think of Jews as a "race" in this sense are somewhat more anti-Semitic than others; and it is significant that this mode of thinking has sharply declined since 1946: Jews are more often viewed now as either a nationality or a religious group.[35] In attitudes toward Negroes, no such shift is discernible. Though it is estimated that 25 percent of the genes in the total gene pool of Negro Americans is Caucasian in origin,[36] Negroes will probably be viewed as a markedly separate "race" for some time to come.

The very different positions of Jews and Negroes in the American social structure are another determinant of their contrasting stereotypes. Jewish Americans are overwhelmingly middle-class. Disproportionately large numbers of them engage in the professions and other white-collar occupations; their median family income easily surpasses the national median, rivaling that of such wealthy religious groups as the Presbyterians and the Episcopalians. Black Americans, on the other hand, are overwhelmingly lower-class. They are found disproportionately often in the service and blue-collar occupations; their median family income is low, barely three-fifths of the national median, and reflects a degree of poverty unequaled among whites except for such destitute groups as the Appalachian mountain folk. There are, of course, poor Jews of lower-class status and prosperous Negroes of middle-class status, but they represent relatively small segments of their respective groups.

There are also differences in the values held by Jews and by Negroes—a natural outcome of their different histories and social positions. The close similarity of the Jews' values and those of the dominant Anglo-Saxon Protestants has been a striking and important aspect of the Jewish experience in America. To use Florence Kluckhohn's convenient scheme, Jewish and Protestant Americans both tend to hold "man-over-nature," "doing," "individualistic" and "future-time" value orientations.[37] Indeed, research on the so-called "Protestant ethic" often finds Jewish subjects far surpassing Protestants in their devotion to such central components of the ethic as achievement values.[38]

The picture is less clear in the case of Negro Americans. The impact of slavery limited the survival of their uniquely African values, so that their value models from the beginning were typically Protestant American. Yet their experience in this country did little to encourage a "man-over-nature," "doing," "individualistic," "future-time" view of life. To be sure, the first moderately prosperous classes of Negroes did evince the Protestant ethic in its purest form.[39] But continued denial of opportunity and increasing racial separation have fostered countervalues among many of the younger, lower-status, less religious Negroes in today's enormous urban ghettos.

The consequences of these differences between Jewish and Negro Americans are vast. To begin with, attitudes toward intermarriage with members of the two groups are markedly different. Stember shows that in 1962 only 37 percent of a nationwide sample stated they "definitely would not marry a Jew," a diminution of 20 percentage points since 1950.[40] In contrast, attitudes toward intermarriage between Negroes and whites have changed very little over the past decades. On the basis of distorted notions of " race," over 80 percent of white Americans opposed interracial marriage in 1963.[41]

A second consequence is that "old Americans," by and large, have responded to Jews and immigrants generally in one way, to Negroes in quite another. In the case of immigrants, including Jews, assimilation was expected; the problem, it was felt, was how to bring them into the mainstream of American life—though "not too fast." In the case of Negroes, assimilation was opposed; the problem, until recently, was defined as how to keep them out of the mainstream. The two contrasting patterns naturally have affected the personalities of individuals in quite different ways. Immigrants and their children have undergone cultural conflicts, painful adjustments in the second generation, and special strains while striving to become "all American." Negroes, on the other hand, have suffered unique identity conflicts, agonizing threats to their survival and dignity, and a crushing sense of rejection and defeat.[42] Significantly, mental illness among Jewish Americans is marked by relatively high rates of neurosis and low rates of psychosis, while among black Americans the reverse seems to be true.[43]

Because of the many differences between Jews and Negroes, prejudices against the two groups relate differently to social class. Stember shows, for example, that anti-Semitism is relatively widespread among individuals of higher status, especially when measured by questions which suggest that Jews are a "race," are "more radical than others," or have "objectionable qualities."[44] By contrast, anti-Negro responses in polls come most frequently from lower-status whites. Thus, as Hyman and Sheatsley have shown, the poorly educated respondents in nationwide surveys favor desegregation of public schools and buses much less often than do the better educated. Apparently, prejudice against Jews or Negroes is most commonly found where a competitive threat is most acutely perceived: anti-Semitism tends to be particularly intense among Christians of a social status similar to that of most Jews, and anti-Negro sentiment is likely to be strongest among whites of a social status similar to that of most Negroes. A revealing exception, however, is to be found in the area of residential segregation: according to Hyman and Sheatsley, the more educated are just as resistant to racially desegregated housing as the less educated.[45]

More surprising are the relationships between group prejudice and political viewpoints, as revealed in attitudes toward Joseph R. McCarthy. A survey conducted in 1954 by the National Opinion Research Center found that persons who favored Senator McCarthy, especially the better educated, were slightly less willing than others to accept Jewish neighbors;[46] on the other hand, a study carried out in the same year by International Research Associates demonstrated that supporters of McCarthy were actually more willing than others to vote for a hypothetical Jewish candidate for Congress.[47] There was, in short, no strong and consistent association between anti-Semitism and McCarthyism. A clearer relationship was evident where attitudes toward Negroes were concerned: a Gallup survey in 1954 noted that opponents of McCarthy approved the recent Supreme Court ruling outlawing segregated schools far more often than did his supporters,[48] though the same poll did not find a consistent relationship between attitudes toward McCarthy and objections to sending children to predominantly Negro schools.[49]

The general tendency of right-wing movements to evince anti-Negro rather than anti-Jewish prejudice became evident again ten years later in the candidacy of Barry Goldwater for the Presidency. Though the candidate, in the new style of "trans-tolerance," insisted throughout that he was not anti-Negro, he and his spokesmen openly rejected the Civil Rights Act of 1964 and attacked racially integrated housing as well as other objectives of the Negro's drive for first-class citizenship. In contrast, no anti-Semitic appeals were broached.

The Jew, then, is no longer a safe target for public attack, while the black still is—in line with the differences between the two types of prejudice which we have noted. Though both types have sharply declined in recent years, anti-Negro prejudice is still far more prevalent than anti-Semitism in the United States today, as is shown in the responses to questions which apply equally to each group. During 1958, roughly two-thirds of the whites in a nation-wide Gallup poll said they would vote for a well-qualified man nominated by their party if he were Jewish; only two-fifths said they would if he were black.[50]

Even sharper differences are found when questions about "social distance" are asked. For instance, surveys of four communities by Cornell University in the early 1950s asked respondents if they would find it "a little distasteful to eat at the same table" with a Negro or a Jew. The percentages of white Christians who said it would be distasteful with a Negro ranged from 50 in Elmira, New York, to 92 in Savannah, Georgia; the percentages saying it would be distasteful with a Jew varied only from 8 in Steubenville, Ohio, to 13 in Savannah.[51] Similar responses were obtained by an additional question about going to a party and finding that most of the people there were Negroes or were Jews. The percentages who disliked the idea of a party attended mostly by Negroes ranged from 80 in Bakersfield, California, to 89 in Steubenville; the percentages for a party attended mostly by Jews ranged from 25 in Steubenville to 34 in Savannah.[52]

More intensive investigations have led to the same conclusion. Bettelheim and Janowitz interviewed in depth 150 white Christians from Chicago, all of them World War II veterans of enlisted rank. Using the same criteria for prejudice against both groups, Bettelheim and Janowitz rated 65 percent of their subjects as either intensely or outspokenly anti-Negro, 27 percent as harboring stereotyped anti-Negro attitudes, and only 8 percent as truly tolerant of Negroes.[53] When it came to attitudes toward Jews, only about half as many were rated intensely or outspokenly prejudiced (31 percent), a similar percentage were rated as holding stereotyped beliefs (28 percent), and five times as many were rated as tolerant (41 percent).[54]

Not only are attitudes toward Negroes more negative than attitudes toward Jews, but they are also far more salient to most Americans. A fairly accurate measure of saliency is provided in polls by the percentage of persons who are uncertain, say they don't know, or otherwise fail to choose one of the offered alternatives. In surveys dealing with prejudice against Negroes, these percentages are generally small; thus, Hyman and Sheatsley report that in four polls from 1942 to 1963, questions on racial desegregation consistently obtained noncommittal responses from only about 4 percent of the samples.[55] With anti-Semitic items, the proportions are generally higher; thus, the 137 percentages of noncommittal replies recorded by Stember range from 1 to 42, with a median of 11.

Anti-Negro and anti-Jewish attitudes, being shaped by somewhat different social forces, do not necessarily rise or fall together. True, both have declined sharply over the past generation in the nation as a whole; but, as is often the case, the South shows a deviant pattern and thereby provides special clues. Anti-Negro sentiments have notably lessened in the South since 1942, actually changing faster in many ways than has been true elsewhere; meanwhile, anti-Semitism seems to have declined at a markedly slower pace in the South than in other regions.

Hyman and Sheatsley's analysis of nationwide surveys from 1942 to 1963 conclusively demonstrates massive shifts in whites' opinions about the Negro in the South.[56] With more room for improvement, the South shows generally higher relative and absolute rates of modification than the North. Thus, the belief of the white public in the equal intelligence of Negroes rose from 21 to 59 percent in the South, and from 50 to 80 percent in the North; support by whites of desegregated public transportation climbed from 4 to 51 percent in the South, and from 57 to 88 percent in the North; and approval by whites of desegregated neighborhoods increased from 12 to 51 percent in the South, and from 42 to 70 percent in the North. In short, the white South, for all its ugly signs of resistance to racial change, is altering its most basic sentiments toward the black.

Anti-Semitism in the South presents a contrasting situation. As was noted briefly in Chapter 6, the South has traditionally been one of the least anti-Semitic regions in the nation, and a considerable body of data suggests that it remained so until the 1940s. Stember shows, for example, that in 1939–1946 Southerners ranked lowest in anti-Semitic responses to six of nine questions.[57] In polls conducted during 1946 and 1947, Roper found the South, together with the Far West, to be among the least anti-Semitic areas of the United States.[58] A study of over 1,000 wartime rumors from all parts of the nation, conducted by R. H. Knapp in 1942, lends further weight to this conclusion.[59] He noted that anti-Semitic stories constituted 9 percent of the rumors in the nation but only 3 percent of the rumors in the South; in contrast, anti-Negro rumors made up over 8 percent of the total for the South but only 3 percent of the total for the nation. Consistent with these data, other inquiries have found large numbers of white Southerners intensely anti-Negro and at the same time highly favorable to Jews.[60]

The last twenty years have witnessed a diminution of anti-Semitism in the South, as elsewhere, but a minimal one compared to other regions. Some institutional indications of the South's earlier relative standing still exist; thus, the Anti-Defamation League of B'nai B'rith, in its exhaustive study of religious barriers in social clubs, found discrimination less prevalent in the South, Southwest, and Far West than in other areas.[61] But Stember's broader data present another picture: in seven of his nine comparisons over time, percentage declines in anti-Semitism between 1939 and 1962 were smaller in the South than in any other region; by 1962, the South ranked slightly above all other areas in anti-Semitic responses to four of the nine questions.[62]

Stember offers a methodological explanation for this regional change. The 1939 survey drew its sample from voters, which limited the participation of Negro respondents, whereas the 1962 survey included Negroes in approximately their true proportion of the adult Southern population. Consequently, Stember suggests, a possible greater degree of anti-Semitism among Negroes might

have distorted the results in the South. Additional data, however, cast doubt upon this explanation. The Cornell survey of Savannah, conducted in the early 1950s, found approximately the same percentages of Negroes and whites responding to stereotype questions about Jews in an anti-Semitic fashion.[63] For instance, 44 percent of whites and 48 percent of Negroes agreed that "Jews are dishonest in their business dealings."[64] Questions about "social distance," such as the one about eating at the same table with a Jew, uncovered somewhat larger differences between races, but the Negroes' greater preference for distance is probably a function more of racial taboos than of religious bigotry. In any event, only two of Stember's nine comparisons deal with social distance, and one of these can be tested for racial differences by combining three national surveys which asked the same question during the early 1950s.[65] When asked, "How would you feel if a Jewish family were going to move next door to you?" 8.7 percent of whites and 8.0 percent of Negroes in the South stated they "wouldn't like it at all"; 15.5 percent of whites and 12.9 percent of Negroes said it "wouldn't matter too much."[66] In other words, roughly one of every four whites but only one of every five Negroes in the South had some qualms about a Jewish neighbor.

The inclusion of more Negro Southerners in the 1962 survey, then, apparently does not explain away the relatively slow decline of anti-Semitism in the South between 1939 and 1962. The deviant pattern of the South—faster diminution of anti-Negro attitudes but slower diminution of anti-Semitism than elsewhere—provides suggestive clues about the different social forces underlying the two types of prejudice. As the region's cities grow into major metropolitan centers, and its expanding industries erode the older agricultural economy, traditional institutions and attitudes are inevitably undergoing drastic alteration. Basically, the South is becoming more American and less Confederate. The deviant pattern described here is part of this process of "deregionalization": the white South, formerly unique in its rejection of the Negro and its acceptance of the Jew, is becoming more and more like the rest of the nation.

Numerous studies have revealed that urbanization and industrialization are significantly associated with marked reductions in racial animosity.[67] As white Southerners rise into the middle class, receive more and better education, and develop into acclimated urbanites, the fears and threats traditionally associated with the Negro lose some of their force. But these changes often perpetuate or even heighten anti-Semitism.

To see the full importance of this point, we must consider the traditional position of Jews in Southern life. Though few in number, they have long occupied prominent roles in the region—from cabinet posts in the Confederate Government to current ownership of the major department stores in virtually every large city. Acceptance of Jews was facilitated by the special emphasis which Fundamentalist Protestants placed on the Old Testament. Moreover, the superego stereotype elsewhere reserved for the Jew was in the South largely projected onto the Yankee, who was caricatured by the poor, defeated, and defensive South as crafty, pushy, materialistic, too successful, and not to be trusted. Most significant of all, the German Jews who constituted the bulk of the earlier Jewish population in the South were an integral part of antebellum and Civil War folklore. I remember well the special respect which the leading Jewish family enjoyed in my Southern home town. Though this family included the foremost bankers and jewelers of the city, the usual anti-Semitic stereotypes were never applied; for, after all, the family's social position was solidly grounded on the fame of its brave Civil War ancestor, Colonel Kahn.[68]

The rapid social changes in today's South are weakening much of this tradition-linked protection against anti-Semitism. An increasing percentage of Southern Jewry is not of pre-Civil War German stock and thus is not draped in the Confederate battle flag. In addition, typical forms of anti-Semitism are being fostered by many of the very processes which reduce anti-Negro feeling—for example, the growth of the middle class, immigration of Northerners, and competitive urban life. The inference is clear: Anti-Semitism and anti-Negro attitudes are by no means shaped by identical social forces; hence, they do not necessarily rise and diminish together.

Do prejudices necessarily replace one another? The many distinctions between anti-Jewish and anti-Negro attitudes raise the question of how hostile sentiments toward various minorities are related to one another. Conventional wisdom holds that a reduction in one type of prejudice invariably leads to an increase in another. But is this true? If prejudice against one minority drops, does prejudice against another necessarily rise?

To tackle this central question, a choice must be made between two contrasting conceptions of aggression. Sigmund Freud and later psychoanalytic writers have generally postulated a closed system on the order of a steam boiler, containing a fixed amount of instinctive aggression which if not released through one outlet will seek and find another. According to this view, society's problem is how to channel aggression through appropriate safety valves. Indeed, creative, constructive work is seen as an important means of sublimating fundamentally aggressive instincts. Gordon W. Allport objects to this conception.[69] He argues that no single closed-system model can account for the vast range of phenomena which Freudians classify under the single instinct "aggression" (from individual rage to war) and under sublimation (from counting up to

ten to painting the *Mona Lisa*). The model he proposes is an open-system, feedback type. Rather than a finite, instinctual force that demands release, aggression in Allport's view is a variable capacity whose expression is governed by both inner and outer conditions; once it is released further aggression is more likely, not less likely, to occur. Creative, constructive endeavors, he maintains, are ends in themselves, meeting specific needs, rather than mere reflections of aggression.

How we answer our question depends on which of these rival models we choose. If we accept the Freudian model, we will expect a reduction of prejudice against one minority to cause an increase of prejudice against another, unless the inevitable flow of aggression finds a different outlet altogether. Prejudice, the old saying goes, will always be with us. Allport's model creates markedly different expectations. From this vantage point, there is nothing inevitable about prejudice. In fact, his feedback model suggests that greater tolerance of one minority would improve the chances for greater tolerance of others. Hence, prejudice need not always be with us; both personal and social conditions can be achieved which essentially eliminate this societal liability.

The available evidence tends to support Allport's more optimistic open-system view. Social-psychological studies of prejudice have repeatedly found hostility toward one outgroup to be highly and positively correlated with hostility toward other outgroups; that is, individuals who are prejudiced against Jews also tend to be prejudiced against Negroes, Catholics, and outgroups in general.[70] One ingenious experiment tested attitudes of students toward the peoples of thirty-two nations and races plus three nonexistent groups ("Daniereans," "Pireneans" and "Wallonians"),[71] and found, as the open-system model would predict, that persons who rejected the real groups tended to reject the imaginary ones as well. Unless we assume that the quantities of instinctual aggression, while finite, vary vastly among individuals, it is difficult to see how a fixed-quantity, closed-system model of aggression could easily account for this well-established finding.

Other data provide further evidence. Anti-Jewish responses to questions asked in polls were most intense during the later stages of the World War II—presumably the high point in the nation's release of aggression. More important, Stember's data, together with those of Hyman and Sheatsley described above, prove that anti-Semitic and anti-Negro attitudes have since then undergone a sharp simultaneous decline. A similar conclusion is reached by G. M. Gilbert, who compared the stereotypes of ten groups as held by Princeton undergraduates of similar backgrounds in 1932 and in 1950:[72] Across the board, stereotypes had "faded" and lost their saliency. Data like these are what we would expect if the open-system model of aggression is correct.

Closed-system theorists might challenge such results on the grounds that the studies did not properly allow for substitute channels of aggression. Thus, some individuals might use prejudice against outgroups as their principal outlet for aggression, while others might channel all their aggressive energies in other directions. But research by Ross Stagner casts doubt upon this method of explaining away the findings of Stember and others.[73] Stagner found that students who channeled aggression in one direction were especially likely to channel it in others as well.

Finally, cross-cultural research further confirms Allport's position. S. T. Boggs found positive relationships between individual, group, and ideological aggression within societies; in war-oriented societies, individuals were inclined to behave aggressively toward one another, and myths and legends tended to be aggressive in content.[74]

Though such evidence is not conclusive, it weighs heavily in favor of Allport's open-system, feedback conception of aggression. We may therefore answer our basic question in the negative: available evidence suggests that a reduction in prejudice against one minority does *not* necessarily lead to any increase in prejudice against another. On the contrary, prejudices against different groups, even when shaped by somewhat different social forces, are likely to decline together.

Note that this expectation rejects only the Freudian closed-system or "drainage" theory, not the more limited displacement theory; it still allows for possible substitution of scapegoats. Just as in the South the Yankee long replaced the Jew as the object of superego stereotyping and hostility, so today the political establishment is perhaps substituting for the Jews as a target of animosity on the national scene. The phenomenon of transtolerance and other aspects of the radical right strongly suggest this possibility.[75] Incidentally, any such anti-elite bias would be noteworthy as evidence against the widely held dogma that scapegoats must be weak and vulnerable. In any event, such substitutions are possible, but not, according to the open-system model, inevitable.

Notes

1. A blatant exception is, of course, the Ku Klux Klan, which is still openly anti-Negro, anti-Jewish, and anti-Catholic. But, significantly, today's Klan is a mere ghost of the Klan of the 1920s; it is isolated in numbers and locale, shunned even by the vast majority of Southern segregationists.

2. D. Bell (ed.), *The Radical Right* (Garden City, N.Y.: Doubleday Anchor Books, 1963), p. 168.

3. *Ibid.*, p. 250.

4. *Ibid.*, p. 256. Similarly, Welch was "pleased" to reprint *Color, Communism and Common Sense* by Manning Johnson, a Negro and former member of the Communist Party.

5. *Ibid.*, p. 445.

6. F. Knebel, "Race Riots: Goldwater Boon," *Look*, September 22, 1964, p. 41.

7. Bell, *op. cit.*, pp. 442, 444.

8. C. H. Stember, *Jews in the Mind of America* (New York: Basic Books, Inc., 1966), pp. 31–47.

9. H. H. Hyman and P. B. Sheatsley, "Attitudes Toward Desegregation," *Scientific American*, July 1964, Vol. 211, No. 1, pp. 16–23.

10. Stember, *op. cit.*, pp. 69, 96, 104.

11. *Ibid.*, p. 81.

12. H. G. Erskine, "The Polls: Race Relations," *Public Opinion Quarterly*, 1962, Vol. 26, p. 139. It should be noted that the failure of this item to provoke different response patterns in 1946 and 1956 does not conflict with the earlier finding that there was a sharp reduction in anti-Negro prejudice. The item does not correlate well with known measures of prejudice.

13. I. de Sola Pool, R. P. Abelson, and S. L. Popkin, *Candidates, Issues, and Strategies: A Computer Simulation of the 1960 Presidential Election* (Cambridge, Mass.: M.I.T. Press, 1965).

14. *Ibid.*, p. 115.

15. G. W. Allport, *The Nature of Prejudice* (Cambridge, Mass.: Addison-Wesley Publishing Co., 1954), pp. 261–282. We shall explore in detail the implications of the latter process in Chapters 11 and 12.

16. See: Anti-Defamation League of B'nai B'rith, "A Study of Religious Discrimination by Social Clubs," *Rights*, 1962, Vol. 4, No. 3; "The Jewish Law Student and New York Jobs," *Rights*, 1964, Vol. 5, No. 4; "Employment of Jewish Personnel in the Automobile Industry," *Rights*, 1963, Vol. 5, No. 2; American Jewish Committee, *Patterns of Exclusion from the Executive Suite: The Public Utilities Industry*, December 1963.

17. H. Cantril, *The Politics of Despair* (New York: Basic Books, 1958).

18. *Ibid.*, p. 71.

19. The "ecological fallacy" is committed when the characteristics or behaviors of individuals (in this case, shifts of their opinion toward being anti-Negro) are inferred from data for groups only (in this case, statewide voting for an anti-Negro candidate). The fallacy is easily recognizable in some instances. For example, when we sample by city-block units, say in Chicago, we will find a high positive correlation between the percentages on each block of adult illiterates and of adult readers of comic books, though these group percentages obviously cannot represent the characteristics of the same individuals. For a thorough discussion of this common fallacy, see W. S. Robinson, "Ecological Correlations and the Behavior of Individuals," *American Sociological Review*, 1950, Vol. 15, pp. 351–357; H. Menzel, "Comment on Robinson's 'Ecological Correlations and the Behavior of Individuals,'" *American Sociological Review*, 1950, Vol. 15, p. 674; H. C. Selvin, "Durkheim's *Suicide* and Problems of Empirical Research," *American Journal of Sociology*, 1958, Vol. 63, pp. 607–619. All three papers may be found in S. M. Lipset and N. J. Smelser (eds.), *Sociology: The*

Progress of a Decade (Englewood Cliffs, N.J.: Prentice-Hall, 1961), pp. 132–152.

20. F. Powledge, "Poll Shows Whites in City Resent Civil Rights Drive," *The New York Times*, September 21, 1964, pp. 1, 26.

21. Information kindly supplied by Professor Peter Rossi, then the Director of N.O.R.C., and used with his permission.

22. This was also suggested in *The New York Times'* results, which showed large majorities of white New Yorkers supporting the employment title of the 1964 Civil Rights Act and stating that they would not be uncomfortable if some "nice" Negro families lived near them. Powledge, *op.cit.*

23. In this particular, too, *The New York Times* poll agreed as far as it went; indeed, a slightly larger majority favored Johnson over Goldwater than had chosen Kennedy over Nixon in 1960.

24. Once again, the findings of *The New York Times* poll agree with those of the more definitive N.O.R.C. study. Fifty-four percent of the New Yorkers interviewed felt the civil-rights movement "should slow down," and 49 percent felt nonviolent demonstrations "hurt the Negro's cause." See also: J. W. Carey, "An Ethnic Backlash?" *The Commonweal*, October 16, 1964, pp. 91–93.

25. For examples of these earlier polls, see S. Alsop and O. Quayle, "What Northerners Really Think of Negroes," *The Saturday Evening Post*, September 7, 1963, pp. 17–21; "How Whites Feel About Negroes: A Painful American Dilemma," *Newsweek*, October 21, 1963, pp. 44–57.

26. Erskine, *op. cit.*

27. American Institute of Public Opinion, press release, July 18, 1963.

28. American Institute of Public Opinion, press release, May 22, 1965. See also: *Integrated Education*, November–December 1969, Vol. 7, No. 6, pp. 51–52.

29. A large body of literature supports the proposition that people who generally do not vote are more apathetic, alienated, authoritarian, and uninformed than those who do. Relevant studies include G. M. Connelly and H. H. Field, "The Non-Voter—Who He Is, What He Thinks," *Public Opinion Quarterly*, 1944, Vol. 8, pp. 175–187; P. K. Hastings, "The Non-Voter in 1952: A Study of Pittsfield, Mass.," *Journal of Psychology*, 1954, Vol. 38, pp. 301–312; and "The Voter and the Non-Voter," *American Journal of Sociology*, 1956, Vol. 62, pp. 302–307; H. H. Hyman and P. B. Sheatsley, "Some Reasons Why Information Campaigns Fail," *Public Opinion Quarterly*, 1947, Vol. 11, pp. 412–423; M. Janowitz and D. Marvick, "Authoritarianism and Political Behavior," *Public Opinion Quarterly*, 1953, Vol. 17, pp. 185–201; S. M. Lipset, *Political Man* (Garden City, N.Y.: Doubleday & Co., 1960), pp. 79–103; F. H. Sanford, *Authoritarianism and Leadership* (Philadelphia: Institute for Research in Human Relations, 1950), p. 168; S. A. Stouffer, *Communism, Conformity, and Civil Liberties* (Garden City, N.Y.: Doubleday & Co., 1955).

30. B. Halpern, "Anti-Semitism in the Perspective of Jewish History," in Stember, *op. cit.*, pp. 273–301; and Stember, *op. cit.*, pp. 31–47.

31. B. Bettelheim and Morris Janowitz, *Social Change and Prejudice* (New York: The Free Press of Glencoe, 1964).

32. *Ibid.*; T. W. Adorno, E. Frenkel-Brunswik, D. J. Levinson, and R. N. Sanford, *The Authoritarian Personality* (New York: Harper & Bros., 1950). Each of these studies provides impressive case and quantitative data in support of this psychoanalytic interpretation of prejudice.

33. Direct evidence on the parallels between the American stereotype of the black and the Northern Italian stereotype of the Southern Italian is provided in M. W. Battacchi, *Meridionali e settentrionali nella struttura del pregiudizio etnico in Italia* [Southerners and Northerners in the Structure of Ethnic Prejudice in Italy] (Bologna: Società Editrice Il Mulino, 1959).

34. S. M. Elkins, *Slavery* (New York: Grosset & Dunlap, 1963).

35. Stember, *op. cit.*, pp. 50, 53.

36. B. Glass, "On the Unlikelihood of Significant Admixture of Genes from the North American Indians in the Crescent Composition of the Negroes of the United States," *American Journal of Human Genetics*, 1955, Vol. 7, pp. 368–385.

37. F. R. Kluckhohn, "Dominant and Variant Cultural Value Orientations," in H. Cabot and J. A. Kahl (eds.), *Human Relations*, Vol. 1 (Cambridge, Mass.: Harvard University Press, 1953), pp. 88–98.

38. B. C. Rosen, "Race, Ethnicity, and the Achievement Syndrome," *American Sociological Review*, 1959, Vol. 24, pp. 47–60.

39. E. F. Frazier, *Black Bourgeoisie* (New York: Collier Books, 1962). However, once socio-economic factors are controlled, there appear to be no sharp value differences between black and white Americans. See: M. Rokeach and S. Parker, "Values as Social Indicators of Poverty and Race Relations in America," *Annals of the American Academy of Political and Social Science*, 1970, Vol. 388, pp. 97–111.

40. Stember, *op. cit.*, p. 106.

41. In the Harris poll of whites in 1963, 84 percent objected to a "close friend or relative marrying a Negro," and 90 percent objected to their "own teen-age daughter dating a Negro." William Brink and Louis Harris, *The Negro Revolution in America* (New York: Simon & Schuster, 1964), p. 148. That these data are largely determined by racial, and not social class, considerations is indicated by similar results of other items which specify upper-status blacks.

42. T. F. Pettigrew, *A Profile of the Negro American* (Princeton, N.J.: D. Van Nostrand Co., 1964), p. 148.

43. *Ibid.*, Chapter IV.

44. Stember, *op. cit.*, p. 227. This is *not* to imply that upper-status individuals tend to be more anti-Semitic across many types of items. In recent years, this trend has if anything lessened, with some studies now showing greater anti-Semitism among lower-status Americans. See: G. J. Selznick and S. Steinberg, *The Tenacity of Prejudice: Anti-Semitism in Contemporary America* (New York: Harper & Row, 1969), Chapter 5.

45. Herbert H. Hyman and Paul B. Sheatsley, "Attitudes Toward Desegregation," *Scientific American*, December 1956, Vol. 195, No. 6, pp. 35–39.

46. Bell, *op. cit.*, p. 416; C. H. Stember, *Education and Attitude Change* (New York: Institute of Human Relations Press, 1961), p. 118.

47. Bell, *op. cit.*, p. 415.

48. Stember, *Education and Attitude Change, op. cit.*, p. 95. This relationship manifested itself strongly among persons with a high school or college education; it was, however, reversed among those with only a grammar school education.

49. *Ibid.*, p. 143.

50. *Ibid.*, pp. 62, 76.

51. R. M. Williams, Jr., *Strangers Next Door* (Englewood Cliffs, N.J.: Prentice-Hall, 1964), p. 52.

52. *Ibid.*

53. Bettelheim and Janowitz, *op. cit.*

54. *Ibid.*

55. Hyman and Sheatsley, *op. cit.* (1964).

56. *Ibid.*

57. Stember, *Jews in the Mind of America, op. cit.*, p. 224.

58. "The Fortune Survey," *Fortune*, February 1946, pp. 257–260; October 1947, pp. 5–10.

59. R. H. Knapp, "A Psychology of Rumor," *Public Opinion Quarterly*, 1944, Vol. 8, pp. 22–37.

60. See, for example, E. T. Prothro, "Ethnocentrism and Anti-Negro Attitudes in the Deep South," *Journal of Abnormal and Social Psychology*, 1952, Vol. 47, pp. 105–108.

61. Anti-Defamation League, "A Study of Religious Discrimination by Social Clubs," *op. cit.*

62. Stember, *Jews in the Mind of America, op. cit.*, p. 224.

63. Williams, *op. cit.*

64. *Ibid.*, p. 50.

65. These data are based on a secondary analysis by the writer of three national surveys by the National Opinion Research Center: Studies No. 294 (November 8, 1950), 342 (June 30, 1953), and 365 (November 26, 1954). The writer wishes to thank the Roper Public Opinion Research Center at Williams College and its director, Professor Philip K. Hastings, for making these studies available.

66. With the three surveys combined, these percentages involve 854 white Southerners and 201 Negro Southerners.

67. T. F. Pettigrew and M. Richard Cramer, "The Demography of Desegregation," *Journal of Social Issues*, 1959, Vol. 15, No. 4, pp. 61–71.

68. Not the actual name. Incidentally, this special role of the Jew provides an additional explanation for Ringer's finding that in the South Jews are generally perceived as being far less in favor of racial desegregation than they actually are. See Stember, *Jews in the Mind of America, op. cit.*, Chapter 9.

69. Allport, *op. cit.*, pp. 354–366.

70. *Ibid.*, pp. 68–81; Adorno, *et al., op. cit.*

71. E. L. Hartley, *Problems in Prejudice* (New York: Kings Crown Press, 1946).

72. G. M. Gilbert, "Stereotype Persistence and Change Among College Students," *Journal of Abnormal and Social Psychology*, 1951, Vol. 46, pp. 245–254.

73. R. Stagner, "Studies of Aggressive and Social Attitudes: 1. Measurement and Inter-relation of Selected Attitudes," *Journal of Social Psychology*, 1944, Vol. 20, pp. 109–120.

74. S. T. Boggs, *A Comparative Cultural Study of Aggression* (unpublished honors thesis, Social Relations Library, Harvard University, 1947).

75. Bell, *op. cit.*

16

A Rap on Race

MARGARET MEAD
AND JAMES BALDWIN

Margaret Mead and James Baldwin met for the first time on the evening of 25 August 1970. The preceding decade had been one of the most momentous in American history: the civil rights movement had brought a mixture of hope, redemption and disappointment. Black Power had, in many ways, superseded the more gradualist approaches of civil rights. The leaders, actual and symbolic, of the two movements had both been assassinated. New laws ending *de jure* legislation and prohibiting racial discrimination had been welcomed before the realization that legal prohibition was not necessarily followed by the disappearance of racism and discrimination. Rather, both assumed new, less obvious forms.

Mead, the noted anthropologist whose research had deepened her familiarity with a variety of cultures, and Baldwin, celebrated author of, among others, *The Fire Next Time, Notes of a Native Son* and *Go Tell It on the Mountain*, agreed to meet and talk about the issue of race in its most general sense. In early phases of their seven-and-a-half hour discussion, Mead brought up the subject of disparities of power in human relationships. It touched off an interesting passage in the discussion which revolved around, as Mead put it, "Power and fear" and which Baldwin linked to his own experiences growing up in Harlem.

This is the burden, in a sense, that in this country the black man and the white woman carried in plantation days. If a white woman made a mistake, or didn't remember who she was every single second, everyone would suffer. So you never forget you must never turn your back, never let anybody steal from you, keep your nerve. You have nothing but nerve to protect you. I lock up the guns when I am alone.

This is what we've had in the South. I'd read all the books, but I'd never gone south until 1942; and when I crossed the Mason-Dixon line I felt I was not in the United States, I was in New Guinea. Because this kind of thing isn't true in the North. It may crop up, but it isn't a Northern feeling, that you have to be aware of what you do every minute, every single minute. I've carried this burden to the point where it meant life and death every second. You think of those early days in the South, and the strongest men were the only ones that survived. Everybody else had died in the slave ships.

BALDWIN: Yes, that's true.

MEAD: So they were the strongest people and, on a plantation twenty miles from anywhere, left in charge of a white woman very often. And she carried everybody's lives in her hands and so did the strongest of the black men. They had to keep things steady.

BALDWIN: It's a devastating relationship, you know.

MEAD: All desperate relationships are devastating. I used to do a lot of lecturing on race in the 1940s, and I had some rules. People had to stand on their two feet to ask questions. To ask me if I wanted my daughter to marry a Negro, they were going to stand up and look me in the eye. And my answer was, "Yes, if she respects him and he respects her."

BALDWIN: Yes.

MEAD: "But," I added, "I think at the present moment that every marriage in Nazi Germany is a very bad marriage, because men don't respect women, and I don't think that any marriage is good unless both partners respect each other."

BALDWIN: That's it, of course.

MEAD: Now when you have any terrific disparity in power it produces terrible relationships.

BALDWIN: Yes. Of course, at the root of all this is power, isn't it?

MEAD: Power and fear.

BALDWIN: Which has become pathological. I went south very late, too. I went south for the first time, I guess, in 1957. I'd never been south before. Now I had, before that.... This was, I guess, my first real encounter with Southern racial terrors, because growing up in Harlem you know very soon why you're there and the white people feel very strange for you and it isn't true in the beginning that you hate them. It's just that you don't know who they are.

MEAD: You don't know who they are and you don't go near them.

BALDWIN: You don't go near them, but you feel menaced by them. All kinds of things happen in Harlem, but Harlem is a colored community. You know, everyone around me was colored. So the white thing didn't really break in completely. What really must have happened, I can see now, is that I blotted a lot of it out, out of pure panic. Because a kid doesn't know how to handle it, really.

My teachers were white, most of them. I didn't like most of them, but it wasn't because they were white that I didn't like them. It was just because they were strange. My favorite teacher happened to be a black lady; then, later on, a white school teacher who was a Communist. In those years everybody had to be a Communist, really, obviously, you know. If I had been three years older, I would have been a Communist, too. But she fed us and took me to the theater and things like that. And she was the first human being to sort of move out of that kind of monolithic mass that is composed of the landlords, the pawnbrokers and the cops who beat you up. She gave me my first key, my first clue that white people were human.

But I didn't keep that key very long, because I started working for the Army during the war. I was working for the first time with Southerners, and I had just never, never encountered this kind of madness before. I was a street boy; I grew up in Harlem. When you're small you've got to be quick and fairly agile and sharp-tongued, and you just didn't let anybody get away with anything, because you'd be dead if you did. So I walked around New Jersey working for the Army with people from Georgia, Alabama, Mississippi. I talked the way I always talked, acted the way I always acted, and I just couldn't believe what happened—the kind of fury that erupted. I told a white man from Georgia once that he was a liar. I wasn't being particularly hostile; I was just—

MEAD: You just thought he was a liar.

BALDWIN: I just thought that he was a liar and told him so. I'll never forget his face. It turned purple. It was the first time I was ever scared in my life, I must say, by another human being. But I saw something happen in his face: first it turned purple, then it turned absolutely white, and something happened in his eyes. I realized I was looking at death. That man wanted to kill me. If I had been alone I think he would have. And he was a much older man than I. I was only seventeen years old; he was about fifty. But a seventeen-year-old boy, because he was black, had managed to overturn his whole universe and he was about to kill me. That was my first rehearsal. That whole year, that whole time, is something that I've never been able to write about.

When I went south, I was a grown man. By this time—it's funny—I had a double reaction. I found myself in Montgomery, Alabama, and it wasn't the spirit of the people which was different or which surprised me, because by the time I was thirty-one I had given up expecting sanity from most white Americans. Essentially, I knew most white Americans were trapped in some stage of infantilism which wouldn't allow them to look at me as though I were a human being like themselves. I didn't expect them to. But I didn't expect what I found in the South, either. What happened to you is almost exactly what happened to me. I felt that I was walking on this rug, this wall-to-wall carpet. Beneath it is a complex system of wires, and one of those wires, if you step on it, will blow up the whole house.

MEAD: That's right.

BALDWIN: And everybody in the South knows where that wire is except me. I've got to cross this rug, too. But I don't know how I'm going to get across it, because every step I take is loaded with danger. Every time I open my mouth I'm wrong. The way I look at people is wrong. The way I sound is wrong. I am obviously not only a stranger in town, I'm an enemy. I've arrived with a bomb, because I'm a black from America in America.

MEAD: You're endangering everybody.

BALDWIN: I'm also endangering everybody else, which gives you another fear. Then you really get scared. When I worked with Medgar Evers for a little while, I would never dare open my mouth in front of other people around him. If he were working on a case or talking with white or black people, I wouldn't open my mouth because I had a Northern accent and I didn't know what that would trigger in the minds and hearts of the people he was talking to and what kind of danger it might place him in. He was already, God knows, in enough danger.

That's a grim, grim pathology. The situation forces you, the black cat in it, to become a party to it, whether you like it or not. You cannot escape the pathology of a country in which you're born. You can resist it, you can react to it, you can

do all kinds of things, but you're trapped in it. And your frame of reference is also the frame of reference of white people, no matter how you yourself try to deal with it. No matter what you tell your children, you're trapped: the despised darker brother in this great white man's house.

And the great, great problem then is how you are going to liberate yourself, first of all in the mind. Every objective fact which surrounds you simply bears witness to your degradation. And how in the world are you going to teach your child to grow up as a man when he sees daily how little anyone respects your manhood? The kid knows very well.

I knew it. I didn't know, I couldn't say, when my father came home from work, what my father's working day was like, but I did know that my father put on his bowler hat and his white shirt and his dark preacher's uniform every morning the Lord sent him, and with his little black lunch box in his hand he went someplace downtown, went to Long Island, where he was working in some factory, doing the most awful kind of hard labor. He made twenty-seven dollars and fifty cents a week all the years that I knew him. And he had nine children. He couldn't feed them, and of course he went—it was absolutely inevitable he would go mad.

How could he bear it? You can't quit the job if you've got those kids to feed. Your wife knows what you're going through, and if she loves you that makes it worse, because there is so little you can to do to protect her. Your children are growing up and they begin to despise you, because they don't think you're a man. And you find yourself, because you happen to be born in the United States of America about two thousand years too early—

MEAD: I don't think it's that long.

BALDWIN: Well, two thousand or two hundred or twenty, it doesn't make any difference if it's one man's life. You go under. The crime or the pathology, which come to the same thing, is that it was not, it is not, being done by accident. It is not bizarre; it is not something like an act of God. It is something that has been done deliberately and is being done deliberately.

MEAD: Well, you know, I think you've got to stop there and think a little bit about history. Just consider for a minute if we never invented boats.

BALDWIN: Yes, where would England be.

MEAD: If we never invented boats, we would never have the problem we have today. If everybody had to walk, because they couldn't walk very far in a lifetime, they would stop and make love to the local girls. And gradually they would have moved from Africa, over Europe, getting paler and paler. But it would take a thousand years, and by the time they got to Sweden and got those pale blue eyes, and light skin so that they would enjoy what sun there was, because there wasn't much there—now, it would have taken thousands of years, and it would have been imperceptible. From the blackest group in Africa all the way up to the blond people up in Scandinavia.

But you see what happened was boats. And people are always taking boats and tearing along coasts and across seas, putting people side by side that contrast so sharply. Now, I think, we have talked a lot in this country.... One of the things I'm not sure of is whether it is one of the things worth discussing here—about generations—but in one way you and I belong to the same generation, in that we're prewar.

BALDWIN: We're pre-atomic age.

MEAD: These are the things we thought about and talked about. And they used to say children don't have any race prejudice. We heard that until the sacred cows screamed.

BALDWIN: "We've got to be taught to hate."

MEAD: That's what people said, that race feeling is all learned. Well, it isn't. It's true, you've got to be taught to hate, but the appreciation and fear of difference is everywhere.

BALDWIN: That's right.

MEAD: And I've seen—plenty of people in this country have seen a white child who got used to a black face and black hands, and then the black person took off his shirt and they screamed because they sort of thought that this black face and black hands belonged to a white body. But I've seen a black child do the same thing with a white man—scream with fear—because, you know, there *is* a conspicuous difference between a black skin and a white skin. In New Guinea the children scream with fear when they first see white people, just as much as white people scream with fear, because the contrast is too great. What we did on this earth with ships was to travel great distances. You could pick up people and take them far away, and as a result we've got these tremendous contrasts that try the souls of people. I think you've got to realize one other thing about white people, and that is that a white skin is a terrible temptation.

BALDWIN: How do you mean, exactly? But I think I know what you mean.

MEAD: Because we look like angels, you know that?

BALDWIN: I was going to get to that. Go on.

MEAD: You see, when those Angles from England were taken to Rome to be sold as slaves—were being sold as slaves in the marketplace—and a pope came along and looked at these slaves and he said, "What are they called?" and somebody said Angles and he said, "Oh, no, not Angles, angels...." Now that meant way back when Christianity was a Mediterranean religion. But angels were white. The dead, you see, are white everywhere, because the bones are white and people associate the dead with skeletons and ghosts. Then you have angels and they are white. Now you get a group of people coming along—

BALDWIN: Who are also white.

MEAD: When the first people landed in Australia, the Australian aborigines thought they were the ghosts of their ancestors coming back. When Cortez landed in Mexico, he was greeted as the fair god; as far as we know there had never been any white people there. This was a dream of the dead. Now, it is not good for people's character—

BALDWIN: To be identified with angels.

MEAD: —to look like angels; it makes them behave very badly.

BALDWIN: That's very strange, because the root of it is somewhere there, it seems to me, and that's deeper, I suppose, isn't it, than one would like to think?

MEAD: That's terribly, terribly deep, I think.

BALDWIN: Deeper than churches.

MEAD: But you know, there is something else about it, too. That is, it makes a difference whether you say white or light or bright. Funny, they all rhyme!

BALDWIN: Yes. "Light, bright and damn near white."

MEAD: You see, I've lived in a place where there wasn't any fire unless you make it with two little pieces of wood, a fire plow. People guard fire very carefully in such a place. And there is no light at night but the little embers of the fire, and you're terribly afraid. You can't make light easily; there is only a little spot of light in the darkness, and so people have been afraid of the dark always.

BALDWIN: Which is also identified with what? With death?

MEAD: Well, you see, with danger.

BALDWIN: With danger, yes.

MEAD: With danger. With terrible danger. Thieves come out of the night when there isn't any moon. Headhunters raid the camps. Wild beasts are only held off by the fire. When there is a moon it is lovely; you can dance all night. But when there is no moon the thieves get you. The enemy gets you. Anything can get you. You don't know what.

Now I think electric lights are going to get rid of that one. Our children aren't afraid of the dark, not the ones who have lived in the city with electric lights. They press a button and the world is flooded, and they don't ever have to grow up with a fear of the dark.

BALDWIN: All that's very gloomy, in a way. It's going to be a very long time before we conquer what is essentially a tribal—

MEAD: It is before tribalism. This is, you know, just peoples' feeling about the way they look themselves. Then you get the contrast between black and white in the same group.

There was a little albino girl in Samoa, and they used to call her my sister. She had pink eyes and pale, blemished skin. To them she looked like me. And there is a strain of people in Samoa with honey-colored hair. Fathers used to grow their daughters' hair and sell it for wigs. Everybody made wigs of this honey-colored hair because people thought it was so beautiful. This went way back before there were any white people there at all. And everywhere one goes there are such contrasts. Now, when it's a little contrast it doesn't matter, but when it is a big contrast people do—

BALDWIN: But nobody knows where they come from really. That's why we have so many—

MEAD: I noticed you used the word ... something about dark deeds.

BALDWIN: That's right. You know, I'm obviously—

MEAD: You're speaking "bloody English."

BALDWIN: I'm working in the English language, yes.

MEAD: But we find it also in African languages, you see. That's the thing that's so strange.

BALDWIN: Yes, or else not strange. That's what you're saying.

MEAD: Well, what I'm saying is it's understandable that this association of white and good and ghosts and all of these things.... And now there are other people: Alvin—

BALDWIN: Poussaint, the black psychiatrist.

MEAD: He makes a great deal about the association between black and dirt.

BALDWIN: Yes, I know another psychiatrist who does, too.

MEAD: But I don't think that's nearly as important. I think the point is brightness versus darkness and the fear of the dark. My little girl once said, "What's fear, what does it mean to be afraid?" She had never recognized anything to be afraid of, and I took her by the hand and stood her in the doorway of a totally dark room. "Look in there," I said. "That's what people mean when they say they're afraid." So I think that one has to consider that white people—Europeans, and this is all Europeans—I mean, just as you recognized in your book, that all Europeans have a deadly temptation to feel a sense of biological superiority.

BALDWIN: What you're saying comes close to suggesting that one of the reasons for the riddle of white supremacy is that all of a sudden there is some universal impulse to identify with light and fire. It is not merely historical—

MEAD: Universal perception.

BALDWIN: Yes. It is not merely an historical or theological aberration, let's say, but it comes out as something profound in everybody's nature.

MEAD: In everybody's nature.

BALDWIN: That's a weird and frightening perspective, isn't it, in a way?

MEAD: You see, I think it can be eliminated, now that we don't have to be afraid of the dark.

BALDWIN: Of course, but we have so many other things to be afraid of.

MEAD: Yes, but just the same, if brightness is something everybody can have from the time they're born—

BALDWIN: But it will be a long time before brightness becomes something everybody can have from the day they're born.

MEAD: We're all moving that way. Most people have electricity, acquaintance with electric lights. In the past no one knew that there was such a thing as immediate light flooding the world with brightness. A bunch of burning coconut leaves doesn't light anything. You know, it just makes a spot. There is no—

BALDWIN: It doesn't illuminate.

MEAD: No illumination.

BALDWIN: White people are in some sense a kind of tragic case.

MEAD: Yes, but you see it's a part of you also. Of course, in any oppressive situation both groups suffer, the oppressors and the oppressed. The oppressed suffer physically: they are frightened, they're abused, they're poor. But the oppressors suffer morally.

BALDWIN: Which is a worse kind of suffering.

MEAD: Because they have to deny something in themselves. Now, one of the things I wanted to ask you about.... I took a friend of mine who lives in Paris to the performance of Genet's *The Blacks* that was given over here. He had seen the performance that was given at the Musée de l'Homme, which was acted by Africans, young Africans—anthropologists, I suppose—and he said it was a sacrament of hate.

BALDWIN: Really?

MEAD: You know, when they gave it over here they kept clowning all the time. Did you see it?

BALDWIN: I saw it here, yes. St. Marks Playhouse.

MEAD: It was just on the edge of clowning all the time.

BALDWIN: Yes, that's true.

MEAD: And they were just the poorest haters I've ever seen loose. They really were!

BALDWIN: That's true. I think that Jean Genet's *Blacks* on some level is a very frightening play. It is a very intimidating play. I was somewhat involved with the production in New York because I knew the director and I knew a lot of people in the cast, and I was over there a few times during rehearsal. I realized that many of the black people in the cast were—or all the black people in the cast had ... how can I put this?—were not exactly ashamed, but there was something in Genet's tone—

MEAD: That was wrong for them.

BALDWIN: There was something that was merciless in the tone of the play and the perceptions of the play. It's a very black play indeed, a much blacker play than any American I know of would be able to conceive or write.

MEAD: That's right.

BALDWIN: *Nobody* gets away, the way he structured it. It's just an absolutely grim circle which is going to go on and on and on and on forever, according to Genet. Whether one agrees with this or not is not the point.

MEAD: But that's what the play is.

BALDWIN: And in order to play it you have to reach a level in yourself which not many people are able to do, really. And the reason I think that it was always on the edge of clowning is because the people in the play, even unconsciously, and perhaps the director too, even unconsciously, had to protect themselves against this really ghastly vision in which everybody after all is utterly condemned. You know, there isn't anybody in that play worth anything. They're all absolute monsters and horrors.

[* * *]

Now, up to about thirty years ago there really were no black people in the South who hadn't received some kindness from white people. There were hardly any black doctors then, or black teachers, or black dentists, or black trained nurses; Huey Long got black nurses into the hospitals by making speeches about all the white nurses nursing black people. Almost everywhere—unless you lived in the very far reaches of some rural area—black people had their wounds bound up by white people.

BALDWIN: And vice versa.

MEAD: It isn't quite vice versa, because there were these pockets of poor whites where there were no blacks at all. These poor whites were caught in the middle because the blacks despised them and the other whites despised them. They just didn't have any life at all. In 1942 I started saying, "We've got to hurry, while there are still people who—"

BALDWIN: Remember this. The kindness.

MEAD: —who remember this, and who have received kindness from each other's hands.

BALDWIN: That's not true anymore. It's not true at all.

MEAD: That's it, you see. This is the thing that's happened. In institutions like Hampton Institute, with its middle-class black students—some quite wealthy—there are many, I believe, who never received a kindness from a white person in their whole lives.

BALDWIN: Didn't know any white people personally—in fact, at all.

MEAD: Never saw them, and this scared them. When they come out into the white world they're able to hate them because they are hating a stranger, and it's very easy to hate a stranger. But it's hard to hate the thing that's close to you, and this was the South thirty years ago.

BALDWIN: Until thirty years ago.

MEAD: Until we began getting a whole educated group of black doctors, black lawyers–

BALDWIN: Until the Second World War, which altered the economy. It shifted everybody's relations and made the whole patriarchal thing, which is what we are

essentially talking about, obsolete. It became obsolete nearly overnight.

MEAD: And the style that those actors were still acting in when they gave The Blacks was in the old style of black-white relations.

BALDWIN: I don't know what would happen if one did that play now. There's a very unfortunate sentimentality that surrounds the whole question of color in America. It's unfortunate. And The Blacks is not in the least sentimental. Yet everyone in America, including black people, has always on some level—or, if not always, often—been necessarily blinded by a kind of hope which was simply sentimental, in that it did not refer to reality. Even the civil rights movement was stained with a kind of sentimentality which sometimes drove me nearly mad. I admired those kids very much. I thought that everybody was possessed with tremendous devotion and tremendous belief. Yet it is a very sentimental country. The American consciousness is sentimental in just as bad a way as the German consciousness, which means that they never see anything clearly. This applies to black people, too. Now I think something else is happening. I think now with The Blacks it might … the production might err in the direction of a kind of sentimentality of rage.

MEAD: It would still be sentimental.

BALDWIN: It would still be sentimental.

MEAD: You know, I put your kind of writing beside Louise Bogan or Will Gibson. They both happen to be Irish people who as children had a living language around them and then just went in and got English literature from nowhere. Louise Bogan's parents were hardly literate, and she used to say that when she was sixteen she walked into the Boston Public Library and took Keats off the shelf.

BALDWIN: It's almost exactly what I did.

MEAD: First you had the liveliness of a living language around you. I think that's necessary. But then you hadn't been corrupted by anything low-level or any nonsense in between, really.

BALDWIN: That's very true. I never thought about it quite that way until much, much later. But in the very beginning I was surrounded by the people in the church and all that music and all that fantastic imagery. Of course, as a kid you don't react to it that way, but it's in you.

MEAD: All the way inside.

BALDWIN: I used to tell my mother, when I was little, "When I grow up I'm going to do this or do that. I'm going to be a great writer and buy you this and buy you that." And she would say, very calmly, very dryly, "It's more than a notion." That kind of dry understatement which characterizes so much of black speech in America is my key to something, only I didn't know it then.

Then I started reading. I read everything I could get my hand on, murder mysteries, *The Good Earth*, everything. By the time I was thirteen I had read myself out of Harlem. There were two libraries in Harlem, and by the time I was thirteen I had read every book in both libraries and I had a card downtown for Forty-second Street, which is where I first encountered a white policeman. But that's another story.

But that has a lot to do with—what I had to do then was bring the two things together: the possibilities the books suggested and the impossibilities of the life *around* me. Of course, by this time I was in some kind of collision without quite knowing it, with the assumptions of the … what we will call the master language and the facts of life as it, life, was being presented to me. Dickens meant a lot to me, for example, because there was a rage in Dickens which was also in me.

MEAD: Well, the subject matter—

BALDWIN: And *Uncle Tom's Cabin* meant a lot to me because there was a rage in her which was somehow in me. Something I recognized without knowing what I recognized, if you know what I mean.

Later on, when I went away to Paris and found myself, I had to think all this through. I found myself in Paris partly because I realized that I couldn't live in America on the assumptions by which I lived really, and quite unconsciously because…. I was very young, and the assumptions of the people by whom I was surrounded, who now were white people, were so fatally different that I was really in trouble. I was in danger of *thinking* myself out of existence, because a black, an unknown helpless black boy, wandering around the way I did and thinking the way I thought, was obviously a dangerous kind of freak. Obviously, you say what you think, and there is no way to hide what you think. People look at you with great wonder and great hostility, and I got scared because I could see that I wouldn't be able to function in this world or even in this language, and I went away.

But I began to think in French. I began to understand the English language better than I ever had before; I began to understand the English language which I came out of, the language that produced Ray Charles or Bessie Smith or which produced all the poets who produced me. A kind of reconciliation began which could not have happened if I had not stepped out of the English language. It's a very strange kind of odyssey, but I think in one way it explains a lot about Black American literature.

For the sake of argument there are two kinds of poets: the kind of respectable poet represented by Countee Cullen, who essentially used a borrowed idiom and did very interesting things with it, but very minor things, and a poet like Gwendolyn Brooks, who really picks up her language out of the streets. She knows Shakespeare and Blake and Milton and she can make marvelous alliterations and marvelous ironies and perceptions, because she lives in both languages. In a sense she's creating—and that's what you're doing anyway if you're a writer—in a sense re-creating the language.

But you can only re-create it out of human speech, so in a sense black poets are putting, for the first time in the history of the world, the experience of black people into what has been essentially a white language. It's one of the great unconscious contributions America has made, because the way Americans speak is really tremendously influenced and stained by their relationship to black men. It has made a whole new language which doesn't yet exist, for example, in

England or anywhere else where English is spoken. And black people elsewhere in the world—I began to realize when I was in London and Africa—black people who come from the colonies are just beginning to feel not exactly at home in the West but uneasy in the West.

17

Portraits of White Racism

DAVID T. WELLMAN

'When people speak of racism they usually mean attitudes rather than institutionally generated inequality,' wrote David Wellmann in the opening chapter of his study *Portraits of White Racism*. The chapter is entitled "Prejudiced people are not the only racists in America" and this conveys precisely Wellmann's central argument. He acknowledged that research on attitudes is a legitimate area of inquiry, but argued that prejudice should not be conflated with racism. If it is, then 'the crucial feature of race relations in America becomes the *ideas* that whites have about others; not their own superior position, the benefits following from their position, or the institutions that maintain this relationship' (p. 21).

His own work attempted to break away from the analytical tradition that 'begins with ideals' and affords those ideals causal primacy. While both Myrdal and his critic Cox anchored their analyses in different spheres, neither managed to escape the tradition. According to Wellmann: 'Cox and Myrdal see different functions performed by prejudiced attitudes; but for Cox, as well as Myrdal, racial antagonisms are set in motion by racist ideas rather than institutionally generated conflict.' Wellmann's focus was on such conflict. His interviews were 'portraits' of racism which collectively formed a wider vista. Gene Danich was one of his subjects. Here he talks about Black Power.

"EQUALITY MEANS AIN'T NOBODY BETTER THAN ANYBODY ELSE"

Gene may be isolated from black people; their problems may not be his own. But he is certainly not insulated from the issues they raise. He is regularly bombarded by radio, television, and newspaper accounts of black power, riots, busing, and Black Panthers. The black men he works with talk about racial issues all the time. Gene relates to these issues in a pragmatic sort of way. He does not really have a distinct, integrated way of seeing the world. Thus he sorts and sifts through issues and topics as they confront him and takes a position based on what he thinks are his best interests in each case.

Gene is no longer the frightened high school youth who saw blacks only in fearful one-dimensional terms. Now he is most impressed by the difficulty of their situation and the unfairness of it all. He thinks blacks have a much "rougher" life than white people. The majority of people in the world are

white and "they're all down on the colored people."
Not all whites, he points out. The majority of whites
are not down on colored people *outwardly*. But
inwardly many of them say "don't let them marry
my sister." The problem is that a lot of people have
"this prejudice inside them which they just keep in
and won't let out." People who let it out, in Gene's
estimation, are "sons of bitches," and he stays away
from them because "I don't like people who are that
radical."

Prejudice is not the main problem facing black
people, in Gene's view. As he sees it "insufficient
education opportunities" is a much more crucial
issue; "all of their problems, as a race and as a
group of people, would stem from that." He knows
that blacks do not have "as good jobs" as white
people, but that is because they are not well educated. And because of that, they get a reputation for
being "crooks." But "what else can a man do?" he
asked. "He's got to have some money." If a man has
no education he cannot get a job; or if "because of
his color" he cannot get a job, he has to get the
money somehow. Sometimes he has to "hit somebody over the head" for it. "That's just the way it
goes." But as far as Gene is concerned, "it ain't
gonna make no difference if he's black or white." If
a man has no education he is going to be "a crook."
The way he figures it, "a man's got to have coins."

Gene is not sure how to solve the problem. He
gets upset by some of the proposals he hears, and by
some of the leaders he reads about or watches on
television. He thinks Malcolm X's separatism is
wrong. Gene breaks the world down in zero-sum
terms; there is only so much to go around. The way
he sees it there cannot be "two wholly separate
communities and both communities have all the
best advantages." As he calculates it, "there aren't
that many best advantages available separately." If
the "best advantages" are put together in a "lump,"
they might cover everybody. "But you can't make
two lumps out of that and have them both be the
same size lumps," he concluded.

The issue of separatism does not excite Gene.
Stokely Carmichael[2] does. "Oh man," he exclaimed,
"I'd shoot that son of a gun dead in the head if I had
half a chance; Carmichael is nothing but a trouble-
maker. You can't name one single thing that
Stokely Carmichael does, that *I* know about, that's
constructive." The only thing Gene has seen him do
is "get that shit stick and stir the pot"; "everything
he does is to tear something down." Gene does not
think that what Carmichael is tearing down is
"right," however. He realizes that sometimes "you
got to tear some things down to build some things

up." But as far as he can tell, Carmichael "isn't
building nothing; he ain't even *trying* to."

Gene does not claim to know much about
Carmichael; just what he reads in the paper and sees
on television. But what he knows he dislikes. All he
sees is Carmichael making "big speeches," "going
to Cuba," and "thumbing his nose" at the United
States. He acts like a lot of other "big shots" who
make his jaws tight. In his estimation, "that dude
Stokely or Malcolm wants to be an all-powerful
being, somebody that's better than me, and he ain't
no more man than me in any way, shape, or form."

Gene is convinced that Carmichael wants to be
the 'all-powerful race messiah of the black people";
he wants to "run everything." Gene "can't go for
that." "Nobody needs to have that kind of power,"
he declared. In his estimation, black people need
money, not a messiah. Blacks have it hard because
they have no money; they have no way to get out of
trouble. If a man has money in the bank he can go
to court and buy his way out. But what does Stokely
Carmichael offer? "Stirring up more shit," he said,
answering his own question.

Gene is not "down on" all black leaders or strategies for racial change. He likes Martin Luther
King, although he is not too familiar with the man's
philosophy. He knows King is nonviolent. But nonviolence itself does not appeal to Gene; that would
be too hypocritical. What he likes best is that King's
approach does not involve him. As he put it, "King
is not trying to be *better* than me."

He has no problem with the idea of black
power, either. As he sees it, black power is black
people "bringing themselves to a position where if
a white man says, 'I'm going to throw you out,'
he can't." Gene defines the idea with one word:
"equality."

His notion of equality is concrete. "It means that
you ain't no different than me; ain't nobody any
better than anybody else." But equality does not
mean intermarriage. As far as Gene can tell, as long
as the earth rolls around, a majority of white people
will be against that. But with regard to other things
in life, like having opportunities, equality means
things will be "even." And black power is the
means for achieving it."

Black power is also an attitude toward white
people. Gene thinks the black man is "registering
his independence; his indignation with his treatment." And where there is a possibility of achieving
this objective, "black power is that group movement." Black power is "the banding together" of
black people. And Gene respects that.

Alex detected a problem with this formulation.
"Do you realize black power originated from
Stokely Carmichael?" he pointed out. Yes, Gene
was aware of that.

"But yet you disagree with Stokely Carmichael
and you prefer Martin Luther King over him. How
do you explain that?"

---

[2] Chairman of the Southern-based Student Nonviolent
Coordinating Committee, or "SNICK," the controversial
Carmichael was considered by many people to have origi-
nated the "black power" slogan.

"Cause Martin Luther King is not trying to be better than me. And hell, King's really a do-nothing. I mean what did the March on Washington do? Wheee. People took a big walk and wore out their shoes. Maybe if he was making shoes and selling them then he'd be doing something. But he's not doing nothing. What's he done?"

"You ain't gonna put me in the bag of having to defend King, man. But what you say raises a problem. I'm talking about what they can do for black people and you're talking in terms of how they relate to you. Now you believe that Martin Luther King isn't doing anything for black people?"

"Right."

"You believe black power *is* doing something for black people?"

"Right."

"But you disagree with Stokely?"

"Right. Look, what I'm saying is that as relates to what either of those two people are doing for black people I feel Stokely is doing more for them by virtue of the fact that he is doing *something*. Even if it's nothing but just stirring up shit – and he's sure doing that! But King? What's King doing? If Stokely's doing anything he's doing more than King."

"I don't understand, man. If you think King ain't doing nothing why do you disagree with Stokely?"

"Because he's trying to be better than me and he's trying to be better than everybody else."

"Why do you say that?"

"I don't really know any specific instances. I just get the feeling from reading about Stokely Carmichael that he wants to be the best of everything, of *everybody*. And everybody includes me. I don't like nobody to think he's better than me. Like big Dave down at the hall; he thinks he's better than everybody, man. As far as he's concerned, his shit don't stink. Big Dave ain't no better than me either."

"I'm having trouble pinning you down, Gene. I'm trying to get at this discrepancy because first you say you believe that he's doing something for black people but then you say what he's doing for black people ain't half as important as what he's saying in terms of being better."

"He's not doing anything constructive that I know about."

"But yet you think that's better than King."

"Yeah. What's King doing for black people? He's doing nothing. At least Stokely's stirring them up; they're getting mad."

"But yet you prefer King over Stokely!"

"Yes."

"So what you're saying is that the most important thing isn't that he's doing something for black people. The most important thing is how he relates to other people – specifically *you*. And you're saying that how he relates to you is more important than what he is doing for black people."

"To me it is, yes."

"Why is that more important than what he's doing for black people? Why should you give a damn *how* Stokely relates to you? Why would you give a damn about how he helps black people? Why would you even concern yourself with Stokely Carmichael and his superiority over everybody? Why, man?"

"Look, man, what Martin Luther King is doing cannot possibly ever come back on me. You see. Because he's not doing nothing. He's leading a march down the street. Well walk down the goddamn street. I don't give a fat rat's ass. But what Stokely Carmichael is doing is better for the black people because he's stirring them up. He gives them energy and ambition to do something. You see? And if I was a black man I would *have* to relate to Stokely Carmichael because he's stirring things up; he's getting me going see? And he's getting all my brothers going. See? He's making things roll. But as he relates to *me*, and *I* am white you know, the way I see what Stokely Carmichael does is stir up a lot of shit that could break out into something that might *involve* me."

"Involve you how?"

"A riot. I'm driving down the street in Oakland and somebody throws a rock through my window. Oh I'd be mad. Ohhh, I'd be mad! Understand? See, I get pretty hot. But I don't mess with nobody else and I don't expect them to mess with me. You see? What Stokely Carmichael does is likely to involve me in something I dislike; something I would definitely not agree with; something I would not want to be a part of. Now that's as opposed to what Martin Luther King does. I don't see any way in the world he can wrap me up in what he's doing. In other words Martin Luther King is not likely to do anything that would involve me in a riot, a fight, burn my house down, or anything like that. Does that make it clear?"

"Yeah. I guess so."

"I hate to make it hard for you man," Gene sighed, "but it ain't easy. I mean it just ain't easy."

For the most part Gene's feelings about racial controversies are ambivalent; his clear-cut attitudes toward King and Carmichael, black power and separatism are exceptions to the rule. When Gene hears people talking about "integration," for example, he thinks of schools. And he has a rather self-serving notion of what that means. It means that kids go to the school "closest" to their homes. If the school system in his town were not integrated, that would mean black kids in his town were being bused to Oakland and white kids living in Oakland were being bused to his all-white town. Gene would be a "mad son of a bitch" if his son had to go to school across town; "someone would pay for it."

Nevertheless, Gene's feelings about the matter are tangled up by conflicting emotions. He feels his kids are "disadvantaged" because they have few opportunities to associate with black children. If they went to integrated schools they would gain "understanding"; something he never had until the Marines. Yet he is not sure he would be willing to have his children bused in order to attend integrated schools. He might be willing if some "purpose was achieved"; if the kids got something out of it. But why pay to send them miles to school and then not get something out of it? He cannot see what is being achieved by busing programs that currently exist. Politicians may get black votes; but he wonders what the children get. He saw an idea on television that he liked. Some black students from a San Francisco high school went down to an all-white school on the peninsula and they all spent the day getting to know each other. Gene thinks "that's great." He would have "given anything" for something like that when he was their age. But busing for its own sake? He "can't go for that."

Integration means schools to Gene; it definitely does not mean interracial marriage. In his estimation, interracial marriage is not a very significant strategy for helping blacks. The way he sees it, if colored people are ever going to have the opportunities other people have – "if my opportunities are yours and if my son's opportunities are your son's," he explained to Alex – "then it's got to be in the schools." As far as Gene can tell, mixed marriage is quite a rare thing. "Nothing that small could ever be as important as something as big as integration in the schools."

Gene has other reservations about interracial marriages. He thinks white people are very sensitive about it. White men feel "impugned" when a white woman goes to bed with a black man. From what he can tell, instead of getting mad at the Negro they get mad at the white girl for even being around a black man.

Gene finds it difficult to talk about the topic; Alex had to push him to be specific. Gene has a daughter of his own and Alex asked what his feelings would be if she were to marry a black man. Gene sighed and then thought about the question. He did not think it would bother him one bit if it happened in the future, some other day and age. He "wouldn't like it to happen right now" and he has one main reason for that feeling. He would worry about her children. From what he gathers, white people "would put them kids down." He is especially concerned about the treatment they might receive at the hands of other kids. He knows kids can be rough on each other and when a couple of them gang up on another, that one has it bad. If his daughter were married to a black man and they had children, other kids' parents would "talk about it." The kids would overhear it and it could only be a "disaster" for his potential grandchildren. He does not want his grandchildren exposed to that.

But what if the children were raised in the black community, Alex wanted to know. That way they might have a place; they might not be ostracized. Gene's voice grew small. "If they had a place that would be great." In his estimation "kids are fabulous, they got to have everything"; kids are "all we got, there ain't nothing else. Once you're gone, that's all you got left." He would be for whatever is "best for kids."

But Gene was not really happy with that formulation. He does not think it is feasible for kids to spend their whole lives "hiding from everything else in the world"; spending their lives in some ghetto so "nobody'll talk about them." What if they just stayed in the ghetto, Alex asked? Gene was not too sure about that either. He wanted to know if the kids could come out one black and one white. "I don't know how they come out," he laughed nervously. "It varies," said Alex. But if one were colored and one white and they brought friends over to the house there would still be problems, Gene insisted. What if they both had dark complexions, Alex countered. That was fine with Gene; those two kids would have a place, a community of their own.

He was not convinced that was possible, however. He could not get a handle on the "full story." "I don't know Negro people," he said, running out of patience, "I don't know how they feel." He was not sure the kids would be accepted in the black community, or even if there was a black community. But he does know how white people feel, and that sooner or later the kids would have to come in contact with them. That would be "disastrous." When Gene thinks about all the possibilities he goes in a circle and ends up where he began. Interracial marriages are possible in the future where they could be a "perfectly normal, natural thing." But not now. The kids would "suffer."

Riots are something else Gene goes round and round about. He has strong feelings about the issues they raise; but nothing as simple as whether he is for or against them. He is not sure that taking things, breaking windows and stealing furniture, is necessary. But he also wonders if there is any other way for people living in riot areas to get "that stuff." He does not know; he has never seen places like Watts or Chicago. So riots might be "all right." He is still troubled by the issue because he knows "it ain't right to steal." He is caught between conflicting senses of morality. Should he evaluate riots by the biblical notion of thou shalt not steal, or by his own standards of fairness? Gene wonders whether the people who own stores in the ghetto have been giving black people a "screwing"; "14 percent every week or something like that." If that is true, the guy is "supposed to get robbed." The way Gene sees it, "he's supposed to be a loser 'cause he's been putting it on people." But he is not really sure which picture is the correct one.

He is convinced about one thing, however. He does not "go for throwing rocks at firemen." "That's crazy"; "it's wrong as two left feet." As Gene sees it, "that cat's in there risking *his* ass to put out *your* fire" and hitting him in the head with a rock is "stupid." What good does it do to shoot him, Gene wonders. "The poor son of a bitch is just doing his job." As far as Gene can tell, all firemen do is put out fires. Shooting at them, throwing rocks, "that ain't right."

Shooting at cops, on the other hand, might be justified in Gene's estimation. He can imagine a situation where a cop gets a couple colored guys "up against the wall" and starts hitting them with his stick. "That cop's *supposed* to be shot," as far as Gene is concerned. He believes black claims about police brutality – "there can't be all that much smoke without some fire" – but he does not accept *all* the talk about police brutality. His younger brother is a policeman in a South Bay town and sometimes Gene can see things from the policeman's angle. He thinks cops are sometimes brutal because they see so much and have to put up with "bull shit" from everybody. As far as Gene can tell, an honest cop's job is "just like riding down a sewer in a glass-bottom boat"; they see all the "worst" society has to offer. He thinks this probably helps make them brutal, but is not really sure it is the only reason. Some of the cops he knows around town are "more interested in being all-powerful unto themselves, like a god, than they are in doing a job."

Their job, as far as he is concerned, is to "protect the property and the lives of those persons who pay taxes in their jurisdiction." Whether Gene consciously meant to exclude people who do not pay taxes is uncertain, but he clearly feels that police should use any means necessary to protect at least the people who do. If somebody beats up on his kid, cops are supposed to "get that stopped," no matter how.

As Gene sees it, the cop's job is "to maintain law and order." And by that Gene does not mean "to keep blacks in their place." He is talking about something that is both more general and more personal than that. Why should certain demonstrations be stopped and not others, he asked. Should they be stopped because they offend the mayor or the police? No. If people are holding a demonstration in a park where no one is being bothered, "well let that one go." "That ain't got nothing to do with law and order." But if people demonstrate in front of the tunnel connecting the East Bay with Walnut Creek, and people cannot get to work, "*that* demonstration got to come to a stop." In Gene's mind, law and order is violated when "something causes trouble for most people." And then the cop's job is to stop it.

Gene feels rather "selfish" on the topic; "if something gets in *my* way," he said, then it is against law and order. When a teenager abandoned his "junk car" across the street from Gene's house, it was offensive – not only to the neighborhood, but to Gene personally. People see the car in front of his house and "relate a bunch of junk" to him. Gene is bothered by that because he has $20,000 invested in the house and does not want people to associate his investment with "junk." Maintaining law and order in this instance means that the police have "got to get that car removed" because it offends Gene and he is a taxpayer.

Gene has not figured out what to make of the Black Panthers; he has not sorted out a stance toward them with which he is comfortable. Compared to his feelings about Martin Luther King, he "totally disagrees" with them. He thinks "they're like the cops; they would rather be god than do a job." He also gets the impression that "they want to be these all-powerful beings." And Gene "just doesn't dig all-powerful beings; that's all there is to it."

But that is not really all there is to it. Gene "kind of goes along with" the Panthers' idea of arming the black community to protect itself. He thinks black people need "to do something" to help themselves. He agreed most with "the original intent" of the idea; it was right for them to "give a guy a twelve-gauge shotgun and teach him how to use it." That way if some "son of a bitch" came in his front door, the guy "knows just what to do"; he could "take care of business." But Gene is strongly opposed to using firearms for any other purpose. "You don't need to go around stirring up shit with a shotgun," in his estimation. People should not take shotguns to demonstrations "like them dudes that went up there to the legislature in Sacramento." Gene thinks that was a "*big* mistake."

Firearms are a big part of his life. He has over forty rifles, pistols, and shotguns in his bedroom. He has had them since he was a kid; they are part of his hobby. He makes his own guns and loads his own ammunition; he "really digs the sport." When Panthers walked into the State Assembly packing shotguns, "putting on a big show," they "messed things up" for Gene. The legislators passed a law saying it was illegal to carry guns "just on account of them dudes that went up there making like gang busters."

EPILOGUE

Were Gene to be interviewed in a survey, he would probably be found ranking high on somebody's prejudice or authoritarianism scale. He certainly has his prejudices; his daughter marrying a black man is one. He also displays streaks of authoritarianism: shit disturbers in his estimation should be shot. We *expect* people like Gene to be prejudiced and/or authoritarian. That is what working-class life in America does to people.

If that was all we said about Gene, what a distorted, oversimplified, caricatured picture of him it would be!

Concepts such as prejudice or authoritarianism fail either to shed very much light on people like Gene Danich, or to describe them accurately. Gene departs from the authoritarian–prejudiced personality prototype in critical ways. He has the ability to criticise his father, for one. While Gene has no hostility toward his father, he is able to say, in terms of an ideal, that he is more of a man than his father. Gene has some anxiety about putting down his father; he stammered and paused a good deal throughout this part of the discussion, but he would not idealize him. Authoritarian people are ostensibly incapable of doing this. They are supposedly unable to be objective or critical of their parents, whom they need to idealize.

Gene's thoughts about black people are also not categorical – another supposed trait of prejudiced–authoritarian thinking. Gene makes distinctions among black people. He is favorably disposed toward blacks who espouse ideas he finds to his liking and adamantly opposes people he feels threatened by. He has no objections to certain black people living next door to him: "people who don't throw their garbage outside." And he would not live in a neighborhood with people who did. Gene does not perceive black people as an undifferentiated mass. He does not generalize about them in the categorical terms we would expect of a prejudiced person.

Rigid thinking may be a defining characteristic of prejudice. It hardly characterizes Gene Danich's thinking, however. If anything, Gene is remarkably open and flexible about some very controversial and emotional subjects. He favors law and order but he feels that policemen who brutalize black people "deserve to be shot at." He is ambivalent about riots. In his estimation people should not steal but there are mitigating circumstances. Businessmen who exploit black people "should" be robbed. His mind is not made up about the Black Panthers arming themselves. He can see a need for black people to know how to protect themselves from abuses of authority. Nevertheless, Panther demonstrations did result in legislation that restricted his use of firearms. We could say many things about Gene's thoughts regarding black people, but one of them would not be that they are rigid.

To talk about Gene Danich in terms of prejudice or authoritarianism would not only be inaccurate – it would also miss, if not obscure, what is essential about him. It would not capture the essence of the dynamic and complicated way in which he relates to the issues posed by black people.

Gene is quite aware of racial inequality in American life. He sees that blacks have a "rougher" time than whites. The jobs they hold are not as good as the ones white people have. They have less money than whites. He does not minimize these facts. Nevertheless, the situation is understandable to Gene; he can explain it. He thinks that the educational opportunities open to black people are "insufficient." He also feels that many whites are "down on" black people; they are prejudiced. In his estimation, these factors explain the situation of black people, and he is opposed to this state of affairs; he does not think it is right that black people should be treated in this fashion. Gene has a very strong commitment to what he considers fair play.

The most compelling feature of his thinking is his intense sense of self-interest. Above all else he is concerned about how issues affect him personally. It is through this lens that he filters all questions. Thus he is able to make the remarkable admission that if he were black he would be a Stokely Carmichael supporter because Carmichael is doing something for black people. He is white, however, and opposes the man because his actions might come back on Gene. The feelings Gene holds toward blacks are thus not dictated by prejudice or authoritarianism. Instead they follow from his evaluation of how his interests are affected. And because Gene recognizes inequality as blocked access, rather than as a form of privilege, he is open to some policies that will change the situation of black people. However, he is only open to policies that do not alter institutions from which he receives benefits: He favors integrated schools as long as busing is not involved; black people should be armed as long as firearms legislation is not increased.

Gene's openness to black power strategies is understandable in this context. As he chooses to understand the strategy, it is a very nonmilitant, nonviolent one. He sees it as equality, as solidarity. It is almost a legalistic, gradual approach to change. Gene can favor such a strategy because it barely affects him. Why he interprets it this way, how he has come to this understanding, is frankly puzzling.

Gene's posture toward black people is somewhat unique among our respondents. Most people develop ways of minimizing racism when they explain the situation of blacks. In this way they put distance between themselves and the problems involved. They get themselves off the hook. But Gene confronts the issues head on. Where there is a conflict between his interests and those of black people, he explicitly opts for his own. He makes no pretense about it and does not "pretty up" his formulations with fancy disclaimers. The uniqueness of Gene's "strategy" for defending his privileges is its simplicity and straightforwardness. He will resist anything that undercuts his self-interest.

This may explain his hostility toward Malcolm X and Stokely Carmichael – but not its intensity. Gene is bothered by their cockiness and what he thinks is their pretension to be all-powerful gods. They behave as if they want to be "better" than he is. The special threat is not because they are blacks who are cocky and arrogant; whites who are arrogant and bossy also bother him. On the other hand, Gene is not at all hostile toward Martin Luther King who he feels is not trying to be better than he. None of this answers the question of why he likes King. Is it because King is not arrogant, or is it because his actions do not affect Gene?

Perhaps Gene's intense feelings about Carmichael are related to his deep desire to remain uninvolved in matters that evoke his violent propensities. After all, many of the key events or turning points in his life have been associated with physical confrontations. At age ten or eleven he defied his father and hit some neighborhood toughs over the head with a board. At sixteen or seventeen he punched a high school teacher and consequently received no diploma. His first personal contact with blacks was a fist in the mouth at age eighteen when he was in the Marines. That resulted in his becoming "prejudiced." A fight with another worker at the farm machinery company made it necessary for him to look for a new job. The job turned out to be the best one he has ever had. Maybe the reason Gene feels so strongly about Carmichael is that he fears the consequences of his involvement in the issues raised. He knows he is prone to violent encounters. He may be trying to conquer this tendency. As he remarked with some relief about longshore work, "you can't fight on the docks."

Gene reflects some of the characteristics sociologists find among working-class men. He is physically expressive; has a sense of fair play; strives for control over his work and dignity in his life; and has a feeling of camaraderie toward his fellow workers. He is an outdoorsman. But there is another side to Gene. A side that is not always associated with working-class life but which may be becoming more and more characteristic of young American workers. It perhaps helps explain Gene's concern about people like Carmichael. Gene may be a member of the working class, but he has a very bourgeois orientation toward life. He is far more concerned about property, property rights, and individual freedom than he is about collective rights or social justice. In this sense he is his father's son. Like his father, he is an intense individualist. Carmichael's appeal to black people as a collectivity is undoubtedly threatening.

Gene's fears are probably attributable, in part, to the process of embourgeoisement that segments of the American working class are experiencing. He earns a comfortable living. He will own his own house in only seven years. He drives a new car. His children go to a good school and have an opportunity to do better than he did if they wish. He has a stake in the process that makes all this possible, and Carmichael is challenging it. Perhaps it is fear of this challenge that Gene expresses when he says, "Carmichael wants to be better than me."

Gene's feelings about racial matters, like so many other issues in his life, mostly boil down to how they affect him personally. In areas where implications for his self-interest are unclear, his feelings are characteristically ambivalent. When an issue appears to involve him, however, Gene's feelings are predictable: He wants to maximize his self-interests as he sees them. If there is a "logic" or "consistency" to Gene Danich's way of handling the world, this is it.

A study of this type cannot assess the extent to which Gene Danich is representative of young American workers. Indeed, that is not its purpose. Nevertheless, Gene's experiences, feelings, and formulations seem quite typical of many workingmen in his generation. Gene is neither authoritarian nor prejudiced. That is too simple. He is terribly ambivalent and confused. He is constantly beset by competing values, loyalties, goals, and realities. He is confronted daily by a world he does not always understand, one which often offends him, but over which he wants to exert a certain degree of control. He knows from experience that social resources are not infinite, that people are competing for them, and that he wants his fair share. His sense of fair play prevents him from relegating black people to perpetual inferiority, yet he is aware that their gain could be his loss. He has worked hard to get where he is and has suffered in the process; he has a great deal invested in what he believes to be America. The contradictions in his life and feelings put him in a difficult position. The only reasonable articulation he can live with is one that combines equality or fair play with his self-interests. It may not be consistent, or even logically possible. But it is honest. It is not the conjured creation of an authoritarian–prejudiced personality.

Personal Concerns and the Commitment to Individualism

The combined and often contradictory ways in which race and class are experienced produce distinctive receptivities to racial change. The changes people find acceptable, in turn, reflect the stakes that are generated for them by the racial and class organization of society. Black people raise issues that often directly affect working-class whites like Danich and Kurier. When the situation of blacks is upgraded, these people feel it first. The issue for working-class whites, then, is a *personal* one: They will feel changes in the racial order personally and directly. Gene Danich is vividly aware of the problem: He favors anything that does not affect him personally. Mrs. Kurier fears that changing the current arrangements may allow blacks to "get even." Despite their personal concerns, these two people are more receptive than the others to strategies like black power and militant leaders like Stokely Carmichael.

Middle- and upper-class whites like Harper and Wilson have other concerns, and they are receptive to other possibilities. The issues posed by blacks do not usually affect them as directly as they do working-class whites. Black demands barely touch Harper. Militancy inconveniences Wilson and makes his job more difficult, but it does not "cost" him anything directly. Thus, for middle-class whites the issue is not a personal one. They feel involved only to the extent that blacks become a "social" problem. Their lack of personal involvement is not translated into neutrality toward black power and militant leaders, however. They are not receptive to either one. Harper and Wilson feel most comfortable with strategies that promote and encourage individual effort. Both agree that blacks need to develop pride in themselves and learn how to work hard. Each feels that his personal experience validates this strategy.

These observations contain an apparent paradox. The two people most personally affected by racial change are the least hostile to militant strategies; the two people least affected are the most hostile. The paradox disappears when we consider what is at stake for each group, which also tells us something about how receptive each is to racial change.

Danich and Kurier are concerned about problems affecting them directly; they are defending personal interests. Blacks can do pretty much what they please, as long as it does not involve them directly. Harper and Wilson, on the other hand, are *not* defending their personal interests; that is not what is at stake for them. They are defending the principle of individualism. They do not object to the black power strategy because of the personal consequences it might have for them: Their class position insulates them from most of the direct effects. Their basic objection to a strategy like black power is that it violates the principle of individualism that guides and justifies their lives. Each of these men is convinced that America does not recognize color, it recognizes only individual achievement; They are deeply committed to it, and they want it to continue. Strategies like black power evoke group solutions to problems that Harper and Wilson attribute to individual deficiencies. Group solutions, however, do more than that: they attack the very basic belief that individuals can succeed if they try hard enough. That is why militant leaders and strategies "burn up" Wilson; that is why Harper rejects militancy with the accurate observation that agitators want to "upset our way of life."

This explains how people who appear the least affected by potential change can be the most hostile to militant strategies. Harper and Wilson actually have more at stake than Danich and Kurier. Their principles are at issue. It is not just a question of immediate personal interest. There is no way group strategies can avoid bumping into the principles of individualism to which these men subscribe. In contrast, the same strategy need not necessarily collide with the personal interests of Danich and Kurier. When it does, it is opposed; when it does not, the problem is minimized.

Another reason why Danich and Kurier are more receptive to black demands is perhaps attributable to the downward pushes of class. Evidently one aspect of working-class experience in America is a heightened awareness of inequality. Along with Wilson, the other person of working-class origin, Danich and Kurier are the most conscious of the inequalities experienced by blacks. Gene would like to see equality achieved in America, and he has concrete ideas about what it would look like. Darlene has similar desires. Nevertheless, neither of them is particularly optimistic about the possibilities. Both are aware of the many obstacles that block the way: They are conscious of power differences and the differences these make in accomplishing something approximating equality. Working-class people like Danich and Kurier, then, recognize and acknowledge differential power and relate these differentials to racial problems. Recognizing that power is involved, they realize there is little blacks can do as individuals to change the situation. Thus they are sensitive to the limits of individual solutions and the advantages of group strategies. Middle-class people, on the other hand, deny that inequality even exists. For Harper there is no issue: Equality is already a fact. While Wilson recognizes that people are treated differently, he argues this is not a function of inequality. It occurs because people are born with different capabilities. He says there is no such thing as equality. Hence Danich and Kurier recognize inequality and attribute it in part to differences in power, under certain conditions they are willing to accept group solutions that involve militancy and invoke power.

But what of the young people, like Roberta, from the counterculture community? How do their racial and class experiences come together in the possibilities they envision for racial change? Roberta combines elements of the stance taken by Danich and Kurier with elements of the Harper–Wilson thrust. Like working-class whites, people in Roberta's situation are directly affected by the actions of black people. Most of them have decided to temporarily give up class-based advantage. They therefore feel the racial pushes from below in much the same way as do working-class people. They are defined by blacks and acted toward as a group. Thus the issue for people like Roberta, with Danich and Kurier, is a personal one and that is the way Roberta sees it: She resents being "hassled by spades." Unlike working-class whites, however, Roberta is not receptive to strategies such as black power. She finds it a "drag." Blacks should be "above" issues like racism and "ignore" the people who dislike them. Like middle-class whites, Roberta is most receptive to individual rather than group strategies for change. In this respect, she sounds a great deal like Harper and Wilson. Roberta may have been able to give up the advantages of class; she certainly has not been able to give up its ideology.

There is a powerful irony contained in her situation. On the surface, people like Roberta appear the least prejudiced of all, and the most interested in creating a new world. The opposite, however, may be in fact the case. Unlike the others, Roberta is defending *both* her personal interests *and* the principles of individualism; she does one in terms of the other. Given the peculiar way in which she experiences race and class, she resists changes that have negative personal consequences and that challenge the principles by which she organizes her life. Thus she may have the most at stake and be the least sympathetic to racial changes.

Does this mean that people like Danich and Kurier, who are the most receptive, are therefore allies of black people in their assault on inequality? The answer is clearly, no. They are sympathetic to group strategies for change; they do not, however, include themselves in the group needing changes. Since working-class people experience the squeezes of class in individual terms, they do not explicitly see themselves as part of a group, much less one that might include blacks. Thus they cannot imagine that the upward push of blacks might not directly conflict with their personal interests. When they feel no conflict they do not oppose blacks, but they cannot see how they can better their own situation if blacks do too. People like Gene and Darlene realize that resources are limited and that they cannot link their problems with the ones experienced by blacks. The problem is not that they have a blind spot, however. Because their lives are demarcated along both racial and class lines, they cannot afford to reduce one to the other. Given their situation, *that* would be irrational.

There is yet another feature of American life that complicates the potential for victims of inequality to direct their energies toward its sources instead of one another. Neither Danich nor Kurier expresses the same kind of commitment to individualistic principles as do Harper, Roberta, and Wilson. Gene and Darlene find group strategies for social problems acceptable under some conditions, but, like the other three, they are committed to the notion that people should be autonomous and independent. They strongly subscribe to this aspect of America's creed and culture. Gene thinks people should be "self-sufficient"; men should have "control over" their work; the job should involve responsibility and initiative. Darlene is firmly convinced that people should have the "freedom" to move wherever they please; people should have their "own rights" to decide what is done with their property. White working-class people like Gene Danich and Darlene Kurier are not only committed to these ideals, they have a stake in them as well. If the ideals did not exist and have meaning for them,

they would be without hope for the future. They would be unable to see a way out from under the downward pushes of class for either themselves or their children. They would have to resign themselves to the present. Danich and Kurier want these ideals to be a reality. It helps them experience class in individual and thus escapable terms.

Black people threaten and challenge these ideals, and thereby Danich and Kurier, on two levels. One: They stand as a living refutation of the ideals. Their situation is testimony that the ideals are applied selectively. Danich and Kurier are aware of this. Blacks, then, open the ideals to suspicion. Two: When blacks make demands on society, they often invoke past denials they have experienced rather than the independent ideals espoused by Danich and Kurier. Blacks, then, are asking to be rewarded on the basis of criteria that conflict with the ideals to which these people are committed. If black people were rewarded on this basis, it would give them some advantages relative to working-class whites. It would do even more than that, however. In effect, it would say to people that the cultural currency they have invested in has been devalued; the rules of the game have been changed. That is something Danich and Kurier will not tolerate; they have too much of themselves invested. Thus they will only support changes that leave intact the cultural rules for competition. Everything else affects them too personally. A radical break with crucial aspects of American culture is therefore necessary for the Daniches and Kuriers to become involved with blacks in a thoroughgoing assault on inequality. There is however, very little in their experience that would support this kind of departure.

CONCLUSION

This is the situation within which racial sentiments are defined, the context within which racial attitudes exist. White people's sentiments toward blacks are not only forged in this context; they reflect it as well. If they oppose black demands for increased equality, it is not because of their personal predispositions or "prejudices." Their refusal is based primarily on their acceptance of American cultural standards. The people with whom we spoke are concerned about the consequences that racial changes will have for American norms and social institutions. They do not oppose demands raised by blacks in racial terms. Their opposition is based on an *acceptance* of and stake in standards and institutional priorities rather than a *rejection* of black people. If anything, they are more concerned about the things black people *lack* – money, education, middle-class values and aspirations – than about black people per se. In some instances, they seem more concerned about what is happening to them than they are about blacks. William Simon and John Gagnon put it the following way:

Change itself becomes the enemy. Much of the current racism may derive not so much from the factors we once associated with prejudice but with the increasing complications that the image of the Negro community now represents the most powerful symbol of "disruptive" changes in their lives (sic) [1970: 49].

Lipset and Raab found this feeling among Wallace voters in 1968: "... it can best be seen as a backlash against change in which there is an almost absolute congruence between the backlash against dreaded change and the backlash targetry, that is, the change bearers" (1970: 341). They conclude that "the nativist bigotry of such whites finds its genesis not so much in hatred of Negroes, but in the felt dimunition of their own status" (1970: 510).

The distinctive feature of racist thinking, then, is not hatred. What sets it off from other thinking is that it justifies policies and institutional priorities that perpetuate racial inequality, and it does so in distinctively American terms. It is not race to which people refer; instead they speak of "larger" societal interests and values, or the inability of blacks – for reasons for which they assume little responsibility – to compete with whites on equal terms.

I do not question the motives of the people expressing these sentiments. In fact, I am willing to grant that in some instances their intentions may be quite noble: They might actually want to see blacks achieve equality. Their motives, however, are irrelevant. Their thinking is based upon assumptions, and their competing priorities are judged within a framework, that usually insure that they will respond to issues raised by blacks in ways that continue their position of social advantage and therefore maintain their privileges. Their assumptions largely determine their solutions. Given the racial and class organization of American society, there is only so much people can "see." The positions they occupy in these structures limit the range of their thinking. The situation places barriers on their imaginations and restricts the possibilities of their vision.

The racist nature of their thinking is not minimized by the fact that white people are often unaware of the extent to which their advantaged position is based on race. The consequence is the same as if they were conscious of it.

REFERENCE

Simon, W. and Gagnon, J. (1970) 'Working-class Youth: Alienation Without an Image', in L. Howe (ed.) *The White Majority*. New York: Vintage Books.

18

Essence, Accident, and Race*

H. M. BRACKEN

The author asks, in essence, is racism accidental? While the great religious traditions have been proselytizing and universal in their appeal, racism, rooted in the belief or attribution of biological inferiority for some groups, is particularistic. How did racism emerge in the context of Judaism, Christianity, and Islam? The author proposes that intellectuals and religious leaders developed the philosophical, linguistic, and pseudo-scientific foundation for racism as a response to colonialism and imperialism emerging fully in the sixteenth century. Despite the claim of Locke, Hume, Descartes, Voltaire, and many others, claiming objectivity, much of their work and statements about racial differences among people justified racism. The author proposes that the philosophical methodology utilized by these thinkers, and defended as objective but yet utilized to attribute biological inferiority to some groups, continues to reflect research about race today.

In this paper I assume that racism is endemic to our culture. I also assume that we wish to reduce its force and hence that as philosophers we are interested in some of the philosophical sources of racism. My concern is with one strand and one strand only within the complex development of our twentieth-century situation. I appreciate that the term 'racism' is so widely and variedly used today that even for the purposes of a paper it is difficult to specify. However, I certainly mean to include the doctrine which a group may articulate in order to justify their oppressing another group by appealing to some putative flaw in the human essence, in recent times usually interpreted as the biological constitution, of the members of the oppressed group. Thus I mean to include within racism

* A revised version of a paper read before the Irish Philosophical Club, Ballymascanlon, December, 1972. I wish to thank Professors Richard H. Popkin (Washington University, St Louis) and David Fate Norton (McGill University) for the contributions they have made to my understanding of eighteenth century racism. I am indebted to Prof. Ó Murchu, Miss Mary Pollard, and particularly to Mr C. J. Benson (all of TCD), for their invaluable assistance in obtaining background material. I wish also to thank Dr John C. Marshall (University of Edinburgh) for giving me access to his unpublished study of Darwinism

Continued

and language. Finally, I profited from discussions with Prof. Roy Edgley and his colleagues in philosophy at the University of Sussex, with Dr Philip Pettit, Trinity Hall, Cambridge, with my colleagues at UCD, Prof. P. Masterson and Mr Denys Turner, and with my colleagues at TCD, Prof. E. J. Furlong, Dr David Berman, and Mr Patrick H. Kelly. Some of the research for this paper was supported by a grant from the Canada Council.

'congenital inferiority' by virtue of skin colour as well as by linguistic differences.

Philosophers are not the only people who have considered language to be a reflection of mind. Anthropologists have often provided linguistic data to show that the speaking of inferior languages is the mark of the inferior minds of inferior people. Just as university language programmes still consider only the superior cultures of superior peoples worthy of study.[1] *Linguistic imperialism* is evident in the use of similar scientific or cultural-political claims concerning the several Celtic languages vis-à-vis English and French. In Canada the injunction 'speak white' means speak English. Here is a statement of colour racism:

> I am apt to suspect the negroes and in general all the other species of men (for there are four or five different kinds) to be naturally inferior to the whites. There never was a civilized nation of any other complexion than white, nor even any individual eminent either in action or speculation. No ingenious manufactures amongst them, no arts, no sciences. On the other hand, the most rude and barbarous of the whites, such as the ancient GERMANS, the present TARTARS, have still something eminent about them, in their valour, form of government, or some other particular. Such a uniform and constant difference could not happen, in so many countries and ages, if nature had not made an original distinction betwixt these breeds of men. Not to mention our colonies, there are NEGROE slaves dispersed all over EUROPE, of which none ever discovered any symptoms of ingenuity; tho' low people, without education, will start up amongst us, and distinguish themselves in every profession. In JAMAICA indeed they talk of one negroe as a man of parts and learning; but 'tis likely he is admired for very slender accomplishments, like a parrot, who speaks a few words plainly.[2]

The author of these lines was a one-time British Under-Secretary of State, in effect for Colonial Affairs, Mr David Hume. It is an unhappy fact that many of the cultural heroes of the Enlightenment were anxious to establish that large numbers of the peoples of the world were somehow less than men. If we will reflect for a moment, we may recall that Hume was no lover of the Irish or of the Catholics either. R. H. Popkin[3] has distinguished a number of rather different racist theories within the eighteenth and nineteenth centuries. For example: (1) non-whites are mentally deficient—a theory which is still advanced; (2) being non-white is a form of degeneracy based on environmental conditions (sun, food, etc.); (3) there are some beings that look human but which are really closer to the apes, a view which was given a 'scientific' basis by Darwinians; (4) the thesis that there were separate creations of mankind, the Adamites and the pre-Adamites.

Thus, as in (2), sometimes a 'cure' for the inferior elements could be provided through the right environment, assimilation, evolutionary up-grading,

etc. More often, 'alien' racial elements were to be driven out or exterminated—policies that were recommended in relation to the Irish and Jews in England in the nineteenth century. We have seen that Hume takes a hard line. So does Voltaire. He rejected the climate theory and opted for listing the negro as a member of a distinct species of man; specifically different because of lack of intelligence (cf. *La philosophie de l'histoire*, ch. ii.). Berkeley supported slavery but he rejected the specific difference thesis (*Works*, ed. A. A. Luce and T. E. Jessop, VII, 122). Darwin is interesting because of the importance he attributes to languages, because he would seek to defend treating separate races as separate species even if they were cross-fertile, and because one of his infrequent lapses from a lofty scientific style occurs when he includes some scurrilous quotations about the Irish.[4]

Racism in the west appears to be a recent phenomenon. Judaism, Islam, and Christianity are universalistic. They sought and seek converts. It is apparently not until the Spanish Inquisition that one finds biological criteria taking precedence over religious conversion with the distinction of 'new' *vs* 'old' Christians. 'New' *vs* 'old' Protestant in eighteenth century Ireland represents a similar move. However, it was the discovery of the New World which gave real scope for racial theory. Despite the arguments of Las Casas, and Pope Paul III's bull *Sublimus Deus*, affirming the true manhood of Indians, the need to exploit two continents seems to have inclined men to prefer the guidance of Aristotle—some men are by nature slaves (although Aristotle was probably not providing an account of the human essence with that remark).

From our point of view, the most significant feature of the shifts in ideas between the sixteenth and nineteenth centuries is that racism not only runs counter to the three major religious traditions which have dominated the west, it runs counter to the doctrines of man still being articulated within the seventeenth century. Notice that if one is a Cartesian, a defender of mind/body dualism, it becomes impossible to state a racist position. Man's essential properties reside finally in his spirit. His colour, his language, his biology, even his sex—are in the strictest sense *accidental*. (From Plato to Descartes sexist doctrines have been more comfortably situated within the Aristotelian tradition than among the dualists.)

I cited a passage from Hume, but in many ways Locke seems to have been the more decisive influence. Recall Locke's views about substance and quality: he devotes considerable energy trying to determine how secondary qualities inhere in primary ones and how qualities generally inhere in substance. His tendency is to say that we do not know the 'real Constitutions of Substances, on which each *secondary Quality* particularly depends', and that even if we did, 'it would serve us only with experimental (not universal) Knowledge; and reach with Certainty no farther, than that bare Instance' (*Essay*, IV, vi, § 7).[5] The *even if* theme is constant, although the emphasis changes. At II, xxxi, § 13, Locke writes that it is 'very evident to the Mind ... that whatever Collection of simple *Ideas* it makes of any substance that exists, it cannot be sure, that it exactly answers all that are in that Substance: Since not having tried all the Operations of all other substances upon it ...' Then Locke adds the *even if* clause: 'And, after all, if we could have, and actually had, in our complex *Idea*, an exact Collection of all the secondary Qualities or Powers of any Substance, we should not yet thereby have an Idea of the Essence of that Thing. For since the Powers or Qualities, that are observable by us, are not the real Essence of that Substance, but depend on it, and flow from it, any Collection whatsoever of the Qualities, cannot be the real Essence of that Thing.' In IV, vi, § 9, he writes: 'I would gladly meet with one general Affirmation, concerning any quality of *Gold*, that any one can certainly know is true.' This is a remarkable claim because it indicates that Locke has no ground for *ex*cluding from the idea of the substance gold, pain—or *in*cluding malleableness *within* the idea of gold. Locke is prepared to grant (cf. IV, iii, § 6) that matter might think.

Thus one side of Locke's discussion of substance constitutes an attack on the model of essential properties which had played a major role within Cartesianism and, for that matter, within Aristotelianism. It then becomes possible to treat any or no property as essential. Within the revised framework it becomes more difficult to distinguish men from the other animals. The older model had the advantage of trying to formulate what was essential to man. In so doing it provided a modest conceptual barrier to treating race, colour, religion, or sex as other than accidental.

Locke, of course, did *not* want to treat these things as accidental. His very considerable involvement in the Revolution of 1688 is still a matter of lively interest for historians. He has acquired a grand reputation as a man of religious tolerance. Yet he apparently had no difficulty in excluding Catholics from the body politic. I find it remarkable that Locke should have been canonized as the father of religious toleration. There were, after all, people around who had expressed genuinely tolerant sentiments. But one should not lose sight of the alteration in thinking about persons introduced by Locke together with his defences of the revolution. Are there connections between Locke's philosophical accounts of the substantial self or person and the ease with which he can treat Catholics as nonpersons? Without answering that, one may consider another aspect of Locke's work. Peter Laslett has noted that Locke became a Commissioner of

Appeals in 1689 and a founding member of the Board of Trade in 1696. 'Locke himself played a large part in the creation of this second body, the architect of the old Colonial System.'[6] Locke indeed does write about slavery'. According to Laslett, §§ 23, 24, and 85 of the *Two treatises* constitute 'Locke's justification of slavery'. It may seem unnecessary, and inconsistent with his principles, but it must be remembered that he writes as the administrator of slave-owning colonies in America. As Leslie Stephen pointed out,[7] the *Fundamental constitutions of Carolina* provide that every freeman "shall have absolute power and authority over his negro slaves"... The Instructions to Governor Nicholson of Virginia, which Locke did much to draft in 1698,[8] regard negro slaves as justifiably enslaved because they were captives taken in a just war, who had forfeited their lives "by some Act that deserves Death" ... Locke seems satisfied that the forays of the Royal Africa Company were just wars of this sort, and that the negroes captured had committed such acts...'[9]

Just war enters because while Locke would not have countenanced slave-taking within the EEC of his day, he seems to have felt that *waste land* was fair game. Waste land was land not being put to proper economic use—i.e. land which was not the property of civilized, defined as money-exchanging, people. By a happy consequence of his universal principle, Africa and the Americas were waste land. If their residents resisted the take-over of these wastelands, they could properly be taken as captives in a just war and made perpetual slaves.[10]

There is another side to Locke's discussion— the concept-acquisition model. The doctrine of substance and the consequent denial of thinking substance is supported by Locke's account of concept-formation. Locke's 'way of ideas' was interpreted by many to provide something like what we might today call a 'meaning criterion'. And Locke found it unintelligible to say with Descartes that the soul always thinks, or that it has innate ideas. Although there are atomistic and corpuscular elements within Locke's theory of knowledge, his position often reads like a variation on the scholastic thesis that there is nothing in the intellect which is not first in the senses. Bishop Stillingfleet pressed Locke quite hard on the intelligibility of the 'way of ideas' and argued that it created some awkward problems for the faithful. It meant that certain faith claims, e.g., that the soul is immortal, would be difficult to talk about since 'soul' had been rendered meaningless on Locke's analysis. Locke appears to respond by holding that since the whole claim is a matter of faith anyway, there should be no difficulties.

For better or for worse, I submit that the issues in the innate idea arguments of Locke, Leibniz, Descartes, etc., are not narrowly or technically philosophical. What is a person? How does a person learn? These are the sorts of questions really being asked. Empiricism and rationalism offer rather different answers. It is my impression that we have observed in the process of time a continual increase in the techniques of manipulation, in the methods of control, and in the efficiency whereby people have been merchandised. I am not claiming that empiricism is responsible for that; or that a return to rationalism would herald a new age of human freedom. The connections between empiricism and the rise of manipulative models of man may be considered historical, not logical.

And yet the rationalists seem to have been more conscious that those features of man which get singled out as essential have a normative moral character.[11] The empiricists understandably saw their accounts as descriptive. Value-free descriptions of certain peoples as essentially inferior, grounded in some 'science', facilitate treating them as inferior. Which is not to say ingenious rationalists could not have articulated racist theories. That is why I hold that the relation between empiricism and racism is historical. But the lack of an 'in principle' argument should not deter us from recognizing that empiricism has provided the methodology within which theories of political control were successfully advanced, and by means of which colour/brain-weight, IQ, etc., correlation studies have been pursued, and in terms of which the liberal ideology has been cast. Hence the role of empiricism has in fact been decisive within the English-speaking community.

If I urge that we look once again at the discarded Cartesian model it is in large measure because I claim it will help us to see more clearly where we stand and to appreciate how deeply rooted in ideological considerations some of our purest philosophical notions really are. We should also be reminded that the discarded model was not conceptually inadequate.

Perhaps because of Locke, we are inclined to think that the defenders of innate ideas were reactionaries to a man. Certainly John Yolton (in *John Locke and the way of ideas*) has produced incontrovertible evidence to show that there were dozens of people defending innate ideas in the very form Locke refutes. Generally, these were people who defended their pet prejudices simply by producing an innateness claim instead of an argument. But there is another side. Jean Calvin used innate ideas as part of his attempt to establish that a mere individual man was inherently capable of questioning a truth grounded in authority or tradition. And among the Cartesians, innate ideas were part of a general attack on any and all empirical accounts of concept-acquisition. For these purposes, an empiricist account is one which establishes that all knowledge is rooted in the senses by asserting that blind men do not know colour. Peter Geach remarked the difficulty about the appeal to the blind man in *Mental acts*. The empiricist point seems to be that if one closes off one sense channel then one cannot talk about things appropriate to that particular sense. In that form, of course, the claim will not stand up. There is ample evidence that blind people not only can learn the language of colour, they can use it in literary contexts in ways that make it impossible for us to identify the author as blind. On the other hand, if one means by blind-men-not-knowing-colour that they cannot, when handed a coloured object, identify its colour—that is a logical truth; it is not, says Geach, the sort of thing we should be citing in defence of an empirical claim about concept-acquisition.

Leibniz in discussing (in the *New essays*) the case cited in Locke's *Essay* of the blind man made to see by the removal of cataracts remarked that blind men could do geometry. A point the Cartesians had already noted. Indeed, the Cartesians had already decided that although we could talk about the same object as perceived through different senses, our actual cognition of the object could hardly be a function of any sort of resemblance holding between physical object and sensory data. Cartesians could not see how our ideas, how our concepts, could be derived from material things. Hence the introduction of innate ideas as a basis for guaranteeing the objectivity of human knowledge. But that is only part of the Cartesian account.

Descartes begins with a primitive awareness that human language is radically different from anything found elsewhere in the animal kingdom. Man's language skill reveals a unique capacity. In brief, man has a mind. And neither machines nor other animals do. A machine might be constructed which could talk, 'But it never happens that it arranges its speech in various ways, in order to reply appropriately to everything that may be said in its presence, as even the lowest type of man can do. The second difference is, that although machines can perform certain things as well as or perhaps better than any of us can do, they infallibly fall short in others, by the which means we may discover that they did not act from knowledge, but only from the disposition of their organs'.[12] Or as it could be put today, human speech cannot be understood in stimulus-response terms. In fact, Descartes argues that our soul is entirely independent of our body. Which may in part be glossed as: we can think and talk about things which are not in front of our noses. In *Meditation* IV, Descartes again refers to man's creative capacity to spin out thoughts as a function of the freedom of the will.

A Cartesian like Louis de La Forge[13] sees an empirical theory of linguistic meaning and of concept-acquisition as providing a foundation for a denial of human freedom. Our mental life is rooted in the mind's own activity, not in what may seem to be impressed via the sense channels. Man's linguistic creativity as a mark of the mental, in particular the non-imitative linguistic creativity of children, is also discussed by Bernard Lamy.[14]

The Port-Royal wing of Cartesianism actually tried to provide a model of the human mind which would capture this radical freedom motif. They sought to produce a grammar which would do for mind what geometry did for matter. Noam Chomsky[15] suggests that they failed because they did not have at their disposal mathematical models which would enable them to characterize the sorts of rules which might make intelligible our infinite capacity to generate sentences.

There is another dimension to the concept-acquisition discussion. The radical freedom thesis offends. The suggestion that people are autonomous is not attractive to those who want to have power over people—or who want to produce theories about how and why people behave in certain ways. In that context there is something re-assuring about applying to humans methods of learning which have apparently been successful in animal experiments. The empirical model seems to reduce the possibility that the natives might get restless. Moreover, thinking of people as condition-able reserves a place for those who must do the conditioning. Which is to say that the empiricist model of man provides room for experts. Once in power they have a clear vested interest in the theories and categories they employ in talking about men and women. Those theories justify the experts' acceptance and use of power. Whereas people who do not behave in accordance with the theories threaten the adequacy of the theories and hence the original licence to power.[16]

In brief, there are a number of reasons—having nothing to do with explanatory adequacy—why the dualist model was rejected in favour of the empiricist. While people spoke of the rights of man in ever grander terms from the eighteenth century onwards, more and more men were being enslaved. Very quickly the various sorts of racism described at the outset became widespread. When Patrick Henry of Virginia made his impassioned plea, 'Give me liberty or give me death', he owned more than a dozen black slaves. There were, of course, occasional voices raised against slavery. But somehow it had become possible to say that there were different *species* of humans. Some were higher on the scale of personhood than others.[17]

The racism of a Voltaire or a Hume became scientifically well-founded in the nineteenth century. The historical antecedent of colour/IQ correlations was the work of the craniologists. 'In the human brain we find those characteristics which particularly distinguish man from the brute creation. The differences between the various races of men are fundamental differences in intellectual capacity, as well as in physical conformation.'[18] Prof. A. H. Keane of University College, London, writes

as follows about the negro in the ninth edition (1884) of the *Encyclopaedia Britannica*:

> Nearly all observers admit that the Negro child is on the whole quite as intelligent as those of other human varieties, but that on arriving at puberty all further progress seems to be arrested ... 'We must necessarily suppose that the development of the Negro and White proceeds on different lines. While with the latter the volume of the brain grows with the expansion of the brain-pan, in the former the growth of the brain is on the contrary arrested by the premature closing of the cranial sutures and lateral pressure of the frontal bone.' [The citation is from Filippo Manetta, *La Razza Negra nel suo stato selvaggio* (Turin, 1864), p. 20.]

Keane comments on the negro's moral status: 'It is more correct to say of the Negro that he is non-moral than immoral.' An indication of negroes' inferior moral situation is that they engage in the slave trade, 'where not checked by European Governments'. Keane later held that the Chinese 'seem in some respects to be almost as incapable of progress as the Negroes themselves, the only *essential* difference being that the arrest of mental development comes later in life for the yellow than for the black man'.[19] The discovery that neolithic and modern Europeans had the same brain capacity inclined him to place his emphasis on brain serra-tures being more complex 'in the higher than in the lower races'. He writes: 'A better index [than cranial volume] between the mental capacity of the various human groups is afforded by the reasoning faculty, of which articulate speech is at once the measure and the outward expression' (p. 193). As to how languages were to be ranked, he had no doubts.

Nott and Gliddon, and Dr Samuel Morton provided evidence on Celtic brain volumes as well as blacks. The data are included in J. B. Davis and J. Thurnam, *Crania Britannica* (London, 1865). The scientific evidence shows that English brains were best with 96 cubic inches and Germans were next with 95. But the 'native Irish' were a mere 87 and the 'native African Family', 83.7. Dr Robert Knox, *The races of man* (London, 1868), p. 12, writes, 'There never was any Celtic literature, nor science, nor arts ...' He advises us that 'the object of [his] work is to show that the European races, so called, differ from each other as widely as the ... Esquimaux from the Basque' (p. 44). Since he speaks of 'exterminating' (e.g. 229 f) various races, it is not surprising to read, 'Sir Robert Peel's Encumbered Estate Bill aims simply at the quiet and gradual extinction of the Celtic race in Ireland: this is its sole aim, and it will prove successful. A similar bill is wanted for Caledonia ...' (p. 27).

John Stuart Mill writes, *England and Ireland* (London, 1865), p. 35, that the Irish have 'yet to prove their possession' of the 'qualities which fit a people for self-government'. Matthew Arnold notes,

'Undoubtedly the native Irish have the faults which we commonly attribute to them,' *Irish essays* (London, 1882), p. 12. The author of *Ireland from one or two neglected points of view* (London, 1888) asserts, 'The cause [of Western Irish turbulence and lawlessness] is lowness of racial character. All the government conciliation in the world will not alter the moral character of a race of men. It is folly to talk of a governing race conciliating a lower one' (p. 43). A few pages later he asks, 'How can the tricks of reading and writing alter the features of the Negro's face with the character that belongs to the features?' (p. 49). The same is presumably intended to hold for the Irish. L. Perry Curtis, Jr, *Apes and angels …* (Newton Abbot, 1971) shows how extensive was the effort to assimilate the Irish to the simian or the black—the black's inferior status already having been scientifically established.

Linguistic appeals have already been mentioned. They had been made in varying ways for several centuries. They had new force in the post-Darwinian world. A. Schleicher writes, 'The development of language has accompanied, step by step, the development of the brain and of the organ of speech … the study of language conducts us unmistakably to the hypothesis of the gradual evolution of man from lower forms', cited by André Lefèvre, *Race and language* (London, 1894), p. 6. Darwinism not only gave added support to the polygenetic theories of man but also to polygenetic theories of language. Since the diversity of languages was taken to support diversity of man, ranking of men by species was paralleled by the ranking of languages; an end to Adam and Eve entails an end to a single pre-Babel language.

A chapter in de Gobineau's *Essai sur l'inégalité des races humaines*, second ed. 2 vols (Paris, 1884), is entitled: 'Les langues, inégales entre elles, sont dans un rapport parfait avec le mérite relatif des races' (ch. xv). W. D. Whitney, in *Language and the study of language* (London, 1867), said, 'It still remains true that, upon the whole, language is a tolerably sure indication of race' (pp. 373–4). Prof. A. H. Sayce entered a demur: 'The spirit of vanity has invaded the science of language itself. We have come to think that not only is the race to which we belong superior to all others, but that the languages we speak are equally superior', *Introduction to the science of language* (London, 1880), II, 66. 'Language', he said, 'is no test of race, only of social contact' (I, 75). But the racial drive was more powerful. On the one hand Indian and African languages were inferior because they were mere extensions of animal noises, on the other hand they were inferior because they were lexically and syntactically too complex. Gaelic was of course also found to be inadequate.

As I mentioned at the outset neither racism nor linguistic racism had to wait for Darwin. The ground had been well prepared for several centuries. But anthropology succeeded in making racism scientifically respectable. It also thereby enhanced the political usefulness of the social sciences. The Canadian linguistic ethnologist, Horatio Hale, held that 'speech alone, rightly studied, will indicate with sufficient clearness the circumstances of the [racial] mixture'.[20] He also wrote, '[Ethnology] is indispensable … to the politician who in any capacity aspires to direct [a nation's] future' (p. 351). The Irish and the negro questions came before the Anthropological Society of London on more than a few occasions. The following two passages suggest what a valuable contribution to the advancement of science anthropologists were making. One paper begins, 'The object of this paper is to show that the peculiarities of the Irish character … are racial, hereditary, and ineradicable'.[21] Another says, 'if only those in authority would but take the trouble to make themselves acquainted with certain race distinctions,—in fact, become anthropologists,—there would be fewer political mistakes than ruled at present; and less pandering to Negroes, the working classes, and the Celtic Irish …'[22]

From the eighteenth century to the present, social scientists have been striving to establish that people may be ranked racially. Hume or Voltaire or Jefferson did not have such elaborate studies at their disposal as later thinkers provided. Craniologists of the nineteenth century did for the cause what twentieth century IQ experts continue to do: produce, under the guise of science, correlations of colour or language with 'intelligence'. But as Chomsky has pointed out, there is no reason to think that there is any intellectual significance in correlating IQ and skin colour, height, etc. Nor would such studies entail any social consequences, 'except in a racist society in which each individual is assigned to a racial category and dealt with not as an individual in his own right, but as a representative of this category'.[23]

In the eighteenth century one ranked people by race. One also finds parallel rankings of languages transparently in terms of their proximity to the pinnacles of civilization—the English, French, and Germans. Craniology provided hard, objective, value-free scientific data. Like philology it was related to man's intellectual activities. Yet taking the measure of a man in terms of his language or brain weight or head shape or IQ is not something which follows from defining man as a rational animal. As I have said, we apparently get into the ranking business in the first place because we want to justify, we want to make morally legitimate, our pushing people around.

The empiricist model of man did not produce the institution of racial slavery or the forms of racism which have been visited upon Ireland and the Americas. However, it made racism easier to justify by providing us with ways of counting colour, head shape, language, religion, or IQ as essential properties of the person. And it allowed us to think that colour/brain and similar correlations were legitimate scientific enquiries.

I began by citing David Hume's expression of racism. I then discussed John Locke's account of substance and essential properties. I advanced the thesis that racism is easily and readily stateable if one thinks of the person in accordance with empiricist teaching because the essence of the person may be deemed to be his colour, language, religion, etc., while the Cartesian dualist model provided what I called a modest conceptual brake to the articulation of racial degradation and slavery. *Secondly*, I have suggested that the empiricist blank tablet account of learning is a manipulative model and that Cartesians rejected the empiricist doctrine of concept-acquisition because they took it to entail a denial of the possibility of human freedom. In modern times the account of concept-acquisition and learning which they rejected has proved itself to be readily compatible with social conditioning and political control. *Thirdly*, I submit that this essence/accident strand within racism is important to us not only because it is rooted in English thought, but also because when taken together with empiricist learning theory and empiricism's fact/value distinction it has been crucial as an ideological bulwark behind which racially biased pseudo-science continues to flourish.

I want now to discuss briefly a quite different area in which differing attitudes may also be considered to be rooted in the empiricism/rationalism debate—insofar as that debate depends essentially on the question of the 'infinite malleability' of man. It may also cast some light on the role of intellectuals in our culture.

For dualism the category of human speech is sharply distinguished from other animal and physical things and activities. Speech is in one sense physical enough, but in another it carries the mark of the mental since man's creativity and freedom show themselves in language. I think that a case could be made that the doctrine of free speech emerges within a dualist context. It is part of the theory that *telling* (to someone) is not a form of *doing* (to someone) insofar as how a person responds to human speech is within the domain of his freedom. The point was pithily expressed in a comment about pornography enforcement by a late Mayor of New York City, James J. Walker: 'No girl was ever seduced by a book.' That view has never won the day, of course. A good deal of human effort has been expended in trying to control mankind by controlling what can be said. This task has been made progressively more easy by treating *talking* as in the same category as *doing*.

I find the obverse of the argument advanced in Québec: it is said that speech which offends is a form of assault—it being granted that talking is doing. Hence one is morally entitled to take defensive measures. Violence must be met with violence; a natural enough move inasmuch as governments tend to consider speech to be action. It is also an argument which is facilitated by the behaviourist picture of the person; because we have talked about and legislated concerning men in terms of that picture. The linguistic behaviourism which has been the hallmark of modern Anglo-American philosophy thus appears to buttress the case of those in political power who seek to retain and increase their control over all forms of human life.

At a 1951 meeting of the Irish Philosophical Club Professor Furlong read a paper entitled 'Professor Ryle's view of man', *Hermathena* 78 (1951), 12–21, in which he expressed some misgivings about the view of man Ryle advanced. Ryle's view is an extension of the doctrine advanced by Locke and Hume. Locke and Hume had political power in their own right. Ryle, and for that matter, Austin and Wittgenstein, exercised their considerable political influence in other ways—as Gellner and Marcuse have discussed. Thus the philosophical doctrines, the techniques of analysis proposed, would 'leave things as they are'—specifically the things outside philosophy. On the other hand, if one thinks back to the medieval debates over universals one can appreciate why philosophers were attacked and condemned. What they were saying cut to the very heart of the entire intellectual enterprise. Recent work in linguistics seems to be making it more difficult to subscribe to empiricist methodology in dealing with the mind. Hence it may be propitious to question the role of the dominant philosophical style. We might even put this as a badly formed transcendental question. How has it been possible for racism to flourish so successfully in our culture?

I have not contributed to the important and difficult question of evaluating the adequacy of a given philosophical method. But if, as I suggest, one important element in modern racism is rooted in the empiricist tradition, then it may be time to turn a critical eye on that tradition and not be deterred by the usual argument that the method is a neutral analytic tool. That is why I included as an illustration a parenthetical remark about free speech. How we talk (or fail to talk) about minds, persons, and actions, will affect the context in which governments move to control us by controlling our words. If we are more than our words we had better begin saying so.

NOTES

1. See my 'Culture *vs* Jewish culture', *Viewpoints: Canadian Jewish quarterly*, III (1968), 42–48.

2. From the essay 'Of national characters'. Cf. Hume's *Essays: moral, political, and literary*, eds T. H. Green and T. H. Grose (London, 1875), I, 252.

3. See 'The philosophical basis of eighteenth-century racism', in *Racism in the eighteenth century* ('Studies in eighteenth-century culture', Vol. III (Cleveland & London, 1973), pp. 245–262.

4. *Descent of man* (2 vols; London, 1871) I, 174. The quotations are from W. R. Greg.

5. Locke citations are from the fifth (1706) edition of the *Essay*.

6. Peter Laslett's Introduction (ch. ii, § 3) to Locke's *Two treatises of government* (rev. ed. New York, 1965), p. 52.

7. In *History of English thought in the eighteenth century* (London, 1902), 11, 139, cited in Laslett, *op. cit.*, p. 325.

8. Laslett cites his 'Locke and the first Earl of Shaftesbury', *Mind*, 1957.

9. Laslett, *op. cit.* Notes to §§ 23–24, pp. 325–6. I have not included all of Laslett's notes to the passages cited.

10. Discussed in detail in M. Seliger, *The liberal politics of John Locke* (London, 1968).

11. See James Ramsay, *An essay on the treatment and conversion of African slaves* (Dublin, 1784). Ramsay, according to the *DNB* a pupil and friend of Thomas Reid, challenged the relevance of Hume's colour/intelligence correlations. Hume might just as well, using his own case in evidence, 'have denied a capacity for metaphysical subtilty to all who wanted these his great bodily attributes',
(p. 182, ch. v, § ii). Ramsay went on to say, 'The soul is a simple substance, not to be distinguished by squat or tall, black, brown, or fair'.

12. *Discourse*, Part V (Haldane and Ross, I, 116).

13. *Traité de l'esprit de l'homme* (Paris, 1666), esp. chs ix and x.

14. *L'art de parler* ... (Paris, 1676), esp. bk I, ch. xiii.

15. Cf. *Cartesian linguistics* (New York, 1966) and *Language and mind* (New York, 1968).

16. See my 'Minds and learning: the Chomskian revolution', *Metaphilosophy*, iv (1973), 229–245.

17. See the discussion of the Chain of Being in Winthrop D. Jordan, *White over black: American attitudes toward the negro, 1515-1812* (Baltimore, 1969).

18. J. C. Nott and George R. Gliddon, *Indigenous races of the earth* ... (London, 1857), p. 221.

19. A. H. Keane, *Ethnology* (Cambridge, 1896), p. 322. My italics.

20. 'Race and language', *Popular science monthly* (January, 1888), 340–351. A version had been presented to the AAAS under the title 'The true basis of ethnology'.

21. J. Gould Avery, 'Civilisation; with especial reference to the so-called Celtic inhabitants of Ireland', *Journal of the anthropological society*, VII (1869), ccxxi f.

22. Report of the discussion following a paper by Capt. Bedford Pim, RN, *Journal of the anthropological society*, VII (1869), p. ccxxxvl.

23. Noam Chomsky, in *Ramparts*, July/August (1972), p. 30. See also his 'Psychology and ideology', *Cognition*, I (1972), 11–46.

19

The Cress Theory
of Color-Confrontation

FRANCES CRESS WELSING

By utilizing Freudian psychoanalysis, Mary Frances Cress contends that the nature and basis of racism against blacks is actually inferiority complexes among whites. She argues that numerical minority status, and the lack of 'color', or melanin, motivates whites to practice racism against blacks. Racism, according to this author, is simply 'psychological defensive maneuvers or defensive mechanism'. As a defensive mechanism, racism on the part of whites generally takes three behavioral forms: repression, reaction formation, and projection. Thus, whites repress the idea that they feel inferior due to relative smallness in their numbers, as well as the lack of melanin, a distinguishing characteristic of the majority of people. But whites also react to this situation by reversing that which is desired, color, into something negative. And finally, according to Cress, whites exhibit behaviors which project their own desires and inadequacies onto blacks. This view has been critiqued by several observers due to its biological determinism and lack of empirical basis. Furthermore, it reduces racism to primarily a psychological issue, while de-emphasizing its structural, institutional, and historical foundations. Dr Cress' theory and related discussion is expounded in a collection of essays, *The Isis Papers*, published by the Third World Press in 1991.

Unlike religion, the body of knowledge known as science takes the position that all observable phenomena can be explained, or, at least, are grist for the mill of investigation, analysis and understanding by the human mind or brain.

Considering that in today's very small world, at least three-quarters of the people are "non-white" and that the totality of the "non-white" majority population is subjected to domination over the entirety of their lives, either directly or indirectly, by a tiny minority of the world's people who classify themselves as white, racism (white supremacy) is revealed as one of, if not indeed, the most important observable phenomenon in the world today for which social, behavioral and all other scientists should still be seeking an explanation.

Heretofore racism has been defined variously and described, (see Gullattee,[1] Comer,[2] Butts[3] and Pinderhughes,[4]) yet in this writer's view, the comment made by Oliver C. Cox in his 1959 award winning text, *Caste, Class and Race*, still obtains:

> It is not ordinarily realized that, of all the great mass of writing on race relations, there is available no consistent theory of race relations. The need for such a sociological explanation is so great that recently, when one author succeeded, with some degree of superficial logic, in explaining the phenomena in terms of caste relations, the college textbooks and social-science journals, almost unanimously and unquestioningly, hurriedly adopted his theory.[5]

Perhaps the failure of social and behavioral scientists to develop a sound and consistent theory of racism may rest with the tendency of these investigators to be less demanding and less stringently disciplined in sticking to observable and measurable data, than the so-called "physical" scientists are required to be in formulating hypotheses.

Not infrequently, contrary to all the basic premises of modern science, statements are made by some of these scientists 'a priori', that is to say, as valid independently of observation.

Similarly, there is less pressure brought to bear by the society in general on the behavioral and social scientists to yield viable theories and definitions that can subsequently stand and function as efficient and effective tools to be utilized by the social engineers as guides while they seek to change the social reality. Indeed, the contrary would seem to be the case. If there is any pressure at all, it is to maintain the social status quo so that what the institutions of the society reward are all too often the superficial, inconsistent and dysfunctional theories of societal dynamics.

Neeley Fuller, in his 1969 copyrighted, *Textbook for Victims of White Supremacy*,[6] recognized the need for a functional statement on racism, one that could be utilized daily by those earnestly seeking to bring about social change. Fuller observed that contrary to most present thinking, there is only one functional racism in the known universe and that is white supremacy. He challenges his readers to identify and then to demonstrate the superiority or functional supremacy of any of the world's "non-white" peoples over anyone including their own self-determination. Concluding that since there is no functional or operational supremacy of any 'colored' people, the only valid operational definition of racism is white supremacy. Fuller observes that in spite of any and all statements that the world's "non-white" peoples may make about themselves, as having economic and/or political independence and the like, in the final analysis, they are all victims of the white supremacy process. He places major emphasis on the present realities of the world that can be verified and tested rather than on what one could imagine to be the case, such as a black or yellow supremacy. He further emphasized the need

of a perspective for those wishing to understand the white supremacy process, which includes viewing the patterns of relationships between whites and "non-whites" throughout the entire known universe as opposed to focusing on individual cases and/or just one specified locality.

Fuller goes further to develop the concept that racism is not merely a pattern of individual and/or institutional practice but is indeed a universally operating "system" of white supremacy rule and domination in which the effective majority of the world's white people participate. He discounts as invalid theories which state that the evolution of economic systems has necessitated or produced this state of affairs. Instead, he turns such theories upside down by suggesting that various economic systems such as capitalism, communism and socialism have been devised, used and refined in the effort to achieve the primary goal of white domination. In other words, the goal of the system of white supremacy is not for anything other than the establishment, maintenance, expansion and refinement of world domination by members of the group which classifies itself as the white "race".

In such a context, Fuller then suggests that the word race in this sense has little biological validity but is more correctly translated as "organization" whose sole purpose for being is to maintain white domination and world or universal control.

Whether or not one can be emotionally comfortable with Fuller's thesis and assessment seems not germane. The question of such comfort has never been the important concern of scientific investigation. What to this writer appears of great significance in Fuller's work is that the description of relationships between "non-white" and white peoples has been defined and elucidated in such a way as to account for and to illuminate many past and present observable patterns of behavior and social practice. Also, it would seem to account for the major fact that in spite of all kinds of programs and pronouncements to the contrary for the past several hundred years, white supremacy social conditions have remained intact as the dominant universal social reality.

Fuller's emphasis on the question of color amplifies a similar emphasis placed as far back in time as 1903 when, perhaps the greatest American social scientist, W.E.B. Du Bois, stated in his book, *Souls of Black Folks*, that the great problem for the 20th century is that of the color-line.

Impressed that the concept of a "system" of white supremacy domination over the world's "non-white" peoples could explain the seeming predicament and dilemma of "non-white" social reality, as a psychiatrist, my thinking tended to focus on what possible motivational force, operative at both the individual and group levels, could account for and explain the evolution of these patterns of social

The Psycho-genetic and Social Dynamic
of Racism (White Supremacy)

Genetic Factor: color inadequacy state (white)
an albinism variant

Individual and Group Psychological Response:
development of psychological
defense mechanisms

Compensatory Logic System: White supremacy

Compensatory Behavioral Practices:
(economics, education, entertainment, labor,
law, politics, religion, sex, war)

↓

White supremacy behavioral "system" and
culture on world-wide scale

↓

Systematic oppression, domination and
inferiorization of all people with the capacity to
produce significant quantities of melanin
skin-pigment: Black, Brown, Red and Yellow
peoples of the earth.

quality of whiteness is indeed a genetic inadequacy or a relative genetic deficiency state or disease based upon the genetic inability to produce the skin pigments of melanin which are responsible for all skin coloration.

The massive majority of the world's people are not so afflicted, suggesting that the state of color is the norm for human beings and that the state of color absence is abnormal. This state of color absence acts always as a genetic recessive to the dominant genetic factor of color production. Color always "annihilates," phenotypically and genetically speaking, the non-color, white. Black people possess the greatest color potential, with brown, red and yellow peoples possessing lesser quantities respectively. This then is the genetic and psychological basis for the Cress Theory of Color-Confrontation and Racism (white supremacy).

The Theory of Color-Confrontation states that the white or color-deficient Europeans responded psychologically with a profound sense of numerical inadequacy and color inferiority upon their confrontations with the massive majority of the world's people all of whom possessed varying degrees of color producing capacity. This psychological response, be it described as conscious or unconscious, was one of deeply sensed inadequacy which struck a blow at the most obvious and fundamental part of their being, their external appearance.

As might be anticipated in terms of modern psychological theories, an uncontrollable sense of hostility and aggression developed defensively which has continued to manifest itself throughout the entire historical epoch of the mass confrontations of the whites with people of color. That the initial hostility and aggression came only from the whites is recorded in innumerable diaries, journals, and books written by whites. It is a matter of record, also, that only after long periods of great abuse have the "non-whites" responded defensively with any form of counter-attack. This phenomenal psychological reaction of whites has been directed towards all peoples with the capacity to produce the melanin skin pigments. However, the most profound aggressions have been directed towards the black, "non-white" peoples who have the greatest color potential and therefore are the most envied and the most feared in genetic color competition.

The sense of numerical inadequacy and genetic color inferiority led to a number of interesting, although devastating to all "non-white" peoples, psychological defensive maneuvers or defensive mechanisms. The initial psychological defensive maneuver was the "repression" of the initially felt thought or sense of inadequacy—being without color and, of secondary importance, being in deficient numbers, both of which were apparently painful awarenesses. This primary ego defense of repression, was then reinforced by a host of other defensive mechanisms.

behavioral practice seemingly functional in all areas of human activity (economics, education, entertainment, labor, law, politics, religion, sex and war).

Whereas Fuller has suggested already that the "system" of white supremacy consists of patterns of thought, speech and action, practiced in varying behavioral-unit quantities by the effective majority of the world's white people, the only comment on etiology that he makes is that:

Most white people hate black people. The reason that most white people hate black people is because whites are not black people. If you know this about white people, you need know little else. If you do not know this about white people, virtually all else that you know about them will only confuse you.[7]

I reasoned then that in the majority of instances any neurotic drive for superiority and supremacy is usually founded upon a deep and pervading sense of inadequacy and inferiority. Is it not true that the white people represent in numerical terms a very small minority of the world's people? And more profoundly, is not white itself or the quality of "whiteness" indeed not a color but, more correctly, the very absence of any ability to produce color? The

One of the most important was a "reaction formation" response whose aim it was to convert (at the psychological level) something that was desired and envied (skin color) but which was wholly unattainable, into something that is discredited and despised. The whites desiring to have skin color but being unable to achieve this end on their own, said in effect, consciously or unconsciously, that skin color was disgusting to them and began attributing negative qualities to color and especially to the state of the most skin-color—blackness.

That whites do indeed desire to have colored skin can be seen by anyone at the very first signs of Spring or Summer when they begin to strip off their clothes, as many pieces as the law will allow, often permitting their skins to be burned severely in an attempt to add some color to their white, pale, colorless bodies, rendering themselves vulnerable to the dreaded skin cancer in the process. Most cosmetics are also an attempt to add color to their skins. Such coloring make-up is even now being provided for the white male. And finally, untold millions are spent annually on chemicals that are advertised as increasing the tanning potential of whites.

The fact that blacks have attempted also to change the color of their skins to white in no way mitigates the force of this argument as it can be demonstrated readily that these "non-whites" are responding to the already established social conditions of white supremacy. Such a process as is seen in black or other "non-whites" may be described as identification with the dominator, the oppressor or the aggressor.

Another example of the "reaction formation" defense can be seen in the elaboration of the myth of white genetic superiority which into the present time is still being assiduously reinforced (note Jensen's latest elaborations and their acceptance at all levels of the white social structure). Being acutely aware of their lack of or inferior genetic ability to produce skin color, whites built the elaborate myth of white genetic superiority. They then set about the long drawn out task of evolving a social, political and economic structure with all attendant institutions, to give blacks and other "non-whites" the appearance of being inferior human beings.

Yet another psychological defense maneuver utilized by whites has been that of "projection". Feeling extreme hostility and hate towards "non-whites", the whites began the pattern of stating that "non-whites," or people with color, hated them. In many instances, this mechanism has served to mitigate the guilt whites occasionally feel for constantly feeling the need to aggress against blacks and other "non-white" peoples.

Interestingly, the term "non-white" itself is a double negative resulting in a positive statement. This is perhaps a Freudian slip wherein the use of language ultimately reveals the primary psychological dynamic.

Another, perhaps, special instance of the use of projection was the great desire on the part of whites for sexual alliances with "non-whites"—something in which the white male has indulged himself throughout the world. This deep desire was then projected onto the black male and female, the projection being that the blacks and other "non-whites", had sexual desires for white males and females. The Color-Confrontation Theory postulates that the whites desired and still do desire sexual alliances with the "non-whites", both male and female, because it is only through this route that the whites can achieve the illusion of being able to produce color. The extreme rage vented against even the idea of a sexual alliance between the black male and the white female, which has long been a dominant theme in the white supremacy culture, is viewed by the Color-Confrontation Theory as resulting from the great fear that the white male has had of the black male's capacity to fulfill the greatest longing of the white female—that of conceiving and delivering a product of color.

There are other sexual behaviors as well, practiced by some whites, which can be illuminated by the Color-Confrontation thesis. For example, Malcolm X, in his autobiography, stated that the sexual perversion which he was asked to perform most often by white men, was for him as a black male to have sexual intercourse with white females in their presence, while they indeed looked on.[8] This behavioral pattern on the part of white males, instead of being dismissed as a perversion, can be understood when viewed as allowing for a fantasized identification on the part of the white male, with the black male's capacity to give a conceptual product of color to the white female, something she desperately desires but which the white male cannot possibly fulfill.

Further vivid testimony is given also in that black males have reported that in having sexual intercourse with white females, a frequent utterance on the part of the latter is that they wish to have a black baby.

The Color-Confrontation Theory sheds light on the fact that the body area attacked during most lynchings of black males by white males is the area of the genitals where the powerful color producing genetic material is stored in the testicles.

The repeated and consistent focus on the size of the black male's phallus by both the white male and female, can be viewed by this Theory as a 'displacement' away from the real and fundamental concern with the genetic color producing capacity residing in the testicles. Since the fact of color envy must remain repressed, color desire can never be mentioned or the entire white psychological structure crumbles and collapses. Therefore, a displacement to a less threatening object or symbol is made.

Finally, the degrading of sex in the thought and logic processes of the whole of white supremacy culture allows for yet another area of insight into the fundamental psychological dynamics of whites and their alienation from themselves as being related most basically to their physical appearance. At a most primordial level, sex can be viewed as the reproduction of one's own image, of self and of kind. According to the Color-Confrontation Theory, white supremacy culture degrades the act of sex and the process of self-reproduction because the whiteness reflective of an inability to produce color, is deeply despised. It is most explicitly stated in the white supremacy religious and moral philosophies.

This degrading of the sexual act is not found similarly in the cultures of peoples of color, in fact the very opposite appears to be the case. The act of reproduction is held in the very highest esteem as reflected in their religious practices and in their arts. The artistic and religious practices of India and Africa give strong and continuous testimony to this fact. In whites, this initial core feeling of alienation from themselves and then from the act that produced their image, then found subsequent expression in their thought processes and their religious and moral philosophies, moral codes, social acts, social practices and entire social systemic structure.

Psychiatrists and other behavioral scientists frequently use the patterns of overt behavior towards others as an indication of what is felt fundamentally about the self. If hate and lack of respect are outwardly manifested towards other, hate and lack of respect are most often found at deeper levels toward the self.

Facets of some of other present behavioral patterns being manifested within the white supremacy cultural framework would seem to be supportive of this thesis. For example, the profound sense of alienation towards themselves that is being experienced and written about by many white writers in all areas of the world. Some of the current political and social behavioral activity against the ideology and values of the white social structure, although not spoken of in the terminology of this writer, can at one level be appreciated as an expression of a manifestation of the same kernel alienation against whiteness. Thus, the hippies and yippies by allowing dirt to accumulate on themselves, in one sense, are adding color to their skins. Also, by allowing their head and facial hair to proliferate, they give expression to covering themselves with the only part of their bodies that does have true substantive color, their hair.

The present frantic attempts to counter this sense of interpersonal alienation in the white culture by free and open sexual practices and sexual orgies, will, in this writer's view, be totally insufficient to stem or quiet this deep sense of alienation because,

again, the core difficulty begins with a fundamental response to and alienation from their colorlessness and secondarily from the social practices and structure whites have built over the centuries around that psychological core.

Racism (white supremacy) having begun as a form of alienation towards the self has now evolved into the most highly refined form of alienation towards others as well. The Theory of Color-Confrontation views all of the present battle-grounds in the world today as vivid reflections of this alienation towards others. The destructive and aggressive behavioral patterns being displayed throughout the world by white peoples towards all "non-white" peoples is the evidence of the inner hate, hostility and rejection felt towards themselves and of the depth of self alienation that evolved from the genetic and psychological kernel of the color inadequacy state of whites.

The mass inability of whites to live and attend school in the presence of "non-whites", manifested by the patterns of black and white housing and education throughout this country and, indeed, throughout the world, is seen in terms of the Color-Confrontation thesis as the apparent total psychological discomfort experienced by whites in situations in which they must daily face their color inadequacy when they confront their neighbors of color. Also the myth of white superiority cannot be maintained and is exploded in the presence of equitable social and economic opportunity.

The white personality in the presence of color can only be stabilized by keeping blacks and other "non-whites" in an obviously inferior position. The situation of mass proximity to blacks is intolerable to whites because the blacks are inherently more than equal. The blacks and other "non-whites" will always have something of the highest visibility that the whites can never have or can never produce and that is the genetic factor of color. In the presence of color, whites will always feel genetically inferior.

The difficulty whites have in according "non-whites" socio-political and economic equality within the white supremacy structure stems then not from a moral issue nor from a political or economic imperative but instead from the fundamental sense of their own unequal situation in regards to their numerical inadequacy and color deficiency state. Their color inadequacy can only be compensated by a socially superior positional opportunity and stance. The color inadequacy state of whiteness not only demands but indeed, apparently necessitates, a white superiority social structure. Only tokenism can be tolerated by such a motivational psychological state wherein the defense mechanism of evolving the mythology of the exceptional black or "non-white" is utilized.

The thrust towards superiority over peoples of color, the drive towards materialism, acquisition and accumulation, the drive towards a technological culture and the drive towards power, all of which are cornerstones of the universal white supremacy culture, are viewed in terms of the Color-Confrontation thesis as responses to the core psychological sense of inadequacy. Inadequacy, not in terms of infant size as compared with that of the adult's, as postulated by Alfred Adler, but an inadequacy sense rooted in the genetic absence of or relative inability to produce the skin pigments of melanin. This genetic state is in actuality a variant of albinism.

The Color-Confrontation Theory postulates that whites are also vunerable to their sense of numerical inadequacy. The behavioral manifestations or expressions of their sense of this inadequacy in their numbers become apparent in the drive or need to divide the massive majority of "non-whites" into fractional as well as frictional minorities. This is viewed as a key and fundamental behavioral response to their own minority status in the known universe. The white "race", collectively representing the world's largest minority grouping, has so structured and manipulated their own thought processes and conceptual patterns, as well as those of the entire "non-whites" world majority, that the real numerical minority (the whites) illusionally feels and represents itself as the world's majority and the true numerical majority (the "non-whites") illusionally feels and views itself as the minority.

Interestingly, the collective white group whenever discussing the question of color, never discusses any of its own particular ethnic groupings as minorities, but constantly and continuously focuses on the various ethnic, language and religious groupings of colored peoples as minorities. Then great efforts are made to initiate conflict between these arbitrary groupings. This is one of the key methodologies by which a minority can remain in power. The 'divide, frictionalize and conquer' pattern, observable throughout the known universe wherever whites are confronted by "non-whites," is seen as deriving at a primary level from the sense of color deficiency and at a secondary level from the sense of the numerical inadequacy of whites in the known universe of 'colored' peoples. This can be seen then as a compensatory adjustment to permit psychological comfort through dominance and control.

The present day frantic focus on birth control for the entire "non-white" world can be viewed as a further example of the conscious or unconscious awareness on the part of whites of their numerical deficiency status. There is never great emphasis on controlling the births of whites and, indeed, there are some white governmental groupings that give dividends to citizens for increased procreation.

The foregoing are but a few of the examples selected by this writer from millions of large and small behavioral patterns practiced by whites in varying behavioral unit quantities which demonstrate the individual and collective neurotic need to focus on. Color, Sex, Genetics, Numbers, Superiority-Inferiority, White Supremacy and Power. The Theory of Color-Confrontation postulates that all of the above can be explained on the basis of the core psychological sense of a color-deficiency, numerical inadequacy state which white or whiteness represents. The individual patterns of behavior which in the course of time evolved into collective, social, institutional and now systemic patterns are seen as making up the "system of white supremacy" which operates at a universal level and is the only effective and functional racism extant in the world today. Further, racism (white supremacy), in this historical epoch, is viewed as a full blown social contradiction and the major social dynamic force superceding all others in influencing universal social practice and social decisions. It is also being viewed as one of the dominating forces determining character development, personality type and formation.

A functional definition of racism (white supremacy) is therefore, for all practical purposes: the behavioral syndrome of individual and collective color inferiority and numerical inadequacy which includes patterns of thought, speech and action as seen in members of the white organization (race).

What then are the practical implications of this theory?

Of major importance, for the first time in centuries, "non-white" peoples throughout the world will have a rational basis for understanding the motivational nuances of individual and collective white behavior.

It is theorized by the Color-Confrontation thesis that the reason that the massive majority of the world's people, who are of various colors, were able to be manipulated into a subordinated position was that they were unprepared psychologically, in terms of their own thought and logic processes and premises, to understand patterns of behavior that were predicated upon a sense of color deficiency and numerical inadequacy because they themselves had never experienced such a state. This is seen as being analogous to the man with two eyes finding it difficult if not impossible to understand the behavioral patterns and motivations of the congenitally one-eyed man who always looked upon the two-eyed state with jealous antagonism and, perhaps, aggression.

Armed with such insight, knowledge and understanding, the "non-white" will no longer be vulnerable to the behavioral maneuverings of the individual white or the collective white group. "Non-whites" will be less vulnerable to the messages of white superiority which radiate throughout the known universe and permeate the present world culture which is dominate by white supremacy systemization. This will have profound effects on the developing ego structures and self images of all "non-white" children which drastically suffer under the white supremacy culture.

All "non-whites" will further understand that whenever they are confronted by the ideology of white superiority and white supremacy, it is only a compensatory psychological adjustment for a genetic numerical deficiency state and the white supremacy message can be more readily evaluated and negated. This then allows for the psychological liberation of "non-whites" from the white superiority ideological domination which has so negatively affected the total functioning of "non-whites." Further, "non-whites" will be less vulnerable to being maneuvered to battle and squabble among themselves thus weakening the continued domination of the world behavioral system of white supremacy.

The white peoples of the world presumably could benefit also from such an awareness and insight into the motivational core behind behaviors which, if they are to be believed, often baffle them. If they are sincere in their attempts to stop the practices of white supremacy (racism), they may be able to find methods to do so, once they understand the possible cause. Perhaps some psychiatrist will develop a method of mass psychotherapy (i.e., therapeutic counter-racist theater), which will help whites become comfortable with their color and their numbers. However, one can foresee a major problem arising from the difficulty he or she may encounter in motivating whites to realize the secondary gains presently derived from the racist system.

Whether the white peoples of the world can accept this analysis of the white problem in human relations is not for me to answer. I do know that the massive majority of the people in the world are looking for an answer to the dilemma that was once called the "American Dilemma." They are looking for a change. Perhaps the Cress Theory of Color-Confrontation will help them to make that change.

In any event, I am reminded of a statement made by Freud's biographer, Ernst Jones: "In the last analysis, the justification of every scientific generalization is that it enables us to comprehend something that is otherwise obscure."[9]

And, as James B. Conant has stated, "The test of a new idea is ... not only its success in correlating the then known facts but much more its success or failure in stimulating further experimentation or observation which in turn is fruitful. This dynamic aspect of science viewed not as practical undertaking but as development of conceptual schemes seems to me to be close to the heart of the best definition of science."[10]

This essay has been an attempt to analyze the unique universal behavioral phenomenon of white supremacy (racism) and to place in a conceptual framework and context of a theoretical formulation the fundamentals in the dynamics inherent in the spectrum of relations, covering all areas of life activity between people who classify themselves as white and/or members of the white "race" and those people whom the whites have classified as the "non-whites."

NOTES

1. A. C. Gullattee, "The Subtelties of White Racism," a paper presented to the American Psychiatric Association Annual Meeting, Miami Beach, Florida, May 1969.

2. J. Comer, "White Racism: Its Roots, Form and Function," *The American Journal of Psychiatry*, Vol. 26: No. 6, December 1969.

3. P. A. Harrison & H. F. Butts, "White Psychiatrists' Racism in Referral Practices to Black Psychiatrists," *Journal of the National Medical Association*, Vol. 62, No. 4, July 1970.

4. Charles A. Pinderhughes, "Understanding Black Power: Processes and Proposals," *American Journal of Psychiatry*, Vol. 125: 1552-1557, 1969.

5. O. C. Cox, *Caste, Class and Race*, New York: Monthly Review Press, 1959 p. ix.

6. N. Fuller, *Textbook for Victims of White Supremacy*, Copyrighted, Library of Congress, 1969.

7. *Ibid.*

8. Malcolm X, *The Autobiography of Malcolm X* (with the assistance of Alex Haley), New York: Grove Press, 1966, p. 120.

9. E. Jones, *Papers of Psychoanalysis*, Boston: Beacon Press, 1961, p. 73.

10. J. B. Conant, *On Understanding Science*, New York: Mentor, 1953.

20

The Declining Significance of Race: Blacks and Changing American Institutions

WILLIAM JULIUS WILSON

This book is now a classic in discussions focusing on the relationship between race and class in the United States, and the significance of racism in defining relations between blacks and whites. Wilson generally argued that the living conditions characteristics of many urban black communities in the United States could not be attributed solely, or primarily to racial discrimination, although this may have been true in earlier periods in the nation's history. He proposed that national economic factors and developments carried far more weight in explaining the continuing deteriorated social status of blacks and their communities. In this selection, Wilson discusses the relationship between race and the changing economic order in US society and its pre-industrial period. It also explains how segregation was essentially a response to changes in the nation's economy as a period of slavery gives way to the rise of a white working-class sector.

In the preindustrial period of American race relations there was of course very little variation in the economic class position of blacks. The system of racial caste oppression relegated virtually all blacks to the bottom of the economic class hierarchy. Moreover, the social definitions of racial differences were heavily influenced by the ideology of racism and the doctrine of paternalism, both of which clearly assigned a subordinate status for blacks vis-à-vis whites. Occasionally, a few individual free blacks would emerge and accumulate some wealth or property, but they were the overwhelming exception. Thus the uniformly low economic class position of blacks reinforced and, in the eyes of most whites, substantiated the social definitions that asserted Negroes were culturally and biogenetically inferior to whites. The uniformly low economic class position of blacks also removed the basis for any meaningful distinction between race issues and class issues within the black community.

The development of a black middle class accompanied the change from a preindustrial to an industrial system of production. Still, despite the fact that some blacks were able to upgrade their occupation and increase their education and income, there were severe limits on the areas in which blacks could in fact advance. Throughout most of the industrial period of race relations, the growth of the black middle class occurred because of the expansion of institutions created to serve the needs of a growing urbanized black population. The black doctor, lawyer, teacher, minister, businessman, mortician, excluded from the white community, was able to create a niche in the segregated black community. Although the income levels and life-styles of the black professionals were noticeably and sometimes conspicuously different from those of the black masses, the two groups had one basic thing in common, a racial status contemptuously regarded by most whites in society. If E. Franklin Frazier's analysis of the very real sense, the current problems of lower-class blacks are substantially related to fundamental structural changes in the economy. A history of discrimination and oppression created a huge black underclass, and the technological and economic revolutions have combined to insure it a permanent status.

As the black middle class rides on the wave of political and social changes, benefiting from the growth of employment opportunities in the growing corporate and government sectors of the economy, the black underclass falls behind the larger society in every conceivable respect. The economic and political systems in the United States have demonstrated remarkable flexibility in allowing talented blacks to fill positions of prestige and influence at the same time that these systems have shown persistent rigidity in handling the problems of lower-class blacks. As a result, for the first time in American history class issues can meaningfully compete with race issues in the way blacks develop or maintain a sense of group position.[31]

CONCLUSION

The foregoing sections of this chapter present an outline and a general analytical basis for the arguments that will be systematically explored in the following chapters. I have tried to show that race relations in American society have been historically characterized by three major stages and that each stage is represented by a unique form of racial interaction which is shaped by the particular arrangement of the economy and the polity. My central argument is that different systems of production and/or different policies of the state have imposed different constraints on the way in which racial groups interact—constraints that have structured the relations between racial groups and produced dissimilar contexts not only for the manifestation of racial antagonisms but also for racial-group access to rewards and privileges. I emphasized in this connection that in the preindustrial and industrial periods of American race relations the systems of production primarily

shaped the patterns of racial stratification and the role of the polity was to legitimate, reinforce, or regulate these patterns. In the modern industrial period, however, both the system of production and the polity assume major importance in creating new patterns of race relations and in altering the context of racial strife. Whereas the preindustrial and industrial stages were principally related to group struggles over economic resources as different segments of the white population overtly sought to create and solidify economic racial domination (ranging from the exploitation of black labor in the preindustrial period to the elimination of black competition for jobs in the industrial period) through various forms of political, juridical, and social discrimination; in the modern industrial period fundamental economic and political changes have made economic class position more important than race in determining black chances for occupational mobility. Finally, I have outlined the importance of racial norms or belief systems, especially as they relate to the general problem of race and class conflict in the preindustrial and industrial periods.

My argument that race relations in America have moved from economic racial oppression to a form of class subordination for the less privileged blacks is not meant to suggest that racial conflicts have disappeared or have even been substantially reduced. On the contrary, the basis of such conflicts have shifted from the economic sector to the sociopolitical order and therefore do not play as great a role in determining the life chances of individual black Americans as in the previous periods of overt economic racial oppression. But these are matters to be explored in greater detail in the following chapters.

2 Slavery and Plantation Hegemony

In the preindustrial period of American race relations, the system of slavery severely restricted black vertical and horizontal mobility. The basic contacts between blacks and whites were essentially those involving the slaves and the small elite class of slave-owners—a relationship that was stabilized and reinforced by the vast discrepancy in racial power resources on the rural farms and plantations. Being symbiotic in nature, these contacts greatly decreased physical distance; however, social distance was enhanced by clearly defined patterns of dominance and subservience which included elaborate rituals of racial etiquette. There were some slight variations to these patterns both in antebellum southern cities and in relationships involving a small number of free blacks and lower-class whites; but because of the interdependent master-slave relationship, the overwhelming number of blacks in the antebellum South experienced only casual contacts with white nonslaveholders. As the institution of slavery grew, it profoundly affected the pattern of life in the South and, to some extent, in the nation generally. One of slavery's most direct and obvious institutional effects was that it provided the base for the enormous accumulation of public power by a small elite, power that was used to shape the economic structure of the South and the political structure of the nation.

THE HEGEMONY OF SOUTHERN SLAVEHOLDERS

Throughout the period of legal servitude, the ownership of slaves was a privilege enjoyed by only a small percentage of free families in the South. Of the 1,156,000 free southern families in 1860, only 385,000 (roughly one-fourth) owned slaves. However, the majority of slaves were owned by families that possessed at least twenty slaves each. Within this "planter class," some ten thousand families, or the "planter aristocracy," owned more than fifty slaves each. The essential point is that, although the great majority of slaveholders owned small farms where a few slaves labored beside their masters, most slaves lived and worked on plantations where cotton, tobacco, sugar cane, or rice were cultivated on a large, commercial scale.[1]

Despite the fact that power, leadership, and influence were concentrated among members of the planter class, slaveholders in general constituted a broad socioeconomic class sharply differentiated from nonslaveholders by social and political behavior and by basic economic interests. "The most advanced fraction of the slaveholders—those who most clearly perceived the interests and needs of the class as a whole," states Genovese, "steadily worked to make their class more conscious of its nature, spirit, and destiny. In the process, it created a world-view appropriate to a slaveholder's regime."[2] By the end of the eighteenth century, the southern slaveholders had clearly established their hegemony as a regional ruling class. The economic system, the political system, and the juridical system in the South were all controlled and shaped by the slaveholding elite. As a socioeconomic class, the slaveholders "used their political power to protect their class interests, the greatest of which was slavery itself."[3] They also shaped the legal system to reinforce these interests.

The southern legal system embodied an implicit duality that recognized the rights of the state over both slave and free individuals on the one hand, and the rights of the masters over their bondsmen on the other. In early Virginia and Maryland, and later in other colonies, as slavery gradually received legal sanction, the laws not only granted masters overwhelming power over their slaves but also codified white supremacy by restricting slave status to nonwhites and prohibiting interracial marriage. In the words of Genovese, "These early Draconian slave codes served as a model for those adopted by new states during the nineteenth century. Over time, they became harsher with respect to manumission, education, and the status of the free Negro and milder with respect to protection for slave life."[4]

Although the legal system helped to enhance the interests of the slaveholders on a regional level, the political system transcended the southern borders and reflected the national influence of the planters. That the slaveholders were highly organized and politically disciplined is evident in the way they protected and promoted their class interests by virtually denying the meaningful exercise of political power to nonslaveholding whites in the South. At the very least, by the nineteenth century, the procedures used to restrict political participation indicated that the slaveholders had been transformed, in the classical Marxist dictum, from a class-in-itself to a class-for-itself. "Tradition, property qualifications for the suffrage, the counting of the slave population for purposes of legislative apportionment, the gerrymandering of legislative districts, to the detriment of poor whites, or as in South Carolina, qualifications which barred office to all but slaveholders," observe Spero and Harris, "made it easy for the master class to control the state and block all unfavorable legislation."[5] And this domination of regional politics provided the foundation for the slaveholders' heavy influence on the federal government in the latter stages of the antebellum period.

In the first half of the nineteenth century, northern opponents of slavery contended, with convincing documentation, that the planters of the South constituted a politically organized "slave power" that was attempting to control the federal government in hope of providing more national support for the institution of slavery. Antislavery Republicans of the North did not hesitate to point out that since 1789 a substantial majority of congressional committee chairmen, chief justices, secretaries of state, and even presidents had been from the South.[6] In 1856, the *New York Times*, echoing the sentiments of antislavery men, editorialized that the southern politicians were "held together like the feudal barons of the middle ages by a community of interests and of sentiment; and [act] together always for the promotion of their common ends."[7]

The southerners' power in Congress and in the electoral college had been increased by the three-fifths clause of the Constitution to the point where they could regulate the policies of the major parties on slavery. Meanwhile, northern sentiment was weakened by fear of southern threats of secession and by a lack of unity on the issue of slavery. A succession of congressional decisions in the decades preceding the Civil War served to dramatize the influence of the planter class on the Federal government and lent strong support to the idea of "slave power." Salmon P. Chase, the influential antislavery leader of Ohio, pointed out in 1854 that the eighteenth-century policy of restricting and denationalizing slavery was seriously undermined when a report dealing with slavery was altered by the very first Congress to satisfy slaveholders' interests, when the fugitive slave law was passed, and when Congress accepted a territorial cession from North Carolina which allowed slavery to exist in the area. He furthermore noted that the creation of slavery and slaveholdings in areas of national jurisdiction continued into the nineteenth century; Florida and Louisiana were purchased with slavery permitted, the Missouri Compromise extended slavery across the Mississippi River, and the annexation of Texas increased slave power in the Southwest.[8] The Kansas-Nebraska Act of 1854, which dramatically opened the West to slavery, and the Dred-Scott Decision of 1857, which provided federal government protection of slavery in the territories, extended southern influence in the federal government and clearly demonstrated the reality of an aggressive slave power.

The hegemony of the southern slaveholders as a regional ruling class and their influence on national politics emanated directly from a slave-based plantation economy which impeded the ability of non-slaveholders to challenge the planters' political and economic stranglehold over the South; it also enabled the slaveholders to develop a regional center of power that was effectively transferred to the national level. As long as the replenishing of the labor supply did not depend on tapping the reservoir of free labor, slavery as a mode of production created a situation in which economic power was consolidated and concentrated in the hands of the slave-holding elite. With slaves providing the bulk of the labor for the plantations and, as we shall see, a good share of the meager industrial labor force, the competitive advantage of free laborers in an essentially preindustrial economy was drastically curtailed. The weak economic position of nonslaveholding whites provided little leverage for generating social and political power and for developing a sufficient political class consciousness. These whites were not even in a position to exert much influence on the pattern of race relations in the antebellum South.

Structural Relations between Masters and Slaves

There are two distinct historical periods marking the relationship between masters and slaves—the period prior to the cessation of the African slave trade in 1808 in which the planters relied partly on external markets for the reproduction of their labor force and the period following the ban on slave trading in which the reproduction of slave labor was based almost exclusively on natural increase. The significance of this distinction is that many historians feel that the treatment of slaves was considerably harsher in the period prior to the United States' official withdrawal from the African slave trade; there was harsher treatment, it is said, primarily because planters were not compelled to devote serious attention to slave reproduction. However, the issues underlying this assumption are fairly complex and deserve at least a brief discussion on the basis of the available, but far from satisfactory, evidence.

Despite the heightened interest in scholarly interpretations of American slavery and the slave experience (generated in large measure by the controversial studies of Stanley Elkins, Eugene Genovese, and Robert Fogel and Stanley Engerman),[9] recent historical debates on the subject have tended to focus more on nineteenth-century slavery (that is, the period following the ban on slave trading) than on the earlier periods. However, an important study by Edmund S. Morgan on slavery in Virginia has helped to fill some of the gaps in our knowledge about the peculiar institution in the colonial period.[10]

If we examine the situation in colonial Virginia (the first colony to officially recognize slavery, with an act passed in 1661 that made an indentured servant who ran away with a slave responsible for the loss incurred by the master during the slave's absence) around the mid-seventeenth century, we see that the conversion to slavery was not only prompted by the heightened concern over a cheap labor shortage in the face of the rapid development of tobacco farming as a commercial enterprise and the declining number of white indentured servants entering the colonies,[11] but also by the fact that the slave had become a better investment than the servant. As life expectancy increased, resulting from the significant decline in the mortality rate from disease, planters were willing to finance the extra cost of slaves. Indeed, during the first half of the seventeenth century, indentured labor was actually more advantageous than slave labor. "Because of the high mortality among the immigrants to Virginia," states Morgan, "there could be no great advantage in owning a man for lifetime rather than a period of years, especially since a slave cost roughly twice as much as an indentured servant. If the chances of a man's dying during his first five years in Virginia were better than fifty-fifty—and it seems apparent that they were—and if English servants could be made to work as hard as slaves, English servants for a five year term were the better buy."[12]

Because the international slave trade had already firmly established a pattern of black enslavement and because there was no deep-seated opposition to the institution of slavery in the colonies, the increased life expectancy during the second half of the seventeenth century just made it a matter of time before slavery would replace indentured servitude as a major source of cheap labor. It was not necessary to enslave anyone to establish slavery in Virginia: "Virginians had only to buy men who were already enslaved, after the initial risks of the transformation had been sustained by others elsewhere. They converted to slavery, simply by buying slaves instead of servants."[13]

Although slaves in the colonies entered a system of production that had already been established, their presence necessitated new methods of disciplining the work force. In Virginia, for instance, masters of slaves soon recognized the need to impose a higher level of pain than did the masters of servants. "Slaves could not be made to work for fear of losing liberty," observes Morgan, "so they had to be made to work for fear for their lives. Not that any master wanted to lose his slave by killing him, but in order to get an equal or greater amount of work, it was necessary to beat slaves harder than servants, so hard, in fact, that there was a much larger chance of killing them than had been the case with servants."[14] Indeed, the Virginia Assembly recognized this fact and in 1669 passed a law which would legally protect the master who in the process of disciplining his slave actually ended up killing him. Later legislation designed to curb the growing problem of runaway slaves stipulated that it would "be lawful for any person or persons whatsoever, to kill and destroy such slaves by such ways and means as he, she, or they shall think fit, without accusation or impeachment of any crime for the same."[15] The law further specified that the master would be compensated with public funds for the loss of any slaves killed under these conditions. Thus, concludes Morgan, "In order to get work out of men and women who had nothing to gain but the absence of pain, you had to be willing to beat, maim, and kill. And society had to be ready to back you, even to the point of footing the bill for the property you killed."[16]

However, colonial laws which allowed masters and other whites to kill slaves were not extended into the nineteenth century. By 1821, all slave states had amended their laws to protect the lives of slaves and to provide murder indictments against slaveholders and others for killing a slave arbitrarily or through excessive punishment. As Genovese points out in this connection, "When whites did find themselves before the bar of justice, especially during the late antebellum period, they could expect greater severity than might be imagined. The penalties seldom reached the extreme or the level they would have if the victim had been white; but neither did they usually qualify as a slap on the wrist. If one murderer in North Carolina got off with only eleven months in prison in 1825, most fared a good deal worse. Ten-year sentences were common, and occasionally the death penalty was invoked."[17]

It is always a precarious practice to infer the actual treatment of human beings from laws that regulate human behavior. However, a comparison of the laws pertaining to the killing of slaves in the colonial period with the more humane laws in the nineteenth century does suggest a change in societal norms regarding slavery, even if one is not willing to grant any significant changes in the actual behavior of white slaveholders. Still, there are other indications that the lot of slaves fared better in the late antebellum period than in the colonial period. But, before examining these other factors, I want to return to the argument concerning the significance of the cessation of the African slave trade—an argument that some historians have used to explain changes in the treatment of slaves.

The closing of the slave trade in the early nineteenth century did not weaken the institution of slavery, as some Americans might have expected. Rather, it had a reverse effect. It increased the financial commitment of slavery. Because slaves could no longer be legally imported from Africa and because the demand for slaves sharply increased both with the opening of new lands in the Southwest and with the expanding of cotton production in the deep South, the price of bondsmen skyrocketed in the nineteenth century. Even those slaveholders who resided in areas such as Virginia and South Carolina where slave labor was no longer as important as it had been in the past, became more firmly committed to slavery as their investment in human property increased in value.[18]

In addition to the increased financial commitment to slavery, the slave-trade ban increased the reliance on natural reproduction for replenishing the slave population. It therefore became increasingly important for slaveholders to give attention to the material conditions of slaves in order to improve the chances for successful childbirth and physical growth to maturity.[19] Recent historical studies by Fogel and Engerman and by Genovese have asserted that the treatment of slaves progressively improved throughout the nineteenth century and that the rapid natural growth of slavery was associated with more humane treatment.[20] Following federal action in 1808, declaring the importation of slaves illegal, the slave population grew, primarily as a result of natural increase, from one million in 1810 to nearly four million in 1860.[21] The South's experience of rapid slave population growth via natural increase was unique. Despite significantly larger importations throughout the eighteenth and nineteenth centuries, Cuba, Brazil, Jamaica, and Santo Domingo struggled simply to maintain their slave populations by balancing imports against mortality.[22] Fogel and Engerman maintain that the slaveholders in the South provided slaves with material conditions that "compared favorably with those of free industrial workers during the first half of the nineteenth century,"[23] including a diet which "actually exceeded modern (1964) recommended daily levels of chief nutrients."[24] Genovese likewise stresses that the slaves were as well off as a substantial portion of Western European peasants and workers and that the slaveholders during this same period came to fully realize that excessive driving jeopardized the slaves' health and, therefore, contributed to capital loss. "They even enlisted racist arguments to advocate a more humane course, explaining that blacks constitutionally could not work as long as whites."[25]

Both the improved treatment of slaves and their rapid natural growth were, however, a function of the increasing value of slave property in the nineteenth century. To repeat, the price of slaves escalated in the face of expanding cotton production in the deep South and the demand for labor in the newly settled territories of the Southwest. It is little wonder, therefore, that the southern slave system "became progressively more humane with respect to the material conditions of life as it became progressively more repressive with respect to manumission."[26] Nearing the eve of the Civil War, slavery had become a very profitable and successful institution and the drive to improve the material conditions of slaves as well as the campaign to decrease their chances of freedom, both of which predated abolitionist pressures, derived from the planters' interests in maximizing profits.

The slaveholders often responded to criticisms of their efforts to maintain blacks in permanent bondage by proclaiming not only that their bondsmen were treated better than any other slaves in the world but also that their conditions compared favorably with those of the workers and peasants in Europe. Their arguments, of course, selectively focused on the material conditions of life. The slaveholders were not inclined to consider the psychological aspects of slavery outlined in the eloquent remarks of W. E. B. Du Bois in 1934:

> But there was in 1863 a real meaning to slavery different from that we apply to the laborer today. It was in part psychological, the enforced personal feeling of inferiority, the calling of another master, the standing with hat in hand. It was the helplessness. It was the defenselessness of family life. It was the submergence below the arbitrary will of any sort of individual. It was without doubt worse in these vital respects than that which exists today in Europe or America.[27]

Whether one focuses on slavery in the colonial period or in the late antebellum period, "the enforced personal feeling of inferiority" was endemic to permanent servitude. The slave was under constant supervision and efforts were consistently made to generate deferential and submissive behavior. The enduring ritual of race etiquette, reinforced by the master at every turn, stipulated that proper behavior and conduct for blacks involved bowing when meeting the master, standing and showing great humility in his presence, accepting floggings from the master's children, and approaching the mansion in the most self-effacing, humble, and beseeching manner. Floggings and other modes of physical punishment were employed by most planters to ensure ritualistic obedience and deference to plantation rules. Slaves were frequently flogged, punished, or disciplined for failing to complete assigned tasks, running away, learning to read, bickering or fighting with whites or with other slaves, stealing, drunkenness, working too slowly, impertinence, asking to be sold, claiming their freedom, and damaging tools or household articles.[28]

But were the bondsmen psychologically devastated by slavery? It is one thing to recognize the group or personal feelings of inferiority that are inevitably produced by prolonged enslavement, it is quite another to postulate, as does Stanley Elkins, that slaves, very much like Jews in the Nazi concentration camps, were reduced to a childlike dependency.[29] A series of historical studies have challenged Elkins' thesis by positing the view that the institution of slavery left enough "breathing space" for slaves to develop mechanisms or strategies of survival to preserve their humanity, to resist complete personal degradation, to prevent total identification with masters, and to stave off infantilism.[30] Historians disagree, however, in their interpretation of just how and in what context these mechanisms were developed. And to get an idea of the level of disagreement, we need only examine the arguments advanced by Eugene Genovese and Herbert G. Gutman, whose works provide two of the most important and persuasive theses on slave strategies of survival.[31]

According to Genovese, the efforts of slaves to preserve their humanity grew out of and were in part based on the unique form of paternalism that characterized antebellum slavery in the South. Encouraged by the physical proximity and continuous interaction between planters and slaves, southern paternalism stressed duties, responsibilities, and reciprocal demands and expectations. The ideological expression of southern paternalism not only justified slave labor as a legitimate exchange for the masters' protection and direction but also, by the doctrine of reciprocal obligations, implicitly acknowledged the slaves' humanity. In fact, the slaves seized on this interpretation and translated paternalism into a doctrine that greatly stressed their human rights. If it were the master's duty to care for his involuntary labor force, then this duty represented the slaves' right. The slaves' acceptance of paternalism, therefore, signified acceptance of imposed white control within which they established limits, affirmed their rights, and spared their self-respect.[32] "By developing a sense of moral worth and by asserting their rights, the slaves transformed their acquiescence in paternalism into a rejection of slavery itself, although their masters assumed acquiescence in one to demonstrate acquiescence in the other."[33]

Genovese maintains that it was the slaves' religion, a complex mixture of African and Christian beliefs, that provided the medium for elaborating this interpretation of paternalism, a religion that created an organized center of resistance within accommodation, a religion, in short, that reflected white hegemony but also established definite limits to that hegemony. "Southern paternalism may have reinforced racism as well as class exploitation," argues Genovese, "but it also unwittingly invited its victims to fashion their own interpretation of the social order it was intended to justify. And the slaves, drawing on a religion that was supposed to assure their compliance and docility, rejected the essence of slavery by protecting their rights and values as human beings."[34]

Whereas Genovese believes that slaves developed mechanisms to preserve their humanity based on continuous interaction with or reaction to the behavior of planters, Gutman argues that the bondsmen were far more independent in the development of slave communities. By reconstructing the slave family and kinship structure through a careful analysis of plantation birth registers, marriage applications received by Union officers following emancipation, and documents containing the direct testimony of former slaves, Gutman attempts to show that an adaptive Afro-American slave culture was created without any significant involvement or influence exerted by the planters. Instead of using cultural forms that emerged from a manipulation of planter paternalism, slaves adapted in fairly uniform ways to diversified forms of enslavement (living on plantations or in farm counties, or in counties in which few or many slaves resided) by developing and using social and cultural arrangements that white planters did not even perceive. Specifically, Gutman maintains that enslaved Afro-Americans independently developed distinctive domestic arrangements and kin networks that fostered a new Afro-American culture, and that both the family system and the slave culture provided the social basis for the creation of Afro-American communities. In other words, the development of inter- and intra-generational linkages, following the emergence of settled Afro-American slave families provided a basis for a sense of community that was extended over time and across space. Thus, conceptions of kin and family obligations among slaves were transformed by the slaves themselves into conceptions of quasi-kin and nonkin social and communal obligations. Slaves in this network of social obligations and attachments exhibited neither the "social isolation" described in Elkins' study of slavery nor the "elaborate web of paternalistic relations,"

that, according to Genovese, allowed the planter class to establish "hegemony over the slaves."[35]

These conflicting interpretations of the slave experience and the master-slave relationship will continue to generate debate among historians until future research sheds additional light on the subject. If blacks were able to develop unique "strategies for survival," whether by a paternalistic compromise or an independent cultural adaptation, they did so in a racial caste system that exploited their labor, restricted their freedom, and virtually eliminated any chances for free and open competition for scarce rewards and privileges. Moreover, regardless of the degree of cultural independence displayed by the slaves, much of their behavior was influenced or determined by their continuous interaction or relationships with slaveholding whites. The very nature of such a relationship (characterized by dominance and subservience, little physical distance but great social distance) would suggest at least a modicum of paternalistic behavior, because, unlike in more competitive systems of race relations, it allowed for close symbiotic relationships without necessarily threatening the norms of racial inequality. Furthermore, as Genovese points out, many of the informal norms of the paternalistic order, norms which stipulated the masters' obligation to care for their slaves in return for explicit duties and services, were actually formalized or embodied in the nineteenth-century slave codes.[36] Finally, even Gutman recognizes that "Paternalist beliefs were widespread among plantation owners on the eve of the Civil War and affected the behavior of many planters." However, he is correct in further pointing out that "no one, including Genovese, has studied how such beliefs and practices developed."[37] Since the available evidence suggests that paternalistic beliefs among planters were more characteristic of the nineteenth century than of the seventeenth and eighteenth centuries, it would not be unreasonable to associate those beliefs with the increasing value of slave property after the closing of the African slave trade.

It could even be argued that the tendency of southern blacks to separate Caucasians into the "respectable" and the "poor white trash" in the late nineteenth and the twentieth centuries was one of the legacies of slave paternalism. Slaves were clearly cognizant of the protection that the paternalistic order provided them against overt attacks by hostile poor whites. Even with the sharp increase in the slave population during the late antebellum period, as long as paternalistic relations between masters and slaves existed, the racial antagonisms of the nonslaveholding whites were held in check. Lynching, which typified the informal violence of the antebellum South, seldom involved blacks. Genovese estimates that less than 10 percent of the more than three hundred lynching victims between 1840 and 1860 were black.[38] The masters had little need to engage in or to support extralegal measures against blacks because of their power not only over their slaves but also in the larger society. If indiscriminate mob violence against slaves was tolerated, the position of the slaveholding class would be challenged as well and the aggressive activities of the white lower class might eventually exceed racial boundaries. "The masters felt that their own direct action, buttressed by a legal system of their own construction, needed little or no support from poor white trash. Order meant order."[39]

The slaves' reliance on their masters for protection established a pattern of group dependency that was to persist several decades after slavery officially ended. And, as we shall see in the next chapter, when this relationship ultimately collapsed in the postbellum period, it paved the way for a century of Jim Crow segregation.

SLAVERY AND SEGREGATION IN THE ANTEBELLUM URBAN SOUTH

Whereas paternalistic relations, reinforced by slaveholder power, tended to characterize black-white relations on the rural farms and plantations, a noticeably different pattern of racial interaction prevailed in the urban areas of the antebellum South where assertive free blacks, insecure underclass whites, and loosely supervised slaves lived and worked. On the farms and plantations, the social distance between the races was wide and secure. Consequently, the system of status inequalities was not threatened by the high degree of black-white contact and interaction. In rather sharp contrast to this rural pattern, roles and statuses attached to race were somewhat ambiguous in the cities of the Old South.

The ambiguity was exacerbated by the presence of free blacks, never more than a quarter million, who tended to reside in the cities of the Upper South, but who were not unnoticeable in certain cities in the Lower South. Moreover, urban slavery differed quite significantly from slavery on the rural farms and plantations because urban slaves were not as closely supervised and therefore experienced much greater mobility.[40] The increasing complexities and changing needs of the urban economy required a continuous reallocation of labor to accommodate the supply and demand. The imperatives of urban life thus produced a flexible system of slave labor, including an arrangement whereby slaves were used not only in the master's home or business but also were hired out to other employers.

The hiring-out system was accomplished in two ways. One involved simply the binding of a slave to another master. This practice was occasionally used in rural areas. The other permitted a slave to work for several masters at different times and occurred exclusively in urban areas. Although the hiring-out system provided the flexibility required in the urban economic order, it created problems that ultimately undermined the authority of the slavery institution. As Richard C. Wade has pointed out:

> Soon owners found it easier and usually more profitable to permit their bondsmen to find their own employment.... This created a new dimension of independence for the Negroes, since it circumvented the elaborate controls municipalities had placed around the hiring process. Under this arrangement, masters told their Negroes to locate a job, make their own agreement on wages, and simply bring back a certain sum every week or month. The slave, moreover, could pocket any profit he made.[41]

The more the slave was permitted to seek his own employment, the further he was removed from close white supervision. Despite public restrictions designed to prevent blacks from hiring themselves out, slaves generally had the liberty to choose their employers and to arrange their own room and board. If a slave made regular payments to his master and if he was able to avoid the attention of the police, he experienced a fair degree of liberty. This was anything but a satisfactory arrangement to nonslaveholders concerned about keeping the black population, slave and free, under control, and it was particularly disturbing to the working-class elements fearful of black competition for jobs.

Prior to the nineteenth century, urban blacks were kept divided and could not develop cohesive groups in the cities of the South. This was achieved by white efforts to prevent the emergence of geographically segregated Negro housing. In every southern city, "blacks and whites lived side by side, sharing the same premises if not equal facilities and being constantly in each other's presence"[42] Even the white nonslaveholders found themselves living near or next to blacks. Slaves who "lived out" and were not under the direct supervision of their masters could not avoid whites as neighbors; furthermore, free blacks were scattered throughout the city.

However, the pressures of urban living gradually altered the residential patterns of Dixie cities. The housing policy, designed to prevent black concentration, required the twenty-four-hour supervision of slave activity. Inevitably, this proved difficult in the cities where human contact was maximized and where slaves developed independence by working away from their masters by being hired out, by living out, and by mixing openly with free blacks. In time, small slumlike sections populated by both slaves and free blacks emerged, usually on the edge of the city.

In the strict sense of the term, "segregation," or separation of the races, had always existed under slavery. In the rural plantation, certain tasks were assigned to slaves, and slave quarters were removed from the masters' quarters, thereby limiting contact during nonworking hours. But racial separation was never a matter of public policy on the rural plantation. The master-servant model clearly established a superordinate-subordinate relationship between whites and blacks, and the manner in which the master handled his slaves in day-to-day discipline was largely a private matter. But, in urban areas, it soon became apparent that the handling of slaves could not be left to the master's discretion. There, spatial relations were significantly different. "Both races were thrown together; they encountered each other at every corner, they rubbed elbows at every turn; they divided up, however inequitably, the limited space of the town site. Segregation sorted people by race, established a public etiquette for their conduct, and created social distance where there was proximity."[43]

But the segregation that existed in the antebellum urban South is significant only to document the effect of different structural relations on the quality and form of race relations. It demonstrates that when paternalistic patterns of the kind manifested in the rural plantations break down, race relations shift to a more competitive pattern. Segregation replaces paternalistic racial etiquette as a symbol of the racial caste barrier and as a form of racial control. Unlike the rural plantation system where the structure of racial inequality is primarily a product of the relationship between the slaveholders and the slaves, in the cities the relationship between blacks, slave and free, and all segments of the white population shaped racial stratification. In the final analysis, however, race relations in the antebellum cities were far from representative of the South. Over 90 percent of the population resided in rural areas by 1860 and was not exposed to public segregation. Despite the fact that the cities had significant influence on southern life, the racial climate below the Mason-Dixon line is more accurately gauged by focusing on the rural rather than on the urban areas. And even in the cities, the pattern of segregation and other manifestations of competitive race relations were never anywhere as harsh or developed as in the postbellum South or even the late antebellum North.

It is true, as discussed above, that urban race relations in the antebellum South were more ambiguous than in the rural areas and that the status of blacks was less clearly defined. But it is also true that the nonslaveholders, the group that had the most to gain by racial segregation, lacked the power or resources to develop the more extensive and pervasive forms of racial separation that would have restricted black employment and more effectively isolated blacks in certain sections of the city. The business class therefore showed little hesitation in tapping the reservoir of cheap black labor for a variety of handicraft and industrial jobs. And the demand for urban slaves, contrary to previous assumptions, actually accelerated as the country approached the eve of the Civil War.[44] Moreover, since the very existence of slavery stigmatized blacks, the pressure to create segregated institutions never reached the heights attained in the period of Jim Crow segregation following the Civil War. In that period, the rise of the white lower class significantly altered the traditional patterns of racial contact in the South. However, one need not turn to the period following the Civil War to gauge the effect of an organized and assertive landless white population on the relationship between blacks and whites. For the kind of racial segregation characteristic of that period had already been demonstrated in the North in the three decades preceding the Civil War. Indeed, in the following chapter, I shall attempt to show that the role of poor whites in shaping racial stratification was as significant in the late antebellum North as in the racially repressive Jim Crow era of the postbellum South.

CONCLUSION

In this chapter, I have attempted to show how the preindustrial system of production shaped the pattern of race relations in the antebellum South. The hegemony of the slave owners as a regional ruling class derived from a slave-based plantation economy which effectively rendered nonslaveholders powerless and thereby enabled plantation owners to develop almost total control of the political and economic life of the South. The slaveholders' domination of southern politics provided the foundation for their strong influence on national politics regarding the issue of slavery, an influence which ultimately contributed to the growth and stability of the "peculiar institution."

Since nonslaveholding whites were stripped of economic and political power, they had little effect on the patterns of race relations in the antebellum South. And since the meaningful forms of black-white contact were between slaves and the elite class of slaveowners, race relations assumed a pattern in which norms, duties, rights, and obligations (whether in the slave community, or the slaveholder community, or the community of masters and slaves) were all defined and elaborated vis-à-vis the exploitation of black labor. These normative expectations tended to change as the institution of slavery assumed a more clear-cut paternalistic pattern in the late antebellum period, but they continued to reflect the enormous power discrepancy between masters and slaves on the rural plantations and farms.

It is true that in the urban South, where many free blacks were concentrated, a more competitive pattern of race relations emerged that led to the development of segregation as a form of racial control; but, as I attempted to show, such patterns were not representative of the region. In short, the antebellum South displayed a pervasive racial caste system created, institutionalized, and rationalized by the white economic elite. The implications of this system of inequality for the previously discussed economic class theories of racial antagonisms is one of the subjects of the following chapter.

3 Segregation and the Rise of the White Working Class

A split labor market along racial lines developed early in the history of the United States as a result of the institutionalization of slavery: split in the sense that slave labor was considered cheaper than free white labor. Aside from the fact that, unlike slaves, white laborers could strike and press for increased wages, thereby narrowing the difference between production cost and profit, the planter and business classes believed that in most situations slave labor was simply a less expensive investment. For example, a Louisiana state senate committee for the construction of canals, levees, and plank roads calculated in 1853 that the state would save $79,140 a year if three hundred slave carpenters and mechanics were used in favor of three hundred white laborers. The figures in Table 1 indicate that if slaves were bought at $1,000 a head, the annual savings on slave labor would actually pay for the original cost in less than four years.[1]

Slaves were trained in virtually every branch of skilled and unskilled labor.[2] Those who were not needed on the plantation at a particular time were hired out to firms for construction work and numerous other semiskilled and unskilled jobs.[3] The more frequent the contact between black slaves and white workers in the labor market, the more the wages of white workers were depressed to the level of the price required for the hire of slaves.[4]

Bernard Mandel, in his impressive book *Labor: Free and Slave*, stated that:

Not only did the laborers have to meet the price of slave labor, but they also had to produce as much as slaves to hold their own in the struggle for existence, and consequently had to deliver a long day's labor. The ten-hour movement never achieved the dimensions that it did in the North, and had little possibility of success in those circumstances. When the journeymen bricklayers of Louisville were struggling for the ten-hour system, they met an insuperable obstacle in the fact that they were replaceable by slaves, so they had to work as many hours as the slaves or abandon their trade. The stonecutters were able to win the ten-hour day because no slaves were employed in that occupation. But when the carpenters and painters called a strike for shorter hours, it was broken by the employment of slaves on their jobs; some strikers went back to work on the old terms, and others, disgusted and demoralized, emigrated from the state.[5]

Table 1 *Annual Net Savings from the Use of Slave Labor over Free Labor*

Free Labor	
300 whites, hired at $30 a month, per year	$108,000
Provisions	18,000
6 superintendents, at $1,000	6,000
Total cost of free labor per year	$132,000
Slave Labor	
(300 slaves, bought at $1,000 each	$300,000)
Interest on investment, at 5%	$15,000
Provisions and clothes	16,500
Loss of slaves by death, etc.	15,000
6 superintendents, at $1,000	6,000
Extra food for superintendents	360
Total cost of slave labor per year	$52,860
Balance in favor of slave labor	$79,140

Source: Roger W. Shugg, *Origins of Class Struggle in Louisiana* (Louisiana State University Press, 1939), p. 89

Herman Schluter perceived the effect of slavery on white labor in much the same way by observing that, whereas in 1852 the wages of free laborers in the cotton mills of Tennessee barely amounted to 50 cents a day for males and $1.25 a week for females in Lowell, Massachusetts, the wages were 80 cents a day and $2.00 a week for men and women cotton-mill workers respectively.[6] And Philip Foner informs us that competition with slave labor reduced wages for southern white workers to the lowest in the nation. "The daily wages in 1860 for day laborers in the North was about $1.11, whereas in most southern states it was between 77 and 90 cents. The daily wage for carpenters in the North for the same year was about $2, while in many states in the South it did not exceed $1.56. While operatives in Georgia cotton factories were earning $7.39 a month, workers in textile mills in Massachusetts doing the same work were getting $14.74."[7]

The threat to hire slaves was used even in industries where they were not employed. White laborers held meetings throughout the South, endorsing resolutions and presenting petitions to state legislatures and city councils describing the disastrous effects of black competition and demanding laws to prohibit the apprenticing of blacks for skilled trades, to restrict the movement of slaves and free blacks seeking jobs, and to exclude slaves and free blacks from mechanical occupations. Among those who protested were: a group of white carpenters in Wilmington, North Carolina, who in 1857 burned a building that had recently been erected by slaves and who threatened to burn all structures built by slaves in the future; a group of unemployed white stonecutters who in 1830 petitioned the Department of the Navy in Washington, D.C., to discontinue using slave labor in the construction of a dry dock for the navy; and a group of white mechanics who petitioned the legislature of Virginia in 1831 to end the competition of slave mechanics.[8] However, except for a few cases where white laborers were successful in getting legislation passed to neutralize both slave and free black competition (in Charleston, South Carolina, legislation was enacted in 1765 restricting the use of free Negroes and slaves as mechanics and handicraft workers, and in Georgia similar legislation was passed in 1758 prohibiting the employment of a black mechanic or mason),[9] laws generated by white workers were confined in their application to free Negroes. The laws wanted most by white laborers—laws to restrict the employment of slaves—were repeatedly defeated in councils and state legislatures because they conflicted with the interests of employers and slaveholders.[10] Organized labor was weak in the face of the overwhelming political and economic resources of the master class. Thus as Schluter has remarked:

> The free white laborer in South Carolina, for instance, could vote, but not for one of his own class; only a slave-owner could be governor; and the Legislature, composed exclusively of slave-owners, appointed the judges, the magistrates, the senators and the electors for President. And as in South Carolina, so approximately in the other states of the South.[11]

On the surface, the class and racial tensions associated with labor market conflicts in the antebellum South seem to correspond with the arguments advanced in the split labor-market theory of worker racial antagonism. The labor market was split along racial lines; the interests of higher-paid white labor were threatened by the employers' wide use of black labor; class conflicts were expressed in racial antagonism. Moreover, in view of the problems slavery created for wage labor, it is not unreasonable to assume that white laborers would have taken steps to prevent the growth of slavery had they the power to do so. The nonslaveholding masses, who constituted three-fourths of all antebellum white southerners, were too politically weak to resist being displaced or undercut by slave labor. All of these facts are consistent with the split labor-market theory.

There is some evidence which challenges aspects of the split labor-market theory and lends support to the orthodox Marxist's explanation of racial antagonism. More specifically, the former's argument that the business class does not purposefully play off one segment of the working class against the other is not upheld when the actions taken by slaveholders to preserve the institution of slavery are examined. Although it is difficult to uphold the Marxist argument that the slaveholders were actually committed to providing a more privileged economic position for white laborers than for slaves, the slaveholders' rhetoric was designed to convince

white laborers that they had a vested interest in the preservation of the system of slavery. After reviewing documentary evidence, Mandel concluded that white laborers "were constantly told that, by confining the hard, menial and low-paid tasks to the slaves, the white workers were enabled to constitute a labor aristocracy which held the best and most dignified jobs, and that the latter were lucrative only because they were supported by the superprofits wrung from the unpaid labor of slaves."[12] In response to the abolitionists' argument that slavery was detrimental to both free and slave labor, the slaveholders argued that, if slavery were abolished, "the whites would have to take over the menial jobs and the emancipated slaves would be able to compete with them in every branch of industry."[13]

Furthermore, the rigid racial caste system of slavery was not the creation of higher-paid white labor opposed to black competition but of a handful of powerful plantation owners who hoped to maximize their economic resources through bound, controlled labor. Finally, the planters created and cultivated the ideology of biological racism, declaring blacks biogenetically inferior to whites, both as a weapon to justify the system of slavery when it was under attack from abolitionists in the later eighteenth and early nineteenth centuries, and in order to generate a spurious race pride among white laborers and thus diffuse labor militancy by stressing color distinctions instead of class distinctions.[14] If nothing else, race relations in the Old South revealed the incredible weakness of the nonslaveholding class and the incredible strength of the ruling planter elite.

So, if the focus is on the antebellum South, the orthodox Marxist's argument that racism and racial stratification were primarily the work of the ruling class is empirically and theoretically sound. A split labor market was created along racial lines, but higher-paid white labor was too powerless to destroy the system of slavery in favor of a racial system that would eliminate or control black competition. The split labor-market theory fails to account for the caste system and the supporting racist ideology imposed by the business elite. But, if the ruling classes were largely responsible for the forms of racial oppression in the antebellum South, it was the workers or nonelite segments of the white population who played a major role in the various forms of racial oppression in the late antebellum North.

RACIAL ANTAGONISM
IN THE ANTEBELLUM NORTH

Recent historical studies lend support to Alexis de Tocqueville's observation during his tour of the United States in the 1830s that "race prejudice seems stronger in those states that have abolished slavery than in those where it still exists, and nowhere is it more intolerant than in those where slavery was never known."[15] Although slavery was abolished in all states above the Mason-Dixon line in the early nineteenth century, this was not the consequence of widespread humanitarian abolitionist sentiment. The downfall of northern slavery was related to more fundamental matters. Unlike in the South, slavery was not central to the more industrial northern economy. The small slave population, which never exceeded seventy thousand in any given period of time, did perform a variety of agricultural and skilled and unskilled mechanical tasks, but slave labor became less essential as cheap European labor became available.[16] Furthermore, only a small percentage of the economically advantaged groups in the North materially or directly benefited from slave labor; therefore, far less pressure was exerted by powerful interest parties for the preservation of slavery. Finally, strong opposition to the use of slave labor in the early nineteenth century came from various groups in the white working population able to develop sufficient power to influence management and political decisions pertaining to the character of the work force. In comparison with their southern counterparts, northern white workers were more concentrated and better organized, and hence more able to protect their economic interests during the antebellum period.[17] The differences in the resources possessed by northern and southern workers were basically related to the different systems of production in the North and in the South. The slave-based plantation economy in the South isolated white workers and facilitated the consolidation of political and economic power among a small elite; in a diversified economy, workers in the North were more centrally involved in the production process, and therefore the power gap between the workers and the capitalist class was not nearly as great.

The abolition of slavery in New England has been attributed largely to the resentment of white labor toward black slaves.[18] Certainly the legislative influence of white labor is well documented. In Pennsylvania, the legislature, reacting to pressure from mechanics, passed a resolution in 1722 decrying the master's custom of hiring out black laborers and mechanics, and in 1726 passed a law prohibiting this practice.[19] The lieutenant governor of New York in 1737 endorsed the complaints of white tradesmen against the use of skilled slave labor and took the matter up with the assembly.[20] In this connection, there has been some speculation that workers formed the backbone of the abolitionist movement to end slavery in the North, but Mandel argues that "the workers had little direct contact with slavery and its consequences, at least until the expansionism of the slaveholder became a

national problem. The problem of slavery and the oppressions of the slavocracy did not have for them the immediacy and urgency that they had for the workers in Dixie."[21] Rather, the most significant opposition to black competition in the Northeastern states occurred after they all had abolished slavery. Violence often flared up where blacks and whites competed for the same jobs, especially during periods of economic depression. Fear of violence and protests by white workers prompted New York City authorities to refuse licenses to black porters and carmen in 1837.[22] Mob protests by unemployed white workers against the hiring of blacks plagued Philadelphia in 1842 and for several years later. These protests inflicted severe economic losses on blacks and "drove so many from the city that the colored population actually showed a decrease at the census of 1850."[23]

The problems faced by northern blacks in the years preceding the Civil War were in no small measure related to the influx of nearly five million European immigrants between 1830 and 1860. The Scandinavian and German immigrants tended to settle on the farmlands in the Midwest and therefore had little direct contact with blacks, but the impoverished Irish immigrants, overwhelmingly concentrated in the slum areas of northern cities, directly competed with blacks for unskilled jobs and cheap housing. The Irish repeatedly voted against proposals to extend political rights to blacks and successfully eliminated blacks from many low-paying occupations. In 1862, for example, "Irish longshoremen informed their employer that all Afro-American longshoreman, dockhands, and other types of workers must be dismissed summarily, otherwise the Irish would tie up the port."[24] After only a few years in the United States, Irish workers gained control of canal and railroad construction and eliminated the black monopoly of the service occupations.[25]

The relative strength of the white laboring class, however, was most clearly evident in the Old Northwest, particularly the states of Ohio, Indiana, and Illinois. The principal settlers of this area were the nonslaveholding whites of the Upper South (Delaware, Kentucky, Maryland, Missouri, North Carolina, Tennessee, and Virginia) who migrated in large measure to escape the political and economic domination of the southern slaveholding elite. Unlike the Lower South (Alabama, Arkansas, Florida, Georgia, Louisiana, Mississippi, South Carolina, and Texas), where nonslaveholding yeomanry tended to be concentrated in the upcountry and the slaves in the rich black belt or in lowland plantation regions, contact between the nonslaveholders and blacks of the Upper South was more frequent and competition was therefore more severe. Artisans and laborers not only had to contend with the problem of slaves undercutting their economic position, but they also had to compete with a free black population that by 1860 was six times as large (224,963) as the free black population of the Lower South (36,955).[26] As artisans, Upper South whites suffered from competition with skilled slaves, as farmers they were unable to compete with slaveholders for the most fertile land, and as laborers they were undercut by both slave labor and cheaper free black labor. In short, they felt that slavery had solidified their subordinate position in southern society.[27] For, as Berwanger has remarked in this connection: "Many settlers from the South seeking broader economic opportunities migrated to the Old Northwest because slavery was not permitted there. Assuming that the land had been reserved for free labor, they had no intention of legalizing slavery and again establishing a kind of monopoly of United States land for the slaveholder."[28] As the careful studies of Berwanger and Voegeli show, not only did these white laborers successfully resist the extension of slavery into the Old Northwest, but they were also successful in having laws enacted to exclude blacks from entering the area and in imposing discriminatory barriers to eliminate any possible economic competition from blacks already residing in the area.[29]

It is important to remember, however, that racial antagonism, although more intense in the Midwest, characterized black and white interaction throughout the North prior to the Civil War. Indeed, by 1840, 93 percent of the northern black population resided in states that virtually denied them the right to vote. Negroes' political and judicial rights were severely circumscribed by statutes and customs, and blacks were relegated to a position of social inferiority by extralegal codes reinforced by biological racist norms. The pattern of segregation experienced by Negroes is summed up vividly by Litwack:

> They were excluded from railway cars, omnibus, stage-coaches, and steamboats or assigned to special "Jim Crow" sections; they sat, when permitted, in secluded and remote corners of theaters and lecture halls; they could not enter most hotels, restaurants, and resorts, except as servants; they prayed in "Negro pews" in white churches, and if partaking of the sacrament of the Lord's supper, they waited until the whites had been served the bread and wine. Moreover, they were often educated in segregated schools, placed in segregated prisons, nursed in segregated hospitals and buried in segregated cemeteries.[30]

Although the fear of black competition in the labor market was most acute among working class groups in the Middle West and on the East Coast, the greatest reason for white laborers' antipathy towards blacks was not so much the presence of blacks in the northern job market but the overriding fear of a black invasion from the South. Indeed, the violent attacks against blacks in the famous draft riots in 1860 were prompted by Irish resentment of being forced to fight a war against the South that would eventually lead to black emancipation, generate a heavy influx of blacks into northern areas, and create a serious labor surplus.[31] Certainly, the political justification of the North's entering the Civil War was not to free the slaves but to restore the Union after several states had seceded. The Emancipation Proclamation was issued to free the slaves in the rebellious states only after northern military and political leaders considered this historic step necessary to hasten the South's military defeat.

Indeed, certain groups of white workmen were so fearful of black competition that they openly opposed the emancipation of slaves. One of the more illuminating statements on this situation has come from Spero and Harris:

> In New York City, the Democratic party ... [which] purported to represent the working class ... opposed the freeing of slaves on the ground that emancipation would result in the migration of thousands of blacks to northern states, increasing competition for jobs and reducing wages even below the level to which an oversupplied labor market had already sent them.[32]

There were, however, groups of workers throughout the North, guided by doctrines of labor solidarity and socialist theory, who were significantly represented in the antislavery movement. Unions representing highly skilled German mechanics with socialist backgrounds experienced very little competition from Negro laborers and were especially antislavery. The same was true of the New England Workingman's Association, which expressed the strongest antislavery sentiment among native American workers. The official philosophy of both the German and New England organizations was that workers should be opposed not only to black slavery but also to the "white slavery" of the wage system. The southern slave system was considered as just one phase of the capitalist exploitation of the working class.[33] However, this philosophy represented a minority view among the working classes. Racial or ethnic antagonism in the antebellum North and in the Midwest was never seriously threatened by worker solidarity.

The relationship between social class and different forms of ethnic antagonism is implicit in the foregoing discussion. In the antebellum South, the plantation elite was powerful enough to impose the system of slavery on southern society even though the system was detrimental to the interests of the nonslaveholding white majority. In the North, the laboring classes had the power resources to at least preserve their interests in the face of black competition—and the form of racial subjugation they used reflected their concern, namely, the elimination or neutralization of blacks as economic competitors or potential competitors. As far as black-white relations are concerned, the effective control of black workers by white workers during this period represents a "victory" for higher-paid labor. Evidence from this period lends little support to Marxian explanations that ethnic antagonisms were initiated by the capitalist class. It is true that blacks were used as strikebreakers in isolated incidents, but, since employers had a continuous supply of European immigrant labor, efforts to divide the white and black working class were rarely made. Accordingly, the racial exclusion laws passed in the Old Northwest, the discriminatory acts and legislation against black competition, the support of laws to deny blacks legal and political rights, the stripping of blacks from certain occupations they previously engaged in, the relegation of blacks to the most menial and unskilled positions, and the violence which forced blacks out of certain areas were mainly initiated not by the exploiters of labor but by the white working class.

The efforts of the white working class to deprive Negroes of economic, social, and political resources were certainly made easier by the relatively small Negro population in the North. As we shall see in the following sections, the presence of millions of free blacks following the Civil War presented the southern white working class with a far more difficult challenge, as it attempted to overcome the effects of a century of economic and political subordination in the South.

THE PLANTER CLASS AND INSTITUTIONALIZED RACIAL INEQUALITY IN THE POSTBELLUM SOUTH

In an argument quite similar to that advanced by Oliver C. Cox in 1948,[34] the Marxist scholars Baran and Sweezy gloss over the mass of historical data with the less than definitive statement that "when Negroes tried to take advantage of their legal freedom to organize along with poor whites in the Populist movement, the planters answered with violence and the Jim Crow system of legalized segregation."[35] As far as the postbellum period is concerned, only if we focus on the period immediately following the Civil War (the period prior to Reconstruction), can we attribute institutionalized racial inequality solely to the planter class. Initial legislation to restrict and control the black population was not generated by white workers, although they were indeed quite concerned about black competition, but by southern planters and their business and political allies.

Immediately following the Civil War, white supremacy, virtually unchallenged during the period of slavery, appeared to be in serious jeopardy. Slaves had been liberated and some were armed. Not only were fears expressed about blacks becoming full citizens and receiving equal political and civil rights, but there was even talk of blacks dividing up the plantation estates. "This was not only competition," states historian C. Vann Woodward, "it looked to many whites like a takeover."[36] More fundamentally, the ruling economic elite was frightened because the southern economy was on the verge of total collapse without slave labor. For the ruling elite, "black freedom" signified not only a threat to white supremacy but also meant the loss of a guaranteed cheap and controlled labor supply for the plantations.

In 1865–66, southern legislatures, still controlled by business and planter groups, were given freedom by Presidents Lincoln and Johnson to devise ways to resolve the problems created by an economy no longer based on slave labor. The legislatures promptly passed a series of discriminatory laws known as the Black Codes. Although the provisions of the codes varied from state to state, one of their primary objectives was to insure an adequate and cheap labor supply for the plantations. Woodward informs us that the "Black Codes of 1865–66 were mainly concerned with forced labor and police laws to get the freedman back to the fields under control."[37] Those blacks without a permanent residence or who were unemployed were classified as vagrants and could be arrested and/or fined, and, if incapable of paying, were bound out to plantations under labor contracts. As a substitute for the social controls of slavery, the codes also restricted black movement, denied blacks political and legal rights, and in some states provided for segregation of certain public facilities.

These escalating efforts to regain control of the black population in the South aroused considerable opposition from many northerners. To some extent, criticism of the Black Codes sprang from lingering abolitionist sentiments generated prior to the Civil War. Northern liberals, in moral indignation, maintained that the Black Codes were a sinister attempt to reestablish slavery. To a greater degree, however, the opposition was political in nature. Benjamin Quarles put the matter squarely:

> As nothing else, the Black Codes played into the hands of the Republicans, who were looking for reasons to postpone the readmission of the southern states. For these states, if readmitted, would elect enough Democrats to insure that party's control of the government. Hence the Republicans were determined to keep the South in political limbo until the ascendancy of their party was assured. To achieve such ascendancy it would be necessary to enfranchise the southern Negro.[38]

In April of 1886, the Republican-controlled Congress nullified the Black Codes by passing a Civil Rights Act which conferred citizenship on ex-slaves and specified that discriminatory acts against them were punishable by fine and/or imprisonment. Black political and civil rights were further protected by the Fourteenth Amendment passed by Congress in June of 1866. After the Republicans, dominated by the radical wing, had gained a two-thirds majority in both houses in the November election of 1866, Congress passed two supplementary Reconstruction Acts in 1867 that divided the ten southern states into five military districts under northern supervision and that granted blacks the right to vote.[39]

In large measure, white reaction to Reconstruction and the specter of black control of the South was shaped by social class interests. Racial tension increased significantly among lower-class whites who perceived more clearly than ever before the impact of large-scale black competition for low-status jobs. Reconstruction did not destroy the landowning white aristocracy. Both poor whites and blacks were dependent on the planter class for their livelihood as tenants and sharecroppers at the very time when these positions were diminishing in the face of gradual industrialization. The evidence is clear that the planter class of the South effectively prevented any economic or political cooperation or class allegiance between poor blacks and poor whites.[40] As long as poor whites directed their hatred and frustration against the black competitor, the planters were relieved of class hostility directed against them. "Indeed, one motive for the Ku Klux Klan movement of these years was a desire by low class whites to remove the Negro as a competitor, especially in the renting of land."[41] The essential point is that, during the first two decades following the Civil War, poor whites lacked the power resources needed to bring about the kind of institutional changes that would have improved their economic lives, namely, segregationist laws restricting black competition. They were concentrated in positions such as tenant farmers and sharecroppers where their economic situation was as precarious in the early postbellum period as it had been during antebellum slavery. Organized labor remained weak in the face of the overwhelming political and economic resources of the master class.

The reaction of the "people at the top" to the changes in race relations brought about by Reconstruction contrasted sharply with that of lower-class whites. Within a few years after Reconstruction, the ruling economic elite realized that their earlier apprehensions concerning the Negro were unwarranted. Northern Republicans gradually focused their attentions away from their platform of radicalism and protection of black freedom to a promotion of eastern capitalistic expansion in the South.[42] There was greater competition between lower-class whites and blacks and therefore increased racial hostility; but the economic and political hold of the privileged classes over southern life was essentially unchallenged. The plantation elite, aligned with the growing industrial

sector, was no longer fearful of a black threat or takeover. Indeed, blacks remained in a dependent economic relationship with this sector. Because of this, and because blacks were anxious about the manifestation of lower-class white reaction to black competition, conservative white rulers virtually controlled the black vote prior to 1890. In this connection, Woodward states:

> It was true that blacks continued to vote in large numbers and to hold minor offices and a few seats in Congress, but this could be turned to account by the conservative white rulers who had trouble with white lower-class rebellion. Black votes could be used to overcome white working-class majorities, and upper-class white protection was needed by blacks under threat of white lower-class aggression. Many reciprocal accommodations between upper-class whites and blacks were possible under the paternalistic order.[43]

THE WHITE LABOR-REFORM MOVEMENT AND JIM CROW SEGREGATION

Changes in the system of production exerted considerable influence on the developing patterns of class and racial tension in the New South. In the antebellum period, public power was so heavily concentrated among large planters and so clearly derived from property in slaves and land that racial stratification increasingly assumed a paternalistic character that was reflected in the relationships between slaveholders and slaves. This relationship persisted through the early years of the postbellum period. However, as the South experienced gradual industrialization in the late nineteenth century, as new economic institutions generated technological development, as expanded modes of communications and elaborate systems of transportation connected cities with farms, not only was the distribution of power significantly altered in the South but race relations increasingly became associated with class conflicts.[44]

After the Civil War, the planters had to share their power with a rising middle class of merchant-bankers and with owners and operators of factories, mines, and railroads.[45] Nonetheless, the members of all of these groups were conscious of their overlapping economic interests and consequently combined to form a disciplined ruling class. They also were mutually apprehensive of the gradual increase in political activity among the white working class in the 1880s and 1890s. Just as changes in the system of production modified the distribution of power among the ruling elite, so too did it place the workers of the South in greater proximity with one another and thus facilitated their mobilization into collective action groups.

The structural changes in the labor market accompanied severe economic dislocations for many workers of the South. During the last quarter of the nineteenth century, lower-class whites found themselves in increasing contact and competition with millions of freed blacks at the very time that a labor surplus developed in the face of enormous population growth in the South.[46] The problem was especially acute in the Lower South. For the first time, blacks and working-class whites of the Lower South, historically separated in the black belt (low-lands) and the uplands respectively, were forced by economic conditions to confront one another, bump shoulders, and compete on a wide scale for the same jobs. Black youths gradually moved from the lowlands to the new mining and industrial towns of the uplands and found menial, dirty, and low-paying work in tobacco factories, mines, and turpentine camps; meanwhile, sons of white farmers, over-whelmed by debts and falling prices, sifted down from the uplands to the lowlands, where they settled for work in the textile mills or drifted into tenancy. A new breed of southern politician, whose style combined the evangelistic fervor of the southern preacher with the racist rhetoric of the upcountry hillbilly, emerged to articulate the feelings and represent the interests of working-class whites. Their pleas for disfranchisement and legal segregation helped to set in motion a movement that produced decades of Jim Crow segregation.[47] When the Farmers' Alliance, a movement consisting of hundreds of thousands of lower-class white farmers and tenants, first exerted its influence in southern state legislatures, Jim Crow segregation laws sprang up all over the South.[48] For example, in 1887 in Florida, in 1888 in Mississippi, in 1889 in Texas, in 1890 in Louisiana, and in 1891 in Alabama, Arkansas, Kentucky, and Georgia, laws requiring separate accommodations in railway stations and in streetcars were enacted. Perhaps C. Vann Woodward comes closest to summarizing the meaning of these developments when he writes:

> It is one of the paradoxes of Southern history that political democracy for the white man and racial discrimination for the black man were often products of the same dynamics. As the Negroes invaded the new mining and industrial towns of the uplands in greater numbers, and the hill country whites were driven into more frequent and closer association with them, and as the two were brought into rivalry for subsistence wages in the cotton fields, mines and wharves, the lower-class white man's demand for Jim Crow laws became more insistent.... The Negro pretty well understood these forces and his grasp of them was one reason for this growing alliance with the most conservative and politically reactionary class of whites against the insurgent white democracy.[49]

Thus, the last decades of the nineteenth century, a period of economic dislocation (caused by industrial capitalism, population pressures, declining farm prices, and exploitative sharecropping) generated a labor reform movement and Jim Crow segregation that grew hand in hand.

DISFRANCHISEMENT AND THE COLLAPSE OF THE ALLIANCE BETWEEN BLACKS AND THE WHITE BUSINESS ELITE

The real concern of the business elite in the decade or two following Reconstruction was the threat to its political and economic power by the rise of the agrarian and labor reform movements. It is ironic but not surprising that both the business elite and the black minority were fearful of the rise in white lower-class power. The unholy alliance between blacks and the white ruling classes prior to 1890 actually prevented the racial code from becoming more severe.

As long as the alliance between blacks and the conservative economic elite existed, the latter frequently denounced Jim Crow laws in aristocratic, paternalistic tones as "unnecessary and uncalled for" and "a needless affront to our respectable and well behaved colored people."[50] According to Woodward, "when the first state Jim Crow law for trains was passed in 1887, a conservative paper rather shamefacedly admitted it was done 'to please the crackers.'"[51]

However, at the very time that Jim Crow legislation was mushrooming throughout the South, some workers in the Populist movement recognized that as long as conservative whites were aligned with blacks, the possibility of a united working-class labor movement to overcome economic exploitation would indeed be difficult. The Populists sought strenuously to create an alliance with poor blacks. Under the leadership of Tom Watson, a substantial Populist appeal to the black man was generated in Georgia. Some successes also occurred in Texas and Arkansas.[52] This was enough to alarm the conservative Democrats representing the southern business interests, and they too increased their drive to attract the support of black voters, using methods that included the stuffing of ballot boxes with fraudulent votes in the black-belt regions. Both the Populists and the Democrats sought to manipulate the black vote, and both finally realized that since neither was assured of controlling the black vote, "it was much better to have clear-cut constitutional disfranchisement of the Negro and to leave the white group to fight elections out among themselves."[53]

The conservative Democrats of the lowland South, who, when they felt secure about the black vote, had placed the blame for the rise of legal segregation on lower-class whites, joined in the movement for disfranchisement as soon as they became apprehensive about the black vote.[54] Meanwhile, white Republicans of the South were divided over the issue of disfranchisement. "The lily-white faction, which gained ground during the nineties, more or less openly welcomed the movement in the belief that the removal of the Negro would make the party respectable in the South and permit white men to divide."[55] Between 1890 and 1910, blacks were systematically disfranchised by various procedures ranging from the revising of state constitutions to requiring poll taxes, literacy tests, and property qualifications, to the creation of the all-white Democratic primary (which was far more important than the general election because the South was dominated by a one-party system)."[56] Accompanying disfranchisement were increased Jim Crow segregation laws in both public and private institutions and facilities and also the virtual collapse of public education and the systematic exclusion by white laborers of blacks from jobs in the skilled occupational ranks they had held since slavery (such as barbering, masonry, bricklaying, carpentry, and the better agricultural jobs).[57] Moreover, the system of Jim Crow segregation was reinforced by extralegal means of intimidation. Whereas, blacks were seldom lynched under the old paternalistic order (e.g., as I indicated in the previous chapter, it is estimated that of the 300 lynching victims between 1840 and 1860 less than 10 percent were black)[58] "in the last sixteen years of the nineteenth century there had been more than 2,500 lynchings, the great majority of which were Negroes, with Mississippi, Alabama, Georgia, and Louisiana leading the nation."[59]

WHITE ECONOMIC CLASS INTERESTS AND BLACK SUBORDINATION

Restrictive arguments that the Jim Crow system was the work of the capitalist class, or was due solely to the victory of higher-paid white labor, obscure the dynamics of the complex patterns of racial inequality in the postbellum South. I have attempted to show, and historical analysis demonstrates, that: (1) the initial form of racial stratification in the postbellum period, formalized and sanctioned by the Black Codes, was based solely on the efforts of the plantation elite to insure an adequate and cheap labor supply for the plantations in the aftermath of slave emancipation. Racial inequality therefore reflected the class interests of the aristocracy and entailed the exploitation of labor. (2) The emergence of initial Jim Crow segregation laws directly parallels the rise of lower-class whites to political power in the labor reform movement. Racial inequality therefore reflected the class interests of white workers and was designed to eliminate black encroachment in a context of competitive race relations. (3) The political alliance and paternalistic bond between blacks and the business classes

deteriorated in the face of the Populist challenge; this deterioration causing the struggle over the black vote to result in a more united white movement to deprive the Negroes of their political rights. (4) The racial caste system which encompassed all aspects of black life was solidified both by the ruling class's support of disfranchisement and by the working class's drive (with tacit approval of the ruling class) toward racial exclusiveness in occupation, education, and political power.

CONCLUSION

In this chapter I have attempted to show how the different contexts of racial antagonism in the preindustrial and early industrial periods restrict the uniform application of the economic class theories discussed previously. Because they do not focus on the influence of different systems of production on the intergroup arena, the economic class theories are unable to account for the fundamental relationship between changes in the power resources possessed by antagonistic classes and changes in the nature of racial interaction. Thus, whereas the orthodox Marxist explanation is restricted to the racial caste system in the antebellum South and the development of the Black Codes in the immediate post-Civil war period, the split labor-market theory can only be used to explain racial stratification in the late antebellum North and the origins of Jim Crow segregation in the postbellum South. Again, the meaningful application of the economic class arguments in any given historical period depends heavily on the knowledge of the constraints imposed by the particular systems of production during that period, constraints that help to shape the structural relations between racial and class groups and which thereby produce different patterns of intergroup interaction.[60]

As long as the reservoir of free white workers was not central to the reproduction of labor supply in the southern plantation economy, slavery as a mode of production facilitated the consolidation and concentration of economic power in the hands of the slaveholders. The control of the economic system was effectively transferred to the control of the political and legal systems as the slaveholders used their political power to protect their class interests in slavery. The polity therefore reinforced and regulated the system of racial caste oppression and made it difficult for either blacks or lower-class whites to mount any serious challenge to the institution of slavery. In short, the economy provided the basis for the development of the racial caste system, and the polity reinforced and perpetuated that system. Moreover, the economy enabled the slaveholders to develop a regional center of power and the polity legitimated that power.

In the antebellum North, where a more industrial system of production enabled white workers to become more concentrated and better organized, laws of racial oppression, especially in the nineteenth century, increasingly reflected the interests of the white working class. The demise of northern slavery was quickly followed by laws to eliminate black competition, particularly economic competition. However, as the economy of the South gradually drifted toward industrial capitalism in the last quarter of the nineteenth century, the white working classes there were finally able to exert some influence on the form and content of racial stratification. White working-class efforts to eliminate black competition generated an elaborate system of Jim Crow segregation that was reinforced by an ideology of biological racism. The white working class was aided not only by its numerical size but also by its increasing accumulation of political resources that accompanied changes in its relations to the means of production; in other words, it was aided by its gradual transformation of increasing labor power into increasing political power.

NOTES

Chapter one

31. The theoretical implications of this development for ethnic groups in general are discussed by Milton Gordon under the concept "ethclass." See Milton M. Gordon, *Assimilation in American Life* (New York: Oxford University Press, 1964).

Chapter Two

1. Kenneth M. Stampp, *The Peculiar Institution: Slavery in the Ante-Bellum South* (New York: Alfred A. Knopf, 1956), pp. 25–31.

2. Eugene D. Genovese, *Roll, Jordan, Roll: The World the Slaves Made* (New York: Pantheon Books, 1974), p. 27. I am indebted to Genovese (especially for part 1 of book 1, *Roll, Jordan, Roll*) for part of the discussion that follows.

3. Eric Foner, *Free Soil, Free Labor, Free Men: The Ideology of the Republican Party before the Civil War* (New York: Oxford University Press, 1970), p. 100.

4. Genovese, *Roll, Jordan, Roll*, p. 32.

5. Sterling D. Spero and Abram L. Harris, *The Black Worker* (New York: Columbia University Press, 1931), p. 7.

6. Foner, *Free Soil, Free Labor, Free Men*, chap. 3.

7. Quoted in ibid., p. 89.

8. Ibid., p. 89.

9. Stanley M. Elkins, *Slavery: A Problem in American Institutional and Intellectual Life* (Chicago: University of Chicago Press, 1959); Genovese, *Roll, Jordan, Roll*; and Robert William Fogel and Stanley L. Engerman, *Time on the Cross: The Economics of American Negro Slavery* (Boston: Little, Brown, 1974), vol. 1.

10. Edmund S. Morgan, *American Slavery, American Freedom: The Ordeal of Colonial Virginia*. (New York: W. W. Norton, 1975).

11. The decline in the number of white indentured servants entering the colonies is possibly related to concern about the conditions that brought about the Bacon's Rebellion and the discontent expressed by servants following that disturbance. Also, Englishmen experienced less pressure to leave home by the third quarter of the century. "Complaints of overpopulation in England had ceased, as statesmen and political thinkers sought ways of putting the poor to work" (ibid., p. 299).

12. Ibid., pp. 297–98.

13. Ibid., p. 297. Also see George M. Frederickson, "Toward a Social Interpretation of the Development of American Racism," in *Key Issues in the Afro-American Experience*, vol. 1, ed. Nathan I. Huggins, Martin Kilson, and Daniel M. Fox (New York: Harcourt Brace Jovanovich, 1971).

14. Morgan, *American Slavery*, p. 312.

15. Quoted in ibid., pp. 312–13.

16. Ibid., p. 313.

17. Genovese, *Roll, Jordan, Roll*, p. 38.

18. Carl N. Degler, "The Irony of American Negro Slavery," in *Perspectives and Irony in American Slavery*, ed. Harry P. Owens (Jackson: University Press of Mississippi, 1976), p. 5.

19. Ibid., p. 6. In this connection, Degler comments that "It is possible that the slave trade was able to be closed only because natural increase had already demonstrated that it was capable of meeting the demand for new slaves. The source of this decision, however, is not as important as the fact that the exigencies of maintaining a slave system without additions from outside the country were such that the physical condition of the slaves had to be more than minimal. And from present knowledge of the law and the actual treatment of slaves in the colonial period and in the years of the nineteenth century after the closing of the slave trade, conditions did improve markedly, if gradually."

20. Genovese, *Roll, Jordan, Roll*; and Fogel and Engerman, *Time on the Cross*.

21. This fact alone leads one to question the relevance of Herbert G. Gutman's argument as far as the southern slave regime is concerned, namely, that "A high reproduction rate does not depend upon 'good treatment,'" and that "A detailed scholarly literature shows that diverse populations with very low standards increase rapidly." See Herbert G. Gutman, *The Black Family in Slavery and Freedom, 1750–1925* (New York: Pantheon, 1976), p. 310.

22. Genovese, *Roll, Jordan, Roll*, p. 57.

23. Fogel and Engerman, *Time on the Cross*, p. 5.

24. Ibid., p. 115.

25. Genovese, *Roll, Jordan, Roll*, pp. 59–60.

26. Ibid., p. 57.

27. W. E. B. Du Bois, *Black Reconstruction* (New York: Harcourt, Brace and Co., 1935), p. 9.

28. John W. Blassingame, *The Slave Community: Plantation Life in the Ante-Bellum South* (New York: Oxford University Press, 1972), p. 160; and Edmund S. Morgan, *American Slavery*, chap. 15.

29. Elkins, *Slavery*. In response to his critics, Elkins now recognizes that his book did not give sufficient attention to the slave culture. On this point, he states: "The movement to explore black folk culture is in itself an exciting and salutary development which promises much in the way of lighting up the past. In the interests of conceptual mobility however, I wonder how exclusively it ought to be tied to the problem of resistance to slavery. The two are certainly related. But there should also be a way of allowing for the ebb and flow of folk culture over time, and of discovering whether there may be conditions under which such culture and the range of its expression flourishes, and other conditions which tend, relatively speaking, to inhibit it" "The Social Consequences of Slavery," in *Key Issues in the Afro-American Experience*, 1:139. See also, Elkins, "On Slavery and Ideology," in Ann Lane, ed., *The Debate over Slavery: Stanley Elkins and His Critics* (Champaign: The University of Illinois Press, l971), pp. 325–78.

30. See for example, the articles in Lane, ed. *Debate over Slavery*, especially the article by Roy Simon Bryce-Laporte, 'Slaves as Inmates, Slaves as Men: A Sociological Discussion of Elkins' Thesis'; Blassingame, *The Slave Community*; Genovese, *Roll, Jordan, Roll*; Fogel and Engerman, *Time on the Cross*; and Gutman, *The Black Family*. For a good discussion of this research, see the review-essay by George M. Fredrickson, "The Gutman Report," *The New York Review of Books*, 23, no. 15 (September 30, 1976):18–22, 27.

31. Genovese, *Roll, Jordan, Roll*; and Gutman, *The Black Family*.

32. Genovese, *Roll, Jordan, Roll*, pp. 3–7.

33. Ibid., p. 658.

34. Ibid., p. 7.

35. Gutman, *The Black Family*, p. 309.

36. Genovese, *Roll, Jordan, Roll*, pt. 1.

37. Gutman, *The Black Family*, p. 310.

38. Genovese, *Roll, Jordan, Roll*, p. 33.

39. Ibid.

40. In the discussion of urban slavery in the South, I am heavily indebted to Richard C. Wade, *Slavery in the Cities: The South 1820–1860* (New York: Oxford University Press, 1964).

41. Ibid., p. 48.

42. Ibid., p. 75.

43. Ibid., p. 277.

44. Fogel and Engerman, *Time on the Cross*.

Chapter Three

1. See Roger W. Shugg, *Origins of Class Struggle in Louisiana* (Baton Rouge: Louisiana State University Press, 1939), pp. 88–89.

2. Sterling D. Spero and Abram L. Harris, *The Black Worker* (New York: Columbia University Press, 1931), pp. 5–9; Bernard Mandel, *Labor: Free and Slave; Workingmen and the Anti-Slavery Movement in the United States* (New York: Associated Authors, 1955), chap. 2; Robert William Fogel and Stanley L. Engerman, *Time on the Cross: The Economics of American Negro Slavery* (Boston: Little, Brown, 1974), 1:38–43.

3. Spero and Harris, *The Black Worker*, p. 9.

4. Mandel, *Labor*.

5. Ibid., p. 31

6. Herman Schluter, *Labor and Slavery: A Chapter from the Social History of America* (New York: Socialist Literature Company, 1913), p. 92.

7. Philip S. Foner, *History of the Labor Movement in the United States* (New York: International Publishers, 1947), 1:260.

8. Spero and Harris, *The Black Worker*, pp. 7–11; Richard B. Morris, *Government and Labor in Early America* (New York: Octagon, 1965), pp. 186–88; Robert R. Russell, *Economic Aspects of Southern Sectionalism* (Urbana: University of Illinois Press, 1923), pp. 219–20; T. M. Whitfield, *Slavery Agitation in Virginia, 1792–1832* (Baltimore: Johns Hopkins University Press, 1930); Schluter, *Labor and Slavery*, pp. 99–100; Foner, *Labor Movement in the U.S.*, pp. 258–64; and Robert S. Starobin, *Industrial Slavery in the Old South* (New York: Oxford University Press, 1970), pp. 211–12.

9. Morris, *Government and Labor*, pp. 185–86; and Foner, *Labor Movement in the U.S.*, p. 262.

10. Mandel, *Labor*, p. 49.

11. Schluter, *Labor and Slavery*, p. 96.

12. Mandel, *Labor*, p. 57.

13. Ibid., p. 57.

14. Cf. William J. Wilson, *Power, Racism and Privilege: Race Relations in Theoretical and Sociohistorical Perspectives* (New York: The Free Press, 1973), chap. 5.

15. Alexis de Tocqueville, *Democracy in America*, ed. J. P. Mayer (New York: Doubleday, 1969), p. 343.

16. Arthur Zilversmit, *The First Emancipation: The Abolition of Slavery in the North* (Chicago: The University of Chicago Press, 1967), p. 53.

17. Mandel, *Labor*, p. 61.

18. Morris, *Government and Labor*, p. 183.

19. W. E. B. Du Bois, *The Philadelphia Negro: A Social Study*, Political Economy and Public Law Series no. 14 (Boston: Ginn, 1899), p. 15; Mandel, *Labor*, p. 63.

20. Leon F. Litwack, *North of Slavery: The Negro in the Free States, 1790–1860* (Chicago: University of Chicago Press, 1961), pp. 5–6.

21. Mandel, *Labor*, p. 61; also see Williston Lofton, "Abolition and Labor," *The Journal of Negro History* 33 (July 1948):249–93.

22. Litwack, *North of Slavery*, p. 159.

23. Spero and Harris, *The Black Worker*, p. 12; also see Du Bois, *The Philadelphia Negro*, p. 33, and idem, *The Negro Artisan* (Atlanta: Atlanta University Press, 1902), pp. 15–16.

24. Herman D. Bloch, *The Circle of Discrimination: An Economic and Social Study of the Black Man in New York* (New York: New York University Press, 1969), p. 34. *See also* Litwack, *North of Slavery*, p. 166.

25. Litwack, *North of Slavery*, p. 166.

26. See Ira Berlin, *Slaves without Masters: The Free Negro in the Antebellum South* (New York: Pantheon Books, 1974), p. 136. Berlin points out that "The great mass of Negro freedmen lived in the tidewater of the Upper

South between Delaware and North Carolina, where the post-Revolutionary manumission movement had flourished. Better than half the free Negroes in the South resided in Delaware, Maryland and Virginia" (p. 179).

27. Ibid., p. 28.

28. Eugene H. Berwanger, *The Frontier against Slavery: Western Anti-Negro Prejudice and the Slavery Extension Controversy* (Urbana: University of Illinois Press, 1967), p. 18.

29. Berwanger, *Frontier against Slavery*, and V. Jacque Voegeli, *Free but Not Equal: The Midwest and the Negro during the Civil War* (Chicago: University of Chicago Press, 1967); see also Emma Lou Thornbrough, *The Negro in Indiana before 1900; A Study of a Minority* (Indiana Historical Collections, vol. 37. Indianapolis: Indiana Historical Bureau, 1957).

30. Litwack, *North of Slavery*, p. 97.

31. See Albon P. Man, Jr., "Labor Competition and the New York Draft Riots of 1863," *The Journal of Negro History* 36 (October 1951):375–405; and Williston Loften, "Northern Labor and the Negro during the Civil War," *The Journal of Negro History* 34 (July 1949):251–73.

32. Spero and Harris, *The Black Worker*, p. 13.

33. Ibid., pp. 13–14; and Schluter, *Labor and Slavery*, pp. 34–84.

34. Oliver C. Cox, *Caste, Class and Race: A Study in Social Dynamics* (Garden City, New York: Doubleday, 1948).

35. Paul A. Baran and Paul M. Sweezy, *Monopoly Capital: An Essay on the American Economic and Social Order* (Harmondsworth: Penguin, 1966), p. 247.

36. C. Vann Woodward, *American Counterpoint: Slavery and Racism in the North-South Dialogue* (Boston: Little, Brown, 1971), p. 251.

37. Ibid., p. 252.

38. Benjamin Quarles, *The Negro in the Making of America* (New York: Collier Books, 1964), p. 131.

39. John Hope Franklin, *From Slavery to Freedom*, 3d ed. (New York: Alfred A. Knopf, 1967); and Peter M. Bergman, *The Chronological History of the Negro in America* (New York: Harper and Row, 1969).

40. E. Franklin Frazier, *The Negro in the United States* (New York: Macmillan, 1957). Frazier points out that "The planter and propertied classes did not fail to take advantage of the traditional prejudices of the poor whites and the competition between the latter and the Negro to destroy any cooperation between the two groups. The poor whites were constantly subjected to propaganda concerning supremacy and purity of the white race" (p. 135).

41. Ray Marshall, "Industrialisation and Race Relations in the Southern United States," in *Industrialisation and Race Relations*, ed. Guy Hunter (London: Oxford University Press, 1961), p. 66.

42. Woodward, *American Counterpoint*, p. 254.

43. C. Vann Woodward, *Origins of the New South, 1877–1913*. (Baton Rouge: Louisiana State University Press, 1951), pp. 254–55.

44. See Otis M. Scruggs, "The Economic and Racial Components of Jim Crow," in *Key Issues in the Afro-American Experience*, ed. Nathan I. Huggins, Martin Kilson, and Daniel M. Fox (New York: Harcourt Brace Jovanovich, 1971), pp. 70–87.

45. Ibid., p. 73.

46. Ibid.; Woodward, *Origins of the New South*; and V. O. Key, Jr., *Southern Politics in State and Nation* (New York: Alfred A. Knopf, 1949).

47. Scruggs, "Jim Crow," p. 81.

48. Woodward, *Origins of the New South*, pp. 211–12, and Scruggs, "Jim Crow," pp. 84–85.

49. Woodward, *Origins of the New South*, p. 211.

50. Quoted in ibid., p. 257.

51. Ibid., p. 257.

52. C. Vann Woodward, *Tom Watson: An Agrarian Rebel* (New York: Oxford University Press, 1938); Carmen J. Owens, "Power, Racism and Coalition Politics: A Re-examination of the Populist Movement in Georgia" (Master's thesis, University of Chicago, 1973); Bergman, *The Negro in America*, p. 310.

53. Franklin, *From Slavery to Freedom*, p. 337.

54. Commenting on the attitude of three of the most powerful Democratic leaders of the Deep South, Woodward states: "As late as 1879, three foremost spokesmen of the South, Lamar of Mississippi, Hampton of South Carolina, and Stephens of Georgia, agreed in a public statement that the disfranchisement of the Negro was not only impossible but undesired. Lamar declared that it was 'a political impossibility under any circumstances short of revolution,' and that even if it were possible the South would not permit it. 'Hampton, who claimed the distinction of being 'the first man at the South' to advocate suffrage for the emancipated slave, remarked that the Negro 'naturally allies himself with the most conservative of the whites'" (*Origins of the New South*, p. 321).

55. Ibid., p. 324.

56. These procedures were so comprehensive that many poor whites were also disfranchised. This led some states in the South to initiate the so-called "grandfather clause," which waived the voting requirements for those citizens whose ancestors had voted in the 1860 election.

57. Cf. Donald Young, *American Minority Peoples: A Study in Racial and Cultural Conflicts in the United States* (New York: Harper, 1932), p. 99; and Fogel and Engerman, *Time on the Cross*, pp. 258–64.

58. Genovese, *Roll, Jordan, Roll*.

59. Franklin, *From Slavery to Freedom*, p. 439.

60. Some readers may take issue with what seems to be a process of mechanical allocation in the application of the economic class theories to different historical periods of American race relations. As pointed out by Professor Jan Dizard in private communication, it may be argued that either both theories are wrong (or are less parsimonious than another as yet unrealized theory) or that historical observation is incomplete, or both. My position is that the application of any given theory to a particular observable situation depends on whether the conditions under which the theory applies have in fact been met. If the conditions for the application of the theory are not present, it certainly does not mean that the theory is necessarily false. It only means that an adequate test of the theory's

scope and validity cannot be made. Specification of the initial conditions for the application of a theory is therefore crucial. And this is exactly what I have in mind when I argue that meaningful application of the economic class theories depends on knowledge of the constraints imposed by the system of production (or even of the arrangement of the polity, as I pointed out in Chapter 1 and will more fully demonstrate in later chapters). Of course, for our purposes, it would be desirable to develop a more comprehensive theory that systematically integrates propositions concerning the role of the system of production with propositions drawn from the economic class theories. Although I do not attempt such an ambitious project in this book, I do believe that my theoretical arguments have sufficient scope to deal with a variety of historical situations and constitute at least an implicit theory of social change and race relations.

21

Introduction to Black Studies

MAULANA KARENGA

This book remains among the most important in presenting an "African-centered" perspective on race and racism. Professor Karenga shows how the dominant intellectual thought and social analysis models in the United States have developed to both suggest and maintain institutionally the inferiority of blacks in this country. European-dominated thought helps to explain the nature of racism in that it presupposes black cultural inferiority. There are at least two important contributions to the discussion of race and racism in this text: first, the theory elaborated by the author and others proposes that it is useful for black political and economic, and psychological liberation from notions of inferiority; second, it approaches the black community as a unit of analysis in the discussion of racism. In other words, racism is not considered in terms of individuals and groups, but also the spatial community which reflects the institutional and social life of black people.

Black Social Organization

Black social organization is essentially the structure and functioning of the Black community as a whole as well as the various units and processes which compose and define it, i.e., family, groups, institutions, relations, views and values, economics, politics, conflict and change, etc. Thus, Black social organization is the subject matter of Black sociology which directs itself to the study of Black social reality from a Black perspective. The need for a Black perspective evolves inevitably from the fact that U.S. society is a society divided and organized along racial lines, that the ideology and/or social theory which rules in academic and social circles is the ideology of the ruling race/class, and that this ideology or social theory is more of an apologia for the established order than a critical analysis of

it. Therefore, it becomes important that Blacks who are concerned with political, economic and cultural emancipation have an emancipatory social science which is Afrocentric. As Staples (1973:168) argues, "If white sociology is the science of oppression, Black sociology must be the science of liberation."

As an emancipatory social science, Black sociology offers both critiques and correctives. Continuing the tradition of Du Bois (1967), Frazier (1957), Cox (1970), and Hare (1965), Black sociology has set for itself several basic aims: 1) to rescue Black life from the racist interpretations which pose it as pathological and pathogenic, and redefine it in its multidimensionality and variousness; 2) to create new concepts, categories, analytical frameworks and bodies of data that enhance understanding of both Black reality and the larger reality of U.S. society; 3) to make ongoing critical analyses of the structure and functioning of U.S. society, especially in terms of race, class and power; 4) to join severe criticism of internal forces negative to Black progress and liberation with criticism of negative external forces; and 5) to discover, develop and reveal possibilities of social change inherent in both the Black community and the larger society (Ladner, 1973; Staples, 1976; Du Bois, 1975).

Since Black sociology is so inclusive a social science, only a small selection of its concerns can be treated in this chapter. Other major concerns such as politics, economics and social psychology of the Black community will be treated in the other appropriate chapters. The selected concerns which follow are fundamental to understanding Black social organization and are also reflective of issues and problems which are directly related to Black subordination and oppression in U.S. society and Black struggle to end this condition.

The Problem of the Ghettoization

The Black community, like other communities is defined by its sharing of common space, experiences, view and value systems, social institutions and self-consciousness. Its common space, however, is a bounded area of living, i.e., a ghetto, which not only closes Blacks in the community, but simultaneously shuts them out from the access and various opportunities available in the larger society. Even when Blacks move beyond the original bounded areas and form what is called "gilded ghettos" in integrated areas, these outskirt communities "also become linked to the central Black area," as whites leave and other Blacks move in (Glasgow, 1981:34). Moreover, even outside the ghetto physically, Blacks are defined and treated as the majority who are still in the ghetto with allowable variations.

W.E.B. Du Bois (1967) pioneered the scientific study of Black urban life with a major work, *The Philadelphia Negro*, in 1899 and in 1945, St. Clair Drake and Horace Cayton (1962) produced the first major study which was a systematic and scholarly investigation of the Black ghetto itself. During the 60's, Kenneth Clark (1965) contributed *Dark Ghetto: Dilemmas of Social Power* which gave an incisive overview of the problems of ghetto life using Harlem as a model.

What appears, then, from Du Bois's, Drake's and Cayton's, and Clark's analyses, along with others is a social reality defined by six basic dimensions. First, the ghetto is territorial, i.e., residential, bounded and segregated. Inspite of Wilson's (1979) findings of increased Black suburbanization, Rose (1976) shows that in five major cities, it was simply the expansion of the central city areas or increase in the Black population already in the suburbs. Moreover,

Clay (1981:89) reports that suburban migration is limited essentially to the middle class and generally "produces a resegregation pattern where Blacks are concentrated in a few suburban enclaves." Secondly, the ghetto is racial/ethnic, i.e., essentially Black and a product of a racist society which poses race as a central criteria for determining lifechances, opportunities, social status and human worth. Thirdly, the ghetto is socio-economic, i.e., marked by what Clark (1965:27ff) calls economic and social decay. Clark lists as symptoms of ghetto life poor education, poor housing, unemployment, drug addiction and alcoholism, frequent illness and early death, and crime, all accented by "the primary affliction" of inferior racial status "in a racist society."

Fourthly, the ghetto is institutional, i.e., it has a complex of community institutions, organizations and enterprises which are both a positive and a negative (Spear, 1967). The positive aspect of them is that they are structures necessary for selfdetermined maintenance and development. But the negative aspect is that they are often not strong enough to fulfill their function or fail to use their strength adequately for social advancement and change.

Fifthly, the ghetto is clearly political, i.e., both an expression and product of Black powerlessness to prevent its establishment or end its existence. This powerlessness is obviously related to the ghetto's structural incapacity to define, defend and develop its interests as alluded to above. For without strong community structures to resist imposition and advance Black interests, external interests will most likely be imposed. Thus, the ghetto is controlled from outside and it is this external control joined with other factors of ghetto life which have led some to argue that it is an internal colony (Cruse, 1968; Clark, 1964).

Finally, the ghetto is psycho-cultural, i.e., defined by views, values and self-consciousness negative to its development and transformation into a free, proud and productive community (Clark, 1965; Karenga, 1980). Although the psychological aspect will be discussed at length in the chapter in psychology, the cultural dimensions which are directly related will be discussed below. In conclusion, then, it is this fact of ghetto life, the negatives which emerge from it and the solutions posed to correct them and develop a higher level of life that form the core of sociological inquiry and prescription.

The Race/Class Question

One of the most pressing questions in Black sociology is the significance of race and class in Black life. The significance of the question rests not only in its relevance to understanding Black oppression, but also in its relevance in developing strategies for liberation. For depending on the weight each or both are given, the Black community correctly or incorrectly grasps the character of its oppression and the theoretical and practical requirements necessary to end it. Thus, since the late Seventies the debate has intensified concerning which is most important—race oppression or class oppression and how the two interact and relate (Washington, 1979; Willie, 1979).

The focus on class as the fundamental unit of social analysis and the key determinant in social life has been provided most definitively by the sociology of Marxism (Bottomore and Rubel, 1964). Marx argued essentially that the shape and functioning of society was determined by its economic foundation and that class, as a socio-economic category, was basic to the understanding of society and history. Furthermore, he contended that productive systems establish given economic roles – farmer, trader, industrialist, worker – and that each group of persons which stands in the same relationship to the means of production (raw materials, factories, machines, etc.) form a class. As a class, each did the same work, had the same basic interests ("real" as opposed to "perceived") and often engage in conflict with other classes. This conflict between classes, he argued, is the motive force of history. Finally, he contended that the economic foundation was the *base* from which the *superstructure* (law, religion, politics, ideology, etc.) rose and upon which it rested.

From this materialistic (economic) interpretation of society and history evolved two basic Marxist interpretations of the interaction of race and class, the orthodox Marxist theory (Cox, 1970; Reich, 1981) and the split labor-market theory (Bonacich, 1972). Orthodox Marxist theory argues that racism is a reflection of the manipulation of workers by the capitalist class to divide them along racial lines and reduce their capacity to struggle against the system. This results in encouraging discrimination against Blacks, arguing their inferiority, use of Blacks as a surplus, marginal low-paid working force, and establishing a privileged better-paid racist white labor force. Thus, racism is a function of class struggle, not an independent variable itself. The split labor-market theory argues that racial antagonism begins in the labor-market split along racial lines when business promotes worker competition to displace higher paid labor. If the labor-market split is along racial lines with whites' being the higher-paid and Blacks being the lower-paid labor, class antagonism is transformed into racial antagonism in which whites fight to neutralize or eliminate occupational competition with Blacks.

Both of these class theories of race fail to perceive that race and class interact dynamically as variables in social conflict and position. Although the orthodox Marxist view blames the capitalist and the split labor-market theory places the essential burden on the white worker, there are clearly cases where both white capitalists and white workers join to oppress or discriminate against Blacks and other Third World people. Moreover, sometimes it is done for reasons of race and other times for reasons of class and still at other times for both reasons of race and class. Also, in a racist society the class position of a person is greatly determined by his/her race. This is what Fanon (1968:40) meant when he wrote that in the racist context of the colony, race is the key determinant.

Blauner (1972:31) also calls attention to the fact that often in a racist society, racial exploitation and/or control becomes "an end itself, despite its original limited purpose as a means to exploitation and privilege." Finally, Turner (1979:31) argues that racism has become so endemic and historically rooted in U.S. society and its institutions that "it exists apart from and in some cases inspite of, the social attitudes of the people who administer these institutions." Thus, the factor of "covert or institutional racism has a dynamic of its own, despite the vagaries of prejudice and bigotry, real as they are." Given all the above contentions concerning race and class and their interaction and relation, it is clear that racism cannot be reductively translated as a function of class or class struggle. Such a position obscures the complexity and variousness of their interplay and their separate relevance as factors in a racist-capitalist society (Turner, 1979).

There are other positions on race and class, but they will be covered in chapter VI on economics. However, it is important to note in conclusion, that one of the reasons many social scientists and others have in identifying racism is that their definition is deficient. Marxists and non-Marxists tend to see racism as simply attitudes or ideology rather than as multi-faceted involving ideology, structure and practice (Allen, 1974).

Racism is essentially a system of denial and deformation of the history and humanity of Third World people (people of color) and their right to freedom based exclusively or primarily on the specious concept of race (Karenga, 1981). Stripped of all its cultural and scientific mystification, race is a bio-social category designed to assign human worth and social status, using Europeans as the paradigm of humanity and social achievement. Racism, then, which begins with the creation and mystification of race, is social thought and practice which expresses itself in three basic ways, i.e., as: 1) imposition, i.e., conquest of a people, and interruption, destruction and appropriation of a people's history and productive capacity in racial terms; 2) ideology, i.e., an elaborate system of pseudo-intellectual categories, assumptions and contentions negative to Third World peoples and serving as justification of the imposition and reinforcement of the institutional arrangement; and 3) institutional arrangement, i.e., a system of political, economic and social structures which insure white power and privilege over Third World peoples.

THE ISSUE OF CULTURE

Although the question of culture had been raised during the Harlem Renaissance in the 20's, it was during the 60's that the Black community became increasingly concerned about the possession, meaning, reappropriation and reconstruction of their culture. The shift away from integration as the main Movement goal and the resurgence of Black nationalism brought with it a renewed interest in Black culture, its role in life and struggle and a profound and pervasive commitment to revitalize, reconstruct and construct it. Expressive of this thrust were the struggle for Black Studies which demanded recognition of Black contribution to society and the world, the look to Africa for inspiration and models and the proliferation of creative artist groups, study groups, literature and institutions which focused on culture. This thrust was both reactive and proactive, defensive and developmental. It sought not only to halt and reverse the racist attempt to negate Black culture, but also to rebuild and build a system of views and values which aided Blacks in their struggle for liberation and a higher level of human life.

Many racist, liberal and Marxist social scientists argued that Blacks had no real culture, that slavery destroyed it, and that what passed as Black culture was simply a pathological reaction to whites, a duplication of them or an expression of lower-class culture rather than a specific Black culture (Liebow, 1967; Berger, 1967). Myrdal (1944:927-930) argued that the Black person is "an exaggerated American" and essentially a "pathological" reaction to whites. Ellison (1966:316-317) responding to Myrdal stated that Myrdal misjudges Blacks' creativity and adaptive vitality. He posited that Blacks could not possibly "live and develop for over three hundred years simply by reacting." On the contrary, Blacks have made self-conscious and self-constructive efforts which have contributed to American culture, not simply borrowed from it.

Glazer and Moynihan (1963:52) argued that the key to understanding Blacks is to recognize they cannot view themselves as other ethnic groups who have a culture. For the Black person "is only an American and nothing else. He has no values and culture to guard and protect." Such a contention was challenged by the Black cultural Revolution of the 60's which not only reaffirmed Black culture and its difference from white culture in terms of life-goals, worldview and values, but also the need to draw on its African and mass sources to recreate and revitalize it and use it as a weapon in the Black Struggle (Kareng, 1967, Gayle, 1971).

Harold Cruse (1967) in his massive study of culture and politics in Harlem, made a profound contribution to the focus on cultural revitalization and struggle. He maintained that cultural oppression is tightly interlocked with political and economic oppression. For cultural control facilitates political control which in turn insures economic control. Thus, he argued instead of placing higher priority on any one of the three factors of culture, politics and economics, the three must be welded together into a dynamic synthesis and social strategy. Stressing the essentiality of culture to political and economical struggle, Cruse (1967:12) maintained that "as long as the (Afro-Americans') cultural identity is in question or open to self-doubt, then there can be no positive identification with the real demands of his political and economic existence." Therefore, Cruse (1967:475) argues that "there can be no real Black revolution in the U.S. without a cultural revolution as a corollary to the scheme of 'agencies for social change'." He concludes, calling on the Black intellectuals to solve their historical crisis, i.e., alternating between integrationist fantasies and nationalist demands when rejected by whites, and guide the masses to liberation and higher levels of life.

As argued in chapter II in the section on the Sixties, Kawaida theory stood out as the most structured and influential theory of the Black Cultural Revolution. Kawaida (Karenga, 1980, 1978b) contends that the key crisis in Black life is the cultural crisis, i.e., a crisis in views and values. This crisis was caused by several factors, among which are enslavement and deculturalization, the ideological hegemony (dominance in the realm of ideas and values of the ruling race/class) and the growth of popular culture at the expense of national culture.

The need then is for a cultural revolution which will prepare the Black masses for a political struggle to end the social conditions which deny and deform their history and humanity. The cultural revolution, Kawaida states, precedes and makes possible the political revolution and also sustains it. By cultural revolution is meant "the ideological and practical struggle to transform persons and people and to build structures to insure, maintain and expand that transformation" (Karenga, 1982:2). Whereas political revolution is the struggle to seize and reorder the unequal power and wealth in society, cultural revolution is the process which makes it possible and sustains it with transformed self-conscious participants, i.e., self-conscious agents of their own liberation.

Cultural revolution implies and also means revitalizing, creating and recreating culture (Karenga, 1967). Kawaida defines culture as the totality of a people's thought and practice, which occurs in seven basic areas: mythology (sacred and secular), history, social organization, economic organization, political organization, creative production (arts and science), and ethos (collective self-definition and consciousness). It is on these seven levels, Kawaida contends, that Black people must rebuild themselves by rebuilding their culture, so that each area is in both their *image* and *interests*. For it is a political fact that the greater the difference between the culture of the oppressed and the oppressor, the greater the difficulty of dominance and the capacity for resistance.

Finally, Kawaida, in the tradition of Du Bois (1969), Frazier (1973), and Cruse (1967), posits that the cultural and political struggle must be led by a self-conscious vanguard who commits class suicide and identifies with the aspirations of the masses. This vanguard will build on the strengths of Black culture, i.e., its adaptive vitality, strong emphasis on expressive values, empathetic sharing, durability, humanism and creativity, and expand them. Moreover, the vanguard must create an Afro-centric ideology or social theory which negates the ruling race/class ideology and provides the basis for a critical Afro-centric conception of reality and the possibilities and methods of changing it. Kawaida contends that this vanguard must also urge the self-conscious creation of a national culture which not only distinguishes Blacks from their oppressor, but also aids them in their rescue and reconstruction of their history and humanity and enables them to contribute to human history and achievement in their own unique way.

THE BLACK FAMILY

At the heart of social organization is the way a people organizes its relationships. In fact, another way to define social organization is as "ways of teaching, structuring, validating, changing and expanding social behavior and relationships" (Karenga, 1980:35). The focus of social organization is thus on the socialization process, i.e., the value and vision orientation designed to instruct and enhance personal and collective behavior and relationships. Nowhere is this more clear than in the discussion of the Black family. For if the Black family is the smallest example of the nation, i.e., Black people, its strengths and weaknesses greatly determine the capacity of Black people to achieve the social tasks they pose for themselves.

The assessment of the Black family's strength and weakness pervade social science literature. In fact, much of the literature, if not most, can be assigned to either one school of thought and research or the other (Willie, 1970; Staples, 1978; McAdoo, 1981). These two approaches to the Black family may be termed the pathological-pathogenic and the adaptive-vitality approaches. The first is predicated on the assumption that the Black family is either pathological or pathogenic or both. That is to say, it is not only a dysfunctional and sick social unit, but produces sick and dysfunctional members of society.

Frazier (1939), unwittingly helped lay the basis for the pathology school in his research on the Black family. He believed that slavery, urbanization and racism prevented perpetuation of the African family relations and forms and imposed severe strains on the Black family's ability to function effectively. Thus, it developed negative situational adaptations to handle this legacy of oppression and exploitation. From this, he notes, came the matriarchal character of the Black family with its strong women and ineffective and marginal men; its unstable marriages; the prevailing norm of casual sex, and the loss of folk culture cohesiveness in the urbanization process.

Daniel Moynihan (1965), using largely census data, tried to confirm Frazier's conception by statistics. Although Frazier had pointed to the social causes of Black family problems, Moynihan blamed social problems on the Black family. Making a generalized indictment of Black families, he (1965:5) argued that "at the heart of the deterioration of the fabric of (Black) society is the deterioration of the (Black) family." Citing Frazier as if to escape the charge of racist sociology, Moynihan charged that the Black community was plagued by pathological and pathogenic families marked by and conducive to matriarchy, broken and ineffective males, delinquency, economic dependency, poor academic performance, unwed motherhood, etc.

The adaptive-vitality school contends that adaptation by Blacks to socio-economic pressures and limitations must not be seen as pathologies, but as strength, i.e., adaptive vitality. Billingsley (1968), Blassingame (1972), Young (1970), Hill (1972), Nobles (1978), Staples (1978) et al. represent this school. Among the propositions they argue are the following: 1) that the Black family is unique and cannot be fitted into a white formula for analysis; 2) that it was not totally destroyed in slavery; 3) that it has proved its durability and adaptive vitality in the face of severe oppression, and thus, is a strong and functional social unit.

Staples (1971:133) notes that one of the major problems with the traditional approaches to the study of the Black family has been their tendency to fix it in a white-middle class formula. He argues that the result of this subjective approach "has been that the Black family continues to be defined as a pathological unit whose unique way of functioning sustains the conditions of its oppression." Billingsley (1970:132-133) also criticized white social science for focusing almost exclusively on lower income families and ignoring the majority of stable Black families and blaming lower-class families for their victimization by society. Although, he concedes lower-class family negatives while praising upper-class positives, he nevertheless argues these negatives are socially-rooted. Moreover, he stresses that many misunderstood features of the Black family are sources of strength and raises questions concerning politically suspect conclusions which have social policy implications.

Although proponents of the adaptive vitality approach do not agree on the degree of African influence on Afro-American culture and family, there is agreement that slavery did not destroy all. Early studies by Du Bois (1969) and Carter G. Woodson (1936), as well as Herskovits (1941) showed a legacy from Africa as well as from slavery in Afro-American culture and social institutions. More recently, Blassingame (1972) found African survivals in courtship practices, dance, familial roles, folktales, language, music, names, proverbs, and religious beliefs and practice. Blassingame asserted that it is important to realize that "Whatever the impact slavery had on (Blacks') behavior and attitudes, it did not force them to concentrate all their psychic energy on survival." On the contrary, they showed remarkable adaptive vitality in the system and inspite of the end of contact with Africa when the slave trade ended, the enslaved African "was able to retain many cultural elements and (for a while) an emotional contact with his motherland."

Nobles (1978, 1981) posits that Africanity or Africaness is clearly evidenced in Afro-American families. He (1978:22) cites "the actuality of black kinship bonds and the sense of extended family" as an example of this as well as an egalitarian quality to relationships and a profound commitment to the survival of the family (ethnic group). Moreover, he sees Africanity in Blacks' affective rather than economic approach to family life and their sense of collectivity rather than the individualism which is endemic to European culture.

Finally, Sudarkasa (1980, 1981) asserts that both African and slavery legacies exist. She (1981:37) states that "just as surely as Black American family patterns are in part an outgrowth of the descent into slavery, so too are they partly a reflection of the archetypical African institutions and values that informed and influenced the behavior of these Africans who were enslaved in America." Also she (1981:39) notes, that although there are "relatively few 'traces' of direct institutional transfer from Africa to America," there are "numerous examples of the institutional transformation from Africa to America." Thus, she tends to support Blassingame's contention that Africans were able to build viable and creative syntheses out of African and European culture. Sudarkasa essentially poses the concept and force of consanguinity or bloodtie kinship as an enduring Africanism as well as the extended family of which it is an expression. "The extended family networks that were formed during slavery by Africans and their descendents were based on the institutional heritage which Africans had brought with them to this continent," she (1981:45) contends. And the specific forms they assumed depend on the cultural, economic and political circumstances in which Blacks found themselves.

The proponents of the adaptive-vitality model and approach are concerned also that the Black family be viewed and studied as a distinct institution with its own historical tradition and characteristics, not as a pathological or defective variation on the Euro-American theme. Although some make a distinction between *alternative* and *adaptive* strategies and forms developed by Black families to meet the challenge of an oppressive social life, that distinction is not made here. As Sudarkasa (1981:31) has noted, the two characterizations of Black families are not mutually exclusive and represent false dichotomies. For adaptive strategies and behavior contribute to the development of alternative formations as the history of the Black family shows. I have used the term adaptive vitality which is the "ability to adjust structurally and ideologically in confrontation with society without losing its distinct character," to absorb stress and strain and bounce back with vigor. It is the ability to push past simple survival and develop continuously (Karenga, 1980:52). It is in the context of the above clarification that the strengths of Black families which proponents of the adaptive-vitality school are presented and have meaning.

Although Staples, Ladner (1972), Billingsley, Nobles and others have listed various strengths of Black families, the classic study on this is Robert Hill's (1978) book of the same title, *The Strengths of Black Families.* Hill (1978:3) defines family strengths as "those traits which facilitate the ability of the family to meet the needs of its members and the demands made upon it by systems outside the family unit." Having done this, he lists five strengths which examination of literature on Black families reveal as having been "functional for their survival, development and stability" (1978:4): 1) strong kinship bonds which is stronger among Blacks than whites and expresses itself by absorption of relatives, especially minors and the elderly in various families; 2) strong work orientation, i.e., "the Black poor still are more likely to work than the white poor"; 3) the adaptability of family roles, i.e., male and female can assume each other's household roles in the event of absence, illness, etc.; 4) high achievement orientation, i.e., the majority of low-income students and their parents have college aspirations; and finally, 5) religious orientation.

In criticism of the adaptive-vitality proponents, Nathan Hare (1976) contends the strength-of-the-family school may have unwittingly created their own negatives while challenging the negatives of the pathology-pathogenesis school. First, he (1976:9) states that strength-of-the-family orientation "prohibits any recognition of pathological consequences of our oppression" and thus, undermines the thrust of corrective action. Secondly, Hare (1976:10) argues that such an approach "fails to incorporate a power-conflict model appropriate to advocates of social change." Finally, Hare (1976:11) contends that the strength-of-the-family approach helps "make it easier for an oppressive society to ignore the heinous conditions it imposes on the Black family." He stresses that he is not advocating victimology, but he has problems with claiming all is well with the Black world at the expense of social criticism.

Hare's contentions point to a serious dilemma of Black scholarship, i.e., how does one prove strength in oppression without overstating the case, diluting criticism of the system and absolving the oppressor in the process? Likewise, the parallel dilemma is how does one criticize the system and state of things without contributing to the victimology school which thrives on litanies of lost battles and casualty lists, while omitting victories and strengths and the possibilities for change inherent in both Black people and society? The answers to these questions are not easily achieved. The tasks of an emancipatory social science are to develop a critical and balanced analysis which reveals Black strengths and weaknesses as well as a prescription for self-conscious action to free themselves and to shape reality into their own image and interests. Such, then, is the central task of an emancipatory Black social science.

REFERENCES

Allen, Robert. (1974) *Reluctant Reformers*, Washington, D.C.: Howard University Press.

Berger, Bennett. (1967) "Soul Searching," *Trans-Action*, (June) 54-57.

Billingsley, Andrew. (1970) "Black Families and White Social Science," *Journal of Social Issues*, 26, 3 (Summer) 127-142.

Billingsley, Andrew. (1968) *Black Families in White America*, Englewood Cliffs, N.J.: Prentice-Hall, Inc.

Blassingame, John. (1972) *The Slave Community*, New York: Oxford University Press.

Blauner, Robert. (1972) *Racial Oppression in America*, New York: Harper & Row, Publishers.

Bonacich, Edna. (1972) "A Theory of Ethnic Antagonism: The Split Labor Market," *American Sociological Review*, 37 (October), 547-559.

Bottomore, T.B. and Maximilien Rubel. (1964) *Karl Marx: Selected Writings in Sociology and Social Philosophy*, New York: McGraw Hill.

Clark, Kenneth. (1965) *The Dark Ghetto*, New York: Harper & Row Publishers.

Clay, Phillip. (1981) "Housing and Neighborhoods," in *The State of Black America–1981*, New York: National Urban League.

Cox, Oliver C. (1970) *Caste, Class and Race*, New York: Monthly Review Press.

Cruse, Harold. (1967) *The Crisis of the Negro Intellectual*, New York: William Morrow.

———. (1968) *Rebellion or Revolution?*, New York: William Morrow.

Drake, St. Clair and Horace R. Cayton. (1962) *Black Metropolis*, New York: Harper & Row, Publishers.

Du Bois, W.E.B. (1969) *The Negro American Family*, New York: New American Library.

———. (1967) *The Philadelphia Negro*, New York: Schocken Books.

———. (1959) "The Talented Tenth," in *The Negro Problem*, (ed.) Ulysses Lee, New York: Arno Press and New York times, pp. 31-76.

Du Bois, W.E.B. (1975) *W.E.B. DuBois on Sociology and the Black Community*, (eds.) Dan Green and Edwin Driver, Chicago: University of Chicago Press.

Ellison, Ralph. (1966) *Shadow and Act*, New York: New American Library.

Fanon, Frantz. (1968) *The Wretched of the Earth*, New York: Grove Press.

Frazier, E. Franklin. (1973) "The Failure of the Negro Intellectual," in *The Death of White Sociology*, (ed.) Joyce A. Ladner, New York: Vintage Books, pp. 52-66.

———. (1939) *The Negro Family in America*, Chicago: University of Chicago Press.

———. (1957) *The Negro in the United States*, New York: Macmillan Company.

Gayle, Addison. (1971) *The Black Aesthetic*, New York: Doubleday & Co.

Glasgow, Douglas. (1981) *The Black Underclass*, New York: Vintage Books.

Glazer, Nathan and Daniel P. Moynihan. (1963) *Beyond the Melting Pot*, Cambridge: M.I.T. and Harvard University Press.

Hare, Nathan. (1965) "The Challenge of a Black Scholar," in *The Death of White Sociology*, (ed.) Joyce A. Ladner, New York: Vintage Books, pp. 67-78.

———. (1976) "What Black Intellectuals Misunderstand About the Black Family," *Black World*, (March) 5-14.

Herskovits, M. (1941) *The Myth of the Negro Past*, New York: Harper & Row, Publishers.

Hill, Robert. (1972) *The Strengths of Black Families*, New York: Emerson Hall.

Jackson, Jacqueline. (1978) "But Where Are the Men?" in *The Black Family: Essays and Studies*, (ed.) Robert Staples, Belmont, Ca.: Wadsworth Publishing Company, pp. 110-117.

Karenga, Maulana. (1978a) *Beyond Connections: Liberation in Love and Struggle*, New Orleans: Ahidiana.

———. (1978b) *Essays on Struggle: Position and Analysis*, San Diego: Kawaida Publications.

———. (1980) *Kawaida Theory: An Introductory Outline*, Inglewood: Kawaida Publications.

———. (1979) "On Wallace's Myths: Wading Thru Troubled Waters," *The Black Scholar*, 10, 8 (May/June) 36-39.

———. (1981) "The Problematic" Aspects of Pluralism: Ideological and Political Dimensions" in *Pluralism, Racism and Public Policy: The Search for Equality*, (eds.) Edwin G. Clausen and Jack Bermingham, Boston: G.K. Hall & Co., pp. 223-246.

———. (1967) *The Quotable Karenga*, (eds.) Clyde Halisi and James Mtume, Los Angeles: Saidi Publications.

———. (1982) "Society, Culture and the Problem of Self-Consciousness: A Kawaida Analysis," in *"Philosophy Born of Struggle: Anthology of Afro-American Philosophy From 1917*, (ed.) Leonard Harris, Dubuque, IA: Kendall/Hunt; pp. 212-228.

Ladner, Joyce. (1973) *The Death of White Sociology*, New York: Vintage Books.

———. (1971) *Tomorrow's Tomorrow: The Black Women*, Garden City, N.Y.: Anchor Books.

Liebow, Elliot. (1967) *Tally's Corner*, Boston: Little, Brown & Co.

Madhubuti, Haki. (1980) "Not Allowed To Be Lovers," *Black Books Bulletin*, 6, 4, pp. 48-57, 71.

McAdoo, Harriette P. (ed.) (1981) *Black Families*, Beverly Hills: Sage Publications.

Moynihan, Daniel. (1965) *The Negro Family*, Washington, D.C.: Office of Planning and Research, U.S. Dept. of Labor.

Myrdal, Gunnar. (1944) *An American Dilemma*, New York: Harper & Row, Publishers.

Nobles, Wade. (1981) "African-American Family Life," in *An Instrument of Culture*, (ed.) Harriette P. McAdoo, Beverly Hills: Sage Publications.

———. (1978) "Africanity: Its Role in Black Families," in *The Black Family: Essays and Studies*, (ed.) Robert Staples, Belmont, Ca.: Wadsworth Publishing Co., pp. 19-25.

Reich, Michael. (1981) *Racial Inequality*, Princeton: Princeton University Press.

Rose, H.M. (1976) *Black Suburbanization*, Cambridge, Mass.: Ballinger.

Shange, Ntozake. (1977) *For Colored Girls*, New York: Emerson Hall.

Sowell, Thomas. (1981a) *Ethnic Minorities*, New York: Basic Books.

———. (1981b) *Markets and Minorities*, New York: Basic Books.

———. (1975) *Race and Economics*, New York: David McKay Company.

Spear, Allen H. (1967) *Black Chicago*, Chicago: University of Chicago Press.

Staples, Robert. (ed.) (1978) *The Black Family: Essays and Studies*, Belmont, Ca.: Wadsworth Publishing Company.

———. (1976) *Introduction to Black Sociology*, New York: McGraw Hill.

———. (1971) "Toward A Sociology of the Black Family: A Theoretical and Methodological Assessment," *Journal of Marriage and Family*, 33, 1 (February) 119-138.

Staples, Robert. (1973) "What is Black Sociology: Toward a Sociology of Black Liberation," in *The Death of White Sociology*, (ed.) Joyce A. Ladner, New York: Vintage Books, pp. 161-172.

———. (1981) *The World of Black Singles*, Westport, Conn.: Greenwood Press.

Sudarkasa, Niara. (1980) "African and Afro-American Family Structure: A Comparison," *The Black Scholar*, 11 (November/December) 37-60.

———. (1981) "Interpreting the African Heritage in Afro-American Family Organization," in *Black Families*, (ed.) Harriette P. McAdoo, Beverly Hills: Sage Publications.

Touré, Sékou. (1959) *Toward Full Re-Africanization* Paris: Présence Africaine.

Turner, James. (1979) "The Political Sociology of Racism and Systematic Oppression: Internal Colonization as a Paradigm for Socio-Economic Analysis," *Studia Africana*, 1, 3 (Fall) 294-314.

Wallace, Michelle. (1979) *Black Macho and the Myth of the Superwoman*, New York: Dial Press.

Willie, Charles. (1979) *The Caste and Class Controversy*, New York: General Hall, Inc.

———. (1970) *The Family Life of Black People*, Columbus, Ohio: Charles Merrill.

Wilson, Franklin. (1979) *Residential Consumption, Economic Opportunity and Race*, New York: Academic Press.

Wilson. William J. (1978) *The Declining Significance of Race*, Chicago: University of Chicago Press.

Woodson, Carter G. (1936) *The African Background Outlined*, Washington, D.C.: Assn. for the Study of Negro Life and History.

Young, Virginia. (1970) "Family and Childhood in a Southern Negro Community," *American Anthropologist*, 72:269-288.

22

Reflections on American Racism

PAUL M. SNIDERMAN AND PHILIP E. TETLOCK

This article is a critique of the proposal that 'symbolic racism' is a new form of racism in the United States. Symbolic racism is similar to what has been described as covert racism, a dynamic that is not expressed in open confrontation or resistance to groups specifically based on race. An example of overt racism would include beliefs and actions directed at the residential, education, or spatial segregation of racial groups. Symbolic racism, on the other hand, may include opposition to bussing without citing that the basis of this position may be opposition to race mixing. Calling for the presumptory arrest of black youth because presumably they tend to be criminally involved is overt racism; but calls for law and order in certain neighborhoods could be symbolic racism. Sniderman and Tetlock contend in essence that it is empirically difficult to distinguish between inherently honest concerns about certain issues, such as opposition to busing, and racism. The authors imply that racism is a serious problem; but arbitrarily claiming that certain policy positions reflect symbolic racism, may guide people away from focusing on real racism.

We are not persuaded by Kinder's defense of symbolic racism and shall try to explain why. But first it may be helpful to the reader—puzzled, perhaps, by the welter of claims and counterclaims of this exchange—to point to some critical issues on which Kinder and we are now close to agreement. Four issues deserve particular note.

Traditional Prejudice

The original claim of Kinder and Sears was extremely ambitious. They claimed to have discovered a new kind of racism: symbolic racism. This discovery,

if genuine, would be of the first importance, partly because of the claim that symbolic racism is new in the American experience and hence a genuine discovery; still more fundamentally because of their further claim that symbolic racism has replaced traditional forms of racial prejudice.

It is worth appreciating how far-reaching was Kinder and Sears' claim. Traditional prejudice, they contended, had evaporated—an extraordinary contention but one that Kinder and Sears nonetheless advanced explicitly and repeatedly. "Segregationist sentiment," they wrote, "has all but disappeared." They also stated that "the white supremacist view has all but disappeared" and that traditional prejudice "no longer can be a major political force." Finally, to make their position quite unmistakable,

We appreciate the assistance of Roger Anderson in the preparation of this manuscript.

they declared that "White America has become, in principle at least, racially egalitarian" (Kinder & Sears, 1981, p. 416).

The original claim, then, was extreme; Kinder has now abandoned it. "We claimed too much," he notes, "when we declared that white America had become, even in principle, racially egalitarian and that traditional forms of racial prejudice had been replaced by symbolic racism.... Old-fashioned racism remains alive and all too well" (Kinder, 1986, p. 161).

Symbolic Racism
and Affirmative Action

There is a second point, as important as the first, though perhaps less obvious. Opposition to affirmative action, Kinder and Sears originally argued, testifies to symbolic racism. So, too, does opposition to busing. The person who disagrees with court-ordered busing or with racial quotas *is* a racist. Racism and opposition to busing in Kinder and Sears' original formulation are literally the same thing; symbolic racism may be operationally defined as opposition to busing or as opposition to affirmative action (Kinder & Sears, 1981, p. 420).

Kinder has now modified this extreme formulation. Instead of claiming that opposition to quotas or to busing is the same thing as racism, he advances a more modest claim: "such opposition [to quotas and forced busing]," he now says, "stems in part ... from symbolic racism" (1986, p. 152). Or, as he suggests later: "There are a number of reasons to oppose affirmative action; racism, and symbolic racism in particular, is just one" (1986, p. 160).

Kinder's reformulation is a helpful step, but it has serious methodological implications: it has the consequence of impeaching many of the previous measures of symbolic racism. It is not logical, after all, to say on the one side that symbolic racism is one of a number of causes of opposition to busing, and to say on the other that opposition to busing is the same thing as symbolic racism.

Measurement Deficiencies

Third, it is also helpful that Kinder makes some (qualified) acknowledgment of limitations in measures of symbolic racism (1986, pp. 155–156). Thus, he notes that the content of symbolic racism measures varies somewhat from study to study. And he agrees with at least some of our specific objections (e.g., to brevity, ambiguity, and lack of face validity)—and indeed, goes so far as to describe, for these reasons, the Sears and Citrin (1982) measure as "presumptuous" (1986, p. 159).

The Label of Symbolic Racism

A final point of agreement deserves mention. Kinder now believes that the term "symbolic racism" is an

"unfortunate choice" (1986, p. 155)—unfortunate because it is misleading. We agree. The term "symbolic racism" blurs the distinction between racist and nonracist sources of opposition to policies to assist minorities.

Remaining Disagreements

Yet disagreements remain. Specifically, Kinder contends the following: (1) measures of symbolic racism are more standardized than we suggested; (2) we incorrectly classified a measure developed by Sears as a measure of symbolic racism; (3) we erroneously suggested that symbolic racism may be a form of covert racism; (4) we were wrong to contend that symbolic and old-fashioned racism have much in common; and (5) we failed to do justice to the root conception of symbolic racism, specifically to appreciate that it involves a "conjunction" of prejudice and values. We address these criticisms and sketch a constructive agenda for future research on racial policy preferences.

Measurement Volatility

Our critique of symbolic racism measures revealed that different studies had operationalized the construct in highly inconsistent and frequently arbitrary ways. Sometimes symbolic racism refers to covert racism, sometimes not. Sometimes it refers to a cause of opposition to busing; sometimes it *is* opposition to busing. And nearly all the time it is measured in different ways.

Researchers are, of course, entitled to refine and improve their measures. But these changes should be grounded in empirical analysis, with the advantages of new measures demonstrated, not merely asserted. Even more obviously, researchers are under an obligation to point out when measures have been changed. Otherwise, the unsuspecting reader, seeing the same name—"symbolic racism"—will assume that the measure is the same when in fact it is not.

In the face of these difficulties, Kinder takes a sanguine view, contending that inspection of the content of symbolic racism measures shows that they "share a good bit in common" (1986, p. 158). It cannot, however, be said that a brief appeal to similarity in face content is a compelling defense of measurement validity: there is a warehouse of evidence on the major effects of even minor variations in question wording and ordering (e.g., Schuman & Presser, 1981; Schuman, Steeh, & Bobo, 1985). In addition, Kinder's enumeration of symbolic racism measures is selective. For example, Kinder and Sears (1981) employed two measures of symbolic racism, both described as measures of symbolic racism, but each utterly unlike the other. In his Table 1, however,

Kinder presents only one of these measures, the one most similar to previous measures of symbolic racism, but does not acknowledge the other.

Kinder, based on his brief tour of measures, does not feel there are grounds for concern, with the possible exception of the Sears–Citrin measure, and even this measure he feels is fundamentally dependable. It is understandable that a developer of a measure should trust it, but Kinder's attitude may be too trusting. In his judgement, none of the failings of the symbolic racism measures—lack of standardization, ambiguity, confounding of independent and dependent variables—are serious. Is it unreasonable to ask, in light of this position, what weakness a measure of symbolic racism would have to suffer for Kinder to reject it?

A Question of Confusion

For our part, we pointed to a general problem in the measurement of symbolic racism. The problem, briefly described, is not that one measure of symbolic racism differs from all the others, but that virtually all of them differ from one another without any justification or even acknowledgement of the differences. Kinder, for his part, asserts that our critique lacks power, not because we were wrong in our characterization of symbolic racism measures in general, but because we made a mistake about one measure in particular. That mistake was to suppose that the Sears et al. measure (1979) is a measure of symbolic racism. We supposed this, Kinder suggests, because we were "confused" (1986, p. 159). If we were confused, we were certainly in good company; so, too, are Bobo (1983), Kluegel and Smith (1983), McClendon, (1985), Schuman et al. (1985), Stinchcombe and Taylor (1982), among others. Indeed, to our knowledge, every commentator on symbolic racism has read Sears's paper as a study of symbolic racism. And there is a good reason for this: Sears says it is. So he writes:

We have described this combination of prejudice and traditional values as "symbolic racism" (Kinder & Sears, 1981) which (along with general political conservatism) in turn has been shown to generate opposition to busing (Sears, Hensler & Speer, 1979; Sears et al., 1980). (Sears & Allen, 1984, p. 126)

For that matter, Kinder himself has classified Sears's busing study as a symbolic racism study. Referring explicitly to the 1979 study, he summarizes its argument as follows: "opposition to busing is regarded as an aspect of symbolic racism" (Kinder & Sears, 1981, p. 425, fn. 2).

Sniderman and Tetlock's indictment rests heavily on the claim that the questions that Sears and his associates (1979) used to measure symbolic racism include the very same questions that McConahay (1982, 1986) used to measure old-fashioned racism, which McConahay,

Sears, and I all insist is different from symbolic racism. Were this charge true, it would be devastating—but it is not true. (p. 158)

The best way to decide whether our contention is true is to look at the Sears et al. (1979) measure (see our Table 3). Support for antimiscegenation laws is a paradigmatic expression of old-fashioned racism, and the Sears measure includes it. Finally, support for the principle of segregation is the very quintessence of old-fashioned racism, and the Sears measure includes it. Nor is there any doubt that the Sears measure, in addition to having questions tapping old-fashioned racism, also includes questions tapping symbolic racism. In fact, Kinder himself has made this exact point elsewhere. Responding to Bobo's (1983) factor analysis of the Sears 1979 measure, he declared:

even the fine details of Bobo's factor analysis results recapitulate our own. His first factor [see his Table 1], called segregationism, closely resembles what we and others have variously called "generalized (in)egalitarianism" (Sears & Kinder, 1971), "redneck racism" (McConahay & Hough, 1976), or "old-fashioned racism" (McConahay, 1982). His second factor, which he labeled civil rights push, or black political push, was based on the same kind of items that we described as "symbolic racism" or "modern racism" (Kinder & Sears, 1981; McConahay, 1982). (Kinder & Sears, 1985, p. 1143, fn. 2).

We see no reason, therefore, to modify our critique of measures of symbolic racism.

Rationalization and Covert Racism

Symbolic racism, Kinder declares, is not disguised racism (1986, p. 155), and we were wrong to suggest that symbolic racism researchers have said that it is. McConahay, however, takes precisely this position:

In the present context, many whites still harbor negative feelings towards blacks, but it is still not fashionable to express these feelings directly. Hence, the feelings are displaced onto busing and busing has come to symbolize what are perceived to be unfair black demands and unfair black gains in status as well as economics. (McConahay, 1982, p. 716)

Sears has also argued that symbolic racism involves rationalization of anti-black affect:

In short, prior socialization produces symbolic predispositions; these in turn generate affective responses to policy issues (such as busing) symbolically linked to the predispositions; and these new symbolic attitudes about policy issues (such as opposition to busing) in turn generate a series of cognitive rationalizations that provide socially desirable justifications for the policy preferences. (Sears & Allen, 1984, p. 126–127).

It is one thing for Kinder to say that he does not believe symbolic racism is covert racism, and quite another to suggest that McConahay and Sears have not said what they manifestly have said.

For our part, we want to make a strictly logical point: the term "symbolic racism" is appropriate only if one adopts the definition that Kinder eschews—a definition that assigns a secondary or justificatory role to values. Otherwise, symbolic racism researchers place themselves in the untenable position of labeling as racist policy preferences largely rooted in values having nothing to do with race.

It is, accordingly, not surprising that we—and many others, as Kinder acknowledges—have made "the mistake" of supposing that symbolic racism involves policy preference (e.g., opposition to busing) based on anti-black affect but rationalized in terms of traditional values. McConahay and Sears have made the same mistake.

Two Types of Racism

Old-fashioned and symbolic racism, Kinder insists, are quite different, and we were supposedly wrong to worry about their possible overlap. Here, Kinder reverses his previous position. Only recently he contended that symbolic and old-fashioned racism were not worth distinguishing (Kinder & Sears, 1985). Indeed, this contention has been a hallmark of the Sears–Kinder approach to symbolic racism. In consequence, their approach has been logically flawed: how can one claim to have discovered a new kind of racism without demonstrating that it is different from the old? Kinder's new position is logically sound, but goes too far in the opposite direction. Kinder now not only claims that symbolic and old-fashioned racism are worth distinguishing; he claims that they have been *proven* to be different. We do not believe available data warrant this conclusion.

Kinder presents two kinds of evidence to support his claim. The first is factor analysis: the two types of racism are, by this criterion, empirically distinguishable. This kind of evidence, however, is equivocal, as Kinder himself has made plain. On the one hand, when Bobo (1983), relying on factor analysis, shows that these two aspects of racism are empirically distinguishable, Kinder acknowledges that the two are indeed separable dimensions—but insists that they are different dimensions of the same thing and so should properly be combined in a single measure (Kinder & Sears, 1985). On the other hand, when we point out that the two types of racism overlap substantially, Kinder turns to the very same factor analysis and argues that the two are clearly different.

The standards for judgment seem highly arbitrary. This arbitrariness is partly built into the problem itself: at what point are two variables so closely correlated that they should be regarded, not as different things, but as different measures of the same thing? But it is also possible to aggravate the problem of arbitrariness. For example, racism and opposition to busing are correlated only moderately, from about .2 to .3, yet Kinder takes this correlation as evidence that the two are literally the same (Kinder & Sears, 1981). By contrast, symbolic and old-fashioned racism are correlated quite strongly,[1] from about .6 to about .7, yet Kinder takes this correlation as evidence that the two "are clearly distinct."

Kinder, moreover, now maintains not only that symbolic and old-fashioned racism scales are factorially distinct, but that these scales have "distinguishable effects" (1986, p. 161). When measures of symbolic racism and old-fashioned racism are pitted against one another, the former predicts opposition to busing, for example, better than the latter.

This claim, it should be emphasized, is quite modest. Kinder is not asserting that symbolic and old-fashioned racism have different effects, only that they have impacts of differing strength. Even so, this second line of reasoning is no more compelling than the first. Every study examining both symbolic and old-fashioned racism has shown them to be strongly correlated. And so they should be. Kinder himself has said that "symbolic racism has its roots in early-learned racial fears and stereotypes …" (Kinder & Sears, 1981, p. 1141), which is, of course, another way of saying that old-fashioned racism is a cause of symbolic racism, as McConahay (1986), for example, acknowledges. But then the regression results that Kinder reports are necessarily misspecified. For, rather than simply pitting a measure of symbolic racism against a measure of old-fashioned racism, it is necessary *first* to calculate the impact of old-fashioned racism and only then to determine the additional impact of symbolic racism. And, given the correlation between the two forms of racism observed in every study, there is little question that the total effect of traditional racism, properly specified, will be substantially larger than Kinder supposes it to be.

This point deserves emphasis. It is an error simply to throw predictors together in a multiple regression, as symbolic racism researchers have done, ignoring the causal connections among them. It is an error also to ignore the multicollinearity problems that arise when highly correlated predictors are placed together in the same regression equation. These errors have serious consequences, leading Kinder to conclude that "the political impact of traditional forms of racial prejudice pale against those due to symbolic racism" (1986, p. 162). This conclusion is quite misleading; misleading because the impression that traditional prejudice is no longer a political force is created by improperly crediting to symbolic racism a part of the causal impact that should be credited to traditional

---

[1] There are at least two kinds of symbolic racism measures—those that assess dislike of blacks directly (e.g., Sears & Kinder, 1971) and those that infer it from policy preferences (e.g., Kinder & Sears, 1981). Here we refer to the first, not the second.

forms of prejudice. The result is to underestimate the tenacity and potency of traditional race prejudice.

What conclusions, then, can be drawn from the existing evidence? We call attention to two points. First, the two forms of racism are strongly correlated. Second, every observed cause of the one has also been found to be a cause of the other; and every observed consequence of one has been found to be a consequence of the other. Hence it is prudent—indeed, necessary—to ask whether the two "types" of racism differ in kind as Kinder contends, or only in degree as we suspect.

Values and Racism

Symbolic racism, Kinder contends, is a "conjunction" of anti-black affect and traditional values. What does it mean to say this?

A useful place to start is to ask what Kinder means by "traditional American values." After all, he supposes that they are a great obstacle to achieving racial equality. In contrast, Myrdal (1944) supposed that they were the great enemy of racial prejudice. But by traditional American values Myrdal meant a belief in equality and liberty. Kinder, obviously, has something very different in mind. "Traditional American values," he contends, include "individualism and self-reliance, the work ethic, obedience, and discipline" (Kinder & Sears, 1981, p. 416). This is a peculiar list. To our knowledge, no one has ever suggested that obedience and discipline are "traditional American values"—Prussian perhaps, but not American.

Kinder's conception of traditional American values is unusual, in part because he runs traditional values and conservative values together as though they were one and the same. But what is the relation between such values and racism? Both, Kinder claims, make up symbolic racism—in fact, symbolic racism is "prejudice *and* values."

This claim is central to Kinder's case. One must therefore ask what justification exists for it. Scarcely any, it turns out. Symbolic racism researchers have not yet analyzed the relation between prejudice and values; indeed, they have not yet measured the traditional values that are supposedly an integral part of symbolic racism.

Instead, Kinder has followed a different tack, contending that symbolic racism measures capture both prejudice and values. Thus Kinder (1986, p. 156) states: "Because we define symbolic racism to be the conjunction of prejudice and values, we have tried to measure symbolic racism with questions that deliberately mix racist sentiments and traditional American values, particularly individualism."

Kinder, then, is arguing that measures of symbolic racism are "double-barreled"; the questions measure—and should measure—both racism and conservative values simultaneously. Kinder,

moreover, produces no evidence that symbolic racism items measure both racism and conservatism; he simply says that they do. But suppose that he is right. Then measures of symbolic racism confound two attributes—conservative values and prejudice—that may well be separate. People can score high on symbolic racism either because they are conservative but not racist, or because they are racist but not conservative. Racists, according to this approach, are by definition conservatives; and conservatives, again by definition, are racists. This methodological approach is extremely difficult to defend; for it amounts to claiming that a key virtue of symbolic racism measures is that they are systematically ambiguous.

What conclusions about symbolic racism should be drawn from this discussion? Originally, Sears and Kinder (1971) contended that conservatism and prejudice were separate and distinct. A decade later, they announced that symbolic racism, at its core, involves a "conjunction," "a blending," a "fusion" of the two (Kinder & Sears, 1981). They have given no explanation for giving up their original contention that prejudice and conservatism each make substantial but separate contributions—their "separate but equal" thesis, so to speak. Nor have they gathered evidence to justify their subsequent "conjunction" thesis.

Reducing the relation between symbolic racism and conservative values to a tautology is not helpful. The relation between the two raises important theoretical questions. Do people use values to cover their racism? Or are conservative values promoting prejudice against blacks? Or, yet again, do racism and conservative values in some sense work together to encourage opposition to efforts to achieve racial equality?

These questions point to alternative, and empirically distinguishable, ways of conceptualizing symbolic racism. We therefore cannot agree with Kinder that it suffices simply to define symbolic racism as a conjunction of prejudice and *traditional* values.

SCIENCE AND VALUES

We strongly support research that systematically attempts to assess the impact of racist motives on support for government programs to assist minorities. We strongly object, however, to treating opposition to such policies as racist *by definition*. And symbolic racism researchers have done precisely that. Kinder has no apparent qualms, for example, about operationally defining symbolic racism in terms of oppositions to busing, quotes, or special government programs for minorities. He maintains that significant correlations between racial prejudice and positions on these issues justify including such items in symbolic racism scales (1986, pp. 158–159). We reject this position on both logical and epistemological grounds. Such items provide at best a very indirect way of measuring the two assumed components of symbolic racism: racial prejudice and traditional values. A person might oppose busing or quotes for a number of reasons, as Kinder is well aware. Why define one's explanatory construct in terms of items that one has only weak correlational grounds for supposing to measure the construct? A more reasonable procedure would be to advance a precise statement of the racist and value components of symbolic racism, and to develop items that adequately capture these components. It might then be possible to assess whether it makes sense to create a superordinate explanatory construct that "fuses" racial prejudice and traditional values.

The research procedure that Kinder advocates also risks politicizing the social science research process. To label someone a racist, or to label support for a particular viewpoint as racist, is to pass moral–political judgment on that individual or viewpoint. Standards of evidence need to be exceptionally clear in passing such judgments—and if our critique has brought out nothing else, it is the conceptual and empirical confusion within symbolic racism research.

It is useful, in this connection, to return to the parable of the "symbolic Marxism" scale (Sniderman & Tetlock, 1986, p. 148). Symbolic racism scales are intended to identify people who dislike blacks and are conservative. One can imagine, correspondingly, a symbolic Marxism scale to identify people who dislike businessmen and are liberal. We asked, in our original paper, how the social science community would react to conservative researchers who operationalized their concept of symbolic Marxism with items that focused on support for the civil liberties of American communists or on opposition to aid to right-wing governments. Such a research undertaking would be scandalous. And the scandal would not be mitigated by insisting that one's item selection procedure was grounded in definitional choices. Nor would the scandal be mitigated by invoking the existence of a positive relation between left-wing political orientation (liberalism) and support for the constitutional rights of American communists. Thus the symbolic Marxism scale would be a clear-cut example of what C. Wright Mills (1940) called "motive-mongering"—in this case, the use of social science research methods to cast aspersions on political viewpoints with which the researchers disagree.

We are not suggesting that symbolic racism researchers deliberately set out to engage in such motive-mongering. But we do want to state emphatically that their approach lends itself to such abuse. What is objectionable is partly what has been done, especially the labeling of particular policy positions and values as racist by definition. But what is still more objectionable is what has not been done—

i.e., the failure to call attention to the dangers inherent in this approach. Kinder's approach raises the risk of branding people as racists who are not in fact racist but merely conservative. It is not within Kinder's power to eliminate this risk—all social measures are imperfect. But he has the means to call attention to the danger. We have been unable to find any expression of concern on his part about this danger, any warning of the risk of branding people as racist because they are conservative. Even in this exchange, he has chosen to ignore it.

A final point deserves note. The failure to guard against such abuse has intellectual costs. For instance, Kinder correctly points out that in our own work we have accented the role of conservative values as a source of resistance to efforts to achieve racial equality (Sniderman & Hagen, 1985; Sniderman, Hagen, Tetlock, & Brady, in press; Sniderman, Brody, & Kuklinski, 1984). Our conclusion, Kinder (1986, p. 6) implies, is very similar to his own. Kinder is mistaken. True, we have demonstrated a connection between commitment to individualism and opposition to achieving racial equality, but we would certainly not conclude that individualism therefore *is* racism.

A RESEARCH AGENDA

What can we learn from this exchange on symbolic racism? How should future research differ from that of the past? Kinder makes a number of valuable suggestions on directions that future research should take. We especially agree with his emphasis on the importance of taking into account a broad range of explanatory factors—ideological, cultural, cognitive, and the like. Here, we limit ourselves to noting two additional sets of issues that deserve attention in research on racial policy reasoning.

Most fundamentally, researchers need to be clear about the nature of the dependent variable. What exactly are we trying to explain? Considerable evidence has accumulated showing that Americans take quite different positions on racial equality, depending on whether they confront it at the level of principle or of policy. And the difference is not merely one of magnitude, of offering more support for equality as an abstract principle than in a concrete situation; the casual factors underlying support for equality as principle and as policy may differ. For instance, education is a major source in promoting support for the principle of racial equality, but it is apparently of minor importance in encouraging support for actual government efforts to achieve racial equality (e.g., Jackman & Muhe, 1984; but see Sniderman et al., 1984).

How should one interpret this principle-policy puzzle of racial attitudes? No shortage of theoretical accounts exists. Jackman and Muhe (1984) have offered a social desirability explanation: white Americans—especially the educated—are willing to offer rhetorical support for equality but shy from doing anything to achieve it. In contrast, Margolis and Hacque (1981) propose that substantial numbers of Americans sincerely support the principle of equality, but oppose efforts to realize it because they believe the federal government has grown too large and intrusive (see also Kuklinski & Parent, 1981). Sniderman and his colleagues have stressed the role of political conservatism as a source of resistance to specific policy proposals, particularly among the educated (Sniderman et al., 1984; Sniderman et al., in press). Levine (1971) has suggested that citizens really object to the "coerciveness" of efforts to assure racial equality. For that matter, the principle-policy puzzle may be tailor-made for a symbolic racism analysis. Symbolic racism may take precisely the form of supporting the principle of equality, but resisting implementation of it.

Whatever combination of explanatory tactics proves most enlightening, we see the principle-policy puzzle as a key to understanding current psychological and political sources of resistance to reducing racial inequalities. But the principle-policy puzzle is not the only problem worth considering. Of the many others, we single out one for particular emphasis: the problem of motive attribution.

Motive Attribution

We have already noted that labeling an individual or viewpoint as racist is a serious matter. In response, it is reasonable to ask of us the following: When would such a motive attribution be justified? What standards of proof is it reasonable to expect of researchers who seek to assess the importance of racist beliefs or motives as determinants of policy preferences? No general guidelines can be offered. On the one hand, the dichotomous "either-or" theory testing strategy of symbolic racism researchers ("is it the buses or the blacks?") raises the risk of concluding that racist motives are at work when investigators have controlled only for tangible, immediate self-interest, itself only one of a number of possible explanatory alternatives. On the other hand, it is easy to go too far in the opposite direction. Insisting on the need to control for all possible explanatory alternatives—cultural and political values, causal attributions, perceived group interests, ideology—would make it extremely difficult to identify the operation of racist motives even when such motives are at work. People may sometimes use values, attributions, and group perceptions to justify racist-motivated policy preferences; statistically controlling for these variables would, from this viewpoint, obscure the influence of racism.

We see at least two possible solutions to this dilemma. One approach is to turn to more sophisticated forms of correlational analysis—to develop a new generation of models that specify the causal relations among the wide range of explanatory constructs for racial policy preferences (e.g., Sniderman, et al., in press). Careful development of operational indicators and conceptual analysis of these constructs are promising avenues to building a cumulative body of knowledge on determinants of racial policy reasoning.

A second, complementary approach should also be identified. Researchers have developed experimental techniques for unobtrusively assessing the impact of racist motives on social behavior (Crosby, Bromley, & Saxe, 1980). It is possible to transplant key features of this experimental approach—controlled manipulation of independent variables and random assignment of respondents to conditions—into survey settings. Sniderman (1984), for example, has combined experimental and survey techniques to explore the extent to which citizens' intuitive theories of political entitlement are universalistic or particularistic. Universalistic theories maintain that the honoring of claims to a public benefit should not be contingent on features of the claimant such as race. Conversely, particularistic theories maintain that the legitimacy of claims to benefits should often depend on who the claimant is. To explore these natural theories of justice, interviewers pose deliberately varied forms of policy questions to respondents empanelled in a conventional, cross-sectional sample. To take a simplified hypothetical example: half the respondents are asked whether the government in Washington should help people who are poor; the other half are asked precisely the same question expect for one difference—the claimants are poor blacks.

In principle, a number of claimant attributes—race, gender, socioeconomic class, and so on—can be varied simultaneously to identify the interactions of characteristics responsible for honoring or rejecting claims to a variety of public benefits. Neither the respondent nor the interviewer is aware of question variations; so, to the extent responses vary, attribution of racial bias will be on firmer ground than hitherto possible.

In concluding, we should emphasize that no one method eliminates the possibility of error in motive attribution. We should also emphasize that it would be wrong to permit such interpretive problems to inhibit research on the sources of resistances to programs to assist minority groups. Kinder portrays us as more pessimistic about research on policy reasoning than we are. We do not believe, and did not say, the "task of determining the sources of public opinion on racial matters is so formidably difficult ... that ... research on the topic should be abandoned" (Kinder, 1986, p. 168). We do believe, however, the task is very difficult. We also believe current research on symbolic racism is so fraught with conceptual and empirical ambiguities that it makes an already difficult task even more problematic.

In the end, the research program on symbolic racism amounts to a recommendation to change the meaning of the concepts of racism. The change, we have become persuaded, would be a change for the worse because it would weaken the meaning of racism. Racism used to refer to genuine prejudice— a deep-seated, irrational insistence on the inferiority of blacks, and contempt and hostility toward them. It still does. It is a mistake to leech away the meaning of racism, to diminish it, by making it merely a synonym for political attitudes with which one happens to disagree.

REFERENCES

Bobo, L. (1983). Whites' opposition to busing: Symbolic racism or realistic group conflict? *Journal of Personality and Social Psychology, 45*, 1196–1210.

Crosby, F., Bromley, S., & Saxe, L. (1980). Recent unobtrusive studies of black and white discrimination and prejudice: A literature review. *Psychological Bulletin, 87*, 546–563.

Jackman, M. R., & Muhe, M. J. (1984). Education and intergroup attitudes: Moral enlightenment, superficial democratic commitment, or ideological refinement? *American Sociological Review, 49*, 751–769.

Kinder, D. O. (1986). The continuing American dilemma: White resistance to racial change 40 years after Myrdal. *Journal of Social Issues, 42*(2), 151–171.

Kinder, D. R., & Sears, D. O. (1981). Prejudice and politics: Symbolic racism versus racial threats to the good life. *Journal of Personality and Social Psychology. 40*, 414–431.

Kinder, D. R., & Sears, D. O. (1985). White opposition to busing: On conceptualizing and operationalizing group conflict. *Journal of Personality and Social Psychology, 48*, 1141–1147.

Kluegel, J. R., & Smith, E. R. (1983). Affirmative action attitudes: Effects of self-interest, racial affect, and stratification beliefs on whites' views. *Social Forces, 16*, 797–824.

Kuklinski, J. K., & Parent, W. (1981). Race and big government: Contamination in measuring racial attitudes. *Political Methodology, 8*, 131–159.

Levine, R. A. (1971). The silent majority: Neither simple nor simple-minded. *Public Opinion Quarterly, 35*, 571–577.

Margolis, M., & Hacque, K. E. (1981). Applied tolerance or fear of government? An alternative interpretation of Jackman's findings. *American Journal of Political Science, 25*, 241–255.

McClendon, M. J. (1985). Racism, rational choice, and white opposition to racial change: A case study of busing. *Public Opinion Quarterly, 49*, 214–233.

McConahay, J. B. (1982). Self-interest versus racial attitudes as correlates as anti-busing attitudes in Louisville. *Journal of Politics, 44*, 692–720.

McConahay, J. B. (1986). Modern racism, ambivalence, and the modern racism scale. In J. Dovidio & S. L. Gaertner (Eds.), *Prejudice, discrimination, and racism: Theory and research*. New York: Academic Press.

McConahay, J. B., Hardee, B. B., & Batts, V. (1981). Has racism declined in America? It depends on who is asking and what is asked. *Journal of Conflict Resolution, 25*, 563–579.

McConahay, J. B., & Hough, J. C., Jr. (1976). Symbolic racism. *Journal of Social Issues, 32*(2): 23–45.

Mills, C. W. (1940). Situated actions and vocabularies of motive. *American Sociological Review, 5*, 904–913.

Myrdal, G. (1944). *An American dilemma: The Negro problem and modern democracy*. New York: Harper & Row.

Schuman, H., & Presser, S. (1981). *Questions and answers in attitude surveys*. New York: Academic Press.

Schuman, H., Steeh, C., & Bobo, L. (1985). *Racial attitudes in America*. Cambridge, MA: Harvard University Press.

Sears, D. O., & Citrin, J. (1982). *Tax revolt: Something for nothing in California*. Cambridge, MA: Harvard University Press.

Sears, D. O., & Kinder, D. R. (1971). *Racial tensions and voting in Los Angeles: Viability and prospects for metropolitan leadership*. New York: Praeger.

Sears, D. O., & Allen, H. M., Jr. (1984). The trajectory of local desegregation controversies and whites' opposition to busing. In N. Miller & M. Brewer (Eds.), *Groups in contact: The psychology of desegregation*. New York: Academic Press.

Sears, D. O., Hensler, C. P., & Speer, L. K. (1979). Whites' opposition to "busing": Self-interest or symbolic politics? *American Political Science Review, 73*, 369–384.

Sears, D. O., Lau, R. R., Tyler, T., & Allen, H. M., Jr., (1980). Self-interest versus symbolic politics in policy attitudes and presidential voting. *American Political Science Review, 74*, 670–684.

Sniderman, P. M. (1984). Racism and political preferences. Proposal to the National Science Foundation.

Sniderman, P. M., & Hagen, M. G. (1985). *Race and inequality*. New York: Chatham House.

Sniderman, P. M., & Tetlock, P. E. (1986). Symbolic racism: Problems of motive attribution in political analysis. *Journal of Social Issues, 42*(2), 129–150.

Sniderman, P. M., Brody, R. A., & Kuklinski, J. H. (1984). Policy reasoning and political issues: The case of racial equality. *American Journal of Political Science, 28*, 75–94.

Sniderman, P. M., Hagen, M. G., Tetlock, P. E., & Brady, H. (in press). Reasoning chains: causal models or racial policy reasoning. *British Journal of Political Science*.

Stinchcombe, A. L., & Taylor, D. G. (1982). On democracy and school integration. In W. G. Stephen & J. R. Feagin (Eds.), *School integration: Past, present, and future*. New York: Plenum.

23

Problems in the Marxist Project of Theorizing Race

E. SAN JUAN, JR

In this article the author raises the long debate between the primacy of race and class and the nature of racism. E. San Juan takes issue with the strictly Marxist interpretation of racism as simply a tool utilized exploitively by wealthy interests. Racism is more complex than this suggests, and its foundation reflects both entrenched racial thinking in society, as well as the interplay of class interests. The author reviews the traditional Marxist explanation of race and racism, highlighting the role that Gus Hall, the General Secretary of the Communist Party USA, and other Left scholars played in this dialogue. More recent scholarship and activism has given emergence to the proposal that race and class are intertwined and it may be illogical and ahistorical within the context of the United States to separate these two concepts. As support for this position the author refers to the classic work by Oliver Cox, *Caste, Class, and Race* (1948). Cox described as symbiotic the proletarianization of blacks in this country, and the building of a social and institutional foundation in support of a racial order. In later years, this relationship has been examined by scholars, but in particular, black and Latino scholars and activists. The author concludes by suggesting that struggles against racism are fundamental and a necessary first step for the success of class struggles.

With the nationwide eruption of racist violence in the last years—witness the Atlanta murders, the furor over Bernhard Goetz from 1984 to 1987, the racial confrontations in university campuses from Stanford and Wisconsin to Massachusetts, the Miami ghetto rebellion (Watts *déjà vu?*), and recently the Central Park gang rape which occasioned the outburst of "lynch mob mentality" and the formulaic invocation of law and order—the centrality of race in any program for socialist transformation can no longer be shirked. Nor can it be dismissed by quoting, for the nth time, Marx's dictum: "Labor cannot emancipate itself in the white skin where in the black it is branded" (Foster 1973, 196). Indeed, class struggle cannot preempt, or leap over, the color line which W. E. B. Du Bois pronounced as the decisive battlefront of this century and surely of the next.

From the thirties to the sixties, Western Marxism has always subsumed racial conflicts to the class problematic. With the post-World War II emergence of Third World nations led by Marxist-inspired vanguards—China, Vietnam, Korea, and later Cuba, Guinea-Bissau, Mozambique, and Angola—and the birth of the Black liberation movement in the sixties, the dialectic of race and class has been catapulted for the first time onto the center stage of the political-ideological arena. The famous 1968 Kerner report on urban riots, the *Report of the National Advisory Commission on Civil Disorders*, in the wake of Martin Luther King's assassination, crystallized the urgency of the issue.

Writing about "Marxism and the Negro," Harold Cruse, among numerous protagonists, lambasted orthodox Marxists (particularly Trotskyites) for "failing to deal with the race question in America" (1968, 151), thus succumbing to "mechanistic materialism." Since then, a raft of Marxist-Leninist organizations, progressive intellectuals, and independent left publications has debated the thematics of the race-class nexus throughout a whole period (see Progressive Labor party [1970] and Loren [1977], among others). Before a resolution could break the impasse, the reactionary tide of Reaganism swept in just as the Empire's outposts were again being challenged in Nicaragua, El Salvador, the Philippines, and South Africa.

1

It might be useful to remind ourselves, at the outset, how the standard Soviet manual, *Fundamentals of Marxism-Leninism*, consistently asserts the primacy of class over nation, race, or ethnicity. Gus Hall, General Secretary of the Communist party USA, condemns racism as "a deliberate strategy [of monopoly capital] for super-profits" (1972, 145) so that to overthrow this racist system, Blacks and other minorities should unite with the majority white working class.

Radical economists also echoed this sacrosanct doctrine. Michael Reich, for example, noted that "racism is a key mechanism for the stabilization of capitalism and the legitimization of inequality"; racial conflict "obfuscates class interests." Rooted in the capitalist system, racism weakens workers' unity and promotes powerlessness and alienation within "an individualistic and competitive ethos" (Reich 1972, 320). Clearly class polarization, not race, is the central determinant.[1] Even younger radical economists, perhaps influenced by Paul Baran and Paul Sweezy's *Monopoly Capital* (1966),

subscribed to the primacy of class over race. Howard Sherman, for instance, concluded his survey of the statistics on Blacks by asserting that the function of racism was "to justify economic exploitation," to find a scapegoat for all social problems, to divide the oppressed so that the elite can rule (1972, 180-81). Sherman urged white radicals to unity with their Black counterparts to build a viable socialist movement, a call echoed by Michael Lerner, a founder of the New American Movement, who noted that "racism in this country has acquired an independent life" (1973, 201). This was preceded by historian Eugene Genovese's 1968 speech to the Students for a Democratic Society where he argued that racism is not just a class question but is implicated in the right of Blacks and other peoples to self-determination (Genovese 1971). Amid the protracted crisis of Western Marxism, in particular the privileging of the proletariat as the chief revolutionary agent for socialist transformation, the salience of race manifested itself in the Left's rhetorical prioritizing of the democratic principle of self-determination for all peoples, especially those subjugated by racist neocolonial elites (Smith 1979).

We can measure the profound mutation of the conventional Marxist tendency to sublate and valorize every social force or phenomenon within a productivist-economistic model in the last three decades by comparing the arguments of two Marxists, Oliver Cromwell Cox's *Caste, Class and Race* (1948) and Robert Blauner's *Racial Oppression in America* (1972), both epochal discourses in the archive of U.S. race relations.

Long acclaimed as the classic Marxist analysis of race relations, Cox's book aimed principally to refute the habitual academic conflation of race with caste (e.g., Montagu 1962), the widely influential Chicago sociology of race relations cycle (Robert Park), and Gunnar Myrdal's thesis of "cumulative causation" propounded in *An American Dilemma* (1944). Cox elaborates his fundamental premise that racial antagonism is essentially political class struggle. Racial categorization arose with capitalism in order to facilitate the differential commercialization and exploitation of the labor of certain racially marked groups. Ultimately race relations are class conflicts. Shackled by this obsolescent if still canonical view of ideology as epiphenomenal superstructure, Cox discounts racism as "a system of rationalization" not worthy of analysis contrasted with the "material social fact" of class relations. Cognized as race prejudice, racism is "the socio-attitudinal concomitant of the racial-exploitative practice of a ruling class in a capitalistic society" (1948, 321, 470). To the Negro people Cox ascribes an "abiding urge…to assimilate" and thus dismisses outright their impulse to solidarity based on religion, culture, or commonality of experience. Michael Banton correctly faults Cox for overestimating "the integration of the capitalist system" and

---

[1] That the program for Black capitalism and independent community development cannot succeed unless "the systemic oppression of the economic system is ended," has been persuasively documented again by William Tabb (1988).

underestimating the "independence of beliefs in social processes" (1987, 152; see also Sweezy 1953).

What is worth exploring, however, is Cox's notion of an ethnic system (based on culture and physical diversity) coexisting with political and social class conflicts which would allow the analyst to appraise how Blacks not only experienced proletarianization but also racialization, and how they responded to these experiences with ethnic-racial solidarity cutting across class barriers. However, as Robert Miles acutely comments, Cox fails to systematically theorize the concrete dynamics of this interaction between two conceptual networks (1980, 175). The reason for this inadequacy, I think, can be attributed to Cox's reductionist reflex which virtually negates the complex mediation of cultural-ideological praxis in *la vie quotidienne*, the overdetermined constitution of subjects (more precisely, subject positions), and conjunctural displacements in the social field. In other words. Cox's limitation inheres in his instrumental conception of racial beliefs and practices which he immediately links with the extraction of surplus value. Dialectics is sacrificed to the expediency, the utopian dream indeed, of gradual assimilation.

With the autonomous mobilization of the Black masses in the sixties under populist leaders critical or suspicious of integration, Cox's otherwise sophisticated conceptual apparatus no longer matched "material social fact" and had to yield to a more totalizing, self-critical registration of specific historical changes then in progress: Blauner's *Racial Oppression in America*. I consider this text a landmark in refining a Marxist phenomenology and political theory of racial formation in U.S. history.[2] Since my main purpose here is not to catalogue in detail the pre-1980s work on this topic, suffice it to describe briefly Blauner's achievement. For the first time U.S. society is defined as a "racial order" and race as an international political force. Conceived as a site of power and privilege, U.S. racial dynamics are firmly situated within the historical specificity of each people's differential incorporation into the labor-market system. Repudiating the prevailing immigrant model of integration (the mainstream ethnicity school now identified with Nathan Glazer, Daniel P. Moynihan, and *The Harvard Encyclopedia of American Ethnic groups*), Blauner contends that race cannot be reduced to class, nor can racism be simply viewed as "subjective irrational beliefs" (1972, 28-29); race and class are dialectically intertwined. Racially

categorized groups like Blacks, Chicanos, Native Americans, and Asians are both exploited as workers and oppressed as colonized peoples. Applying a global Third World perspective never before tried, Blauner devises the concept of "internal colonialism" (ghetto, barrio, reservation) as the mode fusing both moments of the dialectic. More importantly, he focuses on the mechanisms of cultural domination and the response, nationalist or revolutionary cultural resistance, as the key to grasping racism as a "historical and social project" aimed at destroying the humanity of such peoples.

Within this multileveled perspective, Blauner makes the unprecedented move of valorizing Black political history as the substantive core of Black Power, the movement for self-determination, a process of nation-building which is paradoxically enabled by racial (not just class) oppression (1972, 142–43). In so doing, he cogently disintegrates the traditional received opinion (fostered by Myrdal and structural-functionalist sociology) that the Black person is "an exaggerated American" with pathological values. Blauner delineates the genealogy of his insights in the exemplary practice of Black intellectuals like DuBois, Cruse, Stokely Carmichael, and others. Not only does Blauner chart sensitively the complex, fluid, open-ended initiatives of Third World peoples for self-emancipation, but he is also self-critical of his role as a white researcher who, whatever his professional guild's apologetics, nonetheless participates in the victimization of his subjects (Blauner and Wellman 1973).

From the publication of Blauner's book up to the eighties, Marxist theoretical projects on race were eclipsed by the mainstream sociology of ethnicity and minority group relations. Liberal scholars like Gordon Allport, Richard Schermerborn, George Simpson, and J. Milton Yinger dominated the field; finally, the 1975 textbook *Ethnicity Theory and Experience* edited by Glazer and Moynihan and the 1980 *Harvard Encyclopedia* marked the foundational ascendancy of this school. While the doctrines of ethnicity had been seriously undermined by scholars like Genovese (1971), Saxton (1977), Smith (1982), and Mullings (1984), it was not until the absorption of Althusserian and Gramsci-inspired critiques that a renewal of Marxist thinking on race could properly begin. One indication may be glimpsed in the entry on "Race" by John Rex in *A Dictionary of Marxist Thought* which positively stresses "the emergence of independent class struggle mobilized around national, ethnic and race ideologies" (1983, 407; see also Rex 1986). Given this renaissance of an authentically dialectical or rehistoricized materialism in this decade, and the mixed legacy of research assessed earlier, what new directions should a Marxist theorizing of the race-class nexus take? I offer the following comments as pretexts for further discussion and exchange.

---

[2] Despite the provocative criticisms of the "internal colony" model (one motif in Blauner's research) by Wolpe (1986), Burawoy (1981), and others, I find the narrative of his discourse and its synthesizing framework still cogent and viable, with some modifications and updating (see Liu 1976; Wald 1981).

2

Advances in the analytical power of historical-materialist science since World War II allow us to reaffirm the view that Marxism is a theoretical organon or research praxis operating on two interlocking premises: the materialist one which requires the analysis of political and ideological structures to be grounded in their actual conditions of existence, and the historical one which demands that social relations be understood not as a priori deductions from what has been traditionally conceived as "the base" but as forms with historically determinate *differentiae specificae* (Rozat and Bartra 1980). Racism then cannot be understood as an abstract epiphenomenal result of capitalist development (according to an economistic monism which reduces the category of race to class), or as an "ideal type" (Weber) Which aggregates societies using racial ascription to organize the division of labor, the distribution of goods, and so on. Nor can racism be theorized as a universal, albeit plural, given, each manifestation differing from the other, all of them resistant to any conceptualization because of a pervasive diacritical principle, as one finds in the autonomist approach (more on this later).

I endorse Stuart Hall's (1980) main thesis that the most viable project for Marxist research into the status of the category of race vis-à-vis the political agenda for the socialist transformation of capitalism as a global system is to posit historically demarcated racisms and then proceed from there. Using Gramsci's concept of hegemony as an articulating principle of class alliances, Hall proposes this point of departure:

> One must start, then, from the concrete historical "work" which racism accomplishes under specific historical conditions—as a set of economic, political, and ideological practices, of a distinctive kind, concretely articulated with other practices in a social formation. These practices ascribe the positioning of different social groups in relation to one another with respect to the elementary structures of society; they fix and ascribe those positionings in on-going social practices; they legitimate the positions as ascribed. In short, they are practices which secure the hegemony of a dominant group over a series of subordinate ones, in such a way as to dominate the whole social formation in a form favourable to the long-term development of the economic productive base (1980, 338; see also 1978).

Opposing the class reductionism of traditional Marxists who dissolve race into class. Hall suggests that race as a sociohistorical category possesses a distinctive, "relatively autonomous" effectivity, so that defining the economic grounding does not adequately or fully explain how it concretely functions in a specific formation. Conjoined with the materialist premise, the imperative of historical specificity poses certain questions: "One needs to know how different racial and ethnic groups were inserted historically, and the relations which have tended to erode and transform, or to preserve these distinctions through time—not simply as residues and traces of previous modes, but as active structuring principles of the present organization of society" (1980, 339).

One illustration of this sedimentation and deferred efficacy to which Hall refers is the plight of the Filipino nationality (now more than two million). Filipinos entered the United States for the first time in 1907 as manual workers recruited by the Hawaiian Sugar Planters Association to anticipate any labor shortage caused by the Gentlemen's Agreement to restrict the number of Japanese field hands. This came shortly after the ruthless suppression of Filipino revolutionary forces of the first Philippine Republic between 1898 and 1902. The context then was the violent colonization of six million Filipinos by U.S. military occupation forces. When the racial exclusion of Japanese by the Immigration Acts of 1920 and 1924 occurred, the Sugar Planters Association recruited 45,000 Filipinos more, a practice which continued until the anomalous status of the Filipino colonial subject—neither citizen nor alien—ceased in 1934 with the passage of the Philippine Independence Act and the limitation of immigration to a quota of fifty a year (McWilliams 1964; Quinsaat 1976; Melendy 1981). This historical matrix, coupled with the persistence of a subaltern *habitus* (Bourdieu), may elucidate why Filipinos, compared to other Asian Americans and despite higher educational attainment, continue to be segregated in low-paying jobs (Nee and Sanders 1985).

Concrete investigation of various historical conjunctures is needed to answer how the reproduction of social relations operates through race insofar as capitalism, for example, articulates classes in distinct ways at each level (economic, political, ideological) of the social formation. In effect, the schematics of race and its use to ascribe values, allocate resources, and legitimize the social position/status of racially defined populations (in short, racism) centrally affect the constitution of the fractions of Black, Asian, or Hispanic labor as a class. Put another way, the class relations that ascribe race as social/political/economic positioning of the subject (individual and collective) function as race relations. Hall affirms this key insight: "Race is thus, also, the modality in which class is 'lived,' the medium through which class relations are experienced, the form in which it is appropriated and 'fought through...' Capital reproduces the class, including its internal contradictions, as a whole—structured by race" (1980, 341). Within a modified Althusserian positing of society as a complex, contradictory unity structured in dominance (Althusser 1969), Hall's conception of race as an articulating ideological principle deploys Gramsci's notion of hegemony to elucidate its political effectivity, that is, race as the site and stake of class struggle.

Race or racially based political calculations, under specific conditions, may define the content and form of class struggle—if by class struggle we mean the struggle for hegemony. Hegemony here designates participatory moral-intellectual leadership, not the reified mechanical consensus that legitimizes bourgeois authority. Consequently, instead of just being equated with ideas or beliefs tied to state apparatuses (either repressive or ideological), race becomes an integral element of a hegemonic strategy. It becomes part of a principle operated by the bourgeoisie to articulate an ensemble of discourses and practices designed to construct subjects (or subject positions) whose actions will reproduce capitalist relations (Mouffe 1981). Race then should be construed as an epitomizing aspect of social practice which demonstrates an autonomous effectivity, a historically concrete modality in the configuration of everyday experience of groups and individuals. This is what Blauner and others have shown in describing Black or Chicano cultural politics.

What Hall and others have reminded us is that race as a concrete social practice can only be grasped in specific historical conjunctures. It has no transhistorical essence. This follows from Marx's axiom that "the concrete is the outcome of multiple determinations" (Marx and Engels 1968). Circumscribed by a differentiated or decentered totality and overdetermined by heterogeneous (residual, emergent, dominant) tendencies in the formation, race cannot be abstractly conflated with the ideological or political spheres, much less with the economic. Given the extended or integral state of late capitalism, racialization as a part of bourgeois hegemonic strategy informs not only state policies but also institutions and activities of civil society, and in so doing suppresses the potential for expansive democracy by reinforcing racist hierarchy and authoritarian statism founded on national chauvinism.

How does this Gramscian *problématique* compare with other competing neo-Marxist approaches to race as a theoretical construct and historical practice? In his survey of the "Varieties of Marxist Conceptions of 'Race,' Class and the State," John Solomos comments on the race-class dialectic as obfuscating because it "does little to show the specificity of racism" (in Rex and Mason 1986, 103). Hall's influence on the writers of *The Empire Strikes Back* (Centre for Contemporary Cultural Studies 1982), as well as his specific analysis of Caribbean race/ethnic relations, has perhaps been unjustly underestimated by Solomos.

In his review, Solomos refers to the "autonomy model" associated with John Gabriel and Gideon Ben-Tovim who argue that the issue is not the relation between racism and the social totality but "the conceptualization of racism as the object of struggle in historically defined conditions" (104). Solomos agrees with this view when he stipulates that "there can be no general Marxist theory of racism, since each historical situation needs to be analyzed in its own specificity." Meanwhile, he also concurs with Hall and the proponents of the migrant labor model that the problem of race relations cannot be thought of separately from the structural features of capitalist society. His third desideratum for a satisfactory Marxist analytical framework coincides with Hall's theory of articulation, namely, racial and ethnic divisions cannot be reduced to phenomena completely determined by the structural contradictions of capitalism. Maneuvering between the simple pluralism of the autonomy model where struggle "is not located in any social context" and what he labels the orthodox determinist models, Solomos settles on the prospect of further theoretical refinement in clarifying with greater specificity the social relations of racism in specific societies, its interconnections with class and nonclass aspects of complex social realities, in other words, "the construction, mobilization, and pertinence of different forms of racist ideology and structuration in specific historical circumstances" (106). While this compromise between empiricist relativism and deterministic positivism provides a useful disciplinary guideline, it does not seem to me to offer any substantive catalyzing innovation.

3

While these debates on the crisis of Marxist theory vis-à-vis popular protest and resistance against racism have raged in Britain in the last two decades with the imposition of reactionary state policies on rebellious Asian and West Indian immigrants, the situation in the United States may be said to be characterized by the decline of the civil rights movement, the fragmenting of cultural and left nationalists, and the subsiding of mass struggles (with the notable exception of feminist struggles) upon the withdrawal of U.S. forces from Indo-China. The significant Marxist studies on race during this period, in my opinion, were made primarily by Black and Third World activists (to cite only the most accessible, West 1982, 1988; Marable 1980, 1981, 1983). Their polemical if retrospective orientation contributed to establishing the groundwork for a more consistently dialectical reworking of the race/class/gender dialectic. Before the phenomenal rise of Jesse Jackson followed by the redeployment of left energies to the electoral arena (via the Rainbow Coalition), it was remnants of the New Left and a younger generation of activists receptive to the European debates around

Althusser who took up the task of "re-inventing" a nondogmatic Marxism in consonance with the changed milieu and terrain of contestation (Amariglio et al. 1988).[3] In the late seventies, Stanley Aronowitz (1981) and others set the stage for an interrogation of the orthodox understanding of class, the privileging of capital logic over culture, and so on, in the wake of the worldwide renewal of a critical but also anti-Eurocentric—nay, antiracist—Marxism. Aronowitz in fact pushed the renovation beyond the autonomists' limit by postulating that racism, with race functioning as a "transhistorical sign" for the caste-like underclass, "is rooted in the domination that social and economic hierarchies have attempted to inflict upon nature, including human nature, "so that the problematic of racism transcends historical boundaries and seems to demand a prior ontological diagnosis and subsequent ethical resolution.

One of the most innovative and praxis-oriented results of these developments is Michael Omi and Howard Winant's *Racial Formation in the United States from the 1960s to the 1980s* (1986), parts of which first appeared in 1983 in *Socialist Review*. This work is bound to be controversial and deserves extended comment (I have seen only two superficial reviews of the book so far) since I am personally sympathetic to their bold project of giving theoretical primacy to race as "the fundamental axis of social organization in the United States."

The first part of their book sharply criticizes three paradigms of theorizing race: the dominant paradigm of ethnicity, then the class-based and the nation-based ones. I find their critique of ethnicity theory the most useful, though far from original: they point out that the ethnicity school, by ignoring the qualitatively different historical experiences of various minorities, imposes a monolithic immigrant analogy and thus blames the victims. Racial meanings and dynamics are dissolved in a culturalist absolutism: the paradigm is based on white ethnic history, hence its methodological limitation. Of late, the ethnicity ideologues have provided the chief theoretical weapon for the neoconservative policy of the Reagan administration (Bush's election has not signaled any major revision so far) whose impact Omi and Winant rigorously indict as the systematic reversal of the civil rights gains of the sixties and seventies.

As for the class-based paradigm, Omi and Winant discriminate between the market relations approach (neoclassical economics), stratification theory (exemplified by William Wilson's work), and the class conflict paradigm (classified into segmentation theory and the split labor-market model of Edna Bonacich). In all these variations, Omi and

Winant observe the lack of a theory of racial dynamics which determines class relationships and class identities. They argue from recent findings that sectoral demarcations within and among classes are objects of political struggle so that class formation cannot be fully understood without recognizing the racial identification of subjects or actors. Here they allude to the work of Nicos Poulantzas, Adam Przeworski, Ernesto Laclau, and others. While it is correct to note that class-based theories tend to subsume the category of race into class, it is not quite fair to dismiss the class conflict theories as totally reductionist, even though Omi and Winant admit that they do call attention to "the necessity of understanding classes as the 'effects of struggles,'" a theme broached by the autonomy model cited earlier.

It is when Omi and Winant summarize the challenging paradigm of the nation-based theory that I find myself provoked into substantial disagreement for the simple reason that they ignore the two cardinal premises of historical materialism which I stressed at the beginning. They reject the theory of "internal colonialism" by a somewhat fallacious reduction of the analogy to literal correspondence. Ghetto, reservation, and barrio bear affinities with such colonies as Puerto Rico or the Philippines (a neocolony since 1946) in a political-cultural, not geographical, sense. Moreover, Omi and Winant also reject cultural nationalism and its Marxist variants as limited in explaining the vicissitudes of racial dynamics because "the US political scene allows radical nationalism little space" (50). In this discussion, Omi and Winant can be said to demonstrate "bad faith" since later on, in tracing the origin of their privileged historical agent, "the new social movements," they assert that "The black movement *redefined the meaning of racial identity*, and consequently of race *itself*, in American society" (93). Not only do they ignore the historical matrix of Black nationalism which inflected race as a principle of difference in constructing their collective identity through symbolic (cultural) modes. They also refuse to specify the structural or materialist parameters, particularly the Third World resistance of U.S. imperialist aggression in Africa, Latin America, and Asia in the sixties and seventies which precipitated the global crisis of U.S. hegemony consonant with the civil rights movement. Lacking this totalizing perspective of comprehending U.S. imperialism as a worldwide system, Omi and Winant are unable also to appreciate fully the systemic crisis following U.S. defeat in Indo-China, the Sandinista revolution, and U.S. retreat from Iran which are the conditions of possibility for reaction in the Reagan period (Horowitz 1977; Davis 1984).

In explaining the "unitary social and historical problematic" of race which they claim has not been adequately theorized by the paradigms they

---

[3] The vital contribution of academics like Burawoy (1981) and Bonacich (1980) should also be acknowledged.

question, Omi and Winant offer their theory of racial formation:

> The meaning of race is defined and contested throughout society, in both collective action and personal practice. In the process, racial categories themselves are formed, transformed, destroyed and re-formed. We use the term *racial formation* to refer to the process by which social, economic and political forces determine the content and importance of racial categories, and by which they are in turn shaped by racial meanings (61).

Here they approximate in a discursive way the autonomy model mentioned earlier.

Contending that the system of racial meanings and stereotypes, of racial ideology, is a permanent feature of U.S. culture, Omi and Winant define racialization as a historically specific ideological process, the shifting meanings of race being produced by diverse historical practices of various social groups. Racial meanings pervade the whole society, shaping individual identities and structuring "collective political action on the terrain of the state." Race is thus the organizing principle of social relations; it is not a fixed essence. However, its locus of effectivity seems to gravitate around state apparatuses. Omi and Winant emphasize what is unique in their conception of racial formation: we must understand race "as an *unstable and 'decentered' complex of social meanings constantly being transformed by political struggle*" (68). To illustrate this, they chart the trajectory of racial politics by focusing on the emergence of the racial state within the U.S. racial order (they allude to neo-Marxist thinking on the state by Bob Jessop [1978], Theda Skocpol, and others). Nowhere do they state, however, why the state utilizes racial ideology and for what purpose, although they refer to "conflicting interests encapsulated in racial meanings and identities," "political demands," and so on. They focus on the mechanisms of articulation and rearticulation of racial ideology, acknowledging in passing the value of the minority project of "self-determination" (the nation-based paradigm). But they never clarify why and how the state or the dominant/ruling classes employ this racial ideology as a hegemonic principle. When we reach the section on "The Reagan 'revolution,'" Omi and Winant describe the techniques of the "color-blind" policy implemented by the bureaucratic apparatus and the legitimizing rationale supplied by Glazer and other ethnicity apologists. But what is the *differentia specifica* of this new application in terms of the exigencies of capital, of the social totality?

In concentrating on the details of how the New Right rearticulates racial ideology, Omi and Winant appear to have lost sight of the global picture and downgrade the highly intractable and recalcitrant position of those racial groups whom they have celebrated as heroes of "the great transformation." Any strategy for maintaining capitalist hegemony

necessarily entails its contradiction: the counter-hegemonic resistance of the ruled. This dialectical exploration of possibilities, the response of all the subalterns, is absent in the last third of their book. One can grant that indeed, as their conclusion reminds us, their study has underscored race as "a phenomenon whose meaning is contested throughout social life," that "racial meaning and systems are contested and racial ideologies mobilized in *political* relationships" (138). But what effects they produced in recasting the strategy of the power bloc, the global domination of U.S. corporate monopolies, and the whole international system of transnational capital, they do not say. They conclude by stressing the heterogeneity of new and old immigrants as an obstacle to racially based mobilization, while at the same time predicting that colorblind policies will insure the persistence of economic and political inequality. The question of historical agency is elided here:

> For Asian American and Latino communities, the liberalization of immigration laws in the mid-1960s has led to a vast influx of both "old" and "new" groups. Koreans, Vietnamese, Laotians and Filipinos are distinct in ethnic and class composition from each other and from more "established" groups such as Japanese Americans. An increasingly variegated "community" makes it difficult to speak of a shared experience, common sensibility, or unified political outlook. [Here the authors somehow betray the logic of their own approach; those items they find missing are surely results or ends to be struggled for in the process as each democratic demand is articulated in a chain of equivalence in a hegemonic project.] In the face of these realities, political mobilization along presumed "racial" lines becomes an ambiguous project, even though state policy, and the majority of the American public, continues to identify the groups mentioned along racial lines (i.e., as "Asians") (143).

At this juncture, empiricism has superseded dialectical thinking. Perhaps the sudden wobbling of the argumentation here, the abandonment of a processual and heuristic method, may have been induced by the over-valorizing of the power of the racial state in articulating racist ideology and manipulating the institutional apparatuses of consent. Hegemony becomes hypostatized, contrary to Gramsci's caveat (Merrington 1977; Sassoon 1980). A symptom of that error is Omi and Winant's absurd if wish-fulfilling notion that minorities now "have achieved significant (though by no means equal) representation in the political system" (83). But does having Black mayors or Japanese-American senators automatically guarantee that the programs and policies of these officials will promote the welfare of their racial constituents? While emphasizing the centrality of power and conflict, Omi and Winant privilege political institutionalization—the particular weakness of plural society models

(Hall 1977)—as the coordinating or legitimizing principle instead of the process of hegemonic class alliance or the dynamics of a historical bloc (Poulantzas 1968). Further, in over-emphasizing the interventionist state apparatus, Omi and Winant may have avoided the real target of their investigation, namely, the discursive construction of racial meanings, what Laclau (1977) calls the interpellation of subjects in discourse.

A recent essay by Jeffrey Prager, entitled "American Political Culture and the Shifting Meaning of Race," endeavors to theorize the inscription of race in the pursuit of ascertaining functional norms, but this time concentrating on the semiotic function of race. Prager writes: "In place of racism, I prefer to understand race in America as a 'collective' or 'social representation' implying, as Durkheim and neo-Durkheimian social psychologists today suggest, that the racial problem is a function of the American inability to experience blacks in the same way as other members of the political community" (1987, 75; see also 1982). Here we are paradoxically on the margins of psychologistic speculation which can range from the historicized psychoanalysis of Joel Kovel (*White Racism*) to the existentialist phenomenology of Jean-Paul Sartre (*Anti-Semite and Jew*) and Franz Fanon (*Black Masks, White Faces*).[4] What Prager does in an idealistic fashion—namely, analyze racial discourse and the ideological semiotics of racism as they rework the elements of hegemonic ideology (for instance, liberal individualism)—needs to be historically contextualized and transcoded (Therborn 1980; Green and Carter 1988). More useful for our purposes are studies by Wellman (1977) and Gilroy (1982). What Prager succeeds in doing is to reduce everything to "political discourse, or public conversation," as required by the Durkheimain problematic of ideology as collective representations, and precipitates a poststructuralist reductionism which Perry Anderson (1984) calls the "exorbitation" of the linguistic model (see also Pierre-Charles 1980).

The strengths and weaknesses of Omi and Winant's achievement, which I value highly as an original attempt to formulate a nonessentialist or non-reductive theory of racial dynamics within the framework of a broadly progressive coalition politics, stem from the kind of methodological experiment that we find in neo-Marxists like Laclau and Mouffe. One thesis of their book *Hegemony and Socialist Strategy: Towards a Radical Democratic Politics*, if I may oversimplify it, is that we cannot

privilege any a priori historical agent of revolutionary change (e.g., the proletariat) apart from the process of actual political/ideological struggles at specific historical conjunctures.

Now one of the questions raised against this is that if all modes of symbolic articulation are contingent, not necessary, given the polysemous discourse of new social movements (women, youth, racial minorities, etc.), is it conceivable to identify a homogeneous collective subjectivity that would be the effective agent of historical change? What are the points of condensation in this field of mobile heterogeneous drives, the axis where synchronic and diachronic mappings coalesce? What is the criteria, if any, for judging the material adequacy, aptness or effectiveness of various articulations of democratic demands? Mouffe herself answers by proposing a theory of symbolic articulation (such as rearticulating the aspects of equality and justice in democratic ideology versus the liberal-possessive aspect) within the space of an expansive hegemony. For her, the Gramscian concept of "hegemonic principle" (Bocock 1986) refers to a chain of equivalence which links a plurality of democratic projects/demands on which a democratic will can be built even as the autonomy of different groups is preserved and respected within a milieu of solidarity. Consequently, she treats the notion of "collective will" or the national-popular will manifest in the historic bloc (Gramsci 1971, 202-5) as a metaphor. There is for Mouffe no center or party to embody and represent the collective will, just as for Omi and Winant racial discourse is always decentered, relative to competing articulations and the transvaluations of dispersed forces. However, she insists that discourse is not just language or ideas but concrete social practices which are specific to historically determinate societies, following Gramsci's notion that philosophy (worldviews of varying coherence) permeates all levels of consciousness so that "Philosophy is where the categories of thoughts are elaborated, allowing us to speak about our experience" (Mouffe 1988, 104). That is to say, symbolic contingency can metamorphose to nodes of condensation in the social field, as in definite programmatic goals and actions. Because philosophy as the site of conflicting worldviews constitutes political subjects, Mouffe contends that the field of ideological practices/discourses is the decisive site of political struggle (Hänninen and Paldán 1983, 153-54).

Can everything then be reduced to articulation as a symbolic process, as discourse or signifying practice? Hall for his part points out that while there is no social practice outside ideology, not all practice can be reduced to discourse: for example, the practice of labor which transforms raw materials into a product. While labor is within the domain of representation and meaning it is not reducible to discourse.

---

[4] Saxton (1979) gives an excellent critique of various "historical explanations of racial inequality," together with an inventory of research projects (e.g., comparative history of racist practices in the United States), which are desiderata for formulating a radical democratic political agenda today.

It does not follow that because all practices are *in* ideology, or inscribed by ideology, all practices are *nothing but* ideology. There is a specificity to those practices whose principal object is to produce ideological representations. They are different from those practices which—meaningfully, intelligibly—produce other commodities...[Those forms] of practice operate in ideology but they are not ideological in terms of the specificity of their object (1985, 103-4).

That is astutely expressed. But are there articulations identical with representations, for example, the performative speech that transforms a crowd into a revolutionary agent? Or are there objective articulations preceding their representation (ideological relations of gender, race, nationality, causal relations, etc.)? It has been suggested that to discover such "objective articulations" and to find adequate symbolic representations for them so as to make them effective ideological agents, is the task of Marxist theory.

Wolfgang Fritz Haug warns us that in their obsession to purge class reductionism, the neo-Marxists succumb to a politics of articulation unable to make distinctions so that their efforts mimic Hitler's project of articulating new social movements into a fascist brand of "revolutionary populism." He suggests that we remain within "the problematics of the specificity of a *socialist* articulation, which takes into account the existence of long waves in historical development, 'hard cores' within the changing realm of societal differences" (Hänninen and Paldán 1983). I am not sure if this is not just a matter of discriminating and then reconciling the antithetical demands of short-range (transitional) tactics and of long-range (maximalist) strategy. In any case, Haug also proposes that we adhere to the analytical concept of a "working class" as an overall orientation in forging new empirical tools because, in the absence of this differentiating principle, we would not be able to constitute our identity as "socialists" in search of a "structure of hegemony," even though we may subscribe to the antiessentialist position that there is no unitary revolutionary subject.

What I think Mouffe and other postmodernizing radicals would insist on in the light of those reservations is that the orthodox tradition lacks a theory of the imaginary and symbolic process of signification (theorized by Gilles Deleuze, Jacques Lacan, and others) needed to configure the positioning of various subjects vis-à-vis the structuring of production and the reproduction of social relations (Wilden 1972). It is through the process of the symbolic articulation of ideology that race, as well as gender and nationality, can be understood as the defining quality of specific struggles whose necessary autonomy can only be repressed at the sacrifice of the socialist/democratic project. On the other hand, I think Marx's prescient "On the Jewish Question" (1975) already anticipated the need for a nonessentialist inquiry of extraclass determinants long before Gramsci's intervention (Carr 1985).

5

Can any agenda be extrapolated from this brief, necessarily schematic mapping of what has been done so far? Any future Marxist critique of race relations in the United States needs to take as its point of departure the following summations of the collective experience of the victims of racism expressed by Marable and West:

> The most striking fact about American economic history and politics is the brutal and systematic underdevelopment of Black people...Nothing less than the political recognition that white racism is an essential and primary component in the continued exploitation of all American working people will be enough to defeat the capitalist class (Marable 1983, 1, 262).

> Racism has been the most visible and vicious form of oppression in American society...American leftists most give first priority to the most explosive issues in American society, namely, the probability of U.S. participation in international war principally owing to imperialist policies...and the plight of the urban black and brown poor primarily due to the legacy of racism in an ever-changing capitalist economy (West 1984/1985, 18-19).

That granted, I would then urge considering as a methodological imperative the need to formulate a conception of U.S. racism (not a sociology of race relations) as part of a complex historical totality—that is, the United States as a racially ordered capitalist system—where the hegemony of the bourgeoisie has been constructed through the articulation of race, through the production of subjects inscribed in racist discursive and institutional practices. In the process, a national-popular collective will has been generated by the bourgeoisie on the terrain of everyday life where "common sense" (intellectual and moral worldview) is inflected to reproduce racially ordered capitalist relations of production. Racism is then not a fixed or unitary mechanism but an articulating hegemonic principle which involves both the practices of civil society and state apparatuses. Its private nuances and public styles are altered according to varying historical conjunctures; its ensemble of elements is constantly disarticulated and rearranged according to the changing balance of conflicting forces. Racist practices by the state and by various classes exhibit contradictory properties—as various historians like Higham (1971), Jordan (1974), Kolko (1976) testify—overdetermined by and transformed with the larger political-economic structures of the social formation. This follows as a contextual effect of the production and reproduction of U.S. imperialism on the global stage beginning with the genocidal extermination of the Indians, traversing whole epochs marked by the creation of the internal colonies and later the peripheral ones (the South-west, Puerto Rico, Hawaii) or hitherto neocolonized ones (the Philippines, Central America, some Caribbean islands). This assumes the analytical priority of the logic of the capital accumulation process occurring within the uneven, combined development of various modes of production in the U.S. social formation.

Without this global framework inaugurating the rise of capitalism, any account of the tactical and strategic reconstitution of the U.S. racial dispensation would be deficient because, from the onset of chattel slavery and colonial conquests, the U.S. formation has been conditioned, if not determined, by its position in the world market of labor, raw materials, and so on. Within these parameters, racism as the chief hegemonic articulating principle may be grasped as one mediation between the dynamics of the capitalist world economy and the structural crisis of the U.S. social formation. As John Solomos and his colleagues point out, "the links between racism and capitalist development are complex, and conditioned by the specific socio-political circumstances in which they function" so that "ethnic and racial forms of domination" proceed "not in a linear fashion but are subject to breaks and discontinuities" (1982, 12), particularly during periods of crisis. While the historical trajectory of racism in Britain has been ably charted by A. Sivanandan (1982, 1983), the Centre for Contemporary Cultural Studies (1982), and others, a comparative historical account of U.S. racist practices from an international perspective is still to be written (Daniels and Kitano 1970; Saxton 1971). Omi and Winant have described how, under certain conditions, the capitalist state in the seventies and early eighties functioned as the crucial agency for articulating and reproducing ethnic/racial divisions. But the international context, the imperialist dimension, is scarcely registered in its effects on the internal alignment of political forces.

In a provocative essay, Dominique Lecourt (1980) contends that racism as a specific ideological aspect of class struggle in history arose from the logic of capitalist political economy and its foundation in a unitary social subject. The subject category conceals domination and subordination, the actual relations of class exploitation, by a homogenizing strategy (freedom in individual exchange, in consensus) where differences (shades of plural society and ethnic pluralism?) are interpreted and evaluated as a consequence of the calculation of personal advantage. Since Marxism privileges the dialectics of contradiction, not nomadic or aleatory difference, situated in historically defined social formations, Lecourt believes that we cannot enunciate a general Marxist theory of racism. Such a theory can only spring from the bourgeois ideology of humanism

and its premise of a given human nature; therefore, racism or racialism is "the *reverse* side and the *complement* of bourgeois humanism." Lecourt then concludes that historical materialism enables us to see that racism is not "an aberrant epiphenomenon introducing a dysfunctioning into the regular social order, but a particular aspect of the ideological class struggle in the imperialist era" (284). Whatever the seductive potential of poststructuralist discourse theory (Deleuze, Michel Foucault, Jean-François Lyotard, Jean Baudrillard) to supplement Marxism with a theory of symbolic practice—Pierre Bourdieu's "praxeology" (1977; see also Rossi 1983) seems to avoid the subjectivism of phenomenology and the objectivism of structuralism—as a tool in research strategy. Lecourt's intervention is, at this point in my exploration, salutary.

In any case, I would like to conclude these reflections by submitting for further examination Harold Wolpe's criteria for judging the theoretical and practical value of inscribing the race/class dialectic within the all-encompassing project of global socialist transformation:

> The racial order, including "corporate" racial groups, has to be analyzed as the outcome of multiple determinations of which the operation of an economy characterized, in a non-economistic way, by the capital-labor relation and the structure of state power are essential elements—the account cannot be reduced to race, although the process of racial categorization cannot be reduced to "pure" economy... The decisive question for a Marxist analysis is how, in what way and to what extent do the reproduction, transformation and disintegration of the racial order serve to maintain or undermine the relations of capital accumulation (1986, 129)?

This implies that one cannot finally ignore the moment of the totality and its prefigured disintegration in a revolutionary rupture (Lefebvre 1966). But, as this essay insists, the trajectory of this complicated struggle necessarily has to go through the catharsis of destroying racism in all its protean forms. There is no shortcut or detour. Racial politics indeed are a matter of life and death for millions of Blacks, Hispanics, Asians, Native Americans, and other racially defined communities in the United States. So the more urgent and mandatory it is for all progressive forces to confront racism today as probably the hitherto still undiscovered Archimedean point of the class struggle against the domination of capital, against imperialism.

REFERENCES

Althusser, L. 1969. *For Marx*. New York: Pantheon Books.
Amariglio, J.; Resnick, S.; and Wolff, R. 1988. "Class, Power and Culture." In *Marxism and the Interpretation*

of Culture, ed. C. Nelson and L. Grossberg, 487-501. Urbana: University of Illinois Press.

Anderson, P. 1984. *In the Tracks of Historical Materialism*. Chicago: University of Chicago Press.

Aronowitz, S. 1981. *The Crisis in Historical Materialism*. New York: Praeger.

Banton, M. 1987. *Racial Theories*. Cambridge: Cambridge University Press.

Baran, P. A. and Sweezy, P. M. 1966. *Monopoly Capital*. New York: Monthly Review Press.

Blauner, R. 1972. *Racial Oppression in America*. New York: Harper and Row.

Blauner, R. and Wellman, D. 1973. "Toward the Decolonization of Social Research." In *The Death of White Sociology*, ed. J. Ladner, 310-30. New York: Vintage Books.

Bocock, R. 1986. *Hegemony*. London: Tavistock Publications.

Bonacich, E. 1980. "Class Approaches to Ethnicity and Race." *The Insurgent Sociologist* 10 (Fall): 9-23.

Bourdieu, P. 1977. *Outline of a Theory of Practice*. Cambridge: Cambridge University Press.

Buci-Glucksmann, C. 1982. "Hegemony and Consent." In *Approaches to Gramsci*, ed. A. Sassoon, 116-26. London: Writers and Readers.

Burawoy, M. 1981. "The Capitalist State in South Africa: Marxist and Sociological Perspectives on Race and Class." *Political Power and Social Theory* 2:279-335.

Carr, J, 1985. "On the Racism of Colorblindness." *The Eighties* 5 (Winter): 66-96.

Centre for Contemporary Cultural Studies, ed. 1982. *The Empire Strikes Back*. London: Hutchinson.

Cox, O. C. 1948. *Caste, Class, and Race*. New York: Monthly Review Press.

Cruse, H. 1968. *Rebellion or Revolution*. New York: William Morrow and Co.

Daniels, R. and Kitano, H. 1970. *American Racism: Exploration of the Nature of Prejudice*. Englewood Cliffs: Prentice Hall.

Davis, M. 1984. "The Political Economy of Late Imperial America." *New Left Review*, no. 143 (January-February): 6-38.

Edgar, D. 1981. "Reagan's Hidden Agenda: Racism and the New American Right." *Race and Class* 22 (Winter): 221-38.

Foster, W. 1973. *The Negro People in American History*. New York: International Publishers.

Genovese, E. 1971. *In Red and Black*. New York: Pantheon Books.

Gilroy, P. 1982. "Steppin' Out of Babylon—Race, Class and Autonomy." In *The Empire Strikes Back*, ed. Centre for Contemporary Cultural Studies, 276-314. London: Hutchinson.

Gramsci, A. 1971. *Selections from the Prison Notebooks*. New York: International Publishers.

Green, M. and Carter, B. 1988. "'Races' and 'Race-makers': The Politics of Racialization." *Sage Race Relations Abstracts* 13 (May): 4-29.

Hall, G. 1972. *Imperialism Today*. New York: International Publishers.

Hall, S. 1977. "Pluralism, Race and Class in Caribbean Society." In *Race and Class in Post-Colonial Society*, ed. UNESCO, 150-82. Paris: UNESCO.

Hall, S. 1978. "Racism and Reaction." In *Five Views of Multi-Racial Britain*, ed. Commission for Racial Equality, 23-35. London: Commission for Racial Equality.

Hall, S. 1980. "Race, Articulation and Societies Structured in Dominance." In *Sociological Theories: Race and Colonialism*, ed. UNESCO, 305-45. Paris: UNESCO.

Hall, S. 1985. "Signification, Representation, Ideology: Althusser and the Post-Structuralist Debates." *Critical Studies in Mass Communication* 2 (June): 87-90.

Hänninen, S. and Paldán, L. 1983. *Rethinking Ideology: A Marxist Debate*. Berlin: Argument-Verlag.

Higham, J. 1971. *Strangers in the Land*. New York: Atheneum.

Horowitz, I. 1977. *Ideology and Utopia in the United States 1956-1976*. New York: Oxford University Press.

Jessop, B. 1978. "Marx and Engels on the State." In *Politics, Ideology and the State*, ed. S. Hibbin, 40-68. London: Lawrence and Wishart.

Jordan, W. 1974. *The White Man's Burden: Historical Origins of Racism in the United States*. New York: Oxford University Press.

Kolko, G. 1976. *Main Currents in Modern American History*. New York: Harper and Row.

Kushnick, L. 1981/1982. "Parameters of British and North American Racism." *Race and Class* 23 (Autumn/Winter): 187-206.

Laclau, E. 1977. *Politics and Ideology in Marxist Theory*. London: Verso.

Lecourt, D. 1980. "On Marxism as a Critique of Sociological Theories." In *Sociological Theories: Race and Colonialism*, ed. UNESCO, 267-85. Paris: UNESCO.

Lefebvre, H. 1966. *The Sociology of Marx*. New York: Vintage Books.

Lemer, M. 1973. *The New Socialist Revolution*. New York: Dell Publishing Co.

Liu, J. 1976. "Toward an Understanding of the Internal Colonial Model." In *Counterpoint*, ed. E. Gee. 160-68. Los Angeles: UCLA Asian American Studies Center.

Loren, C. 1977. *Classes in the United States*. Davis: Cardinal Publishers.

Marable, M. 1980. *From the Grassroots*. Boston: South End Press.

Marable, M. 1981. "The Third Reconstruction: Black Nationalism and Race in a Revolutionary America." *Social Text* 4 (Fall): 3-27.

Marable, M. 1983. *How Capitalism Underdeveloped Black America*. Boston: South End Press.

Marx, K. 1975. "On then Jewish Question." In *Early Writings*, ed. Penguin Books, 211-41. New York: Vintage Books.

Marx, K. and Engels, F.1968. *Selected Works*. New York: International Publishers.

McWilliams, C. 1964. *Brothers Under the Skin*. Boston: Little, Brown and Co.

Melendy, H. 1981. *Asians in America*. New York: Hippocrene Books.

Merrington, J. 1977. "Theory and Practice in Gramsci's Marxism." In *Western Marxism*, ed. New Left Review, 140-75. London: Verso.

Miles, R. 1980. "Class, Race and Ethnicity: A Critique of Cox's Theory." *Ethnic and Racial Studies* 3 (April): 169-87.

Montagu, A. 1962. *The Humanization of Man*. New York: Grove Press.

Mouffe, C. 1981. "Hegemony and the Integral State in Gramsci." In *Silver Linings*, ed. G. Bridges and R. Brunt, 167-87. London: Lawrence and Wishart.

Mouffe, C. 1988. "Hegemony and New Political Subjects: Toward a New Concept of Democracy." In *Marxism and the Interpretation of Culture*, ed. C. Nelson and L. Grossberg, 89-101. Urbana: University of Illinois Press.

Mullings, L. 1984. "Ethnicity and Stratification in the Urban United States." In *Racism and the Denial of Human Rights: Beyond Ethnicity*, ed. M. Berlowitz and R. Edari, 21-38. Minneapolis: MEP Press.

Nee, V. and Sanders, J. 1985. "The Road to Parity: Determinants of the Socioeconomic Achievements of Asian Americans." *Ethnic and Racial Studies* 9 (January): 75-93.

Omi, M. and Winant, H. 1986. *Racial Formation in the United States from the 1960s to the 1980s*. New York: Routledge and Kegan Paul.

Pierre-Charles, G. 1980. "Racialism and Sociological Theories." In *Sociological Theories: Race and Colonialism*, ed. UNESCO, 69-83. Paris: UNESCO.

Poulantzas, N. 1968. *Political Power and Social Classes*. London: Verso.

Prager, J. 1982. "American Racial Ideology as Collective Representation." *Ethnic and Racial Studies* 5 (January): 99-119.

Prager, J. 1987. "American Political Culture and the Shifting Meaning of Race." *Ethnic and Racial Studies* 10 (January): 62-81.

Progressive Labor Party. 1970. *Revolution Today: U.S.A.* New York: Exposition Press.

Quinsaat, J., ed. 1976. *Letters in Exile*. Los Angeles: UCLA Asian American Studies Center.

Reich, M. 1972. "The Economics of Racism." In *The Capitalist System: A Radical Analysis of American Society*, ed. R. Edwards, M. Reich, and T. Weisskopf, 314-20. Englewood Cliffs: Prentice Hall.

Rex, J. 1983. "Race." In *A Dictionary of Marxist Thought*, ed. T. Bottomore. Cambridge, MA: Harvard University Press.

Rex, J. 1986. *Race and Ethnicity*. Milton Keynes: Open University Press.

Rex, J. and Mason, D., eds. 1986. *Theories of Race and Ethnic Relations*. Cambridge: Cambridge University Press.

Rossi, I. 1983. *From the Sociology of Symbols to the Sociology of Signs*. New York: Columbia University Press.

Rozat, G. and Bartra, R. 1980. "Racism and Capitalism." In *Sociological Theories: Race and Colonialism*, ed. UNESCO, 287-304. Paris: UNESCO.

Sassoon, A. 1980. *Gramsci's Politics*. New York: St. Martin's Press.

Saxton, A. 1971. *The Indispensable Enemy: Labor and the Anti-Chinese Movement in California*. Berkeley: University of California Press.

Saxton, A. 1977. "Nathan Glazer, Daniel Moyaihan and the Cult of Ethnicity." *AmerAsia Journal* 4 (Summer): 141-50.

Saxton, A. 1979. "Historical Explanations of Racial Inequality." *Marxist Perspectives* (Summer): 146-68.

Sherman, H. 1972. *Racial Political Economy*. New York: Basic Books.

Sivanandan, A. 1982. *A Different Hunger: Writings on Black Resistance*. London: Pluto Press.

Sivanandan, A. 1983. "Challenging Racism: Strategies for the 80s." *Race and Class* 25 (Autumn): 1-11.

Smith, A. 1979. *Nationalism in the Twentieth Century*. New York: New York University Press.

Smith, M. G. 1982. "Ethnicity and Ethnic Groups in America: The View from Harvard." *Ethnic and Racial Studies* 5:1-21.

Solomos, J.; Findley, B.; Jones, S.; and Gilroy, P. 1982. "The Organic Crisis of British Capitalism and Race: The Experience of the Seventies." In *The Empire Strikes Back*, ed. Centre for Contemporary Cultural Studies. London: Hutchinson.

Sweezy, P. 1953. *The Present as History*. New York: Monthly Review Press.

Tabb, W. 1988. "What Happened to Black Economic Development?" *Review of Black Political Economy* 17 (Fall): 65-88.

Therborn, G. 1980. *The Ideology of Power and the Power of Ideology*. London: Verso. UNESCO, ed. 1980. *Sociological Theories: Race and Colonialism*. Paris: UNESCO.

Wald, A. 1981. "The Culture of 'Internal Colonialism': A Marxist Perspective." *MELUS [Multi-Ethnic Literature of the U S]* 8 (Fall): 18-27.

Wellman, D. 1977. *Portraits of White Racism*. Cambridge: Cambridge University Press.

West, C. 1982. *Prophesy Deliverance! Toward a Revolutionary Afro-American Christianity*. Philadelphia: Westminster Press.

West, C. 1984/1985. "Reconstructing the American Left: The Challenge of Jesse Jackson." *Social Text* 11 (Winter): 3-19.

West, C. 1988. "Marxist Theory and the Specificity of Afro-American Oppression." In *Marxism and the Interpretation of Culture*, ed. C. Nelson and L. Grossberg, 17-29. Urbana: University of Illinois Press.

Wilden, A. 1972. *System and Structure*. New York: Tavistock Publications.

Wolpe, H. 1986. "Class Concepts, Class Struggle and Racism." In *Theories of Race and Ethnic Relations*, ed. J. Rex and D. Mason, 110-30. Cambridge: Cambridge University Press.

24

Blacks and Other Racial Minorities: The Significance of Color in Inequality

JOE T. DARDEN

By examining the extent and patterns of housing segregation, Darden shows that blacks tend to experience residential discrimination to a far greater degree than other groups, including Latinos, and Asians. The author concludes that discrimination against blacks in the current period is a major problem as it was reported by the Kerner Commission in 1968. But Darden goes further and claims, unlike others like William J. Wilson for instance, that the basis of the continuing discrimination is skin color. He cites two major studies that show 'discrimination based on skin color to be the major factor hampering black Americans from achieving success at the same rate as members of other minority groups living in the United States'. Consistent with a system of skin color as a foundation for racial discrimination, Darden posits that black Latinos suffer from segregation to a significantly higher degree than white Latinos. In fact, the case of black and white Latinos illustrates that skin color may be more significant than ethnicity for this group since 'black Hispanics are more segregated from white Hispanics than they are from non-Hispanic blacks'. This argument is similar to that made by James Jennings in his discussion of racial hierarchy.

The question of why black Americans have not been able to attain the same levels of socioeconomic status as have other racial/ethnic minorities (Asians, Hispanics, and Native Americans) is an issue of both academic and political importance. In 1968, the Kerner Commission issued a statement on this subject. Twelve years later, in 1980, another study, conducted by Lieberson, looked at the same issue applying factors common to each minority group's situation. Ironically, both studies found discrimination based on skin color to be the major factor hampering black Americans from achieving success at the same rate as members of other minority groups living in the United States. Racial discrimination, the Kerner Commission concluded, was a major reason that blacks have not been able to escape from poverty-stricken ghettos as many of the European immigrants were able to do.

The report did not intend to convey that white immigrants did not suffer the inequities associated with discrimination. On the contrary, white immigrants also were subjected to many hardships, but

Table 1   *Population and Racial Minority-Group Segregation in 10 Standard Metropolitan Statistical Areas of the North Central Region, 1980*

SMSA	Black population	Black vs. white	Hispanic population	Hispanic vs. white	Asian population	Asian vs. white	Native American population	Native American vs. white
Cincinnati	173,656	72.3	2,956	30.3	6,115	33.0	1,194	39.9
Chicago	1,427,827	88.5	580,592	64.0	141,339	52.2	10,709	62.1
Cleveland	345,632	87.5	25,920	55.4	13,164	35.8	2,014	62.4
Detroit	890,417	85.8	71,589	43.6	33,257	26.1	12,483	36.3
Flint	78,871	83.3	8,467	33.4	2,084	25.3	3,013	30.0
Indianapolis	157,258	76.2	8,845	33.2	5,437	36.0	1,486	56.3
Kansas City	173,184	78.9	31,820	42.1	8,420	30.8	4,646	26.9
Milwaukee	150,677	83.0	34,343	56.2	7,630	38.6	6,534	45.1
Minneapolis	50,046	68.3	22,271	40.9	19,686	36.9	15,959	42.4
St. Louis	407,734	81.3	22,284	33.9	12,624	32.9	3,268	37.3
Mean	385,530	80.5	80,909	43.4	24,976	34.8	6,131	43.9

Source: Computed by the author from data obtained from U.S. Bureau of the Census, 1980, *Population and Housing, Summary Tape*, File 4, Washington, DC Data User Services, 1983

there was a difference: the level of discrimination experienced was never as pervasive as the color-based prejudice that has consistently narrowed the opportunities and formed barriers to advancement for black Americans (Kerner Commission, 1968, p. 144).

Paralleling the findings of the Kerner Commission (1968), Lieberson (1980) argues that white ethnics did not suffer the same degree of indignities associated with racism, discrimination and differential preferences as did black Americans when they moved from the rural South to the urban North. He further asserts that, although all of the ethnic minority groups were viewed as inferior by the native-born white population, there was clearly a desirability continuum: members of white ethnic groups were viewed as less inferior than Orientals, and the latter were seen as more desirable than blacks. Lieberson concludes that it was the factor of skin color which resulted in discrimination against blacks that was more pervasive than for any other group.

Building on the work of the Kerner Commission (1968) and Lieberson (1980), I argue in this paper that color-based discrimination remains a significant factor in American society today. As large U.S. metropolitan areas have become ethnically more diverse, enormous differences in socioeconomic status attainment have emerged between native minorities (i.e., blacks and Native Americans) and the more recently arriving immigrant minorities (i.e., Asians and Hispanics). Blacks appear to have attained the lowest socioeconomic status, although they arrived in urban America much earlier than some of the other racial ethnic minorities.

I argue specifically that observed disparities in socioeconomic status are due primarily to color-based discrimination in housing which, in turn, has resulted in unequal access to educational opportunities,

employment, and career advancement. Using data from the 1980 Census of Population and Housing (U.S. Bureau of the Census, 1983) and other sources (U.S. Bureau of the Census, 1985a, b) for the ten Standard Metropolitan Statistical Areas (SMSAs) in the North Central Region, I show empirically that contemporary color-based discrimination, not unlike that described by the Kerner Commission (1968) and Lieberson (1980), occurs along a continuum. The levels of discrimination in housing and unequal access to education and employment opportunities increase from Asian to Hispanic[1] to Native American to black.

MINORITY GROUP RESIDENTIAL SEGREGATION AND SUBURBANIZATION

In U.S. metropolitan areas the effect of discrimination in housing is manifested in the varying degrees of minority-group residential segregation and suburbanization. An examination of the residential segregation of each racial/ethnic minority group from the white majority population clearly shows that blacks are the most residentially segregated of all minorities. For the ten SMSAs in the North Central Region (Table 1), the extent of black-white residential segregation compared with that of other minority groups is demonstrated using census tract data and the index of dissimilarity.[2] The mean level of black-white segregation (80.5%) was more than twice the mean level of Asian-white segregation (34.8%). Whites were found to be much less segregated from Hispanics (43.3%) and Native Americans (43.9%) than from blacks.

Table 2   *Percentage of Each Racial Group's Population Living in the Suburbs in Selected Metropolitan Areas of the North Central Region, 1980*

Suburbs of SMSAs	Whites	Asians	Nat. Am. Indians	Hispanics	Blacks	Share of SMSA suburbanized population
St. Louis	87.4*	86.6*	80.4	75.2	49.4	80.8
Cincinnati	79.4*	63.8	64.4	62.1	24.9	72.5
Detroit	87.7*	80.1*	72.6*	59.5	14.8	72.4
Cleveland	79.8*	74.3*	45.7	31.4	27.3	69.8
Minneapolis	71.8*	65.5	28.1	43.7	16.6	69.7
Flint	79.3*	69.6	67.8	53.1	16.2	69.4
Kansas City	72.2*	58.4	65.1	53.8	29.2	66.2
Chicago	71.4*	51.0	43.3	27.3	16.2	57.7
Milwaukee	61.6*	52.8	23.2	24.0	2.5	54.5
Indianapolis	45.9*	30.3	33.1	30.5	2.9	39.9
Average	73.7	63.2	52.4	46.1	20.0	65.3

*Higher than the percentage of the total SMSA population that is living in the suburbs.
Source: Compiled by the author from data obtained from the U.S. Department of Commerce, Bureau of the Census. *1980 Census of Population and Housing*. Advance Reports, various states

Table 3   *The Percentage of Each Racial Group's Population Living in Central Cities and Suburbs of Metropolitan Areas in the U.S. in 1980*

Area	Percentage of total				
	White	Black	Hispanic	Native Am.	Asian
Central City	34.1	71.3	57.4	42.5	50.8
Suburb	65.9	28.7	42.6	57.5	49.2

Source: Computed by the author from data obtained from the U.S. Department of Commerce, Bureau of the Census. *General Social and Economic Characteristics*. U.S. Summary, Washington, DC, U.S. Government Printing Office, 1982

These findings are consistent with a previous study of 12 SMSAs within the state of Michigan, in which the mean level of black-white segregation was found to be 66.8%, compared with an Asian-white level of only 27%. The levels for Hispanics and Native Americans were 36.9% and 34.8%, respectively (Darden, 1986). The continuum pattern of majority-minority group residential segregation is also supported by other studies (Farley, 1986a, p. 18; Massey and Denton, 1987; Woolbright and Hartmann, 1987, p. 145). Using census-tract data and the index of dissimilarity to examine residential segregation of blacks, Hispanics, and Asians in the nation's 11 SMSAs of 2.5 million or more, for example, Farley (1986a) found that the average level of black-white segregation was 79% compared with an average Asian-white level of only 45%. The average index comparing non-Hispanic whites and Hispanics was 51%.

Woolbright and Hartmann (1987) examined patterns of residential segregation in seven SMSAs (San Diego, Phoenix, Miami, Los Angeles, Houston, Denver, and Chicago) using the index of dissimilarity. They concluded that black-white segregation was highest and Asian-white segregation was lowest in each of the SMSAs except for San Diego, where Hispanic-white segregation was slightly lower (41.5%) than Asian-white segregation (45.5%).

Massey and Denton (1987) used the index of dissimilarity to analyze the extent of black, Asian, and Hispanic residential segregation in 60 SMSAs in the United States in 1980. They found that black-white segregation had the highest average level (69.4%), and the lowest average level was between Asians and whites (34.2%). Indeed, the level of black-white segregation was more than twice the level of Asian-white segregation. Hispanic-white segregation at 43.4% ranged between the two extremes found for Asians and blacks.

The color continuum pattern of residential segregation is duplicated in the pattern of suburbanization. Data on the percentage of each racial/ethnic group's population residing in the suburbs in 1980 are presented in Tables 2 and 3. In the selected metropolitan areas of the North Central region and in the nation as a whole, blacks are the least suburbanized. Nationally, less than a third of blacks in SMSAs live in suburbs, compared with approximately half of the Asian population.

According to Massey and Denton (1987), the differential levels of minority-group residential segregation and suburbanization can be explained by examining the process of racial and ethnic integration in postwar America, a process which links residential integration with suburbanization. To the extent that suburban residence may be precluded for some minority groups by discriminatory housing practices, an important avenue of residential integration may be closed off (Massey and Denton, 1987, p. 818).

Such a situation applies to blacks but much less to Asians and Hispanics.[3] Several studies have indicated that the underrepresentation of blacks in the suburbs is not due to the level of black socioeconomic status (Clark, 1987; Hermalin and Farley, 1973; Langendorf, 1969; Logan and Stearns, 1981). On the other hand, both Asian and Hispanic residential segregation and the degree of suburbanization are highly related to socioeconomic status (Massey and Denton, 1987, p. 819). As the socioeconomic status of these groups rises, residential segregation decreases and suburbanization increases. For Asians and Hispanics, suburbanization is a key step in the larger process of spatial assimilation, a process that is largely closed to blacks. The level of black segregation has not been found to be strongly related to socioeconomic status, and the socioeconomic status of blacks is not strongly related to black suburbanization (Massey and Denton, 1987, p. 823). Regardless of socioeconomic status, most blacks remain highly segregated in central cities of metropolitan areas.

The differential patterns of residential segregation and suburbanization documented above impact significantly the educational and employment opportunities available to the various racial/ethnic minority groups. In the section which follows, I assess the consequences of differential access on the social and economic well-being of black Americans.

The Social and Economic Consequences of Black Concentration in Central Cities

The fact that 71% of the black population of the nation's SMSAs reside in central cities (a level higher than that for any other racial/ethnic group) has serious social and economic consequences. Many blue-collar jobs that once constituted the economic backbones of cities and provided employment opportunities for their poorly educated residents have either vanished or been moved to the suburbs (Kasarda, 1989, p. 4). Thus, newer and better job opportunities are locating further away from the places of black residence, forcing black families to spend more time and money commuting to work or looking for work (Darden, 1986, p. 112).

Given that blacks have more restricted residential-location choices than members of other racial minority groups, the cost associated with distance reduces access to some jobs. The net effect of these imposed travel costs is to reduce the effective wage which black central-city workers receive relative to suburban residents. Another cost imposed by the spatial separation of jobs and residences is that which central-city blacks incur when searching for suburban employment, particularly in view of the limited information available about potential job opportunities. In addition, there is a tendency for employers to hire workers who reflect the racial character of the area in which they are located – i.e., there may often also be an indirect effect of housing segregation on employment opportunities (Kain, 1968; McDonald, 1981, p. 28).

The problems of black residents of central cities are intensified by the fact that employment opportunities in blue-collar, semi-skilled, and low-skilled jobs are moving to the suburbs so rapidly that a surplus of labor in these categories has developed in the central city (McDonald, 1981, p. 29). In other words, there has been a substantial shift in the occupational mix of jobs in central cities (Christian, 1975; Fremon, 1970; Kasarda, 1976; Wilson, F. D., 1979). There has been a decline in craftsman, operative, and laborer categories, while professional, sales, clerical, and service employment has increased proportionally in central cities (Wilson, 1979).

The decline of jobs in central cities has been most pronounced in certain cities of the North Central Region. Postwar employment trends in various sectors of the Detroit economy indicate the magnitude of employment decline in the central city. Between the late 1940s and early 1980s, Detroit's share of the metropolitan region's manufacturing employment dropped from 60.3% to 25%, retail trade from 72.6% to 15.4%, services from 75.3% in (1958) to 23.6%, and wholesale trade from 90.1% to 29.6% (Darden, Hill, Thomas, and Thomas, 1987, pp. 22–23; Vernon, 1966). Between 1958 and 1982, Detroit lost 187,100 jobs, mostly in manufacturing and retail trade where blacks were disproportionately concentrated (Darden, Hill, Thomas, and Thomas, 1987, p. 22).

Postwar employment trends in various sectors of the Chicago metropolitan area reveal a similar pattern of decline. In 1947, the city of Chicago accounted for 70.6% of the total manufacturing employment in the metropolitan region. By 1982, its share had eroded to 34.2%. Between 1947 and 1982, factory employment in Chicago dropped from a 20th-century high of 688,000 to 277,000 jobs – a decline of 59% (Squires, Bennett, McCourt, and Nyden, 1987, p. 27). At the same time, suburban Cook County manufacturing jobs increased from 121,000 to 279,000 (a 131% increase), and factory jobs in the other SMSA counties jumped from 64,000 to 189,000 (a 195% increase) (Squires, Bennett, McCourt, and Nyden, 1987, p. 27). Since 1947, the record is one of almost continuous decline of manufacturing employment in the city. The only exception was a slight increase in jobs during the national industrial boom period from 1963 to 1967 (McDonald, 1984, p. 11).

Black workers have borne much of the brunt of Chicago's job losses. For example, between 1963 and 1977, while the city as a whole was experiencing a 29% decline in jobs, available factory jobs in predominantly black West Central and near-South Side neighborhoods dropped by 45% and 47%, respectively (McDonald, 1984, p. 12). In the United States as a whole, nearly a third of all black men working in durable-goods manufacturing lost their jobs between 1979 and 1984, and that figure rose to 45% in Buffalo, Chicago, Cleveland, Detroit, and Milwaukee (Hill and Negrey, 1988, p. 17). Within durable-goods manufacturing, the workers hardest hit by the industrial slump were black male operatives and laborers – for example, nearly 50% of such workers lost their jobs between 1979 and 1984 in the five cities noted above (Hill and Negrey, 1988, p. 17).

The primary reason blacks have been impacted more severely economically is segregation, both occupational and residential. Black workers tend to be concentrated in production jobs, and that is where the biggest industrial losses have occurred. Black production workers tend to be concentrated in older industrial plants, and those are the ones most frequently closed. Finally, blacks tend to be concentrated in older, central-city neighborhoods, and that is where plants and production jobs are disappearing the fastest (Hill and Negrey, 1988, p. 21).

The declining employment situation for blacks has had significant ramifications for the black population and for society at large. Black family incomes have declined and poverty rates have increased. Blacks in every income level, from the poorest to the most affluent, lost ground and had less disposable income (after adjusting for inflation) in 1984 than in 1980 (Center on Budget and Policy Priorities, 1984, p. 1). Also disturbing is the fact that since 1980, the gap between black poverty and white poverty – always large to begin with – has widened further. Of those Americans who fell into poverty since 1980, 22% were black – even though blacks make up only 12% of the U.S. population. Since 1980, blacks have been nearly twice as likely as other Americans to become poor (Center on Budget and Policy Priorities, 1984, p. 4). The proportion of white Americans living in poverty declined significantly during 1987, while the proportion of black poor people increased. The proportion of white Americans who were poor was 10.5%, compared with 11% in 1986. A total of 21.4 million white Americans lived in poverty in 1987, against 22.2 million in 1986.

However, the proportion of black Americans living in poverty was 33.1% – i.e., more than three times the percentage for whites. The percentage of blacks in poverty increased by 2.0 percentage points, up from 31.1% in 1986. A total of 9.7 million blacks lived in poverty in 1987, compared with 8.9 million in 1986 (Tolchin, 1988; U.S. Bureau of the Census, 1988a, 1988b).

There is increasing evidence that the escalation in poverty among blacks is related to the growing numbers of black female-headed households. Poverty rates have traditionally been high and income levels low in families headed by women. In 1984, for example, 52% of the black families with women as head-of-household were below the poverty line, compared with 15% of the black married-couple families (U.S. Bureau of the Census, 1985a, Tables 1 and 15). While similar trends are occurring in white families, there has been a sharper increase in the proportion of blacks living in these female-maintained families which have high poverty rates (Farley, 1986b, p. 17). The number of black families with children under 18 headed by a female increased from 1,063,000 in 1970 to 2,265,000 in 1984 – a rise of 113% (U.S. Bureau of the Census, 1985b).

While the evidence is clear that the number of black female-headed families has increased rapidly in recent years, the reasons for such an increase continue to puzzle researchers. Wilson and Neckerman (1984, p. 15) have addressed the question in the form of three general hypotheses:

1. The increase in extramarital fertility is related to the increasing difficulty that black women have in finding a marital partner with stable employment.
2. There have been changes in social values regarding out-of-wedlock births.
3. Increased economic independence has been afforded women by the availability of income-transfer payments.

Using data from both the 1970 and the 1980 *Census of Population* for the 47 SMSAs with at least 100,000 blacks in 1980, O'Hare (1988) recently tested empirically each of these hypotheses. The results of his multivariate statistical analyses revealed that the increasing difficulty black women have in finding a black marital partner with stable employment is the most important factor contributing to the increase in female-headed families. That is, of all the independent variables tested, the decline in black male labor-force status was the single most important determinant of growth of black female-headed households in the 47 SMSAs examined. Moreover, other studies indicate that when the factor of joblessness is combined with high black-male mortality and incarceration rates, the proportion of black men in stable economic situations is even

Table 4   *Percentage of Female-Headed Households by Race, 1980*

Black female-headed households as percentage of all black families	37.2
Native American female-headed households as percentage of all Native American families	22.7
Hispanic female-headed households as percentage of all Hispanic families	19.4
Asian female-headed households as percentage of all Asian families	10.8
White female-headed households as percentage of all white families	10.8

Source: Computed by the author from data obtained from U.S. Department of Commerce, Bureau of the Census. *General Social and Economic Characteristics*. U.S. Summary, Washington, DC, U.S. Government Printing Office, 1980

Table 5   *Percentage of Families below Poverty in Central Cities and Suburbs by Race, 1979*

	Percentage below poverty level	
Racial/ethnic group	Central cities	Suburbs
Blacks	26.1	19.3
Native Americans	21.5	16.0
Hispanics	24.9	14.3
Asians	13.0	8.0
Whites	7.7	5.2

Source: Computed by the author from data obtained from U.S. Department of Commerce, Bureau of the Census. *General Social and Economic Characteristics*. U.S. Summary, Washington, DC, U.S. Government Printing Office, 1980

Table 6   *Percentage Unemployed by Race in Central Cities and Suburbs, 1980*

	Unemployment rate	
Racial/ethnic group	Central cities	Suburbs
Blacks	12.8	9.6
Native Americans	12.3	11.0
Hispanics	9.3	8.3
Whites	5.7	5.4
Asians	4.8	4.5

Source: Computed by the author from data obtained from U.S. Department of Commerce, Bureau of the Census. *General Social and Economic Characteristics*. U.S. Summary, Washington, DC, U.S. Government Printing Office, 1980

lower than that conveyed in the current unemployment and labor-force figures (Wilson, 1987, p. 83).

The evidence suggests that due to the greater economic stress and hardship placed upon black families (resulting in part from a decline in black male labor-force status), there is a higher percentage of black female-headed households compared with the percentages of female-headed households in other minority groups. As indicated in Table 4. the percentage of black female-headed households as a percentage of all black families was 37.2 in 1980 compared to 22.7 for Native Americans, 19.4 for Hispanics, and 10.8 for Asians. The percentage of Asian female-headed households was equal to that of whites.

A consistent pattern of racial/ethnic stratification along a color continuum is found as one examines other social and economic indicators. The percentage of blacks with incomes below the poverty level in 1980 was twice that of Asians in central cities, and the gap was even greater in the suburbs (Table 5). The black unemployment rate was the highest of any racial/ethnic group (12.8) – indeed, it was almost three times higher than the rate for Asians in central cities (4.8) in 1980. Asians had the lowest rate of unemployment of any racial minority group, lower even than the rate for whites (Table 6).

It is well known that civilian unemployment rates vary substantially among the Asian-American population. The Japanese, for example, with a high percentage of native-born people, had an unemployment rate of only 3%. The Vietnamese, on the other hand, with a high percentage of recent arrivals to the United States, had a rate of 8%. The important fact, however, is that none of the Asian-American subgroups had unemployment rates as high as those for blacks (Gardner and Smith, 1985, p. 33).

The color continuum pattern of racial/ethnic stratification is also evident in figures on self-employment. Blacks are the most underrepresented among all minority groups in terms of the black share of minority-owned businesses compared with the percentage of blacks among the minority population. Asians are the most overrepresented in terms of the Asian share of minority-owned businesses compared to the percentage of Asians among the minority population (Table 7).

In sum, the residential segregation of blacks in central cities has had severe social and economic consequences, contributing to a lower level of social and economic mobility for blacks compared with members of other racial/ethnic minority groups.

EDUCATION: AN IMPORTANT KEY TO ECONOMIC AND SOCIAL MOBILITY

One of the major avenues traditionally used in America to improve social and economic mobility has been education. The quality of educational

Table 7   *Minority-Owned Businesses and Minority Populations: The Extent of Representation*

Racial/ethnic group	No. of businesses in 1982	%	Population in 1980	%	Representation
Black	339,239	42.1	26,495,025	57.6	− 15.5
Hispanic	248,141	30.8	14,608,673	31.7	− 0.9
Asian	204,212	25.3	3,500,439	7.6	17.1
Native American	14,844	1.8	1,420,400	3.1	−1.3
Total	806,436	100.0	46,024,537	100.0	

Source: Computed by the author from data obtained from U.S. Department of Commerce, Bureau of the Census. *General Population Characteristics*. U.S. Summary, Washington, DC, U.S. Government Printing Office, 1980; U.S. Department of Commerce. *1982 Survey of Minority-owned Business Enterprises*. Blacks, Hispanics, Asians, American Indians, and Other Minorities, MB82-1, MB82-2, MB82-3. Washington, DC, U.S. Government Printing Office, 1986

Table 8   *Comparison of Education Indicators in Detroit and its Suburbs*

Indicators	Suburban mean	No. of suburban districts	Detroit	Difference
Local revenue per pupil, 1970–71	$593	31	$441	$152
Local revenue per pupil, 1980–81	$1,821	31	$819	$1,002
K-12 total instructional expenses per pupil, 1970–71	$692	31	$686	$6
K-12 total instructional expenses per pupil, 1980–81	$1,542	31	$1,493	$49
Current operating expenses per pupil, 1970–71	$905	31	$895	$10
Current operating expenses per pupil, 1980–81	$2,576	31	$2,486	$90
School dropout rate, 1970–71	5.7	31	13.7	8.0
School dropout rate, 1980–81	6.5	31	19.4	12.9
Michigan Educational Assessment Mean Composite Achievement Score (7th Grade) 1971–72	50.8	36	42.8	8.0
Michigan Educational Assessment Mean Math Achievement Score (4th Grade) 1981–82	74.7	32	60.7	14.0
Michigan Educational Assessment Mean Reading Achievement Score (4th Grade) 1981–82	72.9	32	50.9	22.0
Michigan Educational Assessment Mean Math Achievement Score (7th Grade) 1981–82	59.1	32	34.4	24.7
Michigan Educational Assessment Reading Achievement Score (7th Grade) 1981–82	74.3	32	52.5	21.8
Michigan Educational Assessment Math Achievement Score (10th Grade) 1981–82	55.8	32	30.5	25.3
Michigan Educational Assessment Mean Reading Achievement Score (10th Grade) 1981–82	74.5	32	55.1	19.4

Source: Michigan Department of Education. Local District Results, 4th Report of the 1971–72 Michigan Education Assessment Program, September, 1972; Local District Results, 1981–82 of the Michigan Education Assessment Program, 1982

Table 9   The Dropout Rate in Metropolitan Detroit by Racial/Ethnic Group, 1985–86

	Counties						Detroit City	
	Macomb		Oakland		Wayne			
Group	N	R	N	R	N	R	N	R
Black	65	9.6	286	5.9	6,954	14.1	6,631	14.8
Native American	8	2.2	22	8.6	26	6.0	24	23.5
Hispanic	14	6.3	64	9.5	216	16.2	168	20.7
Asian	7	1.9	5	0.6	42	6.4	23	10.9
White	1,760	4.6	2,250	4.8	3,182	5.9	691	23.4
Total	1,854	4.7	2,627	4.9	10,420	9.9	7,537	15.4

N = Number of Dropouts.

R = Dropout Rate.

Source: Michigan Department of Education. Office of Research and Information. Dropout Report 2: Michigan Public High School Dropouts by Racial-Ethnic Group, 1985–86 (Grades 9–12). June 29, 1987

opportunities, however, is often related to the place of residence. Clear disparities exist between the quality of education available in central-city schools and schools in the suburbs. As indicated in Table 8, students in the Detroit public schools experience inequities in several areas. All objective educational indicators, from local revenue per pupil to achievement scores, show that the Detroit suburbs have, on the average, a more favorable performance than does Detroit. Also, the gap between Detroit and its suburbs has widened over time. In 1970-71, for example, the difference in local revenue per pupil was $152. By 1980, the gap had widened to $1,002. The gap in K-12 total instructional expenses per pupil increased from $6 to $49 and the gap in current operating expenses per pupil widened from $10 to $90. In the meantime, at grade levels four, seven, and ten, the mean achievement scores of the suburban school districts were higher than those in Detroit. Such disparities in the public schools have an impact on the number and percentage of high-school dropouts. The dropout rate among all racial/ethnic groups is higher in the central-city schools and lower in the suburbs (Table 9).

It appears that residency in the central city lowers the probability that a student will receive an educational opportunity equal to that of a student in a suburban public school. Thus, the chances for improving one's social and economic mobility are reduced. Since blacks (more than any other group) are concentrated in central cities, the prospects for enhancing black social and economic mobility through education will continue to be problematic.

CONCLUSION

The major objective of this paper was to investigate why certain racial/ethnic minority groups (i.e., Asians, Hispanics, and Native Americans) have achieved higher socioeconomic statuses than have blacks. The evidence from census reports and previous research suggests that blacks experience greater discrimination in housing, as demonstrated by the high level of black residential segregation and the low level of black suburbanization. Both factors serve to reduce the employment and educational opportunities available to blacks compared with other racial/ethnic minority groups. This lack of employment and educational opportunities results in a lower level of socioeconomic status.

The opportunities for social, economic, and spatial mobility available to minority groups occur along a continuum. Asians experience the smallest amount of residential segregation from whites, have the highest level of suburbanization, and are provided the greatest opportunity for social, economic, and spatial mobility. Blacks, on the other hand, experience the greatest amount of residential segregation, the lowest level of suburbanization, and the least opportunity for social, economic, and spatial mobility of all racial/ethnic minority groups.

The white majority population appears to use two sets of criteria in evaluating members of the four racial/ethnic minority groups (Blacks, Hispanics, Native Americans, and Asians). The evidence suggests that Asians and white Hispanics are evaluated according to the criterion of ethnicity. This circumstance leads to greater spatial assimilation for Asians and white Hispanics. As social and economic mobility increases, a reduction occurs in residential segregation and an increase in suburbanization. In this sense, the position of Asians and of white Hispanics is similar to that of white ethnic groups from eastern, central, and southern Europe (Massey and Denton, 1987).

Blacks (including black Hispanics), on the other hand, are evaluated according to a racial criterion, a situation in which spatial assimilation is not strongly related to socioeconomic status (Massey and Mullan, 1985). Due to persistent discrimination in housing based on color, blacks are residentially segregated and largely excluded from the suburbs, regardless of their level of education, income, and occupation. Thus, future improvements in the social and economic status of blacks will not necessarily lead to residential integration and greater suburbanization. Such a pattern differs from that of any other minority group and reinforces the significance of color – i.e., black color – in explaining the unequal status of blacks compared with members of the other minority groups. Color, unlike ethnicity, is a perceived difference based on kind rather than degree. Therefore, blacks continue to experience more discrimination and segregation and less suburbanization than other groups. It is the continuing significance of color, more than any other factor, that explains why blacks have not achieved socioeconomic status equal to that of members of the other racial minority groups.

NOTES

1 Since Hispanics may be of any race, the degree of discrimination will vary, depending on racial characteristics. For example, black Hispanics experience more discrimination than white Hispanics and may even experience as much discrimination as non-Hispanic blacks (see U.S. Department of Housing and Urban Development, 1979, p. 3). Furthermore, the patterns of segregation involving white and black Hispanics closely follow the patterns observed for non-Hispanic whites and blacks generally. White Hispanics are highly segregated from blacks and from black Hispanics. On the other hand, white Hispanics are only moderately segregated from non-Hispanic whites (see Massey and Mullan, 1985, pp. 396–397). Apparently color is more significant than ethnicity, since black Hispanics are more segregated from white Hispanics than they are from non-Hispanic blacks.

2 The index ranges from "0," which indicates no residential segregation, to "100," which indicates complete segregation (for computation of the index, see Darden and Tabachneck, 1980).

3 There is some evidence that the situation also applies less to Native Americans, but further research is needed (see Darden, 1983).

REFERENCES

Center on Budget and Policy Priorities, 1984, *Falling Behind: A Report on How Blacks Have Fared Under the Reagan Policies*. Washington, DC: Center on Budget and Policy Priorities.

Christian, Charles, 1975, Emerging patterns of industrial activity within large metropolitan areas and their impact on the central city work force. In G. Gappert and H. M. Rose, editors, *The Social Economy of Cities*. Beverly Hills, CA: Sage.

Clark, Thomas, 1987, The suburbanization process and residential segregation. In Gary Tobin, editor, *Divided Neighborhoods*. Beverly Hills, CA: Sage.

Darden, J. T., 1983, The residential segregation of Native Americans in cities and suburbs of Michigan. *East Lakes Geographer*, Vol. 18, 25–37.

Darden, J. T., 1986, Accessibility to housing: differential residential segregation for Blacks, Hispanics, American Indians, and Asians. In Jamshid Momeni, editor, *Race, Ethnicity and Minority Housing in the United States*. Westport: Greenwood.

Darden, J. T., Hill, R. C., Thomas, J., and Thomas, R., 1987, *Detroit: Race and Uneven Development*. Philadelphia: Temple University Press.

Darden, J. T. and Tabachneck, A., 1980, Algorithm 8: graphic and mathematical descriptions of inequality, dissimilarity, segregation, or concentration. *Environment and Planning A*, Vol. 12, 227–234.

Farley, R., 1986a, Assessing Black progress: voting and citizenship rights, residency and housing, education. *Economic Outlook USA*, Vol. 13, 16–19.

Farley, R., 1986b, Assessing Black progress: employment, occupation, earnings, income, poverty. *Economic Outlook USA*, Vol. 13, 14–19 (third quarter).

Fremon, C., 1970, *The Occupational Patterns in Urban Employment Change, 1965–1967*. Washington, DC: The Urban Institute.

Gardner, R. W. and Smith, P. C., 1985, Paper presented at the annual meeting of the Population Association of America, Boston, MA, March 28.

Hermalin, A. and Farley, R., 1973, The potential for residential integration in cities and suburbs: implications for the busing controversy. *American Sociological Review*, Vol. 38, 595–610.

Hill, R. and Negrey, C., 1988, *Deindustrialization and racial minorities in the great lakes region, USA*. Discussion Paper Series, Vol. 2, Winter. East Lansing, MI: Michigan State University Urban Affairs Programs.

Kain, J., 1968, Housing segregation, Negro employment, and metropolitan decentralization. *Quarterly Journal of Economics*, Vol. 88, 513–519.

Kasarda, J. D., 1976, The changing occupational structure of the American metropolis: apropos the urban problem. In B. Schwartz, editor, *The Changing Face of the Suburbs*. Chicago: University of Chicago Press.

Kasarda, J. D., 1989, Urban industrial transition and the underclass. In W. J. Wilson, editor, *The Ghetto Underclass*. Annals of the Association of Political and Social Science. Beverly Hills: Sage Publications.

Kerner Commission, 1968, *Report of the National Advisory Commission on Civil Disorders*. Washington, DC: U.S. Government Printing Office.

Langendorf, R., 1969, Residential desegregation potential. *Journal of the American Institute of Planners*, Vol. 35, 90–95.

Lieberson, S., 1980, *A Piece of the Pie: Black and White Immigrants Since 1880*. Berkeley: University of California Press.

Logan, J. R. and Stearns, L. B., 1981, Suburban racial segregation as a nonecological process. *Social Forces*, Vol. 60, 61–73.

Massey, D. and Denton, N. A., 1987, Trends in the residential segregation of Blacks, Hispanics, and Asians: 1970-1980. *American Sociological Review*, Vol. 52, 802–825.

Massey, D. and Mullan, B. P., 1985, Commentary and debate: reply to Goldstein and White. *American Journal of Sociology*, Vol. 91, 396–399.

McDonald, J. F., 1981, The direct and indirect effects of housing segregation on employment opportunities for Blacks. *Annals of Regional Science*, Vol. 15, 27–38.

McDonald, J. F., 1984, *Employment Location and Industrial Land Use in Metropolitan Chicago*. Champaign: Stipes.

O'Hare, W., 1988, An evaluation of three theories regarding the growth of black female-headed families. *Journal of Urban Affairs*, Vol. 10, 2.

Squires, G., Bennett, L., McCourt, K., and Nyden, P., 1987, *Chicago: Race, Class, and the Response to Urban Decline*. Philadelphia, PA: Temple University Press.

Tolchin, Martin, 1988 (September 1), Minority poverty on the rise even as white poor decrease in U.S. *New York Times*, B-9.

U.S. Bureau of the Census, 1983, *Population and Housing*, Summary Tape, File 4. Washington, DC: Data Users Services.

U.S. Bureau of the Census, 1985a, *Current Population Reports*. Series P-60, No. 149. Washington, DC: U.S. Government Printing Office.

U.S. Bureau of the Census, 1985b, *Household and Family Characteristics: March 1984. Current Population Reports*. Series P-20, No. 398. Washington, DC: U.S. Government Printing Office.

U.S. Bureau of the Census, 1988a, *Money, Income and Poverty Status in the United States, 1987*. Number 161. Washington, DC: U.S. Government Printing Office.

U.S. Bureau of the Census, 1988b, *Estimates of Poverty Including the Value of Non-Cash Benefits, 1987*. Advance Report, P-60, Number 58. Washington, DC: U.S. Government Printing Office.

U.S. Department of Housing and Urban Development, 1979, *Discrimination Against Chicanos in the Dallas Rental Housing Market*. Washington, DC: Office of Policy Development and Research.

Vernon, R., 1966, The Changing Economic Function of the Central City. In James Q. Wilson, editor, *Urban Renewal: The Record and the Controversy*. Cambridge: Massachusetts Institute of Technology Press.

Wilson, F. D., 1979, *Residential Consumption, Economic Opportunity and Race*. New York: Academic Press.

Wilson, W. J., 1987, *The Truly Disadvantaged: The Inner City, the Underclass, and Public Policy*. Chicago: University of Chicago Press.

Wilson, W. J. and Neckerman, K. M., 1984, *Poverty and Family Structure: The Widening Gap Between Evidence and Public Policy Issues*. Paper presented at the Conference on Poverty and Policy: Retrospect and Prospects, Williamsburg, VA, December.

Woolbright, L. A. and Hartmann, D. J., 1987, The new segregation: Asians and Hispanics. In Gary Tobin, editor, *Divided Neighborhoods*. Beverly Hills: Sage.

25

Scientific Racism: Reflections on Peer Review, Science and Ideology[*]

CHARLES LESLIE

This is a highly technical article written primarily for the benefit of a scholarly network. But the issues raised illustrate that the nature of race and its implications are still being debated. It is the belief of some that linking race to social and cultural characteristics suggesting inferiority for groups on some scale, is patently racist. Anthropologist Charles Leslie contends that the arbitrary and capricious attribution of social and cultural characteristics to certain groups in ways that suggest that race can distinguish human beings, even if defended by scholars, is racism, albeit, 'scientific racism'. The scholars he critiques, particularly J. Phillippe Ruston's work with sociobiology, defend themselves by arguing that their data is objective and significant, and thus should not be accused of racism. Lewis points out that claiming the cloak of objectivity is not ample defense against the charge of racism. Furthermore, these studies are basically reiterative of scholars in earlier periods who proposed that blacks were both different and inferior.

My topic is the community of social scientists and the civilization that maintains it. I will be anecdotal throughout this lecture, so let us begin with a recent event: *Social Science & Medicine* has just published an article that seems to me to be transparent racist pseudo-science. The article is 'Population differences in susceptibility to AIDS: an evolutionary analysis,' by two psychologists at the University of Western Ontario, J. Philippe Rushton and Anthony

F. Bogaert [1]. The problem that I want us to consider is why Peter McEwan and the scholars he asked to evaluate the manuscript did not consider it to be transparent racist pseudo-science? Peter told a Canadian newspaper reporter who phoned him about the matter that the manuscript was read by a sociologist, a psychologist and a physician, and that "The reviewers and I share the view that the case was sufficiently respectable scientifically to merit publication. We are open to all shades of opinion. The only thing we require is that the material be of sufficient high quality" [2].

Before I read the essay, or had even heard of it, I got a letter from a Canadian anthropologist returning a manuscript on Africa that he had agreed to

[*] This is an edited version of the invited Opening Address at the *XIth International Conference on the Social Sciences & Medicine* held at Leeuwenhorst Congress Center, The Netherlands, 24–28 July, 1989.

evaluate, and saying that he would not act as a reviewer for a journal that published Rushton's work. He enclosed a clipping from a Toronto newspaper that reported the interview with Peter I have just quoted. This seemed to me to be a bit hotheaded, but I answered immediately saying that I would send copies of his letter and my reply to Peter. I told him that if the article was, as reported, about racial differences, then Peter should have sent it for evaluation to an anthropologist or biologist who specialized in research on human evolution and the genetics of racial variation. In any case, I reminded him that peer review is often imperfect, and that he did his Africanist colleague a disservice by refusing to review his entirely unrelated manuscript.

In the following days I received long distance phone calls from two Advisory Editors for the journal who were outraged that it was publishing an article by Rushton, though neither one of them had read it, and were responding to discussions with colleagues in Canada. I was surprised that someone I had never heard of was so infamous, but argued that no matter how bad the article might turn out to be, my callers were wrong to assert that it would corrupt the people who read *Social Science & Medicine*. Nevertheless, I agreed to fax the letter I had mailed to Peter, with a note asking whether publication could be reconsidered. I did not realize that the essay had already been published.

Fax is a wonderful technology. Peter's answer arrived within twenty-four hours.

With regard to the Rushton paper, it is too late to prevent publication even if we wished. The paper was accepted because following two extensive revisions it presented a case that, however contentious, justified consideration. I am guided by the principle that there must be no sacred cows—all reasoned argument has the right to enter the general arena of discourse even if at times this provokes outrage in one quarter or another.... It was obvious from the moment of its arrival that Rushton's paper dealt with a highly sensitive issue and his writings have been the subject of heated controversy in several other places, but this was no reason for evasion. Critics should address the substance of the paper rather than its publication; the weaker they believe it to be the easier should be the task of demolition. Shrill denunciation is no more convincing than bald assertion. I believe we have a duty to defend the bastions of freedom of legal expression, however provocative this may occasionally seem to those within whom prejudice masquerades as given truth.

Peter's eloquence struck home, for I subscribe wholeheartedly to the principles of free speech and scientific discourse, but seemed in this case to have advocated censorship and closure, particularly since I still had not read the Rushton essay. Reading it was a shock, for it was worse than I had expected. It convinced me that in evoking noble sentiments about scientific publication, Peter had missed the point. He and his reviewers had simply failed to recognize the character of the work. Its disingenuous underpinnings and inherently racist premises were transparent to me, but not to them. Why? What appealed to these social scientists so that garbled biology and sociology appeared to be "sufficiently respectable scientifically to merit publication", and racism appeared to be "reasoned argument"?

To answer this question we must summarize the Rushton essay and relate it to the discourse on race in biocultural studies of human adaptation and evolution, and in our society at large. But as I do this you should remember that our topic is the community of social scientists: How does it work? and What is the nature of the civilization that nurtures it? Whether or not you have read the Rushton essay, I expect that my story so far resembles some pattern of events that you have observed or gossiped about on other occasions, and thus has elements familiar to you. We are looking, as Aristotle said, for the general in the particular. To give Rushton's work context I will recount my own reasons for becoming an anthropologist, and speak personally from a career of teaching, research and editorial work. I invite you to compare your experiences and conception of the social sciences to mine, for we have lived through a good portion of the twentieth century and share memories of it, and we participate together in the enterprise that Peter McEwan heads, helping to edit *Social Science & Medicine*, evaluating manuscripts sent to us in its peer review process, publishing in it ourselves, and attending its conferences. This work is continuous with our work in universities, professional associations, governmental agencies and so on, forming a community of scholars divided on regional, national, disciplinary and linguistic lines. The civilization that encompasses and sustains this heterogeniety is never far from our minds.

Rushton is part of our community. He is a member of the psychology department at a good university. He wrote the article in *Social Science & Medicine* while a Fellow of the Guggenheim Foundation, and he cites other articles he has published in respected scientific series, including the *Proceedings of the National Academy of Sciences, U.S.A.* Thus, his work has successfully undergone peer review by numerous institutions. When we look for the general in the particulars of his work we are not looking at another culture alien to our own, but at the culture of our own community.

Rushton and Bogaert's argument is straightforward (From now on I will only refer to the senior author since the flap that has developed in Canada about this work centers on Rushton. Also, I will use his categories and generalizations and comment on them after the summary). The AIDS virus infects Negroid populations more than Caucasoids, and Caucasoids more than Mongoloids. In Africa,

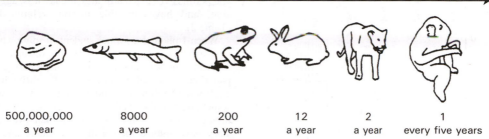

| 500,000,000 | 8000 | 200 | 12 | 2 | 1 |
| a year | a year | a year | a year | a year | every five years |

Figure 1   *Reproductive strategies in the animal world go all the way from extreme 'r', the strategy that relies on maximum egg output and no parental care, to extreme 'K', in which nearly all emphasis is on care and the birthrate is reduced to minimum [1, p. 1214]*

where it originated and is transmitted by heterosexual intercourse as well as by other practices, it is more widespread than in other parts of the world. In North America and other dominantly Caucasian populations, where the primary modes of transmission are homosexual intercourse and intravenous drug use, the sector of the population with African ancestry is much more infected than the Caucasians. The lowest rates of infection are in the Mongolian populations of Asia, and among minority peoples of Mongolian ancestry in other regions. This epidemiological pattern corresponds to racial differences in temperament and behavior that increase the risk of AIDS infection. Rushton does not argue that the three races differ in biological resistance to the virus, with the Mongoloids most resistant and the Negroids most susceptible. The difference in susceptibility that he tries to prove resides in genetically grounded social behavior—in qualities of intellectual and moral life. This difference arose in the course of human evolution through the processes that differentiated Mongoloid, Caucasoid and Negroid racial types.

Rushton's ideas are largely summarized in a drawing, a table and a chart that he borrowed from other scholars to explain the distinction between *r* and *K* selection, and finally, a table that he created to apply this distinction to human races. The distinction between *r* and *K* selection was new to me, but the general concept in these borrowed items was familiar.

The drawing suggested a scale between 4 animal groups represented by an oyster, a fish, a frog, and 3 orders of mammals, a rabbit (Lagomorpha), tiger (Carnivora) and baboon (Primate) (Fig. 1). Actually, Rushton modified the drawing from the original, where the last two animals were a lion and a gorilla. At the *r* end of the scale the reproductive strategy is prolix, producing tiny eggs of which relatively few mature to reproduce, and at the *K* end the strategy involves prolonged uterine development, single birth and slow maturation. Table 1 spells out the distinction between *r* and *K* life styles [1, p. 1215].

Table 1   *Some life history, social behavior, and physiological differences between r- and K-strategies [1, p. 1215]*

r-Strategist	*K*-Strategist
Family characteristics	
Large litter size	Small litter size
Short spacing between births	Long spacing between births
Many offspring	Few offspring
High rate of infant mortality	Low rate of infant mortality
Low degree of parental care	High degree of parental care
Individual characteristics	
Rapid rate of maturation	Slow rate of maturation
Early sexual reproduction	Delayed sexual reproduction
Short life	Long life
High reproduction effort	Low reproduction effort
High energy utilization	Efficient energy utilization
Low intelligence	High intelligence
Population characteristics	
Opportunistic exploiters of environment	Consistent exploiters of environment
Dispersing colonizers	Stable occupiers of habitat
Variable population size	Stable population size
Competition variable, often lax	Competition keen
Social system characteristics	
Low degree of social organization	High degree of social organization
Low amounts of altruism	High amounts of altruism

The chart, taken from Lovejoy [4, p. 342], shows *K* selection within the Primate Order, revealed by a pattern of prolonged development which is most advanced among hominids (Fig. 2).

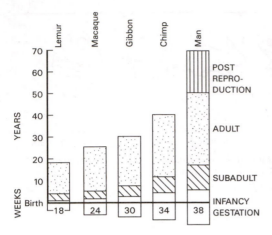

Figure 2   *Progressive prolongation of life phases and gestation in primates [4]*

This was familiar ground, the stuff I used to teach undergraduates and that one encounters in articles on human evolution in popular science magazines or on educational television. It was the story of arboreal adaptations followed by a shift to ground dwelling bipedalism, with the opposable thumb, stereoscopic vision, hand–eye coordination, omnivorous diet and single births described as primate adaptations to an aboreal habitat, and with specialized hind limbs adapted to bipedal locomotion that freed the arms to carry food, babies and weapons, and with these adaptations in turn accompanied by displacement of the estrus cycle by continuous sexual receptivity, pair bonding and parental cooperation in raising fragile infants. The story continues with increasing brain size and selection for complex behavior, including tool production, linguistic symboling, and the control of fire. Throughout this evolutionary story I would emphasize the reciprocal relationship between biological and cultural mechanisms of adaptation. The omnivorous diet including increasing consumption of animal tissue, but mediated by cultural adaptations in tool production and cooking so that carnivore diet occurred without carnivore biological specializations in jaws and teeth. The whole sequence characterized by neoteny, a change in growth pattern that lengthened the period of childhood dependency and learning, giving rise to the ultimate species specific behavior of grammatical speech.

Rushton's chart showing that hominids are *K*-selected was familiar scientific discourse, but his use of the *r-K* distinction to describe racial variation was something else, also quite familiar, for here were the racist premises that I grew up with in the American south, the assertion that Negroes have small brains, low intelligence, big sex organs, mature rapidly, have exaggerated sexual impulses,

and permissive sexual attitudes, are lawless, aggressive, and have unstable marital relationships (Table 2).

When I phoned a former student of mine who is now a biological anthropologist at a distinguished medical school to ask his advice in preparing this paper, he compared my problem to the difficulty of confronting religious fundamentalists who want something that they call 'creation science' taught in biology courses, rather than Darwinian evolution. They have studied the scientific literature and use language borrowed from it along with scattered facts to prove a Biblical view of the world. If you can't just say flat-out that this is a spurious enterprise, as I would like to say of Rushton's article, then refuting their work step by step, my friend said, is "like trying to shovel manure from the barn with a teaspoon."

So many things are wrong with Rushton's article that I despair of ever persuading the author that this science is spurious. Like the fundamentalists who cloth their religious cosmology in a scientific vocabulary, Rushton's agenda lies outside the work itself. But I am constrained to shovel away for awhile just because we are in the barn on our own farm, and I must try to persuade Peter McEwan and his reviewers that we are not in the parlour having tea with a scholar whose work merits publication in our favorite scientific journal. I do not despair of the enterprise because I have worked harmoniously on the journal with Peter for more than a decade, and know him to be fair minded.

The distinction between *r*-selected species and *K*-selected species was first made by Robert H. MacArthur and Edward O. Wilson in an innovative book that has stimulated mathematical formulations of the demographic characteristics of island biotas. *K* is defined as "The 'carrying capacity of the environment.' i.e., the number of individuals in a population of a given species at the population equilibrium" [3]. And *r* is "The 'intrinsic rate of increase,' the per capita rate of net increase in a given environment" [3, p. x]. A high rate of increase will help a species colonize an island, but when it reaches the carrying capacity of the habitat, crowding will increase competition and *K*-selection will favor genotypes that most efficiently use resources. *r*-selection favors the ability to increase the size of the population and thus to take advantage of increased resources, and to recover from temporary environmental insults. MacArthur and Wilson wrote:

In defining the peculiarities of post-colonization evolution, a fundamental distinction was made between *r* selection and *K* selection. The intrinsic rate of population increase, *r*, is likely to be increased in the earliest stages of colonization, when population growth is unrestricted. Moreover, *r* will be held at a high value by those species whose histories include frequently repeated colonizing episodes. But most species occupying stable habitats, once they have attained their

Table 2   *Ranking of populations on r/K associated attributes [1, p. 1216]*

	Mongoloids	Caucasoids	Negroids
Brain weight and intelligence			
Cranial capacity	1448 cm^3	1408 cm^3	1334 cm^3
Brain weight at autopsy	1351 g	1336 g	1286 g
Millions of 'excess neurons'	8900	8650	8550
IQ test scores	107	100	85
Maturation rate			
Gestation time	?	Medium	Fast
Skeletal development	?	Medium	Fast
Age of walking	Slow	Medium	Fast
Age of first intercourse	Slow	Medium	Fast
Age of first pregnancy	Slow	Medium	Fast
Brain weight decline begins	Age 35	Age 25	?
Life-span	Long	Medium	Short
Personality and temperament			
Activity level	Low	Medium	High
Aggressiveness	Low	Medium	High
Cautiousness	High	Medium	Low
Dominance	Low	Medium	High
Impulsivity	Low	Medium	High
Sociability	Low	Medium	High
Reproductive effort			
Multiple birthing rate	Low	Medium	High
Size of genitalia	Small	Medium	Large
Secondary sex characteristics	Small	Medium	Large
Intercourse frequencies	Low	Medium	High
Permissive attitudes	Low	Medium	High
Sexually transmitted diseases	Low	Medium	High
Androgen levels	Low	Medium	High
Social organization			
Law abidingness	High	Medium	Low
Marital stability	High	Medium	Low
Mental health	High	Medium	Low

maximum population size, K, will tend once again to reduce r. There will be a simultaneous tendency to increase K through finer adaptation to the local environment. Thereafter, the relative amounts of r selection and K selection will be determined by the stability of the local environment [3, p. 178].

Rushton's characterization of human races as r-selected or K-selected does not come from MacArthur and Wilson, but appears to be derived from evolutionary theorizing by the anthropologist, C. Owen Lovejoy [4], whose ideas were popularized in a best selling book about the discovery of an extraordinary Australopithecus fossil [5]. Table 3 contrasts Hominid and Pongid adaptations. Although the K strategy of adaptation is a general mammalian trait, and well developed among the primates, Lovejoy argued that Hominids diverged from the Pongids through an adaptive strategy that involved r-selection to reduce the period between births (K-selection would have increased the length of time between births).

Birth spacing is one of five demographic variables in equilibrium when a population reaches the carrying capacity of the environment (Fig. 3). Actual longevity—the probability of surviving—depends on genetic life potential and on interaction with the environment such as avoiding predators and securing food. The higher primates enhance survivorship, e.g. reduce environmentally induced mortality, by "strong social bonds, high levels of intelligence, intense parenting, and long periods of learning" [4, p. 343]. The success of Hominids in changing the ecological niche they inhabit through cultural adaptations, and in colonizing new environments could only have occurred by altering two of the five demographic variables, survivorship and birth interval. The other demographic variables are "direct linear functions of mammalian development physiology" [4, p. 344].

Lovejoy observed that Hominid evolution involved the novelty among the large primates of r-selection for decreased birth intervals which allowed more rapid population increases than would otherwise be the case, and thus facilitated the

Table 3   *Hominid and Pongid adaptations [5, p. 338]*

Hominid	Pongid (Ape)
Exclusively ground-dwelling	Some predominantly in trees. Some predominantly on the ground. None exclusively terrestrial.
Bipedal	Not bipedal
Pair-bonded, leading to establishment of nuclear families	Not pair-bonded. No nuclear families except in gibbons
Increasing immobility of females and young. Possibility of a home base	Females move to secure food and take infants with them. No home base
Food sharing	No food sharing
Beginnings of tool use and tool making	Tool use absent or inconsequential
Brain continues to enlarge	Brain does not enlarge
Continuous sexuality	Sexuality only during estrus
Multiple infant care	Single infant care

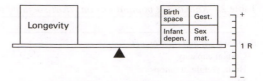

Figure 3   *Mechanical model of demographic variables in hominoids. The R is the intrinsic rate of population increase (1 = static population size). An increase in the lengths of the four periods on the bar to the right (birth space, gestation, infant dependency, and sexual maturity) is accompanied by a comparable shift of longevity to the left, but without realization of that longevity, prolonged maturation reduces R and leads to extinction or replacement by populations in which life phases are chronologically shorter. Of the four variables on the right, only birth space can be significantly shortened (shifted to the left) without alteration of primate aging physiology [4, p. 343]*

colonization of new environments. He described this novel pattern as a complex of feedback relationships between common mammalian behavioral elements and selection for bipedalism, pair bonding and intensified sexuality.

Bipedalism occurs early in the fossil record, and it freed the arms to carry food. Provisioning is a primary parental strategy of canids (dogs, wolves, foxes) and of birds, but among large primates it is peculiar to ourselves, where adults provision each other as well as infants. The arms were also freed to carry altricial infants, thus inhancing the survivorship of fragile genotypes. A sexual division of labor, with male and female provisioning and continuous sexuality, rather than arousal limited to estrus, favored pair bonding and formation of nuclear families with shorter birth intervals and multiple dependent offspring. This evolving social matrix nurtured the prolongation of growth and learning and more efficient exploitation of the environment.

Here is the ground for Rushton's perversion of the distinction between *K*-selection and *r*-selection in Hominid evolution. Lovejoy observed that we display "a greater elaboration of epigamic characters than any other primate," and he goes on to say that among Hominids

> marked epigamic dimorphism is achieved by elaboration of parasexual characters in both males and females, rather than in males alone. Their display value is clearly cross-sexual and not intrasexual as in other primates. It should be stressed that these epigamic characters are highly variable and can thus be viewed as a mechanism for establishing and displaying individual sexual

uniqueness, and that such uniqueness would play a major role in the maintenance of pair bonds [4, pp. 346–347].

Lovejoy is describing the peculiar character of human sexual attraction and love. Without clothing male genitals are large and prominently displayed, compared to other primates, and they are decorated on our naked bodies with pubic hair of various patterns and thickness. Female breasts are relatively prominent and variously shaped, and male beards vary in thickness and pattern along with other parasexual traits in the somatic profiles of both sexes. This pronounced sexual dimorphism and polymorphism facilitates the individualized and intense sexual preferences and attachments involved in human pair bonding, short birth intervals, and effective parenting of several highly dependent children at the same time. In other words, a dash of *r*-selection was an essential element in the distinctive evolutionary pattern of our species. Rushton garbled the concept of Hominid *r*-selection for birth spacing by identifying it with an alleged racial pattern of psychological and social traits that he associated with a small brain and large genital phenotype.

My God, must I go on? I must go on.

To the contrasting pole of *K*-selection, expressed somatically in big brains and small genitals, Rushton attributed the racial character of law abidingness, low aggression and low dominance. He identified the Mongoloids with this pattern, despite the long history of Asian violence, including Japanese military conquests in this century, beginning with their defeat early in the century of Czarist Russia and bloody participation in the first and second World Wars. Are we to consider the Communist revolution in China and its sequalae up to the current executions of workers and students, or the activities of Mr Pol Pot and his followers, to illustrate racial law abidingness, low aggression and low dominance? Rushton gives no reasons at all for attributing these character traits to Mongoloids in his *Social Science & Medicine* article, but in an earlier essay in another journal from which he recycled the tables and charts he used in *Social Science & Medicine*, he cited psychology observations of babies, and personality tests administered to students [6]. How this justified an aggregate description of hundreds of millions of people with highly differentiated cultural traditions he does not say. Instead, he gives us *K*-selected Asian sexual inhibition which he says is expressed in Chinese and other Asian worry about premature ejaculation and the culture-bound syndrome of *Koro*, anxiety about the disappearance altogether of their little penises.

Of course, the real crunch of Rushton's argument is his *r*-selected pole of uninhibited black sexuality. He tells us that a review of sex therapy in Britain revealed that Asian immigrants suffered from premature ejaculation, and that this was not a concern of blacks. But his clinchers on black sexuality are United States rape statistics, a study of child abuse in Philadelphia, and statistics on sexually transmitted diseases. What can I say after all the years of social science research on race issues? It is like trying to correct Rushton's view of racial differences on I.Q. tests, which he associates with the sizes of brains and genitals. Shall we enquire how the female organs were measured? and whether penises were measured from the tip of the foreskin, or the tip of the glans? Shall we discount the racial brain comparisons by observing that brain size is related to body size and that the average differences between male and female brains is greater than the differences he asserts between big and small brain races? What is the use?

I can't go on. I must go on.

One last teaspoon full! Rushton says that he predicted racial differences in *r/K* sexual strategies

> because human populations are known to differ in egg production ... the rate per 1000 of diazygotic twins (the *r*-strategy, caused by production of two eggs at once ...) among Mongoloids is 4, among Caucasoids, 8, and among Negroids, 16, with some African populations having rates as high as 57/1000 [1, p. 1215].

When I consulted Rushton's source [7], it turned out that the reliability of the African statistics was low, for they were all based on hospital reports in the 1950s and 60s in societies where an unrepresentative and a limited segment of the black population used hospitals for birthing. From my own observations in Mexico and India, I am skeptical about the accuracy of provincial hospital records in Third World countries. Even so, Rushton ignored the author's reasoning about dizygotic twinning. Bulmer, the study's author, wrote that since birthing itself is hazardous,

the mother of twins is at a selective disadvantage to the mother of a single baby, except under modern conditions of delivery and prenatal care. He asks, Why wasn't twinning eliminated through natural selection? He reasons that genetic drift in small populations of prehistoric times might have been more important than natural selection, and that this might explain different rates of twinning in modern populations. This is certainly an alternative to Ruston's hypothesis, but Bulmer himself sets it aside because it contradicts the "general feeling among human geneticists that genetic drift has not played an important part in human evolution" [7, p. 180].

It occurred to neither Bulmer or Rushton, so far as I can tell, that twinning may be evidence of more effective parenting. The norm for primates is single births, but for Marmosets the modal birth is dizygotic twins. This *r*-selected trait is facilitated among these small South and Central American monkeys by pair bonding and K-selection for males who provide extensive paternal care for the young [4, p. 345]. Thus, *r*-selection and *K*-selection are complementary processes, rather than polar opposites, in the evolution of this reproductive strategy. The same possibility is suggested by Lovejoy's theoretical reconstruction of the role of sexuality and birth spacing in human evolution. This turns Rushton's argument on its head, for the higher rates of twinning among blacks would be evidence that more effective nuclear families reduced the mortality rates of the mothers of twins, and nurtured offspring who carried this trait to reproductive age.

Bulmer's second speculation about why natural selection did not eliminate dizygotic twinning was that it indicated "a balanced polymorphism due to heterozygote advantage" on the model of sickle-cell genes and resistance to malaria [8, p. 181]. Selection for balanced polymorphism is quite a different interpretation than Rushton's pattern of *r*-selected racial traits, but that Rushton ignored Bulmer's hopothesis is consistent with the manner, or rhetoric, of his essay. It is the manner of a debater making as forceful appearing a case as he can. It is a rhetoric that picks and chooses evidence, that ignores alternative hypotheses, that elides issues. In short, the essay is not constructed in the spirit and manner of a scientific argument, but instead is an ideological tract. We social scientists are not good at telling the difference.

Indeed, most of the most influential work in the social sciences is ideological, and most of our criticisms of each other are ideologically grounded. Non social scientists generally recognize the fact that the social sciences are mostly ideological, and that they have produced in this century a very small amount of scientific knowledge compared to the great bulk of their publications. Our claim to being scientific is one of the main intellectual scandals of the academic world, though most of us live comfortably with our shame.

We do like the appearance of being scientific. It is our way of being respectable, and in applied work our bread depends upon it because the people who hire us expect us to produce data and language that will help them implement and justify programmatic goals. George Bush and Margaret Thatcher look for the economist who will tell them what they want to hear, or Deans and Department Chairmen for the psychologist or sociologist who has the right theoretical orientation to meet their requirements. Still, totalitarian countries have less use for the social sciences than liberal democracies. The kind of work published in *Social Science & Medicine* does not thrive in Communist or Fascist dictatorships, or in countries ruled by religious ideologues. By and large, we believe in, and our social science is meant to promote, pluralism and democracy.

These pronouncements may seem terribly excathedra to you. Let me give particulars from personal experience so that you can see how I arrived at them.

When the Japanese bombing of Pearl Harbor brought the United States into the Second World War, I was an 18-year-old freshman at a small Southern college. I liked to party, and I liked girls, but I was, and I was generally thought to be, a sissy. I thought that I was hopelessly homosexual. I wrote poetry, liked art, and was filled with vague ambitions to be a great man, to make something beautiful, to do something noble. I read about the University of Iowa in *Life* magazine, where artists were awarded Ph.D. degrees for writing novels and painting pictures. So I persuaded my father to let me go to Iowa by working the next summer at an incendiary bomb plant to defray the expense. At Iowa I met two Jewish girls and dated one of them. The other one dated a boy from Texas. My attitudes confirmed their opinion of Southerners, and they were astonished at themselves for having anything to do with me.

Despite unhappiness with my own family and community, and desire to escape them, I had no other culture than the one that I had grown up with. Over half the population in my home town was black, before I started to school I had a black nanny, and we always had a black cook. The African Americans were called Niggers, and lots of jokes described their sexual powers and simple-mindedness. Our schools were segregated, as were all other public facilities, and where there was only one, like the public library, black people were not allowed to use it. At the movies they had a separate entrance and a blocked off section of the balcony.

Jews also lived in my town, and owned the most prominent clothing and jewelry stores on Main Street, but they were not allowed to join the Country Club, and jokes about Jews were as frequent and as demeaning as those about African Americans.

My Jewish girlfriend considered me an exotic creature, for she and her roommate were from Brooklyn in New York City, and they were Communists. One day Gert, who was truly in love

with the boy from Texas, was crying because he told her that other men in his rooming house had teased him about having a kike girlfriend. For me, this was an epiphany. It revealed the world of suffering we inflict on each other with our thoughtless conventions. I realized that we are both tormented and tormentors.

I had to do something with this new knowledge, so I absconded to Chicago to become a Communist. I arrived in November, shortly after my 19th birthday, found a full-time job, a rooming house, and a Communist night school that opened just after Christmas. I subscribed to *The Daily Worker*, and registered for a course on race relations. Meanwhile, my father agreed to pay my tuition at the nearby night school of the University of Chicago, where I registered for an introductory anthropology course. I did not know what it was, but the lady at the desk recommended it.

The race relations course at the Abraham Lincoln School had readings from Stalin, Lenin, Marx and Engels, and discussed the way that leaders in the Soviet Union had solved the 'nationalities question'. I failed to connect their example with the life I had lived on the Mississippi Delta.

The anthropology course was quite different. The teacher had been an expert witness for the defense in the Scopes trial, where a teacher in Tennessee broke the law by teaching evolutionary biology. It was against the law in my home state as well, so I had read *The Origin of Species* in high school on my own, as a banned book. Now in Chicago I learned the names and characteristics of human fossils from an expert. Sinanthropus, *Pithecanthropus erectus*, Neanderthal, Cromagnon—the scientific words rolled on my tongue like delicious fruit. Here was evolutionary data to shock the folks back home. Here was another culture to learn, one dedicated to a critical search for truth, and romantic to boot, for it promised adventure in far off places searching for the reasons we are the kind of animal we are.

But more at hand, and in contrast to the Marxist course, here was a scientific way to study racial variation, and to reject the pervasive racism of American society.

I realize now that the anthropology I learned in the spring of 1943 was inadequately grounded in evolutionary theory, and that even it was tainted with racist misconceptions, but it is useful to describe its argument on race as the background for Rushton's essay.

This is from memory after nearly fifty years, but because the science I learned was ideologically important to me, I believe that my recall is essentially correct. My teacher was Fay-Cooper Cole, who had been trained by Franz Boas, the founder of academic anthropology in the United States. Like Rushton, Cole accepted the division of our species into three racial groups. He might have used the terms 'basic races', or 'primary races'. Let me illustrate

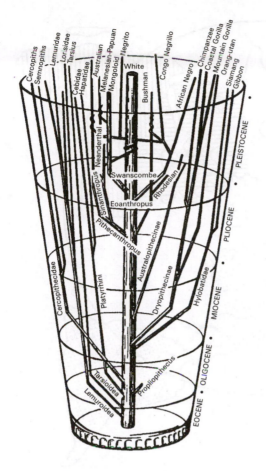

Figure 4 *Family tree of the primates [8, p. 411]*

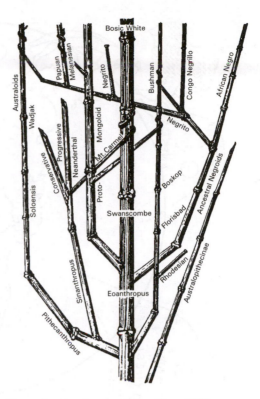

Figure 5 *Family tree of man [8, p. 413]*

the kind of thinking that was involved with two phylogenetic charts from a famous textbook. Notice in the 'Family tree of the primates' (Fig. 4) that the core line for all primate evolution is represented by the white race from which all other members of the order diverge. The anthropocentricism and racism are astonishing to me now, but in 1943 this sort of thing seemed reasonable, as did the 'Family tree of man' (Fig. 5) [8]. I now cringe at the sexism of the title, though I was taken with 'the science of man' in my youth. Here again the 'Basic White' race is the main line of evolution, with the two other 'primary races' branching from it:

1. The 'Ancestral Negroids' who led directly to the modern African population, and a branch that accounts for the pygmies (Congo Negrillo), Southeast Asian Negritos, and the Melanesians.
2. The Mongoloids, whose miscegenation with whites and Melanesians is represented by tendrils.

Then, two minor racial lines are represented by small peripheral populations, the Australian aborigines and the Bushmen of the Kalahari desert.

Unlike Rushton's use of the three race scheme, Fay-Cooper Cole emphasized the extremely heterogeneous nature of these categories, and their conventional or arbitrary character. The last point was made by telling us that well-qualified anthropologists disagreed with each other about the number of races that they counted. For example, they disputed about whether the Australian aborigines were a separate race, or represented a 'primitive Caucasoid' population, along with the Veddas, a tribal people in Sri Lanka, and 'the hairy Ainu' of Northern Japan. This was my first lesson in scientific nominalism, that scientific categories are our own constructions and not 'God's truth'.

Stanley Garn's map (Fig. 6) [9] showing nine races will remind anyone familiar with human variation of the regional differences in physical appearance between populations in different parts of Europe, North Africa and the Near East, which are here lumped together as one area, as are regions that extend from Siberia through China to Indonesia, here shown to be the area of a single Asiatic race.

Fay-Cooper Cole emphasized the extreme heterogeneity encompassed by each category when humanity was reduced to three races. One was obliged in this case to acknowledge local populations of Caucasoids who were as dark skinned, or darker, than local groups of Negroids in Ethiopia.

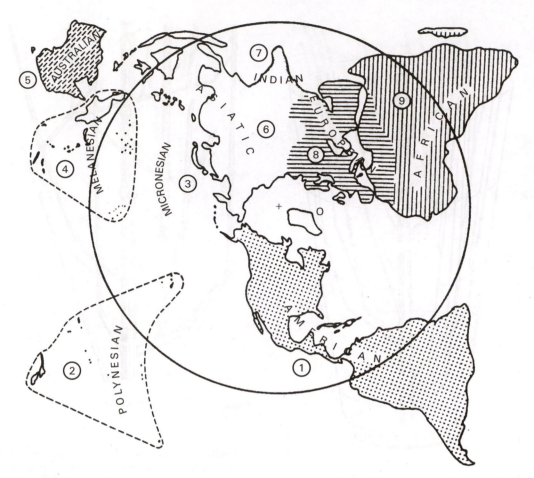

Figure 6   *Polar projection map of the world showing the approximate limits of the geographical races described in the text. This spread-out view shows that large areas of ocean have contributed to reproductive isolation while contiguous land masses allow for easier gene flow*

This provided a debator's point against white racists I grew up with. Cole provided similar debator's points with reference to variations in head form, height, and other somatic features, and reasoned from this that races should be defined by trait complexes for which single traits varied in ways that prevented drawing racial boundaries. Rushton's typological use of race categories, which follows the norm of popular culture and social science usage, sorts people into a simple set of contrasting boxes, yet the geographical reality is a continuous distribution of variable traits that blend with each other as one moves from one region to another.

The central lesson on typological thinking was directed by Cole at the concept of a pure race, and at the supposedly negative effects of race mixture. Rather than dealing with the continuous distribution of physical variations in Europe, three races, Nordic, Alpine, and Mediterranean, were said to compose the Caucasian stock. With photographs of

these types, and anthropometric charts, scientists were supposed to be able to sort people out who were racially pure, or one of a great variety of mixtures of these types. This same idea is expressed by the tendrils in Hooton's phylogenetic chart. Like Rushton's work, the European racial types were said to possess well defined intellectual and moral qualities. Culture, language and religion were garbled with biology by labeling Jews a mongrel race, and calling Nordics an Aryan race. The whole enterprise was transparently wicked to all of us in Fay-Cooper Cole's class for what I still believe to be good scientific and moral reasons. My conviction, then and now, is that the moral and scientific reasons were complementary, that good judgment in the social sciences depends on moral knowledge and sensibility as well as on the critical use of scientific reasoning.

A final point. The variability of physical traits such as skin color, height and head form was said to show that they were adaptive to environmental differences in nutrition, exposure to sunlight, and so on. Dolicocephalic, brachycephalic, the words that anthropologists used to describe these variations were scientific music to my ears, in comparison to Stalin and Lenin on the nationalities problem. Cole described Boas's research on generational changes in the head form of European immigrants to America as evidence that basic physical measurements used by German medical scientists (anthropology was a branch of medicine in Germany) were subject to environmental variations unrelated to genetic change. Thus, with the war on in Europe and the Pacific, part of the refutation of Nazi pseudo-science that I learned argued that racial classifications should give greater weight to non-adaptive than to adaptive traits. We were shown in class how to sort out skulls according to these traits. The Mongoloids, for example, had shovel-shaped incisor teeth, wide zygomatic arches, smooth frontal bones with no supraorbital ridge, and a characteristic difference from other races in the sutures joining the bones of the cranium. This emphasis on non-adaptive traits discounted the Darwinian notion that natural selection gave rise to racial variation through adaptations to different environments.

With this small start on a career in anthropology, I joined the army air corps and became a bomber pilot. It was in the last group of cadets at most of the installations where we were trained. By the time we graduated the army had more pilots than it could use, and the war was ending. One evening at the movies the newsreel showed concentration camps being liberated—the mounds of shoes, the bleached cadavers, the barracks and barbed wire. It was too awful for us to have imagined, but seeing that it had happened, I knew that I and my family and the people in my home town and the soldiers I had trained with could have done it instead of the Germans. Our pride, like theirs was our racism and antisemiticism. The army air corps was entirely segregated, and the only black soldiers on our base were assigned exclusively to unskilled service jobs. The medical corps kept separate blood supplies for black and white troops. A pamphlet by the anthropologist. Ruth Benedict, on human races was banned from distribution on military posts. The Germans had outdone us, but they were our kind.

German medical scientists and anthropologists took an important role in the Holocaust [10]. Eugen Fischer, Director of the Kaiser Wilhelm Institute for Anthropology, was an enthusiastic advocate of the Nazi racial ideology, and was elected Rector of the University of Berlin soon after Hitler gained power. With other medical anthropologists, he helped to design and implement the ostensibly therapeutic program of eugenics of the German government [11]. But scientific racism was not a German aberration, it had a long and respectable career within the international communities of medicine,

biology and the social sciences. From its origins in the nineteenth century until the second World War, it was as at home in France, England, Japan and the United States as it was in Germany.

The politicalization of scientific racism by the Nazis, and the shock of the full revelation at the end of the war of its consequences, were critical events in the history of twentieth century science, and led to an international effort to ground biocultural research on racial variation in more adequate scientific theory and a more humane ethic. UNESCO formed a committee of social scientists for this purpose in 1949. Ashley Montagu, an American anthropologist, wrote the first position paper made public in 1950. Then, a second committee was formed of biologists and anthropologists who worked with Ashley Montagu to revise the statement on race, and circulate it among other scientists for peer review so that a final version could be released in 1951 [12]. This effort to reach a scientific consensus that would turn away from the social ideology, garbled biology and typological thinking that had proven to be so disastrous, emphasized that the real units of human evolution are not racial types but local interbreeding populations. Variation within these populations is the key fact to be studied, not typological uniformity, since variation provides the stuff that allows processes of natural selection to operate.

The theory that guided the UNESCO statement on race is often referred to as 'the neo-Darwinian synthesis'. The rediscovery of Mendelian genetics at the beginning of this century seemed to many scientists to displace the theory of natural selection. The neo-Darwinian synthesis was mainly the work of geneticists and other biologists in Britain and America in the second quarter of this century who reformulated Darwinian thinking in the light of developing genetic knowledge and methods of research.

Soon after I returned to the university to start my education over again, first in its liberal arts college, and then in its graduate department of anthropology, Chicago hired Sherwood Washburn from the Columbia University medical school. He initiated and led a program that revolutionized biocultural anthropology in the United States. He called it "the new physical anthropology", and like the UNESCO statement on race, it was grounded in the neo-Darwinian synthesis. The old preoccupation with classification and anthropometry was shown to be a dead science that generated no useful hypothesis, a waste of time based on an inadequate grasp of functional anatomy, or downright foolish typological thinking that garbled evolutionary concepts.

Now here is the point, from Washburn's perspective, a good deal of what I had learned about human evolution and race was wrong. I had to unlearn some things that had been liberating at the time I chose between becoming a communist or an anthropologist.

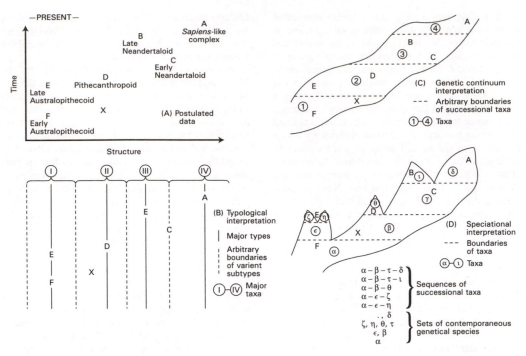

Figure 7   *Postulated data (simplified and generalized) and three possible taxonomic interpretations of known hominide [13]*

For example, Fay-Cooper Cole exphasized the importance of non-adaptive traits in racial variation, but Washburn taught on the contrary, that the adaptiveness of physical traits was the main issue in evolution, and to say that a trait was non-adaptive was either to say that it was unimportant, or that you were ignorant about its adaptive significance.

In challenging anthropologists to assimilate the advancing skills and problem solving theories of research that had created the neo-Darwinian synthesis, Washburn brought a new professionalism and rigor to the discipline. A major problem was to bring taxonomic order to the fossil record. For example, *Pithecanthropus erectus* and *Sinanthropus pekinensis* were assigned different generic and specific names by their discoverers, but in fact they belonged to a single species which is now called *Homo erectus*. Another problem was to clarify the theoretical grounds for different interpretations of the fossil record. Figure 7 [13] is from a symposium that Washburn organized for this purpose. The upper left chart represents the fossil data, and the one below it shows a typological interpretation that avoids inferences about genetic relationships. The phylogenetic charts on the right side of Fig. 7 should be compared to Figs 4 and 5 from Hooton's textbook, which made racial variations in modern populations the central fact of hominid evolution. The interpretation on the lower right of Fig. 7 makes speciation processes a prominent feature of Hominid

evolution, as did Hooton, but modern racial variations disappear entirely in it and in the chart on the upper right that emphasizes genetic continuity. The reason for this is that modern races are taxonomic subdivisions of *Homo sapiens sapiens*, and thus they evolved *after* the emergence of this species. With proper taxonomy and evolutionary reasoning they are not relevant to the evolution of earlier hominids.

The new physical anthropology shifted research after World War II from concern for racial variation to questions of functional anatomy and hominid adaptation. This required new research on primate ecology and behavior so that the distinctive features of hominid adaptations could be analyzed in the larger context of primate and other mammalian adaptive patterns. A burst of innovative work in primate ethology was particularly exciting in the 1950s and 60s, but *ad hoc* speculation about the adaptive significance of racial variation also fluorished in this period, and Washburn criticized it in his Presidential address to the American Anthropological Association.

When I was a student, there were naive racial interpretations based on the metrical data. When these became unacceptable politically the same people used naive constitutional correlations to reach the same conclusions of social importance. Today we have naive concepts of adaptation, taking the place of the earlier interpretations, and a recrudescence of the racial thinking [14].

Washburn addressed the topic of race because the Executive Board of the association requested that he do so. The civil rights movement was gathering force, and Carlton Coon, a renowned anthropologist at a leading American university, had just published a book that scandalized his colleagues when portions of the text were leaked before publication to opponents of civil rights legislation. They also considered Coon's theory of separate evolutionary development for different racial groups, which resembles Rushton's thinking, to be genetically improbable. Washburn asserted,

> There are no three primary races, no three major groups. The idea of three primary races stems from nineteenth-century typology ... If we look to real history we will always find more than three races, because there are more than three major areas in which the raciation of our species was taking place [14, p. 523].

He illustrated the nonsense of much speculation about racial adaptations by analyzing the claim that Mongoloids were an arctic-adapted race. Their short limbs, flat noses and stocky build were supposed to resemble the cold adaptations of some other arctic mammals, and their dark complexion was said to be an adaptation to intense arctic sunlight. Yet in Europe blond complexion and narrow noses were correlated with cold climate, and in Asia a great many Mongoloids have lived for millenia in hot, moist climates. With respect to noses, Washburn wrote

> Let us look at it differently. The nose is the center of a face. Most of a face is concerned with teeth, and bones, and muscles that have to do with chewing. The Mongoloid face is primarily the result of large masseter muscles and the bones from which these muscle arise (malar and gonial angles). This is a complex structural pattern related to the teeth, and a superficially very similar pattern may be seen in the Bushman, whose facial form can hardly be attributed to adaptation to cold [14, p, 525].

Washburn's point was that anthropologists had to learn functional anatomy if they wanted to reason about anatomical adaptations, and that they should not ignore data that did not support their reasoning.

The overall point of Washburn's Presidential Address was that race was of minor importance for understanding the great span of human evolution. It only concerned adaptations during the late Middle and Upper Paleolithic periods, after the emergence of *Homo sapiens sapiens*. Besides that

> The conditions under which the races evolved are mainly gone, and there are new causes for mutation, new kinds of selection, and vast migration. Today the numbers and distribution of the peoples of the world are due primarily to culture. Some people think the new conditions are so different that it is better no longer to

use the word race... but I personally think this confuses more than it clarifies [14, p. 527].

Despite Washburn's misgivings about biologists who wanted to abandon the concept of race, this is the direction that physical anthropology took in the following decades. The units of evolution were populations, not racial types. Thus, variations between populations were the objects of study, and the shift in thinking as the term 'population' displaced the term 'race' was fully in line with neo-Darwinian theory. A more radical shift focused research on the distribution of frequencies of separate genetic traits to reveal biological gradients, or clines. In this work race simply disappeared because the gradients for different traits did not correspond. Finally, advances in biochemistry led to the analysis of geographically localized genetic clusters of largely non-adaptive molecular traits, and this is the cutting edge of current work in what used to be called (and is still sometimes called) racial variation. The geneticist, Cavalli-Sforza, at Stanford University is a leader in this research, yet he and his colleagues reprimanded critics of one of their publications a few weeks ago by asserting, "We never spoke of 'races', a concept which, for humans, is devoid of a useful scientific definition" [15].

Littlefield *et al.* [16] analyzed American textbooks in physical anthropology published between 1932 and 1979 to document the potential demise of the race concept in this discipline. the whole system of higher education expanded rapidly after World War II. The eleven graduate programs in anthropology in 1950 had grown to eighty by 1975, and well over a thousand colleges and universities hired their first anthropologists in this period. The number of physical anthropologists was small, compared to those who specialized in social anthropology or archaeology, but as we joined the faculties of small liberal arts colleges (I was the first anthropologist in 1956 to join the Pomona College faculty in Claremont, California) we taught some biological anthropology along with our own specialties.

Nine textbooks were published in physical anthropology between 1932 and 1960, and three authors wrote six of them [15, p. 642]. One of these authors was Ashley Montagu, who wrote the UNESCO Statement on Race. He took the lead in arguing that biologists should abandon the race concept in dealing with human variation because the assumptions embedded in common social usage made it unsuitable for scientific discourse. He was joined by other leading physical anthropologists as the debate continued through the 1960s. Joseph Birdsell, for example, used a neo-Darwinian definition in the first edition of his textbook, saying that "A race is an interbreeding population whose gene pool is different from all other populations," but in a second edition he declared that "The use of the term race has been discontinued because it is scientifically undefinable and carries social implications that are harmful and disruptive" [16, p. 643].

The expansion of instruction led to the publication of 49 textbooks in physical anthropology between 1960 and 1979. Littlefield *et al.* document a change in the treatment of race as this occurred, and as the debate came to a head in the 1960s.

Of the books included in our study 20 were published between 1932 and 1969, and 13 of these expressed the prevailing outlook that races exist. Only 3 rejected the race concept; the race concept was not mentioned in 2, both published in the late 1960s, and in two cases the panel was unable to reach agreement on the text's classification.... The picture changes dramatically after 1970. Of the 38 texts published in the 1970s, only 12 supported the race concept while 14 opposed it .... This shift became especially pronounced in 1975–79, when the view that races do not exist was expressed in 10 textbooks and became the modal position, with only 5 texts arguing that races are "real" [16, p. 642].

With this background, you can see how shocking Rushton's essay would be to me personally, and as a professional anthropologist. It is doubly offensive because he is a knowledgeable man. He uses neo-Darwinian terminology in referring to r/K selection, and in using 'population' rather than 'race' in the title, 'Population differences in susceptibility to AIDS'. Rushton's sophistication is the reason that I call his work disingenuous and pseudoscientific, rather than simply erroneous. Let me explain.

Medical researchers in the United States have been astonished over the past two decades by the exposure of one case after another of fraud, plagerism and deceit at Harvard, Yale, Stanford, the Sloan Kettering Institute and other centers for scientific work [17]. Representative John Dingell is currently holding a series of Congressional hearings on scientific misconduct. These hearings have involved David Baltimore, a Nobel laureate at MIT, who published a paper with colleagues, one of whom is accused of contributing fraudulent work.

The scientific community is concerned about the potential threat of political interference if attempts are made to legislate processes of peer review and other aspects of scientific work. The Harvard biologist, Steven Jay Gould, has just published an editorial in the *New York Times* to refute the notion in these hearings that error in scientific work forms a continuum from relatively innocent sloppiness and fudging to more serious misconduct. On the contrary, Gould asserts, "Fraud and error are as different as arsenic and apple pie. The first is a pathology and a poison, the second an unavoidable consequence of any complex human activity" [18]. Congressman Dingell's legislative concern to regulate scientific work to reduce or eliminate error is wrongheaded, according to Gould, because such work involves theoretical controversies, disagreements about the facts, inevitable slips of reasoning and observation,

and these errors stimulate other scientists to correct them. In the spirit of Peter McEwan's reaction to objections to the publication of Rushton's article, Gould quotes Darwin's famous observation, "False views, if supported by some evidence, do little harm, for every one takes a salutary pleasure in proving their falseness" [18].

But criticizing errors in Rushton's essay afford no pleasure. Analyzing them is a chore that does not advance the scientific understanding of AIDS, or of racial variation and evolutionary theory. Refutation is a duty because in my opinion his essay is poison. The way that he compounds errors of fact and theory is not a sign of intellectual daring, bold new insights, original observations and new lines of thought. It is familiar racist thinking, a part of our popular culture, and as scientific as the astrological advice in our morning newspapers.

Why did Rushton's essay seem "respectable enough as science" and "reasonably argued" to Peter and the outside reviewers? Of course, I cannot answer for them, but I can guess. To be brief, I will number my speculations and not elaborate on them.

1. Almost all of the contributors to *Social Science & Medicine* are positivists. We like what we call hard data, and Rushton's article, with its maps, tables and charts, looked like the work of a positivist. Perhaps, also, its scientific vocabulary sounded persuasive. Someone who writes about r/K selection, and holds a Guggenheim fellowship, sounds like he knows what he is talking about. We social scientists like the sound and appearance of the natural sciences.

2. Rushton's paper may have appealed to the reviewers because it affirmed a commonsense way of thinking about race. Our popular culture convinces us that people come in types, and that the types correspond to larger groupings that we recognize by skin color, hair form and so forth. Newspapers and television, sociology and police reports sort people by these folkloric typologies. We understand them, and we experience the world this way. Many of us may not be able to tell one Chinaman from another, but we can readily tell a Chinaman from a Nigerian. Thus, Rushton's aggregation of hundreds of millions of people with very different cultures and physical characteristics into three races, and his allegation that these three types differ in characteristic ways in intelligence, growth pattern, sexuality and temperament exactly corresponds to our everyday interaction with each other. Our epidemiologists and social scientists regularly use these racial categories, so it may have been hard for those who reviewed Rushton's manuscript to see that this whole edifice is built on sand.

3. With Peter McEwan, we subscribe to liberal principles of discourse with multiple, conflicting

voices. Also, on the whole we trust each other. Our conflicted community is built on trust that peer review will be even-handed, that we will not violate confidentiality, and that we will study and write in an honest manner. When someone is a member of our community, it is very hard for us to think of his work as disingenuous. Perhaps elements in Rushton's essay seemed doubtful to Peter and the reviewers, but they thought that this was the apple pie of error that could be corrected by others in a fruitful scientific exchange. Thus, their good faith may have prevented them from seeing the reality that I have tried to expose. This is cruel work. We should not be too polite in getting it done. The issue is obvious to members of the scientific community when astrology is involved. If Rushton had submitted a paper on 'Astrological susceptability to AIDS'. Peter and the outside reviewers would have agreed that it was inappropriate for *Social Science & Medicine*. I doubt that Peter would have bothered to send it out for peer review. We no longer have the burden of refuting astrologers because we agree that their pretense to science is fraudulent. Clearly, the scientific tradition in which Rushton's article is written does not yet evoke this degree of consensus. We should all be disturbed and puzzled about why this is so.

Peer review is the most neglected topic in the sociology of science [19, 20], perhaps we feel a taboo against studying this aspect of our community because it is so important to our careers. Its anonymity allows scholars with little power to judge the work of those superior to them without fear of reprisal, but just this confidentiality invites abuse, and we often hear complaints of this nature. Public Citizen, Inc., a public interest law firm organized by Ralph Nader, is presently trying to persuade the National Science Foundation "to run its peer reviews a bit more like a judicial proceeding, with open files, an opportunity for applicants to rebut their critics, and a clear system of appeals" [21]. This legalistic transformation of a communal process that is supposed to run on good faith is likely to be resisted by the scientific community. My own experience editing the anthropology for *Social Science & Medicine*, and twenty books in the University of California Press series. *Comparative Studies of Health Systems and Medical Care*, has been that the vast majority of reviewers are conscientious and fair. The occasional biased review sticks out from other reviews of the same manuscript. The most common problem I have encountered is the reviewer who is too lenient on poorly written or inadequately argued work.

I have worked hard on occasion to see a book through review that had been rejected by another publisher. On occasion, a manuscript I asked the author to revise was published elsewhere without this additional work. Similarly, a journal editor once observed that *Social Science & Medicine* had published articles that he had rejected, and in the very next issue the lead article of his journal was one that I had rejected after it had been through peer review twice and twice rewritten. We are fortunate to have a number of journals and book publishers, a number of places where scholars can apply for research funding or fellowships or jobs, and that the peer review process works as well as it does to uphold standards of performance. But we really don't know very well how it works, and its failures are not well documented.

Finally, I cannot close this essay without thanking Peter McEwan for inviting me to work for his journal. I have always felt that its excellence was due to his intelligence and generosity. And I want to thank him and other members of the planning committee for inviting me to give this talk. I disappointed Peter, who did not think that the address was suitable for the occasion, but I tried to speak from an informed heart, and in the end that is the only worthwhile thing we can do.

Acknowledgements—Karen Rosenberg, Mary B. Williams, Matt Cartmill, Allan Young, Margaret Lock and Lee Mullett helped me with references and critical advice and moral support in writing this paper. I am grateful to them.

REFERENCES

1. Rushton J. P. and Bogaert A. F. Population differences in susceptibility to AIDS: an evolutionary analysis. *Soc. Sci Med.* **28**(12), 1211–1220, 1989.

2. Helwig D. Rushton opens wounds again. *The Globe and Mail* (Toronto, Canada) 13 May, 1989.

3. MacArthur R. H. and Wilson E. O. *The Theory of Island Biogeography*, p. ix. Princeton University Press, Princeton, NJ, 1967.

4. Lovejoy C. Owen, The origin of man. *Science* **211**(4480), 341–350, 23 Jan., 1981.

5. Johanson D. and Maitland E. *Lucy: The Beginnings of Humankind*. Simon & Schuster, New York, 1981.

6. Rushton J. P. Race differences in behaviour: a review and evolutionary analysis. *Person. Individ. Diff.* **9**(6), 1009–1024, 1988.

7. Bulmer M. G. *The Biology of Twinning in Man.* Clarendon Press, Oxford, 1970.

8. Hooton E. A. *Up From the Ape*, Revised Edition. Macmillan, New York, 1947.

9. Garn S. M. *Human Races*, 3rd edn. Thomas, Springfield, IL, 1971.

10. Proctor R. *Racial Hygiene: Medicine Under the Nazis.* Harvard University Press, Cambridge, MA, 1988.

11. Proctor R. From Anthropologie to Rassenkunde in the German anthropological tradition. In *Bones,*

Bodies, Behavior: Essays on Biological Anthropology (Edited by Stocking G. W.), pp. 138–179. University of Wisconsin Press, Madison, WI, 1988.

12. Haraway D. J. Remodelling the human way of life: Sherwood Washburn and the New Physical Anthropology, 1950–1980. In *Bones, Bodies, Behavior: Essays on Biological Anthropology* (Edited by Stocking G. W.), pp. 206–259. University of Wisconsin Press, Madison, WI, 1988.

13. Simpson G. G. The meaning of taxonomic statements. In *Classification and Human Evolution* (Edited by Washburn S.), Viking Fund Publications in Anthropology, No. 37, New York, 1963.

14. Washburn S. L. The study of race. *Am. Anthrop.* **65**, 521–531, 1963.

15. Cavalli-Sforza L. L., Piazza A., Menozzi P. and Mountain J. Genetic and linguistic evolution. *Science* **244**, 1128, 9 June, 1989.

16. Littlefield A., Lieberman L. and Reynolds L. T. Redefining race: the potential demise of a concept in physical anthropology. *Curr. Anthrop.* **23**(6), 641–655, 1982.

17. Broad W. and Wade N. *Betrayers of the Truth: Fraud and Deceit in the Halls of Science*. Simon & Schuster, New York, 1982.

18. Gould S. J. Judging the perils of official hostility to scientific error. *New York Times*, Section E, p. 6, 30 July, 1989.

19. Lock S. *A Difficult Balance: Editorial Peer Review in Medicine*. ISI Press, Philadelphia, PA, 1986.

20. Ciba Foundation Conference. *The Evaluation of Scientific Research*. Wiley, Chichester, 1989.

21. Marshall E. NSF peer review under fire from Nader Group. *Science* **245**, 250, 21 July, 1989.

Comments

J. PHILIPPE RUSHTON

In an autobiographical tone Leslie [1] describes the development of his opposition to the widespread judgement of the community in which he was raised that Negroids were, on averge, more criminal, less intelligent and more sexual than Caucasoids. His resistance was strengthened when he took courses first in Marxism and then in anthropology, and he eventually rejected the utility of the concept of race for science. Leslie is pessimistic about the possibility of objectivity in a field marred by political ideologies; to him, the "fakery and racism" of my paper is "transparent" and he cannot comprehend why the intuitive obviousness of this is not more widely shared. For Leslie, the study of human behaviour is as much a moral political enterprise as it is a scientific one; it "is meant to promote, pluralism and democracy".

AIDS and race: more information. Our 1989 paper [2] discussed the worldwide racial distribution of the 100,410 cases of AIDS that had been reported as of 1 July 1988 to the World Health Organization (WHO). By 1 April 1990 that figure had grown to 237,110 showing an 18 month doubling time and a crystallization of the racial pattern of the pandemic. New calculations show that black Caribbean countries have as big an AIDS problem as do African countries. When the figures are worked out on a per capita basis, the three most affected countries in the world are in the Caribbean—Bermuda, the Bahamas' and French Guiana. In this region AIDS is transmitted primarily through heterosexual intercourse and there is little intravenous drug use.

The data in Table 1 were collated by me from official statistics published by the World Health Organization as of 1 April 1990 (World Health Organization Update, Global Programme on AIDS). The number of AIDS cases per million population was computed to give an indication of the relative seriousness of the epidemic between countries with different sizes of populations after excluding countries reporting fewer than 100 cases. The population size of the country was taken from estimates standardized for mid-1987 by the United Nations using data available as of 1 April 1989 [3]. On this measure Canada has an AIDS rate of 139 per million making it the 25th most affected country in the world. Of the other top countries, 12 are in Africa, 9 are in the Caribbean, 2 are in Europe, and the other is the United States. It must be kept in mind that for every person officially diagnosed with the AIDS disease there are at least 25 others with the contagious HIV virus. Although the figures in Table 1 must be read with caution, especially those from countries with less than a million population, where a few cases can disproportionately affect the per capita total, nonetheless the racial pattern of the pandemic seems established. Indeed, given the underreporting from African and Caribbean countries, the figures in Table 1 must be considered conservative estimates.

Additional evidence for the racial pattern comes from finer grain analysis of the data from within the United States to 1 March 1990 (Centers for Disease Control, HIV/AIDS Surveillance, Report, March 1990) where Negroids are overrepresented in every

Table 1   *The 25 countries most affected by AIDS based on per capita cumulative cases reported to the World Health Organization as of 1 July 1990*

Country	Date of report	Cumulative number of cases	Population in millions (as of mid-1987)	Cases per million
1. Bermuda	31.12.89	135	0.056	2411
2. French Guiana	31.12.89	191	0.086	2221
3. Bahamas	31.12.89	437	0.240	1821
4. Congo	31.12.89	1940	1.837	1056
5. Malawi	08.01.90	7160	7.499	955
6. Uganda	31.12.89	12,444	16.599	750
7. Burundi	31.12.89	2784	5.001	557
8. U.S.A.	31.06.90	133,889	243.934	549
9. Guadeloupe	31.12.89	182	0.337	540
10. Barbados	31.03.90	122	0.254	480
11. Trinidad	31.12.89	567	1.241	449
12. Haiti	30.09.89	2331	5.438	429
13. Zambia	07.05.90	3000	7.563	397
14. Martinique	31.03.90	125	0.334	374
15. Zaire	31.01.90	11,732	32.461	361
16. Rwanda	31.12.89	2285	6.529	350
17. Cote D'Ivoire	01.02.90	3647	11.142	327
18. Zimbabwe	31.03.90	2357	8.640	273
19. Tanzania	01.03.90	6251	23.217	269
20. Kenya	30.06.89	6004	22.936	262
21. Central African Republic	31.12.88	662	2.703	245
22. Switzerland	30.04.90	1280	6.545	196
23. Dominican Republic	31.03.90	1262	6.716	188
24. France	31.03.90	9718	55.632	175
25. Canada	03.05.90	3818	25.652	119

exposure category. If the U.S.A. were racially divided into separate countries, the approx. 30 million Afro-Americans (12% of total) with 34,431 cases of AIDS would have a rate of 1148 per million, equivalent to other Negroid populations in Africa and the Caribbean.

One point often made is that blacks in the United States have AIDS primarily because of intravenous drug use. Although 39–46% of adult American blacks who acquired AIDS did so through drug use, between 48 and 55% acquired it through sexual transmission, 11% heterosexually (compared to 2% of whites). Of all 6027 adult AIDS cases transmitted heterosexually (5% of total), 3747 or 62% involved blacks, with another 17% being Hispanic. Hispanics, of course, are a linguistic group; racially, a proportion is black or partly black, especially in New York. Blacks are also overrepresented in the 'male homosexual/bisexual contact' exposure category (17% versus a population expectation of 12%). Overall, in the last two years, blacks in the United States increased their total share of the AIDS figures from 26 to 27.6%, Hispanics increased from 14 to 15.6%, Mongoloids stayed in at less than 1%, and whites decreased from 59 to

56%. It would have been instructive to compare these figures with those in Canada but the Federal Centre in Ottawa does not break down the figures by race. The prediction is that if they did, as in other multi-racial societies, the pattern would be Orientals < whites < blacks.

In Canada, some reports do not indicate that blacks are disproportionately more infected with HIV, but this is so controversial that authorities are apparently afraid to record the race of AIDS victims. Stories in *The Globe and Mail* (1 July, 1989; 23 December, 1989) showed that by the beginning of May 1989, 116 of the 40,000 people in Quebec who had been born in Haiti had come down with the disease, an incidence of 2900 per million, higher than any country's official report to WHO (Table 1). Of the heterosexuals in Quebec who had contracted the disease, 25 (58%) did so by having sex with a person from Haiti. Similar figures are emerging in the Province of Ontario: A story in *The Toronto Star* (26 July, 1989) indicated that the number of black people in Toronto with AIDS had grown in the previous three months from 39 to 54—an increase of 38%. Of these 54 black people, 12 (22%) were women. Because only 49 of 1102 white HIV carriers were women (4%) the figures suggested that in Canada, as elsewhere, AIDS among blacks is being spread heterosexually.

Racial and political sensitivities, in part, also fuel reluctance to openly discuss matters elsewhere in the world. African countries report only a small proportion of their cases, partly out of concern that the West will perceive Africans as promiscuous [4]. In Durban, South Africa, following the recognition of black STD clinic attendees as being at risk for HIV infection, testing was suspended by the city's health department; the racial disparities also being clear from blood donor data [5]. Cuba claims a much lower rate of AIDS than elsewhere in the intensely affected Caribbean despite (a) the perceived necessity for universal testing and quarantine, (b) the hundreds of thousands of military personnel who have rotated to duty in Central Africa with concomitant increments of syphilis and gonorrhea, and (c) the studies of refugees in the U.S. showing high infection rates as early as 1980 [6].

Following my work with Bogaert on race differences in sexual behaviour [7, 8], some critics have argued [9] that little evidence exists that the races differ in sexual activities because of biases in the data and because the data are not based on random samples. It may come as a surprise to learn that we don't need random samples and that, in fact, very few hypotheses are tested this way: we often need only to hold the setting constant and select from groups not too extreme on the distributions. Following this procedure, I have conducted several as yet unpublished interview studies with young Mongoloids, Caucasoids and Negroids in cities from Canada and the United States, asking questions about their age of first sexual intercourse and the total number of their sexual partners. I have consistently found that the *average* black person reports having an earlier age of first intercourse and more sexual partners than does the *average* white person who reports having an earlier age of first intercourse and more sexual partners than does the *average* Oriental person. I stress the word average since there is much variation in each group. These results thus join those already published [7, 8, 10–12] showing that the racial differences in sexuality are widespread and relatively easy to determine.

The Reality of Race

Although the topic of race differences abounds with ideological minefields, it is possible to rise above them. Imagine that a team of extra-terrestrial biologists arrived on earth to study humans. Would they not quickly observe that, like many other species, humans showed considerable geographical variation in morphology? Surely three major geographical populations or 'races' would be identified immediately and investigation mounted into how many others existed. Questions about the origin of

the body types would be asked and also whether they covaried with life history variables including reproductive tactics in particular. If these scientists had a solid understanding of evolutionary biology, they would also investigate if these populations differed behaviourally, for example with respect to parental investment and social organization and, if they did, how these differences might have evolved. Such an approach has proved very fruitful for population biologists studying other animals, particularly since E. O. Wilson's [13] synthesis of sociobiology. If we are as interested in gaining knowledge as would be these 'extra-terrestrials', then we should apply similar procedures to our study of *Homo sapiens*.

The existence of genetic variation both within and between populations is, in fact, the first postulate of Darwinian theory. Without variation, natural selection would have nothing to work on. (The second postulate of evolutionary theory is that some parts of the variation are more successful at replication than are others.) Thus, from a sociobiological point of view, it is predictable that separate breeding populations will come to differ, genetically, in the mechanisms underlying their behaviour. This is because populations adapt to their environments behaviourally, as well as morphologically [13].

Behavioural, physiological and anatomical differences among the races follow a remarkable pattern [14, 15], a summary of which was presented as Table 3 by Rushton and Bogaert [2] and repeated as Table 2 by Leslie [1]. The observation that on over 60 different variables including brain size and intelligence, rate of maturation, sexuality, personality and social organization, Caucasoids average consistently *between* Mongoloids and Negroids, offers an array of theoretical and empirical problems for analysis.

The predictive nature of race undermines Leslie's argument that racial terminology is poorly justified. Similarly devalued must also be the judgement of influential anthropologist Ashley Montagu [16] who, as Leslie documents, successfully advocated the substitution of the phrase "ethnic group" for "race" in order to shift the emphasis away from a "question begging ... biologistic bias" (p. 697).

The scientific devaluation of the Leslie–Montagu position must occur because it obfuscates higher level conceptual order. For example, the rate of dizygotic twinning per 1000 births among Mongoloids is < 4, among Caucasoids, 8, and among Negroids, > 16, regardless of which country the samples are taken from, with some African populations having twinning rates as high as 57 per 1000 [17, 18]. The incidence of non-monozygotic triplets and quadruplets shows comparable rank orders [17, 18]. The tendency to multiple ovulation is inherited largely through the race of the mother, independently of the race of the father, as observed in Mongoloid–Caucasoid crosses in Hawaii and Caucasoid–Negroid crosses in Brazil [17]. It is misleading of Leslie to suggest that Bulmer's [17] data on racial group differences in twinning are unreliable; many additional surveys on multiple birthing support this epidemiological pattern [18–20] as well as the relation of multiple birthing to r/K reproductive strategies [21]. Perhaps as a result of matching evolutionary processes to ovarian production, parallel differences in testes size have been found among the races. The difference is twofold lower in Mongoloids than in Caucasoids (9g vs 21g), too large a dissimilarity to be accounted for in terms of body size [22, 23]. Although the data are much less conclusive, larger testes have sometimes been found in Negroids than Caucasoids [22, 24].

The efficient unit of analysis, therefore, is the higher order concept of race, within which cluster the different ethnic groups and, ultimately, individuals. Leslie's claim that the concept of race is not useful for human populations not only obscures higher level conceptual order and ignores the approach of population biologists studying other species but also neglects recent developments in the field of medicine and social science. Biomedical-anthropology is a new discipline to study race × diet interactions. For example, the ability of adults to easily digest milk is largely limited to Caucasoids and a lack of knowledge here may have increased mortality among the needy in Third World countries who were inadvertently provided with milk products to alleviate hunger. Other researchers are considering whether there are racial differences in susceptibility to drug addiction; for example, some 80% of Mongoloids become flushed when given alcohol.

The Origin of Human Races

The behavioural and morphological data—in which Caucasoids consistently average *between* Negroids and Mongoloids—can be used to help decide between the various reconstructions of human evolution which Leslie finds so problematic. Current thinking, especially among those physical anthropologists who use molecular biology (blood group, serum protein, mtDNA and nuclear DNA) to buttress the more usual data from paleontology, involves a single origin model for the emergence of modern humans instead of the alternative multiregional models. An African origin is envisaged, perhaps even as recently as 140,000 to 290,000 years ago, with an African–non African split 110,000 ± 34,000 years ago, and a European–Asian split 41,000 ± 15,000 years ago [25–27]. Thus the sequence in which the races emerged in earth history matches the phased linearity of the suite of r/K characters. This parallel is not readily predictable from multiregional origin models based on long periods of separation, in which no consistent pattern of character appearance is expected.

The genetic evidence in favour of the single origin model is that (a) rates of change in mtDNA place the modern human origin at 140,000 to 290,000 years ago; (b) genetic variation is greatest within African populations, which is predictable if they appeared earliest; (c) protein analyses date a Negroid–non Negroid split at 110,000 ± 34,000 years ago and a Caucasoid–Mongoloid split at 41,000 ± 15,000 years ago; (d) blood group data indicate that Caucasoids are intermediate to Negroids and Mongoloids in genetic distance; (e) genetic variation between human populations is low in comparison with variation within populations or with that found in other hominoids thus suggesting a short time period of geographical differentiation [25]. Paleontological data are consistent with the foregoing because the oldest human fossils (92,000 years) have been found in Africa and/or the Middle East, which is the likely pathway from Africa into Eurasia [26].

But why would Mongoloids have ended up the most K-selected? As populations moved north they encountered more predictable and yet more challenging environments, including the ice ages which ended only about 10,000 years ago. Predictable environments are one ecological precondition for K-selection. Tropical savannahs, due to sudden droughts and devastating viral, bacterial and parasitic epidemics, are generally less predictable for long lived species than are temperate and Arctic conditions. Although the Arctic climate varies greatly over one year, it is highly stable among years. The harsher yet more predictable the environment the more stringent would have been the selection pressures for intelligence, forward planning and sexual and personal restraint.

Conclusion

Many of the differences between the races summarized in Leslie's Table 2 appear to confirm the averaged perceptions of the community of Leslie's youth. Although many have striven to dismiss all these as 'stereotypes', the psychometric evidence shows that when human judgements are aggregated and calibrated against other criteria, they are typically found to be valid. This appears to be as true of judging intelligence and social behaviour, where converging evidence can be marshalled to assess 'construct validity', as it is of judging temperature and weights where objective standards can be applied [28]. As a starting point for scholarly discourse, the statistically significant average differences between the races in AIDS, as well as other traits of longer standing, must be acknowledged to exist, even when their interpretation is problematic.

If observed racial differences in crime, educational achievement and sexual behaviour are hypothesized to be due entirely to environmental differences such as "the consequences of living in a racist society", objections are seldom made. If evolutionary and genetic hypotheses are suggested, then *ad hominem* attacks follow almost inevitably. Thus it is not the *data* that are controversial but rather their explanation. The only way to minimize ideological bias is to scrutinize the goodness of fit between data and theory. Which of the alternative theories, then, is more powerful and best fits the total array of assembled data?

REFERENCES

1. Leslie C. Scientific racism: reflections on peer review, science and ideology. *Soc. Sci. Med.* **31**, 891–905, 1990.
2. Rushton J. P. and Bogaert A. F. Population differences in susceptility to AIDS: an evolutionary analysis. *Soc. Sci. Med.* **28**, 1211–1220, 1989.
3. United Nations. *Population and Vital Statistics Report.* United Nations, New York, 1989.
4. Kingma S. AIDS brings health into focus. *New Scient.* **119**, 37–42, 1989.
5. O'Farrell N. AIDS and academic boycotts. *Lancet* **1989-II**, 386, 1989.
6. Anderson W. H. AIDS in Cuba. *Lancet* **1989-II**, 512, 1989.
7. Rushton J. P. and Bogaert A. F. Race differences in sexual behavior: testing an evolutionary hypothesis. *J. Res. Personal.* 21, 521–551, 1987.
8. Rushton J. P. and Bogaert A. F. Race versus social class differences in sexual behavior: a follow up test of the *r/K* dimension. *J. Res. Personal.* **22**, 259–272, 1988.
9. Lynn M. Criticisms of an evolutionary hypothesis about race differences: a rebuttal to Rushton's reply. *J. Res. Personal.* **23**, 21–34, 1989.
10. Weinberg M. S. and Williams C. J. Black sexuality: a test of two theories. *J. Sex Res.* **25**, 197–218, 1988.
11. Hofmann A. Contraception in adolescence: a review. I. Psychosocial aspects. *Bull. Wld Hlth Org.* 63, 151–162, 1984.
12. Konings E., Anderson R. M., Morley D., O'Riordan T. and Meegan M. Rates of sexual partner change among two pastoralist southern Nilotic groups in east Africa. *AIDS* 3, 245–247, 1989.
13. Wilson E. O. *Sociobiology: The New Synthesis.* Harvard University Press, Cambridge, MA, 1975.
14. Rushton J. P. Race differences in behaviour: a review and evolutionary analysis. *Personal. Individ. Diff.* **9**, 1009–1024, 1988.
15. Rushton J. P. The reality of racial differences: a rejoinder with new evidence. *Personal. Individ. Diff.* **9**, 1035–1040, 1988.
16. Montagu M. F. A. *An Introduction to Physical Anthropology*, 3rd edn. Thomas, Springfield, IL, 1960.
17. Bulmer M. G. *The Biology of Twinning in Man.* Clarendon Press, Oxford, 1970.
18. Nylander P. P. S. Frequency of multiple births. In *Human Multiple Reproduction* (Edited by MacGillivray I., Nylander P. P. S. and Corney G.). Saunders, Philadelphia, PA, 1975.
19. Allen G. The non-decline in U.S. twin birth rates, 1964–1983. *Acta genet. med. gemell.* **36**, 313–323, 1987.
20. Allen G. Frequency of triplets and triplet zygosity types among U.S. births, 1964. *Acta genet. med. gemell.* **37**, 299–306, 1988.
21. Rushton J. P. Toward a theory of human multiple birthing: sociobiology and *r/K* reproductive strategies. *Acta genet. med. gemell.* **36**, 289–296, 1987.
22. Short R. V. Sexual selection and its component parts, somatic and genital selection, as illustrated by man and the great apes. In *Advances in the Study of Behavior* (Edited by Rosenblatt J. S., Hinde R. A., Beer C. and Busnell M.-C.), Vol. 9, pp. 131–158. Academic Press, New York, 1979.
23. Harvey P. H. and May R. M. Out for the sperm count. *Nature* **337**, 508–509, 1989.
24. Ajmani M. L., Jain S. P. and Saxena S. K. Anthropometric study of male extended genitalia of 320 healthy Nigerian adults. *Anthropol. Anzeiger* **43**, 179–186, 1985.
25. Stringer C. B. and Andrews P. Genetic and fossil evidence for the origin of modern humans. *Science* **239**, 1263–1268, 1988.
26. Simons E. L. Human origins. *Science* **245**, 1343–1350, 1989.
27. Cavalli-Sforza L. L., Piazza A., Menozzi P. and Mountain J. Reconstruction of human evolution: bringing together genetic, archaeological and linguistic data. *Proc. Natl. Acad. Sci. U.S.A.* **85**, 6002–6006, 1988.
28. Rushton J. P., Brainerd C. J. and Pressley M. Behavioral development and construct validity: the principle of aggregation. *Psychol. Bull.* **94**, 18–38, 1983.

C. OWEN LOVEJOY

In order to 'enter the scientific arena', a manuscript should clearly demonstrate that its subject is important and relevant to the journal's audience, the data accurate, the methods appropriate, the exposition clear, and the logic and reasoning sound. In an ideal world, reviewers acting on behalf of a scientific journal would measure each submission solely on the basis of these criteria, and our research publications would consistently be filled with good science. Unfortunately, reviewers can sometimes be careless, politically motivated, and cavalier. As a consequence, submissions which lack at least one of the above criteria are often accepted for publication.

As Professor Leslie notes, one area in which the review process is often deficient is its critical response to style and form. He points out that substandard ideas often receive unwarranted attention simply because they have been cloaked in the language of science; creationists, among others, succeed in impressing the naive by adopting 'a scientific vocabulary to translate their cosmology'. We are all familiar with this special language, because we are all forced to use it; not to do so would place us in jeopardy with reviewers. This special language can take the ordinary and make it appear profound. Most of us are familiar with 'translation' sheets periodically devised by students who have 'discovered' the language and, even though they are about to adopt it (their dissertations would be in peril if they did not), nevertheless take great satisfaction in pointing out its excessive pomposity: for 'the solute was hydrated and vigorously agitated' read 'I put the stuff in water and shook it'. There are some legitimate reasons for using a more formal scientific language. It is less ambiguous than ordinary language. It is free of idiomatic reference and therefore more universally understood (scientific French is easier to read than common French). But it is also a two-edged sword. How often has mediocre science been allowed to parade as cogent analysis simply because it has been cloaked in scientific parlance?

The manuscript by Rushton and Bogaert was written in the dialect of evolutionary biology. *When translated into common parlance, however, it is virtual nonsense*. Its reviewers were either unfamiliar with the language in which this nonsense was versed, or were overly impressed by it. The *science* being proffered in the Rushton and Bogaert paper, however, as Professor Leslie has elegantly established, is utterly transparent. Let us suppose, for a moment, that they were to submit a similar paper to a journal of mammalian behavior not on human behavior, but that of yellow marmots. Would they be allowed merely to state that "aggressiveness" could be classified in categories of "low, medium, and high" without definition of the specific behavioral criteria on which it was judged? Would they be allowed to lump all secondary sex characters and report them as "small, medium, or large", without accompanying explanation? Would they be allowed to use age-at-death, or age at first intercourse, as measures of *maturation rate* when a host of more direct and vastly more appropriate indices are available? In Table 3 of the Rushton and Bogaert paper "life span" is listed as "long" for "Mongoloids", "medium" for "Caucasoids", and "short" for "Negroids". What reviewer could be so unaware of even the most basic rudiments of environmental determination of human demographic response not to be in awe of such biological naivete? Did no one read this table? It is a hodgepodge of species characters and behaviors which are obviously learned, with levels of generalization too gross to even be

considered ordinal in most cases! Did no social scientist read this paper? We are told that Chinese and Japanese inexperience with "premarital sex" and their lack of permissiveness and concern with sexual display are heritable; that 52% of British female university students "think about sex everyday", but only "1% of Japanese female students did so". These examples are from a subsection of the paper which attempts to establish that they (and a host of other equally ludicrous examples) are manifestations of *genotypic variation* in reproductive strategy! I am particularly interested in Rushton and Bogaert's (presumably) polygenic models for the inheritance of "social organizational complexity", and their projections as to the prospect of identifying which chromosome bears the loci which lead to "decentralized organizations with weak power structures". Perhaps these are pleiotropic characters of a single dominant gene? Those of us interested in social insects look forward with anticipation to their further clarification of these models.

It would seem that in recent years we have become progressively more accepting of mediocre analyses and substandard ideas simply because they are written in the increasingly complex dialects of science. It seems to me that publication of the Rushton and Bogaert manuscript is as much a reflection of this general reduction in standards as it is a failure of the review process to prevent publication of racist views. When the editorial process fails to systematically reject poor quality science, racist tracts are more likely to pass through such porous filters. As McEwan points out, this is but one of a series of Rushton manuscripts.

With the proliferation of scientific jargon comes an ever increasing need for reviewers who are familiar with that jargon. Otherwise it will become increasingly easy to use it as a means to successfully publish in journals whose primary audience is unfamiliar with it. I could suggest the analogy that we do not publish papers by Russian authors merely because they are written in Russian, and we therefore cannot expect effective reviews of Russian manuscripts by those who do not read the language. This analogy, however, is inappropriate: Russian language journals are intended for Russian scholars—non-Russian speakers are not expected to profit from them. If the use of dialect and jargon is sufficient to mask the fundamental science of a manuscript, then the manuscript must be rejected *on those grounds alone*. Good quality science can be made understandable to a wide audience, just as poor quality science can be hidden from that same audience.

McEwan tells us that "critics should address the substance of the [Rushton and Bogaert] paper rather than its publication". Yet it contains no objective measures of behavior, nor evidence of inheritance pattern, nor reliable indices of supposed evolutionary correlates. The paper is simply a compendium of 'bald assertions' which should have been rejected by its reviewers. Otherwise such papers become the focal point of spiraling assertions and counter-assertions. Not even the 'softest' science, i.e. one whose data are derived principally from the reports of trained observers, can survive such editorial laxity. In short, if reviewers consistently employed the same standards that allowed publication of the Rushton and Bogaert paper, the effects on virtually all branches of biosocial science, whether sociology or mammalian behavior, would be devastating.

Poor science is becoming increasingly prevalent precisely because the review process is increasingly ineffective. If we do not reject papers whose underlying deductive and/or inductive processes are transparently artless and naive, then we must expect to see more Rushton-styled analyses in our journals. It is not just scientific racism that must be weeded out by the reviewers, but shoddy science. Let me close with an example. In the *most recent issue* of an anthropology journal one can find the following equation for human cranial capacity:

$$cm^3 = 1{,}274 - 10.9 \text{ (gathering)} + 2.4 \text{ (latitude)}$$

along with a description of its potential use:

… This equation indicates that each 10% of subsistence coming from gathering reduces cranial capacity by 10.9 cm^3. Each degree of latitude increases the cranial capacity by 2.4 cm^3.

If we admit this quality of analysis to our major journals, can we not expect transparent racism to be far behind?

GLENN D. WILSON

There may be many criticisms to be made of Rushton's paper but it surely merits a more reasoned and less personal attack than that of Leslie. His emotional tirade, although motivated by humanitarian considerations with which I have much sympathy, does disserve to the advancement of social science.

Leslie's essay is so rambling that it is difficult to know what he is trying to say or what he believes to be the truth. There are also striking logical lapses: for example, he questions the brain size data by pointing out that larger brains usually go with larger bodies, apparently failing to appreciate that this reinforces Rushton's argument, since Mongoloids (who have the biggest brains) have smaller bodies than Negroids (with the smallest brains).

The idea that humans have large, prominent genitalia in order to promote pair bonds he attributes to a 1981 paper by Lovejoy. This makes me wonder where he was in 1967 when Desmond Morris wrote *The Naked Ape*. Anyway, the trouble with this idea is that humans are not characteristically pair-bonding animals. Gibbons and marmosets may be, but real pair-bonding is seen mostly in birds. Generally speaking, humans mix the promiscuity of chimpanzees with the harem-building of gorillas and the rapist tactics of orangutans (not surprisingly, our nearest relatives). The idea that humans are at the apex of an evolutionary development towards monogamy is a fantasy deriving more from moral hopes than behavioural observation. Scientists should be concerned with what *is*, not what they *would like* to be.

But herein lies the real problem with Leslie's article. He seems to argue that social science can never be value free and therefore we should abandon attempts to make it so. Since this is his own position, he then projects the same attitude onto Rushton and presumes that he is engaged in deliberate mischief-making. I suspect the accusations of 'fraud' are probably actionable but that is Rushton's business.

Another thing that Leslie seems to be saying (insofar as anything he says is clear) is that race does not exist. In reply to this I will adopt his anecdotal approach and tell a story of my own. When I first taught at a California University I had to subject myself to finger-printing and answer many questions that I considered impertinent, including 'what is your religion?' and 'what is your race?'. Finding this slightly offensive, I answered 'none' to both questions, whereupon the Mexican girl behind the desk scratched out my second answer and wrote 'Caucasian'.

My question to Leslie is this: how did she know I was Caucasian if race does not exist, and how are government agencies able to use it as a basis for affirmative action?

The fact that any categorization is arbitrary at its borders does not negate its descriptive usefulness. People vary continuously on many traits, but psychologists still find it useful to compare groups of, say, typical extraverts and introverts. (My resistance to the Californian exercise was based on what I perceived as a political rather than scientific motive for making racial categorizations.) And if there are group differences, shouldn't we be able to study them scientifically even if the results concur with unflattering stereotypes. Evil-intentioned people might quote these results for their own purposes but ignorance of the truth will not rid the world of evil people.

PETER J. M. McEWAN

Any hypothesis which seeks to relate racial and sexual variables is certain to arouse the most profound reactions. Its examination is likely to test to the limit, if not beyond, the individual human capacity to exercise objective judgement. For this reason it is imperative that debate be addressed dispassionately in a manner appropriate to a genuine search toward truth rather than demagogically as in some political debate.

The Rushton paper demanded a cool, reasoned rebuttal. Unhappily, when the rejoinder came it was in the form of an Address to an international meeting which had a quite different agenda, and it was couched in language and presented in the kind of inflammatory manner that the subject, being so susceptible to excite, needed so much to avoid.

Leslie's response raises a number of important, separate but related issues which need to be unravelled. The first is the substantive question: is the Rushton hypothesis viable? There is no doubt that the dialect of evolutionary biology used in the original paper has been widely discredited and that some of the behavioural variables quoted by Rushton are highly suspect. It is understandable that these flaws should be scornfully rejected by his critics. But questions remain. To reinforce criticism alternative explanations for apparently legitimate variations should be provided. Why is it, to take an example from the physical domain, that there appears to be variation in gamete production, and, to take a behavioural example, variation in patterns of premarital coitus? How should it be that variations in cranial capacity and brain weight have been recorded and that there is evidence for gross variation in sexual activity? It is not enough to cry wolf. Can variations such as these be explained away as artefacts of faulty methodology? If so, the faults should be explicated and thus laid to rest. Variations that appear valid should be recognised and where appropriate replicated or confirmed.

The whole concept of race needs more careful and close analysis. Is it so objectively dubious a construct in human affairs as never to be used? If not, in what areas of for example epidemiology or social science is it a relevant or useful explanatory variable? How should it be defined? Such questions are at the heart of the Rushton–Leslie divide yet one noted scholar invited to comment told me he found "each deserving of severe criticism … Rushton is without rigour … Leslie's criticism is clearly 'over the top' and seems also to be totally misdirected". That such observations are possible demonstrates the need for more dispassionate

enquiry and debate which can only illuminate, but censorship distinguish.

It may be that whatever physical or behavioural variations can be confirmed are as irrelevant to epidemiological or psycho-social understanding as skin colour. But the argument needs to be stated and defended, not assumed as a holy tenet which it is scientific heresy to question. Alternative explanations will then be advanced to account for whatever variations may remain. As matters stand, there is a danger that certain branches of science, by fearing to enter the arena, fail to meet their obligation.

I have a more general concern. The social sciences are often by necessity inexact. Complex relationships can be considered in a *confirmatory* mode of enquiry or in an *inquisitive* mode. The former selects data and arbitrary interpretations in order to confirm an *a priori* view of the world. The latter postpones interpretation and is reluctant to ascribe causal relationships without the most undeniable evidence. One guides the data to confirm the conclusion, the other permits the conclusion to be guided by the data. One presents itself more definitely, more stridently, the other can be hesitant, conditional, tentative. But this is not all. The confirmatory mode is generally permeated by a moral, political or religious stance, and is thereby deeply emotive, the other is motivated by a spirit of genuine enquiry. One is manipulative, using enquiry to bolster its own presuppositions and employing every gambit to gain acceptance, the other may at times appear ideologically barren, preferring only the gentler voice of reason. Most of us have had experience of both modes of approach and the depth of passion and power play that can erupt when the confirmatory line is even questioned.

The second issue implicit in Leslie's paper raises the question of censorship in general and whether, in this particular case, publication was justified. There is the closely related matter of the use of the emotive term 'racism'.

In a recent balanced and telling critique of Rushton's general position, James Flynn has written "As the Canadian media over the last few months amply demonstrate, Rushton has been the target of much abuse and labelled a racist. There is a real danger that his future work will not get a hearing, thanks to outlets being intimidated by the fear of unwelcome press scrutiny. This is wrong in itself and it is worth remarking that the truth can never be racist, nor can telling the truth as you see it, assuming there is no evidence of wilful neglect of evidence, an accusation Rushton need not fear. Suppressing Rushton's views also means that those who believe they can make a reasoned case against him are silenced, for lack of dialogue, which is to say everyone is the loser" [1].

I believe a journal has a duty never to allow preconception or prejudice to influence publication. In the long term, truth is unassailable and what is false will be condemned. Condemned not by derision, not by censorship, but by reason.

If courage and intellectual integrity are needed to examine certain aspects of the world that we desperately hope are not as they might at first appear then the requisite courage and integrity must be forthcoming.

Racism is by definition prejudiced; the only way to decide whether an hypothesis is or is not racist is to give it the opportunity to present itself so that it can be openly examined. Only then, if it is universally rejected, should it and its proponents be labelled racist. It was, after all, social science that first drew attention to the blind captivating power of labelling.

The question of peer review is raised. After twenty-five years of observing the process in operation I have come to the conclusion that, like democracy, it may not always be effective in achieving its ends but it is the best method available. It would help to balance its most serious blunders if journals, especially those like *Social Science & Medicine* that deal with different disciplines and subjects, published more commentaries immediately following contentious material. The difficulty is the purely practical one of obtaining a fair representation of different perspectives in reasonable time. In the present case, for example, several leading scholars declined (for contrasting reasons) to comment and it has taken several months to assemble the comments that now appear.

However, there is to my mind, a far more serious threat to standards than the occasional lapse of peer review. This is the unceasing proliferation in the number of journals, increasing at the rate of more than one a day. There is less and less time to review, more and more chance to publish; less and less time to read, more and more material needing to be read. The grave responsibility of those launching new journals should be as carefully measured as should the judgement of librarians forced to select from an ever widening choice out of a steadily contracting budget. It is the kind of real world dilemma that some

of our more inward-looking colleagues tend to overlook, but it is one that requires urgent reappraisal.

My last point is that, as my old friend and editorial colleague Charles Leslie knows, I regarded his choice of subject for an invited opening Address at an international conference with a prepared agenda as inappropriate and mischievous. It was inappropriate for a number of reasons: it did not bear upon any conference theme; at the time only a very few of the audience would have seen the Rushton paper; it raised questions of peer review which were not directly the concern of an international audience gathered to consider some of the most important topical problems affecting the social sciences and their relation to medicine and medical care; no-one present could have been expected to harbour any racial prejudice; it was designed for the hustings and to pre-empt conference discussion away from all designated themes. It was a privileged occasion, with publication provisionally guaranteed (without peer review!). But, most important, in so far as it concerned the problem of AIDS, it deflected attention away from such pressing global issues as raised, for example, by the influential views of Mr Abdullah al-Mashad, head of Egypt's Fatwa Committee, as quoted in the *London Times* shortly before the meeting opened: "We must purge society of the Aids patient and those like him, because his existence causes public harm". According to the report, Mr Mashwad then "suggested starvation and denial of medicine as the means of killing the patients. (He) added that pregnant women with Aids must have abortions even if the foetus was more than four months old" [2].

In short, I found it profoundly disappointing that such a strong and deserving case, and one that needed to be presented in the same dispassionate style as its adversary, was handled in such an unfortunate manner.

REFERENCES

1. Flynn J. R. The psychologist. *Bull. Br. Psychol. Soc.* 9, 363, 1989.
2. *London Times* 4 July, 1989.

Rejoinder

CHARLES LESLIE

The comments on my essay speak for themselves in a manner that will not be misunderstood by most readers, and I hope that what I have written is equally clear. For example, I do not myself deny the reality of racial variation, but simply give a narrative account of changes in the ways variations between and within populations are analyzed by human biologists. In fact, I welcome and enjoy racial variations, along with cultural and individual variations, but with a profound sadness that Peter McEwan, despite my efforts, is not persuaded that Rushton's work is a corruption of science. Opinions vary, and his is that my address is written in an inflammatory manner, while Rushton's essay is a genuine scientific effort. He quotes an unnamed scholar as saying that my essay is "totally misdirected", yet he judges Rushton's work to deserve "dispassionate enquiry". Readers will realize that an essential part of my argument is that scientific work requires passion. Particularly in the social sciences we must examine what we are passionate about, and how our passions influence our work.

26

There's More to Racism Than Black and White

ELIZABETH MARTINEZ

In this article the author reminds the reader that racial relations and racism in the United States is not simply an issue of black and white. There are other racial and ethnic groups in this society that are not of European descent and have experienced racial and ethnic discrimination. Although this is not a new development in the history of the United States, it has been generally overlooked by scholars and others concerned with race issues. In fact, this country has been racially and ethnically polyglot from its very beginning. Greater attention is being paid to racism and how it impacts groups other than Blacks or African-Americans due, in part, to the changing demography of the nation, where communities of color are increasing rapidly *vis-à-vis* whites. Martinez focuses on some Chicano experiences to illustrate another facet of racism, but her exposure of this issue is relevant for other communities of color, as well.

The small brown woman with a serious face stood on the curb almost motionless as thousands of people marched by her in a line that stretched 22 blocks. Amidst huge banners and hundreds of big colorful signs, her hand-lettered words on corrugated paper had a haunting simplicity:

> We were here
> We are here
> This was our land
> is still our land
> Stand up for your rights.

It was August 25, 1990, in Los Angeles and people—mostly Mexican American—were marking the 20th anniversary of the Chicano Moratorium against the war in Vietnam. We assembled at the same park as we did two decades ago and marched the same route to the same park for a rally. As the *señora's* sign indicated, the struggle goes on and in many ways conditions have worsened for Latinos— La Raza—over the past 20 years. At the same time, the Moratorium reflected important, complex, and often positive new developments. Finally, for the U.S. left in general, the event carried a message that cannot be ignored.

On August 29, 1970, some 20,000 mostly Chicano people came from all over the country to protest the Vietnam war and especially the fact that our casualties were running at a much higher rate than the Mexican American proportion of the U.S. population. As the rally began around midday, a minor scuffle near the edge of the park served as the excuse for a massive police attack. Tear gas filled the air as 500 officers charged the youth, families, and elderly who had been sitting on the grass and drove out the panicked crowd. I remember running with a dozen other people into a nearby house to get away from the tear gas. Friends and relatives were scattered; my daughter, for one, could not be located until ten o'clock in the evening.

Three Chicanos died that day as a result of the police repression: Angel Diaz, Ruben Salazar and Lynn Ward. The best-known was journalist Salazar, who had been investigating and writing a series of articles on recent cases of police brutality for *The Los Angeles Times*; he had reportedly become radicalized in the process. After the attack in the park he had stopped with a friend at the nearby Silver Dollar cafe and was sitting at the bar. From the sidewalk outside, a sheriff's deputy fired a 10-inch tear-gas projectile into the cafe, which almost blew off Salazar's head. Later claiming they had received reports of an armed man in the bar, police said that before firing they had told all occupants to leave; witnesses said they heard no such warning.

That evening the sky over East Los Angeles turned black with smoke as protesters selectively torched many buildings. Sirens wailed for hours; barricades everywhere made "East Los," as it's called, look like an occupied territory. In the weeks that followed, the District Attorney refused to prosecute Salazar's killer despite an inquest damaging to the Sheriff's Department. Protesters demonstrated over the next few months; at one event, when officers again fired on the crowd with tear gas, some people hurled objects at them. Police killed one man, an Austrian student who looked Chicano, and left 19 wounded by buckshot.

At this year's Moratorium police seemed to keep a relatively low profile. News reports said 6,000 people came, mostly from the Southwest with a sprinkling of Chicago and New York participants. It looked like more, and it certainly felt like more because of the high spirits and energized mood. Was it yet another Day of Nostalgia in the current era of 1960s anniversaries? Yes, but mostly no.

Moratorium organizers had said the day's goal was not just to commemorate a historic event but to protest conditions now facing the overwhelming majority of La Raza. The excellent, thoughtful tabloid *L.A. Moratorium*, published by the organizing committee, pointed to the elimination of Chicano studies, attacks on bilingual education, "English Only" laws, terror from police and immigration officers, attacks by the Klan and skinheads, youth killing one another, the dumping of toxic wastes in Raza communities, and CIA/FBI imported drugs. (One might add a recent statistic: the infant mortality rate among Latinos in Los Angeles County has risen by over a third since 1987.) At the same time, the tabloid said, "the ability of the Movement to defend its people's rights is

extremely limited or nonexistent" and the lack of organization also prevents effective support for Native American struggles and against U.S. colonialism in Central America.

The rally program sustained these themes. Although activists with long histories of struggle were featured, like Dolores Huerta of the United Farm Workers and Professor Rudy Acuña, they never lingered on "the wonderful 1960s." This was no mere pep rally. Instead they and other speakers talked eloquently about domestic issues as well as U.S. militarism and intervention, democracy in Mexico, and opposition to the 1992 quincentenary to "celebrate" Christopher Columbus's arrival in 1492.

What about lessons to be drawn from the past, or a longrange strategy and developed vision for the future? The rally itself did not go much beyond calling for greater activism. Still something was being born, something new and very young was in the air.

About half the Moratorium participants seemed to be under 25, including many college as well as high school students. A major force in mobilizing the youth was MEChA (Movimiento Estudiantil Chicano de Aztlan, the Chicano Student Movement of Aztlan). Born in 1969, its strength ebbed in later years. By 1985, according to one MEChA leader, much of the organization was splintered by ideological debate; activism revived in response to worsening socioeconomic conditions. Today divisions still exist on such issues as a strictly Chicano vs. broader Latino focus, and the merits of affiliation with nonstudent, left organizations. Still, MEChA has lasted far longer than most student groups and retains a certain moral authority.

Many of the Chicano youth marching on August 25 were not even born when the first Moratorium took place, and most schools teach little about the extraordinary struggles of the 1960s worldwide. At its best MEChA helps to fill this void, serving as a transmission belt from past to present, with faculty members who were 1960s activists sometimes providing continuity as well as inspiration. The youth on the march seemed to be learning their history and respecting it. You could feel a thrill ripple through the crowd when one speaker said: "20 years ago they tried to destroy the Chicano movement. 20 years later we are here to tell them they failed!"

All that week and through September, events related to the Moratorium took place in Los Angeles: several days of extensive TV coverage; a photo exhibit; two plays, one of them a re-enactment of the killing of Salazar staged in the Silver Dollar itself and another called "August 29." A major exhibition, "Chicano Art: Resistance and Affirmation" (CARA) from 1965-1985 opened at the University of California, with many special cultural events scheduled around it.

"We want to pass on our history," said one student at the Moratorium and the spirit that visibly animated the youth that day was indeed nationalist. Dozens of times the 1960s cry of "Chicano Power!" rang out. But the words seem to have a different meaning today—more concrete and more complex than yesterday's generalized rhetoric.

"'Chicano Power' is different now because people realize we will be the majority in a few years," said a young Chicana from Fresno. "The next step will be to turn those numbers into political and economic power, to take over our communities. For example, in the valley in Fresno the people are 80 percent Chicano and Mexicano. The mayor and the school board should reflect that. When it happens, it will be a real affirmation of Chicano Power".

A second meaning of Chicano Power today lies in its implicit rejection of "Hispanic" as a label imposed by the dominant society and adopted by many Latinos themselves—especially those sometimes called Chuppies or Buppies—Chicano or Brown yuppies. "Hispanic" is a fundamentally racist term which obliterates the Native American and African American heritages of La Raza in favor of the white European component from Spain. The August 25 march countered this distortion with a contingent of Native Americans at the head of the line. Others carried signs rejecting "Hispanic" and affirming "Chicano."

That message also came across while people assembled to march, when the group Culture Clash performed and "Slick Rick" did his bilingual Chicano rap songs. He chided: "Chicanos who are wearing blue contact lenses today—forget it, you're Chicano. Don't try to be white, they do it better!" And: "The 1980s were supposed to be the 'Decade of the Hispanic' but that turned out to be an event sponsored by Coors beer." In other words: the concept "Hispanic" emerged as a marketing tool to conveniently target all Spanish-speaking cultures at once.

The Chicano/Latino/Raza versus "Hispanic" debate is about more than terminology or even racism. It also concerns values, politics, and class: the Raza tradition of collectivity and sharing versus the individualism and consumerism that intensified during the 1980s. In that decade, for example, we saw one "Hispanic" art exhibit after another, often with corporate sponsors and usually apolitical in content. But the new exhibit, CARA, is consciously entitled "Chicano Art" and is not by chance much more political than its predecessors. CARA organizers also say they sought to avoid commercialization and cultural homogeneity. Further, the show was organized by means of an unusually collective approach—regional committees rather than a single curator—so as to promote the empowerment of community people rather than professional elitism.

In these and other ways, the nationalism that ran strong on August 25 has an implicitly or overtly anticapitalist thrust. Any denunciation of capitalist exploitation brought strong cheers from the rally audience. The presence of organized labor at this year's Moratorium also seemed stronger than 20 years ago, in part because of militant struggles that have been recently waged by workers like Janitors for Justice. Mostly Central Americans, they have attracted wide support from many groups with their courage, determination, imaginative tactics—and by winning a major victory. The extremely brutal police attack on their peaceful demonstration at Century Plaza earlier this year further generated solidarity.

A NEW INTERNATIONALISM

Above all, the Moratorium emanated an internationalism much stronger than 20 years ago. Some of us had wondered if it would address current U.S. policy in the Persian Gulf. We need not have doubted. Signs everywhere, and not just from predominantly white left formations, called for an end to U.S. militarism in the Middle East. "The oil belongs to the people, not Texaco!" got some of the loudest applause at the rally.

There was also a much stronger Mexican presence than in 1970, which speaks to the ever-growing Mexican population. Their numbers are rising so rapidly that formerly Chicano neighborhoods are now Mexican (the different terms here meaning, simplistically, born in the U.S. as opposed to born in Mexico). A well-known Mexican socialist leader, Heberto Castillo of the Democratic Revolutionary Party (PRD), spoke eloquently at the rally, stressing the crucial links between today's struggle for democracy in Mexico and action by Mexican-origin people here.

In another kind of internationalism not seen 20 years ago, a group from the Nation of Islam attended the rally and one of the best-received speakers came from the African People's Socialist Party. This spirit may be drawing encouragement from cross-cultural developments like the black-inspired Chicano rap music from Culture Clash, Kid Frost's *Hispanic Causing Panic* album, and other singers. Finally, a small Korean contingent marched in the Moratorium—a welcome sight.

The National Chicano Moratorium Committee, which worked on the event for many months at the national and regional levels deserves much credit for its success. "The most democratic mobilization effort in my memory," Professor Rudy Acuña called it, despite having disagreed with members at times. Its commitment to combat sectarianism paid off well, judging by the wide variety of politics represented. The banner of the Mothers of East Los Angeles, a strong community organization, could be seen not far from a small sign proclaiming "Mao—hoy mas que nunca" (Mao, today more than ever). Although the "Principles of Unity" limited membership on the organizing committee to Chicano/Mexican organizations, anti-white feeling seemed absent.

When it came to gender roles, the committee showed little progress over 20 years ago. Women held the posts of—guess what—secretary and treasurer, plus one youth coordinator. All four media liaisons were men. Rally speakers had a better balance: far from equal but solid, and women's participation in the movement was not trivialized by tokenistic recognition. In addition to Dolores Huerta, Nita Gonzales of Denver (longtime community organizer and daughter of "Corky" Gonzales) spoke as did Juana Gutierrez of the Mothers of East Los Angeles and Patricia Marin of Orange County MEChA.

On the march itself you could see a Chicana women's consciousness that was absent 20 years ago. Signs like "Vote Chicano—Vote Chicana" may not have been numerous, but they wouldn't have been seen at all before. Activist women agree it's time for the decline of the "CPMG," a species identified by several Chicanas talking in the Silver Dollar after the Moratorium: the Chicano Person Movement Guy. The generation of women now in college may bring major changes. In recent years, for example, it has not been unusual to find a woman heading a MEChA chapter or women outnumbering the men on a MEChA board. A future Moratorium organizing committee should find more women with experience, in their 30s and 40s like much of the current committee, and ready at least to run more of the show.

How shall White Leftists Relate to a New Movimiento?

Some of us felt a new Chicano movement being born last Aug. 25. The day made it clear that sooner or later this will happen—a Latino movement, I would hope. An old question then arises: how will leftists relate to it? Past experience has been so poor that for many Latinos—not to mention other people of color in the U.S.—"the left" has often come to mean white folks. In the next era, will so much of the Anglo left continue to minimize the Mexican American struggle?

At the heart of the problem is a tendency to see race relations and the struggle against racism primarily or exclusively in terms of black and white. Every week articles or books appear that claim to address racial issues like Affirmative Action but contain not a single word about any population except the African American. In the histories of the 1960s by white authors, although the treatment of

black struggle is never adequate one can at least find Martin Luther King, the Black Panthers, and a few other references. But in 25 such books reviewed by this writer, the massive Chicano movement of the 1960s and early 1970s might never have happened. (See "That Old White (Male) Magic," Z, July-August 1989.)

To criticize this blindness is not to deny the primacy of African American struggle: the genocidal nature of enslavement, the constant resistance by slaves, the "Second Reconstruction" of the 1960s and its extraordinary leaders, and today's destruction of black youth if not black males in general. Also, African Americans up to now remain the largest population of color in this country. I began my own political work in the black civil rights movement because it was so obviously on the cutting edge of history for all people of color, for the whole society. Many white progressives also gave support, sometimes even their lives, to that movement. But somehow, while combating the symbolism of blacks as "the Invisible Man" they overlooked new "invisible" men—and women—of other colors.

One apparent exception to the left's myopia about Mexican Americans surfaced during the party-building movement of the 1970s. A flurry of Marxist-Leninist position papers about Chicanos descended, telling us that we were a nation and should secede from the U.S. (wha?), or that we were a national minority whose goal should be regional autonomy (wha?), or that we were a nothing more than part of the U.S. working class (wha?), or that we were a racial but not a national minority (hunh?!). Those we called the Alphabet Soup came to visit Chicano groups in New Mexico at different times. Their organizational positions were unrelated to the realities we knew, concoctions that seemed to have sprung full-grown from their heads, nourished by theory alone. This could only leave us feeling a lack of respect for our history, culture, and struggle.

Earlier the Communist Party had done better and provided courageous leadership to labor struggles involving Mexican or Chicano workers. But here too Raza who were in the party have their stories to tell of an alienating chauvinism. All in all, left organizations too often use that demeaning stock phrase: "African Americans and other minorities" or "African Americans and other Third World people" or "African Americans and other people of color."

Even when Anglo leftists do study Raza culture and history, the problem remains of demonstrating support for Latinos abroad rather than at home. Many Anglos have worked hard on solidarity with Central America and against U.S. intervention. They learn Spanish, embrace the culture, pass hard and often dangerous time in Central American countries. But, except for the issue of refugees and sanctuary, this has rarely translated into support for domestic struggles by Latino peoples—for example, Chicanos/Mexicans or Puerto Ricans in the U.S. Intentions aside, a romanticized and in the end paternalistic view of Latinos tends to prevail all too often.

Anglos are not alone in showing little effort to understand the history, culture, and struggles of Mexican Americans. Peoples of color can also be blind. Among blacks, for example, author Manning Marable is one of the few who regularly brings Latinos into his worldview. Even within the same population, class differences make some Chicanos want racism exposed, while others prefer to maintain a pretense of "No problem." Some will affirm their brownness proudly while others prefer to pass for white if possible.

Up to now the dominant society has had no interest in teaching our unknown histories to anyone and preferred to leave in place the melting-pot model. The burden then falls on the rest of us to work for internationalism inside—not just outside—U.S. borders. We have to teach and learn from each other, we have to develop mutual knowledge of and respect for all our cultures. A new kind of U.S. left will not be born otherwise, as activist/author Carlos Muñoz emphasized in a recent hard-hitting *Crossroads* article.

1992: A Chance to Sing "De Colores" as Never Before

The upcoming quincentenary offers a once-in-500-years chance to pull our colors together in common protest. Christopher Columbus's arrival on this continent has meaning, usually deadly, for all people of color and many others. In the face of what will be constant, repugnant official celebrations of 1492, we can together mount educational events and demonstrations of all kinds with great scope and impact. The symbolism begs for sweeping protest, a protest that will not merely say "No" to what happened 500 years ago but affirm the infinite treasure-house of non-European cultures and histories, then and now.

For Native Americans, of course, Columbus's arrival meant instant genocide. Today indigenous peoples all over the continent are already planning domestic and international actions. Europe's colonization also paved the way for the enslavement of Africans by the million, brought here to build vast wealth for others with their blood and sweat. At the same time, colonialism launched the birth—by conquest and rape—of a whole new people, La Raza, who combine the red, white, and black in what we may still call a bronze people.

On the backs of all these colors was constructed the greatest wealth ever seen in the world, a wealth that soon came to need more slaves of one kind or another. This time it drew them from the East: Chinese, Japanese, Filipino, Pacific peoples, and many others. Ultimately the whites failed to protect many of their own children from an inhuman poverty and contempt.

So we can come together on this, if we choose. We can make 1992 a year that THEY will remember. We can, in gentler terms, make it the year of "De Colores," of new alliances, in the spirit of the old song by that name: "*Y por eso los grandes amores de muchos colores me gustan a mi*" ("*And so the loves of many colors are pleasing to me.*")

27

Shadows of Race and Class

RAYMOND S. FRANKLIN

While William J. Wilson implies that race and class can be approached separately in another selection in this reader, Franklin argues that these two concepts are fundamentally intertwined. In order to understand how racism operates in the United States it is critical to note that a significant sector in the black community is also poor. In the author's opinion, it is inaccurate to examine and analyze race or racism, without also focusing on or emphasizing class dynamics. Thus, racism is not simply a racial issue, but a class one, as well. He concludes, 'The over representation of black males in the lower classes, a condition that reproduces itself in a variety of institutionally determined ways, is intimately associated with race, affecting the status of blacks other than those in the lower class … In this way, race–class connections determine not only the myopic perceptions of the white community *vis-à-vis* the black community but also divisions and attitudes within the black community itself.' The author suggests that racism is facilitated against black people because society also exhibits class prejudice.

Is the subordinate position of the black population ultimately derived from the stigma of color, or is it due to the black population's inferior class or economic position?[1] Even when both the race and class categories are employed, either the question of primacy is raised or class and race are affirmed simultaneously without a coherent statement about their interaction. Race is frequently employed to include unique historical roots and culture; class is often enlarged to embrace a variety of economic characteristics. The choice of category or emphasis forms the basis of arguments about the determinants of black status and the nature of discrimination. It also determines the kinds of policies and strategies advocated to eliminate racial injustices. The race–class arguments take place, moreover, within the African-American community, between whites and blacks, and among radical, liberal, and conservative scholars and leaders. Finally, and most important in my view, the race–class dialogue is transacted daily through the mass media, inside our institutions, and on the streets of our major metropolises. Lurking beneath many individual experiences and incidents, both within the separate communities and between them, are judgments that are linked, knowingly or otherwise, to either class or race logic or some confused combination of both.

When white Americans think about black criminals and hardened youth, about black dope addicts and unwed black teenage parents, about black basketball players and professional black fighters, about black intellectuals who head African-American studies programs in our academies, about the overrepresentation of graduating black seniors majoring in education, about conspicuous consumption patterns among different segments of the black population, what kinds of mind-sets are employed to cast their interpretations? Are they class and economic or race and cultural ones?

Do members of the white professional class interpret the black underclass differently from members of the black professional class? If so, is this difference in interpretation due to race or to class? Why were privileged white radical students who smashed windows on university campuses in the late sixties and early seventies castigated as spoiled brats who grew up with too much privilege, while black militants who also smashed windows were often classified as animals?[2] Is looting by blacks seen or remembered differently from that perpetrated by whites? When a black medical intern coming off duty from New York Hospital on the upper East Side spends ten to twenty minutes more per day trying to catch a cab than his white cohort, and when black cab drivers as well as white ones consciously avoid the pickup, is this rejection based on race, class, or the assumed ghettoized place of residence where race and class are often fused?

Answering these and similar questions is the task I undertake in this essay. To do so involves the synthesis of a wide range of historically rooted materials and experiences, and the application of theory in a form that captures the texture of black–white contemporary experiences in post-World War II American society.

What I find inadequate in most broad historical and theoretical perspectives is their abstractness or distance from the web of social and economic realities that I observe, encounter, and know exist. Even when statistical data are presented in abundance, they often fail to capture what black–white, subordinate–dominate relations are about and miss much of what we should be trying to understand. Since I pose my own race–class interactionist perspective as an alternative to a number of major contending views, I shall proceed by first depicting those major perspectives that I reject. There are three: *rational individualism, class determinism,* and *non-Eurocentric culturalism.* All these foundation perspectives are implicitly or explicitly in battle with each other; all have a view about the nature of the social science enterprise that is used to explain black–white relations and the overall status of African-Americans.

RATIONAL INDIVIDUALISM

Gary Becker's influential book, *The Economics of Discrimination,* was the first endeavor systematically to use mainstream microeconomic theory to explain income differences between groups associated with discrimination.[3] The book's impact was perhaps related more to this fact than to what Becker actually proved through evidence about discrimination. Economists, not unlike other academic professionals, readily see truth in models they have been trained to use and aesthetically appreciate. Becker starts his argument with a notion he identifies as the "taste for discrimination" (subjective states of mind decision makers employ to guide market choices). Development of tastes is an individual affair and has no explicit source. Beginning on the demand side of the market, employing blacks or working with blacks or living next door to blacks has a disutility (negative feeling) to whites that leads to racial inequalities. In the absence of skill and educational differences (the economist's definition of productivity), additional psychic costs are incurred or experienced by whites when they must relate to blacks on equal terms. Whites, therefore, seek to avoid extra costs or seek compensation when they occur. In Becker's model, racially guided decisions are not fundamentally different from those that determine why some individuals prefer apples to oranges and, thereby, discriminate against orange growers when apples are selected:

> Discrimination and prejudice are not usually said to occur when someone prefers looking at a glamorous Hollywood actress rather than some other woman; yet they are said to occur when he prefers living next to whites rather than next to Negroes. At best calling just one of these actions "discrimination" requires making subtle and rather secondary distinctions.[4]

From this and related kinds of individual choice-theoretic hypotheses, statistical inquiries are made to explain income, wage, employment, or residential location differentials which are unrelated to productivity per se. Whites exclude blacks or demand extra compensation if required to associate with them. Underlying Becker's reasoning is an effort to equate discrimination with tastes that guide choices made by consumers or other economic agents, choices not necessarily related to the absence of knowledge about the products or factors. They are related, as I have emphasized, to individual values or psychic expressions.

The labor market is the pool from which labor is recruited and in which labor is disposed when it is no longer needed. Individuals who recruit and exclude in such markets are assumed to make decisions guided by narrow economic interests. Broader social and political ramifications of individual decisions are ignored, analyzed separately from each other, and viewed to be part of another sphere in the social structure. The differences in economic well-being between the races that cannot be explained by "objective" factors often have been taken to represent discrimination, or the economic costs of being black.[5] If some assumed cultural traits, independent of the conditions that determine the black population's status due to discrimination, are considered, income differences related to race may statistically disappear.[6] "If the school system fails to educate blacks and businesses refuse to employ blacks because of their lack of education, economic discrimination does not appear in the equation. Blacks can then be legitimately rejected on the basis of productivity per se.

The sources of individual taste differences are not examined or sought; tastes, at best, are relegated to unexplained vagaries of culture that exist outside the economic order and are taken as given. In this sense there is no account taken of the possible repercussions of a "discriminatory" wage or the exclusion by the dominant group. Motivation and diligence are assumed to remain constant despite the injustices experienced by blacks. The fact that black workers may become less productive as a result of discrimination against them is a dynamic not part of Beckerian reasoning.[7]

Rational individualism avoids tracing the way organizational hierarchies constrain individual action and affect incentives.[8] Deficient educational systems, chronic economic instability, ghettoization the absence of interclass contacts, and general subordination in the distribution of power produce individual modes of adaptation and lifestyles that are not considered by analysts who simply aggregate outcomes from aggregating individual decisions.

Becker and his numerous followers, in equating "race tastes" with general kinds of "tastes," avoid the question of why they are unable to predict or explain whether one prefers apples to oranges by observing one's skin color, but would not hesitate to predict the color of one's marriage partner through such an observation. The reason is simple: choices guided by race are not trivial, secondary distinctions derived from the vagaries of culture; they are not randomly distributed like other market values in the society, but are already patterned by institutionally determined practices.

When we switch from the demand to the supply side where human capital theorists make a case, the emphasis is on the characteristics of individuals (skills, education, work experience, work attitudes, etc.). Blacks have accumulated less human capital than whites and, therefore, do less well in the labor market. Blacks structure themselves, like whites, through investment in human capital. This occurs as a result of the individual's own calculated interests and those derived from investment by "familial, educational, or other background [sources surrounding] ... individuals who are unevenly distributed" in the economic order.[9] Individual decision makers among blacks and whites are aggregated and group differences in income, employment, occupations, and other factors are carefully measured. How these aggregated differences are interpreted among rational individualists varies; some may attribute them to genetic factors

(see chap. 3) and others to deeply rooted cultural traditions that somehow have become divorced from current circumstances and systematic discriminatory practices.[10] If blacks invest less in themselves, it may be due to their own limitations. Or it may be due to a variety of rational considerations such as those located in the capital markets run by individual decision makers who also are behaving rationally when they either refuse loans to blacks or charge blacks higher interest rates.[11] In the final analysis, given the consideration of a large variety of factors, conservative rational individualists reduce discrimination to a minor part of current black–white economic differences in status. Since significant differentials appear to exist and persist – in spite of the legal and social egalitarian policies in effect for the past forty years – they are seen as due to variables independent of race per se (e.g., cultural patterns, genetics, work habits, the momentum of history, and, not least, slothfulness created by dependence on the welfare state).[12] Perhaps what distinguishes conservative from liberal rational individualists is the point at which they cease to add variables to eliminate unexplained residuals; the latter are then examined to explain discrimination based on race. Liberals are hesitant to view such factors as marital status, work attitudes, cultural patterns, and welfare dependency as race free. Race, in liberal formulations, is embedded in these factors, and therefore must be addressed by interventionist policies.

CLASS DETERMINISM

John E. Roemer, a leading American Marxist theoretician, argues that "Marxist theory ... remains in a state of relative vagueness" with regard to the nature of racial discrimination at the level of the individual firm.[13] In correcting this condition, Roemer develops a theoretical model that proves why it is in the employer's rational self-interests to nurture racial discord or take advantage of existing racial disharmony among workers: namely, it weakens the collective bargaining power of workers as a whole and thereby lowers the wage bill for individual maximizing capitalists. Roemer admits that examining racial discrimination at the firm level provides only a partial insight. "A full Marxian or radical treatment," he adds, "would inquire into what institutions and practices in capitalist society are responsible for endowing workers [or others with racial prejudices]."[14]

This fuller statement represents a counterpoint both to Becker's neoclassical treatment that takes "tastes for discrimination" as given or outside the economic domain, and to the "human capital" position that puts a great burden on the individual's own rational understanding of self-interest. Instead, the radical argument claims that circumstances or tastes are "manipulated in such a way as to produce an equilibrium outcome beneficial to the capitalists."[15] This capacity to control the economy emanates from the definition of the dominant class and its derived power from the ownership of the means of production. Ownership carries with it domination; its absence leads to subordination. Since the African-American population is void of a capital-owning class, it is axiomatically positioned like all other workers or wage earners in the system. Blacks have shared economic interests that will eventually, it is assumed, find common ground for them with white workers. Rationality for the individual in this model involves discovering class interest rather than self-interest.

Racism leading to forms of discrimination in the radical or Marxian account is commonly focused on work site relations and is assumed beneficial to the capitalist class as a whole, a class that has the interests and power to reproduce the racial climate conducive to its profit-driven needs. The bottom line in this argument is that racism is determined by the dominant class in order to protect its interests and privileges.[16] White workers who are persuaded or conditioned to "think race" are assumed to be irrational or to suffer from "false consciousness." In a similar vein, black Marxists, one study concluded, believed in

> the causal priority of economic factors in explaining racial bigotry in America.... The rights of individual workers, regardless of gender, race, religion, or ethnicity, are realized in and through the working class.... When workers are exploited economically they suffer culturally as well. The difficulties experienced by women, blacks, and other victims of discrimination are, in the last resort, caused by worker exploitation.[17]

Erik Olin Wright, another well-known Marxist and influential scholar, in seeking to avoid class reductionism maintains nevertheless that class structures constitute the central organizing principles of societies; they shape the range of possible variations in race, ethnic, and gender relations.[18] While he finds that black–white returns to education tend to disappear when class is considered,[19] Wright nevertheless seeks to escape, albeit awkwardly, from class reductionism by suggesting that "it would be a mistake to interpret the results ... as indicating that all racial discrimination is really disguised class oppression.... Social processes ... distribute people into class positions in the first place."[20] This need to maintain a primacy of class, even when social relations appear to be its determinant, stems from a fear that without a class analysis social science is likely to slide into the "multiple oppressions" approach to understanding society. Societies, in this view, are characterized by a plurality of oppressions, each of which is rooted in a different form of domination – sexual, racial,

national, economic, and so on – none having any explanatory priority over any other. Class, then, becomes just one of many oppressions, with no particular centrality to social and historical analysis.[21]

There are many unattended questions in the Marxian perspective that will be addressed in subsequent chapters on a different level. Suffice it for now to suggest that racial discord in the nonwork sphere may be more important than that found in the work sphere.[22] What values people bring to work may be as relevant as those determined by work. Furthermore, discordant relations that weaken the collective interests of workers at the firm level may lead to production disruptions and problems that raise costs. It does not follow that "divide and conquer" tactics are axiomatically in the economic interests of capitalists. As a matter of fact, the desire and capacity of white workers to exclude blacks from some industries or occupations may increase white wages more than it lowers black ones and thereby increase the total wage bill. More important, white and ethnic workers did not need capitalists to divide them from black workers; the history of organized labor from its inception to its present struggle against affirmative action has an indigenous voice.[23] White ethnic workers did their excluding job more thoroughly than any capitalist could ever have imagined. Finally, racially oriented thinking may be driven by social, moral, and cultural interests that cannot be subsumed solely under the economic structures related to profit maximization, "objective" material interests, or economic exploitation. They may even have social costs that are not beneficial to the business system as a whole.

NON-EUROCENTRIC CULTURALISM

In contrast to the above orientations – that racial inequalities are the result of the aggregation of rational, individual decision makers or that they are derived from individual enterprise's objective needs in the work site that are aggregated to serve the general class interests of the whole business system – a cultural and/or non-Eurocentric perspective has also developed.[24] The cultural and non-Eurocentric categories at times overlap. Some, but not all, proponents of this view initiate their position by criticizing Marxism or some variant of class reductionism: "Marxism is inadequate because it fails to probe other spheres of American society where racism plays an integral role – especially the psychological and cultural spheres."[25] Or, in the words of two radical culturalists seeking to break away from Marxism, it is believed by many radicals (Marxists et al.) that "the focus on class ... could permit communication across the chasms and gulfs that separate minority communities and racial minorities as a whole from the white working class."[26] Radicals, in this critique, "failed to grasp the comprehensive manner by which race is structured into the U.S. social fabric."[27]

The culturalists (race advocates), in the course of rejecting class reductionism, also reject the liberal, pluralistic methodology that emphasizes a multiple number of factors without any one necessarily being central. Like the Marxists, the culturalists, at the extreme, argue for the primacy idea, which, of course, is race rather than class:

[Race] is a fundamental organizing principle of social relations.... At the micro-level, race is a matter of individuality, of the formation of identity. The ways in which we understand ourselves and interact with others; the structuring of our practical activity – in work and family, as citizens and as thinkers.... At the macro-level, race is a matter of collectivity of the formation of social structures: economic, political and cultural/ideological.[28]

Pushing the argument beyond the boundaries of the United States and the history of capitalism, Cornel West reminds us that racism predates capitalism: "Its roots lie in the earlier encounters of Europe, Africa, Asia and Latin America.... Racist folktales, mythologies, legends, ends, and stories that function in the everyday life of common people predate the 17th and 18th centuries."[29] This mode of approaching racism casts a very wide net; it sees racism as part of a Eurocentric civilization that embraces "three discursive logics: Judeo-Christian, scientific, and psycho-sexual discourses [that] ... have been employed to justify racist practices."[30]

From Eurocentric religion we learn that "black skin is a divine curse."[31] From scientific logic, which promotes, among other things, the "activities of observing, comparing, measuring, and ordering physical characteristics of human bodies," we acquire notions of "black ugliness, cultural deficiency, and intellectual inferiority."[32] From Eurocentric psychosexual discourse, we acquire the view that Africans are imbued "with sexual prowess [and that non-Europeans are] either cruel revengeful fathers, frivolous carefree children, or passive long-suffering mothers.... Non-Europeans (especially black people) [are associated] with dirt, odious smell, and feces."[33] The race advocates, when generalized, argue that "racist practices directed against black, brown, yellow and red people are an integral element of U.S. history, including present day American culture and society."[34]

This extreme historicism, with its trans-epocal view of racial categorizing by white Europeans, not only leads to a rejection of many current tenets of Western civilization, but it comes close to suggesting that white supremacy is biosocially determined. Such a pure race emphasis necessarily leads to nationalist exhortations, strategies, and programs. More problematic is the fact that "people of color" are called upon – as if minorities of color had common grievances – to oppose Eurocentric civilization and/or U.S. hegemony. Native Americans, Hispanics, Puerto Ricans, Asian-Americans, and others are thematically clustered and identified as being oppressed and culturally dominated by a common white source.[35]

Each of these foundation approaches is muted in practice and often, depending upon the context, is combined with the others in inconsistent ways; for example, a class emphasis, often used for political reasons, leads to race-specific programs.[36] Nationalist ideologies frequently require policies dependent on white transfers or benign white cooperation.[37] These inconsistencies are not necessarily wrong if they are understood as part of the paradoxes of liberal, democratic social orders. But the advocates of one-dimensionally driven perspectives are not comfortable with such paradoxes or contradictions and rarely respect the social orders in which they articulate their case.

Each of the foundation perspectives is driven by an initial assumption that ultimately derails the perspective from a compelling analysis with appropriate strategies and policies. Rational individualists begin with the axiom Know Thyself and neglect the institutions that determine the self. Class determinists begin with the need to know "thy" economic class and neglect other collectivities that determine conflict and affect change. And non-Eurocentric culturalists affirm the necessity to know "thy" cultural or geographic roots and neglect the need to use existing institutions and circumstances that are unrelated to the historically determined trajectories. Each of these primary launching assumptions is inadequate and tends to take the social science enterprise down a path that makes it less useful than it might otherwise be. They tend to create models or orientations that are removed from the real experience of the subjects whom they are seeking to understand. While each provides partial insights, none generates clear strategies and interventionist policies appropriate to a liberal, democratic market system like our own.

Having eliminated from consideration the three major perspectives – rational individualism, class reductionism, and non-Eurocentric culturalism – it is legitimate to ask what remains. The answer is to focus on the wide repercussions of a chronic condition: consequential portions of the black population have been historically and are at present overrepresented in subordinate economic and social positions. By concentrating on the nature of subordination that defines black–white relations, it becomes possible to integrate history, theory, and experience in ways that address the enduring economic and social injustices inflicted on African-Americans.

Race–Class Interactionism

There is a dynamic and reactive interplay between race and class that is frequently absent in the analysis of black–white relations. Central to my analytical framework is how race relates to class and class to race over time and in varying social and organizational contexts. This book, therefore, is not about a narrow range of economic differences per se, nor about how race and class each separately determine differences in black–white conditions. In this sense my orientation differs from authors whose works either avoid the race–class nexus by focusing on individual-level characteristics or proceed from assumptions that either emphasize class domination in work site relations or race degradation as rooted in Eurocentric history and culture.

My alternative approach is developed in less universal or global terms; its backdrop is specific to the United States. This is not to reject comparative analysis as a matter of principle, but I believe that black–white relations in the United States can be explored more insightfully by emphasizing their unique dimensions. African-American uniqueness, in my judgment, is more profound than similarities employed to demonstrate commonalities.

This more circumscribed focus is justified for a number of reasons. First, the history of African-Americans from enslavement to the present has a presence in the larger drama of American life that makes the historical relevance of black–white relations qualitatively different from that of other racial minorities. As a group in struggle for social justice, African-Americans have induced periodic constitutional and social crises responsible for shifting the whole direction of our national deliberations about ourselves as a nation and a democracy.

Second, whites in all strata of American society manifest perceptions of a distorted and misanthropic nature that have a greater breadth, depth, and durability than those held about other discriminated-against minorities who constitute the American mosaic. African-American biological features, when associated with class and cultural differences, are more indissoluble than ethnic differences in the absence of biological ones. Race ideology as it applies to African-Americans, we are reminded, is ever present and "helps insiders make sense of the things they do and see – ritually, repetitively – on a daily basis."[38] Race thinking and interpretations of events, even when incorrect, provide coherence to both whites and blacks, albeit for different reasons. In other words, race ideology and its everyday uses and validation may be false from a scientific view, but they are socially real and cannot be readily ignored as long as the actual routines and activities of everyday life are maintained. Breaking away from the perennial patterns of activity is a necessary precondition to eliminating the ideological categories that explain and justify the animosities embedded in everyday practices.

Third, while race categorizing is sociohistorically rooted, in the United States it is almost exclusively reserved for African-Americans to signify status and not physical features.[39] Thus, "havin' a little Negra blood in ya' – just one little teeny drop and a person's all Negra."[40] What this means when applied to African-Americans is complex. Physical features are instrumental to status degradation because African-American features have social associations and meaning to both whites and blacks. "Blood" ancestry is also relevant – even without identifiable physical features – if the ancestry is African-American. Yet, the story of one's status changes if one's accent is foreign. Foreign blacks are identified by their national origin. This problem becomes manifest for U.S. census takers when they survey Hispanics. Members of the same family may well fall under three different categories: white, Hispanic, or black.[41]

Finally, the larger arena of oppressed ethnic-racial communities embracing Caribbeaners, Latinos, Asian-Americans, Filipinos, and others, does not constitute a seamless or interrelated web, a cohesive social and political group with shared sentiments toward whites. The system of chauvinism that has affected their respective well-being is not shared with each other or with African-Americans. In many vital respects, a number of these oppressed minorities in fact possess racist sentiments toward African-Americans. Recent slurs by the Japanese and the black conflict with Korean grocery-store owners are just the tip of the iceberg.[42] Just as African-Americans who visit Kenya learn that they are viewed as American tourists, Caribbeaners make distinctions as revealed by a Haitian college student's comment: "When I am with whites, I am black. When I am with blacks [African-Americans], I am Haitian."[43] And, in a pilot survey aimed at measuring race or class reactions to ambiguous situations that involved some form of discrimination, West Indian blacks overwhelmingly interpreted the situation in terms of class bias or as class and a "little" race bias, whereas African-Americans almost uniformly saw race as the only factor in their interpretation.[44] Class as used here, and as I use it throughout this book, perhaps needs to be defined before I proceed to delineate the structure of my framework.

Class is not an a priori abstraction defined by relations in the work sphere independent of its meaning in everyday routines and perceptions. In this sense, airline pilots who sell their labor power to private companies for $40,000 or more per year are not in the same class as those who sell their labor power for much less. Their structural "togetherness" has no social meaning for my purposes here. While I am closer to the Weberian definition of market capacity to command income in the labor market, either as an individual or as an affiliate of an organized group, this definition is also too restricted for my interests.

Class, for the purposes at hand, constitutes the individual's or group's average ability (actual or potential) to communicate command capacity in three spheres: the labor market, the consumer market, and the internal market of enterprises. It should be further noted that actual capacities may be more or less than those communicated, or they may be communicated in ways detrimental to the individual's success. Actual capacities may also be at variance with the way the dominant group evaluates what is communicated by the subordinate one. Black families whose incomes are identical to those of whites may be forced to communicate their consumption capacities in ways that have differential consequences. A big, fancy car driven by a black person is not interpreted by whites in the same way that whites interpret "their own" conspicuous forms of "making it."

While the different spheres of communicating command capacities are related, the attributes that determine the actual or potential communication of command capacity vary and can be known only through empirical investigation. Communicating a command capacity to acquire entry into an enterprise does not mean that the same attributes will work inside the enterprise as one seeks to enhance one's career. Individuals with identical incomes may not have the identical communication capacities to purchase the same bundle of goods related to well-being. The individual's group identity, or its absence, will affect the capacity to communicate command. An aggressive white male inside an enterprise may be seen as having the kind of attributes that are valued; the same attributes for an African-American may serve as a barrier. The inability to buy a home through the capital markets in a desirable location, however adequate the income and secure the employment, could well determine one's accumulation of wealth and thereby eventually affect one's communication of command capacity in other spheres in which individuals or groups must function.

Since the communication of command capacity differs systematically when race becomes one of its determining attributes, race and class are defined in relation to each other. But to understand the dynamic and reactive interplay of the race–class nexus, to view its operation and trace its varying patterns, one needs not only to differentiate among kinds of markets, but also to examine some subtle differences within similar markets.

SHADOWS OF RACE AND CLASS

African-Americans themselves – religious and secular leaders, scholars and writers, middle-class professionals, workers, welfare recipients – have a history of engagement and struggle over the meaning of the American experience in its various modes and of the uses to which the social sciences are put in the exploration of issues concerned with family, community, education, intelligence, values, class, and race. This long-standing engagement is unlike that of any other ethnic-racial group. That is why

> in the United States, there are scholars and black scholars, women and black women. Saul Bellow and John Updike are writers; Ralph Ellison and Toni Morrison are black writers. George Bush and Michael Dukakis were candidates for president; Jesse Jackson was a black candidate for president.[45]

Or as John Hope Franklin further remarked upon publication of his most recent book, *Race and History: Selected Essays, 1938–1988*, when he was asked what role race has played in determining his specialization as a historian,

> It's often assumed I'm a scholar of Afro-American history, but the fact is I haven't taught a course in Afro-American history in 30-some-odd years. They say I'm the author of 12 books on black history, when several of those books focus mainly on whites. I'm called a leading black historian, never minding the fact that I've served as president of the American Historical Association, the Organization of American Historians, the Southern Historical Association, Phi Beta Kappa, and on and on. The tragedy ... is that black scholars so often have their specialities forced on them.[46]

However accomplished John Hope Franklin may be – as a historian, as a historian of the whole South or of the whole nation – and whatever division of labor he may wish to project as constituting his identity, he is forced to reflect the shadow cast upon his black self that W. E. B. Du Bois's oft-repeated observation revealed:

> The Negro is ... born with a veil, and gifted with second sight in this American world – a world which yields him no true self-consciousness, but only lets him see himself through the revelation of the other world. It is a peculiar sensation, this double consciousness, this sense of always looking at one's self through the eyes of others, of measuring oneself by the tape of a world that looks on in amused contempt and pity.[47]

The shadow cast on individual blacks emanates from the group characteristics of "all" blacks. This process has many consequences and a variety of dimensions. It constitutes one of the main dynamics of the race–class nexus that I develop in chapter 6. The race–class connection itself emerges from the aggregation of dominant–subordinate relations in most spheres of American life. This is explored in chapter 4.

The general proposition that I demonstrate involves how the overcrowding of blacks in the lower class – which thoughtful whites often identify as a "pure" class issue derived from the deficiency of skills, education, and so on – casts a shadow on middle-class members of the black population that have credentials but are excluded or discriminated against on racial grounds. Middle-class black reactions to this shadow vary: they have internal and external dimensions. The internal dimension involves examining the intraclass and gender differences in well-being and outlook among blacks themselves. The external dimension requires an examination of the debates between the races. The internal and external debates are not similar. Thus, understanding the race–class nexus requires an examination of race relations between the populations and the interplay of class differences within the separate racial communities. White middle-class responses to upward mobility endeavors by the black middle class are often related to concerns about the black lower class. In a similar vein, the black middle-class outlook is frequently conditioned by the status of the black lower class.

The dynamics of the race–class nexus, it should be further noted, unfold differently in varying contexts. The variations in labor markets, the internal markets of enterprises, and sites in which consumption patterns are communicated limit or extend the impact of the race–class dynamics with regard to the allocation of blacks and whites in the microspheres of society. In these latter spheres, dominant–subordinate rule tends to be followed. But dominant–subordinate patterns vary in subtle ways and depend upon variations in the mechanisms, sources, and forms of discrimination on the one hand, and types of commodities produced or sold and the technologies used in production on the other. The micropatterns established along a dominant–subordinate axis determine and are determined by the interplay between race and class on the more aggregate level; both inform each other in the course of their related movements.

The nature of dominant–subordinate relations and of the race–class connections is embedded in black affirmations, white reactions, and black–white debates over a range of issues that make up the history of the past forty years. These center on the civil rights and black power movements, white backlash, the legacy of slavery, scientific IQism, rules governing black–white economic relations, the status of the black middle class, the rise of the black underclass, the central city/suburban division along racial lines, and a range of issues focused on community, family, and gender.

The concluding arguments of this book extend the implications of my analysis in the context of the central city's decline. I develop an agenda concerned with rescuing our cities from decay, building communities, and restructuring family life in ways that embrace the needs of African-Americans and the larger white society.

NOTES

1. I endeavor in this chapter to extend the debate stimulated by William Julius Wilson in *The Declining Significance of Race: Blacks and Changing American Institutions* (Chicago and London: University of Chicago Press, 1978).

2. This characterization was made at a Queens College administrative meeting dealing with student demonstrations on campus, Spring 1971.

3. Gary S. Becker, *The Economics of Discrimination* (Chicago: University of Chicago Press, 1957).

4. Ibid., p. 5.

5. William Darity, Jr., "What's Left of the Economic Theory of Discrimination," in *The Question of Discrimination: Racial Inequality in the U.S. Labor Market*, ed. Steven Shulman and William Darity, Jr. (Middletown, Conn.: Wesleyan University Press, 1989), p. 336.

6. Ibid., p. 337; see also Thomas Sowell, *Ethnic America* (New York: Basic Books, 1981).

7. Raymond S. Franklin, "A Framework for the Analysis of Interurban Negro-White Economic Differentials," *Industrial and Labor Relations Review* 21, no. 3 (April 1968): 368.

8. Shulman and Darity, Jr., "Introduction," in *Question of Discrimination*, p. 3.

9. Ibid., p. 2.

10. Hylan Lewis, *Blackways of Kent* (Chapel Hill: University of North Carolina Press, 1955); Oscar Lewis, *La Vida: A Puerto Rican Family in the Culture of Poverty* (New York: Random House, 1966); Lee Rainwater, *Behind Ghetto Walls: Black Life in a Federal Slum* (Chicago: Aldine, 1970).

11. James P. Smith, "Career Wage Mobility," in Shulman and Darity, Jr., *Question of Discrimination*, pp. 112–13.

12. Charles Murray, *Losing Ground: American Social Policy, 1950–1980* (New York: Basic Books, 1984).

13. John E. Roemer, "Divide and Conquer: Micro-Foundations of a Marxian Theory of Wage Discrimination," *Bell Journal of Economics* 10, no. 2 (Autumn 1979): 695–96.

14. Ibid., p. 704.

15. Ibid.

16. Paul Baran and Paul Sweezy, *Monopoly Capital* (New York: Monthly Review Press, 1966), pp. 263–64.

17. Robert A. Gorman, "Black Neo-Marxism in Liberal America," *Rethinking Marxism* 2, no. 4 (Winter 1982): 119

18. Erik Olin Wright, *Classes* (London and New York: Verso, 1985), pp. 31–32.

19. Erik Olin Wright, *Class Structure and Income Determination* (New York: Academic, 1979), p. 197.

20. Ibid.

21. Wright, *Classes*, p. 31.

22. Ira Katznelson, *City Trenches: Urban Politics and the Patterning of Class in the United States* (New York: Pantheon, 1981), chaps. 2, 8.

23. Herbert Hill, "Black Labor and Affirmative Action: An Historical Perspective," in Shulman and Darity, Jr., *Question of Discrimination*, pp. 190–267.

24. Molefi Asante, *The Afrocentric Idea* (Philadelphia: Temple University Press, 1987).

25. Cornel West, *Toward a Democratic Socialist Theory of Racism* (New York: Institute for Democratic Socialism, 1988, pamphlet), p. 3.

26. Michael Omi and Howard Winant, *Racial Formation in the United States: From 1960 to the 1980s* (New York and London: Routledge, 1986), p. 106.

27. Ibid., p. 107.

28. Ibid., pp. 66–67.

29. West, *Theory of Racism*, p. 3.

30. Ibid., p. 4.

31. Ibid.

32. Ibid.

33. Ibid.

34. Ibid.

35. Omi and Winant, *Racial Formation*, p. 138.

36. Stephen Steinberg, "The Underclass: A Case of Color Blindness," *New Politics* 11, no. 3 (Summer 1989): 42–60.

37. Thomas Vietorisz and Bennett Harrison, *The Economics of the Development of Harlem* (New York: Praeger, 1970); see esp. chap. 4.

38. Barbara Jeanne Fields, "Slavery, Race, and Ideology in the United States of America," *New Left Review* 181 (1990): 110.

39. Ibid., pp. 97–100. See also Omi and Winant, *Racial Formation*, pp. 58–64.

40. A line from the movie *Raintree Country*, quoted by Edward D. C. Campbell, Jr., *The Celluloid South: Hollywood and the Southern Myth* (Knoxville: University of Tennessee Press, 1981), pp. 168–70.

41. Fields, "Slavery Race, and Ideology," p. 98.

42. David E. Sanger, "Japanese Offers Apology for Slur, *New York Times*, October 18, 1990, sec. A.

43. This comment was made by a Haitian graduate student at City University of New York in 1984.

44. Raymond S. Franklin, "Race and Class Attitudes among Adult Worker District-65" (a pilot survey of some UAW District-65 adult evening students con New York, 1978).

45. Fields, "Slavery, Race and Ideology," p. 98.

46. Quote cited by John McGurl in a review by Drew Gilpin Faust, "Unpollsion," *New York Times Book Review*, June 3, 1990, p. 13.

47. W. E. B. Du Bois, *Souls of Black Folk: Essays and Sketches* (Greenwich: Fawcett, 1961), pp. 16–17.

28

The Race Relations Problematic

MICHAEL BANTON

The author takes issue with conceptual limitations regarding the approaches to understanding and defining race relations. He begins by describing briefly earlier attempts to provide an intellectual and conceptual framework for the study of race relations. Such attempts were dominated by theories stating major biological differences between racial groups and attributing, on this basis, cultural superiority to white groups. Although the term 'race relations' has evolved in terms of what it includes, it is still limited and confusing in its applicability. For example, the term implies that race is similar to how color and skin pigmentation are utilized in discriminatory situations. The term race relations also assumes that differences between blacks and whites are always more significant than differences among blacks, or among whites, from different groups. Discrimination could also be based on a person or a group's ethnic or national origins. Thus, race relations is not as neat a category as it is assumed in public discourse, or research.

In 1965 the British parliament passed the first anti-discrimination statute and called it a Race Relations Act. The name was unfortunate since it suggested that each individual could be assigned to a race, and that relations between persons of different race were necessarily different from relations between persons of the same race. In 1975 a further anti-discrimination statute was called the Sex Discrimination Act, so the revised 'race' act passed in the following year could well have been called the Race Discrimination Act, or the Prevention of Racial Discrimination Act, recalling the name of the statute against terrorism. Instead, the earlier title was used again. The official endorsement of the concept of 'race relations' has surely influenced the ideas and behaviour that are part of sociology's research agenda. This article seeks to show how developments in the law can help resolve sociological problems in the conceptualization of racial relations.[1]

ORIGINS

The first recorded use of the expression 'race relations' dates from 1911 when it was used, in the title only, of a study of the economic status of Negroes in various Georgia counties.[2] Yet the intellectual origins of the expression go back to a small number of pre-Darwinian theorists who argued for the permanence of racial types. Within the genus *Panthera*, lions, tigers and leopards were distinct species.

Relations between animals of different species differed from relations between animals of the same species. Blacks, whites and yellows were represented as different species within the genus *Homo*. So racial relations among humans were to be identified by objective phenotypical characters. Nature had made black-white relations different from black-black relations. The pre-Darwinian version of permanent types later gave place to a post-Darwinian variant which represented blacks, whites and yellows as subspecies at different stages of evolution.[3]

After the First World War it was argued that the racial classifications of everyday life were social constructions based in the popular consciousness. Racial relations were therefore to be identified by shared subjective definitions.[4] One version held that such definitions were generated by situations of conquest, imperial rule and group privilege.[5] Variants of this view traced racial or ethnic antagonism to a split labour market and to the differential incorporation of groups into state structures.[6] Where the objective conception of racial relations envisaged a racial equilibrium as biologically maintained, the second perspective saw any equilibrium as politically maintained. The first way of identifying a racial relation led to a conception of racial relations as the study of the relative positions of collectivities in a natural order. The second way switched to a social order but still assumed that any relation between phenotypically distinctive individuals was a racial relation. Even if an individual realized that there was no objective basis for the distinction, and that appearances were socially generated, he or she was regarded as still trapped by others' perceptions.

After the Second World War commentators were as ready to talk of a 'colour problem' as of a 'race problem'. Both expressions made it sound as if the source of tension lay in biological differences rather than in the social use of them. My generation of sociologists after 1950 wished to stress the importance of studying the relations between individuals assigned to categories and to draw upon US research into what was later called the prejudice-discrimination axis. The first anti-discrimination bill, proposed by a Member of Parliament in 1951 but not debated, was called a Colour Bar Bill. From the middle 1950s, however, the idiom of race became more popular than that of colour. Some sociologists started to turn their attention to elements that were common to what were identified as racial conflicts in the USA, South Africa and other countries. Others, and particularly those with a historical orientation, objected to this enterprise. They started from the observation that the significance attached to phenotypical variation differs from one society to another and changes over time. Since racial classification and its associations were not constant, it was possible to understand racial relations only within the history of particular societies or regions. There is truth in such a contention, yet anyone who

has got used to life in a racially divided society is likely to interpret observations about divisions in other societies, or their absence, in terms of the racial ideas of his or her own society. Comparison may be tricky, yet it is unavoidable and it generates transcultural folk concepts that cannot well be ignored. Comparative study can be directed to the answering of limited questions. It does not have to seek the same kind of comprehensive understanding that is commonly sought in historical study.

THE PROBLEMATIC AND ITS CRITIC

By the end of the 1960s what Robert Miles calls a race relations problematic had taken shape. The annual conference of the British Sociological Association in 1969 was designed 'to contribute to the wider move on the part of some sociologists to integrate race relations into general sociological theory and discussion'.[7] Research based on the prejudice-discrimination axis could not account for the black mobilization movement of the 1960s in the USA. Nor did it seem adequate to an analysis of the racial element in British immigration policy of the same decade. Two components of the attempt to develop relevant theory were my account of the use of race as a role sign and John Rex's description of six structures of social interaction associated with the notion of racial differentiation.[8] My argument was too condensed because it led Julian Pitt-Rivers[9] to infer that I thought of a biological conception of race as constituting the role sign. So I replied: 'People do not perceive racial differences. They perceive phenotypical differences of colour, hair form, underlying bone structures and so on. Phenotypical differences are a first order abstraction, race is a second order abstraction. It is phenotypical differences which are used as role signs'.[10] Rex and I wished to keep the focus of attention on the analysis of interaction between racialized categories. I described my strategy as anascopic (looking up from the 'micro') and his as catascopic (looking down from the 'macro'). Marxist writers subsumed a catascopic interpretation within a philosophy of history addressed to current political issues.

In *Racism and Migrant Labour*, Robert Miles[11] argued that while the idea of race relations was present in popular consciousness it was misleading. To use it as the starting point for a problematic was to reflect back the phenomenal, everyday world, and, in so doing, legitimate the world of appearances. In particular, it could reinforce the false notion that the human species consists of a number of distinct races, each separately endowed with special cultural qualities and capacities. By a problematic I understand a set of questions of interest to scholars who share views about the best ways to answer the questions. In Miles' argument the essential relations were those of class, overlaid by the distortions of racism as a historical complex generated within and by capitalism. Other sociologists of his generation agreed with him in using 'racism' as an *explanandum*, a definer of a field of study, rather than as an *explanans*, as had been the practice of the previous generation. Seen from my standpoint, the new approach, in most of its varied developments, tended to neglect interpersonal relations, to aggregate aspects of behaviour that were best examined separately, and to represent racism as something with a life of its own that changed form as circumstances changed.

In Miles' writing on this topic there is a strongly prescriptive element: black-white relations in Britain should be seen in terms not of race relations but of racism and labour migration. His problematic is presented as one that should supersede mine, which is described as 'phoney'. My view is less doctrinaire. I shall argue for the race relations problematic without denying that there may also be a legitimate racism problematic. As I see them, the former is anascopic, the latter catascopic; they address different questions and could well develop side by side.

RACE AND COLOUR IN LAW

Recent decisions in the courts show that the law can take account of the influence upon popular behaviour of beliefs or assumptions about race without relying upon a zoological classification of races. The law is developing a vocabulary to cover the whole process of discrimination. I argue that social scientists can learn from this, and that they should take over legal definitions unless there are good reasons to the contrary.

The Race Relations Act of 1976 uses the words 'racial group' to define a class of protected persons consisting of five sub-classes. Race is used to define both the class and one of the sub-classes. According to section 3

> 'racial group' means a group of persons defined by reference to colour, race, nationality or ethnic or national origins, and references to a person's racial group refer to any racial group into which he falls.

I propose to discuss the distinction at the level of the sub-class between discrimination on grounds of colour and discrimination on grounds of race.[12] Before doing so, I would note that British law is not unique in dividing the class of protected persons into sub-classes. The International Convention on the Elimination of Racial Discrimination lists race, colour, descent, national and ethnic origin. The European Convention on Human Rights lists race and colour as two among ten grounds of prohibited discrimination. All the main international human rights conventions and British anti-discrimination policy statements list race and colour separately.

The leading case on the interpretation of 'ethnic origins' is that of *Mandla v Dowell Lee*.[13] The issue was whether a Sikh father who wished his son to be able to wear a turban as a pupil in a private school was entitled to the law's protections against indirect discrimination. The House of Lords decided in his favour. The court held that for a group to constitute an 'ethnic group' for the purposes of the 1976 Act it had to regard itself, and be regarded by others, as a distinct community by virtue of certain characteristics, two of which were essential. First it had to have a long shared history, of which the group was conscious as distinguishing it from other groups, and the memory of which it kept alive, and second it had to have a cultural tradition of its own, including family and social customs and manners, often but not necessarily associated with religious observance. Characteristics of geography, language, literature, religion and minority status (as either an oppressed or a dominant group) might be relevant though not essential. Gypsies and Rastafarians have since been held to be groups which meet what are now called 'the *Mandla* conditions'.[14]

In contemporary speech the expressions race and colour are frequently synonymous. It is therefore of interest that the 1976 Act specifies two sets of circumstance in which it is permissible to discriminate on grounds of race 'defined otherwise than by reference to colour'. The exceptions concern admission to clubs, and charitable instruments. They enable Laurence Lustgarten[15] to conclude that

> the Indian Workers' Association need not admit English or Pakistani applicants, and a bequest to establish an old people's home for Jews may still be given legal effect. It remains impermissible to establish a scholarship fund for whites only – which in this context is not a 'race' but a 'colour'.

It is permissible to establish a scholarship fund for people of a particular descent even though they are likely to be all of similar colour.

Clubs and charities have to work from written documents that can be subject to legal scrutiny. Members of the public may have difficulty envisaging circumstances in which someone may be said to have discriminated on grounds of colour but not of race. Simple if somewhat unusual examples are provided by cases in which a person's skin colour has changed because of a medical condition. White people may become dark because of a kidney disorder, or the removal of their adrenal glands, or Nelson's disease following an attack of jaundice. The kidneys fail to break down the melanocyte-stimulating hormone from the pituitary glands. As a result, English people find themselves regarded as Asians or blacks, and suffer discrimination. They have not changed their race. The discrimination is a reaction to skin colour. There are also changes in the opposite direction when Asian and black people contract forms of vitiligo and their skin lightens.

There have been press reports of Afro-Americans in the USA with this condition who suffer because blacks believe them to be white.[16] In Britain an Indian businessman whose skin lightened found that this helped him in his business life. By calculating the monetary value of such a change, or the costs borne by whites whose skin darkens, it might be possible to estimate the financial cost of being non-white in modern Britain.[17]

There are pharmaceutical products which enable pale-skinned people to acquire a sun tan more quickly, either by an artificial application of colour or by screening out ultra violet rays and increasing the melanin in their skin. There are others used by some black people which contain hydroquinine. This lightens their complexion by destroying the melanocyte. Very recently it has become possible by genetic engineering to switch on genes in plant cells so that they produce more melanin. Since changes in the earth's ozone layer are causing an increase in skin cancers, there should be a big market for new products enabling whites to darken their skin.[18] The same techniques could presumably be used to reduce melanin, so that before long skin colour may be a matter of personal choice. Questions of discrimination on grounds of colour as opposed to race may in the future have an actuality they have lacked in the past.

Whether they do or not, there is reason to look more closely into the distinction between colour and race implicit in the present law. Allegations of discrimination are heard in the civil courts and do not have to meet the same criteria as to intention as actions in the criminal courts. Before reaching a finding of discrimination a court or tribunal has nevertheless to be satisfied as to the subjective ingredient. This was stated by Mr. Justice McCullogh in a sex discrimination case as follows:

> To determine whether a woman has been treated less favourably 'on grounds of her sex' it is necessary to consider why she was so treated. This will involve a consideration of the state of mind of the alleged discriminator, but only so far as necessary to discover whether the factor which brought about the difference in treatment was that she was a woman and not a man ...[19]

What is the factor that leads an English person to deny a job or a service to a person of African or Asian origins when it would not have been denied to a similarly qualified person of English origins? When should that factor be identified as colour and when as race? In most circumstances it will not be necessary for a court or tribunal to address the second question. It can announce a finding of racial discrimination without specifying whether it occurred on grounds of colour or race or both. Only if someone suffering from Nelson's disease or in comparably unusual circumstances sought relief might it be necessary to consider whether the aggrieved person was within either of the first two protected sub-classes, and in this way sharpen their definition.

The factor which causes discrimination will vary from case to case. It might be a belief that someone belonged to a particular race and would therefore possess or lack particular qualities. This would exemplify an ideological source of discrimination. Since 1945 there has been significant progress in the struggle against racial ideology. As the controversies over questions about race in the Census indicate, there is now widespread doubt among white English people, as well as minority members, about the validity of racial classifications. Yet if the remains of racial ideology were to be eliminated forthwith, physical differences such as skin colour would still be present and would still be used, often unreliably, in reaching assumptions about personal qualities.

RACIAL GROUNDS

Sociologists who presented racial relations as distinguished by shared subjective definitions did not investigate the extent to which these were actually shared. This makes it the more interesting to note an observation by Oliver Cox [20]

> ... by race relations we do not mean all social contact between persons of different 'races', but only those contacts the social characteristics of which are determined by a consciousness of 'racial' differences. Two people of different 'race' could have a relation that was not racial.

This last sentence was important from both a scientific and a political point of view. To determine when two such people could have a relation that was not racial would delimit racial from non-racial relations. To discover the conditions under which such a relation could be attained would point to a strategy for reducing racial tension. Cox did not elaborate the reasoning that lay behind his sentence. Perhaps its truth seemed self-evident to him and to others, so its significance was not appreciated. It seems to have been assumed that a relation which was not racial was not, for these purposes, a social problem. Any suggestion that there could be good racial relations appeared to be a contradiction in terms.

A clear-cut answer to the question of what is a racial relation is now not only possible but relevant to an understanding of the place of law in measures to eliminate racial discrimination. The British acts since 1965 have prohibited actions 'on racial grounds' in specified fields or circumstances. The International Convention on the Elimination of All Forms of Racial Discrimination defines as discrimination 'any distinction, exclusion, restriction or preference based on race, colour, descent, or national or ethnic origin which has the purpose or effect of nullifying or impairing the recognition, enjoyment or exercise, on an equal footing, of human rights and fundamental freedoms in the political, economic, social, cultural and any other field of public life'. The expression 'based on ... race' is virtually identical with the British 'on racial grounds'.[21]

In determining whether someone has acted on prohibited grounds it is necessary, as Mr. Justice McCullogh indicated, to consider the state of mind of the alleged discriminator. Since it is unlawful in Britain to discriminate against a Jewish man on the grounds of his race or ethnic origins, but not unlawful to do so on the grounds of his religion, a court may one day have to decide whether someone who has discriminated against a Jew, and claims to have acted on religious grounds, is trying to excuse unlawful behaviour. It is also possible for a man to discriminate against another on racial grounds because he believes him to be of a particular race even though the man is not of that race. In the discussion of the causes of behaviour it is often useful to distinguish between intent and motive. When someone acts in order to achieve a particular objective that person's intention can be inferred. Intention is often conscious and it directs action towards particular objectives. On the other hand, ambition, avarice, jealousy, and so on, are motivations which may give rise to a continuing pattern of action and thereby make particular intentions more comprehensible. To decide if someone has acted on racial grounds it may be necessary to relate an action in question to such a continuing pattern. A particular action will often be shaped by a mixture of motives; it can be found discriminatory, despite the presence of some good motives, if a person of one race is treated less favourably than someone of a different race would have been. The case of *R v Commission for Racial Equality ex parte Westminster City Council*[22] is helpful in this connection because the judges in the Court of Appeal disagreed about whether, before issuing a notice to cease discrimination, the CRE needed evidence of racial motivation on the part of the alleged discriminator or whether someone who reluctantly acted in conformity with the racial motivations of *other* people might be found to have acted on racial grounds. The majority took this latter view. In this somewhat extended sense, racial motivation constitutes the subjective ingredient of the offence of racial discrimination when direct discrimination is in question.

To establish unlawful racial discrimination three requirements have to be fulfilled.[23] Firstly, there has to be an action or omission within a protected field. Secondly, there has *either* (if it is a case of direct discrimination) to be evidence that the defendant acted on prohibited grounds, *or* (if it is a case of indirect discrimination) that an unjustifiable condition had been imposed which was more difficult for members of a given racial group to meet. Thirdly, the action or omission has, as a result, to be to the detriment of a person or persons affected. The definition of direct discrimination points to a definition of racial relations. Racial relations are constituted by a wider range of actions and omissions in that they can be established in any sphere of social life. A racial relation's defining characteristic is the second requirement for direct racial discrimination, that of grounds. Racial relations are relations in which behaviour is racially motivated. That is to say, they are relations in which the parties' behaviour is influenced by their assigning one another to racial roles. When a man defines someone as belonging in a racial category other than his own, he regards that person as having rights and obligations in some way different from those of a person belonging to the same racial category as himself (otherwise there would be no separate categories). In Britain at the present time popular definitions of race will comprehend the first two sub-classes and at times the others also. In unequal relations, the dominant party may force the weaker party to accept a racial definition of the relation between them. The second requirement is therefore crucial, whereas the third one does not have to be met at all. Racial relations are not necessarily detrimental to anyone. A racial motivation can lead to someone's being treated more favourably.

Cox's sentence can now be explicated. Two persons of different 'race' can have a relation that is not racial whenever their behaviour towards one another is not racially motivated. Implicit in this argument is a distinction between relations and relationships. Relations exist between individuals, relationships between roles. When two individuals interact, they can do so on the basis of alternative relationships: man and woman; senior and junior; employer and employee; landlord and tenant; black and white; English and Nigerian; Christian and Muslim; one sporting enthusiast to another, and so on. Inter-personal relations are many-stranded; the parties can switch from an interaction based upon a relationship of employment to one based upon gender, and so on. Which relationship is to be the base for their interaction is a matter for negotiation. One party may have greater power in this respect. For example, a male employer might attempt to shift his relation with his secretary from the basis of employment to one of gender, but such an attempt will not necessarily succeed. There are also parties of indeterminate status who may sometimes but not always succeed in getting themselves accepted in a preferred role. In the circumstances envisaged by Cox, two men who might be regarded by others as being of different race could establish a relation. This could be conducted on the basis of different relationships, one of which would be a racial relationship, but if neither of them was influenced by any notion that the physical differences were relevant to conduct, the relation between them would not be racial. Of course, it may not be possible to determine whether such an influence was present in a particular instance.

THE DEFINITION OF 'RACIAL'

The law has been running on parallel courses in Britain and the USA. Two cases were decided by the US Supreme Court in 1987 which bore on the reach of anti-discrimination legislation.[24] In one, the Shaare Tefila congregation instituted a civil rights action against eight men accused of defacing their synagogue with antisemitic slogans. The first court dismissed their suit, holding that discrimination against Jews is not racial discrimination, and this view was upheld on appeal. In the other case, Saint Francis College defended itself against a suit brought by a professor who claimed that he had been denied tenure because of his Arab origin and Muslim religion. The first court dismissed their suit, holding that the law did not cover claims of discrimination based upon ancestry, but this was reversed on appeal. The two further appeals were argued on the same day and decided in sequence. Counsel for the congregation did not argue that Jews were a separate race, but that the animus against them had been racial; since whites who had been victimized by other whites for giving support to the rights of blacks had been given the Court's protection, so should her clients. This raised the question of whether an alleged discriminator was mistaken in identifying the victim racially. Seeking criteria for who was protected by reference to race, the justices asked about the relation of race to national origin, colour, ethnicity, physiognomy, ancestry and stock. A unanimous Supreme Court later decided that for a charge of racial discrimination to be made out it was necessary to demonstrate not only that the defendants were motivated by racial animus but also that the animus was directed toward the kind of group that Congress intended to protect in 1866 when it passed the statute. Jews and Arabs could bring suit because they were among the peoples considered to be distinct races when the statute was enacted, whether or not these groups could be considered racial in modern scientific theory. A distinctive physiognomy was not essential to qualify for protection. Discrimination based upon ancestry or ethnic characteristics could be racial discrimination in law.

The House of Lords decision in the *Mandla* case is in line with present popular usage and much social scientific usage. The adjective racial is used to identify groups distinguished by physical characters and the adjective ethnic for groups distinguished by cultural characters. Racial minorities are thought to be groups based on involuntary and ethnic minorities upon voluntary identification. This usage has several disadvantages. It does not allow for the possibility that a group may be both a racial minority, because it experiences discrimination related to its members' physical characteristics, and an ethnic minority, because of its cultural distinctiveness. It overlooks the evidence that in everyday life racial assignment follows cultural rules which regulate the classification of anomalous persons. The same person may be assigned to different racial categories in different countries and the definition of those categories changes over time. The significance of physical characters is culturally defined. The popular usage also has the unfortunate consequence that ethnicity is often thought to be an attribute of minorities alone. Those features of majorities which might otherwise be considered ethnic are instead identified as cultural or national. The features of minority culture which differ from majority culture and lead to the former being called ethnic, derive either from the way of life in the area where the minority people or their ancestors used to live, or they derive from the structure of majority-minority relations in their present location.

In the *Mandla* case the judgments in both the Court of Appeal and the House of Lords were unanimous in declaring that the words 'colour, race, nationality or ethnic or national origins' were to be interpreted in terms of their meaning to the general public and not in any technical sense. The days in which anthropologists could claim to be experts able to define race objectively are over. Social scientists can follow the courts and acknowledge that in different countries the general public varies in its use of the idea of race as a pointer to classification. There are also changes over time both in the meaning attributed to the word and in its relation to other classifiers.

RACE AND COLOUR IN SOCIETY

Skin colour is a feature which varies along a continuous scale when measured by a light meter, but in social life it is used either as a discontinuous or a continuous variable in ordering social relations. In the first case it is used, together with other phenotypical features, to assign an individual to a racial category. Racial categories are discontinuous, so rules have to be developed to determine how individuals of anomalous appearance are to be classified. By deciding that anyone with more than a given degree of pigmentation is coloured rather than white, a continuous scale is split into two. This kind of assignment gives rise to categorical relations. In the second case, colour is used to assign an individual to a place in a scale of continuous differentiation. Usually, however, it is not taken in isolation but is perceived as a factor, which, together with wealth, education, accent, demeanour, etc., decides where an individual should be placed in a scale of social status. This process gives rise to status relations both between and within racial categories.

The classic analyses of black-white relations in the Deep South associated with W. Lloyd Warner,[25] illustrate these distinctions. Colour was in the first place a racial sign used to assign individuals to either the black or the white category. This might decide whether they could vote, sit in a restaurant, try on clothes in a department store, and so on. These were situations governed by the principle of social inequality. There were other situations governed by the principles of good business. In these colour was one status sign among others. Blacks were always subordinated to whites by racial criteria but some blacks could be ranked above some whites by status criteria. Whites sometimes disagreed about whether a particular inter-category relation was to be defined in terms of race or status. Calculations of status also governed relations within racial categories. All groups have ideas about what defines beauty and who is to be accounted good-looking. They have what has been called a somatic norm image.[26] Complexion may be an important element. The whites in the Deep South may not have varied greatly in colour but someone of darker hue may have needed to explain that, for example, it derived from a Spanish grandparent. The blacks in the Deep South did vary greatly in colour and employed a series of adjectives to designate differences of shade. In the northern cities there was greater spatial segregation; a black person encountered racial discrimination in fewer circumstances and the black population had more freedom to service itself in an economy that offered greater opportunities. Colour was still used to assign individuals to racial categories but the implications of categorization were less far-reaching. Considerations of social status were more important in both inter- and intra-category relations so there was no reduction in the relevance of colour as a status sign.

The same physical features do not have the same social significance in different settings. Anthropological studies in Northeastern Brazil have shown that there differences in colour are used to place individuals on a scale but that this placement has little influence upon access to privilege or resources.[27] There are no racial categories, though the same cannot be said for all parts of Brazil. In a cosmopolitan milieu, like that of Geneva, where there are many people involved with the UN, colour may have little or no sign value because by itself it gives no indication as to the likelihood that a person speaks French or English, holds a high position or a low one, and so on. Nor does everyone read the signs in the same way. Prior experience, education, political identification and personality traits may all affect the outcome. The number and nature of racial categories, if any, depends partly upon the size and

composition of groups and their position in the economic structure, but it is also a product of the political relations between them.

In Britain the social significance of skin colour has changed over the last forty years, reflecting changes in the size of the minority groups and the patterns of majority-minority interactions. Up to the middle of the century, skin colour was in the first place a territorial sign, designating a colonial visitor or a temporary and somewhat exceptional resident. Since a dark-skinned man could be a maharajah, an African chief, a doctor, student or seaman, colour by itself had little value as a sign of status. But with the increase in working-class immigration from the colonies the association of a dark colour with a low social status was strengthened.

This is to view matters from a white perspective. With the build-up of minority communities in the 1960s, minority self-definition became more important. Many minorities, particularly those from South Asia, sought to preserve distinctive cultural features; they wished the majority to respect those features and allow minorities to cultivate their own identities. West Indians wanted whites to respect black pride. The hitherto prevailing practice of using the adjective coloured as a category name was disparaged. In order to combat racial disadvantage new forms of categorization were introduced which are better described as ethnic than as racial. Whereas racial assignment in the Deep South was imposed on the weaker section by the stronger, ethnic categorization is negotiated between groups. It endorses cultural difference and is justified as being, on balance, important to the reduction of disadvantage.

The present position in Britain therefore requires a complex framework of analysis, one which, I believe, can constitute an improved race relations problematic. In the first place there is the conscious or unconscious assignment of individuals to racial categories. This is primarily a matter of whites denying services to non-whites on racial grounds as these are defined in law. There is a series of important questions to be answered about the situations in which discrimination of various kinds occurs most frequently, why it occurs, and the variations between its forms. There is also an assignment, which is frequently a self-assignment to ethnic categories, which extends the protections of the law to groups which are culturally but not physically distinguishable in circumstances in which they are treated less favourably than members of the discriminating group. This opens a further range of questions about group characteristics.

In the second place there is a largely unconscious tendency for whites to place other whites on a continuous scale of social status. A person's physical appearance is one element in this appraisal and skin colour is important to the white somatic norm image. In inter-category relations whites usually judge the status claims of non-whites by the criteria determining status within the white category. Social psychologists have investigated some of the factors involved. In one study samples of people were shown photographs of eighteen men and asked to evaluate each face for intelligence, honesty, social class, political inclination and attractiveness.

> Their judgments of which political party a person supported were related to how attractive and intelligent they judged that person's face to be and from which social class they believed that person to come. These judgments were affected neither by the raters' political inclinations, nor by their sex.

The higher the faces were rated for these qualities, the more likely were they thought to be photographs of Conservatives.[28] Facial appearance was a trigger evoking prior shared ideas relating to status differences. The social significance of differences in styles of speech has been examined in a variety of studies. Those who use Received Pronunciation are rated more highly than those who use a regional style. This influences the effectiveness of communication between the parties. Consistent findings have been reported for other cultures. An up-to-date review has concluded

> many recent studies have shown that standard listeners infer from non-standard speech style not only that such speakers would be unsuitable as partners in close personal relationships but would likely hold many dissimilar beliefs from them and are also perceived as being less in control communicatively.[29]

Speech can be another trigger or sign that guides conduct. This line of research should be extended to cover the significance of colour in relation to other attributes of appearance and speech. It should also cover the significance attached to colour differences within the minorities. The black pride movement challenged the negative evaluation of a dark colour and sought to persuade people that black could be as beautiful as white. Those who sympathize with this aspiration should be interested to learn in what circumstances, in both inter- and intra-category relations, people currently act on this premiss.

In some circumstances the appropriate course of conduct is defined by the context of the encounter. Hospitals provide a good example, for though the patient and the doctor may be assigned to different races, the relations between them are defined by their roles and not by race. It is possible that racial consciousness is most effectively reduced when individuals see one another as playing occupational roles. It may be as important to study situations in which discrimination is absent as those in which it is present.

CONCLUSION

The 'race relations problematic', should be seen as an examination of the changing significance of colour, descent, national and ethnic origins as well as of race, and as one set among the many kinds of grounds on which people draw distinctions. In Britain, the growth in numbers of persons of partly European and partly Asian or Afro-Caribbean ancestry will add to other tendencies making it necessary to allow for inter-individual variations in the significance attached to skin colour and in ideas about racial categorization. Racial relations are to be identified by the subjective meaning attached to differences, but that meaning is by no means completely determined by structurally generated forces. Miles' claim that the sociology of race relations necessarily reifies race has not been substantiated, and the racism problematic has difficulties of its own. If racism is directed only against physically distinctive categories of people, then this concept also can reinforce notions of biological differences. In penalizing action 'on racial grounds' the law does not 'reflect back' or legitimate false ideas. To the contrary, it stigmatizes them and is starting to change 'the phenomenal, everyday world'. In determining the scope of the protected class and in examining behaviour that springs from mixed motives, the law is defining key terms with greater precision than many of those used in the socio-scientific study of inter-group relations. Sociologists are often more interested in large-scale social trends, but if the importance of these is to be established it should be possible to identify their influence at the interpersonal level. The law relating to racial discrimination shows some of the ways in which this can be done.

NOTES

1. This article condenses arguments advanced in two presidential addresses to the Royal Anthropological Institute and separately published by the Institute: *Which Relations Are Racial Relations?*, 1988, and *Science, Law and Politics in the Study of Racial Relations*, 1989.

2. R. P. Brooks, 'A Local Study of the Race Problem: Race Relations in the Eastern Piedmont Region of Georgia', *Political Science Quarterly*, vol. 26, 1911, pp. 193–221.

3. Sir Arthur Keith, *Ethnos or The Problem of Race*, London, Kegan Paul, 1931.

4. Robert E. Park and E. W. Burgess, *Introduction to the Science of Sociology*, Chicago, University of Chicago Press, 1921.

5. Oliver C. Cox, *Caste, Class, and Race: a study in social dynamics*, New York, Monthly Review Press, 1948.

6. Edna Bonacich, 'A Theory of Ethnic Antagonism: The Split Labor Market', *American Sociological Reveiw*, vol. 37, 1972, pp. 547–59; Leo Kuper, *Race, Class and Power. Ideology and Revolutionary Change in Plural Societies*, London, Duckworth, 1974.

7. Sami Zubaida (ed.), *Race and Racialism*, London, Tavistock, 1970.

8. John Rex, 'The Concept of Race in Sociological Theory', in Zubaida, *op. cit.*, pp. 35–55.

9. Julian Pitt-Rivers, 'Race Relations as a Science: A Review of Michael Banton's "Race Relations"', *Race,* vol. 11, 1970, pp. 335–42.

10. Michael Banton, 'Analytical and Folk Concepts of Race and Ethnicity', *Ethnic and Racial Studies*, vol. 2, 1979, pp. 127–38.

11. Robert Miles, *Racism and Migrant Labour*, London, Routledge, 1982.

12. Anthony Dickey, 'The Race Formula of the Race Relations Acts', *The Juridical Review*, 1974, pp. 282–97.

13. 1983 All England Law Reports: 1062–72.

14. Michael Banton, 'Are Rastafarians an Ethnic Group?' *New Community*, vol. 16, 1989, pp. 153–7.

15. Laurence Lustgarten, *Legal Control of Racial Discrimination*, London, Macmillan, 1980.

16. E.g. Evelyn Irons, 'The White Negroes', *Sunday Times Magazine*, 17 January, 1971.

17. Cf. Michael Banton, *Racial Minorities*, London, Fontana, 1972, pp. 97–8.

18. John Elkington, 'The Melanin Message in the Bottle', *The Guardian*, 29 November, 1988.

19. 1988 Industrial Relations Law Reports at 99.

20. *Op. cit.*, p. 320.

21. The seventh preambular paragraph of the Convention uses the expression 'on the grounds of race'. In the French and Spanish texts (which are equal in authenticity to the English text) the same words are used in the preambular paragraph and in the definition in article 1(1).

22. 1985 Industrial Relations Law Reports: 426–34.

23. Not all acts of discrimination are unlawful. The British legislation protects people from discrimination in employment, education, and the provision of goods, facilities, services and premises. It does not extend to employment in a private household. It would not affect the decision of a father who disinherited his daughter for marrying someone of another race. Discrimination is permissible 'where being of a particular racial group is a genuine occupational qualification for the job'. The stock example used to be the Chinese restaurant with a Chinese decor and Chinese cuisine which wished to employ only waiters of Chinese physiognomy, but Section 5(2)(d) is now used to advertise for black social workers on the grounds that they can deal more effectively with the needs of black people. Since only the Commission for Racial Equality is empowered to bring proceedings in respect of discriminatory practice, it has on occasion brought actions against local authorities making questionable use of Section 5(2)(d).

24. 107 Supreme Court 2019 (1987); 107 Supreme Count 2022 (1987). Also *The United States Law Week* March 3, 1987, vol. 55(34) 3579–81.

25. W. Lloyd Warner, *The Structure of American Life*, Edinburgh, Edinburgh University Press, 1952, pp. 15–27.

26. H. Hoetink, *Caribbean Race Relations: A Study of Two Variants*, London, Oxford University Press, 1967, pp. 120–26. (orig. pub., in Dutch, in 1962).

27. Marvin Harris, 'Racial Identity in Brazil', *Luso-Brazilian Review*, vol. 1, 1964, pp. 21–8.

28. Ray Bull and Nichola Rumsey, *The Social Psychology of Facial Appearance*, New York, Springer Verlag, 1988, pp. 55–6.

29. Howard Giles, Miles Hewstone, Ellen B. Ryan and Patricia Johnson, 'Research on Language Attitudes', pp. 585–97 in Ulrich Ammon, Norbert Dittmar & Klaus J. Mattheier, *Sociolinguistics*, Berlin, de Gruyter, 1987 at pp. 590–1.

29

Dysconscious Racism: Ideology, Identity, and the Miseducation of Teachers

JOYCE E. KING

Joyce E. King describes another manifestation of racism which she describes as 'dysconscious racism'. She proposes that dysconscious racism prevents a full and sincere embrace of the celebration of racial and ethnic diversity in US society. This kind of racism 'tacitly accepts dominant white norms and privileges. It is not the *absence* of consciousness (that is, not unconsciousness) but an *impaired* consciousness or distorted way of thinking about race as compared to, for example, critical consciousness)' (p. 135). In a study of undergraduate students' perceptions about racism, she found that invariably white students attribute the current social and economic problems of blacks, and black children in particular, to slavery. Thus, slavery in US history becomes a mechanism by which to overlook contemporary factors contributing to racial social and economic disparities. Commentary about US institutions reflects a strong belief among the students in the racial fairness and neutrality of such. But King contends that these mechanisms serve to defend and apologize for a system built on white privilege.

They had for more than a century before been regarded as ... so far inferior ... that the negro might justly and lawfully be reduced to slavery for his benefit .... This opinion was at that time fixed and universal in the civilized portion of the white race. It was regarded as an axiom in morals as well as in politics, which no one thought of disputing ... and men in every grade and position in society daily and habitually acted upon it ... without doubting for a moment the correctness of this opinion. (*Dred Scott v. Sanford*, 1857)

Racism can mean culturally sanctioned beliefs which, regardless of the intentions involved, defend the advantages whites have because of the subordinated positions of racial minorities. (Wellman, 1977, p. xviii)

The goal of critical consciousness is an ethical and not a legal judgement [*sic*] about the social order. (Heaney, 1984, p. 116)

CELEBRATING DIVERSITY

The new watchwords in education, "celebrating diversity," imply the democratic ethic that all students, regardless of their sociocultural backgrounds, should be educated equitably. What this ethic means in practice, particularly for teachers with little personal experience of diversity and limited understanding of inequity, is problematic. At the elite, private, Jesuit university where I teach, most of my students (most of whom come from relatively privileged, monocultural backgrounds) are anxious about being able to "deal" with all the diversity in the classroom. Not surprisingly, given recent neoconservative ideological interpretations of the problem of diversity, many of my students also believe that affirming cultural difference is tantamount to racial separatism, that diversity threatens national unity, or that social inequity originates with sociocultural deficits and not with unequal outcomes that are inherent in our socially stratified society. With respect to this society's changing demographics and the inevitable "browning" of America, many of my students foresee a diminution of their own identity, status, and security. Moreover, regardless of their conscious intentions, certain culturally sanctioned beliefs my students hold about inequity and why it persists especially for African Americans, take White norms and privilege as givens.

The findings presented herein will show what these beliefs and responses have to do with what I call "dysconscious racism" to denote the limited and distorted understandings my students have about inequity and cultural diversity—understandings that make it difficult for them to act in favor of truly equitable education. This article presents a qualitative analysis of dysconscious racism as reflected in the responses of my teacher education students to an open-ended question I posed at the beginning of one of my classes during the fall 1986 academic quarter to assess student knowledge and understanding of social inequity. Content analysis of their short essay responses will show how their thinking reflects internalized ideologies that both justify the racial status quo and devalue cultural diversity. Following the analysis of their responses and discussion of the findings I will describe the teaching approach I use to counteract the cognitively limited and distorted thinking that dysconscious racism represents. The concluding discussion will focus on the need to make social reconstructionist liberatory teaching an option for teacher education students like mine who often begin their professional preparation without having

ever considered the need for fundamental social change (see also Ginsburg, 1988; and Ginsburg & Newman, 1985).

Critical, transformative teachers must develop a pedagogy of social action and advocacy that really celebrates *diversity*, not just random holidays, isolated cultural artifacts, or "festivals and food" (Ayers, 1988). If dysconscious racism keeps such a commitment beyond the imagination of students like mine, teacher educators need forms of pedagogy and counter-knowledge that challenge students' internalized ideologies and subjective identities (Giroux & McLaren, 1988). Prospective teachers need both an intellectual understanding of schooling and inequity as well as self-reflective, transformative emotional growth experiences. With these objectives in mind, I teach my graduate-level Social Foundations of Education course in the social reconstructionist tradition of critical, transformative, liberatory education for social change (see Gordon, 1985; Freire, 1971; Giroux & McLaren, 1986; Heaney, 1984; Shor, 1980; Searle, 1975; Sleeter & Grant, 1988). In contrast to a pedagogy for the oppressed, this course explores the dynamics of a liberatory pedagogy for the elite. It is designed to provide such teacher education students with a context in which to consider alternative conceptions of themselves and society. The course challenges students' taken-for-granted ideological positions and identities and their unquestioned acceptance of cultural belief systems which undergird racial inequity.

Thus, the course and the teaching methods I use transcend conventional social and multicultural Foundations of Education course approaches by directly addressing societal oppression and student knowledge and beliefs about inequity and diversity. By focusing on ways that schooling, including their own miseducation, contributes to unequal educational outcomes that reinforce societal inequity and oppression, students broaden their knowledge of how society works. I offer this analysis of dysconscious racism and reflections on the way I teach to further the theoretical and practical development of a liberatory praxis that will enable teacher education students to examine what they know and believe about society, about diverse others, and about their own actions.

Dysconsciousness is an uncritical habit of mind (including perceptions, attitudes, assumptions, and beliefs) that justifies inequity and exploitation by accepting the existing order of things as given. If, as Heaney (1984) suggests, critical consciousness "involves an ethical judgement [*sic*]" about the social order, dysconsciousness accepts it uncritically. This lack of critical judgment against society reflects an absence of what Cox (1974) refers to as "social ethics"; it involves a subjective identification with an ideological viewpoint that admits no fundamentally alternative vision of society.[1]

Dysconscious racism is a form of racism that tacitly accepts dominant White norms and privileges. It is not the *absence* of consciousness (that is, not unconsciousness) but an *impaired* consciousness or distorted way of thinking about race as compared to, for example, critical consciousness. Uncritical ways of thinking about racial inequity accept certain culturally sanctioned assumptions, myths, and beliefs that justify the social and economic advantages White people have as a result of subordinating diverse others (Wellman, 1977). Any serious challenge to the status quo that calls this racial privilege into question inevitably challenges the self-identity of White people who have internalized these ideological justifications. The reactions of my students to information I have presented about societal inequity have led me to conceptualize dysconscious racism as one form that racism takes in this post-civil rights era of intellectual conservatism.

Most of my students begin my Social Foundations course with limited knowledge and understanding of societal inequity. Not only are they often unaware of their own ideological perspectives (or of the range of alternatives they have not consciously considered), most are also unaware of how their own subjective identities reflect an uncritical identification with the existing social order. Moreover, they have difficulty explaining "liberal" and "conservative" standpoints on contemporary social and educational issues, and are even less familiar with "radical" perspectives (King & Ladson-Billings, 1990). My students' explanations of persistent racial inequity consistently lack evidence of any critical ethical judgment regarding racial (and class/gender) stratification in the existing social order; yet, and not surprisingly, these same students generally maintain that they personally deplore racial prejudice and discrimination. However, Wellman (1977) notes that this kind of thinking is a hallmark of racism. "The concrete problem facing white people," states Wellman, "is how to come to grips with the demands made by blacks and whites while at the same time *avoiding* the possibility of institutional change and reorganization that might affect them" (p. 42). This suggests that the ability to imagine a society reorganized without racial privilege requires a fundamental shift in the way White people think about their status and self-identities and their conceptions of Black people.

For example, when I broach the subject of racial inequity with my students, they often complain that they are "tired of being made to feel guilty" because they are White. The following entries from the classroom journals of two undergraduate students in an education course are typical of this reaction[2]:

> With some class discussions, readings, and other media, there have been times that I feel guilty for being White which really infuriates me because no one should feel guilty for the color of their skin or ethnic background. Perhaps my feelings are actually a discomfort for the fact that others have been discriminated against all of their life [*sic*] because of their color and I have not.

> How can I be thankful that I am not a victim of discrimination? I should be ashamed. Then I become confused. Why shouldn't I be thankful that I have escaped such pain?

These students' reactions are understandable in light of Wellman's insights into the nature of racism. That White teacher education students often express such feelings of guilt and hostility suggests they accept certain unexamined assumptions, unasked questions, and unquestioned cultural myths regarding both the social order and their place in it. The discussion of the findings that follows will show how dysconscious racism, manifested in student explanations of societal inequity and linked to their conceptions of Black people, devalues the cultural diversity of the Black experience and, in effect, limits students' thinking about what teachers can do to promote equity.

THE FINDINGS

Since the fall academic quarter 1986 I have given the student teachers in my Social Foundations course statistical comparisons such as those compiled by the Children's Defense Fund (Edelman, 1987) regarding Black and White children's life chances (e.g., "Compared to White children, Black children are twice as likely to die in the first year of life"; see Harlan, 1985). I then ask each student to write a brief explanation of how these racial inequities came about by answering the question: "How did our society get to be this way?" An earlier publication (King & Ladson-Billings, 1990) comparing student responses to this question in the fall 1986 and spring 1987 quarters identifies three ways students explain this inequity. Content analysis of their responses reveals that students explain racial inequity as either the result of slavery (Category I), the denial or lack of equal opportunity for African Americans (Category II), or part of the framework of a society in which racism and discrimination are normative (Category III). In the

---

[1] It should be noted that dysconsciousness need not be limited to racism but can apply to justifications of other forms of exploitation such as sexism or even neocolonialism—issues that are beyond the scope of the present analysis.

[2] I want to thank Professor Gloria Ladson-Billings, who also teaches at my institution, for providing these journal entries. See her discussion of student knowledge and attitudes in this issue of the *JNE*.

present article I will again use these categories and the method of content analysis to compare student responses collected in the 1986 and 1988 fall quarters. The responses presented below are representative of 22 essay responses collected from students in 1986 and 35 responses collected in 1988.

Category I explanations begin and end with slavery. Their focus is either on describing African Americans as "victims of their original (slave) status," or they assert that Black/White inequality is the continuing result of inequity which began during slavery. In either case, historical determinism is a key feature; African Americans are perceived as ex-slaves, and the "disabilities of slavery" are believed to have been passed down intergenerationally. As two students wrote:

> I feel it dates back to the time of slavery when the Blacks were not permitted to work or really have a life of their own. They were not given the luxury or opportunity to be educated and *each generation passed this disability on* [italics added]. (F6–21)[3]

> I think that this harkens [sic] back to the origin of the American Black population as slaves. Whereas other immigrant groups started on a low rung of our economic (and social class) ladder and had space and opportunity to move up, Blacks did not. They were perceived as somehow less than people. This view may have been passed down and even on to Black youth ... (F8–32)

It is worth noting that the "fixed and universal beliefs" Europeans and White Americans held about Black inferiority/White superiority during the epoch of the Atlantic slave trade, beliefs that made the enslavement of Africans seem justified and lawful, are not the focus of this kind of explanation. The historical continuum of cause and effect evident in Category I explanations excludes any consideration of the cultural rationality behind such attitudes; that is, they do not explain *why* White people held these beliefs.

In Category II explanations the emphasis is on the denial of equal opportunity to Black people (e.g., less education, lack of jobs, low wages, poor health care). Although students espousing Category II arguments may explain discrimination as the result of prejudice or racist attitudes (e.g., "Whites believe Blacks are inferior"), they do not necessarily causally link it to the historical fact of slavery or to the former status of Black people as slaves. Rather, the persistently unequal status of African Americans is seen as an *effect* of poverty and systemic discrimination. Consider these two responses from 1986 and 1988:

> ...Blacks have been treated as second class citizens. Caucasians tend to maintain the belief that Black people

are inferior ... *for this reason* [italics added] Blacks receive less education and education that is of inferior quality .... less pay than most other persons doing the same job; (and) live in inferior substandard housing, etc. (F6–3)

> Because of segregation—overt and covert—Blacks in America have had less access historically to education and jobs, which has led to a poverty cycle for many. *The effects described are due to poverty* [italics added], lack of education and lack of opportunity. (F8–7)

In addition, some Category I and Category II explanations identify negative psychological or cultural characteristics of African Americans as effects of slavery, prejudice, racism, or discrimination. One such assertion is that Black people have no motivation or incentive to "move up" or climb the socioeconomic ladder. Consequently, this negative characteristic is presumed to perpetuate racial inequality: Like a vicious cycle, Whites then perceive Blacks as ignorant or as having "devalued cultural mores." The following are examples of Category II explanations; even though they allude to slavery, albeit in a secondary fashion, the existence of discrimination is the primary focus:

> Blacks were brought to the U.S. by Whites. They were/are thought to be of a "lower race" by large parts of the society .... society has impressed these beliefs/ideas onto Blacks. (Therefore) Blacks probably have lower self-esteem and when you have lower self-esteem, it is harder to move up in the world .... Blacks group together and stay together. Very few move up ... partly because society put them there. (F6–18)

> Past history is at the base of the racial problems evident in today's society. Blacks have been persecuted and oppressed for years ... Discrimination is still a problem which results in lack of motivation, self-esteem and hence a lessened "desire" to escape the hardships with which they are faced. (F8–14)

In 1986 my students' responses were almost evenly divided between Category I and Category II explanations (10 and 11 responses, respectively, with one Category III response). In 1988 all 35 responses were divided between Category I (11) and Category II (24) responses, or 32% and 68%, respectively. Thus, the majority of students in both years explained racial inequality in limited ways—as a historically inevitable consequence of slavery or as a result of prejudice and discrimination—without recognizing the structural inequity built into the social order. Their explanations fail to link racial inequity to other forms of societal oppression and exploitation. In addition, these explanations, which give considerable attention to Black people's negative characteristics, fail to account for White people's beliefs and attitudes that have long justified societal oppression and inequity in the form of racial slavery or discrimination.

---

[3] This and subsequent student comment codes used throughout this article identify individual respondents within each cohort. "F6–21," for example, refers to respondent 21 in the fall 1986 academic quarter.

DISCUSSION

An obvious feature of Category I explanations is the devaluation of the African American cultural heritage, a heritage which certainly encompasses more than the debilitating experience of slavery. Moreover, the integrity and adaptive resilience of what Stuckey (1987) refers to as the "slave culture" is ignored and implicitly devalued. Indeed, Category I explanations reflect a conservative assimilationist ideology that blames contemporary racial inequity on the presumed cultural deficits of African Americans. Less obvious is the way the historical continuum of these explanations, beginning as they do with the effects of slavery on African Americans, fails to consider the specific cultural rationality that justified slavery as acceptable and lawful (Wynter, 1990). Also excluded from these explanations as possible contributing factors are the particular advantages White people gained from the institution of racial slavery.

Category II explanations devalue diversity by not recognizing how opportunity is tied to the assimilation of mainstream norms and values. These explanations also fail to call into question the basic structural inequity of the social order; instead, the cultural mythology of the American Dream, most specifically the myth of equal opportunity, is tacitly accepted (i.e., with the right opportunity, African Americans can climb out of poverty and "make it" like everyone else). Such liberal, assimilationist ideology ignores the widening gap between the haves and the have nots, the downward mobility of growing numbers of Whites (particularly women with children), and other social realities of contemporary capitalism. While not altogether inaccurate, these explanations are nevertheless *partial* precisely because they fail to make appropriate connections between race, gender, and class inequity.

How do Category I and Category II explanations exemplify dysconscious racism? Both types defend White privilege, which, according to Wellman (1977), is a "consistent theme in racist thinking" (p. 39). For example, Category I explanations rationalize racial inequity by attributing it to the effects of slavery on African Americans while ignoring the economic advantages it gave Whites. A second rationalization, presented in Category II explanations, engenders the mental picture many of my students apparently have of equal opportunity, not as equal access to jobs, health care, education, etc. but rather as a sort of "legal liberty" which leaves the structural basis of the racial status quo intact (King & Wilson, 1990). In effect, by failing to connect a more just opportunity system for Blacks with fewer white-skin advantages for Whites, these explanations, in actuality, defend the racial status quo.

According to Wellman, the existing social order cannot provide for unlimited (or equal) opportunity

for Black people while maintaining racial privileges for Whites (p. 42). Thus, elimination of the societal hierarchy is inevitable if the social order is to be reorganized; but before this can occur, the existing structural inequity must be recognized as such and actively struggled against. This, however, is not what most of my students have in mind when they refer to "equal opportunity."

Category I and Category II explanations rationalize the existing social order in yet a third way by omitting any ethical judgment against the privileges White people have gained as a result of subordinating Black people (and others). These explanations thus reveal a dysconscious racism which, although it bears little resemblance to the violent bigotry and overt White supremacist ideologies of previous eras, still takes for granted a system of racial privilege and societal stratification that favors Whites. Like the Whites of Dred Scott's era, few of my students even think of disputing this system or see it as disputable.

Category III explanations, on the other hand, do not defend this system. They are more comprehensive, and thus more accurate, because they make the appropriate connections between racism and other forms of inequity. Category III explanations also locate the origins of racial inequity in the framework of a society in which racial victimization is *normative*. They identify and criticize both racist ideology and oppressive societal structures without placing the responsibility for changing the situation solely on African Americans (e.g., to develop self-esteem), and without overemphasizing the role of White prejudice (e.g., Whites' beliefs about Black inferiority). The historical factors cited in Category III explanations neither deny White privilege nor defend it. I have received only one Category III response from a student at the beginning of my courses, the following:

> [Racial inequity] is primarily the result of the economic system ... racism served the purposes of ruling groups; e.g., in the Reconstruction era ... poor Whites were pitted against Blacks—a pool of cheap exploitable labor is desired by capitalists and this ties in with the identifiable differences of races. (F6–9)

Why is it that more students do not think this way? Given the majority of my students' explanations of racial inequity, I suggest that their thinking is impaired by dysconscious racism—even though they may deny they are racists. The important point here, however, is not to prove that students are racist; rather, it is that their uncritical and limited ways of thinking must be identified, understood, and brought to their conscious awareness.

Dysconscious racism must be made the subject of educational intervention. Conventional analyses—which conceptualize racism at the institutional, cultural, or individual level but do not address the cognitive distortions of dysconsciousness—cannot help students distinguish between racist justifications of the status quo (which limit their thought, self-identity, and responsibility to take action) and socially unacceptable individual prejudice or bigotry (which students often disavow). Teacher educators must therefore challenge both liberal and conservative ideological thinking on these matters if we want students to consider seriously the need for fundamental change in society and in education.

Ideology, identity, and indoctrination are central concepts I use in my Social Foundations of Education course to help students free themselves from miseducation and uncritically accepted views which limit their thought and action. A brief description of the course follows.

The Cultural Politics of Critiquing Ideology and Identity

One goal of my Social Foundations of Education course is to sharpen the ability of students to think critically about educational purposes and practice in relation to social justice and to their own identities as teachers. The course thus illuminates a range of ideological interests which become the focus of students' critical analysis, evaluation, and choice. For instance, a recurring theme in the course is that of the social purposes of schooling, or schooling as an instrument of educational philosophy, societal vision, values, and personal choice. This is a key concept about which many students report they have never thought seriously. Course readings, lectures, media resources, class discussions, and other experiential learning activities are organized to provide an alternative context of meaning within which students can critically analyze the social purposes of schooling. The range of ideological perspectives considered include alternative explanations of poverty and joblessness, competing viewpoints regarding the significance of cultural differences, and discussions of education as a remedy for societal inequity. Students consider the meaning of social justice and examine ways that education might be transformed to promote a more equitable social order. Moreover, they are expected to choose and declare the social changes they themselves want to bring about as teachers.

The course also introduces students to the critical perspective that education is not neutral; it can serve various political and cultural interests including social control, socialization, assimilation, domination, or liberation (Cagan, 1978; Freire, 1971; O'Neill, 1981). Both impartial, purportedly factual information as well as openly partisan views about existing social realities such as the deindustrialization of America, hunger and homelessness, tracking, the "hidden" curriculum (Anyon, 1981;

Vallence, 1977), the socialization of teachers, and teacher expectations (Rist, 1970) allow students to examine connections between macrosocial (societal) and microsocial (classroom) issues. This information helps students consider different viewpoints about how schooling processes contribute to inequity. Alongside encountering liberal and conservative analyses of education and opportunity, students encounter the scholarship of radical educators such as Anyon (1981), Freire (1971), Kozol (1981), and Giroux and McLaren (1986), who have developed "historical identities" (Boggs et al., 1978) within social justice struggles and who take stronger ethical stances against inequity than do liberals or conservatives. These radical educators' perspectives also provide students with alternative role models; students discuss their thoughts and feelings about the convictions these authors express and reflect upon the soundness of radical arguments. Consequently, as students formulate their own philosophical positions about the purposes of education, they inevitably struggle with the ideas, values, and social interests at the heart of the different educational and social visions which they, as teachers of the future, must either affirm, reject, or resist.

Making a conscious process of the struggle over divergent educational principles and purposes constitutes the cultural politics of my Social Foundations course. In this regard my aim is to provide a context within which student teachers can recognize and evaluate their personal experiences of political and ethical indoctrination. In contrast to their own miseducation, and using their experience in my course as a point of comparison, I urge my students to consider the possibilities liberatory and transformative teaching offers. To facilitate this kind of conscious reflection, I discuss the teaching strategies I myself model in my efforts to help them think critically about the course content, their own world view, and the professional practice of teaching (Freire & Faundez, 1989). To demonstrate the questions critical, liberatory teachers must ask and to make what counts as "school knowledge" (Anyon, 1981) problematic, I use Freire's (1971) strategy of developing "problem-posing" counter-knowledge. For example, I pose biased instructional materials as a problem teachers address. Thus, when we examine the way textbooks represent labor history (Anyon, 1979) and my student teachers begin to realize all they do not know about the struggles of working people for justice, the problem of miseducation becomes more real to them. Indeed, as Freire, Woodson (1933), and others suggest, an alternative view of history often reveals hidden social interests in the curriculum and unmasks a political and cultural role of schooling of which my student teachers are often completely unaware.

Analysis of and reflection on their own knowledge and experience involves students in critiquing ideologies, examining the influences on their thinking and identities, and considering the kind of teachers they want to become. I also encourage my students to take a stance against mainstream views and practices that dominate in schools and other university courses. Through such intellectual and emotional growth opportunities, students in my course re-experience and re-evaluate the partial and socially constructed nature of their own knowledge and identities.

My approach is not free from contradictions, however. While I alone organize the course structure, select the topics, make certain issues problematic, and assign the grades, I am confident that my approach is more democratic than the unwitting ideological indoctrination my students have apparently internalized. For a final grade, students have the option of writing a final exam in which they can critique the course, or they may present (to the class) a term project organized around an analytical framework they themselves generate.

Toward Liberatory Pedagogy in Teacher Education

Merely presenting factual information about societal inequity does not necessarily enable preservice teachers to examine the beliefs and assumptions that may influence the way they interpret these facts. Moreover, with few exceptions, available multicultural resource materials for teachers presume a value commitment and readiness for multicultural teaching and antiracist education which many students may lack initially (Bennett, 1990; Brandt, 1986; Sleeter & Grant, 1988). Teacher educators may find some support in new directions in adult education (Mezirow, 1984) and in theories of adult learning and critical literacy which draw upon Freire's work in particular (Freire & Macedo, 1987). This literature offers some useful theoretical insights for emancipatory education and liberatory pedagogy (Heaney, 1984). For example, the counter-knowledge strategies I use in my Social Foundations course are designed to facilitate the kind of "perspective transformation" Mezirow (1984) calls for in his work. It is also worth noting that a tradition of critical African American educational scholarship exists which can be incorporated into teacher preparation courses. Analyses of miseducation by Woodson (1933), DuBois (1935), and Ellis (1917) are early forerunners of critical, liberatory pedagogy. This tradition is also reflected in contemporary African American thought and scholarship on education and social action (see Childs, 1989; Gordon, 1990; Lee et al., 1990; Muwakkil, 1990; Perkins, 1986).

As Sleeter and Grant (1988, p. 194) point out, however, White students sometimes find such critical, liberatory approaches threatening to their self-concepts and identities. While they refer specifically to problems of White males in this regard, my experience is that most students from economically privileged, culturally homogeneous backgrounds are generally unaware of their intellectual biases and monocultural encapsulation. While my students may feel threatened by diversity, what they often express is guilt and hostility. Students who have lived for the most part in relatively privileged cultural isolation can only consider becoming liberatory, social-reconstructionist educators if they have both an adequate understanding of how society works and opportunities to think about the need for fundamental social change. The critical perspective of the social order offered in my course challenges students' world views as well as their self-identities by making problematic and directly addressing students' values, beliefs, and ideologies. Precisely because what my students know and believe is so limited, it is necessary to address both their knowledge (that is, their intellectual understanding of social inequity) and what they believe about diversity. As Angus and Jhally (1989, p. 12) conclude, "what people accept as natural and self-evident" is exactly what becomes "problematic and in need of explanation" from this critical standpoint. Thus, to seriously consider the value commitment involved in teaching for social change as an option, students need experiential opportunities to recognize and evaluate the ideological influences that shape their thinking about schooling, society, themselves, and diverse others.

The critique of ideology, identity, and miseducation described herein represents a form of cultural politics in teacher education that is needed to address the specific cultural rationality of social inequity in modern American society. Such a liberatory pedagogical approach does not neglect the dimension of power and privilege in society, nor does it ignore the role of ideology in shaping the context within which people think about daily life and the possibilities of social transformation. Pedagogy of this kind is especially needed now, given the current thrust toward normative schooling and curriculum content that emphasizes "our common Western heritage" (Bloom, 1987; Gagnon, 1988; Hirsch, 1987; Ravitch, 1990). Unfortunately, this neoconservative curriculum movement leaves little room for discussion of how being educated in this tradition may be a limiting factor in the effectiveness of teachers of poor and minority students (King & Wilson, 1990; Ladson-Billings, 1991). Indeed, it precludes any critical ethical judgment about societal inequity and supports the kind of miseducation that produces teachers who are dysconscious—uncritical and unprepared to question White norms, White superiority, and White privilege.

Myths and slogans about common heritage notwithstanding, prospective teachers need an alternative context in which to think critically about and reconstruct their social knowledge and self-identities. Simply put, they need opportunities to become conscious of oppression. However, as Heaney (1984) correctly observes: "Consciousness of oppression can not be the object of instruction, it must be discovered in experience" (p. 118). Classes such as my Social Foundations course make it possible for students to re-experience the way dysconscious racism and miseducation victimize them.

That dysconscious racism and miseducation of teachers are part of the problem is not well understood. This is evident in conventional foundations approaches and in the teacher education literature on multiculturalism and pluralism which examine social stratification, unequal educational outcomes, and the significance of culture in education but offer no critique of ideology and indoctrination (Gollnick & Chinn, 1990; Pai, 1990). Such approaches do not help prospective teachers gain the critical skills needed to examine the ways being educated in a racist society affects their own knowledge and their beliefs about themselves and culturally diverse others. The findings presented in this article suggest that such skills are vitally necessary. The real challenge of diversity is to develop a sound liberatory praxis of teacher education which offers relatively privileged students freedom to choose critical multicultural consciousness over dysconsciousness. Moving beyond dysconsciousness and miseducation toward liberatory pedagogy will require systematic research to determine how teachers are being prepared and how well those whose preparation includes critical liberatory pedagogy are able to maintain their perspectives and implement transformative goals in their own practice.

REFERENCES

Angus, I., & Jhally, S. (Eds.). (1989). *Cultural politics in contemporary America*. New York: Routledge.

Anyon, J. (1979). Ideology and U.S. history textbooks. *Harvard Educational Review, 49*, 361–386.

Anyon, J. (1981). Social class and school knowledge. *Curriculum Inquiry, 11*, 3–42.

Ayers, W. (1988). Young children and the problem of the color line. *Democracy and Education, 3*(1), 20–26.

Banks, J. (1977). *Multiethnic education: Practices and promises*. Bloomington, IN: Phi Delta Kappa Educational Foundation.

Bennett, C. (1990). *Comprehensive multicultural education: Theory and practice*. Boston: Allyn & Bacon.

Bloom, A. (1987). *The closing of the American mind*. New York: Simon & Schuster.

Boggs, J. et al. (1978). *Conversations in Maine: Exploring our nation's future*. Boston: South End Press.

Brandt, G. (1986). *The realization of anti-racist teaching*. Philadelphia: The Falmer Press.

Cagan, E. (1978). Individualism, collectivism, and radical educational reform. *Harvard Educational Review, 48*, 227–266.

Childs, J. B. (1989). *Leadership, conflict and cooperation in Afro-American social thought*. Philadelphia: Temple University Press.

Cox, G. O. (1974). *Education for the Black race*. New York: African Heritage Studies Publishers.

Du Bois, W. E. B. (1935). Does the Negro need separate schools? *Journal of Negro Education, 4*, 329–335.

Edelman, M. W. (1987). *Families in peril: An agenda for social change*. Cambridge, MA: Harvard University Press.

Ellis, G. W. (1917). Psychic factors in the new American race situation. *Journal of Race Development, 4*, 469–486.

Freire, P. (1971). *Pedagogy of the oppressed*. New York: Harper & Row.

Freire, P., & Faundez, A. (1989). *Learning to question: A pedagogy of liberation*. New York: Continuum.

Freire, P., & Macedo, D. (1987). *Literacy: Reading the word and the world*. South Hadley, MA: Bergin & Garvey.

Gagnon, P. (1988, November). Why study history? *Atlantic Monthly*, pp. 43–66.

Ginsburg, M. (1988). *Contradictions in teacher education and society: A critical analysis*. Philadelphia: The Falmer Press.

Ginsburg, M., & Newman, K. (1985). Social inequalities, schooling and teacher education. *Journal of Teacher Education, 36*, 49–54.

Giroux, J., & McLaren, P. (1986). Teacher education and the politics of engagement: The case for democratic schooling. *Harvard Educational Review, 56*, 213–238.

Gollnick, D., & Chinn, P. (1990). *Multicultural education in a pluralistic society*. Columbus, OH: Merrill.

Gordon, B. (1985). Critical and emancipatory pedagogy: An annotated bibliography of sources for teachers. *Social Education, 49*(5), 400–402.

Gordon, B. (1990). The necessity of African-American epistemology for educational theory and practice. *Journal of Education, 172*, in press.

Harlan, S. (1985, June 5). Compared to White children, Black children are ... *USA Today*, p. 9–A.

Heaney, T. (1984). Action, freedom and liberatory education. In S. B. Merriam (Ed.), *Selected writings on philosophy and education* (pp. 113–122). Malabar, FL: Robert E. Krieger.

Hirsch, E. D. (1987). *Cultural literacy: What every American needs to know*. New York: Houghton Mifflin.

Howard, B. C. (1857). *Report of the decision of the Supreme Court of the United States and the opinions of the justices thereof in the case of Dred Scott versus John F. A. Sandford, December term*, 1856. New York: D. Appleton & Co.

King, J., & Ladson-Billings, G. (1990). The teacher education challenge in elite university settings: Developing critical and multicultural perspectives for teaching in a democratic and multicultural society. *European Journal of Intercultural Studies, 1*(2), 15–30.

King, J., & Wilson, T. L. (1990). Being the soul-freeing substance: A legacy of hope in Afro humanity. *Journal of Education, 172*(2), in press.

Kozol, J. (1981). *On being a teacher*. New York: Continuum.

Ladson-Billings, G. (1991). Beyond multicultural illiteracy. *Journal of Negro Education, 60*(2), 147–157.

Lee, C. et al. (1990). How shall we sing our sacred song in a strange land? The dilemma of double consciousness and complexities of an African-centered pedagogy. *Journal of Education, 172*, (2), in press.

Mezirow, J. (1984). A critical theory of adult learning and education. In S. B. Merriam (Ed.), *Selected writings on philosophy and adult education* (pp. 123–140). Malabar, FL: Robert E. Krieger.

Muwakkil, S. (1990). Fighting for cultural inclusion in the schools. *In These Times, 14*(37), 8–9.

O'Neill, W. F. (1981). *Educational ideologies: Contemporary expressions of educational philosophy*. Santa Monica, CA: Goodyear.

Pai, Y. (1990). *Cultural foundations of education*. Columbus, OH: Merrill.

Perkins, U. E. (1986). *Harvesting new generations: The positive development of Black youth*. Chicago: Third World Press.

Ravitch, D. (1990). Diversity and democracy. *The American Educator, 14*, 16–20.

Rist, R. (1970). Student social class and teacher expectations. *Harvard Educational Review, 40*, 411–451.

Searle, C. (Ed.). (1975). *Classrooms of resistance*. London: Writers and Readers Publishing Cooperative.

Shor, I. (1980). *Critical teaching in everyday life*. Boston: South End Press.

Sleeter, C., & Grant, C. (1988). *Making choices for multicultural education: Five approaches to race, class and gender*. Columbus, OH: Merrill.

Stuckey, S. (1987). *Slave culture: Nationalist theory and the foundations of Black America*. New York: Oxford University Press.

Vallence, E. (1977). Hiding the hidden curriculum: An interpretation of the language of justification in nineteenth-century educational reform. In A. Bellack & H. Kliebard (Eds.), *Curriculum and evaluation* (pp. 590–607). Berkeley, CA: McCutchan.

Wellman, D. (1977). *Portraits of White racism*. Cambridge, MA: Cambridge University Press.

Woodson, C. G. (1933). *The miseducation of the Negro*. Washington, DC: Associated Publishers.

Wynter, S. (1990, September 9). *America as a "world": A Black studies perspective and "cultural model" framework*. [Letter to the California State Board of Education.]

30

Origins of the Myth of Race

DOUG JENNESS

The author argues that racism, or racial hate, or 'racial prejudice' emerged during the fifteenth and sixteenth centuries as a justification for institutional slavery. Jenness states that 'the myth of a black race that is inferior was developed to rationalize the institution of enslavement of blacks from Africa'. Initially, the justification for racism was that blacks, and also Indians, and others were not Christian, but infidels. But this justification was not effective because it placed a burden on Christians to convert non-Christians and ultimately to treat new converts equally. Thus, skin color, became a convenient mechanism for the enslavement of millions of laborers. Racial categorization of some laborers was also functional during the imperialism that emerged in the nineteenth and twentieth centuries. Today, racial hate and prejudice, similarly continue to keep people divided along a socially constructed line, called race. This serves the interests of groups that exploit poor people, and working-class people.

The following is the text of a talk given at a December 28–29 regional socialist educational conference in St. Paul, Minnesota. The gathering, which drew participants from cities in Minnesota, Illinois, Missouri, Iowa, and Nebraska, also discussed topics ranging from the political situation in the United States to the origins of women's oppression and why working people should defend immigrants' rights.

In Dubuque, Iowa, during the last six months there have been 14 incidents of cross burnings with 20 crosses burned. Right-wing racist forces on a national scale have decided to put a spotlight on integration plans in Dubuque and have called for a march January 18 in support of what they call "white rights."

For the last several weeks newspapers in Dubuque have given regular, matter-of-fact coverage to this proposed action. A headline from a recent issue of Dubuque's *Telegraph Herald* reads, "White Rights Group Plans January March." No quote marks are placed around "white rights." This tends to legitimize the notion that there is such a thing as "white rights" that this white supremacist organization is championing. The National Association for the Advancement of White People, another racist outfit, has announced its support for the January 18 march. Some civil rights supporters are calling for protests against the actions by the ultra-rightists.

Here in the Twin Cities we have a small formation called the White Student Union. Its members are attempting to start an organization at the University of Minnesota. The group has attempted to draw in reactionary fascist skin-heads from East St. Paul to conduct thug attacks on antiracist fighters. This has generated protests by students and others, not only at the University of Minnesota, but at other campuses in the area as well.

I'd like to describe what this organization sees as its purpose. A flier distributed by the group says:

"What's the purpose of the White Student Union? To protest affirmative action and quotas and to promote white culture. What is white culture? Each race is naturally predisposed to its own set of values. White values are reflected in such time-tested cultural expressions as classical music, canonized literature, a representative form of government, a free market economic system, Western medicine, romantic love, and the nuclear family. Whites tend to value a specific kind of analytical thinking based on logic rather than intuition, 'knowledge,' or dogmatic adherence to preset rationales.

Continuing, the White Student Union states, "Western white thinking consists of analytical observation, detailed intellectual exploration, effectively explicit social discourse, and inner gratification arising from increased understanding about life. Whites structure their lives as if time is objectively real and ultimately linear, setting high goals and aspiring to accomplish them through tenacious hard work: In a free market system, where they can set their own goals, whites value their personal ambitions deeply, and thus find great satisfaction in striving towards excellence with every resource they can tap ..." The leaflet goes on in that strain.

"Isn't everybody equal? Equal according to what values? Would you judge a raccoon as if it were a canary? Everyone is different. If people were all the same, it would never matter whether one talked to one person rather than another. It is preferable to be free to aspire to achieve one's full cultural potential in a community which reflects one's own natural cultural values."

Then the flier, referring to quotas and affirmative action, asks, "What characteristics does the White Student Union hope to find and foster in its members? Primarily the White Student Union welcomes people who are pro-white. We protest racism against whites, and adhere to white values in our lives. We work with a strong will, consciously avoiding such defeatist attitudes as cynicism and despair.

"We are heterosexual, and happy about it. We strive to promote white culture, to observe honestly what directions it is taking, and to preserve the ideals we value most within it."

In an earlier article, White Student Union leader Tom David describes who he considers to be part of the "white race," making it explicit that Jews are not part of it. He didn't explain what "race" they are part of.

Is there a 'White Race?'

These two recent examples from Dubuque and the Twin Cities reflect an increasing ideological offensive by right-wing and fascist-type organizations that utilize reactionary demagogy. They pose important questions that working people and youth must answer: Is there such a thing as a "white race" with distinct "white rights?" Is there a white culture? Does affirmative action for Blacks and other oppressed nationalities harm workers with white skins? Is there a Black race with rights? Are there races at all? If so how are they determined, by what criteria? How many are there?

To pose these questions is to implicitly ask if there are parts of the human population that can be identified as belonging to distinct and inferior races.

Is the question of whether or not the White Student Union should be officially recognized as a campus organization the same as whether or not a Black student union should be recognized?

What about antihate laws? Is the hatred of oppressed Blacks against their oppression the same as the hatred expressed by Tom David, David Duke, Patrick Buchanan, and so on?

These questions can't be pooh-poohed, dismissed, or just answered superficially. Clear, scientific answers are needed to counter the demagogy of the ultra-right and fascist elements— not to convince the cadre elements of fascist organizations, but because these ideas have confused thousands of workers, farmers, students, and others. The question of race, of nation, of country have been the stock and trade of fascist demagogy for decades. Right-wing demagogues also charge defenders of a woman's right to choose abortion with tearing apart the family. What answer should class-conscious workers give to that? Should the family be torn apart? Should it be allowed to disintegrate? To answer this you have to go deeper than defending abortion rights as just a matter of democratic rights.

Another theme rightists hammer away at is that of "country." We're citizens of this country, of the "American nation," we're told. Our government, they say, has a responsibility to defend the rights of our citizens to jobs ahead of those rights for immigrant workers from other countries. How do we answer that?

These themes that fascists and right-wingers raise require deeper explanations,—scientific explanations. They pose questions that can't just be set aside. It is not enough to simply say "we're for immigrant rights, Black rights, abortion rights," and so on in order to effectively arm others to see the dangers in and be able to effectively counter the rightist and fascist arguments.

In this presentation I'll take up the question of race. This afternoon there will be a class on immigrant rights and tomorrow the questions of the origin of women's oppression and the family will be discussed.

Origins of the Concept of Race

Because racial prejudice is so deeply embedded in our society, it usually comes as a surprise to many people to learn that the concept of races is a social construct, and a recent one in human history. It did not emerge until the early days of capitalism, when the institution of chattel slavery was introduced.

The myth of a Black race that is inferior was developed to rationalize the institution of enslavement of Blacks from Africa.

The merchant capitalists of the 15th, 16th, and 17th centuries needed massive quantities of labor power in the New World—more than they could get from just utilizing white indentured servants or from the indigenous populations of the Americas— of whom millions were wiped out in just a few years from diseases brought from Europe.

In *Capital*, Karl Marx explained what steps the early capitalists took to gather the necessary capital together to get their system off the ground, a process called primitive accumulation. In Europe they drove peasants off the land and into factories in the newly emerging cities. This was done at a forced pace and with a great deal of human misery. Another central aspect of the primitive accumulation of capital was the introduction of the slave labor system: utilizing a form of labor from an earlier epoch of human society—that reached its most developed form in ancient Greece and Rome. They introduced it into the capitalist system where the slave produced commodities for a capitalist market.

First the Indians and then Blacks were enslaved. They justified this slave system on the basis that Blacks and Indians weren't Christians, that they were infidels. One of the big tasks of the Christian world was to convert non-Christian peoples to Christianity, thereby integrating them into and making them part of the western Christian world.

This ideological rationalization didn't stand the test of time because as Indians and Blacks became Christians, it could no longer justify keeping them in bondage.

In its place a more insidious and long-lasting edifice was built: the concept of race. Blacks were identified as a biologically inferior race—one naturally suited to slave labor. A whole different set of behavioral patterns were assigned to Blacks, such as temperament or ability to withstand hard work and heat, that suited them to slave labor.

Black Skin Branded

The emerging capitalist class needed a rationalization that made Blacks not only temporarily inferior but one with which they would remain inferior generation after generation. The concept of race supplied that. Skin color was the physical characteristic singled out to brand an entire part of the human race. Like ranchers would put a brand on cattle. It made it hard for Blacks to escape the slaveholder. Everyone in society knew that if you had black skin you were a slave, or could be enslaved. White indentured servants could escape and go off into the woods somewhere in the spacious unsettled lands of the Americas. For Blacks it was nearly impossible. A brand was placed on this sector of society by the British, the French, the Belgian, the Dutch, the Spanish, the Portuguese, and later the U.S. merchant and planting capitalists.

All the capitalist politicians, the preachers, and the academicians rallied their efforts behind this justification. After Charles Darwin presented the theory of natural selection for the evolution of species in 1859—a gigantic conquest in scientific thinking—a raft of so-called scientists were brought in to give the notion of racial inferiority a "scientific" veneer. This spurious effort attempted to prove that it was through natural selection and evolution that Blacks were closer to the apes in the evolutionary chain.

Enormous battles have been waged by working people in the United States over the past 150 years, struggles that put an end to chattel slavery and brought down the system of legalized segregation that arose in its place. But the myth of race, constructed to justify an inhuman social system, still gets an echo today, as can be seen from the literature of the White Student Union and others.

The myth of race, and the superiority of one race over another, has not only been used to justify slavery in the United States. It is the cornerstone of the apartheid system in South Africa, where the wealthy capitalist ruling class constructed a state of the "white race." Nelson Mandela accurately characterized this system as a "crime against humanity." After decades of brutal suppression of the struggle to bring down the hated system, the Pretoria regime has also been pushed into an historic retreat. In its place a new nation is being forged, one made up of all Blacks and whites who want to live in a democratic republic. As the African National Congress explains, they are fighting for a "democratic, nonracial, nonsexist South Africa."

But some of you may be asking: wasn't there prejudice based on race or a concept of race in earlier periods of human history, especially where slavery existed? In ancient Greece, slavery was the main mode of production. The Greeks sent their armies to capture slaves far and wide. The people who weren't Greek were considered barbarians. But barbarians weren't a race. They came in many colors, cultures, backgrounds, and varying geographical areas.

In the later stage of the Greek empire, under the reign of Alexander the Great, the Greeks aimed to make the peoples they conquered part of Greek culture. At the same time they sought to merge major features of other cultures with theirs and urged the intermarriage of people of different cultures and backgrounds.

In Rome, another society in which slavery was the main mode of production, slavery was not based on the color of a person's skin either. There was no real conception of race at that time. Slaves in Rome came from the British Isles, Ethiopia, Persia, Greece, and elsewhere. They ranged from being artisans and poets to mine workers and field workers.

Those from Britain were of more dubious value because they were more culturally backward. Cicero explained, for example, that they didn't know much about art or music and weren't really good as slaves.

It's worth reading Julius Caesar's account of his first invasion of Britain and his description of what he saw as the cultural level of the Britons. He says they were a strange people—they were terrifying—but they were odd. The men shaved all their hair off, except that on their head which was kept long. They went into battle virtually naked, with blue tattoos on their bodies. Caesar describes it as a terrifying sight.

Medieval society was similarly not divided on the basis of race. It was divided between Christians and infidels, Christians and Jews, and Christians and Muslims.

RADICAL RECONSTRUCTION IN THE US

Coming back to the United States and the struggle against slavery, it is worthwhile to point out that even many abolitionists assumed that Blacks were inferior. They reasoned, though, that even an inferior people should not be enslaved and treated like livestock. The abolition of slavery was a result of the Second American Revolution, which was without question the most important revolution of the 19th century anywhere in the world. But it didn't bring an end in anti-Black racism and prejudice.

There was a possibility that a major fight along this course could have been waged. After the defeat of the Confederacy in 1865, and under Radical Reconstruction, revolutionary popular governments were established in many of the former slave states. The most advanced ones were based on an alliance of poor whites and former Black slaves. Many Blacks participated in these governments and held leading elected offices as senators, congressmen, and state representatives—positions that even today they do not hold in some states.

During Radical Reconstruction, the potential power of working people began to be felt. Blacks won self-confidence, broke down erroneous conceptions of what Blacks were capable of doing, and smashed racist barriers. Strides forward in areas such as public education were made.

But Radical Reconstruction was smashed by the industrial capitalists. Blacks were never granted their central demand of 40 acres and a mule. At the same time tens of thousands of white settlers were getting tracts of land through the Homestead Act adopted in 1862. This denial of land of Blacks and the smashing of Reconstruction governments were major setbacks for the struggle against the oppression of Blacks and for the fight of all working people against exploitation.

The capitalist class halted and then reversed Radical Reconstruction through a bloody reign of terror. They feared the convergence of these revolutionary governments with the rise in the labor movement and the massive protests of working farmers in the South and in the Midwest that were beginning to take place in the 1870s.

JIM CROW SEGREGATION

After a period of several decades of reaction a system of legal segregation was imposed in the 1890s and the early years of the 1900s in the former slave states throughout the South. It took some time between the smashing of Radical Reconstruction in the late 1870s and early 1880s, and the codification of what became the Jim Crow system of legal segregation, a system backed by state and extralegal terror.

Establishing this system went hand in hand with the emergence of imperialism at the turn of the century. The depth and scope of the imposition of the segregation laws was part and parcel of, and drew sustenance and strength from, the development of imperialist domination of other countries by the U.S. ruling families.

It went hand in hand with the need of the ruling class to use racism to justify imperialist oppression and conquest and the horrible atrocities that went along with it. The period was marked by imperialist wars, invasions, and subjugation of the Philippines, Cuba, Puerto Rico, Hawaii, and other lands. The "white race" was presented as having the burden of helping to civilize the "inferior peoples." This was extended to all people of color.

Pseudo-scientific arguments were developed to justify this oppression. These tried to show that there is a genetically superior white race. This ideology and so-called science were not only used to justify imperialist aggression, conquest, and oppression but was also retained inside the imperialist countries. The concept of race that had developed with the origin of slavery was kept in place as an instrument of class exploitation inside the United States. It became deeply enmeshed in capitalist exploitation, primarily as a measure to divide working people. The intended effect was not just to squeeze proportionally more profits from the labor of workers with black skins, but to squeeze more from the working class as a whole.

Do Human Features Determine Race?

But the question of the existence of races isn't disproved by simply describing the origin and development of anti-Black prejudice and the institutionalization by capitalists of racial division. We have to step back and take a closer look at the structure of the ideology that has been set up. For instance, someone could argue that there is a biological basis to race. If there is, doesn't that affect behavior patterns and aren't there really some very distinct races with distinct biological foundations and distinct social behavior? It's important to get at the biological arguments because they are the foundations on which the sociological conceptions of race are built.

The attempt to define biological races of human beings has almost always been done to show that some genetic basis exists for differences in human behavior. The reason that a larger percentage of Blacks than whites are poor and live on welfare, the argument goes, is due to character traits that are determined by their biological and genetic make-up. This view, in some form or fashion, is not uncommon. According to Tom David, people who aren't part of "white culture" aren't capable of understanding classical music. There are different levels of intelligence and capacity for culture. Blacks just aren't biologically quite up to it.

The white Student Union says in its leaflet that people from each race have their own culture and they should stick to that culture. We should keep them separate, David says; it's natural. He states "each is separate" and he doesn't try to say that one is better than the other. But this is all malarkey. We know this in this country that "separate but equal" is the most transparent cover for maintaining the superiority of whites over Blacks and other people of color.

The problem with trying to establish a biological criterion is that biologists and physical anthropologists have a difficult time coming up with any kind of objective criteria for defining races. What set of physical features can be used that would have any kind of genuine social meaning? Should it be eye color, color-blindness, skin color, hair color or texture, average height, average weight, length of the limbs, shape of the nose, brain size, or toe size? Those kinds of measurements have been taken as part of this pseudo-science. And applying them is not just a theoretical matter. For the past several decades the South African government has used such characteristics to define each and every new-born baby by "race," be it white, Indian, Colored, or African.

With one or more of these characteristics they've come up with anywhere from three to scores of different races in the world. It's hard to get a handle on it when you have so many different races. When I was in school, I think I was taught that there were five races. It was common for a long time for people to say that there were three: Caucasian, Negroid, and the Mongoloid. But of course if you have three main races where does that leave all the other people? What about Puerto Ricans? There are a lot of indigenous peoples in Mexico, a lot of immigrants from Europe, and a large number of people—probably the majority—who are a mixture of European and Indian. What race would Mexicans be? Negroid? Caucasian? Mongoloid? Mongrel?

Are pygmies in Africa Negroid? Are Bushman in Africa? Are aborigines in Australia? What race do the Sami people, who we know as Laplanders in northern Norway, Sweden Finland, and Russia come from?

Well, that's why people started getting long lists of races. Melanesian, Polynesian, Arabs, and the list goes on. The fact is that variation is very great in the human species. Moreover it is not static. What might have been considered races, 5,000 years ago are different from the way the same person would construct them today. There have been migrations, intermarriage, and colonial settlements for thousands of years. And these have intensified in the last few centuries. So the complexion of the human race is going to keep changing.

Scientific Conclusions

In the mid-19th century, even one of the most accomplished scientists, Louis Aggasiz, argued that Blacks and whites are separate species. Other scientists argued that different races are sub-species of the human species. But in recent years an increasing number of biologists and physical anthropologists have rejected the notion that there is any meaningful definition of race.

One of the most prominent is the anthropologist Ashley Montagu. In 1964 he edited a book called *The Concept of Race*, which contained a series of articles by anthropologists and biologists rejecting the concept of race.

The same year he gave a series of lectures published in a book, *The Idea of Race*. In this volume he noted:

"All human beings and all human groups differ from one another in one or more genes. That is a fact; and it is also a fact that when such individuals or groups are classed into arbitrary subdivisions called 'races' no matter what the criteria for such subdivisions may be, these classifications are arbitrary and correspond to nothing in reality. What is more important, such arbitrary subdivisions cannot be regarded as units of evolution either in space or in time. In the particular case of man, the 'races' that have been arbitrarily recognized are from a few to scores. What is obscured by such arbitrary definitions of 'race' are the facts. First, that the very idea of 'race' exists only in the mind of the definer, that it is an abstraction; second, that it in fact corresponds to nothing in reality; and third, that it obscures the real meaning of population variability. In short the biological concept of 'race' is an obfuscating one."

In the mid-1970s biologist and paleontologist Stephen Jay Gould wrote an article entitled, "Why we should not name human races—a biological view." It is included in his book, *Ever Since Darwin*. In rejecting the concept of race he noted that more sophisticated techniques of measuring variability in a species "show a continuous pattern of variation."

In his book on *Afro-American History* Malcolm X said, "And actually Caucasoid, Mongoloid, and Negroid—there's no such thing. These are so-called anthropological terms that were put together by anthropologists who were nothing but agents of the colonial powers, and they were purposely given that status, they were purposely given such scientific positions, in order that they could come up with definitions that would justify the European domination over the Africans and the Asians."

Even Adolf Hitler, who wrote and spoke extensively about the virtues of the "Aryan race" and the inferior nature of other races admitted in 1930: "I know perfectly well that in the scientific sense there is no such thing as race. But a farmer can't get his breeding right without the concept of race. And I as a politician, need a conception which enables the order that has hitherto existed on a historical basis to be abolished, and an entirely new and antihistoric order enforced and given an intellectual basis, and for this purpose the conception of race serves me well."

This underlines the cynical character of much of fascist demagogy.

We might face a totally different situation if it could be scientifically established that persons with particular physical characteristics were mentally or physically more limited than other humans. But this has never been established. All the measurements of brain size, IQ, and so on have not shown this. An excellent book by Stephen Jay Gould, *The Mismeasure of Man*, effectively debunks the notion that there is any relationship between brain size and intelligence, and IQ tests and intelligence, in human beings or that there is some pattern of brain size that proves Blacks are inferior.

Racial differentiation only serves the purpose of justifying oppression and superexploitation. It is a fiction, a form of mystification.

What's real and what isn't a mystification is that humanity with a Black skin and all people of color have been branded by capitalism as subject to oppression. This common oppression of Blacks in the United States has led to a common consciousness as a people facing the same struggles. The crushing of Radical Reconstruction and the subsequent struggle by Blacks against their oppression laid the basis for the forging of a nationality.

Nationality is a political characterization. It describes a people who are fighting for political equality up to and including self-determination, a people struggling for full equality in relation to the state and society, and for rights such as equal opportunities for jobs, education, and housing.

The fight for Black rights is progressive and the gains that have been won have aided all working people. There is no oppression of human beings based on white skin color. Most whites are workers or farmers and are exploited, but not because they are white. There is no oppressed white nationality and no fight for "white rights" that can be progressive. A struggle for white rights can only be a fight to preserve oppression of Blacks and other people of color.

That's why there is no parallel between a Black student union and a white student union. One is fighting to extend equality, the other to maintain inequality. One should be given campus recognition the other should not. We reject the idea that the campus is not part of the world or a part of the class struggle. Campus resources, such as those given to recognized student organizations, should be used to advance working-class interests, not to oppose those interests.

Now, does affirmative action take away the rights of workers who are white; does it come at their expense? This is an important question because if it did we would have to oppose it. Affirmative action is the recognition that special steps are necessary to win equal opportunities for Blacks.

A vigorous fight for this will benefit all workers—Blacks, whites, and Latinos—because it draws them closer together and it is the road to unity in political struggle. That's why the question of affirmative action is ultimately a class question, not a race question.

Karl Marx, in the first volume of *Capital*, wrote, "In the United States of America, every independent workers' movement was paralyzed as long as slavery disfigured a part of the republic. Labor in a white skin can't emancipate itself where it is branded in a black skin."

He was talking about the period just after slavery had been abolished and was hopeful that the branding of labor in a Black skin was going to be ended. But as I have explained, it hasn't and Marx's statement still rings true today. Notice that Marx starts with labor, with the working class. He talks about labor that has been branded, not about race.

Now finally I'd like to conclude with a word on the antihate ordinances. Here in St. Paul, we have an antihate ordinance and it's being tested right now before the U.S. Supreme Court. It was adopted back in 1982. There are similar laws in other cities and some states.

Their alleged aim is to generally outlaw expressions of hate. Some, like the one here, have amendments outlawing certain actions such as cross burning. In general, though, the measures are against hate. Hatred by whom, against whom, is left open.

And that's a problem. Because there are different kinds of hate. I hate the capitalist ruling class. If you really start to think about what they've done in the world in the last century, the people they've slaughtered, you can really work yourself into a hate.

It's important to do that from time to time because it helps give you some revolutionary energy. Malcolm X and others expressed a real hatred of this racist system.

Such expressions by our class are considered "hate" under this law. The law doesn't have any class content. An equal sign is put between the hatred by Blacks of racism and the hatred expressed by white racists when they burn crosses on people's front yards. That's one problem.

The second, related problem is that it outlaws expression and ideas. It not only addresses actions, but speech. You don't need an antihate law to outlaw cross-burning. To terrorize somebody by burning a cross on their yard is against the law right now. You don't need some special antihate law to make it illegal. It's against civil rights laws, it's against trespass laws, and it should be outlawed. You shouldn't be able to go burn crosses on somebody's yard to scare the hell out of them and drive them out of the neighborhood.

Any kind of racist intimidation, should be against the law. A gang of racist hooligans shouldn't be able to circle a couple of Blacks on the street and start yelling at them. That's not freedom of speech but threatening behavior, violent behavior. But expressions of "hatred" in newspapers or public meetings are prohibited under the antihate ordinances as well. I could probably be indicted for what I've just said about the ruling class, if the authorities were to choose to do so.

As with all kinds of laws like this that restrict freedom of speech and expression, the authorities may use them to go after some racists or antilabor hooligans. But that's all cover for going after the real targets: militant unionists, Black rights fighters, communists, and other fighters for social justice.

Chris Nisan, a leader of the Young Socialist Alliance here in the Twin Cities, has been doing some work on these laws for a *Militant* article. One study he found showed that the majority of the people who have been found guilty of violating antihate codes adopted on many college campuses over the last several years have been Blacks. This was usually for opposing Zionism. By opposing the Zionist capitalist government in Israel, you can be charged with being anti-Semitic.

These are things working people should oppose. Moreover, it gets off the crucial foundation of who is responsible for oppression. Is it some individual who is expressing some hateful ideas? Is that the problem we face in the United States? It gets away from the fact that there is a political and economic system that is responsible for racism, brought it into the world, and benefits from it. That is what must be opposed and fought against.

Clarity on all these questions and explaining them as clearly as we can, helps to give us more confidence that racial prejudice is not some innate part of human nature. Instead, it has a clear historical origin and is rooted in a specific social system. It benefits a distinct class, the billionaire ruling families. Looking at this crucial issue historically and scientifically helps us see the solid basis that exists for uniting working people of all backgrounds to overturn capitalist rule and thereby lay the basis for ending the scourge of racism once and for all.

31

Talking about Race, Learning about Racism: The Application of Racial Identity Development Theory in the Classroom

BEVERLY DANIEL TATUM

While some people would acknowledge, as does Beverly Daniel Tatum, that racism is a 'pervasive aspect of US socialization' and molds significantly social, economic, and political relations, others would deny this reality. In the latter case there may be individuals and groups who resent even the raising of the possibility of racism, and resist talking about this problem. Beverly Daniel Tatum examines how racism is raised and discussed in the classroom. She identifies several presumptions about race and racism that make it difficult for US students to discuss this topic openly and honestly. One obstacle is that race should be treated as a taboo subject; a second is the belief that society is basically a just one, guided by a fair and race-neutral meritocracy; a third obstacle is personal denial of any connection to racism. These kinds of obstacles reflect how people view the issue of racism.

As many educational institutions struggle to become more multicultural in terms of their students, faculty, and staff, they also begin to examine issues of cultural representation within their curriculum. This examination has evoked a growing number of courses that give specific consideration to the effect of variables such as race, class, and gender on human experience—an important trend that is reflected and supported by the increasing availability of resource manuals for the modification of course content (Bronstein & Quina, 1988; Hull, Scott, & Smith, 1982; Schuster & Van Dyne, 1985).

Unfortunately, less attention has been given to the issues of process that inevitably emerge in the classroom when attention is focused on race, class, and/or gender. It is very difficult to talk about these concepts in a meaningful way without also talking and learning about racism, classism, and sexism.[1] The introduction of these issues of oppression often generates powerful emotional responses in students that range

---

[1] A similar point could be made about other issues of oppression, such as anti-Semitism, homophobia and heterosexism, ageism, and so on.

from guilt and shame to anger and despair. If not addressed, these emotional responses can result in student resistance to oppression-related content areas. Such resistance can ultimately interfere with the cognitive understanding and mastery of the material. This resistance and potential interference is particularly common when specifically addressing issues of race and racism. Yet, when students are given the opportunity to explore race-related material in a classroom where both their affective and intellectual responses are acknowledged and addressed, their level of understanding is greatly enhanced.

This article seeks to provide a framework for understanding students' psychological responses to race-related content and the student resistance that can result, as well as some strategies for overcoming this resistance. It is informed by more than a decade of experience as an African-American woman engaged in teaching an undergraduate course on the psychology of racism, by thematic analyses of student journals and essays written for the racism class, and by an understanding and application of racial identity development theory (Helms, 1990).

SETTING THE CONTEXT

As a clinical psychologist with a research interest in racial identity development among African-American youth raised in predominantly White communities, I began teaching about racism quite fortuitously. In 1980, while I was a part-time lecturer in the Black Studies department of a large public university, I was invited to teach a course called Group Exploration of Racism (Black Studies 2). A requirement for Black Studies majors, the course had to be offered, yet the instructor who regularly taught the course was no longer affiliated with the institution. Armed with a folder full of handouts, old syllabi that the previous instructor left behind, a copy of *White Awareness: Handbook for Anti-racism Training* (Katz, 1978), and my own clinical skills as a group facilitator, I constructed a course that seemed to meet the goals already outlined in the course catalogue. Designed "to provide students with an understanding of the psychological causes and emotional reality of racism as it appears in everyday life," the course incorporated the use of lectures, readings, simulation exercises, group research projects, and extensive class discussion to help students explore the psychological impact of racism on both the oppressor and the oppressed.

Though my first efforts were tentative, the results were powerful. The students in my class, most of whom were White, repeatedly described the course in their evaluations as one of the most valuable educational experiences of their college careers. I was convinced that helping students understand the ways in which racism operates in their own lives,

and what they could do about it, was a social responsibility that I should accept. The freedom to institute the course in the curriculum of the psychology departments in which I would eventually teach became a personal condition of employment. I have successfully introduced the course in each new educational setting I have been in since leaving that university.

Since 1980, I have taught the course (now called the Psychology of Racism) eighteen times, at three different institutions. Although each of these schools is very different – a large public university, a small state college, and a private, elite women's college – the challenges of teaching about racism in each setting have been more similar than different.

In all of the settings, class size has been limited to thirty students (averaging twenty-four). Though typically predominantly White and female (even in coeducational settings), the class make-up has always been mixed in terms of both race and gender. The students of color who have taken the course include Asians and Latinos/as, but most frequently the students of color have been Black. Though most students have described themselves as middle class, all socioeconomic backgrounds (ranging from very poor to very wealthy) have been represented over the years.

The course has necessarily evolved in response to my own deepening awareness of the psychological legacy of racism and my expanding awareness of other forms of oppression, although the basic format has remained the same. Our weekly three-hour class meeting is held in a room with movable chairs, arranged in a circle. The physical structure communicates an important premise of the course – that I expect the students to speak with each other as well as with me.

My other expectations (timely completion of assignments, regular class attendance) are clearly communicated in our first class meeting, along with the assumptions and guidelines for discussion that I rely upon to guide our work together. Because the assumptions and guidelines are so central to the process of talking and learning about racism, it may be useful to outline them here.

Working Assumptions

1. Racism, defined as a "system of advantage based on race" (see Wellman, 1977), is a pervasive aspect of U.S. socialization. It is virtually impossible to live in U.S. contemporary society and not be exposed to some aspect of the personal, cultural, and/or institutional manifestations of racism in our society. It is also assumed that, as a result, all of us have received some misinformation about those groups disadvantaged by racism.

2. Prejudice, defined as a "preconceived judgment or opinion, often based on limited information," is

clearly distinguished from racism (see Katz, 1978). I assume that all of us may have prejudices as a result of the various cultural stereotypes to which we have been exposed. Even when these preconceived ideas have positive associations (such as "Asian students are good in math"), they have negative effects because they deny a person's individuality. These attitudes may influence the individual behaviors of people of color as well as of Whites, and may affect intergroup as well as intragroup interaction. However, a distinction must be made between the negative racial attitudes held by individuals of color and White individuals, because it is only the attitudes of Whites that routinely carry with them the social power inherent in the systematic cultural reinforcement and institutionalization of those racial prejudices. To distinguish the prejudices of students of color from the racism of White students is *not* to say that the former is acceptable and the latter is not; both are clearly problematic. The distinction is important, however, to identify the power differential between members of dominant and subordinate groups.

3. In the context of U.S. society, the system of advantage clearly operates to benefit Whites as a group. However, it is assumed that racism, like other forms of oppression, hurts members of the privileged group as well as those targeted by racism. While the impact of racism on Whites is clearly different from its impact on people of color, racism has negative ramifications for everyone. For example, some White students might remember the pain of having lost important relationships because Black friends were not allowed to visit their homes. Others may express sadness at having been denied access to a broad range of experiences because of social segregation. These individuals often attribute the discomfort or fear they now experience in racially mixed settings to the cultural limitations of their youth.

4. Because of the prejudice and racism inherent in our environments when we were children, I assume that we cannot be blamed for learning what we were taught (intentionally or unintentionally). Yet as adults, we have a responsibility to try to identify and interrupt the cycle of oppression. When we recognize that we have been misinformed, we have a responsibility to seek out more accurate information and to adjust our behaviour accordingly.

5. It is assumed that change, both individual and institutional, is possible. Understanding and unlearning prejudice and racism is a lifelong process that may have begun prior to enrolling in this class, and which will surely continue after the course is over. Each of us may be at a different point in that process, and I assume that we will have mutual respect for each other, regardless of where we perceive one another to be.

To facilitate further our work together, I ask students to honor the following guidelines for our discussion. Specifically, I ask students to demonstrate their respect for one another by honoring the confidentiality of the group. So that students may feel free to ask potentially awkward or embarrassing questions, or share race-related experiences, I ask that students refrain from making personal attributions when discussing the course content with their friends. I also discourage the use of "zaps," overt or covert put-downs often used as comic relief when someone is feeling anxious about the content of the discussion. Finally, students are asked to speak from their own experience, to say, for example, "I think …" or "In my experience, I have found …" rather than generalizing their experience to others, as in "People say …".

Many students are reassured by the climate of safety that is created by these guidelines and find comfort in the nonblaming assumptions I outline for the class. Nevertheless, my experience has been that most students, regardless of their class and ethnic background, still find racism a difficult topic to discuss, as is revealed by these journal comments written after the first class meeting (all names are pseudonyms):

The class is called Psychology of Racism, the atmosphere is friendly and open, yet I feel very closed in. I feel guilt and doubt well up inside of me. (Tiffany, a White woman)

Class has started on a good note thus far. The class seems rather large and disturbs me. In a class of this nature, I expect there will be many painful and emotional moments. (Linda, an Asian woman)

I am a little nervous that as one of the few students of color in the class people are going to be looking at me for answers, or whatever other reasons. The thought of this inhibits me a great deal. (Louise, an African-American woman)

I had never thought about my social position as being totally dominant. There wasn't one area in which I wasn't in the dominant group.... I first felt embarrassed.... Through association alone I felt in many ways responsible for the unequal condition existing in the world. This made me feel like shrinking in a hole in a class where I was surrounded by 27 women and 2 men, one of whom was Black and the other was Jewish. I felt that all these people would be justified in venting their anger upon me. After a short period, I realized that no one in the room was attacking or even blaming me for the conditions that exist. (Carl, a White man)

Even though most of my students voluntarily enroll in the course as an elective, their anxiety and subsequent resistance to learning about racism quickly emerge.

SOURCES OF RESISTANCE

In predominantly White college classrooms, I have experienced at least three major sources of student resistance to talking and learning about race and racism. They can be readily identified as the following:

1. Race is considered a taboo topic for discussion, especially in racially mixed settings.
2. Many students, regardless of racial-group membership, have been socialized to think of the United States as a just society.
3. Many students, particularly White students, initially deny any personal prejudice, recognizing the impact of racism on other people's lives, but failing to acknowledge its impact on their own.

Race as Taboo Topic

The first source of resistance, race as a taboo topic, is an essential obstacle to overcome if class discussion is to begin at all. Although many students are interested in the topic, they are often most interested in hearing other people talk about it, afraid to break the taboo themselves.

One source of this self-consciousness can be seen in the early childhood experiences of many students. It is known that children as young as three notice racial differences (see Phinney & Rotheram, 1987). Certainly preschoolers talk about what they see. Unfortunately, they often do so in ways that make adults uncomfortable. Imagine the following scenario: A White child in a public place points to a dark-skinned African-American child and says loudly, "Why is that boy Black?" The embarrassed parent quickly responds, "Sh! Don't say that." The child is only attempting to make sense of a new observation (Derman-Sparks, Higa, & Sparks, 1980), yet the parent's attempt to silence the perplexed child sends a message that this observation is not okay to talk about. White children quickly become aware that their questions about race raise adult anxiety, and as a result, they learn not to ask the questions.

When asked to reflect on their earliest race-related memories and the feelings associated with them, both White students and students of color often report feelings of confusion, anxiety, and/or fear. Students of color often have early memories of name-calling or other negative interactions with other children, and sometimes with adults. They also report having had questions that went both unasked and unanswered. In addition, many students have had uncomfortable interchanges around race-related topics as adults. When asked at the beginning of the semester, "How many of you have had difficult, perhaps heated conversations with someone on a race-related topic?", routinely almost everyone in the class raises his or her hand. It should come as no surprise then that students often approach the topic of race and/or racism with both curiosity and trepidation.

The Myth of the Meritocracy

The second source of student resistance to be discussed here is rooted in students' belief that the United States is a just society, a meritocracy where individual efforts are fairly rewarded. While some students (particularly students of color) may already have become disillusioned with that notion of the United States, the majority of my students who have experienced at least the personal success of college acceptance still have faith in this notion. To the extent that these students acknowledge that racism exists, they tend to view it as an individual phenomenon, rooted in the attitudes of the "Archie Bunkers" of the world or located only in particular parts of the country.

After several class meetings, Karen, a White woman, acknowledged this attitude in her journal:

> At one point in my life – the beginning of this class – I actually perceived America to be a relatively racist free society. I thought that the people who were racist or subjected to racist stereotypes were found only in small pockets of the U.S., such as the South. As I've come to realize, racism (or at least racially orientated stereotypes) is rampant.

An understanding of racism as a system of advantage presents a serious challenge to the notion of the United States as a just society where rewards are based solely on one's merit. Such a challenge often creates discomfort in students. The old adage "ignorance is bliss" seems to hold true in this case; students are not necessarily eager to recognize the painful reality of racism.

One common response to the discomfort is to engage in denial of what they are learning. White students in particular may question the accuracy or currency of statistical information regarding the prevalence of discrimination (housing, employment, access to health care, and so on). More qualitative data, such as autobiographical accounts of experiences with racism, may be challenged on the basis of their subjectivity.

It should be pointed out that the basic assumption that the United States is a just society for all is only one of many basic assumptions that might be challenged in the learning process. Another example can be seen in an interchange between two White students following a discussion about cultural racism, in which the omission or distortion of historical information about people of color was offered as an example of the cultural transmission of racism.

"Yeah, I just found out that Cleopatra was actually a Black woman."

"What?"

The first student went on to explain her newly learned information. Finally, the second student exclaimed in disbelief, "That can't be true. Cleopatra was beautiful!" This new information and her own deeply ingrained assumptions about who is beautiful and who is not were too incongruous to allow her to assimilate the information at that moment.

If outright denial of information is not possible, then withdrawal may be. Physical withdrawal in the form of absenteeism is one possible result; it is for precisely this reason that class attendance is mandatory. The reduction in the completion of reading and/or written assignments is another form of withdrawal. I have found this response to be so common that I now alert students to this possibility at the beginning of the semester. Knowing that this response is a common one seems to help students stay engaged, even when they experience the desire to withdraw.

Following an absence in the fifth week of the semester, one White student wrote, 'I think I've hit the point you talked about, the point where you don't want to hear any more about racism. I sometimes begin to get the feeling we are all hypersensitive." (Two weeks later she wrote, "Class is getting better. I think I am beginning to get over my hump.")

Perhaps not surprisingly, this response can be found in both White students and students of color. Students of color often enter a discussion of racism with some awareness of the issue, based on personal experiences. However, even these students find that they did not have a full understanding of the widespread impact of racism in our society. For students who are targeted by racism, an increased awareness of the impact in and on their lives is painful, and often generates anger.

Four weeks into the semester, Louise, an African-American woman, wrote in her journal about her own heightened sensitivity:

Many times in class I feel uncomfortable when White students use the term Black because even if they aren't aware of it they say it with all or at least a lot of the negative connotations they've been taught goes along with Black. Sometimes it just causes a stinging feeling inside of me. Sometimes I get real tired of hearing White people talk about the conditions of Black people. I think it's an important thing for them to talk about, but still I don't always like being around when they do it. I also get tired of hearing them talk about how hard it is for them, though I understand it, and most times I am very willing to listen and be open, but sometimes I can't. Right now I can't.

For White students, advantaged by racism, a heightened awareness of it often generates painful feelings of guilt. The following responses are typical:

After reading the article about privilege, I felt very guilty. (Rachel, a White woman)

Questions of racism are so full of anger and pain. When I think of all the pain White people have caused people of color, I get a feeling of guilt. How could someone like myself care so much about the color of someone's skin that they would do them harm? (Terri, a White woman)

White students also sometimes express a sense of betrayal when they realize the gaps in their own education about racism. After seeing the first episode of the documentary series *Eyes on the Prize*, Chris, a White man, wrote:

I never knew it was really that bad just 35 years ago. Why didn't I learn this in elementary or high school? Could it be that the White people of America want to forget this injustice? ... I will never forget that movie for as long as I live. It was like a big slap in the face.

Barbara, a White woman, also felt anger and embarrassment in response to her own previous lack of information about the internment of Japanese Americans during World War II. She wrote:

I feel so stupid because I never even knew that these existed. I never knew that the Japanese were treated so poorly. I am becoming angry and upset about all of the things that I do not know. I have been so sheltered. My parents never wanted to let me know about the bad things that have happened in the world. After I saw the movie (*Mitsuye and Nellie*), I even called them up to ask them why they never told me this.... I am angry at them too for not teaching me and exposing me to the complete picture of my country.

Avoiding the subject matter is one way to avoid these uncomfortable feelings.

"I'm Not Racist, But ..."

A third source of student resistance (particularly among White students) is the initial denial of any personal connection to racism. When asked why they have decided to enroll in a course on racism, White students typically explain their interest in the topic with such disclaimers as, "I'm not racist myself, but I know people who are, and I want to understand them better."

Because of their position as the targets of racism, students of color do not typically focus on their own prejudices or lack of them. Instead they usually express a desire to understand why racism exists, and how they have been affected by it.

However, as all students gain a better grasp of what racism is and its many manifestations in U.S. society, they inevitably start to recognize its legacy within themselves. Beliefs, attitudes, and actions based on racial stereotypes begin to be remembered and are newly observed by White students. Students of color as well often recognize negative attitudes they may have internalized about their own racial group or that they have believed about others. Those who previously thought themselves immune to the effects of growing up in a racist society often find themselves reliving uncomfortable feelings of guilt or anger.

After taping her own responses to a questionnaire on racial attitudes, Barbara, a White woman previously quoted, wrote:

> I always want to think of myself as open to all races. Yet when I did the interview to myself, I found that I did respond differently to the same questions about different races. No one could ever have told me that I would have. I would have denied it. But I found that I did respond differently even though I didn't want to. This really upset me. I was angry with myself because I thought I was not prejudiced and yet the stereotypes that I had created had an impact on the answers that I gave even though I didn't want it to happen.

The new self-awareness, represented here by Barbara's journal entry, changes the classroom dynamic. One common result is that some White students, once perhaps active participants in class discussion, now hesitate to continue their participation for fear that their newly recognized racism will be revealed to others.

> Today I did feel guilty, and like I had to watch what I was saying (make it good enough), I guess to prove I'm really *not* prejudiced. From the conversations the first day, I guess this is a normal enough reaction, but I certainly never expected it in me. (Joanne, a White woman)

This withdrawal on the part of White students is often paralleled by an increase in participation by students of color who are seeking an outlet for what are often feelings of anger. The withdrawal of some previously vocal White students from the classroom exchange, however, is sometimes interpreted by students of color as indifference. This perceived indifference often serves to fuel the anger and frustration that many students of color experience, as awareness of their own oppression is heightened. For example, Robert, an African-American man, wrote:

> I really wish the White students would talk more. When I read these articles, it makes me so mad and I really want to know what the White kids think. Don't they care?

Sonia, a Latina, described the classroom tension from another perspective:

> I would like to comment that at many points in the discussions I have felt uncomfortable and sometimes even angry with people. I guess I am at the stage where I am tired of listening to Whites feel guilty and watch their eyes fill up with tears. I do understand that everyone is at their own stage of development and I even tell myself every Tuesday that these people have come to this class by choice. Some days I am just more tolerant than others.... It takes courage to say things in that room with so many women of color present. It also takes courage for the women of color to say things about Whites.

What seems to be happening in the classroom at such moments is a collision of developmental processes that can be inherently useful for the racial identity development of the individuals involved. Nevertheless, the interaction may be perceived as problematic to instructors and students who are unfamiliar with the process. Although space does not allow for an exhaustive discussion of racial identity development theory, a brief explication of it here will provide additional clarity regarding the classroom dynamics when issues of race are discussed. It will also provide a theoretical framework for the strategies for dealing with student resistance that will be discussed at the conclusion of this article.

STAGES OF RACIAL IDENTITY DEVELOPMENT

Racial identity and racial identity development theory are defined by Janet Helms (1990) as

> a sense of group or collective identity based on one's *perception* that he or she shares a common racial heritage with a particular racial group... racial identity development theory concerns the psychological implications of racial-group membership, that is belief systems that evolve in reaction to perceived differential racial-group membership. (p. 3)

It is assumed that in a society where racial-group membership is emphasized, the development of a racial identity will occur in some form in everyone. Given the dominant/subordinate relationship of Whites and people of color in this society, however, it is not surprising that this developmental process will unfold in different ways. For purposes of this discussion, William Cross's (1971, 1978) model of Black identity development will be described along with Helms's (1990) model of White racial identity development theory. While the identity development of other students (Asian, Latino/a, Native American) is not included in this particular theoretical formulation, there is evidence to suggest that the process for these oppressed groups is similar to that described for African Americans (Highlen, et al., 1988; Phinney, 1990).[2] In each case, it is assumed that a positive sense of oneself as a member of one's group (which is not based on any assumed superiority) is important for psychological health.

Black Racial Identity Development

According to Cross's (1971, 1978, 1991) model of Black racial identity development, there are five

---

[2] While similar models of racial identity development exist, Cross and Helms are referenced here because they are among the most frequently cited writers on Black racial identity development and on White racial identity development, respectively. For a discussion of the commonalities between these and other identity development models, see Phinney (1989, 1990) and Helms (1990).

stages in the process, identified as Preencounter, Encounter Immersion/Emersion, Internalization, and Internalization-Commitment. In the first stage of Preencounter, the African American has absorbed many of the beliefs and values of the dominant White culture, including the notion that "White is right" and "Black is wrong." Though the internalization of negative Black stereotypes may be outside of his or her conscious awareness, the individual seeks to assimilate and be accepted by Whites, and actively or passively distances him/herself from other Blacks.[3]

Louise, an African-American woman previously quoted, captured the essence of this stage in the following description of herself at an earlier time:

> For a long time it seemed as if I didn't remember my background, and I guess in some ways I didn't. I was never taught to be proud of my African heritage. Like we talked about in class, I went through a very long stage of identifying with my oppressors. Wanting to be like, live like, and be accepted by them. Even to the point of hating my own race and myself for being a part of it. Now I am ashamed that I ever was ashamed. I lost so much of myself in my denial of and refusal to accept my people.

In order to maintain psychological comfort at this stage of development, Helms writes:

> The person must maintain the fiction that race and racial indoctrination have nothing to do with how he or she lives life. It is probably the case that the Preencounter person is bombarded on a regular basis with information that he or she cannot really be a member of the "in" racial group, but relies on denial to selectively screen such information from awareness. (1990, p. 23)

This de-emphasis on one's racial-group membership may allow the individual to think that race has not been or will not be a relevant factor in one's own achievement, and may contribute to the belief in a U.S. meritocracy that is often a part of a Preencounter worldview.

Movement into the Encounter phase is typically precipitated by an event or series of events that forces the individual to acknowledge the impact of racism in one's life. For example, instances of social rejection by White friends or colleagues (or reading new personally relevant information about racism) may lead the individual to the conclusion that many Whites will not view him or her as an equal. Faced with the reality that he or she cannot truly be White, the individual is forced to focus on his or her identity as a member of a group targeted by racism.

Brenda, a Korean-American student, described her own experience of this process as a result of her participation in the racism course:

> I feel that because of this class, I have become much more aware of racism that exists around. Because of my awareness of racism, I am now bothered by acts and behaviors that might not have bothered me in the past. Before when racial comments were said around me I would somehow ignore it and pretend that nothing was said. By ignoring comments such as these, I was protecting myself. It became sort of a defense mechanism. I never realized I did this, until I was confronted with stories that were found in our reading, by other people of color, who also ignored comments that bothered them. In realizing that there is racism out in the world and that there are comments concerning race that are directed towards me, I feel as if I have reached the first step. I also think I have reached the second step, because I am now bothered and irritated by such comments. I no longer ignore them, but now confront them.

The Immersion/Emersion stage is characterized by the simultaneous desire to surround oneself with visible symbols of one's racial identity and an active avoidance of symbols of Whiteness. As Thomas Parham describes, "At this stage, everything of value in life must be Black or relevant to Blackness. This stage is also characterized by a tendency to denigrate White people, simultaneously glorifying Black people...." (1989, p. 190). The previously described anger that emerges in class among African-American students and other students of color in the process of learning about racism may be seen as part of the transition through these stages.

As individuals enter the Immersion stage, they actively seek out opportunities to explore aspects of their own history and culture with the support of peers from their own racial background. Typically, White-focused anger dissipates during this phase because so much of the person's energy is directed toward his or her own group- and self-exploration. The result of this exploration is an emerging security in a newly defined and affirmed sense of self.

Sharon, another African-American woman, described herself at the beginning of the semester as angry, seemingly in the Encounter stage of development. She wrote after our class meeting:

> Another point that I must put down is that before I entered class today I was angry about the way Black people have been treated in this country. I don't think I will easily overcome that and I basically feel justified in my feelings.

At the end of the semester, Sharon had joined with two other Black students in the class to work on their final class project. She observed that the three of them had planned their project to focus on Black people specifically, suggesting movement into the Immersion stage of racial identity development. She wrote:

---

[3] Both Parham (1989) and Phinney (1989) suggest that a preference for the dominant group is not always a characteristic of this stage. For example, children raised in households and communities with explicitly positive Afrocentric attitudes may absorb a pro-Black perspective, which then serves as the starting point for their own exploration of racial identity.

We are concerned about the well-being of our own people. They cannot be well if they have this pinned-up hatred for their own people. This internalized racism is something that we all felt, at various times, needed to be talked about. This semester it has really been important to me, and I believe Gordon [a Black classmate], too.

The emergence from this stage marks the beginning of Internalization. Secure in one's own sense of racial identity, there is less need to assert the "Blacker than thou" attitude often characteristic of the Immersion stage (Parham, 1989). In general, 'pro-Black attitudes become more expansive, open, and less defensive" (Cross, 1971, p. 24). While still maintaining his or her connections with Black peers, the internalized individual is willing to establish meaningful relationships with Whites who acknowledge and are respectful of his or her self-definition. The individual is also ready to build coalitions with members of other oppressed groups. At the end of the semester, Brenda, a Korean American, concluded that she had in fact internalized a positive sense of racial identity. The process she described parallels the stages described by Cross:

> I have been aware for a long time that I am Korean. But through this class I am beginning to really become aware of my race. I am beginning to find out that White people can be accepting of me and at the same time accept me as a Korean.
>
> I grew up wanting to be accepted and ended up almost denying my race and culture. I don't think I did this consciously, but the denial did occur. As I grew older, I realized that I was different. I became for the first time, friends with other Koreans. I realized I had much in common with them. This was when I went through my "Korean friend" stage. I began to enjoy being friends with Koreans more than I did with Caucasians.
>
> Well, ultimately, through many years of growing up, I am pretty much in focus about who I am and who my friends are. I knew before I took this class that there were people not of color that were understanding of my differences. In our class, I feel that everyone is trying to sincerely find the answer of abolishing racism. I knew people like this existed, but it's nice to meet with them weekly.

Cross suggests that there are few psychological differences between the fourth stage, Internalization, and the fifth stage, Internalization-Commitment. However, those at the fifth stage have found ways to translate their "personal sense of Blackness into a plan of action or a general sense of commitment" to the concerns of Blacks as a group, which is sustained over time (Cross, 1991, p. 220). Whether at the fourth or fifth stage, the process of Internalization allows the individual, anchored in a positive sense of racial identity, both to proactively perceive and transcend race. Blackness becomes "the point of departure for discovering the universe of ideas, cultures and experiences beyond blackness in place

of mistaking blackness as the universe itself' (Cross, Parham, & Helms, 1991, p. 330).

Though the process of racial identity development has been presented here in linear form, in fact it is probably more accurate to think of it in a spiral form. Often a person may move from one stage to the next, only to revisit an earlier stage as the result of new encounter experiences (Parham, 1989), though the later experience of the stage may be different from the original experience. The image that students often find helpful in understanding this concept of recycling through the stages is that of a spiral staircase. As a person ascends a spiral staircase, she may stop and look down at a spot below. When she reaches the next level, she may look down and see the same spot, but the vantage point has changed.[4]

WHITE RACIAL IDENTITY DEVELOPMENT

The transformations experienced by those targeted by racism are often paralleled by those of White students. Helms (1990) describes the evolution of a positive White racial identity as involving both the abandonment of racism and the development of a nonracist White identity. In order to do the latter,

> he or she must accept his or her own Whiteness, the cultural implications of being White, and define a view of Self as a racial being that does not depend on the perceived superiority of one racial group over another. (p. 49)

She identifies Six stages in her model of White racial identity development: Contact, Disintegration, Reintegration, Pseudo-Independent, Immersion/Emersion, and Autonomy.

The Contact stage is characterized by a lack of awareness of cultural and institutional racism, and of one's own White privilege. Peggy McIntosh (1989) writes eloquently about her own experience of this state of being:

> As a white person, I realized I had been taught about racism as something which puts others at a disadvantage,

---

[4] After being introduced to this model and Helms's model of White identity development, students are encouraged to think about how the models might apply to their own experience or the experiences of people they know. As is reflected in the cited journal entries, some students resonate to the theories quite readily, easily seeing their own process of growth reflected in them. Other students are sometimes puzzled because they feel as though their own process varies from these models, and may ask if it is possible to "skip" a particular stage, for example. Such questions provide a useful departure point for discussing the limitations of stage theories in general, and the potential variations in experience that make questions of racial identity development so complex.

but had been taught not to see one of its corollary aspects, white privilege, which puts me at an advantage.... I was taught to see racism only in individual acts of meanness, not in invisible systems conferring dominance on my group. (p. 10)

In addition, the Contact stage often includes naive curiosity about or fear of people of color, based on stereotypes learned from friends, family, or the media. These stereotypes represent the framework in use when a person at this stage of development makes a comment such as, "You don't act like a Black person" (Helms, 1990, p. 57).

Those Whites whose lives are structured so as to limit their interaction with people of color, as well as their awareness of racial issues, may remain at this stage indefinitely. However, certain kinds of experiences (increased interaction with people of color or exposure to new information about racism) may lead to a new understanding that cultural and institutional racism exist. This new understanding marks the beginning of the Disintegration stage.

At this stage, the bliss of ignorance or lack of awareness is replaced by the discomfort of guilt, shame, and sometimes anger at the recognition of one's own advantage because of being White and the acknowledgement of the role of Whites in the maintenance of a racist system. Attempts to reduce discomfort may include denial (convincing oneself that racism doesn't really exist, or if it does, it is the fault of its victims).

For example, Tom, a White male student, responded with some frustration in his journal to a classmate's observation that the fact that she had never read any books by Black authors in any of her high school or college English classes was an example of cultural racism. He wrote, "It's not my fault that Blacks don't write books."

After viewing a film in which a psychologist used examples of Black children's drawings to illustrate the potentially damaging effect of negative cultural messages on a Black child's developing self-esteem, David, another White male student, wrote:

I found it interesting the way Black children drew themselves without arms. The psychologist said this is saying that the child feels unable to control his environment. It can't be because the child has notions and beliefs already about being Black. It must be built in or hereditary due to the past history of the Blacks. I don't believe it's cognitive but more biological due to a long past history of repression and being put down.

Though Tom's and David's explanations seem quite problematic, they can be understood in the context of racial identity development theory as a way of reducing their cognitive dissonance upon learning this new race-related information. As was discussed earlier, withdrawal (accomplished by avoiding contact with people of color and the topic of racism) is another strategy for dealing with the discomfort experienced at this stage. Many of the previously described responses of White students to race-related content are characteristic of the transition from the Contact to the Disintegration stage of development.

Helms (1990) describes another response to the discomfort of Disintegration, which involves attempts to change significant others' attitudes toward African Americans and other people of color. However, as she points out,

due to the racial naivete with which this approach may be undertaken and the person's ambivalent racial identification, this dissonance-reducing strategy is likely to be met with rejection by Whites as well as Blacks. (p. 59)

In fact, this response is also frequently observed among White students who have an opportunity to talk with friends and family during holiday visits. Suddenly they are noticing the racist content of jokes or comments of their friends and relatives and will try to confront them, often only to find that their efforts are, at best, ignored or dismissed as a "phase," or, at worst, greeted with open hostility.

Carl, a White male previously quoted, wrote at length about this dilemma:

I realized that it was possible to simply go through life totally oblivious to the entire situation or, even if one realizes it, one can totally repress it. It is easy to fade into the woodwork, run with the rest of society, and never have to deal with these problems. So many people I know from home are like this. They have simply accepted what society has taught them with little, if any, question. My father is a prime example of this.... It has caused much friction in our relationship, and he often tells me as a father he has failed in raising me correctly. Most of my high school friends will never deal with these issues and propagate them on to their own children. It's easy to see how the cycle continues. I don't think I could ever justify within myself simply turning my back on the problem. I finally realized that my position in all of these dominant groups gives me power to make change occur.... It is an unfortunate result often though that I feel alienated from friends and family. It's often played off as a mere stage that I'm going through. I obviously can't tell if it's merely a stage, but I know that they say this to take the attention off of the truth of what I'm saying. By belittling me, they take the power out of my argument. It's very depressing that being compassionate and considerate are seen as only phases that people go through. I don't want it to be a phase for me, but as obvious as this may sound, I look at my environment and often wonder how it will not be.

The societal pressure to accept the status quo may lead the individual from Disintegration to Reintegration. At this point the desire to be accepted by one's own racial group, in which the overt or covert belief in White superiority is so prevalent, may lead to a reshaping of the person's belief system to be more congruent with an acceptance of racism. The guilt and anxiety associated with Disintegration may be redirected in the form of fear and anger directed toward people of color (particularly Blacks), who are now blamed as the source of discomfort.

Connie, a White woman of Italian ancestry, in many ways exemplified the progression from the Contact stage to Reintegration, a process she herself described seven weeks into the semester. After reading about the stages of White identity development, she wrote:

> I think mostly I can find myself in the disintegration stage of development.... There was a time when I never considered myself a color. I never described myself as a "White, Italian female" until I got to college and noticed that people of color always described themselves by their color/race. While taking this class, I have begun to understand that being White makes a difference. I never thought about it before but there are many privileges to being White. In my personal life, I cannot say that I have ever felt that I have had the advantage over a Black person, but I am aware that my race has the advantage.
>
> I am feeling really guilty lately about that. I find myself thinking: 'I didn't mean to be White, I really didn't mean it." I am starting to feel angry towards my race for ever using this advantage towards personal gains. But at the same time I resent the minority groups. I mean, it's not our fault that society has deemed us "superior." I don't feel any better than a Black person. But it really doesn't matter because I am a member of the dominant race.... I can't help it ... and I sometimes get angry and feel like I'm being attacked.
>
> I guess my anger toward a minority group would enter me into the next stage of Reintegration, where I am once again starting to blame the victim. This is all very trying for me and it has been on my mind a lot. I really would like to be able to reach the last stage, autonomy, where I can accept being White without hostility and anger. That is really hard to do.

Helms (1990) suggests that it is relatively easy for Whites to become stuck at the Reintegration stage of development, particularly if avoidance of people of color is possible. However, if there is a catalyst for continued self-examination, the person "begins to question her or his previous definition of Whiteness and the justifiability of racism in any of its forms...." (p. 61). In my experience, continued participation in a course on racism provides the catalyst for this deeper self-examination.

This process was again exemplified by Connie. At the end of the semester, she listened to her own taped interview of her racial attitudes that she had recorded at the beginning of the semester. She wrote:

> Oh wow! I could not believe some of the things that I said. I was obviously in different stages of the White identity development. As I listened and got more and more disgusted with myself when I was at the Reintegration stage, I tried to remind myself that these are stages that all (most) White people go through when

dealing with notions of racism. I can remember clearly the resentment I had for people of color. I feel the one thing I enjoyed from listening to my interview was noticing how much I have changed. I think I am finally out of the Reintegration stage. I am beginning to make a conscious effort to seek out information about people of color and accept their criticism.... I still feel guilty about the feeling I had about people of color and I always feel bad about being privileged as a result of racism. But I am glad that I have reached what I feel is the Pseudo-Independent stage of White identity development.

The information-seeking that Connie describes often marks the onset of the Pseudo-Independent stage. At this stage, the individual is abandoning beliefs in White superiority, but may still behave in ways that unintentionally perpetuate the system. Looking to those targeted by racism to help him or her understand racism, the White person often tries to disavow his or her own Whiteness through active affiliation with Blacks, for example. The individual experiences a sense of alienation from other Whites who have not yet begun to examine their own racism, yet may also experience rejection from Blacks or other people of color who are suspicious of his or her motives. Students of color moving from the Encounter to the Immersion phase of their own racial identity development may be particularly unreceptive to the White person's attempts to connect with them.

Uncomfortable with his or her own Whiteness, yet unable to be truly anything else, the individual may begin searching for a new, more comfortable way to be White. This search is characteristic of the Immersion/Emersion stage of development. Just as the Black student seeks to redefine positively what it means to be of African ancestry in the United States through immersion in accurate information about one's culture and history, the White individual seeks to replace racially related myths and stereotypes with accurate information about what it means and has meant to be White in U.S. society (Helms, 1990). Learning about Whites who have been antiracist allies to people of color is a very important part of this process.

After reading articles written by antiracist activists describing their own process of unlearning racism, White students often comment on how helpful it is to know that others have experienced similar feelings and have found ways to resist the racism in their environments.[5] For example, Joanne,

---

[5] Examples of useful articles include essays by McIntosh (1988), Lester (1987), and Braden (1987). Each of these combines autobiographical material, as well as a conceptual framework for understanding some aspect of racism that students find very helpful. Bowser and Hunt's (1981) edited book. *Impacts of Racism on Whites*, though less autobiographical in nature, is also a valuable resource.

a White woman who initially experienced a lot of guilt, wrote:

> This article helped me out in many ways. I've been feeling helpless and frustrated. I know there are all these terrible things going on and I want to be able to do something.... Anyway this article helped me realize, again, that others feel this way, and gave me some positive ideas to resolve my dominant class guilt and shame.

Finally, reading the biographies and autobiographies of White individuals who have embarked on a similar process of identity development (such as Barnard, 1987) provides White students with important models for change.

Learning about White antiracists can also provide students of color with a sense of hope that they can have White allies. After hearing a White antiracist activist address the class, Sonia, a Latina who had written about her impatience with expressions of White guilt, wrote:

> I don't know when I have been more impressed by anyone. She filled me with hope for the future, She made me believe that there are good people in the world and that Whites suffer too and want to change things.

For White students, the internalization of a newly defined sense of oneself as White is the primary task of the Autonomy stage. The positive feelings associated with this redefinition energize the person's efforts to confront racism and oppression in his or her daily life. Alliances with people of color can be more easily forged at this stage of development than previously because the person's antiracist behaviors and attitudes will be more consistently expressed. While Autonomy might be described as "racial self-actualization, ... it is best to think of it as an ongoing process ... wherein the person is continually open to new information and new ways of thinking about racial and cultural variables" (Helms, 1990, p. 66).

Annette, a White woman, described herself in the Autonomy stage, but talked at length about the circular process she felt she had been engaged in during the semester:

> If people as racist as C. P. Ellis (a former Klansman) can change, I think anyone can change. If that makes me idealistic, fine. I do not think my expecting society to change is naive anymore because I now *know* exactly what I want. To be naive means a lack of knowledge that allows me to accept myself both as a White person and as an idealist. This class showed me that these two are not mutually exclusive but are an integral part of me that I cannot deny. I realize now that through most of this class I was trying to deny both of them.
>
> While I was not accepting society's racism, I was accepting society's telling me as a White person, there was nothing I could do to change racism. So, I told my self I was being naive and tried to suppress my desire to change society. This is what made me so frustrated – while I saw society's racism through examples in the readings

and the media, I kept telling myself there was nothing I could do. Listening to my tape, I think I was already in the Autonomy stage when I started this class. I then seemed to decide that being White, I also had to be racist which is when I became frustrated and went back to the Disintegration stage. I was frustrated because I was not only telling myself there was nothing I could do but I also was assuming society's racism was my own which made me feel like I did not want to be White. Actually, it was not being White that I was disavowing but being racist. I think I have now returned to the Autonomy stage and am much more secure in my position there. I accept my Whiteness now as just a part of me as is my idealism. I will no longer disavow these characteristics as I have realized I can be proud of both of them. In turn, I can now truly accept other people for their unique characteristics and not by the labels society has given them as I can accept myself that way.

> While I thought the main ideas that I learned in this class were that White people need to be educated to end racism and everyone should be treated as human beings, I really had already incorporated these ideas into my thoughts. What I learned from this class is being White does not mean being racist and being idealistic does not mean being naive. I really did not have to form new ideas about people of color; I had to form them about myself – and I did.

IMPLICATIONS FOR CLASSROOM TEACHING

Although movement through all the stages of racial identity development will not necessarily occur for each student within the course of a semester (or even four years of college), it is certainly common to witness beginning transformations in classes with race-related content. An awareness of the existence of this process has helped me to implement strategies to facilitate positive student development, as well as to improve interracial dialogue within the classroom.

Four strategies for reducing student resistance and promoting student development that I have found useful are the following:

1. the creation of a safe classroom atmosphere by establishing clear guidelines for discussion;
2. the creation of opportunities for self-generated knowledge;
3. the provision of an appropriate developmental model that students can use as a framework for understanding their own process;
4. the exploration of strategies to empower students as change agents.

Creating a Safe Climate

As was discussed earlier, making the classroom a safe space for discussion is essential for overcoming students' fears about breaking the race taboo, and will also reduce later anxieties about exposing one's own internalized racism. Establishing the guidelines of confidentiality, mutual respect, "no zaps," and speaking from one's own experience on the first day of class is a necessary step in the process.

Students respond very positively to these ground rules, and do try to honor them. While the rules do not totally eliminate anxiety, they clearly communicate to students that there is a safety net for the discussion. Students are also encouraged to direct their comments and questions to each other rather than always focusing their attention on me as the instructor, and to learn each other's names rather than referring to each other as "he," "she," or "the person in the red sweater" when responding to each other.[6]

The Power of Self-Generated Knowledge

The creation of opportunities for self-generated knowledge on the part of students is a powerful tool for reducing the initial stage of denial that many students experience. While it may seem easy for some students to challenge the validity of what they read or what the instructor says, it is harder to deny what they have seen with their own eyes. Students can be given hands-on assignments outside of class to facilitate this process.

For example, after reading *Portraits of White Racism* (Wellman, 1977), some students expressed the belief that the attitudes expressed by the White interviewees in the book were no longer commonly held attitudes. Students were then asked to use the same interview protocol used in the book (with some revision) to interview a White adult of their choice. When students reported on these interviews in class, their own observation of the similarity between those they had interviewed and those they had read about was more convincing than anything I might have said.

After doing her interview, Patty, a usually quiet White student, wrote:

> I think I learned a lot from it and that I'm finally getting a better grip on the idea of racism. I think that was why I participated so much in class. I really felt like I knew what I was talking about.

Other examples of creating opportunities for self-generated knowledge include assigning students the task of visiting grocery stores in neighborhoods of differing racial composition to compare the cost and quality of goods and services available at be two locations, and to observe the interactions between the shoppers and the store personnel. For White

students, one of the most powerful assignments of this type has been to go apartment hunting with an African-American student and to experience housing discrimination firsthand. While one concern with such an assignment is the effect it will have on the student(s) of color involved, I have found that those Black students who choose this assignment rather than another are typically eager to have their White classmates experience the reality of racism, and thus participate quite willingly in the process.

Naming the Problem

The emotional responses that students have to talking and learning about racism are quite predictable and related to their own racial identity development. Unfortunately, students typically do not know this; thus they consider their own guilt, shame, embarrassment, or anger an uncomfortable experience that they alone are having. Informing students at the beginning of the semester that these feelings may be part of the learning process is ethically necessary (in the sense of informed consent), and helps to normalize the students' experience. Knowing in advance that a desire to withdraw from classroom discussion or not to complete assignments is a common response helps students to remain engaged when they reach that point. As Alice, a White woman, wrote at the end of the semester:

> You were so right in saying in the beginning how we would grow tired of racism (I did in October) but then it would get so good! I have *loved* the class once I passed that point.

In addition, sharing the model of racial identity development with students gives them a useful framework for understanding each other's processes as well as their own. This cognitive framework does not necessarily prevent the collision of developmental processes previously described, but it does allow students to be less frightened by it when it occurs. If, for example, White students understand the stages of racial identity development for students of color, they are less likely to personalize or feel threatened by an African-American student's anger.

Connie, a White student who initially expressed a lot of resentment at the way students of color tended to congregate in the college cafeteria, was much more understanding of this behavior after she learned about racial identity development theory. She wrote:

> I learned a lot from reading the article about the stages of development in the model of oppressed people. As a White person going through my stages of identity development, I do not take time to think about the struggle people of color go through to reach a stage of complete understanding. I am glad that I know about the stages because now I can understand people of color's

---

[6] Class size has a direct bearing on my ability to create safety in the classroom. Dividing the class into pairs or small groups of five or six students to discuss initial reactions to a particular article or film helps to increase participation, both in the small groups and later in the large group discussions.

behavior in certain situations. For example, when people of color stay to themselves and appear to be in a clique, it is not because they are being rude as I originally thought. Rather they are engaged perhaps in the Immersion stage.

Mary, another White student, wrote:

I found the entire Cross model of racial identity development very enlightening. I knew that there were stages of racial identity development before I entered this class. I did not know what they were, or what they really entailed. After reading through this article I found myself saying, "Oh. That explains why she reacted this way to this incident instead of how she would have a year ago." Clearly this person has entered a different stage and is working through different problems from a new viewpoint. Thankfully, the model provides a degree of hope that people will not always be angry, and will not always be separatists, etc. Although I'm not really sure about that.

Conversely, when students of color understand the stages of White racial identity development, they can be more tolerant or appreciative of a White student's struggle with guilt, for example. After reading about the stages of White identity development, Sonia, a Latina previously quoted, wrote:

This article was the one that made me feel that my own prejudices were showing. I never knew that Whites went through an identity development of their own.

She later told me outside of class that she found it much easier to listen to some of the things White students said because she could understand their potentially offensive comments as part of a developmental stage.

Sharon, an African-American woman, also found that an understanding of the respective stages of racial identity development helped her to understand some of the interactions she had had with White students since coming to college. She wrote:

There is a lot of clash that occurs between Black and White people at college which is best explained by their respective stages of development. Unfortunately schools have not helped to alleviate these problems earlier in life.

In a course on the psychology of racism, it is easy to build in the provision of this information as part of the course content. For instructors teaching courses with race-related content in other fields, it may seem less natural to do so. However, the inclusion of articles on racial identity development and/or class discussion of these issues in conjunction with the other strategies that have been suggested can improve student receptivity to the course content in important ways, making it a very useful investment of class time. Because the stages describe kinds of behavior that many people have commonly observed in themselves, as well as in their own intraracial and interracial interactions, my experience has been that most students grasp the basic conceptual framework fairly easily, even if they do not have a background in psychology.

Empowering Students as Change Agents

Heightening students' awareness of racism without also developing an awareness of the possibility of change is a prescription for despair. I consider it unethical to do one without the other. Exploring strategies to empower students as change agents is thus a necessary part of the process of talking about race and learning about racism. As was previously mentioned, students find it very helpful to read about and hear from individuals who have been effective change agents. Newspaper and magazine articles, as well as biographical or autobiographical essays or book excerpts, are often important sources for this information.

I also ask students to work in small groups to develop an action plan of their own for interrupting racism. While I do not consider it appropriate to require students to engage in antiracist activity (since I believe this should be a personal choice the student makes for him/herself), students are required to think about the possibility. Guidelines are provided (see Katz, 1978), and the plans that they develop over several weeks are presented at the end of the semester. Students are generally impressed with each other's good ideas, and, in fact, they often do go on to implement their projects.

Joanne, a White student who initially struggled with feelings of guilt, wrote:

I thought that hearing others' ideas for action plans was interesting and informative. It really helps me realize (reminds me) the many choices and avenues there are once I decided to be an ally. Not only did I develop my own concrete way to be an ally, I have found many other ways that I, as a college student, can be an active anti-racist. It was really empowering.

Another way all students can be empowered is by offering them the opportunity to consciously observe their own development. The taped exercise to which some of the previously quoted students have referred is an example of one way to provide this opportunity. At the beginning of the semester, students are given an interview guide with many open-ended questions concerning racial attitudes and opinions. They are asked to interview themselves on tape as a way of recording their own ideas for future reference. Though the tapes are collected students are assured that no one (including me) will listen to them. The tapes are returned near the end of the semester, and students are asked to listen to their own tapes and use their understanding of racial identity development to discuss it in essay form.

The resulting essays are often remarkable and underscore the psychological importance of giving students the chance to examine racial issues in the classroom. The following was written by Elaine, a White woman:

> Another common theme that was apparent in the tape was that, for the most part, I was aware of my own ignorance and was embarrassed because of it. I wanted to know more about the oppression of people in the country so that I could do something about it. Since I have been here, I have begun to be actively resistant to racism. I have been able to confront my grandparents and some old friends from high school when they make racist comments. Taking this psychology of racism class is another step toward active resistance to racism. I am trying to educate myself so that I have a knowledge base to work from.
>
> When the tape was made, I was just beginning to be active and just beginning to be educated. I think I am now starting to move into the redefinition stage. I am starting to feel ok about being White. Some of my guilt is dissipating, and I do not feel as ignorant as I used to be. I think I have an understanding of racism; how it effects [*sic*] myself, and how it effects this country. Because of this I think I can be more active in doing something about it.

In the words of Louise, a Black female student:

> One of the greatest things I learned from this semester in general is that the world is not only Black and White, nor is the United States. I learned a lot about my own erasure of many American ethnic groups.... I am in the (immersion) stage of my identity development. I think I am also dangling a little in the (encounter) stage. I say this because a lot of my energies are still directed toward White people. I began writing a poem two days ago and it was directed to White racism. However, I have also become more Black-identified. I am reaching to the strength in Afro-American heritage. I am learning more about the heritage and history of Afro-American culture. Knowledge = strength and strength = power.

While some students are clearly more self-reflective and articulate about their own process than others, most students experience the opportunity to talk and learn about these issues as a transforming process. In my experience, even those students who are frustrated by aspects of the course find themselves changed by it. One such student wrote in her final journal entry:

> What I felt to be a major hindrance to me was the amount of people. Despite the philosophy, I really never felt at ease enough to speak openly about the feelings I have and kind of watched the class pull farther and farther apart as the semester went on.... I think that it was your attitude that kept me intrigued by the topics we were studying despite my frustrations with the class time. I really feel as though I made some significant moves in my understanding of other people's positions in our world as well as of my feelings of racism, and I feel very good about them. I feel like this class has moved me in the right direction. I'm on a roll I think, because I've been introduced to so much.

Facilitating student development in this way is a challenging and complex task, but the results are clearly worth the effort.

IMPLICATIONS FOR THE INSTITUTION

What are the institutional implications for an understanding of racial identity development theory beyond the classroom? How can this framework be used to address the pressing issues of increasing diversity and decreasing racial tensions on college campuses? How can providing opportunities in the curriculum to talk about race and learn about racism affect the recruitment and retention of students of color specifically, especially when the majority of the students enrolled are White?

The fact is, educating White students about race and racism changes attitudes in ways that go beyond the classroom boundaries. As White students move through their own stages of identity development, they take their friends with them by engaging them in dialogue. They share the articles they have read with roommates, and involve them in their projects. An example of this involvement can be seen in the following journal entry, written by Larry, a White man:

> Here it is our fifth week of class and more and more I am becoming aware of the racism around me. Our second project made things clearer, because while watching T.V. I picked up many kinds of discrimination and stereotyping. Since the project was over, I still find myself watching these shows and picking up bits and pieces every show I watch, Even my friends will be watching a show and they will say, "Hey, Larry, put that in your paper." Since they know I am taking this class, they are looking out for these things. They are also watching what they say around me for fear that I will use them as an example. For example, one of my friends has this fascination with making fun of Jewish people. Before I would listen to his comments and take them in stride, but now I confront him about his comments.

The heightened awareness of the White students enrolled in the class has a ripple effect in their peer group, which helps to create a climate in which students of color and other targeted groups (Jewish students, for example) might feel more comfortable. It is likely that White students who have had the opportunity to learn about racism in a supportive atmosphere will be better able to be allies to students of color in extracurricular settings, like student government meetings and other oganizational settings, where students of color often feel isolated and unheard.

At the same time, students of color who have had the opportunity to examine the ways in which racism may have affected their own lives are able to give voice to their own experience, and to validate it rather than be demoralized by it. An understanding of internalized oppression can help students of color recognize the ways in which they may have unknowingly participated in their own victimization, or the victimization of others. They may be able to move beyond victimization to empowerment, and share their learning with others, as Sharon, a previously quoted Black woman, planned to do.

Campus communities with an understanding of racial identity development could become more supportive of special-interest groups, such as the Black Student Union or the Asian Student Alliance, because they would recognize them not as "separatist" but as important outlets for students of color who may be at the Encounter or Immersion stage of racial identity development. Not only could speakers of color be sought out to add diversity to campus programming, but Whites who had made a commitment to unlearning their own racism could be offered as models to those White students looking for new ways to understand their own Whiteness, and to students of color looking for allies.

It has become painfully clear on many college campuses across the United States that we cannot have successfully multiracial campuses without talking about race and learning about racism. Providing a forum where this discussion can take place safely over a semester, a time period that allows personal and group development to unfold in ways that day-long or weekend programs do not, may be among the most proactive learning opportunities an institution can provide.

REFERENCES

Barnard, H. F. (Ed.). (1987). *Outside the magic circle: The autobiography of Virginia Foster Durr*. New York: Simon & Schuster. (Originally published in 1985 by University of Alabama Press)

Bowser, B. P., & Hunt, R. G. (1981). *Impacts of racism on whites*. Beverly Hills: Sage.

Braden, A. (1987, April-May). Undoing racism: Lessons for the peace movement. *The Nonviolent Activist*, pp. 3–6.

Bronstein, P. A., & Quina, K. (Eds.). (1988). *Teaching a psychology of people: Resources for gender and sociocultural awareness*. Washington, DC: American Psychological Association.

Cross, W. E., Jr. (1971). The Negro to black conversion experience: Toward a psychology of black liberation. *Black World*, *20*(9), 13–27.

Cross, W. E., Jr. (1978). The Cross and Thomas models of psychological nigrescence *Journal of Black Psychology*, *5*(1), 13–19.

Cross, W. E., Jr. (1991). *Shades of black: Diversity in African-American identity*. Philadelphia. Temple University Press.

Cross, W. E., Jr., Parham, T. A., & Helms, J. E. (1991). The stages of black identity development: Nigrescence models. In R. Jones (Ed.), *Black psychology* (3rd ed., pp. 319–338). San Francisco: Cobb and Henry.

Derman-Sparks, L., Higa, C. T., & Sparks, B. (1980). Children, race and racism: How race awareness develops. *Interracial Book for Children Bulletin*, *11*(3/4), 3–15.

Helms, J. E. (Ed.). (1990). *Black and white racial identity: Theory, research and practice*. Westport, CT: Greenwood Press.

Highlen, P. S., Reynolds, A. L., Adams, E. M., Hanley, T. C., Myers, L. J., Cox, C., & Speight, S. (1988, August 13). *Self-identity development model of oppressed people: Inclusive model for all?* Paper presented at the American Psychological Association. Convention, Atlanta, GA.

Hull, G. T., Scott, P. B., & Smith, B. (Eds.). (1982). *All the women are white, all the blacks are men, but some of us are brave: Black women's studies*. Old Westbury, NY: Feminist Press.

Katz, J. H. (1978). *White awareness: Handbook for anti-racism training*. Norman: University of Oklahoma Press.

Lester, J. (1987). *What happens to the mythmakers when the myths are found to be untrue?* Unpublished paper, Equity Institute, Emeryville, CA.

McIntosh, P. (1988). *White privilege and male privilege: A personal account of coming to see correspondences through work in women's studies*. Working paper, Wellesley College Center for Research on Women, Wellesley, MA.

McIntosh, P. (1989, July/August). White privilege: Unpacking the invisible knapsack. *Peace and Freedom*, pp. 10–12.

Parham, T. A. (1989). Cycles of psychological nigrescence. *The Counseling Psychologist*, *17*(2), 187–226.

Phinney, J. (1989). Stages of ethnic identity in minority group adolescents. *Journal of Early Adolescence*, *9*, 34–39.

Phinney, J. (1990). Ethnic identity in adolescents and adults: Review of research. *Psychological Bulletin*, *108*(3), 499–514.

Phinney, J. S., & Rotheram, M. J. (Eds.). (1987). *Children's ethnic socialization: Pluralism and development*. Newbury Park, CA: Sage.

Schuster, M. R., & Van Dyne, S. R. (Eds.). (1985). *Women's place in the academy: Transforming the liberal arts curriculum*. Totowa, NJ: Rowman & Allanheld.

Wellman, D. (1977). *Portraits of white racism*. New York: Cambridge University Press.

32

The Retreat of Scientific Racism: Changing Concepts of Race in Britain and the United States between the World Wars

ELAZAR BARKAN

The author examines the development of racism between the First and Second World Wars. It is during this period that racism emerged as a major political and scientific issue. The rise of Nazism and 'Aryan science' generated an intellectual movement challenging notions of natural racial orders. This movement was led by individuals like Franz Boas in the United States. In Britain the movement to counter scientific racism was more diffuse. Although some British scholars who earlier espoused validity for natural racial orders began to change their thinking during the 1930s as a result of international developments, 'staunch racists' like G.H.L.F. Pitt-Rivers, and Reginald Ruggles Gates, continued to be dominant academic figures. The fulcrum of the political struggles in Britain between intellectuals considered racists and anti-racists, was the debate about the validity of biological evidence purporting to show the existence of a natural racial order.

Confronting Racism: Scientists as Politicians

1933 – EARLY HESITATIONS

Following Hitler's accession to power on January 30, 1933, the fight against racism became a primary concern for a small but growing number of scientists. The 1920s saw scientists moderating their earlier racial enthusiasm and moving in an egalitarian direction, becoming skeptical of racial typologies and beginning to contest the capability of contemporary scientific knowledge to resolve the heredity versus environment debate. The urgency of dealing with racist doctrines became more compelling with the rise of Nazism, and anthropologists found themselves at the center of public demand to rebuke "Aryan science." Most scientists, excluding rightwing radicals, dismissed Nazi scientific racism as mere nonsense right from 1933, as is evident from their correspondence. Their public commitment, however, differed according to their social and intellectual affinities, and prior to the late 1930s only a minority explicitly opposed racism. Consequently, the period can be subdivided into three phases.

The first, which occurred during 1933-34, included several initiatives motivated by the plight of refugees and the question of anti-Nazism, but in general the issue of race was faced only indirectly. The second phase amounted to a stalemate up to 1938; while efforts to counter racism through institutionalized scientific channels were frustrated anti-racist publications by individuals became popular. It was during the third period, however, from 1938 on, that the scientific community declared itself against racism. Since the 1950s, public memory has been that the rejection of Nazism led to the refutation of scientific racism,[1] but as discussed in the introduction was not a foregone conclusion. It took great efforts and political manoeuvering by committed scientists to facilitate this rejection of racism.[2] Most scientists were hesitant to join the political frontier in the intellectual battle to discredit racism. The first to do so were those who were already prepared; left-wingers, liberals and Jews. Despite an initial response of disbelief, a small contingent mobilized itself and became a focal point of rallying against Nazism. Their numbers increased slowly and their commitment grew. Before 1938 attempts to publish joint scientific anti-racist statements to represent the discipline's position

foundered and it was left to individual efforts to fill the gap through books and articles. While an institutional committee in England failed to reach a consensus to condemn racism, collective efforts never even reached the point of trying to formulate an official position in America. From December 1938 onwards, following the aggravation of the political situation and the growing impatience with Nazism in the West, earlier campaigns materialized in a number of anti-racist declarations. These included statements by the American Anthropological Association, the executive council of the Society for the Psychological Study of Social Issues, and a group of distinguished geneticists at the International Congress of Genetics in Edinburgh, which became known as the Geneticists' Manifesto.[3] All of them asserted the principle of opposing Nazi racial theories, but did not go far towards defining race in egalitarian cultural terms. This was postponed until UNESCO initiated its first statement on race in 1950.

The single most active American scientist to combat racism in science was Franz Boas who remained the central figure of American anthropology up to his death in 1942. During the thirties his main contribution became more political, primarily in assisting refugees from Germany and fighting against scientific and political racism. In 1933, at the age of seventy five, Boas was still teaching full time at Columbia, where he supervised more (and better) PhD.s in anthropology than found at any other school in the country. Reputedly, his hopes of early retirement did not materialize due to the Depression and Columbia's refusal to hire replacements, especially Boasians. A veteran of many public campaigns, with contacts mostly in Europe and few in England, Boas suddenly found himself in the midst of a new turmoil, combating prejudice and conducting an intensive research program in an endeavour that continued literally till the last day of his life, ten years later.[4]

For more than a decade before 1933, Boas was active on behalf of German-American cooperation, especially in science. Although he visited Germany in 1932, and kept up his activities in the Germanistic Society of America, he did not comment on the internal politics of the country prior to March 1933. He seemed reluctant to adopt a position of blank opposition to the regime of a country with which he

---

[1] This account is agreed upon by those, including Stocking, who subscribe to the present egalitarian consensus as scientifically correct (G. Stocking, "Lamarckianism," in *Race, Culture, and Evolution* (1968; Chicago: University of Chicago Press, 1982, pp. 234–238), and by those including John Baker who bemoan equality. For Baker since 1928 no ideas against equality of races could be voiced. Sorokin's *Contemporary Sociological Theories* "marked the close of the period in which both sides in the ethnic controversy were free to put forward their views, and authors who wished to do so could give objective accounts of the evidence pointing in each direction. From the beginning of the thirties onwards scarcely anyone outside Germany and its allies dared to suggest that any race might be in any sense superior to any other, lest it should appear that the author was supporting or excusing a Nazi cause. Those who believed in the equality of all races were free to write what they liked, without fear of contradiction ... Sorokin's chapter is well worth reading today, as a reminder of what was still possible before the curtain came down." John R. Baker, *Race* (Oxford: Oxford University Press, 1974), p. 61. See also Stepan, *The Idea of Race in Science: Great Britain 1800–1960* (Hamden, Conn.: Archon Books, 1982).

[2] Peter J. Kuznick (*Beyond the Laboratory: Scientists as Political Activists on 1930s America* (Chicago: Chicago University Press, 1987), describes the campaign against Fascism and pays attention to the fight against racism. See especially chs. 7–8.

[3] Ruth Benedict, *Race: Science and Culture* (1940: New York: The Viking Press, 1943), pp. 195–199. "Geneticists' Manifesto at the International Congress of Genetics in Edinburgh," *Journal of Heredity*, 30 (1939), 371–374. Diane Paul, "Eugenics and the Left," *Journal of the History of Ideas*, 45 (1984), 567–590. William B. Provine, "Geneticists and Race," *American Zoologist*, 26 (1986), 857–887.

[4] Herskovits, *Franz Boas: The Science of Man in the Making* (New York: Scribner's 1953.)

retained a profound cultural identification. During March and April 1933, requests for help from Germany started to accumulate in Boas's files, but despite his efforts to help, he felt "hopeless." The crisis came to dominate Boas's work. The first initiative for international cooperation was coordinated from London, where a committee to help the German refugee scientists was formed under the chairmanship of Gilbert Murray, and included Sir William Beveridge, Sir Gowland Hopkins (President of the Royal Society) and George Trevelyan. Boas organized the American side,[5] neglecting his scientific activity as well as many of his previous social interests, including his involvement with minorities questions in the United States. By May 1933, Boas found himself engaged both in helping individuals find haven in the United States and in organizing opposition to anti-Semitism and racism. This was part of the wider response to the refugees' plight, and it is in this context that peer pressure upon biologists and anthropologists to renounce the scientific credentials of racism became critical.

Boas joined the American Committee Against Fascist Oppression in Germany when it was organized in March. His first public act was to address an open letter to President Hindenburg on March 27, which became the manifesto of Boas's later work. In his political activities Boas continued to apply rigid standards of accuracy, and refused to support propaganda which he believed did not measure up to these standards. When the Committee published a "Black Book of German Fascist Atrocities," Boas withdrew from the Committee because he believed these did not represent a systematic policy, only "unfavorable ruffianism in days of revolution."[6] By late April he had tried to get the Council of the National Academy of Sciences to pass a resolution against "the tendency to control scientific work from non-scientific viewpoints that are [sic] spreading particularly among the nations of Europe." Such an unspecified target was to be used often in resolutions over the next few years because it could be seen as "directed [not] against Germany alone, but equally against Italy or Russia or any other state that is guilty of the same offense." When this effort failed, Boas sought to have a similar resolution passed by the American College of Physicians and Surgeons.[7] As more detailed reports of the "utter despair of all classes of Jews in Germany" began to reach him, and as he became aware of "a well organized attempt in New York, and probably in other parts of the country, to propagate anti-Semitism," his Jewish commitment overshadowed any prior loyalties to Germany. In June, he took the lead in

organizing the Lessing League to combat "the anti-Semitic agitation which is being carried on in this country by the Silver Shirts Party."[8] Boas, who had devoted so much of his life to liberal causes and campaigned incessantly to influence public opinion, was realistic and skeptical about the impact of such efforts through writing because, he commented sadly, "only people who agree will read it."[9] Here, nonetheless, his contributions turned out to have a lasting importance. Boas undertook a systematic effort to "counteract the vicious, pseudo-scientific activity of so-called scientists who try to prove the close relation between racial descent and mental character." He launched a research program aimed at providing data to "attack the racial craze" by "undermin[ing] its alleged scientific basis" and creating opportunities to combat racist fallacies in an educational campaign.

Boas recognized that he would be considered a partisan in conducting an investigation on racial questions, specifically if it involved the Jewish question, and therefore organized a committee which consisted largely of non-Jews. Financial support, however, was mostly Jewish since non-Jews had declined solicitations. The enterprise was carried out under the auspices of the Council of Research of the Social Sciences at Columbia University, which included the sociologist Robert MacIver, the psychologist A. T. Poffenberger and the geneticist Leslie Dunn, all nationally prominent. The committee was largely a facade for the work of Boas and his students.[10] For some time the council had been supporting the research of Otto Klineberg, who demonstrated the predominant role of environment in determining the mental characteristics of American blacks. Boas's goal was to show that "individual heredity and racial heredity are entirely different things and that while we may find that certain characteristic traits are inherited in a family, the race is altogether too complex to infer that racial characteristics as such

---

[5] Boas to R. Pound, May 23, 1933. FBP.

[6] Boas to M. Trent, April 23; to M. Butler, May 3, FBP.

[7] Boas to C. Abbott, April 17; Boas to M. Butler, May 3; Boas to H. Cushing, April 25. FBP.

[8] B. Liebowitz to E. Boas, May 4; Boas to L. Posner, May 26, FBP.

[9] Boas to Kaempfert, *New York Times* Science Editor, April to, 1933. Boas to W. M. Wheeler, Harvard, May 23, 1933. FBP.

[10] Boas called for a meeting at the City Club in November 1933, to organize the campaign, aiming to raise $10.000 annually to study "Racial and Social Differences in Mental Ability," and refute alleged racial characteristics. The American Museum of Natural History declined the invitation, Frederick Osborn would not help financially, and Boas had to rely on Jewish financial support. Since June 1934, Dunn was away, and gave Boas an official *carte blanche* in running the committee. Boas to M. Warburg, Dec. 29, 1933; to F. Warburg, Nov. 24, 1933. Other non-Jews who were suggested included, in psychiatry William A. White (Washington). Macfie Campbell (Boston). See E. M. Friedman to Boas, Nov. 13. FBP.

are inherited."[11] The essential aim of the Council was to achieve wide publicity, hoping to shorten the time lag of publication by issuing pamphlets. The council also planned to publish books of which Boas's *Anthropology and Modern Life* [1928] was the model. Boas paid great attention to media coverage, and invested much effort in writing letters to editors and issuing press releases. His article "Aryans and Non-Aryans" was submitted to the *Atlantic Monthly, Harper's, Scribner's* and *Esquire*, before being finally published in June 1934 in *Mercury*, eight months after the initial attempt.[12] Boas even explored the possibility of producing an educational movie to combat anti-Semitic propaganda, to be based on his studies of gestures of Jewish and Italian immigrants.[13] He also tried to mobilize scientists to speak out publicly against scientific assumptions underlying racism and insisted that even popular publications, devised only as propaganda tools, should be accurate in content. On similar grounds he opposed Ignaz Zollschan over the years, as being too much of a Jewish nationalist.[14]

Perhaps the most telling of Boas's commitments to civil rights was his struggle to give fair protection to Nazis in the U.S.[15] Boas refrained from party politics, but was very active on public issues. This included membership in many organizations, among them the American Committee Against Fascist Oppression in Germany, the National Committee for the Defence of Political Prisoners, and a committee for civil rights of Indians. In addition, he served as the national chairman of the American Committee of Democracy and Intellectual Freedom and of the Committee on Race

Relations of the Society of Friends. He also corresponded with many political organizations, recruiting participants and speakers on their behalf. At Columbia he was involved with the branch of The League of Struggle for Negro Rights (1933) as well as with defence of academic freedom. Occasionally, Boas became an advocate for the rights of minorities, such as the Korean students, who rarely captured public attention.[16]

His political experience during the thirties made him into a sophisticated political observer.[17] Despite repeated disappointments, and echoing Tocqueville's fear of democracy, Boas maintained a belief in the impact of words, and in the ability of the individual to shape society:

> I do not believe that the simple term 'Democracy,' which we connect with intellectual freedom, applies to every kind of democracy, because … an intolerant or bigoted democracy may be as bad as any form of absolutism … My own personal experience has been that on account of my consistent stand for intellectual freedom I have been ostracized by the American democracy in 1919, by Russian scientists in 1932, and by Germany at the present time.[18]

Aside from general political anti-fascist activity, there was very little organized response to Nazism among scientists and almost none from official scientific institutions. Scientists reserved their

---

[11] Boas to F. Warburg, Oct. 9, 1933. FBP.

[12] Boas to Sadgwick, Nov. 8, 1933; Marion Sanders to Boas, Dec. 20, 1933.

[13] Boas to Harry Warner, June 30, 1938.

[14] Boas to the members of the Council, April 21, 1933. On the Council's plans, Boas, circular, n.d. (1935?). Boas asked Hooton to find an opportunity to publish an anti-racist statement and arranged the contacts with media agencies to assure coverage. Boas to Berneys, Jan. 27, 1936; For a session at the National Academy of Science Boas solicited interviews by journalists for himself, Hrdlicka, Todd and Hooton, April 13, 1936. The "gestures" study was targeted to the Sunday Magazine of the *New York Times*. On Zollschan, see below pp. 318–325.

[15] He demanded that "proper public judicial procedure" should also be applied in the case of those "guilty of the numerous outrages." Boas withdrew from the National Committee for the Defence of Political Prisoners because they declared their intention of not defending a Nazi group, and he supported the appointment of Furtwaengler as Director of the New York Philharmonic Orchestra, because opposition to it was based solely on political motives. Boas to Hirsch, Jan. 15, 1935; to the Editor, *New York Times*, March 2, 1936.

[16] Boas to S. Dickstein, Jan. 16, 1940. It is interesting to note that he was totally unaware of racial discrimination against the Japanese on the West Coast. Boas's "Japanese sources" ascribed anti-Japanese sentiments and actions to be politically motivated, not racially (Boas to M. Hillyer, April 29, 1942). Boas's support of the black minority was long and extensive. In this context it should be mentioned that he supported political efforts to combat anti-black legislation, affirmative action in education" in principle and in practice – by giving blacks the opportunity to participate in anthropological and psychological studies of their own people. His participation in a symposium of Fascism and Lynch-terror emphasized his twofold opposition to racism ("Leipzing and Scottsboro – A Tale of Two Cities." Dec. 6, 1933, FBP) as did his activities in combating racial legislation on the state level. For The League of Struggle for Negro Rights see FBP, Nov. 25, 1933. He was particularly influential in the State of Washington where the anti-racial-miscegnation bill was finally defeated in 1939. Boas testified, and urged others to do the same. Boas and M. Jacobs correspondence, especially March 21, 1939. FBP.

[17] Previously Boas had been politically naïve, as his correspondence with the Soviet Union and Germany suggests, but in this he was not alone. Until his breach with Germany, his correspondence does not include any comments on the political situation in Germany, where he summered in 1932. His remarks concerning the Soviet Union display ignorance.

[18] Boas to Schneiderman, May 15, 1939. FBP.

comments, and except for excluding a small number of investigations financed at Columbia, no organized initiative was taken to undermine the scientific claims of Nazi racism. While racism was on the wane in American science, little immediate response to the Nazi threat emerged among scientists.

BRITAIN – RACE AND CULTURE COMMITTEE

In contrast to the United States, where the Boasian critique of racial typology had been central to the formation of anthropology during the first three decades of the century, in Britain the question of race did not become prominent until after 1933, before that date the primary debate had been over class relations.[19] Functional and social anthropology became the dominant form of the discipline more by secession from nineteenth century evolutionary tradition than by confrontation. Rather than being marginalized by institutional anthropology in the 1920s, as were the American hereditarians, British racialists remained respected figures in the profession and dominated the Royal Anthropological Institute into the thirties. Consequently egalitarianism was almost non-existent among the British.[20] It was only when British liberals were forced to reconcile their overall world-view with their racial prejudices and had to wrestle with their long accepted social intellectual conventions that they began to advocate anti-racism. A few of those who had displayed ugly racism at an earlier date, such as Julian Huxley or J. B. S. Haldane, began to shift in an anti-racist direction around 1930 and within few years became the symbols of anti-racism. Others, however, committed themselves to the nonracist position only later. In 1931 Arthur Keith updated his 1916 theory of racial antagonism as part of human nature. John Linton Myres called it "provocative" in a review for *Man* but did not confront it critically.[21] Keith's position sparked a minor controversy, but it was not until three years later, and under different circumstances, that the anthropology community embarked on its first institutionalized attempt to face racism.

By the spring of 1934, British scientists had encountered the question of a response to Nazism – privately or in scientific circles – either in regard to the immigration of persecuted fellow scientists or as a political question. Left-wingers and liberals voiced a growing demand for an active response, part of which was reflected in the political tension and internal pressure, which led the Royal Anthropological Institute with the support of the Institute of Sociology, to establish on April 24, 1934, a committee to study the "racial factor in cultural development." Among the British anthropologists, the driving force to form the Race and Culture Committee seems to have been Charles Seligman. A major stimulus from outside the anthropological establishment had come from Ignaz Zollschan, a Czechoslovakian Jewish physician then in Britain as part of his European tour in a personal campaign to combat Nazi anti-Semitism.

The Race and Culture Committee was established under constraints which made its task impossible. When, in the spring of 1936, the committee published what it called an interim report,[22] even the editorial in the moderate *Nature* had some harsh comments: it had taken the committee two years to deliberate on the question of "a simple definition of race to serve as a guide to the general public in the discussions of the problems of to-day," and then it did not deliver. "Not only are alternative definitions offered, but also several members append observations which at times almost amount to minority reports." *Nature* found the two definitions "inexceptionable," and added: "these definitions are far from being generalizations from concrete realities and empirical, [these] are no more than logical concepts, postulated for the purpose of classification and investigation." Examining the existing distribution of physical characters among the population groups of the world, *Nature* remarked that "race is pure abstraction." Taken at face value, this view would have placed *Nature* among later date extreme anti-racialists. But this was not so much a result of *Nature*'s egalitarianism as a display of its frustration with the committee's work; impatience which resulted from the recognition that "racial distinctions have emerged from the sphere of intellectual inquiry and have been made the practical basis of discrimination." Consequently it was the task of scholars to agree upon and publish a resolution which

---

[19] Kevles, *Eugenics*; Stepan, *Race*; Paul, "Eugenics and the Left."

[20] G. Stocking (ed.), *Functionalism Historicized. Essays on British Social Anthropology*, History of Anthropology II (Madison: University of Wisconsin Press, 1984).

[21] Sir Arthur Keith, *Ethnos, or the Problem of Race* (London: K. Paul, 1931). Keith's public stature was enhanced by his official role in the Royal College of Surgeons in London and his position as Rector of the University of Aberdeen. He first formulated his nationalistic theory in 1916, under the impact of World War I, and the updated version received publicity in two distinguished lectures: his Huxley memorial lecture, and the

Continued

Rectorial address in Aberdeen. Myres, *Man*, 32 (1932), 246. Keith's position promised that the theory would continue to arouse public opinion throughout the 1930s (see correspondence in *Man*, March-June 1940), and even in the post-war period.

[22] Royal Anthropological Institute and the Institute of Sociology. *Race and Culture* (London: Le Play House, 1936).

would return the debate to its appropriate domain.[23] The visibility of the racial question turned anthropology into a popular topic and this, coupled with a belief in objectivity and rationality, united the anthropologists under the auspices of the Royal Anthropological Institute to solicit contributions for studies on the racial history and population of Britain, justified by the claim that Britain lagged behind many other countries in such studies. The list of twenty signatories appended to the request included Gates, Huxley, Keith and Seligman.[24] *Nature's* editorial displayed the misconception that a scientific debate can return the spectre of racism to its previously "respected" dimensions. Anthropologists and biologists were presumed objective in their scientific analysis of the question of race, and there was not even a hint that the reverse might be the case, namely that prejudice was the source of scientific justification and that scientists were trapped by the same blindness as the public at large. *Nature's* "objectivity" was illustrated in several editorials such as "The Aryan Doctrine," which attacked German dogmatism, and in the same spirit reproached the Americans (by implication, Boas and his disciples) who resorted to the easier alternative of egalitarianism, following the "voice of the facile theorist ... while the scientific investigator of race, who refrains from dogmatism pending fuller inquiry, is still crying in the wilderness."[25]

This middle-of-the-road attitude was also manifested in a letter to *The Times* from Alfred Haddon, Sir Gowland Hopkins, the President of the Royal Society, and J. B. S. Haldane, in which they admonished Sir John Simon, a Cabinet Minister, for exhibiting his Aryan extraction.[26] The editorial emphasized the widespread ignorance among the public concerning the race issue, and partially blamed the divided anthropologists for being unable to communicate a clear message to the public. After explaining the Nordic and Aryan theories, the editorial concluded: "Such dogmatic assumptions, unfortunately have their attraction for the political doctrinaire and the agitator; and it is perhaps to be regretted therefore, that the International Congress of Anthropological and Ethnological Sciences did not see its way to promote investigation into such racial problems on broad lines. The machinery may seem over-weighty; but at least the truth would have been made available in authoritative form to all."[27] The hopes of the summer of 1934 evidently did not materialize: by 1936 the

Race and Culture Committee showed that a clear authoritative statement in the name of the profession was unattainable.

Professional politics rendered the Race and Culture Committee's efforts futile. The most prominent racist among British anthropologists was Arthur Keith, and the staunch racists on the committee were G. H. L. F. Pitt-Rivers, and Reginald Ruggles Gates, all of whom belonged to the mainstream of the profession. Despite the relatively few records pertaining to the Race and Culture Committee, the cooperation between Pitt-Rivers and Gates in presenting a racist front is clear. The anti-racists on the committee, however, were certainly better represented. The classification of British scientists as anti-racists in the mid-thirties, when a formalist approach to race was still widespread and the Boasian critique hardly present, may cast doubts on the whole exercise. Yet if the definition employed is narrow enough and politically oriented, it is possible even at this stage to distinguish racists from anti-racists. Anti-racists included scientists who opposed political racism, classified themselves as such and objected to the use of scientific theories to justify racial discrimination. The members of the Race and Culture Committee who published such views before World War II included the chairman G. Elliot Smith, the anatomist Le Gros Clark, the geographer Herbert J. Fleure, the cultural anthropologist Raymond Firth, the biometrician Geoffrey Morant and the biologist J. B. S. Haldane.

This narrow definition of anti-racism has to be understood in its historical context, one that excluded Jews from the Committee because they were deemed too subjective to participate in such a scientific elucidation. Simplistic objectivism was the norm to such a degree that even liberals and the victims themselves, in this case the Jews, accepted ostracism; and so because of Gates's opposition, the sociologist Morris Ginsberg was not included.[28] The same attitude of appeasement guided the British opposition to a Czech initiative to organize an international race congress. John Linton Myres, the British diplomat of anthropology, consented to such congress if it could be kept "strictly scientific." But in his view, this was unlikely since "it appears at present to be sponsored by Czechoslovakia, Austria and France," countries which, as victims, were expected to retaliate. A further prerequisite was the inclusion of the Germans who, Myres thought were unlikely "to come to a Prague-Vienna-Paris enterprise."[29] Surely Myres did not expect that the inclusion of an official German delegation was to turn a race congress into a

---

[23] *Nature*, 137 (April 18, 1936), 635–637.

[24] *Times*, March 13, 1935, also published in *Man*, 35 (April 1935).

[25] "The Delusion of Race," *Nature*, 137 (April 18, 1936), 635–637. "Genetics and Race," *Nature*, 137 (Dec. 12, 1936), 998–999.

[26] Quoted in, *Nature*, 134 (August 7, 1934).

[27] "The Aryan Doctrine," *Nature*, 134 (August 18, 1934), 229–231.

[28] Seligman to Gates, April 22, 1935. RRGP.

[29] Myres to Farquharson, confidential (March 1934?) 121 fol. 106: Myres to Fleure, March 10; 1934, 121 fol. 112. JLMP.

dispassionate scholarly enterprise. At least by implication, he claimed that as a result of the political
situation the topic evaded scientific analysis.

Although the culture of British science was very
formal, disagreements among scientists often
reached the public domain. Individually, several
scientists entertained themselves by engaging in
lively disputes, which included much correspondence with the editors of the *Times* and *Nature*. Yet
the British scientific establishment was almost
sacred, or at least tried to present itself as such. Its
best strategy for preserving unity was to *avoid* issues
that could not be settled peacefully. Scientific legitimacy stemmed from very few tradition-bound
institutions and societies. Oxford, Cambridge, and
London were the only centers that mattered; other
universities only counted when they conformed.
Opposition was never meaningful if mounted from
the provinces. The key to success was incorporation
and accommodation. As long as no viable institutional alternative existed, everyone had to fall in
line, even the "Visible College."[30] The Race and
Culture Committee should therefore be viewed as
an effort in accommodation.

If the fear of Nazism motivated left-wingers to
establish the Committee, right-wingers were encouraged by the Nazi success to increase their activities.
Gates's xenophobia, for example, was manifested in
his anti-miscegenation campaign, which he began in
1933. Although his aim was to show that "there is no
method of knowing how many [colored people] are
born" in Britain, he defined it as "an increasingly difficult" problem. Undaunted by this lacuna in knowledge, he based his argument on studies that included
500 children – "no doubt a very small fraction of the
whole number." Gates was worried "that the only
force against [racial] crossing is that of social
ostracism which can be evaded in various ways,"
especially in port towns where colored people had
their own streets.[31] Like other racists Gates denied
that his views had any connection with Nazi doctrines, and Seligman even solicited, perhaps perfunc-
torily, his cooperation in the campaign against
German racism. Ostensibly there was no institutional
cleavage between racists and anti-racists in British
science, but in the case of the Race and Culture
Committee this overzealousness in pursuing a consensus where none existed became self defeating.[32]

Gates's comments for the Race and Culture
Committee presented adequately his disagreement
with other members. Gates believed that "in the
taxonomy of animals and plants the conception of
groups within groups had long held sway and it is
difficult to see how it could be otherwise with man
if evolution has taken place."[33] From this basic
analogy the rest followed. Because Gates looked
for "groups within groups," and applied the same
terminology to mankind as to the rest of nature, he
chose to speak about species and races "or smaller
population groups." He considered fertility an
"obsolete" criterion for a species and therefore "if
an Australian aborigine and an Eskimo were bred
together there is no reason to doubt that they would
show full fertility, but this is not a sufficient reason
for placing them in one species. If the same criteria
of species were applied to mankind as to other
mammals, it appears that the White, Black and
Yellow types of man at least would be regarded as
belonging to separate species." Gates thought that
anthropological data which showed no considerable
geographical area to be inhabited exclusively by
any one race did not "nullify the value of these
types as anthropological conceptions," and concluded: "It appears clear that within historical times
the reverse process of racial migration and intermixture has been taking place at an even accelerat-
ing rate ... This process has led not merely to an
undoing of the evolution which has taken place
under condition of geographical isolation. Evolution
has not ceased, but intermixture has largely taken
the place of isolation as an evolutionary factor."[34]

The other racist on the Committee was Captain
George H. L. F. Pitt-Rivers, the grandson of the
founder of the Pitt-Rivers Museum at Oxford. After
a career in the army and the colonial service,
H. L. F. Pitt-Rivers became active in anthropological circles in the 1920s, as well as a close friend of
Bronislaw Malinowski. Author of the influential
volume on *The Clash of Culture and the Conflict
of the Races*, Pitt-Rivers was a member of the
Eugenics Society and Secretary-General and
Honorary Treasurer of the International Union for
Scientific Investigation of Population Problems
from 1928 to 1937. His support for Nazi Germany
went a long way beyond mere vocal Aryanism. He
taught in Germany during the 1930s, and following
the outbreak of the war was held a political prisoner

---

[30] Gary Werskey, *The Visible College* (London: Allen
Lane, 1978), uses the term with regard to the left, though
Werskey does not make this particular analysis. For
Huxley's case, see above, chapter 5.

[31] Gates's views were too "outspoken" for the
Nineteenth Century, which declined the contribution.
Fleming to Gates, Oct. 13, 1933: Gates to Blacker, Oct.
16, 1933. RRGP.

[32] Seligman introduced Zollschan, an anti-racist activist,
to Gates in the spring of 1934. Seligman to Gates, March

Continued

15, 1934. RRGP. Did Seligman actually believe that Gates
would cooperate in such an effort? One would doubt that,
but perhaps Seligman's intention in soliciting Gates was to
deter him from public opposition.

[33] Gates, "The Conception of Race," August 6, 1934, in
the Bodleian, Ms. 121 f. 162–3. JLMP. Published in the
report as his addendum.

[34] Gates, "The Conception of Race."

in England during 1940–1942. The scientific contribution he treasured most was the science of "ethnogenics," a method for the study of the "inter-action of race, population and culture." Among his recreations he listed "refuting politicians," and it is evident why Pitt-Rivers spared no efforts to have his racial views aired in the Committee's report.[35]

Pitt-Rivers's concern was that "the looseness with which the term race is used" obscures "the process of race-extinction." He accepted that migration confused the linkage of race with a geographical region, and therefore replaced traditional race formalism with rigid ethnic identity and "race-types" which were dissociated from their customary "geographical habitats." In this context, the important distinction was culture. Pitt-Rivers described the "Nordic," "Alpine" and "Mediterranean" as standardization of the characteristics of existing race-types although, as he added, these were arbitrary. The meaningful distinction lay in a "race-cultural complex" of "People" – namely, Celtic, Aryan, English. This critique of traditional racial divisions from a racist perspective shows that the answer to cultural relativism and biological complexity was not necessarily egalitarian. Pitt-Rivers credited Arthur Keith as the writer who had refuted the idea of the fixity of race-types not from an egalitarian, but from a nationalist and racialist, perspective. An evolutionary view of race implies continuous development; where Gates emphasized the biological aspect alone, Pitt-Rivers combined it with the cultural.

Even when the Committee managed to agree on an abstract principle, political compromise remained a constant impediment.[36] Of the report's twenty-three pages, only the three pages of the preamble were agreed upon by all of the members, but even these reflected disagreement. Although Boas's article in the *Encyclopedia of Social Sciences* on "Race" was given as a bibliographical source, Pitt-Rivers suggested a critical addendum to the effect that Boas's approach was "not compatible with the most recent approach of human ecologists or of ethnologists." The compromise was a supplementary reference to a recent book on human ecology.[37] The Committee debated Boas's work, and Elliot Smith requested from Boas for the Race and Culture Committee thirty copies of his essay "Aryans and Non-Aryans": "As chairman I want all the members to read your pamphlet before we draft our final report." It was in Elliot Smith's opinion "extremely valuable at the moment when I am deeply involved in the task of trying to combat the racial non-sense that now plays so large a part in current journals and discussions."[38]

The committee in effect offered two definitions of race: nominalist and realist, emphasizing the limitation of scientific knowledge of the physical aspects of human groups, and suggesting only that "innate psychological characters may later be found to differentiate them." The nominalist definition called for caution in the use of statistical averages based on "descriptive and measurable characters" (i.e., phenotype) which might in fact "obscure … several diverse strains" (i.e., genotype). An alternative definition emphasized the condition of continuous isolation and spoke of "genetical characteristics" that distinguished different groups. The geographical factor, a source of disagreement, was absent. The committee's mandate had been to define "how far particular races and populations are actually linked with particular cultures or culture elements," but the members could never agree on this question. Instead they appended seven individual definitions which reflected the various currents in the anthropology community.[39]

While the conflict between racists and non-racists was evident, the nonracist members of the committee also disagreed on method and content. Morant argued from a biometrician's perspective that biological knowledge was not sufficient for any practical application. He minimized the role of paleontology and archeology in favor of methods which are "essentially descriptive" and "do not presuppose any particular theory of individual or racial inheritance."[40] This inexplicable definition of race and the overall political impotency of scientists, was later regretted by Morant. Following the outbreak of World War II, he expressed remorse that anthropologists had failed to oppose racism earlier.

Though Morant did not find an institutional niche for himself in the post-war years, he certainly represented a respectable and viable position during the thirties.[41] This illuminates two points: first that it was still possible in England during the 1930s to be at the center of scientific activity, to deal with

[35] *Who Was Who*, 1961–1970: "A. H. L. F. Pitt-Rivers," *Dictionary of Scientific Biography*. The centrality of the *Journal of the International Union for Scientific Investigation of Population Problems* is attested by the contributors to its first issue. These included among others J. Huxley, Carr-Saunders, and Crew.

[36] Such was the case when Seligman tried to persuade Gates to endorse a call from the International Institute for Intellectual Cooperation for "a general investigation of the anthropological and ethnological basis of Western civilization." Seligman, assured of the support of Malinowski, Elliot Smith, Myres and Firth, added that on the Continent "considerable progress seems to have been made … in the organization of research groups" on similar matters. Seligman to Gates, March 17, 1935. RRGP.

[37] The book was E. J. Bews, *Human Ecology* (London: Oxford University Press, 1935). Pitt-Rivers to Gates, Dec. 15, 1935. RRGP.

[38] G. E. Smith to Boas, Oct. 8, 1934; Sept. 26, 1934. FBP.

[39] *Race and Culture*, pp. 3–4.

[40] G. M. Morant "Biometrician's View of Race in Man." in *Race and Culture*.

[41] On Morant's work see above, pp. 158–162.

inheritance and to reject genetics; and second that there was no correlation between a progressive scientific method and its application to social issues. Morant's biometric method was leading to a dead end, but his conclusions were context dependent and anti-racialist in content. Similarly, Elliot Smith's only scientific instructive comment was that biologically the contemporary usage of "races" was the equivalent of Linnaeus' "species." The rest was a rehearsal of his earlier diffusionism. Yet Smith fought racism, both Nazi theories and the overtones of Arthur Keith's "nationalism," until his death in 1937. The geographer and anthropologist H. J. Fleure described the inadequacy of biological or statistical methods in a language which discloses his anti-racialist position only to a careful and attentive reader. While on other occasions he was more direct as, for example, in a lecture to the Royal Anthropological Institute, in the report he concluded that "the averaging of whole populations regardless of these diversities of strain or breed obscures important biological facts and gives results which are sometimes too abstract to be of great value." This was not quite the dynamite that could serve an egalitarianist political campaign.[42]

J. B. S. Haldane and Raymond Firth criticized racism from what might be considered the frontier of knowledge. Haldane argued that any definition of race must include a reference to geographical distribution as well as to human characters. Due to immigration, the geographical aspect should relate to a certain past. Recognizing obvious differences, Haldane focused on populations with overlapping characters. His insistence that biological, and therefore racial, differences are due to genes was almost unique in the committee. Firth approached the question from the perspective of a cultural anthropologist. He minimized the influence of physical characters on cultural achievements and rejected the assumed importance of race. Yet his anti-racist position can only be appreciated in its historical context. In substance, Firth, like other anti-racist members of the Committee, could have endorsed modern sociobiology, and conceded that "consideration of temperament" played a part in the "acquisition of culture," although science has no way of obtaining information "in substantiation of this general impression."[43] Despite their willingness to entertain racial conjectures, their position elucidated the unscientific nature of such hypothesis.

Gates and Pitt-Rivers used the terminology of genetics to support their idiosyncratic racial typologies, an approach which lent their theories an appearance of scientific progressiveness and respectability. They differed with other members on two issues: firstly that races did not mean

geographical isolation, and secondly that racial mixture was an evolutionary force which, in Gates's words, "produced many new races." Pitt-Rivers advocated his own "ethnogenics" to cover the combination of genetics with the "study of human history in terms of changing race, population and culture." He explicitly opposed Smith but accepted diffusionism and claimed that the racial transfer of cultural elements by borrowing is a process which involves selection and therefore implies inner capacity. These scientific theories accentuated the racialist interpretations and hence were compatible with Gates's and Pitt-Rivers's political alliances. They drew comfort from Germany, and from the German anthropologist Eickenstedt, who also refrained from addressing the geographical origin.[44] The growing political crisis of the 1930s was not a congenial atmosphere for compromise, and the confrontation became more fierce. The decision of the Race and Culture Committee to publish an unsatisfactory report was the only alternative to a declaration of failure, which was inadvisable since an agreement was needed for professional and political reasons. The small anthropological profession was suddenly given center stage in defining the "truth" of the burning political question of race, an importance it had never attained before. The benefits and publicity were tempting, as was the moral and political responsibility. While the Committee failed to reach a consensual statement on race, the pressure of international events made further attempts in other arenas inevitable.

One such instance was the joint session at the annual meeting of the British Association at Blackpool (1936) of the zoology and anthropology sections, which debated the definition of race. *Nature* supported the scientists' efforts to face "the exploitation of the race concept by politicians" and concluded that it "behoves all scientific workers … to respond for the demand of the general public for guidance" in these matters. Perhaps more important, at the end of the article came a call for scientists to "relinquish" the scientific use of the term race because the politicians had "appropriated the term." In this it echoed Huxley's and Haddon's recently published *We Europeans*. *Nature*'s traditional emphasis on the objectivity of science and its role in guiding the public was being contradicted by political events. Though the magazine did not explicitly change its perceptions of the social relations of science, it implied that scientific terms were influenced and shaped by public opinion.[45] The public demand was for anthropology to define race scientifically and rename it. Most anthropologists followed this intellectual trend against racism and

---

[42] For Fleure's comments, see *Race and Culture*, pp. 6–8.
[43] Firth's comments in *Race and Culture*.

[44] Pitt-Rivers to Gates, Dec. 15, 1935. RRGP.
[45] "Genetics and Race," *Nature*, 137 (Dec. 12, 1936), pp. 998–999.

shifted the subject matter of their research from the biological to the cultural. For many the transformation preceded World War II, but the British scientific community followed the government's policy of appeasement, and prevented the shift against rigid racial typology and, by implication, against racism, from receiving formal approval.

33

When Black First Became Worth Less

ANTON L. ALLAHAR

In another selection in this anthology the query is raised, is racism accidental? This article poses a related question, why does racism remain as a social force? Anton Allahar intentionally sidesteps the issue of whether or not differences between black and white people are real and measurable. Instead he states that regardless of the answer to this issue, people act towards each other in certain situations as if perceived racial differences were based on reality. The author begins the essay by showing that oppression was not necessarily racial in earlier historical periods. Even slavery, according to some observers, predates the emergence of racism. The early basis of racism includes religious assertions and involvement in slavery and ideological justifications for colonialism. But as these factors disappeared from society, racism continued due to the functional role it played in maintaining power relations born in the earlier periods. The author shows how plantation owners in the Caribbean, for example, relied on racism and sexism directed against black women in particular, to maintain control over blacks since such control was directly tied to profits and wealth.

Whether or not "black" people and "white" people actually exist is not as important as the fact that human beings *behave* as if they do. Peoples' colours are seen to be associated with their races; they are thus identified, and they identify themselves, as lying somewhat along a colour continuum that runs from blue-black to pinkish-white. The number of races that it is possible to identify today is correspondingly very large. Indeed it is so large that the term "race" has itself become quite meaningless. Robert Miles says it best when he asserts that 'race' is "an idea that should be explicitly and consistently confined to the dustbin of analytically useless terms" (1989:72).

The reality of the situation, however, is that it has not been so confined, and colour and race continue to act as key social markers that provide individuals and groups with packaged meanings of themselves and others. The attribution of such meanings linked to physical and genetic characteristics is the basis on which categorizations are made with their attendant expectations as to what various individuals and groups are like, what they are capable of, and even about their morality. When such categorizations are informed by negative meanings, and when those meanings serve to relegate people to subordinate positions in a system of hierarchical social rankings, racism is the result. For along with its ideological message, racism is the practice of including and excluding individuals and groups from participating fully in the social economy on the basis of some imputed racial similarities or differences, and their denial of access to certain services and resources.

Visible physical differences among people are impossible to deny. They have existed throughout history and have been used positively and negatively depending on the circumstances. In a very general sense, those who are phenotypically different are presumed to be socially and culturally different, and to have different religious and political beliefs and practices. This makes it possible to set them apart completely as outsiders, as belonging to distinct nations, tribes, races, and so on. And further, when military strength is combined with the ideologies of nationalism, tribalism, and racism, the possibilities for widespread conflict and domination are created. But, as we said, these will all vary depending on the context. Thus, while human beings have always operated with the ideas of the "in-group" and the "out-group," the actual mechanics of inclusion and exclusion have run the gamut from total assimilation to outright extermination. Always, however, the members of the in-group, those in the powerful positions, have used ideological justifications or rationalizations for their actions. In the case of racism, one often hears references to their so-called *natural* superiority as a group.

My aim is to explore some of the roots of those rationalizations, and to draw attention to the fact that, like any other ideas, those developed around the question of race can, and have assumed a life of their own, divorced from the original context in which they arose. They have been applied in different ways throughout history and have served diverse ends. Thus, whether or not the ancient Egyptians were racist towards the Ethiopians, or the colour symbolisms of the Old Testament were meant literally, these considerations served greatly to inform the later practices of slavery and colonialism, and to justify to the slave owners and colonizers their historic actions.

It is in this sense that .Miles regards racism as a relation of production; for it was an indispensable aspect of the process of primitive accumulation of colonial capital, which was vital to the consolidation and development of capitalism at the global level, and which saw the Africans' enslavement as "the appropriate position for a population at a different stage of human development, for a different (and inferior) kind of human being" (Miles, 1989:111). As will be seen, however, the roots of such a rationalization antedated African slavery by several millennia, and throughout the post-slavery period down to the present day, have continued to shape, albeit in altered form, the processes of labour recruitment and exploitation in an age of late capitalism.

RACISM

Students of Cuban history are familiar with the figure of Juan Gregorio de Neyra, the richest mulatto in Cuba during the first half of the eighteenth century. Desirous of eliminating the stigma of having "black blood"[1] the descendants of Juan Gregorio chose only to marry white spouses, so that by the early nineteenth century we are told that the de Neyra family had managed to achieve total whiteness. In 1802, however, a social and political scandal was created when one of the descendants, María Josefa de la Luz Hernández, had her marriage stopped by the local authorities on the grounds that she had "tainted" blood. And around the same time, in Havana's leading newspaper, *Papel Periódico*, the following appeared, aimed apparently at the de Neyra family:

> if a rich dark man
> confesses that his grandpa was black,
> nothing wrong with that.
> But if he thinks his cash
> makes him a dark gentleman,
> it doesn't follow.[2]

Where does this all begin? When did black people come to be worth less than others? Why? Who is black? And how black is black? It may not be possible to answer all these questions, but hopefully by posing them some insight into the phenomenon of racism will be afforded; and by extension, some understanding of the politics of race will be gained.

Contrary to popular belief, racism did not *cause* black people to be oppressed and enslaved. "Slavery was not born of racism," Eric Williams tells us, "rather, racism was the consequence of slavery" (1966:7). And further, slavery was not to be identified solely with the African and his or her subjugation by the white European. For long before Europeans went to Africa, (white) slavery was commonplace in ancient Greece and Rome, Asians had invaded and conquered other Asians, and often with the help of black African rulers, Edward Shils reminds us, "Arabs had exploited and enslaved black Africans" (1968:2). Slavery, therefore, was neither unique nor peculiar to the African, since we also know, together with the indigenous inhabitants of the Americas, poor whites from Europe were among the first to experience the privations of human freedom in the "New World."

For Williams, therefore, slavery was more of an economic than a racial phenomenon *per se*: "... it had to do not with the color of the laborer, but with the cheapness of the labor" (Williams, 1966:19). Where in history, then, does the concern with blackness or negritude arise? If slavery is not to be wholly or exclusively associated with blacks, whence arose the socio-religious ideas that blacks were evil and sinful, and that enslavement was their just punishment? (Moreno Fraginals, 1976:53; Lewis, 1983:139). Partial answers to this question may be sought in many places, including the history of art and literature, and the rise of Christianity as a religion that was embraced by white Europeans as a counter to Islam.

THE HISTORY OF THE IDEA

If we are to accept the views of Frank M. Snowden Jr., the writings that cover the period from the pharaohs to the Ceasars are to be noted for the rather accurate and benign portrayal of blacks in the ancient world. To be sure, differences between blacks (Ethiopians) and others (primarily the Egyptians) were noted, but according to Snowden there was no attempt to link phenotypical characteristics with social standing. This may have been due to the fact that "from earliest times Egyptians had been acquainted with blacks, and had fought alongside black mercenaries at least as early as 2000 B.C." (Snowden, 1983:5). Throughout most of this period blacks were seen as formidable, keen soldiers who defended their interests, national and personal, and who protected their own territory, as expertly and as skilfully as others. Whether as ally or as enemy they were roundly respected.

But the question is, can the views of Snowden be uncritically accepted? After all, he is the same person who defends as non-racist those classical authors who showed a decisive preference for northern or "white" beauties over their southern or "dark" counterparts. And as part of that defense he offers the intellectually feeblest comment to the effect that "it is questionable whether individuals should be called racist because they accept the aesthetic cannons prevailing in their country" (1983:63). He also chides modern scholars for seeing "color prejudice where none existed" (*Ibid:*64) in the paintings, sculptures, and engravings of the period. Among those singled out are C.T. Seltman (1920:14) who challenges the unquestioned portrayal of the Negro as ugly in works of art; Arthur Lane (1971:55) who rejects the depiction of the Negro as grotesque; and D. von Bothmer (1963:161) who opposes the image of black people in classical art as purely comical caricatures.

For Snowden, however, any focus on ugliness and comic distortion is largely the product of projection on the part of modern commentators – a product of the mind of the beholder. On this score he continues to support his assertion in an earlier work that extended into the Greco-Roman period: "There is nothing in the evidence to suggest that the ancient Greek or Roman established color as an obstacle to integration into society" (1970:217-218). Because he did not find any evidence, however, does not mean that none existed.

A somewhat different view is presented by John Block Friedman who surveys the period from antiquity through the Middle Ages with a view to identifying both the existence of "race" prejudice and its origin. For Friedman, the search is centred on medieval art and thought, and concerns what were called the "monstrous races." Beginning with the writings of Homer as early as the ninth century B.C., and going all the way down to Virgil in the last century B.C., and even in the travel reports of such men as Alexander the Great, Pliny the Elder, Ctesias and Megasthenes, one finds a virtual obsession with the strange or "monstrous races" that were supposed to live on the margins of the Greco-Roman world.[3] For like any other tightly-knit culture, the Hellenes were xenophobic, fearful, and suspicious of outsiders whom they tended to view as inferior and untrustworthy barbarians.

The Ethiopians were the first to be so viewed. Derived from the Greek word *Aethiops*, which literally meant "burnt-faced," the Ethiopians of earliest times were seen not only to be different, but also to be inferior, savage, and lacking in morals. Indeed, so powerful was this image, that even the famous Father Bartolomé de las Casas, who was sent to the West Indies to protect the native Indians from complete extinction at the hands of the Spanish *conquistadores*, could have held the view that among the African slaves some were "as black as Ethiopians, so malformed in their faces and bodies that they appeared to those who looked at them to be the image of another and lower hemisphere" (Quoted in Wagner, 1967:247). It is, thus, not too difficult to understand why Friedman could argue that, "color polarities were easily interchanged with moral polarities" and in time being black came to signify inferiority and immorality just as being white implied salvation (1981:26; 64-65). He even goes on to document the fact that the homiletic writers of the period associated blackness with sin, vice, and the Devil. Blackness was the punishment meted out to them by God.

This was the message of such men as Paulinus of Nola and Fulgentius of Ruspe, the latter of whom saw the Ethiopian as "one not yet whitened by the grace of Christ shining upon him;" and then there was Theodulus' definition of the word *Ethyopum*:

> Ethiopians, that is sinners. Indeed, sinners can be rightly compared to Ethiopians who are black men presenting a terrifying appearance to those beholding them (Quoted in Friedman, 1981:65).

Even Snowden, in his apology for the racism that was rife in classical antiquity, notes the generally accepted view at the time which held that later "Christ came into the world to make blacks white" (1970:217). He tries to put a good face on this otherwise outrageous claim, however, by stating that the Ethiopian, the blackest and most unusual of all men, was used merely as a symbol of the evil and the lack of grace that characterized all those in need of salvation, and was not meant to refer to black people alone. But this only begs the crucial question of why, in the first place, were blacks in need of salvation?

During this period, given the overall state of ignorance and confusion that abounded in the areas of geography, biology, and science in general, the popular imagination was filled with ideas of strange and monstrous peoples that lived on the periphery of the then-known world. And along with Amazons, Cyclopes and others, black people came to be viewed as just another such race or people. Since their pigmentation, hair texture, and facial features differed radically from the norm, they were seen as deviating from the natural order of things or going against nature, and throughout the Middle Ages were generally regarded with the fear, suspicion, and intolerance that are born of ignorance. Black people, thus, became anomalies, prodigies, and portents from God. It was a time when "natural events considered to be indicators of God's intentions towards human beings were defined as *portenta* or *monstra*" (Miles 1989:16).

Although these terms were used synonymously at times, the former retained its meaning of "warning" and the latter its meaning of "demonstration" or "revelation." This notwithstanding, the term *monstra* soon came to be used by Greek travellers in reference, not only to the "anomalous" Indian and African races, but to all peoples and cultures that appeared in any way different from the western norm, clearly linking or equating it with the idea of "monster." And throughout the ages its different uses and meanings were consistent in that they all seemed to carry negative connotations that were usually meant to indicate a warning from God that all was not well. In this context the influential writer Isidore of Seville, who made the first leap from individual monstrous births (for example Siamese twins or children born with physical deformities), to entire monstrous races, is a good case-in-point. Arguing that such anomalous births signified a message from God, he goes on to assert that: "Just as among individual races there are certain members who are monsters, so also among mankind as a whole, certain races are monsters..." (Quoted in Friedman, 1981:116).

While Isidore of Seville does not mention blacks or Ethiopians specifically, he clearly leaves the door open for others to make the link. For again, given the time periods with which we are dealing, and the rampant xenophobia that attended the encounters between different peoples, it was not long before those in the majority came to develop rationalizations—scientific and theological—of their realities. As we know, the "scientific" explanation for the monstrosity of blackness was the environmental theory which had certain peoples living too close to the sun and as a consequence developing their unique burnt colour, their "unusual" hair, and a whole host of anomalous physical and facial features. In all of this, however, the important point to note is that the skin pigmentation and deviant (in the statistical sense) physical appearances of black peoples set them apart from the norm in Greco-Roman society and automatically cast them in a negative light. As Miles observes, "monstrousness,

sin, and blackness constituted a rather different form of Trinity in the European Christian culture in this period" (1989:17). Coupled with their physical appearance, the unfamiliar social conventions and cultural practices of the blacks (and other "barbarian" peoples elsewhere), especially their preferences for wearing little or no clothing, rendered them not only savage, but also cannibalistic, immoral, and, like animals, sexually uninhibited (Jordan, 1968:4; Sanders, 1978:211-225; White, 1972:21-22).

IDEOLOGICAL CONTEXT

At the ideological level it is possible to understand such representations of blacks in two ways. The first concerns the image of blacks that resided principally in the minds of the European travellers, who, according to Philip Curtin, were imbued with a very deep sense of curiosity for the exotic lives of non-Europeans. Further, and right into the modern period of European colonization of the New World, much of this curiosity was sexually voyeuristic and concentrated on "a libidinous fascination for descriptions of other people who break with impunity the taboos of one's own society" (Curtin, 1964:24). Thus, in the case of the Africans, one can understand the numerous references to their nakedness, the size of their genitalia, their frequency of sexual intercourse, and even their supposed mating with apes (Jordan, 1968:151-159; Fryer, 1984:138-140, 159). As a result, a great deal of the travellers' reports concerning the peoples they encountered emphasized those social and cultural practices that were most different and outrageous in comparison to their own societies and cultures, while generally tending to ignore the similarities that suggested a common human link between themselves and the Africans: "... the reporting often stressed precisely those aspects of African life that were most repellent to the West and tended to submerge the indications of a common humanity" (Curtin, 1964:23).

The second ideological context in which the European mentality was formed relates to the politico-religious opposition between Islam and Christianity. For while the wider world beyond Europe may have been unknown to Europeans, the Islamic world as represented by the Middle East, North Africa, and India, was not. This was due to the fact that for centuries prior to the colonization of the New World, Europeans, particularly the Iberians, had come into contact and conflict with the Moslems (Moors), who had occupied parts of the Iberian Peninsula for some 700 years. Up to this point the vast majority of the Moslems were seen to be Arabs, and the strength of Islamic belief among the darker-skinned Arabs, coupled with the occupation, made Europeans both fearful and resentful of the Arab peoples. Add to this the significant economic might of the mercantile and commercial interests in the Islamic countries and one gets a clear idea of why their counterparts in Christian Europe would be moved to employ whatever means, ideological and military, to combat them.

Because it is customary for the enemy to be portrayed in as negative a light as possible, Muhammad, the prophet of Islam, and indeed the entire religion, were depicted by the Christian Europeans "as barbaric, degenerate and tyrannical," given to much violence, polygamy, sodomy, and general sexual promiscuity (Miles, 1989:18). As a consequence, the leading European economic interests used the pretext of defending Christianity to launch the so-called Crusades or Holy Wars against the Islamic infidels (Saracens), and during the entire period of Reconquest those wars were legitimized in Christ's name. In other words, what was at root an economic conflict, became cast as a battle between rival religions and "races." Thus, Daniel writes:

> In a period when Europe was in a mood of aggression and expansion, its surplus energy created an attitude to its Arab and Arabic-speaking neighbours which was based, not on what the Arabs were like, but on what, for theological reasons, they ought to be like (1975:248).

Much of that fear and suspicion of Moslems and Arabs has been passed down to the present.

RACE, COLOUR, AND CHRISTIANITY

Unlike the supporters of scientific and environmental explanations of human physical differences, Christians were committed to the notion of monogenesis and a common human origin. This is related to the question of "creationism" according to which all human beings are created by God and descended from Adam and Eve. The creationist doctrine, nevertheless, encountered a special difficulty when it came to accounting for the infinite variety of the human species. In other words, if all humans have common ancestors, whence arose the vast physical differences that characterize the species?

Uncomfortable with standard scientific explanations, many of which challenged and controverted biblical claims, Christians had to look elsewhere for answers to such questions as related to the different "races" and colours of human beings. And, like the Greeks and Romans before them, a great deal of myth and fantasy attended their responses. Thus, for example, we have stories of Cain and Abel, the sons of Adam and Eve, and of Noah and his son Ham. As we know, both Cain and Ham were guilty of misdeeds and disobedience for which God punished them. We also know that, along with being exiled from the kingdom of God, other punishments were meted out to them. Consequently Cain, we are told, was often seen as the parent of the monstrous races in early Christian commentary; and it was very common to assume that the monstrous races inherited Cain's curse and all the torments associated with exile from the kingdom of God.[4]

In the case of Ham, the association between blackness, evil, and punishment is made more explicit. In *Genesis* 9:21 we are presented with a scene of a drunken Noah (one of his jobs was that of tending a vineyard), who, having fallen asleep naked, was happened upon by Ham. Instead of covering up his father as any dutiful and loyal son would have done, Ham, who had been chastised by his father for sexual incontinence on the Ark, called his brothers to witness the sight and proceeded to mock Noah. Japheth and Shem, however, refused to countenance their brother's behaviour and covered their father's naked body. Once awakened, Noah realized what had happened, whereupon he again chastised Ham and asked God's curse on him.

According to several popular biblical interpretations (Utley, 1941:243) the curse, which was to extend to all Ham's descendants, was that they be forever (a) black and (b) servants (and eventually slaves) of his brothers' children. Thus, Friedman quotes an eleventh century traveller who presents us with a vivid portrait of Ham's son (Canaan) "as having black skin, red eyes, a deformed body, and horns on his forehead..." (Friedman, 1981:101). And in a more contemporary illustration of this same point Georg Gerster, writing for the *National Geographic* in 1975, reports on an interesting exchange between an apparently light-skinned nomadic Tuareg *marabout* (holy man) and a group of Moslem Songhais travellers on a boat in the Niger river. Given the fact that, according to Gerster, "some Moslems have tied the genealogy of all black people to Ham," the holy man sought to argue his racial and moral superiority over his fellow travellers by proclaiming that "the black race suffers the curse of Ham." But, we are told, when one of the Songhais, "Koran in hand, proved that the holy book of Islam sustained none of his claims," the Tuareg *marabout* "would not budge from his position" and a very heated argument resulted (Gerster, 1975:174).

The key point to be made here (and it must be strongly emphasised), refers to W.I. Thomas' oft-repeated statement to the effect that "if men define the situations as real they are real in their consequences" (1928:572). The crucial issue, then, is not so much the actual punishment meted out by God to Cain and Ham, but rather, the fact that later Christians came to understand that punishment in a specific way and *acted on the basis of that understanding*. This is similar to Max Weber's discussion of the Calvinist belief in predestination, which, even if it were not true, was nevertheless accepted as such by the believers, and came to have a direct impact on the conduct of their daily lives. Thus, in the same way that non-Calvinists later came to share the belief in the doctrine of predestination, so too non-Christians came in time to associate the idea of blackness with wrong-doing and the more sinister aspects of human existence and life in general.

As we know, in numerous later interpretations of *Genesis*, Ham's link with evil and sin was routine and unquestioned, and was also frequently used as a moral justification for the enslavement of black people. Friedman cites three major works in support of this contention. In the first, *Lebor Gabála*, he recalls Noah's indignation toward Ham (who was assigned to repopulate the continent of Africa) and the above-noted call for him to become the "slave of his brethren." More the point, however,

> ... in the Adrian and Epictetus dialogue the question is raised, "From whence and in what manner are slaves made?" The reply is "from Ham." In the translation of and commentary on *The City of God* made by Raoul de Presles, the author observes ... "Thus it can be seen how the line of Ham was evil, for from it descended servants" (Friedman, 1981:101-102).

This reading of the literature is quite at odds with the interpretation of Frank Snowden Jr. (1970 and 1983) who, while acknowledging the existence of black demons and the association of black with death and ill omens, nevertheless insists on the generally favourable view of black people in antiquity. He is also adamant about the fact that "the early Christians did not alter the classical color symbolism or the teachings of the church to fit a preconceived notion of blacks as inferior, to rationalize the enslavement of blacks... [I]n the early church, blacks found equality in both theory and practice" (1983:107-108). Nowhere, however, does Snowden deal with the above-discussed interpretations related to Cain and Ham or with the entire question of "monstrousness" as treated by J.B. Friedman.

RACE AND CHRISTIANITY IN COLONIAL TIMES

For a comparatively more recent insight into the symbolic dimension of race and colour in the context of Christianity, Roger Bastide is most instructive. Though not going as far back as the above authors, Bastide seems to favour the view that Christianity as a doctrine or body of thought is replete with examples of racial stratification and colour prejudice. "Christianity," he states, "has been accompanied by a symbolism of color. This symbolism has formed and cultivated a sensitivity to color that extends even to people who claim to be detached from religion" (1968:35). Hence, this author is in essential accord with Weber and the foregoing argument which holds that an ideology, once having taken root in a concrete context, can develop a life of its own and spread to encompass different individuals and groups in different situations that are far removed from the original context in which the ideology developed; hence, he writes:

"It is not surprising, then, that a symbolism of color association could survive the disappearance of its mystical Christian roots" (1968:48); even to the point of permeating the consciousness of non-Christians, who, through the years, have applied it in social contexts that have nothing to do with God and religion.

This is the sense in which we can understand the close relationship between slavery and racism in the Americas. In their desire to justify the enslavement of African blacks in the New World, Catholic monarchs, the Church, and all manner of Christian (Catholic and Protestant) slave-owning planters relied heavily on the claim that the blacks were evil, cursed by God, and fully deserving of punishment (enslavement) for their reported sins and misdeeds in biblical times. It is in this vein that the historian, Manuel Moreno Fraginals, when commenting on the situation in Cuba between the years 1760 and 1860, observes that the local Church there had built up an elaborate body of doctrine justifying slavery. "It was based on the belief that the chief reason for bringing the black savage from Africa was to redeem him by work and teach him the road to Christian salvation" (1976:53). In other words, slavery was a necessary penance if the African were ever to become civilized.

The Church, therefore, which participated in, and sanctioned, the institution of slavery, was warmly embraced by certain fractions of the slave-owning plantocracy; and given the practical necessity to maintain social order and control within their enterprises, the latter, in turn, found a ready-made ally in the Church. Both groups invoked the medieval Christian notion that man will earn his bread only by the sweat of his brow, and applied it generously to the slaves. In this way, the consciences of both planter and priest could be soothed by regarding the entire socio-economic complex of sugar and slavery almost as a redemptive undertaking, while the slave trade itself could be recast as an unselfish missionary activity.

Thus, although it would not be accurate to argue that Christianity caused racism against blacks, it is not difficult to sustain the position that it lent a unique ideological justification to the enslavement of black Africans. Through its unmistakable colour symbolisms, Christian teachings (both Catholic and Protestant) aided greatly in the establishment of the secular institution of African slavery and gave a spiritual impetus to those who benefited from the odious trade in human flesh. According to those symbolisms "white" is used to express the idea of purity and innocence as associated with the Virgin Mary[5], while "black" is symbolic of the Devil and his agents[6]. The ideological implications are very evident; and their consequences for black people did not disappear when slavery ended. For the symbolisms of colour and race have remained with Christianity to the present, manifesting themselves in both the sacred and secular domains.

One has only to consider the figure of Christ himself, who is supposed to transcend all colours and races; but in the contemporary Western imagination, in paintings, sculptures and so on, Christ has become rather Aryanized. For his presumed Jewish origins are now quite difficult to detect phenotypically[7], owing to "the deliberate whitening or bleaching effort that changed Christ from a Semitic to an Aryan person" (Bastide, 1968:37). Thus, the dark hair Christ is thought to have had is now rendered as sandy-brown or blonde, while his once-matching dark eyes have become blue. And Harold Ladoo echoes the exact sentiments when he speaks of Jesus as the King of the Jews, but "he was a Jew in the English fashion: blonde hair, blue eyes, red beard and a pink face" (1974:39).

Owing to the colour symbolisms that were so widely used at the time, this metamorphosis of Christ from Semite to Aryan was seen as quite necessary, for as the incarnation of God on earth he had to be distanced, as far as was possible, "from everything that could suggest darkness or blackness, even indirectly" (Bastide, 1968:37). Ironically, then, it seems that the old Christian belief that God made man in his own image and likeness has been reversed: man (white man) is now seen to have remade God in his own image and likeness. Once performed, this act of spiritual hygiene ramified throughout much of the world; for it is now the case that black Christians everywhere worship Christ in his Aryan incarnation.

This is not to imply, however, that Church lore failed to positively recognize the contributions made by black and coloured individuals. For as the Christian church emerged from the Middle Ages and greater knowledge of those peoples who lived beyond the borders of the then-known Christian world began to grow, the odd coloured or black person was admitted to the sainthood. Thus, along with the famous Black Madonnas of Medieval times, Wolfgang Seiferth talks of St. Mauritius, who, though initially conceived as white and later as a Moor, had, by the thirteenth century, come to be depicted as a Negro (1941:370-376). Then there was the case of St. Benedict of Palermo, also known as St. Benedict the Moor, who was long ignored by the Church, but who, with the colonization of Africa and the development of slavery, was finally given official recognition.[8] To this list one could add St. Iphigenia the Mulatto, St. Balthasar the Negro King, and perhaps the best known, St. Martin de Porres, who was beatified in 1837 and later canonized in 1962.

These individuals notwithstanding, the Church has continued to show little sensitivity to the black members of its flock. A recent instance of this concerns the December 1990 canonization of a white, Canadian, female saint (Marguerite D'Youville 1701-1771), who was widely known to have owned and sold hundreds of slaves. It must not be thought,

however, that all discrimination was limited to race; for together with the racial factor, it also embraced the issues of sex or gender, as they affected the so-called woman of colour.

CHRISTIANITY, COLONIZATION, AND THE WOMAN OF COLOUR

In most discussions of colonialism and racism attention has been focused on men: white masters and black male slaves. But the enterprise embraced a great deal more than an intra-male dialectic, for from its very inception, miscegenation or race mixing (which necessitates the involvement of women), was as much a part of the process as was slavery, violence, and plunder. At the outset, the primary ethnic elements were clearly distinct from each other: Iberians, native Indians, and Africans. It was not long, however, before sexual pairings among these three groups served to produce entirely new ethno-racial categories of people. The general pattern was one in which the white male, given his position of dominance, took the initiative vis-à-vis the Indian and African women; and from their liaisons were derived *mestizo* (white-Indian) and *mulatto* (white-African) offspring. A third combination known as the *zambo* in Spanish America (or *cafuso* in Brazil), resulted from the union of Africans and Indians.[9] And this was not all, for as could be imagined, further complexities arose when, for example, a *zambo* and a *mulatto* would have a child – *calpanmulato*; or a Spaniard and a *mulatto* – *morisco* etc.[10]

In the present context the most relevant of these inter-racial relationships concerned the white male and the Indian or African female. Since the idea of empire was conceived and executed by men, it is no great surprise that women, white women, played such a relatively minor role in the entire undertaking. Certainly, in the first century or so of the colonization of the New World, whether as wives, mistresses, or servants, white women were largely absent, and white men freely sought the companionship of those women who were available. Once begun, the practice occasioned numerous myths concerning the unbridled sexual passion, the sheer capacity for orgasm, and the very morality of these women. Colonial Brazil was a case in point. As Simon Collier observes, the "dark-skinned woman seemed to have enjoyed an excellent reputation as a source of erotic satisfactions" (1974:149); while Bastide reports on how black people were viewed in general and on their lack of morality concerning the Holy Sacrament of marriage: "the black woman will make love at anytime, and with anyone... making love to a colored woman does not mean anything, will have no consequences, for 'the blacks don't marry, they just pair off'" (1961:11-12).

It was not long before greatly embellished stories began to make their way back to Europe, and as early as 1512 the King of Spain, Ferdinand, ordered the authorities at the *Casa de Contratación* to make provision for sending white Christian female slaves to the colonies (Hoetink, 1973:59) to temper the miscegenative practices of the Spanish colonizers. It would seem, therefore, that the Spanish crown was equally concerned with the questions of race and religion, but less so with civil status. For like the Amerindian and African concubines of the colonists, the white Christian females were also slaves.

Though obeyed, the King's order did not result in the large-scale migration of white women, slave or free, Christian or non-Christian. In fact, for most of the colonial period, especially the first one hundred years, European women were vastly outnumbered by their Amerindian and African counterparts; and as a consequence, during the sixteenth century, the *mestizo* and *mulatto* populations grew at an amazing rate. The following statement attributed to one of the *conquistadores* of Chile, Francisco de Aguirre (1508-1581), who claimed to have fathered over fifty *mestizo* children, sums up well the mentality of the day: "... the service rendered to God in engendering *mestizos* is greater than the sin incurred in so doing" (Ojeda, 1929:31).

The religious justification, however, was not the only one used. For by the early nineteenth century in Cuba, the planter class was caught in an interesting bind. On the one hand, they were concerned about the acute shortage of labour, and on the other, they were cognizant of the risks involved in having the black population grow too large. Thus was born the plan of having white men mate with slave women to increase the ranks of the workers and simultaneously "whiten" the population:

> The idea was not crossing black men with white women, but white men with black women... the white women must not obstruct the island's whitening process by having mulatto children; the black woman on the other hand, would procreate mulattos and thereby hasten the process (Moreno Fraginals, 1976:134).

To these considerations one must add the special enchantment the Indian woman held for the Iberian man (Freyre, 1964:19) and the almost mystical allure of the African woman (Collier, 1974:145). For, as Freyre argues, the principal reason why these women appeared so desirable to the Iberians had to do with the latter's long contact with the Saracens (Moslems who had invaded and occupied the Iberian Peninsula), which left in them a sense of romantic adventure involving "... the idealized figure of the enchanted Moorish woman, a charming type, brown-skinned, dark-eyed, enveloped in sexual mysticism, roseate in hue" (1964:19). But very importantly, the attraction was not limited to

the lay colonist, for there were many more than a few priests whose sexual fantasies were fuelled by the innocence and powerlessness of these women, and who, while eagerly granting absolution to their fellow compatriots for their sexual promiscuity, were quick to forego their own vows of chastity and were also living in the same manner. Thus, in his inimitable style, Freyre tells us that "in place of ascetics austerely concerned with their vows of virginity there flourished formidable stallions in clerical garb," themselves fathering *mestizo* and *mulatto* children. He even relates the case of a Jesuit priest who one day asked his congregation for a "Hail Mary for the bishop's woman who is in labour" (1964:391).

In their New-World adventure, both the Catholic Spaniard and Portuguese, priest and layman, were able to free themselves of the restrictions imposed by their socio-religious upbringing on the enjoyment of sexual intercourse. According to that upbringing, sex (which is forbidden to the priest), is "dirty" and is only to be engaged in for the purpose of procreation. However, removed from the religious-cultural baggage of their homelands, where sex and marriage were limited largely to one's own colour and where "a too carnal enjoyment of the wife would have taken on the aspect of a kind of incest, degrading to both the white man and the white woman" (Bastide, 1968:40), European males regarded the woman of colour as a legitimate outlet for all that they were taught was sexually perverse, but nonetheless totally desirable and satisfying.[11]

In this context, therefore, the sexism directed at the woman of colour has to be seen as fundamentally political in that it involved the white man's abuse of *power* over the latter, and the use of 'race' to justify such abuse. For especially in the case of the priests (who were probably not entirely innocent with regards to the white women in their own societies), it is clear that they felt a great deal freer to act with impunity against the woman of colour since she was really of no consequence, and had no social base on which to call them to task. It was, thus, possible for them to become openly sexually engaged with the woman of colour, who was, by definition, less socially empowered than her white European counterpart.

CONCLUSION

The discrimination against the woman of colour, therefore, was very much like the discrimination against the Indian or the African. It appears as part of a set of Old-World beliefs and attitudes used to buttress a set of New-World practices. White Europeans saw themselves as having an inherent capacity and desire for democracy and freedom, while non-Europeans, particularly Africans, were thought to be a lower order of human being, and not really capable of appreciating "true" freedom. Power, in this case both economic and political, was the driving rationale, and the biological conception of race was confused with its social definition.

Biology and race became independent variables that explained the rate of social advancement and economic progress; and the religious ideology of Christianity was the justification or pretext used to explain away any guilt that might have been incurred along the way. In the process, however, as the historical roots of racism disappeared, racism itself did not. Rather, new racist ideas have evolved all the way from classical antiquity, utilizing the images of medieval thought and the colour symbolisms of Christianity to inform discriminatory practices right into the modern period. For although races are socially imagined and not biologically real categories, human beings continue to act as if they were real; and as long as they do so, race becomes real in its consequences.

Notes

1 This reflects the Spanish concern at the time for what was called *limpieza de sangre* (purity of blood), and is captured by Harold Benjamin, who speaks of the admission requirements at the University of San Gregorio in Quito, Ecuador, during much of the colonial period: "Applicants for entrance had to establish by a detailed legal process 'the purity of their blood' and prove that none of their ancestors had engaged in trade" (1965:16). This last stipulation was aimed principally at those of Moslem and Jewish ancestry, and harkened back to the 700-year foreign occupation of the Iberian peninsula, when such economic activities were considered dirty by the Church, and, hence, came to be dominated by non-Christian elements in the society (Allahar, 1986:565).

2 Cited in Manuel Moreno Fraginals (1976:155), along with *Expediente promovido contra Maria Josefa de la Luz Hernández para evitar su casamiento*. Archivo General de Indias; sección 11 (Cuba), leg. 1956.

3 In the popular historical accounts one finds reference to the so-called "Plinian races," named after the Roman author, Pliny the Elder, who was an avid compiler of documents related to, among other things, the great variety of human beings who were supposed to inhabit far away places such as India, Ethiopia, Albania, and Cathay. Many of these "races" later appeared in common folk talks and epic stories of the time. For example, there is Alexander the Great's contact with the *Amazons*, warlike women who live without men and who cut off their right breasts in order to draw their bows more powerfully; Pliny's *Androgini*, who have the genitals of both sexes and are to be found in Africa, and the *Blemmyae* of the Libyan deserts, who have no heads or necks and whose faces are found on their chests; Ctesias' *Cynocephali* or dog-headed men who lived in the mountains of India; *Cyclopes*, the

one-eyed giants of Homer and Virgil also to be found in India and parts of Sicily. These, along with scores of other hairy, tall and short, ugly, black, speechless, and savage peoples, actual and imagined, comprised the monstrous races of antiquity.

4 What is important here is not the exact nature of the term "curse" as reported in the Bible; but rather the interpretations of it by Old Testament scholars and Christians alike. And one of the popular interpretations that is relevant to the present argument concerns the question of equating punishment, evil, and sin with negritude. Thus, we are told that God placed a mark (or horns as some interpretations have it), on Cain and his progeny so that they would be easily recognised as trouble-makers, wrong-doers, and as receivers of God's wrath. For many that mark or curse was a black skin (Bastide, 1968:36).

5 One commonly speaks of something being "as pure as the driven snow," which refers to white snow that is clean or unsoiled.

6 Here one hears of those whose "souls are black" or who commit "dark deeds." And it is also possible for one who is "blackened by sin" to be "bleached" of that sin.

7 While there is an obvious difficulty with regard to stereotyping people on the basis of phenotypical characteristics, this reference is to the time of Christ when long-distance travel and extensive contacts between those peoples who differed radically in physical appearance were not common and, consequently, discreet populations did not reflect the rich variety that today is found in most parts of the world.

8 The stigma associated with black skin came into play with St. Benedict the Moor, who, it appears, was something of a womanizer and also not entirely unattractive to women; but he was supposedly also a very devout man, and "wishing to escape from feminine temptations, St. Benedict prayed to God to make him ugly – so God turned his skin black" (Bastide, 1968:39).

9 In the case of the *zambo* it is not too clear who "took the initiative" since, according to Simon Collier "the African proved extremely attractive to the Indian woman" (1974:150).

10 As Angel Rosenblat (1954:168-79) indicates, the possibilities were infinite, and the designations of the offspring from such unions were as imaginative as they were funny. Thus, we are told that the child of a *calpanmulatto* and a *zambo* was known as a "tente en el aire" (hold your head high) implying pride in some degree of blood purity, while the child of a "tente en el aire" and a mulatto was known as a "no te entiendo" (I don't understand your make-up). Similarly, if a *morisco* mated with a *mulatto* the issue was called a "salto atras" (a jump backwards) owing to the implied darkening of the skin that resulted from such a pairing.

11 This is the source of many of the sexual myths and delights surrounding the woman of colour, whose unbridled sexuality was constantly compared to the white woman's. The sheer voluptuousness of the woman of colour, Bastide tells us, is viewed as sexually enticing to men. Her slightest gesture "such as the balanced sway of her body as she walks barefoot, is looked upon as a call of

the female sex to the male." At the other extreme, however, "the white woman is desexualized, if not disincarnated or at least dematerialized" (1968:40). Thus, Collier (1974:149) recalls a popular jingle in Brazil which holds that:

Moça morena é quitute; moça branca é canja fria. [A dark girl is a delicious titbit; a white one like cold chicken soup].

References

Allahar, Anton L. 1990 *Class, Politics, and Sugar in Colonial Cuba.* New York: Edwin Mellen Press.

Allahar, Anton L. 1986 "Historical Patterns of Change and Development," in *The Social World.* Lorne Tepperman and R.J. Richardson (eds). Toronto: McGraw-Hill Ryerson.

Bastide, Roger 1968 "Color, Racism, and Christianity," in *Color and Race.* J.H. Franklin (ed). Boston: Houghton Mifflin.

Bastide, Roger 1961 "Dusky Venus, Black Apollo," in *Race,* Vol. 3.

Benjamin, Harold 1965 *Higher Education in the American Republics.* New York: McGraw-Hill.

Collier, Simon 1974 *From Cortes to Castro: An Introduction to the History of Latin America 1492-1973.* New York: Macmillan.

Curtin, Philip D. 1964 *The Image of Africa: British Ideas and Action, 1780-1850.* Madison: University of Wisconsin Press.

Daniel, N. 1975 *The Arabs and Medieval Europe.* London: Longman.

Franklin, John Hope (ed) 1968 *Color and Race.* Boston: Houghton Mifflin.

Freyre, G. 1964 *The Masters and the Slaves.* (S. Putnam trans). New York: Knopf.

Friedman, John Block 1981 *The Monstrous Races in Medieval Art and Thought.* Cambridge: Harvard University Press.

Fryer, P. 1984 *Staying Power: The History of Black People in Britain.* London: Pluto Press.

Gerster, Georg 1975 "River of Sorrow, River of Hope," in *National Geographic* 148: August.

Hoetink, H. 1973 *Slavery and Race Relations in the Americas.* New York: Harper and Row.

Jordan, Winthrop D. 1968 *White Over Black: American Attitudes Toward the Negro, 1550-1812.* Chapel Hill: The University of North Carolina Press.

Ladoo, Harold "Sonny" 1974 *Yesterdays.* Toronto: Anansi.

Lane, Arthur 1971 *Greek Pottery.* 3rd ed. London: Faber.

Lewis, Gordon K. 1983 *Main Currents in Caribbean Thought.* Baltimore: The Johns Hopkins University Press.

Miles, Robert 1989 *Racism.* London: Routledge.

Moreno Fraginals, Manuel 1976 *The Sugarmill: The Socio-Economic Complex of Sugar in Cuba.* New York: Monthly Review Press.

Ojeda, Tomás Thayer 1929 "Francisco de Aguirre," in *Revista Chilena de Historia y Geografia.* No. 64.

Rosenblat, Angel 1954 *La Población, Indigena y el Mestizaje en América.* 2 Vols. Buenos Aires.

Sanders, R. 1978 *Lost Times and Promised Lands: The Origins of American Racism.* Boston: Little, Brown and Co.

Seiferth, Wolfgang S. 1941 "St. Mauritius, African," in *Phylon* 4.

Seltman, C.T. 1920 "Two Heads of Negresses" in *American Journal of Archaeology* 24.

Shils, Edward 1968 "Color, the Universal Intellectual Community, and the Afro-Asian Intellectual," in *Color and Race.* J.H. Franklin (ed). Boston: Houghton Mifflin.

Snowden, Frank M. Jr. 1983 *Before Color Prejudice: The Ancient View of Blacks.* Cambridge: Harvard University Press.

Snowden, Frank M. Jr. 1970 *Blacks in Antiquity: Ethiopians in the Greco-Roman Experience.* Cambridge: Harvard University Press.

Thomas, W.I. and Dorothy, S. 1928 *The Child in America.* New York: Alfred Knopf.

Utley, Francis Lee 1941 "Noah's Ham and Jansen Enikel," in *Germanic Review* 16.

Von Bothmer, D. 1961-2 "A Gold Libation Bowl," in *Bulletin of the Metropolitan Museum of Art.* No. 21.

Wagner, Henry Raup 1967 *The Life and Writings of Bartolomé de las Casas.* Albuquerque: University of New Mexico Press.

White, H. 1972 "The Forms of Wildness: Archaeology of an Idea," in *The Wild Man Within: An Image in Western Thought from Renaissance to Romanticism.* Pittsburgh: University of Pittsburgh Press.

Williams, Eric 1966 *Capitalism and Slavery.* New York: G.P. Putnam's Sons.

34

Conceptualising Racisms: Social Theory, Politics and Research

JOHN SOLOMOS AND LES BACK

This paper includes an overview of how racism has been conceptualized in the last several decades. The authors point out that debates about the nature of racism have been intense and based on differing theoretical foundations and assumptions, and paradigms. Reference is made to Michael Banton's *Race Relations* as an example of the earlier concepts of race relations during the 1960s. In this book, Banton argued the existence of six kinds of racial orders: institutionalized contact, acculturation, domination, paternalism, integration and pluralism. Another important contribution to our understanding of racism is represented by the work of Frederik Barth who showed ethnicity and racial identification is not necessarily less salient in multi-ethnic social settings. Class dynamics in the development of racism are emphasized in the work of John Rex, *Race Relations in Sociological Theory*. This kind of analysis was then extended by Robert Miles in his work, *Racism and Migrant Labour*. Here, Miles proposed that racism and racial conflict are functional as ideology in support of certain economic interests. The politics associated with racism, was touched upon in the work of the Centre for Contemporary Cultural Studies captured in publication, *The Empire Strikes Back* (1982). This approach facilitated a look at the political foundations of gender discrimination and sexism, as well.

Solomos and Back offer a number of more recent concepts and ideas not fully analyzed in the past studies. These new ideas are again reformulating our understanding of racism. Such ideas include: re-examination of traditional Marxism based on political movements motivated and activated by identity other than class; the impact of enduring ethnicity and culture; the utilization of non-racial language and codes to maintain racial orders; the role of the media and popular outlets in the definition and re-definition of racism; the emergence of racialized nationalism in Europe; analyzing the role and nature of 'whiteness'; these issues must be integrated in contemporary dialogue and analysis of racism according to the authors.

During the past twenty years theoretical and political debates have raged over how to conceptualise racism and the status of race as a social and analytical concept. At the same time the analysis of race and racism has become an established field of study in a number of social science disciplines, most notably in sociology, political science, economics, anthropology, cultural studies and geography (Rex and Mason 1986; Goldberg 1990). In this paper we want to examine the range of disputes which have taken place. In particular we will focus on the 'race relations problematic' and the developments that have occurred in the last ten years. Our aim is to position and evaluate these debates within particular historical contexts. What we want to argue is that a series of political strategies are encoded within these academic debates.

The central question which has bedevilled critical analysis is what kinds of meanings can be given to the category race? Equally, how should racism be identified as a political force within European societies, the United States and South Africa? In the past twenty years writing in this area has fragmented into entrenched theoretical paradigms. What we shall suggest is that it is necessary to radically evaluate these conceptual critiques and begin to explore a new research agenda that breaks out of the paradigmatic confines of 'race relations'.[1] In order to begin this process of discussion we shall review some of the key areas of debate in recent years, before moving on to outline our own perspective.

RACE AND SOCIOLOGICAL THEORY

The early attempts to theorise racial and ethnic relations in Britain emerged from two concerns. First, the patterns of immigration and incorporation in social and economic relations of black and other ethnic communities. Second, the role of colonial history in determining popular conceptions of colour, race and ethnicity. The early studies were carried out in the 1950s and 1960s by scholars such as Michael Banton, Ruth Glass, John Rex and Sheila Patterson.[2] These studies concentrated on the interaction between minority and majority communities in employment, housing and other social contexts. What is interesting in hindsight, given the virulence of some of the theoretical debates of the past decade, is the relative absence of a clear theoretical perspective about: i) what constituted the object of analysis of these specific studies; and, ii) the absence of a wider socio-political perspective about the interplay between 'race relations' and other kinds of social relations. The crucial question which these studies failed to address in detail was the ontological status of race as a social construct.

By the 1960s, however, there was a noticeable growth of interest in the theorisation of the study of both the new forms of migration and settlement as they were being experienced in Britain and elsewhere and other types of 'race relations'. Michael Banton's book on *Race Relations* represents a good example of texts from this period. It looked at race relations from a global and historical perspective, concentrating particularly on situations of cultural contact, beliefs about the nature of race, and the social relations constructed on the basis of racial categories. By looking at the experience of changing patterns of interaction historically Banton argued that six basic orders of race relations could be delineated: namely, institutionalised contact, acculturation, domination, paternalism, integration and pluralism (Banton 1967). It was during the period of the 1960s that what Banton and others have called the 'race relations problematic' became the dominant approach in this field (Banton 1991).

While often utilising racial classifications, this literature also incorporated anthropological perspectives on ethnicity and social boundaries. Richard Jenkins (1986:172–178) has shown that there is a direct continuity between the methodological and theoretical approach applied to tribal societies and their 'modern' equivalent – *ethnic groups*. However, considerable confusion exists over exactly what constitutes an ethnic group and whether such an approach can cope with the complex cultural processes occurring in British cities.

The early studies of ethnicity in multi-ethnic contexts were highly influenced by the work of Frederik Barth (1959, 1969). Barth observed that social boundaries were enduring in ethnically plural contexts and that cultural contact does not result in the lessening of cultural diversity. For Barth the nature of interaction between social systems cannot be explained by simply describing the internal workings of each cultural system; rather what needs to be discussed is the social activity at the boundary. Barth's major contribution was the insistence that ethnic groups are essentially social constructs. His starting point is that ethnic groups are categories of ascription and identification. As a result, ethnic categories constitute 'organisational vessels' into which a range of symbols and markers can be poured. These may be significant for all social behaviour or they may be confined to specific situations (Barth 1979:14). Barth's situational model of ethnicity was most clearly incorporated by Michael Banton (1983) and Sandra Wallman (1979).

The major weaknesses of this approach are two-fold. First, there is a contradiction between the situational emphasis on identity ascription and the tendency to define ethnicity in a static way. This is particularly evident in the way Sandra Wallman has utilised Barth's framework (Wallman 1986). Ethnicity remains something which is either active or inactive. The result is that there is not enough room to explore the ways in which the cultural expression of ethnicity changes through time because it is defined as primordial (Cohen 1974). Second, the situational ethnicity model does not articulate the micro structure of the boundary system with the macro context of class-divided metropolitan situations. This is perhaps the most profound limitation of this approach.

In the context of the sociology of race John Rex has made the most sustained effort to bring a class perspective to the study of ethnic relations. Rex's text on *Race Relations in Sociological Theory* has exercised a major influence over this field since its appearance and it remains one of the most ambitious attempts to provide a theoretical grounding for research in this field. According to Rex's analytic model, the definition of social relations between persons as race relations is encouraged by the existence of certain structural conditions: e.g. frontier situations of conflict over scarce resources, the existence of unfree, indentured, or slave labour, unusually harsh class exploitation, strict legal intergroup distinctions and occupational segregation, differential access to power and prestige, cultural diversity and limited group interaction, and migrant labour as an underclass fulfilling stigmatised roles in a metropolitan setting (Rex 1970). From this perspective the study of race relations is concerned with situations in which such structured conditions interact with actors' definitions in such a way as to produce a racially structured social reality.

These are the concerns which Rex articulated clearly in two studies of race relations in Birmingham during the 1960s and the 1970s. In the study conducted by Rex and his associates in Handsworth during the mid-1970s (Rex and Tomlinson 1979), the basic research problem was to explore the degree to which immigrant populations shared the class position of their white neighbours and white workers in general. The substance of the analysis goes on to outline a class structure in which white workers have been granted certain rights which have been won through the working class movement via trade unions and the Labour Party. The result in the 1970s was a situation of class truce between white workers and subordinate classes. The position of migrant workers and their children is located outside the negotiation that had taken place between the white workers and capital. They experience discrimination in all the areas where the white workers had made significant gains, i.e. employment, education, housing. It follows from this that the position of migrant workers placed them outside of the working class in the position of an 'underclass':

> The concept of underclass was intended to suggest ... that the minorities were systematically at a disadvantage compared with their white peers and that, instead of identifying with working class culture, community and politics, they formed their own organisations and became effectively a separate underprivileged class (Rex and Tomlinson 1979:275).

From this point Rex and Tomlinson develop a model of political action and even a political agenda for black populations as they become a 'class for themselves'. Immigrant minorities are forced into a series of reactive/defensive political strategies. This process takes on different forms within Asian and West Indian communities. Within Asian communities this results in a concentration on capital accumulation and social mobility. In the West Indian community it takes the form of withdrawal from competition altogether with an emphasis on the construction of a black identity. This all leads to what Rex refers to elsewhere as the 'politics of defensive confrontation' (Rex 1979).

NEO-MARXISM AND RACISM

The early 1980s saw the emergence of a number of substantial criticisms of the research agenda on 'race relations', written largely from a neo-Marxist perspective. Such criticisms were influenced both by theoretical and political considerations, and they helped to stimulate new areas of debate. One of the first attempts to provide a theoretical critique of the approaches of both Banton and Rex is to be found in the work of Robert Miles since the early 1980s. The starting point of Miles's critique was his opposition to the existence of a sociology of race, and his view that the object of analysis should be racism, which he viewed as integral to the process of capital accumulation (Miles 1982, 1986). His analysis was first articulated in *Racism and Migrant Labour* and it is perhaps the most sustained attempt to include the study of racism within the mainstream of Marxist social theory. His empirical research has focused specifically on the situation in Britain and the rest of Europe, and has looked at the role of political, class and ideological relationships in regulatory power within society. Analytically, race constitutes a paper tiger (Miles 1988) that may be a common term of reference within everyday discourse, but which presents a serious theoretical problem. It is here where Miles diverges from what he sees as the race relations problematic. While Rex is concerned with models of social action (i.e. for Rex it is enough that race is utilised in everyday discourse as a basis for social action) Miles is concerned with the analytical and objective status of race as a basis of action (Miles 1982:42). Race is thus an ideological effect, a mask which hides real economic relationships (Miles 1984). Thus the forms of class consciousness which are legitimate for Miles must ultimately be reduced to economic relations which are hidden within the regulatory process of racialisation.

For Miles the process of racialisation is interrelated with the conditions of migrant labourers. Its effects are the result of the contradiction between

> on the one hand the need of the capitalist world economy for the mobility of human beings, and on the other, the

drawing of territorial boundaries and the construction of citizenship as a legal category which sets boundaries for human mobility (Miles 1988:438).

Within the British setting this ideological work conducted primarily by the state acts as a means of crisis management and results in racialising fragments of the working class. Race politics are thus confined to the forces of regulation. For Miles the construction of political identities which utilise racial consciousness play no part in the development of a progressive politics.

Miles raises some fundamental questions about the nature of political action within communities of migrant labour. The most important of these is the degree to which black and minority politics are really distillations of class conflict. If this is true any movements away from class based political action (i.e. movements towards any notions of black community politics) are doomed to failure (Miles 1988; Miles 1989a). If one takes this argument further, class based political action is ultimately in opposition to any sort of sustained political organisation around a notion of race. For Miles the politics of race is narrowly confined to the struggle against racism. This is neatly captured in the way he uses Hall's (1980:341) statement on the relationship between class and race. He concludes that it is not race but racism which can be the modality in which class is lived and fought through (Miles 1988:447).

Miles's insistence that racial differentiations are always created in the context of class differentiation (Miles 1989a) is a core feature of his critique of the work of Banton and Rex. However, his position results in a kind of class reductionism which ultimately limits the scope of theoretical work on conceptualising racism and racialised social relations. For example, in some contexts class exploitation may be incidental to the construction of situations of racial dominance (Goldberg 1992). However, the greatest contribution that Miles makes is his insistence that 'races' are created within the context of political and social regulation. Thus 'race' is above all a political construct. It is within this context that the concepts of *racial categorisation* and *racialisation* have been used to refer to what Robert Miles calls 'those instances where social relations between people have been structured by the signification of human biological characteristics in such a way as to define and construct differentiated social collectivities' (Miles 1989a:75). His work constitutes an attempt to reclaim the study of racism from an apoliticised sociological framework and locate it squarely in a Marxist theorisation of social conflict.

Another influential critique of the sociology of race in the early 1980s emanated from the Centre for Contemporary Cultural Studies (CCCS) in Birmingham. The work of the CCCS Race and Politics Group during this period was particularly concerned with the changing nature of the politics of race during the 1970s and the development of new forms of racial ideology. The theoretical approach of the CCCS Group was influenced by the work of Stuart Hall in particular (Hall 1980). They were critical of the arguments of both the sociologists of race and of Miles.

The work of the Group resulted in the publication of *The Empire Strikes Back* (CCCS 1982). This volume attracted widespread attention at the time and it still remains a point of reference in current debates. Two of the contributors to this volume have subsequently attempted to develop substantive studies derived from it (Gilroy 1987; Solomos 1988, 1989). A major concern of the CCCS Group was the need to analyse the complex processes by which race is constructed as a social and political relation. They emphasised that the race concept is not simply confined as a process of regulation operated by the state but that the meaning of race as a social construction is contested and fought over. In this sense they viewed race as an open political construction where the political meaning of terms like black are struggled over. Collective identities spoken through race, community and locality are for all their spontaneity powerful means to co-ordinate action and create solidarity (Gilroy 1987). This work shares Rex's concern with social action but rejects his sociological framework as being at best ill-founded and at worst politically spurious.

Within this model of political action a multiplicity of political identities can be held. An inclusive notion of black identity can prevail and at the same time allow heterogeneity of national and cultural origins within this constituency (Gilroy 1987:236). Gilroy, for example, argues that the crucial question here is the extent to which notions of race can be re-forged into a political colour of opposition. He holds little hope that this process can be developed within the arena of representative democracy. Instead he views pressure group strategies which have evolved out of community struggles that utilise a specifically black political vernacular as the way forward. Gilroy argues for a racial revision of class analysis in metropolitan contexts. He suggests that political identities which are spoken through race can be characterised as social movements which are relatively autonomous from class relations.[3]

It should also be noted that *The Empire Strikes Back* was one of the first books on race relations in Britain to look in any depth at the question of gender and the role of sexism in the context of racialised relations. The contributions of Hazel Carby and Pratibha Parmar to this volume provided a point of reference and debate in the debates about the interplay between race, class and gender during the 1980s. They also highlighted the relevance of looking at this dimension of racial relations in a context where the bulk of research ignored gender.

In exploring these issues *The Empire Strikes Back* acted as a catalyst to a politicisation of debates about the role of research in relation to race relations. In a sense the political struggles that were occurring within black communities during the 1980s were being echoed in the context of the production of knowledge about racism. The sociology of race relations stood accused of being implicitly conservative and unable to articulate the theorisation of racism with the nature of a class divided and structural inequalities in power. On the other hand, the sociologists of race and ethnic relations were also criticised for letting their theoretical imaginations be coloured by an implicit eurocentrism. The result was that the sociological literature demonstrated an inability to record the experiences of the black people in Britain in a sympathetic way (Lawrence 1981). These challenges marked an attempt to articulate the theoretical debates about how to understand racism with the political urgencies of economic crisis and the ideological challenge of the Conservative New Right. The point that we want to emphasise here is that this debate needs to be situated within the political conjuncture of the early 1980s. It is quite clear that the preoccupation with prioritising the analysis of racism was linked to a concern to fix the theoretical debate on questions of power and inequality. However, in making the conceptualisation of racism a priority, these critiques failed to develop a theoretical framework for an elaborated analysis of wider social and cultural processes. It is this issue which has become one of the central theoretical questions of recent years.

New Ethnicity, New Racism: Reclaiming Culture and the Politics of Identity

The debates of the early 1980s continue to influence research agendas. However, a number of recent developments have meant that the neo-Marxist critiques of the early eighties have not been able to cope with the complexities of theorising racism in the 1990s. The first of these is the crisis within Marxism itself. In this context some have called for a radical revision of class analysis (Castells 1983; Gilroy 1987; Anthias 1992) in order to incorporate political movements which mobilise around forms of identity other than class. Others have suggested a need for a move away from Marxism as a framework of analysis and have taken on board some of the concerns of post-structuralism and postmodernism (Gates 1986; Goldberg 1990).

One of the results of this shift is the growing concern with the status of cultural forms and a return to an analysis of the nature of ethnicity in metropolitan settings. The political naivety of the early work on ethnicity meant that for much of the 1980s the analysis of cultural processes and forms was rejected in favour of a focus on the politics of racism. The rejection of 'culture' was tied up with the notion that the culturalist perspective of the 1970s did little more than blame the victims of racism (Lawrence 1982). However, the question of cultural production and the politics of identity are fast becoming an important area of contemporary debate. New perspectives are being developed which examine the ways in which cultural forms are being made and re-made producing complex social phenomena (Hewitt 1991). These new syncretic cultures are being plotted within the global networks of the African and South Asian diaspora (Gilroy 1987; Bhachu 1991).

The process of reclaiming 'culture' in critical debate has simultaneously involved a re-examination of how racism is conceptualised. These contributions engage in one way or another with the arguments of post-structuralism and postmodernism and they point to the need to avoid uniform and homogeneous conceptualisations of racism. Although not yet part of the agenda of mainstream research on race relations, a range of studies of racialised discourses in the mass media, literature, art and other cultural forms have begun to be produced. Reacting against what they see as the lack of an account of cultural forms of racial discourse, a number of writers have sought to develop a more rounded picture of contemporary racial imagery by looking at the role of literature, the popular media and other cultural forms in representing changing images of race and ethnicity.

As David Goldberg has pointed out, 'the presumption of a single monolithic racism is being displaced by a mapping of the multifarious historical formulations of *racisms*' (Goldberg 1988). In this context it is perhaps not surprising that a key concern of many recent texts in this field is to explore the interconnections between race and nationhood, patriotism and nationalism rather than analyse ideas about biological inferiority. The ascendancy of the political right in Britain during the 1980s prompted commentators to identify a new period in the history of English racism. The 'new racism', or what Fanon (1967) referred to as 'cultural racism', has its origins in the social and political crisis afflicting Britain (Barker 1981; Gilroy 1990). Its focus is the defence of the mythic 'British/English way of life' in the face of attack from enemies *outside* ('Argies', 'Frogs', 'Krauts', 'Iraqis') and *within* ('black communities', 'Muslim fundamentalists'). Paul Gilroy points to an alarming consequence of new racism where blackness and Englishness are reproduced as mutually exclusive categories (Gilroy 1987:55–56).

The new cultural racism points to the urgency of comprehending racism and notions of race as changing and historically situated. As David Goldberg has pointed out, it is necessary to define race conceptually by looking at what this term signifies at different times (Goldberg 1992). Thus the question of whether 'race' is an ontologically valid concept or otherwise is side stepped in favour of an interrogation of the ideological quality of racialised subjectivities. The writing on new racism shows how contemporary manifestations of race are coded in a language which aims to circumvent accusations of racism. In the case of new racism race is coded as culture. However, the central feature of these processes is that the qualities of social groups are fixed, made natural, confined within a pseudo-biologically defined culturalism (Barker 1981). What is clear from these writings is that a range of discourses on social differentiation may have a metonymic relationship to racism. The semantics of race are produced by a complex set of inter-discursive processes where the language of culture and nation invokes a hidden racial narrative. The defining feature of this process is the way in which it naturalises social formations in terms of a racial/cultural logic of belonging.

With the widening of theoretical concerns has come a literature which looks at the aesthetic elements of the culture of racism. This is an area which has been neglected within the discussions of race and social theory in the field of race relations. Equally, with a number of notable exceptions (Cohen 1988a,b, 1991; Cohen and Bains 1988), the emerging discipline of cultural studies has also been curiously silent on the issue of how to understand the cultural dynamics of racism. There is an important intellectual and theoretical project in' interrogating the historical, cultural, literary, and philosophical roots of ideologies of race.

The role of the press and other popular media in shaping social images about racial and ethnic minorities has been a particular focus. A number of detailed studies have, for example, looked at how press coverage of racial questions can help to construct images of racial minorities as outsiders and as a threat to social cohesion (Hall *et al.* 1978; van Dijk 1991). One important example of this process was the furore about Salman Rushdie's *The Satanic Verses* and the response of some Muslim political leaders to its publication. The attempt by some Muslim community leaders to use the affair as a means of political mobilisation received wide coverage in the media and led to a wide ranging debate about the 'future of race relations' in British society (Asad 1990). Sections of the press used the events surrounding the Rushdie affair to question the possibility of a peaceful transition towards a multi-racial society. Hostile media coverage of the events surrounding the political mobilisations around the Rushdie affair thus served to reinforce the view that minorities who do not share the dominant political values of British society pose a threat to social stability and cohesion. The affair also gave added impetus to debates about the multiple cultural and political identities that have been included in the broad categorisation of 'black and ethnic minority communities'.

One of the weaknesses of the literature which looks at media and political discourses is that it has not attempted to look at how these ideological forms manifest themselves at the local level within specific communities. The question remains as to how pervasive is the 'new racism'? Or, how do these national discourses relate to the particularities of a specific social context? Gilroy, for example, alludes to a new kind of cultural politics which defies new racism and develops a political and cultural aesthetic that is both black and English. Stuart Hall, returning to the flag metaphor refers to a shift in his own thinking:

> Fifteen years ago we didn't care, or at least I didn't care, whether there was any black in the Union Jack. Now not only do we care but we must (Hall 1990:30).

A series of empirical studies have shown evidence that significant dialogues are taking place within multi-ethnic communities of working class youth (Hewitt 1986; Jones 1988). In the encounter between black young people and their white inner city peers: 'Black culture has become a class culture ... as two generations of whites have appropriated it, discovered its seductive forms of meaning for their own' (Gilroy 1990:273). The result is that it is impossible to speak of black culture in Britain separately from the culture of Britain as a whole. These processes have important implications for developing an analysis of racism which is socially, politically, and even geographically situated. The local context has important effects resulting in complex outcomes where particular racisms may be muted while others flourish (Back 1993).

Another focus within the emerging literature on the cultural politics of racism has been the social construction of race and difference in literature and the cinema. This has been a neglected area of research, but in recent years this has been remedied by the publication of a number of important studies of race, culture and identity. Originating largely from the United States such studies have looked at a number of areas, including literature, the cinema and other popular cultural forms. They have sought to show that within contemporary societies our understandings of race, and the articulation of racist ideologists, cannot be reduced to economic, political or class relations.

This type of approach is in fact more evident outside of sociology. The work of literary and cultural theorists in the United States and Britain has in recent years begun to explore seriously the question of race and racism, and has led to a flowering of studies which use the debates around post-structuralism and postmodernism as a way of approaching the complex forms of racialised identities in colonial and post-colonial societies (Gates 1986, 1988; Goldberg 1990).

There has also been a growth of interest in historical research on the origins of ideas about race and in the dynamics of race, class and gender during the colonial period (Ware 1992). This has been reflected in important and valuable accounts of the changing usage of racial symbols during the past few centuries and in accounts of the experiences of colonialism and their impact on our understandings of race and culture. The work of Gayatri Spivak has helped to highlight, for example, the complex processes of racial and gender identification experienced by the colonised during the colonial and post-colonial periods (Spivak 1987). Other studies have sought to show that the oppressed themselves have produced their own discourses about race and identity in the context of their own experiences of domination and exclusion (Bhabha 1990; Young 1990).

Equally, it has become clear that there is a need to shed the narrow confines of the race relations problematic and develop a more sophisticated analysis of the impact of various racisms on the white majority. An embryonic literature exists on the politics of whiteness which is attempting to develop such a focus of inquiry. However, there are immediate difficulties with this endeavour, as Richard Dyer (1988) has shown in his discussion of film representations. Dyer contends that white ethnicity in the cinema is implicitly present but explicitly absent and as a result it has 'an everything and nothing quality'. In these representations whiteness is equated with normality and as such it is not in need of definition. Thus 'being normal' is colonised by the idea of 'being white'. From a different perspective bell hooks has graphically discussed the terrorising effect that 'whiteness' has on the black imagination. Writing on her experience of growing up as a black woman in the American South she comments: 'whiteness in the black imagination is often a representation of terror' (hooks 1992:342). Clearly there is a need for a research agenda which looks at the way white subjectivities are racialised, and how 'whiteness' is manifested in discourse, communication and culture.

This turn within critical writing has important implications. One of the fundamental criticisms of the sociology of race and ethnic relations is that it has too often focused on the victims rather than the perpetrators of racism. Prioritising whiteness as an area of critical endeavour has the possibility of disrupting the sociological common sense which equates the discussion of racism with the empirical scrutiny of black communities. Toni Morrison in her analysis of whiteness in American novels comments:

> My project is an effort to avert the critical gaze from the racial object to the racial subject; from the described and imagined to the describers and imaginers; the serving to the served (Morrison 1992:90).

Stuart Hall[4] has pointed out the urgency of deconstructing the meanings of whiteness, not just in order to counter racism but that it is also important for the wellbeing of the African and Asian diaspora living in Britain.

I think for black people who live in Britain this question of finding some way in which the white British can learn to live with us and the rest of the world is almost as important as discovering our own identity. I think they are in more trouble than we are. So we, in a curious way, have to rescue them from themselves – from their own past. We have to allow them to see that England is a quite interesting place with quite an interesting history that has bossed us around for 300 years [but] that is finished. Who are they now?

There is already an emerging literature which is trying to answer the rhetorical question which Hall has asked (Back 1993; Jones 1988). However the connection between race and nation may well be eclipsed in the 1990s by the spectre of an integrated and racialised Europe.

While racialised nationalisms may prove pervasive and inhibiting with regard to progress towards European unification, it is clear that the European community also share a racialised identity – a pan-European whiteness. This was clearly evoked by the former Prime Minister of Britain Margaret Thatcher during a speech given in Bruges in 1988. She stated:

> Too often the history of Europe is described as a series of interminable wars and quarrels. Yet from our perspective today surely what strikes us most is our common experience. For instance, the story of how Europeans explored and colonised and – yes, without apology – civilised much of the world is an extraordinary tale of talent, skill and courage.

While much of the debate on racism in the 1980s focused on the relationship between nationhood and racism, it may be that in the 1990s racialised discourses will focus on the 'natural Europe home' and attempt to define who belongs there. Alarming traces of these processes can already be seen in the European Community publication *Living in Europe: A Handbook for Europeans* (1989). Scanning the pages of this guide to the 'new Europe' one is struck by the overwhelming paleness of the images presented of European citizens.

Theoretically comprehending 'whiteness' is certainly an important intellectual project. However, there are a number of possible shortcomings. In the hurry to shift the critical gaze there is always a danger of suspending reflection on the analytical terms of this project. Like many of the debates on the ontological status of culture, there is a danger of reifying whiteness and reinforcing a unitary idea of 'race'. In order to avoid this it is crucial to locate any discussion of 'whiteness' in a particular empirical and historical context. Equally, one must insist that whiteness is a political definition which regulates the consent of white subjects within the context of white supremacy. Additionally, any discussion of whiteness must incorporate an appreciation of how gendered processes are inextricably articulated with the semantics of race (Ware 1992;

Back forthcoming). We are arguing that interrogating whiteness as a form of identity and a political discourse must: i) focus on de-colonising the definition of 'normal'; and, ii) simultaneously prohibit the reification of whiteness as a social identity.

In summary, we are suggesting that the theoretical engagements of the early 1980s cannot adequately conceptualise racism in the 1990s. The political struggles which underscored these debates have moved on. In many ways the turn towards the conceptualisation of culturally defined racisms and the politics of identity has been led by the political events of the late eighties. In particular the continuing hegemony of the Conservative right in Britain has challenged theorists to reappraise the usefulness of Marxist orthodoxy. This is perhaps best exemplified by the debate over the *New Times* thesis (see Hall and Jacques 1989; Sivanandan 1990), which suggests that a range of sites for social antagonism and resistance exist within contemporary Britain which cannot be conceptualised within a conventional class analysis. Equally, in the context of the complex forms of identity politics the semantics of race cannot be confined to the politics of regulation (Miles 1989b). The controversy over the publication of Salman Rushdie's book *The Satanic Verses* has provided a warning that the politics of culture cannot be appreciated within the conceptual language of the 1980s.

Questions of cultural production and change must be integrated within a contemporary conceptualisation of racism. Thus we are suggesting that these theoretical debates need to be contextualised within a shifting political context. The certainties of the critique of the race relations problematic are no longer tenable. What seems to characterise the contemporary period is, on the one hand, a complex spectrum of racisms, and, on the other hand, the fragmentation of the definition of blackness as a political identity in favour of a resurgence of ethnicism and cultural differentiation. At the same time, and perhaps paradoxically, new cultures and ethnicities are emerging in the context of dialogue and producing a kaleidoscope of cultural syncretisms.[5] There may well be contradictory trends emerging, but neither the *race relations problematic* of the 1970s nor the *racism problematic* of the 1980s are equipped to deal with the contemporary situation. In the final section we want to make some suggestions as to how these conceptual problems might be resolved.

CONCEPTUALISING RACISMS AND RACIAL DISCOURSE

The politics of race and racism has undergone numerous transformations in recent decades. Debates about the ontological status of race, the object of investigation and the agenda for research in this field are partly the result of these transformations. While some authors writing in the tradition of race and ethnic relations studies have been careful to separate the research process from political action, such a separation is in some ways impossible and even undesirable. This is why the political agendas involved in conceptualising racism need to be made explicit.

It is perhaps because analytical debates necessarily involve political disputes that no one theoretical perspective is dominant at the present time. Indeed much of the mainstream research in this field is not theoretically informed in any substantial way. There is a need for greater theoretical clarity on key concepts and a broadening of the research agenda to cover issues that have been neglected, such as the politics of culture and identity. In this sense Banton may well be right in his contention that different theoretical paradigms may be able to contribute their own distinctive accounts of the processes which involve the attribution of specific meanings to racial situations (Banton 1991). However, the point that Banton misses is that the various paradigms which are adopted within this area of research contain an implicit or explicit political position *vis à vis* the politics of knowledge production. In this case it is not a matter of choosing appropriate analytical tools from some diverse theoretical bag, but rather it is necessary to situate these paradigms in relation to each other and to political debates over what could or should be the focus of analysis.

The question of how to conceptualise racism is not purely an academic matter, it is connected with a wider political culture in any given historical conjuncture. Our own awareness that this is the case has been heightened by our current research into local politics and racism in Birmingham and the dilemmas we are facing with regard to the relationship between research and political interventions (Back and Solomos 1992). One of the starting points of this research is that race is foremost a political construct. As a result racialised assertions need to be located within processes of social regulation and identity formation. In the course of our research, however, it has become clear that racism manifests itself in plural and complex forms. In this situation the logic of racism needs to be appraised in what we shall call *metonymic elaborations*. This means that racisms may be expressed through a variety of coded signifiers. We have already discussed one such elaboration, i.e. the coding of race as culture. Contemporary racisms have evolved and adapted to new circumstances. The crucial property of these elaborations is that they can produce a racist effect while denying that this effect is the result of racism. For example, the new racisms of the 1980s are coded within a cultural logic. As a result the champions of this racism can claim that they are protecting their way of life and that the issue of colour or phenotype is irrelevant.

In this context unitary or simplistic definitions of racism become hard to sustain. However, it seems clear that contemporary racisms share some central features. They attempt to fix human social groups in terms of *natural* properties of belonging within particular political and geographical contexts. The assertion that racialised subjects do not belong within – say British society – is then associated with social and cultural characteristics designated to them within the logic of particular racisms.

It follows from the above argument that racist discourses need to be rigorously contextualised. This means that racisms need to be situated within specific moments. The effect of a particular racist discourse needs to be placed in the conditions surrounding the moment of its enunciation. This means irrevocably crossing the analysis of racism with other social relations surrounding gender and sexuality or the culture of institutional politics. For example, in our work in Birmingham we have identified particular elaborations of racism which are being mobilised against black politicians within the context of democratic politics. In Birmingham there has been a significant increase in political participation in the Labour Party from within black communities and in particular Muslims originating from Kashmir and Pakistan. In this changing context black politicians are often accused of fostering duplicitous political affiliation. It is asserted that an 'Asian Mafia' exists within the context of Birmingham's Labour Party. This is underscored by a construction of 'subcontinent politics' which are corrupt, violent and incompatible with Britain's democratic process. This demonstrates a moment where the political mobilisation of black communities is racialised. In this context the truth or falsehood of particular events or assertions become irrelevant. What is significant is that these discourses make accusations of impropriety believable with regard to all people designated as 'Asian politicians'.

The claim that a 'white mafia' exists simply does not resonate with racialised discourse in the same way as that we have described above. What this particular form of political racism does is: i) undermine the political struggles for representation being waged within 'Asian' communities; and, ii) legitimate resistance to political representation in terms of cultural incompatibility of 'sub-continent culture' with 'British culture'. This is an example of the metonymic elaboration of race where race is coded as culture. When people utilising these ideas are challenged they claim that this is not racism, but merely reflects and provides 'evidence' of deficiencies within the political culture of black communities.

In this context, the meanings of race and racism need to be located within particular fields of discourse and articulated to the social relations found within that context. It is then necessary to see what kinds of racialised identities are being formed within these contexts. Birmingham has also been a focus of the debate around whether 'Asian' communities should be defined as 'black'. With regard to the ontological status of these classifications, we view them as political constructions of identity that need to be situated within specific social and discursive contexts. We in no way accept that these identifications relate to 'natural communities', or that one notion is more politically legitimate than others. Rather they constitute moments where community and identity are defined: manifestations of racial and ethnic closure. We are suggesting a position which builds into any analysis a rigorous scrutiny of racialised definitions, whether they are operated by the local state or the range of political mobilisations that are occurring around racial and ethnic identities within black communities. This approach seeks to decipher the meanings of racialised identities without attempting to prioritise one classification as more legitimate than another.

We are suggesting a model for conceptualising racisms which is: i) sensitive to local and contextual manifestations of racist discourse; and, ii) able to connect local manifestations with wider or national public discourses. As yet the theoretical work on racism has produced accounts of racism which derive contemporary forms of racism from public political discourse. This evidence is then used to generalise about broad trends within British society. We are suggesting that there is a need to situate racisms within particular settings, before moving towards a more general account of their wider significance.

In summary, we are suggesting that racism needs to be conceptualised as multiple and metonymically elaborated. The analysis of contemporary racisms needs to be situated within particular discursive contexts. Racism cannot be reduced to class relations but neither can it be seen as completely autonomous from wider social relations such as gender and sexuality. We are arguing for a more rigorous analysis of the semantics of race and the elaboration of racisms. It is clear that the 1990s will pose serious questions with regard to the way racism is conceptualised. In this context the orthodoxies of the last ten years may prove inappropriate when attempting to meet these challenges.

NOTES

1. This paper explores some of the theoretical issues we are facing in writing up our research on 'The Politics of Race and Social Change in Birmingham', which was financed by the Economic and Social Research Council under award number R 000 23 1545 from 1989 to 1992. We are grateful to the ESRC for their support.

2. In this paper we do not provide a discussion of these early studies, though any rounded overview of the origins of the sociological study of race would have to include them.

Similarly we do not attempt to explore the relationship between research agendas and public policy discourses.

3. A similar position also emerged in the United States during the early 1980s and also took as their starting point the interrelationship between relations of politics, power and racism. The most influential of these was a study by Michael Omi and Howard Winant of the processes of 'race formation' in the United States. They put particular emphasis on the role of political and legal relations in defining the existence of racial categories and defining the social meanings of notions such as racial inequality, racism and ethnicity (Omi and Winant 1986).

4. Taken from 'After Dread and Anger' BBC Radio 4, 1989.

5. Here we are thinking particularly of the hybrid cultural forms that are being generated within inner city communities of young people. In particular, the fusion of Caribbean and South Asian musical elements in Birmingham and in the music of Apache Indian, Bally Sagoo and Johnny Z.

References

Anthias, F. 1992. 'Connecting "Race" and Ethnic Phenomena'. *Sociology* 26, 3:421–438.

Asad, T. 1990. 'Ethnography, Literature, and Politics: Some Readings and Uses of Salman Rushdie's *The Satanic Verses*'. *Cultural Anthropology* 5, 3:239–269.

Back, L. 1993. 'Race, Identity and Nation within an Adolescent Community in South London'. *New Community*, January.

Back, L. Forthcoming. 'Cultures of Racism, Rituals of Masculinity: Mutual Crossings of Racism and Gender' in N. Lindisfarne and A. Cornwall *The Meanings of Masculinity*. London: Routledge.

Back, L. and Solomos, J. 1992. 'Doing Research, Writing Politics: The Dilemmas of Political Intervention in Research on Racism'. Unpublished paper.

Banton, M. 1983. *Racial and Ethnic Competition*. Cambridge: Cambridge University Press.

Banton, M. 1987. 'The Battle of the Name'. *New Community* 14, 1/2: 170–175.

Banton, M. 1991. 'The Race Relations Problematic'. *British Journal of Sociology* 42, 1:115–130.

Barker, M. 1981. *The New Racism*. London: Junction Books.

Barth, F. 1959. *Political Leadership Among Swat Pathans*. London: Athlone Press.

Barth, F. 1969. *Ethnic Groups and Boundaries: The Social Organisation of Cultural Difference*. London: George Allen and Unwin.

Bhabha, H.K. 1990. 'Interrogating Identity: The Postcolonial Prerogative' in D.T. Goldberg (ed.) *Anatomy of Racism*. Minneapolis: University of Minnesota Press.

Bhachu, P. 1991. 'Culture, Ethnicity and Class Amongst Punjab Sikh Women in 1990s Britain'. *New Community* 17, 3:401–412.

Castells, M. 1983. *The City and the Grassroots*. London: Edward Arnold.

Centre for Contemporary Cultural Studies. 1982. *The Empire Strikes Back*. London: Hutchinson.

Cohen, A. 1974. 'Introduction: The Lesson of Ethnicity' in A. Cohen (ed.) *Urban Ethnicity*. London: Tavistock.

Cohen, P. 1972. 'Subcultural Conflict and Working Class Community'. *Working Papers in Cultural Studies* 2, University of Birmingham.

Cohen, P. 1988a. 'Popular Racism, Unpopular Education'. *Youth and Policy* 24:8–12.

Cohen, P. 1988b. 'Tarzan and the Jungle Bunnies: Class, Race and Sex in Popular Culture'. *New Formations* 5, Summer: 25–30.

Cohen, P. 1991. *Monstrous Images, Perverse Reasons: Cultural Studies in Anti-Racist Education*. Centre for Multicultural Education, Institute of Education, University of London, Working Paper 11.

Cohen, P. and Bains, H. (eds.) 1988. *Multi-Racist Britain*. Basingstoke: Macmillan.

Commission of the European Communities. 1989. *Living in Europe: A Handbook for Europeans*. Brussels: ECSC.

van Dijk, T.A. 1991. *Racism and the Press*. London: Routledge.

Dyer, R. 1988. 'White'. *Screen* 29, 4:44–45.

Fanon, F. 1967. *Towards the African Revolution*. New York: Monthly Review Press.

Gates, H.L. 1988. *The Signifying Monkey*. New York: Oxford University Press.

Gates, H.L. (ed.) 1986. *'Race', Writing and Difference*. Chicago: University of Chicago Press.

Gilroy, P. 1987. *There Ain't No Black in the Union Jack*. London: Hutchinson.

Gilroy, P. 1990. 'One Nation Under a Groove: The Cultural Politics of "Race" and Racism in Britain' in D.T. Goldberg (ed.) *Anatomy of Racism*. Minneapolis: University of Minnesota Press.

Gilroy, P. 1991. 'It Ain't Where You're From, It's Where You're At ... The Dialectics of Diasporic Identification'. *Third Text* 13:3–16.

Goldberg, D.T. 1992. 'The Semantics of Race'. *Ethnic and Racial Studies* 15, 4:543–569.

Goldberg, D.T. (ed.) 1990. *Anatomy of Racism*. Minneapolis: University of Minnesota Press.

Hall, S. 1980. 'Race Articulation and Societies Structured in Dominance' in UNESCO (1980). *Sociological Theories: Race and Colonialism*. Paris: UNESCO.

Hall, S. 1988. 'New Ethnicities' in K. Mercer (ed.) *Black Film British Cinema: ICA Documents* 7. London: British Film Institute.

Hall, S., Critcher, C., Jefferson, T., Clarke, J. and Roberts, B. 1978. *Policing the Crisis: Mugging, the State, and Law and Order*. London: Macmillan.

Hall, S. and Jacques, M. 1989. *New Times: The Changing Face of Politics in the 1990s*. London: Lawrence and Wishart.

Hewitt, R. 1986. *White Talk, Black Talk: Inter-Racial Friendship and Communication Amongst Adolescents*. Cambridge: Cambridge University Press.

Hewitt, R. 1991. *Language, Youth and the Destabilisation of Ethnicity*. Paper given at the 'Conference on Ethnicity in Youth Culture: Interdisciplinary Perspectives', Fittjagard, Botkyrka, Sweden, 3–5 June, 1991.

hooks, b. 1992. 'Representing Whiteness in the Black Imagination' in L. Grossberg, C. Nelson and P. Treichler (eds.) *Cultural Studies*. London: Routledge.

Jenkins, R. 1986. 'Social Anthropological Models of Inter-Ethnic Relations' in J. Rex and D. Mason (eds.) *Theories of Race and Ethnic Relations*. Cambridge: Cambridge University Press.

Jones, S. 1988. *Black Culture, White Youth: the Reggae Tradition from FA to UK*. Basingstoke: Macmillan.

Lawrence, E. 1981. 'White Sociology, Black Struggle'. *Multi-Racial Education* 9, Summer: 3–17.

Lawrence, E. 1982. 'In the Abundance of Water the Fool is Thirsty: Sociology and Black "Pathology" in CCCS *The Empire Strikes Back*. London: Hutchinson.

Miles, R. 1982. *Racism and Migrant Labour*. London: George Allen and Unwin.

Miles, R. 1984. 'Marxism Versus the "Sociology of Race Relation"?' *Ethnic and Racial Studies* 7, 2:217–237.

Miles, R. 1986. 'Labour Migration, Racism and Capital Accumulation in Western Europe'. *Capital and Class* 28:49–86.

Miles, R. 1988. 'Racism, Marxism and British Politics' . *Economy and Society* 17, 3:428–460.

Miles, R. 1989a. *Racism*. London: Routledge.

Miles, R. 1989b. 'From Where We Have Come to Where We Are Going: Reflections on Racism and British Politics, 1945–2000'. Paper presented at the Political Studies Association at the University of Warwick, 4–6 April 1989.

Miles, R. and Phizacklea, A. 1979. 'Some Introductory Observations on Race and Politics in Britain' in R. Miles and A. Phizacklea (eds.) *Racism and Political Action in Britain*. London: Routledge and Kegan Paul.

Miles, R. and Phizacklea, A. 1984. *White Man's Country: Racism in British Politics*. London: Pluto Press.

Omi, M. and Winant, H. 1986. *Racial Formation in the United States*. New York: Routledge and Kegan Paul.

Phizacklea, A. and Miles, R. 1980. *Labour and Racism*. London: Routledge and Kegan Paul.

Reeves, F. 1983. *British Racial Discourse: A Study of British Political Discourse about Race and Race Related Matters*. Cambridge: Cambridge University Press.

Rex, J. 1968. 'The Sociology of the Zone of Transition' in R. Pahl (ed.) *Readings in Urban Sociology*. London: Pergamon Press.

Rex, J. 1970. *Race Relations in Sociological Theory*. London: Weidenfeld and Nicolson.

Rex, J. 1973. *Race, Colonialism and the City*. London: Routledge and Kegan Paul.

Rex, J. 1979. 'Black Militancy and Class Conflict' in R. Miles and A. Phizacklea (eds.) *Racism and Political Action in Britain*. London: Routledge and Kegan Paul.

Rex, J. 1986a. *Race and Ethnicity*. London: Open University Press.

Rex, J. 1986b. 'The Role of Class Analysis in the Study of Race Relations – a Weberian Perspective' in J. Rex and D. Mason (eds.) *Theories of Race and Ethnic Relations*. Cambridge: Cambridge University Press.

Rex, J. 1988. *The Ghetto and the Underclass: Essays on Race and Social Policy*. Aldershot: Avebury.

Rex, J. 1989. 'Some Notes on the Development of the Theory of Race and Ethnic Relations in Britain'. Unpublished discussion document, Centre for Research in Ethnic Relations.

Rex, J. 1990. 'The Relationship Between Theoretical and Empirical Work in the Centre'. Unpublished discussion document, Centre for Research in Ethnic Relations.

Rex, J. and Mason, D. (eds.) 1986. *Theories of Race and Ethnic Relations*. Cambridge: Cambridge University Press.

Rex, J. and Moore, R. 1967. *Race, Community and Conflict*. London: Oxford University Press.

Rex, J. and Tomlinson, S. 1979. *Colonial Immigrants in a British City*. London: Routledge and Kegan Paul.

Sivanandan, A. 1990. 'All That Melts into Air is Solid: The Hokum of New Times'. *Race and Class* 31, 3:1–30.

Solomos, J. 1988. *Black Youth, Racism and the State*. Cambridge: Cambridge University Press.

Solomos, J. 1989. *Race and Racism in Contemporary Britain*. Basingstoke: Macmillan.

Spivak, G.C. 1987. *In Other Worlds*. London: Methuen.

Wallman, S. (ed.) 1979. *Ethnicity at Work*. London: Macmillan.

Wallman, S. 1986. 'Ethnicity and Boundary Process in Context' in J. Rex and D. Mason (eds.) *Theories of Race and Ethnic Relations*. Cambridge: Cambridge University Press.

Ware, V. 1992. *Beyond the Pale: White Women, Racism and History*. London: Verso.

Young, R. 1990. *White Mythologies: Writing History and the West*. London: Routledge.

35

The Invention of White Race:
Racial Oppression and Social Control

THEODORE W. ALLEN

As Louis Kushnick (see the collection of his works in *Race, Class, and Struggle* [1998]) did many years earlier, the author explores the relationship between racism, ethnicity, and its impact on working-class consciousness. Allen extends the discussion by utilizing Irish history to illustrate that as race is a social construction, so is 'white'. Allen does this by giving ample examples of the 'racial oppression' faced by Irish tribes at the hands of the English. This racial oppression is similar in some ways to that experienced by African tribes by European powers in the colonization of Africa. But when Irish immigrants arrive in the United States throughout various periods, it becomes clear that coopting them as 'white' is a way of maintaining a social and wealth status quo beneficial to the very powerful and rich. This cooptation is adequate to neutralize political and ideological opposition from the Irish, but concomitantly prevent the emergence of cross-racial/ethnic class-based alliances. The whitinization of Irish immigrants is utilized by former slaveholders as well as the new industrial managers seeking to control unionization and the push for higher wages and improvement in living conditions. Although the Irish immigrants are highlighted in this study, the author states that dynamics associated with the invention and appointment of whiteness apply to other groups as well.

The Anatomy of Racial Oppression

However one may choose to define the term "racial", it concerns the historian only as it relates to a pattern of oppression (subordination, subjugation, exploitation) of one set of human beings by another. Orlando Patterson, in his *Slavery and Social Death*, takes "the racial factor to mean the assumption of innate differences based on real or imagined physical or other differences."[1] But, as I have pointed out in the Introduction, such an assumption does not an oppressor make; presumably the objects of racial oppression (however the term is defined) are capable of the same sorts of assumptions. David Brion Davis, explaining slavery in the United States, says, "racial dissimilarity [was] offered as an excuse" for it.[2] That is true enough and consistent with Patterson's definition of "the racial factor." But again, excuses are not an automatic promotion to oppressor; before racial oppression is excused, it must first be imposed and sustained. That is what needs to be explained.

Unfortunately, "racial dissimilarity" in the conventional phenotypical sense proves to be more banana peel than stepping stone. Historically, "racial dissimilarities" have not only been artificially used, they are themselves artificial. In colonial Hispanic America, it was possible for a person, regardless of phenotype (physical appearance), to become "white" by purchasing a royal certificate of "whiteness."[3] With less formality, but equal success, one may move from one "racial category" to another in today's Brazil where, it is said, "money whitens."[4] On the other hand, in the United States the organizing principle of society is that no such "whitening" be recognized – whether "whitening" by genetic variation or by simple wealth. In 1890, a Portuguese emigrant settling in Guyana (British Guiana) would learn that he/she was not "white." But a sibling of that same person arriving in the United States in that same year would learn that by a sea-change he/she had become "white."[5] In the last Spanish census of Cuba, Mexican Indians and Chinese were classified as "white", but in 1907 the first United States census there classed these groups as "colored."[6] According to Virginia law in 1860, a person with but three "white" grandparents was a Negro; in 1907, having no more than fifteen out of sixteen "white" great-great-grandparents entitled one to the same classification; in 1910, the limit was asymptotic: "every person in whom there is ascertainable any Negro blood ... [was to] be deemed a colored person."[7] As of 1983, the National Center for Health Statistics was effectively following the 1910 Virginia principle by classifying any person as black if either of the parents was black. At the same time, in Texas the "race" classification was determined by the "race" of the father.[8] Prior to 1970, a set of Louisiana court decisions dating back to the late 1700s had upheld the legal concept that "any traceable amount" of African ancestry defined a "Negro." In 1970, "racial" classification became the subject of hard bargaining in the Louisiana state legislature. The Conservatives held out for 1/64, but the "more enlightened" opposition forced a compromise at 1/32 as the requisite proportion of Negro forebears, a principle that was upheld by the state's Supreme Court in 1974.[9]

By considering the notion of "racial oppression" in terms of the substantive, the operative element, namely "oppression," it is possible to avoid the contradictions and howling absurdities that result from attempts to splice genetics and sociology.[10] By examining racial oppression as a particular system of oppression – like gender oppression or class oppression or national oppression – we find firmer footing for analyzing racial slavery and the invention and peculiar function of the "white race," and for confronting the theory that racial oppression can be explained in terms of "phenotype" – the old ace-in-the-hole of racist apologetics. This approach also preserves the basis for a consistent theory of the organic interconnection of racial, class, national, and gender oppression.[11]

THE IRISH ANALOGY

To our conditioned minds, the attitude and behavior of Anglo-Americans toward African-Americans and American Indians have the readily recognizable character of racial oppression. But when racial oppression is defined in terms of its operational principles, the exclusion of the Irish case is seen to be wholly arbitrary. The exclusion is especially deplorable when practiced by European-American scholars, because it ignores a case where "white" consciousness on the part of the observer is least likely to affect the drawing of conclusions. A "need to know they were white"[12] cannot possibly serve to explain the attitude of the English toward the Irish. The history of English rule in Ireland, and of the Irish in America, presents instructive parallels and divergences for the understanding of "race" as a sociogenic rather than a phylogenic category; and of racial slavery as a system of social control.

HISTORIANS AND THE ANALOGY

Even as the nineteenth-century imperialist "scramble for Africa" was unfolding, resonances of English abolitionism and Chartism, and of the great Civil War and Emancipation in America, still thrilled somewhere in the collective consciousness of historians toiling to interpret the past to the present. One such, the distinguished English historian and abolitionist Henry Hallam (1777–1859), pointed out the racist affinity of the Spanish genocide of the Christian Moors and the English oppression of the Irish.[13]

The pre-eminent Anglo-Irish historian William Edward Hartpole Lecky (1838–1903) noted how the people of the English Pale in Ireland came to "look upon the Irish as later colonists looked upon the Red Indians."[14] Or consider the remarkable insight of W. K. Sullivan, Irish historian and President of Queen's College, Cork, who analogized the social role of the non-gentry Protestants in Ireland and the "poor whites" in America.[15] Karl Marx applied the analogy in pursuit of the unity of working people of all countries:

> The ordinary English worker hates the Irish worker ... [and] in relation to the Irish worker he feels himself a member of the *ruling* nation.... His attitude is much the same as that of the "poor whites" to the "niggers".[16]

The most depraved derivation of the analogy was voiced by the English historian Edward A. Freeman (1823–92) during a visit to America in 1881. The United States, he said, "would be a grand land if only every Irishman would kill a negro, and be hanged for it."[17]

World War Two had an obvious effect on consciousness of the analogy among historians concerned with the problem of slavery and racism. They have devoted considerable attention to the attitudes of the English in the Tudor and Stuart periods toward the Irish, as homologues of the general European attitude toward the Indians of the Americas.[18] In his richly documented exposition of the close relation of the images of the Irish and the American Indians and Africans, David Beers Quinn claims that this closeness revealed "what some Englishmen thought about some Irishmen and about Irish society."[19] Historians such as Quinn, Jones, Canny and Muldoon argue effectively that racism among Europeans is not limited to their relations with non-Europeans, but that it can exist in the most extreme form between one European nation, such as England, and another, such as Ireland. To that extent they make a worthy contribution to the analysis of the societies based on lifetime bond-labor in the Americas, and of the Anglo-American continental plantation colonies in particular.

Since their studies center mainly on Elizabethan times, they give no particular attention to the white-supremacism directed particularly against African-Americans that is of central importance for the study of American history. The same circumstance forecloses any close examination and analysis of the parallels between white supremacy in Anglo-America and the religio-racial oppression of the Irish resulting from the Cromwellian English conquest in 1652 and the Penal Laws of the eighteenth-century Protestant Ascendancy. Finally, this limitation of perspective leaves unconsidered the case of the Irish immigrant who, however poor, Catholic and racially oppressed he/she might have been in Ireland, could emerge in Anglo-America as an ordained member of the "white race" along with Anglo- and other European-Americans, with all the privileges, rights and immunities appertaining thereto. This peculiar social transition is instructive in the principle of the relativity of "race." It certainly was a thing not dreamt of in the philosophy of the English planters of Munster.

Some historians accept the parallels so far as the American Indians are concerned, but do so in such a way as to deny their relevance to the white-supremacist oppression of African-Americans. They cite the opinion of certain seventeenth-century Englishmen to the effect that Indians are born "white" and only become "tawny" by prolonged exposure to the elements.[20] Muldoon, for example, taking note of the English way of lumping the Irish and the Indians together as "savages", asserts,

"Crucial to this comparison was the belief that Indians were white men …"[21]

George M. Frederickson defines "racism" in such a way as to exclude extension of the parallel between Irish and Indians to the African-American. While noting that the English justified their genocidal treatment of the Irish and the American Indians by classing them as "savages," he maintains that this did not involve "a 'racial' concept in the modern sense" because it was "not yet associated with pigmentation."[22]

Nicholas P. Canny, developing the lead provided by David Beers Quinn, documented and analyzed significant parallels in the attitudes taken by the Elizabethan English ruling classes toward the Irish and the American Indians. English executors of American colonial projects, Professor Canny writes, brought "the same indictments against the Indians and later the blacks in the New World that had been brought against the Irish." It was his specific aim "to show how the justification for colonization influenced or reflected English attitudes toward the Gaelic Irish and, by extension, toward the imported slave and the indigenous populations in North America."[23] While Canny does not undertake a treatment of the parallel between the Irish and African-Americans, it is not because he considers it irrelevant. Quite the contrary; he writes: "We find the same indictments being brought against the Indians, and later the blacks, in the New World that had been brought against the Irish."[24]

Michael Hechter makes a special contribution by explicitly challenging, in the context of the same parallel, the dominance of the "phenotype" fixation.

Anglo-Saxons and Celts cannot be differentiated by *color*. Despite this, however, racism came to flower [in Ireland] as well. I think that Americans have come to realize how this is possible by following the recent events in Northern Ireland.[25]

THE ANALOGY AS PRACTICE

The chronology of English colonial exploits being what it was, Professor Quinn found that the Irish became the "standard of savage or outlandish" social behavior for interpreting African and American Indian societies.[26] In its sameness with respect to the Irish and to American Indians and African-Americans, this ideology and practice was not concerned with "phenotype," color, etcetera, but rather with the "uncivilized ways" of the victims.[27] Once categorized as "uncivilized," they were regarded by the ruling class as doubtful prospects, at best, for admittance to the "Christian" establishment. Resistance to conquest and the ways of colonial exploitation was interpreted in terms of an incapacity for civilization, and this exclusion from

"Christian civilization" served to excuse further oppression.[28]

Walter Devereux (1541–76), the first Earl of Essex, who unsuccessfully attempted to plant an English colony in Ulster in 1573, envisaged Ireland as England's Indies, and he predicted that the English government would soon be forced to restrict emigration to Ireland just as the Spanish imposed restraints "for going to the Indies."[29] Another early English conquistador was Robert Dudley (1532–88), first Earl of Leicester. The Irish were "a barbarous people," said Leicester, and the English should deal with them as other Christian colonizers did with barbarians elsewhere in the world.[30] This theme, repeated with variations, supplied a continuing rationale for English oppression of the Irish.

At the time of the plantation of Ulster launched in 1609, the English appealed to Christian fellowship in urging the Spanish government not to give aid and comfort to the Irish resistance. Addressing the Spanish Lords of Council in Madrid, the English ambassador, Sir Charles Cornwallis, asserted that the Irish were "so savage a people" that they long ago deserved the same treatment "used by the Kings of Spain in the Indies, or those employed with the Moors … scattering them in other parts."[31]

Nearly two centuries later Dublin-born Edmund Burke, then the preeminent British statesman, observed that the English Protestant Ascendancy regarded the Irish "as enemies to God and Man, and indeed, as a race of savages who were a disgrace to human nature."[32]

English practice in Ireland included elements that are counterposed in the experiences of the Indians and of the African-Americans: namely the expropriation of the lands of the former, and the super-exploitation of the labor and the incorporation-without-integration of the latter. In the one case, "Irish land might be confiscated without much more scruple than the land over which the Red Indian roves."[33] In the other, "The poor people of Ireland [in the eighteenth century] are used worse than negroes by their lords and masters, and their deputies of deputies of deputies."[34]

In 1814, the great Irish leader Daniel O'Connell, himself a staunch abolitionist, wishing to express his disappointment with his English Whig friends for lapsing into chauvinism toward the Irish people, chose to base his comment on the same analogy. "I did imagine," he said, "we [Catholic Irish] had ceased to be whitewashed negroes, and had thrown off for them [the Whigs] all traces of the colour of servitude."[35]

The Whig baron Henry Brougham, for all of his avowed abolitionism, found reason to protest in the House of Lords when Robert Tyler and then his father, United States President John Tyler of Virginia, spoke out in favor of repeal of the Union of Britain and Ireland. It was, Brougham said:

> … as if the Queen of this country, like the President, were to say she had her heart and soul in the cause of the Carolina and Virginia negroes, and that she hoped ere long to see a white republic in the north, and a black republic in the south.[36]

THE HALLMARK OF RACIAL OPPRESSION

The assault upon the tribal affinities, customs, laws and institutions of the Africans, the American Indians and the Irish by English/British and Anglo-American colonialism reduced all members of the oppressed group to one undifferentiated social status, a status beneath that of any member of any social class within the colonizing population. *This is the hallmark of racial oppression* in its colonial origins, and as it has persisted in subsequent historical contexts.

The African-Americans

Of the bond-laborers who escaped to become leaders of maroon settlements before 1700, four had been kings in Africa. Toussaint L'Ouverture was the son of an African chieftain, as was his general, Henri Christophe, a subsequent ruler of Haiti, who died in 1820.[37] It is notable that the names of these representatives of African chieftaincy have endured only because they successfully revolted and threw off the social death of racial oppression that the European colonizers intended for them. One "Moorish chief," Abdul Rahamah, was sold into bondage in Mississippi early in the nineteenth century.[38] Abou Bekir Sadliki endured thirty years of bondage in Jamaica before being freed from post-Emancipation "apprenticeship" in Jamaica. The daughter of an "Ebo" (Ibo?) king and her daughter Christiana Gibbons were living in Philadelphia in 1833, having been freed from chattel bondage some time earlier by their Georgia mistress.[39] We can never know how many more Africans were stripped of all vestiges of the social distinction they had known in their homelands by a social order predicated upon "the subordination of the servile class to every free white person," however base.[40]

In taking note of the plight of Africans shipped as bond-laborers to Anglo-American plantations and deprived of their very names, Adam Smith in 1759 touched the essence of the matter of racial oppression. "Fortune never exerted more cruelly her empire over mankind," he wrote, "than when she subjected those nations of heroes to the refuse of Europe."[41] A century later the United States Supreme Court affirmed the constitutional principle that any "white" man, however degraded, was the social superior of any African-American, however cultured and independent in means.[42]

This hallmark of racial oppression in the United States was no less tragically apparent even after the abolition of chattel bond-servitude. In 1867, the newly freed African-Americans bespoke the tragic indignation of generations yet to come: "The virtuous aspirations of our children must be continually checked by the knowledge that no matter how upright their conduct, they will be looked upon as less worthy of respect than the lowest wretch on earth who wears a white skin."[43]

The American Indians

In 1831 a delegation of the Cherokee nation went to Washington to appeal first to the Supreme Court and then to President Andrew Jackson to halt the treaty-breaking "Indian Removal" policy, designed to drive them from their ancestral homes. The delegation included men who were not only chosen chiefs of their tribe but had succeeded in farming and commerce to become "Cherokee planter-merchants."[44] Their appeals were rebuffed; President Jackson was well pleased with the decision of the Supreme Court denying the Cherokees legitimacy as an independent tribal entity in relation to the United States.[45]

This was a culmination, as well as a beginning. Proposals made over a period of two decades by church groups and by the Secretary of War for the assimilation of the Indians by intermarriage had been rejected.[46] At the same time, the independent tribal rights of the Indians were challenged by United States "frontier" aggression. As a consequence of this rejection on the one hand and the disallowance of tribal self-existence on the other, the individual American Indian, or whatever degree of social distinction, was increasingly exposed to personal degradation by any "white" person. In 1823, the Cherokee leader John Ridge (son of Major Ridge), a man of considerable wealth, supplied out of his own experience this scornful definition of racial oppression of the Indian:

An Indian ... is frowned upon by the meanest peasant, and the scum of the earth are considered sacred in comparison to the son of nature. If an Indian is educated in the sciences, has a good knowledge of the classics, astronomy, mathematics, moral and natural philosophy, and his conduct equally modest and polite, yet he is an Indian, and the most stupid and illiterate white man will disdain and triumph over this worthy individual. It is disgusting to enter the house of a white man and be stared at full face in inquisitive ignorance.[47]

The Irish

From early in the thirteenth century until their power entered a two-and-a-half-century eclipse in 1315,[48] the English dealt with the contradictions between English law and Irish tribal Brehon law by refusing to recognize the latter, at the same time denying the Irish admittance to the writs and rights of English law.[49]

In 1277, high Irish churchmen, having secured support among powerful tribal chieftains, submitted a petition to the English king Edward I, offering to pay him 8,000 marks in gold over a five-year period for the general enfranchisement of free Irishmen under English law. The king was not himself unwilling to make this grant of English law. But he thought he ought to get more money for it, and so the Irish three years later raised the offer to 10,000 marks.[50]

What was being asked was not the revolutionary reconstitution of society but merely the abandonment of a "racial" distinction among freemen ruled by English law in Ireland. In the end the king left the decision to the Anglo-Norman magnates of Ireland, and they declined to give their assent. Referring to a replay of this issue which occurred some years later, Sir John Davies concluded, "The great [English] Lordes of Ireland had informed the king that the Irishry might not be naturalized, without damage and prejudice either to themselves, or to the Crowne."[51]

Irish resentment and anger found full voice in the wake of the Scots invasion effected in 1315 at the invitation of some Irish tribes. In 1317, Irish chieftains led by Donal O'Neill, king of Tyrone, joined in a Remonstrance to John XXII, Pope to both English and Irish. In that manifesto the Irish charged that the kings of England and the Anglo-Norman "middle nation" had practiced genocide against the Irish, "enacting for the extermination of our race most pernicious laws."[52] The manifesto presented a four-count indictment: (1) Any Englishman could bring an Irishman into court on complaint or charge, but "every Irishman, except prelates, is refused all recourse to the law by the very fact [of being Irish]"; (2) "When ... some Englishman kills an Irishman ... no punishment or correction is inflicted;" (3) Irish widows of English men were denied their proper portion of inheritance; and (4) Irish men were denied the right to bequeath property.

Whatever exactly the remonstrants meant by their word "race," their grievances, like those of the African-Americans and the American Indians I have cited, bore the hallmark of racial oppression. From the Petition of 1277 to the Remonstrance of 1317, it was specifically the legal status of the free Irish men, rather than the unfree, which was at issue.

The really peculiar feature about the situation in Ireland is that the free Irishman who had not been admitted to English law was, as far as the royal courts were concerned, in much the same position as the betagh [the Irish laborer bound to the land].[53]

From Analogy to Analysis: Colony
versus Tribe

In each of these historical instances, a society organized on the basis of the segmentation of land and other natural resources under private, heritable individual titles, and having a corresponding set of laws and customs, acting under the direction of its ruling class brings under its colonial authority people of societies organized on principles of collective, tribal tenure of land and other natural resources, and having their respective corresponding sets of laws and customs.[54] In each of these confrontations of incompatible principles, the colonizing power institutes a system of rule of a special character: designed to deny, disregard and delegitimate the hierarchical social – tribal, kinship – distinctions previously existing among the people brought under colonial rule. The members of the subjugated group, stripped of their tribal and kinship identity, are rendered institutionally naked to their enemies, completely deprived of the shield of social identity and the corresponding self-protective forms of the tribal and kinship associations that were formerly theirs. Although not all are to be made slaves of the colonizing power, the object is social death for the subjugated group as a whole, whether individually and in groups they are forcibly torn from their home country to serve abroad among strangers, or they are made strangers in their own native land.[55] They are "desocialized by the brutal rupture of the relations which characterize the social person," the tribal, kinship and even the unit family relationships that constituted their social identity. They are to be allowed only one social tie, that which "attache[s] them unilaterally to" the colonizing power.[56]

Once the conquest is complete, the "clash of cultures" takes on the flesh-and-blood form of a host of colonists with newly acquired property claims.[57] These interests, and their concomitant social and legal attributes, once more bar the subject people from admittance to the common law of the colonizing power, although tribal and kinship-group law and custom have been overthrown.

The social death of the subjugated people is followed by social resurrection in new forms from which they take up the task of overthrowing racial oppression. In some cases, the ruling power is able to maintain its dominance only by co-opting a stratum of the subject population into the system of social control. In thus officially establishing a social distinction among the oppressed, the colonial power transforms its system of social control from racial oppression to national oppression. In the nineteenth century, the Haitian Revolution represented the failure of this colonial policy of co-optation; British policy in the West Indies, and the policy of Union

with Britain and Catholic Emancipation in Ireland, represented its success. On the other hand, in continental Anglo-America and in the Union of South Africa, the colonial power succeeded in stabilizing its rule on the foundation of racial oppression.

The Assault on Tribal Relations among Africans

The English and other Europeans, and in time European-Americans, first came to Africa as traders and raiders, not as colonists. The colonial option was not theirs, since the people of subequatorial Africa, universally organized as tribal societies made up of kinship groups, were then too strong and independent to allow the seaborne Europeans any other course.[58] For that reason the inherent contradiction of the tribal relations of the African peoples and the European relations based on individual ownership of land and other natural resources remained a latent factor offering no serious obstacle to the development of the enterprises characteristic of that period of the history of that region.[59]

But upon those millions, mainly from West Africa and Angola, who were transported as captive bondmen and bondwomen to the plantation Americas, the clash of cultures was visited with the abruptness of a thunderclap, undiminished by time, and with the harsh and stifling cruelty of exile in chains. In America the colonial employers made "detribalization" a deliberate part of the "seasoning" process undergone by all newly arriving bond-laborers.[60] Colonial authorities made it a matter of policy to frustrate bond-labor rebelliousness by segregating laborers of the same language or other affinity groups from each other. The Coromantees and the Ashanti were particularly feared, it was said.[61]

The acquisition of African bond-laborers for American plantation colonies was made exclusively by capture and abduction. The consequent destruction of their family ties was unaccompanied by the gloss of Christian preachments on the "heathenism" of kinship group and marriage customs, such as were directed at the Irish and the American Indians.

The Assault on American Indian Tribal Relationships

Whilst United States policy very early showed a disregard for the rights of Indian tribes, the avowed determination to destroy Indian tribal relations did not become the dominant theme until after the Civil War. Prior to that time, "Indian policy" moved in a three-phase cycle – massive treaty-breaking incursions by Americans on Indian lands; war; and then another "treaty" involving "cessions" of Indian lands – systematically repeated, until finally the Indians had been "ceded" into the confines of "reservations."[62]

The direct assault on tribal relations had been anticipated by half a century; in 1830 the Georgia state legislature nullified Indian tribal laws within the state's boundaries. This legislation was condemned by its critics as an attack against "the entire social existence of the [Cherokee] tribe." The exiling of thousands of the Cherokee people over the Trail of Tears in 1838 was justified on the grounds that "Common property and civilization cannot coexist."[63] In 1854 (the year of the passage of the Kansas–Nebraska "squatter sovereignty" law) the Omaha Indians "ceded" 10,000,000 acres of land to the United States in a "treaty" which, for the first time, provided for the breaking up of the tribe's remaining lands into individual allotments.[64] The treaty was hailed as giving hope that soon all Indian lands would be "thrown open to the Anglo-Saxon plough."[65]

To the extent that they were consulted in the matter, the Indians overwhelmingly rejected the "severalty" (individual ownership) option for cancelling tribal land rights. If, in the end, their wishes were ignored, it was not because the Indian point of view was not understood. As the ethnologist J. W. Powell of the Smithsonian Institution informed the United States Congress:

> In Indian tribes individual or personal rights and clan rights are very carefully differentiated. The right to the soil, with many other rights, inheres in the clan. Indian morality consists chiefly in the recognition of clan rights; and crime in Indian society chiefly consists in the violation of these clan rights. In Indian society the greatest crime is the claim of an individual to land, and it is also a heinous sin against religion.[66]

"Citizenship," he concluded, "is incompatible with kinship society."

By 1859, a general assault on tribal ownership of land was under way, which would become the central feature of United States "Indian policy" and its "civilizing mission." The legislative culmination of that assault came with Congressional passage in 1887 of the Dawes General Allotment Act. Its purpose and rationale were articulated with drumfire consistency and remarkable clarity. In his 1859 annual report to Congress, US Indian Affairs Commissioner Charles E. Mix advocated converting reservation lands to individual allotments. Indian "possession of large bodies of land in common" was the root of what Mix saw as "habits of indolence and profligacy."[67] A Congressman cited Mix's report in arguing that "the first step to be taken" in the execution of Indian policy was in "uprooting the community of property system [and] ... extinguishing or modifying the tribal relation."[68] In the course of the 1866 debate on relations with the

Sioux, Representative Burleigh of Dakota recalled that, as United States Indian Agent there in 1862, he "did advocate the removal of the [Sioux] women and children with a view to wiping out the tribe."[69]

While the Paris Commune was yet within living memory, in the era of Haymarket and the robber barons,[70] the destruction of tribal relations was polemically associated with the threat of socialism and communism. In the year the Second Socialist International was formed, Indian Commissioner T. J. Morgan showed, more than most socialists did, an instinctual grasp of the vital link between white supremacy and anti-socialism. "The Indians," Morgan said, "must conform to 'the white man's ways,' peaceably if they will, forcibly if they must. The tribal relations should be broken up, socialism destroyed and the family and the autonomy of the individual substituted." The year before, Commissioner Oberly had pointed out the great moral gulf fixed between the two societies. He condemned "the degrading communism" of Indian tribal ownership, where "neither can say of all the acres of the tribe, 'This is mine.'" With the allotment to individuals of Indian tribal lands, he theorized, the Indian would be able to emulate "the exalting egotism of American civilization, so that he will say 'I' instead of 'We,' and 'This is mine,' instead of 'This is ours.'" If the Indians rejected this tutelage, he concluded, it should be forced on them, as it were, for their own good.[71]

The Assault on Irish Tribal Relationships

The conflict between colonizing powers, on the one hand, and African and American Indian societies, on the other, is a familiar story (however distorted); indeed, it is still not completely played out. Not so with Irish tribal society, which was finally and completely destroyed even as the first English settlers were setting foot outside Europe. For that reason, and because everything that is "white" in our historiography instinctively rejects the notion of an affinity of non-European and Irish tribal societies, it seems necessary to treat the Irish case in somewhat greater detail.[72]

In ancient Ireland, that is, up to the invasion of the Norsemen in the middle of the ninth century, "The legal and political unit ... was the *tuath*, ruled by the tribal king," writes D. A. Binchy, "and though the number of tribes tended to vary with the vicissitudes of Irish and political history, it never fell below one hundred."[73] The *tuath*, though tribal,[74] that is, a kinship society, was characterized by a highly developed class differentiation, originating perhaps in the differential disposition of spoils from inter-tribal raids and wars, and in adventitious turns of fortune. However class differentiation began, it represented a contradiction within tribal society. The general evolutionary course of Irish tribal life, as it was at the time of the Anglo-Norman invasion in 1169, appears to have been shaped by this internal contradiction along the following lines: (1) there was a predominant tendency toward downward social mobility;[75] (2) although only a small proportion of the land was held as private property by generations of individual chieftain families,[76] a much larger proportion of the cattle, the main form of wealth, was owned by these nobles (*flaiths*) and by cattle-lords (*boaires*);[77] (3) these chiefs were able to "leverage" (as we might say today) certain factors, such as relative over-population[78] and the recruitment of laborers and tenants (*fuidirs*) from "kinwrecked" remnants of broken tribes, in a way that enhanced the social power of the chieftain class relative to the generality of tribe members;[79] (4) increasing numbers of tribe members, from the lower category of tenant and share-herder (the *daer-chele*) on down were very poor and dependent,[80] and increasingly reduced to the serflike status of the *sen-cleithe*, who made up the common labor class known to the Anglo-Normans as the *betagh*.[81]

This process of class differentiation took place within the matrix of tribal kinship relationships, the basic social unit of which was the *fine*, more particularly the *derbfine*.[82] Each *derbfine* was made up of all the males patrilineally descended from the same great-grandfather. The *derbfine* was the most basic form of the *fine*; although the latter term is given a wide-ranging application, it always signifies "kinship group." The *fine*, more particularly the *derbfine*, was the radial center of the obligations and loyalties of the individual tribe members, and the sanctuary of that member's rights.

Each *derbfine* occupied its land by assignment from the tribal authority. Upon the death of the great-grandfather there would be, let us say, four surviving grandfathers (his sons). Each of these, then, would be the peak of a new *derbfine*, and usually its chosen chief. Or, at the other extreme, the appearance of a new generation, being a fresh set of great-grandsons, would create, let us say, four new or immanent *derbfines*. Consequently, at regular intervals a redistribution of the lands of the old *fine* was necessary, according to the prescribed schedule of apportionment. (The same schedule governed the distribution of the *derbfine*'s share of booty from cattle raids, and of the lands and property of any deceased member of the *derbfine*.)

The tribal form circumscribed and inhibited the process of class differentiation. For instance, since the *derbfine* was collectively responsible for default by any of its members, no member could become a "free" client of a lord belonging to another *derbfine*, without the collective consent of the *derbfine* as a whole. Likewise, the chief of the *derbfine* could not enter into any external contract without the consent of the entire *derbfine*. Or

again, in the exceptional case of the individual acquisition of land by means other than through *derbfine* distribution, the land could not be sold by its acquirer without the consent of the full membership of the *derbfine* – an unlikely prospect. Nor could an individual member of the *derbfine* dispose of his inherited land without the consent of the full membership of the *derbfine*. In general, to the maximum possible extent trade or contract relations were to be entered into only with fellow *derbfine* members. In a society in which the members of the noble (chieftain) class derived their main support from the contracted services of share-herders, such tribal principles obviously would present barriers to class differentiation.[83]

A small proportion of the land was possessed and passed down from generation to generation by chieftains and by certain professional families (families of historians, poets, judges, artisans, physicians). But the vast majority of the land belonged to the tribe as a whole, and not to any individual.

Out of the tribal lands, arable land was assigned by the tribal council to the respective kinship groups as their own, to be used and periodically redistributed among their members as described above. The largest part of the land (which later appeared in the records as "waste, woods, bog, and mountain land") was common land, open without artificial or legal barrier for the free use of all members of the tribe, according to established practices, for grazing cattle, finding fuel, hunting, and whatever other advantages it might offer.[84]

The general tendency of the development of the contradiction between the tribal principles and class differentiation, along the lines noted above, culminated in the emergence of a handful of chieftains, who not only dominated their respective *tuaths* but also subordinated weaker tribes simply by *force majeure*. The eleventh and twelfth centuries, up to the coming of the Anglo-Normans, were consumed by this internecine struggle of these overkings, some of whom aspired to the eminence of high king (*ard-ri*) over all Ireland.

To what extent – if any – did the emergence of provincial tribal powers and their struggles for dominance affect the basic tribal constitution of Irish society? Was history working its purpose out and "a race evolving its monarchy" so far toward a European-style Irish feudal order that "[t]ribes had ceased to exist ... the Brehon law did not check kings; the tribal control had ceased; old rules and customs were inapplicable to the new order of things"?[85] Was this century and a half of ceaseless war and destruction preparing Ireland to "join Europe" under Anglo-Norman and papal sponsorship?[86] Or did "The structure of [Irish] society ... [retain] a recognizable identity throughout the first half of Irish history, up to the coming of the Normans,"[87] despite this bloody epoch of "centralization" by battle-axe? Was Otway-Ruthren's verdict still correct?

... the structure of Celtic society differed far more widely from the general continental pattern than had that of Anglo-Saxon England [at the time of the Norman Conquest], while by the later twelfth century the new Anglo-Norman society was setting on lines which had been so marked a feature of the Norman conquest of Wales and Italy.[88]

If we are to grant political economy its dominion, at the root of the question lies the fact that whereas the English economy was based mainly on land cultivation, the Irish economy was primarily based on cattle-herding. England's Domesday Book, compiled about 1086 to estimate the national wealth for royal tax purposes, was essentially a survey of cultivable landholdings and resources for their cultivation. A century later in Gaelic Ireland, hides, wool and meat were still the essentials of commerce, and animals and animal products supplied the staples of everyday existence.[89] The main demands of the English Peasant Revolt of 1381 were for an end to the serf's bondage to the land, and for the limiting of rent to four pence per acre. (See Volume Two.) The main problem of the Irish tenant (client) family (along with just surviving the perils of the depopulating random wars) was that of keeping up with the annual rent on the cattle advanced on loan by the chief, which was to be paid back out of the increase and produce of their cattle.[90]

The difference between herding and tillage produced a corresponding variation in the manner of holding and distributing land. Herds vary in extent within very elastic limits, according to their rate of natural increase. They are not fixed in one place, except by the daily care of the herders. Otherwise they rove over the land, no respecters of plot markers, guided by their own feeding and sheltering instincts, their scope limited only by seasonal changes, natural variations of terrain, and grass yield. The net product is measured in terms of the natural increase and produce of the herd. Land, by contrast, is a limited, specific, fixed portion of the earth's surface. For cultivation purposes, it lends itself to parcelling on virtually permanent lines, and to the exclusive use of the parcels by individual production units, where some enforceable advantage is seen in it, according to the differential rent – the marginal yield per unit of labor per measured unit of land.

In Gaelic Ireland, whatever the form of landholding, an individual could not own a large tract of land "in the same sense that he might own a knife or a spade ... [L]ordship of the land belonged to the political rather than the economic order of ideas. It implied authority rather than ownership."[91] Under English (Anglo-Norman) law every inch of land was either held directly by the king or held in fee from the king by private individuals.[92] The colonizers coming from England

... believed that they were acquiring a rigid, complete and perpetual ownership of the "land" from the zenith to the uttermost depths – an ownership more complete than that of any chattel – an ownership which they imagined to be self-existing even when the person in whom it should be "vested" was unknown or unascertained. They called this sort of ownership an "estate," i.e., a status, something that stood of its own virtue.[93]

Out of this basic divergence arose a set of superstructural dissonances with regard to principles of marriage and family, post-mortem reversion of property, succession as chief or king, and the conduct of war, to say nothing of other lifestyle and cultural values.[94] There were two conflicting rules of inheritance: gavelkind (an English word adapted for a much different Irish custom) and English primogeniture; two laws of succession: the Irish "tanistry" and the English royal primogeniture; two marriage forms: polygyny for men of the Irish noble classes, and the formally strict but strictly formal monogamy of the English man; two concepts of criminal justice: the adjudication of compensatory liability for particular individual damages, as determined by Irish judges, known as Brehons; and the English public law of offenses against "the king's peace"; and two styles of war: Irish cattle-raiding and tribal political alliances, but non-interference in internal affairs,[95] in contrast to the English territorial conquest and possession under new, presumably permanent sovereignty and land title.

Under the custom of Irish gavelkind, a deceased man's partible wealth – most notably his cattle and assigned cultivable land – was distributed among the surviving men of his particular kinship group, numbering perhaps four to the fourth power,[96] according to a prescribed order of apportionment up and down the generation ladder. Brotherless daughters had restricted rights of inheritance.[97] By English feudal, and later bourgeois, law, the first-born son was the sole heir, and in the case of "a failure in the male line" the inheritance belonged to the widow, or to the daughters equally. Upon the subsequent marriage of such a female heir, her "estate" became the husband's.

Upon the death of an Irish king or tribal chief, his wealth was disposed of by gavelkind in the same way as that of any other man so summoned. His successor in office was chosen from the ranks of the most influential kinship group, by election of all the enfranchised members of the tribe. This man also succeeded to the perquisites of office, including free entertainment as he travelled the territory, and the use of mesne land cultivated by "base clients" or bond-laborers. In England, at least from the thirteenth century onward, whenever succession to the throne was orderly it was by the rule of primogeniture, and carried with it, of course, private ownership of royal property.

A man of an Irish tribe typically sought to have a large number of sons to add to the strength of his *fine* as a part of his tribe.[98] To that end, the man of sufficient wealth might have a plurality of wives. "Irish law, even in the Christian period," Binchy writes, "extends a limited recognition to other types of union [other than the one with the *cetmuinter*, the "head wife"] of varying degrees of social standing (*lanamnas*), which are neither permanent nor monogamous."[99] The sons of each wife enjoyed equal social standing. The exception was the son of a slave woman, who was barred from inheriting not because the union was any less legitimate than any other, but because the slave was not a member of the kinship group.[100]

The feudal order that the Anglo-Normans brought to Ireland was conceived of as a pyramid of authority and obligation radiating from the king down through various grades of lordship and vassalage, and based on the principle that every rood of ground was privately owned, whether the owner be the king himself or a holder "in fee" from the king. Great lords then let out their lands to lesser lords, and ultimately to the laboring people of various degrees. Given this pyramid of power, the benefits (then as now) were apt to be greater as one rose in the scale of power. Under the terms of the "fee," the land was held "in perpetuity," to be passed undiminished from generation to generation and, more particularly, from eldest son to eldest son. This principle was intended to promote and preserve the stability of the pyramid of authority, which it was thought would be weakened by the division of the land among several heirs. And when a father or other male guardian was negotiating an alliance by the marriage of a prospective heir, a son or a brotherless daughter, there was advantage in brokering for a whole inheritance rather than by fractions of it. Thus entrenched, the principle of primogeniture produced by logical extension the extreme feudal cult of bridal virginity, the chastity-belt mentality, and the illegitimizing of "bastards" in order to assure the integrity of the inheritance.

The contrasting English and Irish laws of inheritance appear to be at the root of one of the most remarkable of the ineluctable contradictions between the two social systems. Under English law, children of wealthy fathers were hostages to their inheritances.[101] The eldest son was the heir; a younger son might move into that position by the death of an elder brother; daughters were to be assigned "marriage portions." Orphan children of the wealthy classes were assigned as "wards" of male "guardians" who exercised the legal authority of parents over them, including the privilege of disposing in marriage of the orphans along with their inheritances or "portions." Where estates of the greatest extent were involved, the marriage engagement of orphans became a source of enrichment for monarchs, at first, and then of the members of a Court of Wards. Whatever the circumstance, it was an essential principle of estate management to preserve a male heir and the virginity of daughters. Consequently, the closest supervision over the children was enforced by the father or the guardian who had the disposal of the estate and the marriage portions. It would have been unthinkable for an English lord to give complete custody of his children to another lord, to be reared and educated from the age of seven until the girls reached the age of fourteen and the boys seventeen.

But in Ireland just such a system of fosterage (called by the English "gossipred") was practiced.[102] For all its formal resemblance to hostage-giving,[103] it was something quite different; it bound rich families to each other in strong fraternal relations. The foster children were cared for with such affection and concern that the foster family ties became as close as those within their own respective families. But whatever might by accident befall the foster child, the disposition of the inheritance among the father's kinship group would not otherwise be affected.

Except for high political offenses such as treason, crimes under the laws of Celtic Ireland were treated as private, personal grievances, indeed like civil suits. The aim was to provide satisfaction for the aggrieved party, and thereby to prevent resort to vengeance. What was denied to the victims, the state did not arrogate to itself. There was, therefore, no capital punishment,[104] no jail, no sheriff, no special instrument of punishment touching life or limb. Complaints originated exclusively with the suit of the aggrieved party, who if successful was awarded reparations assessed by the Brehon. If the guilty party defaulted, his kinship group was liable. English law, by contrast, was aimed at maintaining "the king's peace." Crimes against individuals were breaches of that peace, and subject to public prosecution under public law. Having assumed the role of aggrieved party, the English state, "the crown," substituted public vengeance for private vengeance, and imposed it by means of chains, stocks and prisons, but most commonly the gibbet. In appropriate cases the estate of the guilty party was also subject to heavy fines or escheat to the crown.

Four and a half centuries of coexistence of Gaels with the foreigners, from Henry II to Henry VIII, added force to the transforming effect on the tribal system of the internal contradiction of developing class differentiation. Yet there remained at the end a residue of deep-rooted conflicts between the constitutional principles of the Gaelic and English systems: (1) corporate ownership of land by agnatic descent groups (the *derbfines*) as against individual ownership with testamentary rights; (2) tanistry and election against primogeniture in choosing kings; (3) crimes as torts, and collective liability, in contrast to private liability, the concept of "crown" against the individual for breach of "the king's peace"; (4) inheritance by gavelkind as against primogeniture.

There can be no doubt that the constitutional differences of the Celtic Irish and the English social orders were regarded by the English as a fundamental barrier to colonization. The need for English colonialism to destroy Irish tribal forms and ways was analyzed by Sir John Davies (1569–1626) in his *A Discovery of the True Causes why Ireland was never entirely Subdued ...*, written in 1612.[105] Davies's career uniquely qualified him to observe the course of English interests in Ireland, as he had already served King James I there as Solicitor-General for three years (1603–1606), and then as Attorney-General. He made a thorough research of the records of all reigns from the Anglo-Norman invasion of Ireland in 1169 to the Plantation of Ulster in 1609. In the course of his study he presented the case against the laws and customs of the Irish tribes, which in the English fashion he called "septs."

Tribal customs, Davies said, necessarily tended to cause the Irish to be "Rebelles to all good Government," to "destroy the commonwealth wherein they live, and bring Barbarisme and desolation upon the richest and most fruitfull Land of the world."[106] Unlike "well-governed Kingdomes and Commonweals," Ireland lacked the death penalty, and consequently the strong might freely prey upon the weak.[107] Tanistry made for unstable government because chieftaincy was not a hereditary estate, and election was to the "strong hand."[108] Gavelkind, made more ruinous by the equal standing of "bastards," was the root cause of the "barbarous and desolate" condition of the country. It fragmented estates and made titles transitory, impoverishing the nobility, who nevertheless would not engage in trade or mechanical arts.[109] It was all of a piece with the Irish family form, with its "common repudiation of their wives," the "promiscuous generation of children," and the "neglect of lawful matrimony."[110] The solidarity of the kinship groups, doubly reinforced by the close-as-blood affinities of fosterage, had made it impossible, Davies said, for English authorities to prosecute Irish malefactors.[111]

But as experience in Scotland and Wales would show, and as Davies himself pointed out, such a clash of systems did not make racial oppression the only option. The papal assignment of "lordship" over Ireland to the English in about 1155 did not envisage any such a socio-political monstrosity as racial oppression, but merely the imposition of conformity in Christian practices.[112] For their part, the Anglo-Normans under kings Henry II and John were prepared to proceed in Ireland as they had in Scotland. There they had supplanted tribal organization with feudal power vested in the Scottish chieftains Malcolm Canmore and David I in the late eleventh and the early twelfth centuries.[113] In such proceedings, intermarriage linking families of the respective upper classes was a normal, indeed essential, part of the process. So it began in Ireland. The first of the Anglo-Norman arrivers, Richard Fitzgilbert (Strongbow) de Clare, agreed in 1169 to assist an Irish king, Diarmuit Macmurchada, to regain the domains from which he had been driven by rival Irish chieftains, but only on condition that Strongbow take Macmurchada's daughter in marriage. In 1180 Hugh de Lacy, then chief bearer of King Henry's authority in Ireland, married the daughter of another Irish king, Ruaidri Ua Conchobair. In both cases King Henry reacted with suspicion, sensing a threat to his authority in Strongbow and de Lacy thus independently becoming heirs to Irish lands.[114] Both the marriages and the king's suspicions were rooted in recognition of the legitimacy, in Anglo-Norman terms, of class distinctions among the Gaelic Irish. For the first fifty years of the Anglo-Norman incursion, the English government under three successive kings held to this policy of "assimilating [Gaelic] Irish local government to the system prevailing in England," even though, as I have suggested, it seemed to be learning that this clash of social orders was perhaps more profound than that which the Normans had faced when they invaded England a century before.[115]

Why then was the tested Scottish policy of over-lordship abandoned in favor of an attempt to rule in Ireland by racial oppression? Sir John Davies, looking back, ascribed the decision to power jealousy on the part of the Anglo-Norman lords toward any rivalry for royal favor that might evolve among native Irish.[116] A recent study suggests a more particular, that is, economic, basis for the case against the Anglo-Norman lords, along the following lines.[117]

The change of policy began with the death of the English king, John, in 1216, followed by the installation of the Anglo-Norman triumvirate – William Marshal, Geoffrey de Marisco and Archbishop Henry "of London" – in charge of Irish affairs. By that time European grain prices had been rising sharply for fifty years to a level which remained high throughout the thirteenth century.[118] The merchant-connected palatinate Anglo-Norman lords, headed by the aggressive triumvirate, reacted to the prospects for profit to be made by a change from herding to tillage by becoming impatient with the slow-moving, more civil policy of converting the Irish to European ways. William Marshal himself was one of those who profited by switching the land he seized from herding to tillage, and his labor supply from Irish herders to English tillers.[119] We may well believe that such motives were a sharp spur to the abandonment of the policy of assimilation and to the turn to the abortive but historically instructive first attempt to impose racial oppression in Ireland.

How well, if at all, this economic determinist thesis will stand the test of focused research must be left to Irish scholars to decide. That the change was being made with regard to priests was evident by 1220. In June of that year, Pope Honorius III replaced his papal legate in Ireland, Henry of London, for complicity in an English decree "that no Irish cleric, no matter how educated or reputable, is to be admitted to any ecclesiastical dignity."[120] Whatever the explanation – Anglo-Norman power jealousy or high grain prices or a combination of these, and/or possibly still other factors – a pope is our witness that this turn to racial oppression was made by deliberate ruling-class decree, rather than by compulsive fulfillment of some gene-ordained "need to know they were English."

COMPELLING PARALLELS

Given the common constitutional principles of the three cases – the Irish, the American Indian, and the African-American – the abundant parallels they present are more than suggestive; they constitute a compelling argument for the sociogenic theory of racial oppression.[121]

If from the beginning of the eighteenth century in Anglo-America the term "negro" meant slave, except when explicitly modified by the word "free,"[122] so under English law the term "hiberni-cus," Latin for "Irishman," was the legal term for "unfree."[123] If African-Americans were obliged to guard closely any document they might have attesting their freedom, so in Ireland, at the beginning of the fourteenth century, letters patent, attesting to a person's Englishness, were cherished by those who might fall under suspicion of trying to "pass."[124] If under Anglo-American slavery "the rape of a female slave was not a crime, but a mere trespass on the master's property,"[125] so in 1278 two Anglo-Normans brought into court and charged with rap-ing Margaret O'Rorke were found not guilty because "the said Margaret is an Irishwoman."[126] If a law enacted in Virginia in 1723 provided that "manslaughter of a slave is not punishable,"[127] so under Anglo-Norman law it sufficed for acquittal to show that the victim in a killing was Irish.[128] Anglo-Norman priests granted absolution on the grounds that it was "no more sin to kill an Irishman than a dog or any other brute."[129] If the Georgia Supreme Court ruled in 1851 that "the killing of a negro" was not a felony, but upheld an award of damages to the owner of an African-American bond-laborer mur-dered by another "white" man,[130] so an English court freed Robert Walsh, an Anglo-Norman charged with killing John Mac Gilmore, because the victim was "a mere Irishman and not of free blood," it being stipulated that "when the master of the said John shall ask damages for the slaying, he [Walsh] will be ready to answer him as the law may require."[131] If in 1884 the United States Supreme Court, citing much precedent authority, including the Dred Scott decision, declared that Indians were legally like immigrants, and therefore not citizens except by process of individual naturalization,[132] so for more than four centuries, until 1613, the Irish were regarded by English law as foreigners in their own land. If the testimony of even free African-Americans was inadmissible,[133] so in Anglo-Norman Ireland native Irish of the free classes were deprived of legal defense against English abuse because they were not "admitted to English law," and hence had no rights that an Englishman was bound to respect.

A minor proportion of the Irish were enfran-chised in that two-thirds to three-fourths of Ireland where English law prevailed at the height of the Anglo-Norman era.[134] Members of five noble Irish families were granted procedural standing in English courts. Designated the "Five Bloods," they were the O'Neills of Ulster, the O'Connors of Connaught, the O'Melaglins of Meath, the O'Briens of Munster and the M'Murroughs of Leinster.[135] The inclusion of the M'Murroughs and the O'Connors in this list suggests that these excep-tions were made, in part at least, to protect land titles and ancillary rights deriving from some of the previously mentioned early intermarriages between Irish and English. Just as in Jamaica centuries later individual free "persons of color" might be enfran-chised by "private bills" approved by the colonial authorities, just as prospering individuals of African or Indian descent in colonial Spanish-America could buy royal certificates of "whiteness,"[136] so in the thirteenth century individual free Irishmen might occasionally purchase admission to English law. However, in the three years when this form of enfranchisement was most used, only twenty-six Irish were enrolled. Whilst the number enfranchised is said to have been greater than the number for-mally enrolled in that status, the generality of the free Irish remained outside its protection.[137] However, unlike the Jamaica and Spanish-America instances, events in Ireland aborted the initial possi-bility of the emergence of an Irish buffer social con-trol stratum for the English.

THE PERSISTENCE OF RACIAL
OPPRESSION – BY POLICY DECISION

The renewal of English efforts to reduce Ireland to its control in the latter part of the sixteenth century coincided with the full and final commitment of England to the Reformation.[138] Since the twelfth century the English had operated in Ireland under papal authorization; now that benign relationship came quickly to an end, emphasized by continual English Crown expropriations of Church property in Ireland. Not only was Ireland made the object of a more aggressive English colonial expansionism, it became a particular focus of the rivalry between Protestant England and Catholic Spain, then England's chief colonial competitor. In this historical context the Protestant Reformation worked its purpose out by recasting anti-Irish racism in a deeper and more enduring mold. What had fed primarily on simple xenophobia now, as religio-racism, drank at eternal springs of private feelings about "man and God." The historian and member of the British House of Commons Thomas Babington Macaulay would say that the Reformation "brought new divisions to embitter the old ... a new line of demarcation was drawn; theological antipathies were added to the previous differences, and revived the dying animosities of race."[139]

For more than two centuries, Anglo-Irish and native Irish over almost all of Ireland had coexisted in a "nonracial" symbiosis. But now increasing English colonial expansionism and desperate Irish resistance culminated in the nine-year Tyrone War, 1594–1603, over the issue of the very existence of Celtic society. The spiral of history had come full circle. "The issue in the Nine Years War," writes Sean O'Domhnaill, "was knit as never before in any war in Ireland since the days of Edward Bruce." It was not merely a matter of the English "breaking the great lords"; in so doing they had "to subjugate the Irish people."[140] "Neither the Irish nobles nor their followers," writes O'Domhnaill, "wanted innovations in religion, or laws which were not of their own making, or a centralised system of government based on a kingship which had its origin and being in another country."[141] This supreme historic effort of Celtic Ireland by its forces alone to throw off English colonialism ended in defeat.

Before, Irish chieftains had retained sufficient initiative to strengthen their tribal authority by the opportune exploitation of relationships with the English (or with the Spanish). But their social base remained the tribe, with its basic principles of land-holding, inheritance and succession.[142] In the decades of "the king's peace" that followed the Tyrone War, however, the English social order in Ireland demonstrated the advantages it held for economic survival and advancement in the context of the emergent modern capitalist commodity production system. The English landlord system was more profitable for the exploitation of Irish tenants and laborers than the Irish tribal system. It was a period of economic undermining of the Celtic system, marked by steady English pressure in the form of "plantation" projects, and by a degree of assimilation of the Irish chieftains into the English system through leasing and mortgaging.[143] It would seem that such erosive factors account in part for the fact that when Irish rebellion was renewed in 1641, rather than being an independent Gaelic struggle it became a subordinate component of the Royalist side in the War of the Three Kingdoms, which grew out of the English Civil War of Crown and Parliament.

Besides the Celtic Catholic Irish, there were the "Old English" Catholics, descended mainly from pre-seventeenth-century settlers. Although they used Gaelic extensively, rather than English, as their everyday language, they sought to assure Protestant English authorities of their loyalty to the mother country and their abhorrence of the ways of the native Irish.[144] Even so, they were stigmatized and penalized as "recusants" for refusing to abandon the faith of their fathers. In 1628 Charles I, hard pressed by the sea of troubles that would eventually topple his throne, sought to raise money by selling certain concessions, called Graces, to the Catholic Anglo-Irish. These dispensations were to include: security of the land titles of Catholics in possession for sixty years or more; permission for Catholic lawyers to represent clients before the courts; and an easing of the pressure to conform to Protestant forms of worship. In return, Anglo-Irish Catholics fulfilled an undertaking to provide he king with £120,000 sterling in three annual installments. But within a few years the king, having spent the money, lost all interest in giving the Graces the promised force of law.

The royal repudiation of the Graces was the culmination of a long train of slights, disabilities and confiscations endured by the Catholic Old English under Protestant English monarchs and the Church of England. Yet despite Charles's bad faith, when the choice was to be made between an Anglican king and Establishment and various kinds of no-bishop Puritans, the Catholic Anglo-Irish became involved for some period and to some extent on the losing royal side in alliance with the native Irish.

The Irish phase of the War of the Three Kingdoms ended in 1652 with complete English Parliamentary victory and conquest. The terms of the English Act of Settlement of 1652 and the Act of Satisfaction of the following year[145] resounded in Celtic Ireland like clods on a coffin lid. Irish rebellion having become fatally involved in the English Civil War, the complete extirpation of Celtic society was made an integral part of the settlement imposed by the Parliamentary Party even though its members might engage in the most bitter polemics over aspects of its implementation. In 1655 a pamphlet by Vincent Gookin, a Cromwellian adviser and functionary in Ireland, called for a tempering of the wholesale uprooting of the Irish under the English "transplantation" policy as set down in the 1652 Act of Settlement.[146] Colonel Richard Lawrence, a member of the parliamentary commission charged with carrying out the transplantation policy, was a Cromwellian settler in Ireland and a leading spokes- man for the military party in regard to Irish affairs. Apparently offended by what he considered Gookin's unwarranted interference with his execution of his duties, Lawrence charged Gookin with launching "poisoned arrows against authority ... intended to wound and weaken the English government [in Ireland]."[147] But on the matter of completing the destruction of the Irish tribes, he and Gookin were as one. The Irish, Gookin said, must above all be prevented from "knitting again like Worms, their divided septs and amities." Lawrence declared that the first requirement of a successful Irish policy was to:

> break or (at le[a]st) much weaken and limit that great spreading interest of the Irish, (viz.) their spreading Septs, which have been hetherto the very seed spots and nurseries of all factions and Rebellions, and (withal) the preservers of all their old Heathenish, wicked Customs and Habits, which are like the Humane, Jewish and Popish Traditions (though generally of a more wicked nature and tendentie) recommended from father to son, and so rivited into them by the reputation of Antiquity that there is little hope of reclaiming them while those Septs continue.[148]

Not only were previous social distinctions among the Irish to be ignored by English colonial law; now the English proceeded unrelentingly to decimate the Irish tribal lords by exile. Within a space of some twenty-four months, 35,000 to 40,000 Irish men – that is to say, one out of every six men over the age of about twenty-five – were sold in groups to serve as soldiers in foreign armies, chiefly the Spanish.[149] Vincent Gookin noted with satisfaction that "the chiefest and eminentest of the nobility and many of the Gentry" had been driven into exile.[150] As for those that remained, one colonial administrator was overheard to say, they "must ... turn into common peasants or die if they don't."[151]

A CLASSIC CASE OF RACIAL OPPRESSION

Before the outbreak of the rebellion in 1641, the Celtic, "native" Irish Catholics, the Old English Catholics and the Protestant "New English" shared possession of Irish lands in roughly equal proportions.[152] Under the Act of Settlement all persons, except such as could prove they had maintained "constant good affection" toward the English Parliamentary government between 1642 and 1652, were to be totally expropriated and evicted from their holdings. Such of the "ill-affected" as were not under sentence of death or banishment, were nevertheless also to be expropriated of their lands. They, however, were to be assigned some fractional equivalent of their original acreage in Connaught and County Clare. Catholics, according to their degree of "guilt," were to receive from one-half to one-third portions. "Ill-affected" Protestants were to forfeit only one-fifth of their estates, and were allowed to relocate outside of Connaught.[153] More than half the land in Ireland fell under this attainder; of Catholic landlords, only twenty-six out of a total of around ten thousand were excepted.[154] As for the native Irish, whatever distribution of their lands might subsequently be made, it would be done according to English law. This expropriation meant, therefore, the destruction of Celtic tribal landholding, and of Celtic society, even in its last stronghold west of the Shannon. Except for the Royalist Protestants,[155] those of the attainted class who were not hanged or exiled or otherwise debarred were – much like American Indians of the nineteenth century – assigned to live on some fractional equivalent of their former holdings in Connaught and in Clare where they found "not wood enough to hang a man, water enough to drown him, nor earth enough to bury him."[156] Of the ten thousand Catholic landholders of 1641, no more than four thousand qualified for any such land assignment at all; only one in five of the original ten thousand was actually assigned land west of the Shannon; and of these about six hundred were in possession twenty years later.[157]

About five out of every eight acres of profitable land were held by Catholics in 1641; by 1654 that share was reduced to one out of twelve.[158] The restoration of Charles II to the English throne in 1660 was followed by some restitution of Catholic lands, to a total of two out of every nine acres.[159] The defeat of Ireland's last great trial at arms, 1689–91, under the banner of the deposed English Catholic king, James II,[160] was made the occasion for the final swamping wave of expropriations, until in 1703 Catholics, who were fifteen out of every twenty in the population, held no more than one acre in nine of the profitable land; within another fifty years the Penal Laws operated to reduce the share to one out of every sixteen acres.[161] Four centuries before, the Anglo-Normans had refused to share English law with the Irish; now the English refused to share Irish land with the Irish. There was to be no new ascendance of assimilation and equality such as the amities of the fourteenth and fifteenth centuries might have promised. From 1652 onward, racial oppression, written into every new title deed, was anchored in the very bedrock of the Irish colonial economy. It was "The Act [of Settlement] by which most of us hold our Estates," said Chancellor John Fitzgibbon with painful candor. "... [E]very acre of land which pays quitrent to the Crown is held by title derived under the Act of Settlement."[162]

The native or, as they were termed, the "mere" Irish had been "admitted to" English law in 1613 (11 James I c. 5 [Irish Statutes]), only to be outlawed as "Papists," the common English epithet for Roman Catholics, in 1641. In December of that year the English Parliament in a joint declaration of both Houses had vowed unalterable determination to prevent the practice of the "Popish" religion in Ireland.[163] Now, in the aftermath of the rebellion, the Catholic Anglo-Irish landlords – no less "Popish" than the native Irish – were to suffer under the same religio-racist interdictions as did the Irish chiefs and lords, tenants and laborers.[164] The ancient amities of Anglo-Irish and native Irish survived only in the common fate of Catholics.

When the historian W. F. T. Butler concluded that "A common misfortune had welded all these [Catholics – Old English and native Irish] into one race,"[165] he was not referring to a genetic "merger" of Old English and Irish Catholics, nor to the appearance of some new Irish phenotype. He was affirming, rather, that that which in Ireland took the form of anti-Popery, and in time would be officially known as the Protestant Ascendancy, was a classic system of racial oppression.

NOTES

1. "A great deal, of course, depends on what one means by race. I take the racial factor to mean the assumption of innate differences based on real or imagined physical or other characteristics" (O. Patterson, *Slavery and Social Death* [New York, 1990], p. 176). What other, "non-physical," characteristics are meant, Patterson does not say at this point (pp. 176–8) in his discussion. Elsewhere his presentation may justify the inference that he had in mind considerations of presumed mental, temperamental, or moral attributes.

2. David Brion Davis, *The Problem of Slavery in Western Culture* (Ithaca, 1966), pp. 23–4. Davis makes this comment in the context of a critical examination of the views of George Bancroft as expressed in his *History of the United States, from the Discovery of the American Continent*, 10 vols, 14th edn (Boston, 1850–74). Davis cites from 1:159–61, 2:451. Bancroft (1800–91), a fervent Jacksonian and US expansionist, served as Secretary of the Navy, 1845–46, and was Ambassador to Britain from 1846 to 1849.

3. Charles Edward Chapman, *Colonial Hispanic America: A History* (New York, 1933), p. 118.

4. Marvin Harris, *Patterns of Race in the Americas* (New York, 1964), p. 59.

5. US Department of Commerce, Bureau of the Census, *Historical Statistics of the United States, 1789–1945* (Washington, DC, 1975), Series B 40–47 and n. 1. Walter Rodney, *A History of the Guyanese Working People, 1881–1905* (Baltimore, 1981), p. 143.

6. Franklin W. Knight, "Cuba," in David W. Cohen and Jack P. Greene, *Neither Slave Nor Free* (Baltimore, 1972), p. 280, n. 8.

7. Cited in June Purcell Guild, *Black Laws of Virginia* (1936, Negro Universities Press reprint, 1969), from the Virginia Statutes for the given years.

8. "What Makes You Black?", *Ebony*, 38:115–16 (January 1983).

9. *Boston Globe*, 17 September 1983. In an apparent misprint, the *Globe* says the Conservatives took their stand on "1/164," which I have taken the liberty of inferring to have intended "1/64." I do so not out of any pro-Conservative bias, but simply because of the fact that 164 is not a power of two. See also the *New York Times*, 6 July 1983.

10. In Louisiana in 1970 a lawyer went down to the Legislature to lobby for a definition of "Negro" sufficiently limited to leave a client of his on the "white" side of the line. "I got into a hassle with some of them," he later said; "... they started off at one one-hundred-and-twenty-eighth, and just to have some bargaining power I started off with ... an eighth. We finally struck the bargain at one thirty-second, and it sailed through" (*New York Times*, 30 September 1982).

11. The essential difference between racial and national oppression is the following. In the system of racial oppression, social control depends upon the denial of the legitimacy of social distinctions within the oppressed group. In the system of national oppression, social control depends upon the acceptance and fostering of social distinctions within the oppressed group.

12. See my discussion of Winthrop D. Jordan's view in the Introduction.

13. Henry Hallam, *Constitutional History of England from Henry VII to George II* (London, 1827), 3:401.

14. William Edward Hartpole Lecky, *A History of England in the Eighteenth Century*, 8 vols (New York and London, 1878–90), 2(1882):103.

15. W. K. Sullivan, *Two Centuries of Irish History, 1691–1870*, Part I, *From the Treaty of Limerick to the Establishment of Legislative Independence, 1691–1782*, edited by James Bryce (London, 1888), pp. 39–40.

16. Letter from Marx (London, 9 April 1870) to S. Meyer and A. Vogt, revolutionary German exiles in the United States (*Karl Marx and Friedrich Engels on Britain* [Moscow, 1962], pp. 551–2); emphasis in original.

17. Lewis P. Curtis, *Anglo-Saxons and Celts* (Bridgeport, Connecticut, 1968), p. 81, citing W. R. W. Stephens, *The Life and Letters of Edward A. Freeman*, 2 vols (London, 1895), 2:242.

18. Notable contributions to this field of study include: David Beers Quinn, "Sir Thomas Smith and the Beginning of English Colonial Theory," *Proceedings of the American Philosophical Society*, 89:543–60 (1945); David Beers Quinn, "Ireland and Sixteenth-century European Expansionism," in T. Desmond Williams, ed., *Historical Studies*, 1:20–32 (Papers Read before the Second Irish Conference of Historians, London, 1958); David Beers Quinn, *The Elizabethans and the Irish* (Ithaca, 1966); Howard Mumford Jones, 'The Origins of the Colonial Idea in England," *Proceedings of the American Philosophical Society* (1949); Howard Mumford Jones, *O Strange New World: American Culture, the Formative Years* (New York, 1964); Nicholas P. Canny, "The Ideology of English Colonization: from Ireland to America," *William and Mary Quarterly*, 3rd series, 30:575–98; Nicholas P. Canny, *The Elizabethan Conquest of Ireland: A Pattern Established, 1565–76* (New York, 1978); and James Muldoon, "The Indian as Irishman," *Essex Institute Historical Collections*, 3:267–89 (October 1975).

19. Quinn, *Elizabethans and the Irish*, p. vii. See particularly pp. 20–27 for an example of Quinn's presentation of this point.

20. Wesley Frank Craven, *White, Red, and Black: The Seventeenth-century Virginian* (Charlottesville, 1971; New York, W. W. Norton reprint, 1977), pp. 39–40.

21. Muldoon, p. 270.

22. George M. Frederickson, *White Supremacy: A Comparative Study in American and South African History* (London University Press, 1981), p. 15.

23. Canny, "Ideology of English Colonization," p. 596 (repeated almost verbatim in his *Elizabethan Conquest of Ireland*, pp. 160, 576).

24. Canny, "Ideology of English Colonization." p. 596.

25. Michael Hechter, *Internal Colonialism: The Celtic Fringe in British National Development, 1536–1966* (Berkeley, 1975), pp. xvi–xvii. Cf. Raymond Crotty, *Ireland in Crisis: A Study in Capitalist Colonial Undevelopment* (Dover, New Hampshire, 1986), p. 38. Sociologist Richard Williams makes a signal contribution along this line by bringing a study of history to a trenchant critique of misleading American sociological categories, which he believes impede the struggle for equality. He starts with the proposition that "race and ethnicity are social designations rather than natural categories" (Richard Williams, *Hierarchical Structures and Social Value: The Creation of Black and Irish Identities in the United States* [New York, 1990], p. ix).

26. Quinn, *Elizabethans and the Irish*, p. 26.

27. In 1978, Alden Vaughan questioned the validity of the Irish parallels, but he found no satisfactory alternative rationale for the contempt shown by Elizabethan Englishmen toward the American Indians. But whatever it may have been, he is convinced that it was not a matter of color prejudice, "for Englishmen believed the Virginia Indians to be approximately as white as themselves" (Alden T. Vaughan, "'Expulsion of the Savages': English Policy and the Virginia Massacre of 1622." *William and Mary Quarterly*, 3rd series, 35:57–84 [January 1978], p. 59, n. 3). Might it not have been that the earliest Anglo-Americans "believed the Virginia Indians to be as white as themselves" for the simple reason that they had not yet identified themselves as "whites"? Later, Vaughan returned to the subject, and noted a shift in the English color perception of Indians beginning in the late seventeenth century, corresponding to the beginning of the usage "white" to distinguish Europeans and European-Americans from Indians; but he excludes African-Americans in making this observation, implying that where European-Americans and African-Americans were involved the former were immemorially designated "whites" (Alden T. Vaughan, "From White Man to Redskin: Changing Anglo-American Perceptions of the American Indian," *American Historical Journal*, 87:917–53 [October 1982]. For his exclusions of African-Americans from his generalization, see p. 931). Instances in which the seventeenth century Virginia court records seem to contradict him in this regard will be considered in Volume Two of this study. It is encouraging to note that by 1989 Vaughan had come to believe in the germaneness of "possible parallels and contrasts between English–African and English–Irish relations" (Alden T. Vaughan, "The Origins Debate," *Virginia Magazine of History and Biography* 97:311–54 [July 1989], p. 353, n. 129).

28. Canny, "Ideology of English Colonization," pp. 575–6, 588–92.

29. Canny, *Elizabethan Conquest of Ireland*, pp. 133–4, citing Essex to Privy Council, Additional Manuscripts 48015, fols 305–14.

30. Canny, *Elizabethan Conquest of Ireland*, p. 134, citing a letter of Leicester to (Sir William?) Fitzwilliam, 24 August 1572. Canny also cites another Elizabethan as likening Sidney's mission in Ireland to that of the Spanish in America, as one of "brideling the barbarous and wicked."

31. Cornwallis to the Spanish Council, 16 October 1609. Great Britain Public Record Office, *Calendar of State Papers relating to Ireland of the Reign of James I*, vol. 3 (1608–10) (London and Edinburgh, 1874), edited by C. W. Russell and John P. Prendergast, 3:83. When it had suited their Reformationist purposes a quarter of a century earlier, however, the English ruling class published the writings of Bartolomeo de las Casas exposing and condemning the usages of the Christian conquistadors in the Americas (Bartholomew de Las Casas, *The Spanish Colonie, Or Briefe Chronicle of the Acts and gestes of the Spaniards in the West Indies, called the newe World for the space of xl yeeres* [London, 1583; Readers Microprint Corporation, 1966; see the Foreword for the history of the appearance of this English edition of writings of Las Casas]. See, for instance, sigs A, A2, B2, B3).

32. In a letter to Hercules Langrishe, 3 January 1792, *The Works of the Right Honorable Edmund Burke*, 6th edition (Boston, 1880), 12 vols, 6:305.

33. Lecky, *History of England*, 2:280.

34. Philip Dormer Stanhope, Fourth Earl of Chesterfield (1694–1773), who had served as Lord Lieutenant of Ireland (1745–46), writing to the Bishop of Waterford on 1 October 1764 (cited in Philip Henry Lord Mahon, *History of England from the Peace of Utrecht to the Peace of Versailles*, 7 vols [London, 1858], 5:123).

35. From a speech given at a meeting of the Catholic Board, Shakespeare Gallery, Exchequer Street, Dublin, 8 January 1814 (*Select Speeches of Daniel O'Connell. M. P.*, edited with historical sections by his son John O'Connell, Esq., 2 vols [Dublin, 1865], 1:408).

36. *Hansard's Parliamentary Debates*, 3rd series, 71:391 (8 August 1843). Brougham, an English abolitionist but an opponent of Irish independence, knew that the slaveholding Tyler family was playing politics with the repeal issue in the United States (see Chapter 8).

37. Richard Price, ed., *Maroon Societies: Rebel Slave Communities in the Americas* (Garden City, New York, 1973), p. 20; C. L. R. James, *The Black Jacobins: Toussaint L'Ouverture and the San Domingo Revolution* (revised edition, New York, 1963), pp. 17, 19.

38. Alfred H. Stone, "The Mulatto Factor in the Race Problem," *Atlantic Monthly*, 91:658–62 (1903), p. 660. Stone pegged his thesis on a distinction between "mulattoes" and "negroes." However, his awareness of social distinctions among Africans who were to be declassed in plantation America is worth noting. Terry Alford's *Prince Among Slaves: The True Story of an African Prince Sold into Slavery* (New York, 1977) is the history of Ibrahim, who is identified (p. 61) as "Rahahma" in a context which makes it apparent that he is the same person to whom

Alfred H. Stone referred as "Rahamah." Stone also mentions "Otman dan Fodio, the poet chief of the Fulahs" as among distinguished Africans brought as slaves to plantation America.

39. E. S. Abdy, *Journal of a Residence and Tour in the United States of North America, from April 1833 to October 1834*, 3 vols (London, 1835), 3:346–8.

40. H. M. Henry, *Police Control of the Slave in South Carolina* (Emory, 1914), p. 11, citing Nott and McCord (Law): *Witsell v Parker;* and 2 Strobhart (Law), 43: ex parte Boylston.

41. Adam Smith, *Theory of Moral Sentiments*, 6th edition, 2 vols (London, 1790), 2:37

42. US Supreme Court decision in *Dred Scott v. Sanford*, March 1857.

43. *Address of the Colored Convention to the People of Alabama.* published in the *Daily State Sentinel*, 21 May 1867 (James S. Allen, *Reconstruction: The Battle for Democracy [1865–1876]* [New York, 1937], pp. 237–8).

44. Major Ridge, who was not the richest man in the Cherokee nation, and who was not on the delegation, had an estate at this time of $22,000, not counting his thirty African-American bond-laborers and his interest in a trading post business (Thurman Wilkins, *Cherokee Tragedy: The Story of the Ridge Family and the Decimation of a People* [New York, 1970], pp. 183–4). An official census in 1835 found that of the population of the Cherokee nation (in contiguous areas of Georgia. North Carolina, Alabama and Tennessee) numbering 17,000, 1,600 were African-American bond-laborers (Samuel Carter III, *Cherokee Sunset, A Nation Betrayed: A Narrative of Travail and Triumph, Persecution and Exile* [Garden City, 1976], p. 22). The phrase "Cherokee planter-merchant" is Carter's (p. 23).

45. Opinion of Chief Justice John Marshall in *Cherokee Nation v. State of Georgia*, 30 US (1831), in Wilcomb E. Washburn, *The American Indian and the United States: A Documentary History*, 4 vols (New York, 1973), p. 2558. On Jackson's attitude, see ibid., pp. 2352–3, 2461–2, 2554, 2603; and Carter, pp. 216–17.

46. The Methodists having first taken the lead, the Moravians, Baptists, Congregationalists and Presbyterians, in concert, denounced the "white" incursions against Cherokee tribal lands and individual rights, attacks that became especially aggressive after the discovery of gold on Cherokee land in 1828. These Christian missionary workers "attached value to intermarriage as a force for improvement" (Wilkins, pp. 35, n. 58, 202–3, 219).

In 1815, William H. Crawford of Georgia, Secretary of War in Madison's cabinet, proposed a policy of merger by intermarriage of European-Americans and American Indians (see Introduction, n. 54). See Wilkins, p. 145, citing *Christian Herald*, Vol. 10, p. 468 (20 December 1823).

47. Wilkins, p. 145, citing *Christian Herald*, Vol. 10, p. 468 (20 December 1823).

48. "The [Scots] invasion [of Ireland] by Edward Bruce in 1315 has been recognized as the turning point of English influence in medieval Ireland" (G. H. Orpen, *Ireland Under the Normans*, 4 vols [Oxford, 1911–20], 4:160).

49. In a Gaelic-language article, a modern Franciscan historian, Canice Mooney (Cainneach O Maonaigh) finds in this Anglo-Norman policy a "racist" precedent of what occurred "yesterday in Birmingham, Alabama, or earlier in Sharpeville, South Africa" ("Racialism and nationalism in the Irish church, 1169–1534," *Galvia*, 10:4–17 [1954]). I am indebted to Brother Quinn of Iona College for translating this article for me. F. X. Martin characterizes Mooney's article as an "Irish nationalist interpretation" ("John, Lord of Ireland, 1185–1216," in *A New History*, 2:147, n. 3). The abbreviation *A New History* is used throughout this work to refer to *A New History of Ireland, under the auspices of the Royal Irish Academy*, planned and established by the late T. W. Moody 10 vols (Oxford, 1976–), of which all but vols 1, 6, and 7 were published as of 1992. The volumes composed by a select group of Irish scholars, are variously edited thus far by Art Cosgrove, T. W. Moody, F X. Martin, F J. Byrne, W. E. Vaughan. The citations will note the name of the contributor and the contribution, with locations cited by volume number and page number.

50. Jocelyn Otway-Ruthven, "The Request of the Irish for English Law, 1277–80," *Irish Historical Studies*, 6:261–70 (1948–49), pp. 264–5; Jocelyn Otway-Ruthven, "The Native Irish and English Law in Medieval Ireland," *Irish Historical Studies*, 7:1–16 (1950–51), pp. 14–15.

51. Sir John Davies, *A Discovery of the True Causes why Ireland was never Entirely Subdued ...* (London, 1612; 1969) p. 116. Orpen noted that Davies's comment was even more applicable to the earlier rejection of the Irish petition for enfranchisement (*Orpen*, 4:23, n. 3).

52. Edmund Curtis and R. B. McDowell, eds, "Remonstrance of the Irish Princes to Pope John XXII, 1317," in *Irish Historical Documents* (London, 1943), p. 41.

53. Otway-Ruthven, "Native Irish and English Law," p. 6. The complaint of the Irish "free" classes of the thirteenth century was despairingly echoed five centuries and three conquests later, during the early years of the Penal Laws era, by a Gaelic poet raging against a trinity of oppressions: the poverty from which escape was forbidden; the systemic frustration of all hope of social recognition; and, above all, "the contempt that follows it, for which there is no cure" (cited and translated in T. W. Moody and J. C. Beckett, *Ulster Since 1800, second series, a social survey* [London, 1957], p. 171).

Daniel O'Connell, looking back in about 1815, reminisced: "It was easy to tell a Catholic in the streets by his subdued demeanour and crouching walk. So deeply had the iron of oppression entered into their souls" (a paraphrase given by Robert Dunlop, *Daniel O'Connell* [New York, 1908], p. 45).

54. Speaking of kinship societies in general, Orlando Patterson says, "Land was corporately owned" (Patterson, *Slavery and Social Death*, p. 241). A fairly recent comprehensive bibliography makes it manifest that the central problem of "land reform" in colonial, neo-colonial and post-colonial Africa is the conversion from tribal land ownership to individual (corporate or personal) title (*Land Tenure and Agrarian Reform in Africa and the Near East: an Annotated Bibliography*, compiled by the staff of the

Land Tenure Center Library, Madison, Wisconsin, under the direction of Teresa Anderson, Librarian [Boston, 1976]). For the view of an early Pan-Africanist and pioneer of "African socialism," see J. E. Casely-Hayford (African name, Ekra Agiman), *The Truth about the West African Land Question* (London, 1971), with an Introduction by E. U. Essien-Udom, Department of Political Science, University of Ibadan. Casely-Hayford (Ekra Agiman) was "a member of the Anona clan, Ghana." "He was not opposed to modernization as such, but he wanted it to take place within the framework of 'African humanism'" (Professor Essien-Udom's Introduction). See also the Senate testimony of Major J. W. Powell of the American Bureau of Ethnology, Smithsonian Institution, at hearings on the Allotment Act of 1881 (Washburn, pp. 1751–2). The Irish case is discussed at length below.

55. The term and concept "social death," credit for which is given to Michel Izard, was used in a seminar on slavery in pre-colonial Africa held in Paris in 1971 under the auspices of the Institut international africain. Orlando Patterson found it appropriate to his general critique of slavery, to which he gave the title *Slavery and Social Death*. See Claude Meillassoux, ed., *L'Esclavage en Afrique précoloniale* (Paris, 1975), pp. 21–2.

56. The quoted phrases are in Meillassoux, p. 21.

57. "… colonists soon enough develop a sense of their own interests" (Liam de Paor, *Divided Ulster* [Harmondsworth, 1970], p. 24).

58. See Appendix C.

59. "By the sixteenth century, for example, much of the land of Europe was in the private possession of a landowning class. In West Africa, even today, most of the land is not so divided" (Basil Davidson with F. K. Bush and the advice of Ade Adayi, *A History of West Africa to the Nineteenth Century* [New York, 1966], p. 176).

See also Williams, *Hierarchical Structures and Social Value*, pp. 55–6.

60. Orlando Patterson, "Slavery and Slave Revolts: A Sociological Analysis of the First Maroon War, 1665–1740," in Richard Price, ed., *Maroon Societies*, p. 283. Patterson's article was originally published in *Social and Economic Studies*, 19:289–325 (1970).

In contrasting the situation of the African captives and the American Indians in the Anglo-American colonies, Phillips notes that the former were more vulnerable because "they were completely broken from their tribal stems" (Ulrich Bonnell Phillips, *Life and Labor in the Old South* [Boston: Little, Brown and Company, 1929], p. 160).

61. "The chief circumstance upon which the planters based their hope of security was the diversity of language and race among the negroes" (Vincent T. Harlow, *A History of Barbados, 1625–1685* [Oxford, 1926], p. 325). See Patterson, "Slavery and Slave Revolts," pp. 256, 261, 263, 282–3.

62. After the war against the Powder River Sioux in 1866, General John Pope testified on the basis of his own personal participation in this cynical program of spoliation of the Indian: "… the peace commissioners promise the Indians, in the first place, that the whites shall not go into the Indian country, knowing well that it is impossible to fulfill any promise of the sort; the parties who make these treaties know they must be broken; I have broken them, and I have known for twelve months that war would come out of it" (Washburn, *American Indian and the United States*, pp. 1508, 1522).

63. Ibid., pp. 1134, 1158. In December 1827 the Georgia legislature nullified the treaty-based land rights of the Cherokees and declared them tenants-at-will subject to dispossession by the colonists (Wilkins, *Cherokee Tragedy*, p. 196). This reduction of natives to colonial tenants-at-will was a re-enactment of the treatment of the native Irish under the Plantation of Ulster (see Chapter 5). Ulster Protestant settlers were numerous in the original Cherokee territory, but whatever record there may be of contemporary references to this parallel has escaped this author.

64. Washburn, p. 2484.

65. Ibid., quoting an editorial in the St Louis *Republican*.

66. Ibid., p. 1752.

67. Ibid., p. 68.

68. Ibid., p. 1230.

69. Ibid., p. 1429.

70. Haymarket Square in Chicago was the scene of a rally on 4 May 1886, held in support of the eight-hour-day campaign and specifically to protest the police brutality against an assembly of strikers on the previous day. A large contingent of armed police came to stop the meeting. A bomb went off, resulting in the death of eight of the police. Eight anarchist leaders were convicted, who became known to labor history as the "Haymarket martyrs." Of the eight, four were hanged and one died in jail, a suicide it was said. In 1893, the remaining three were freed from prison by Illinois Governor Peter Altgeld, who declared that they had been tried unfairly.

In the United States the term "robber barons" is applied to capitalist entrepreneurs who, in the latter part of the nineteenth century, accumulated (and occasionally lost) vast fortunes by unabashed fraud, bribery and force, including the brutal repression of working-class resistance. There were railroad barons, timber barons and cattle barons, who were licensed by a corrupt Congress and state legislatures to privatize (as today's Conservatives would say) public lands taken by force and fraud from Indian tribes, and to loot the public treasury. They enacted a reversion to the primitive accumulation period of the English enclosures of the sixteenth century and the plunder of Aztec and Inca treasures by the conquistadors. The reader is referred to the old but still champion history of this United States phenomenon, Gustavus Myers, *History of the Great American Fortunes* (New York, 1907, republished 1937). See also Matthew Josephson, *The Robber Barons: The Great American Capitalists, 1861–1901* (New York, 1934).

71. Washburn, 1:422. Morgan's views can be found in ibid., pp. 1:424–5.

72. Graven in my consciousness is the caution offered by Professor Eoin MacNeill regarding "the sort of fallacy common enough when the history of a nation or description of its customs is undertaken by foreigners" (Eoin MacNeill, *Celtic Ireland* [Dublin, 1921], p. 116). I am a student of

Irish history, but not a scholar in it as those whose works I cite are. I have tried to stay clear of controversies in this field. In some instances, where it appears that I am involved willy-nilly, I have sought to present the contrary views fairly, and to defend my own. My focus here is always on the nature and extent of the structural differences. between the Anglo-Norman social order and the Gaelic–Celtic social order as they confronted each other in Ireland – and their significance for an understanding of racial oppression.

73. D. A. Binchy, "Ancient Irish Law," *Irish Jurist*, new series, 1:85–92 (1966), p. 89. Estimates of the number of *tuaths* for later periods may reflect a demise of weaker tribes, as cattle raids concentrated wealth in the hands of the strong tribes (Kenneth Nicholls, "Gaelic Society and Economy in the High Middle Ages," in *A New History*, 2:414–15.

74. Professor Eoin MacNeill, who made some of the most important investigations of the records of ancient Ireland argued that the term "tribe" should not be applied to early Irish society because he thought it invidiously suggested a comparison with the societies found among the "Australian or Central African aborigines" in the modern day (Eoin MacNeill, *Phases of Irish History* [Dublin, 1919], pp. 288–9; Eoin MacNeill, *Early Irish Laws and Institutions* [Dublin, 1935], pp. 24–5). MacNeill categorized the ancient Irish as "European white men" (*Celtic Ireland*, Preface). P. W. Joyce regularly used the term "tribe," although he made reference only to "Aryan" parallels (*A Social History of Ancient Ireland* [1913], 1:167). Kenneth Nicholls, however, points a footnote at an African parallel ("Gaelic Society and Economy in the High Middle Ages," p. 425). Students of early Irish history will recognize the validity of the parallels with Africa apparent in *Land Tenure and Agrarian Reform in Africa and the Near East*, the bibliography cited in n. 54.

Other Irish historians, before and after MacNeill, who have found the terms "tribe" and "tribal" appropriate include: D. A. Binchy, cited above, n. 73; W. K. Sullivan ("permission of the tribe council"), cited by his contemporary George Sigerson at p. 8 of *History of the Land Tenures and Land Classes of Ireland with an account of the Various Secret Agrarian Confederacies* (London, 1871), a work recommended highly by MacNeill; Sigerson himself ("another tribe" [ibid., p. 9]); Alexander George Richey, ed., *Ancient Laws of Ireland* (Dublin and London, 1879), Vol. Vl, Glossary (*fine* = "tribe"; "it is probably impossible to use any word in translation that will not be liable to a misconception; the translator renders it mostly by tribe, but also by family"); ibid., Vol. IV. *Brehon Law Tracts*, p. cxvii ("a system of tribe law"); Standish O'Grady, in "The Last Kings of Ireland," *English Historical Review*, 4:286–303 (1899), uses "tribe," "tribal," "clan"; Irish Texts Society, *A Smaller Irish– English Dictionary, for the Use of Schools* (1932) (*fine* = "tribe; family"); and *A New History*, 8:11 (*tuath* = "people, tribe, tribal kingdom ...").

75. Gearoid Mac Niocaill, *Ireland Before the Vikings* (Dublin, 1972), p. 67; Nicholls, pp. 397–8.

76. In Gaelic Ireland in the sixteenth century, the chiefs exercised their privileges in the matter of the customary land redistribution in ways that "tended to concentrate land ownership" in their own hands. Furthermore, the conveyance of land rights, by inheritance or otherwise, was subject to such heavy assessments by the chiefs that the land in question often passed into the hands of the chief. Most common of all was the takeover of lands that the landholder had mortgaged to a chief (lord) for stock. If the charges were not met, the client (tenant) lost his holding. Whilst the tenant had a theoretical right to pay up and reclaim his land, "the conditions for redemption were ... often virtually impossible of fulfillment" (D. B. Quinn and K. W. Nicholls, "Ireland in 1534," in *A New History*, 2:34–5). See also: Joyce, 1:186–7; and George Sigerson, pp. 6–7.

77. Joyce, 1:156–60,1:194–5.

78. Mac Niocaill, pp. 68–9.

79. Joyce, 1:163–4.

80. Ibid., 1:193, 1:195. Mac Niocaill, pp. 63, 65.

81. For all its Gaelic appearance, the term *betagh* does not seem to have appeared until it was used by the Anglo-Norman settlers to describe the native Irish of the laboring classes, who like the English villein (serf) were *adscriptus glebae*, that is, not free tenants for a term of years or at-will, but bound hereditarily to the land of their lord.

82. This section on the *derbfine* is based on (1) Mac Niocaill, pp. 49–53; (2) MacNeill, *Celtic Ireland*, p. 151; (3) MacNeill, *Phases of Irish History*, pp. 296–7; and (4) Sigerson, pp. 8–11.

83. "This constitution of the clans was one of the evils of ancient Ireland. It weakened the power of the kings or supreme chieftains" (James Henthorne Todd, ed., *The War of the Gaedhil with the Gaill; or the Invasion of Ireland by the Danes and other Norsemen* [originally a twelfth-century work], in *Chronicles and Memorials of Great Britain and Ireland during the Middle Ages* [London, 1867], vol. 48, p. cxviii).

84. See Joyce, 1:187–8, 2:282–4, for a discussion of the practical arrangements for sharing the use of common lands.

85. Standish O'Grady, "The Last Kings of Ireland," pp. 287, 291. This view is supported by Brian Cuiv in *The Course of Irish History* (Cork, 1967), pp. 120–22; and by F J. Byrne, "The Trembling Sod," in *A New History*, 2:4–5.

86. In 1155, or within a few years thereafter. Pope Adrian, the only Englishman ever elected pope, in an act that came to be known as the Donation of Adrian granted Ireland to Henry II and commanded the Irish to submit to the English king. Rome was particularly interested in rooting out unacceptable practices by the Celtic clergy, such as rejection of celibacy, and the hereditary succession to office. In parallel with the temporal authorities, this pope intended to secure "the abandonment of features of Gaelic society going back to pre-Christian times" (F. X. Martin, "Diarmait Mac Murchada and the Coming of the Anglo-Normans," in *A New History*, p. 56).

87. Kathleen Hughes, Introduction to Jocelyn Otway-Ruthven, *A History of Medieval Ireland* (New York, 1986), p. 14.

88. Otway-Ruthven, *History of Medieval Ireland*, p. 102. It is interesting to note that during the Norse

occupations of parts of Ireland, from the end of the eighth century to the middle of the eleventh, though many were the battles between the "Gaedhil" and the "Gaill," the Irish and the foreigners, land tenure principles were not at issue. Possibly that was in part due to the fact that the Scandinavians were primarily raiders and traders rather than cultivators. But it would seem equally due to the fact that "The Norse system [of land tenure] resembled the Irish in a marked manner" (Sigerson, p. 12).

The French views of land tenure certainly differed from those of the Algonkian people inhabiting Canada in the two centuries after the French made their first appearance on that coast in 1504. But since the French were soon primarily concerned first with fishing and then with the fur trade, their relations with the Algonkians were little troubled by land tenure issues (Gary B. Nash, *Red, White, and Black: The Peoples of Early America* [Englewood Cliffs, NJ, 1974], pp. 107–8). See also Alfred G. Bailey, *The Conflict of European and Algonkian Cultures. 1504–1800* (St John, New Brunswick, 1937), and William Eccles, *The Canadian Frontier, 1534–1670* (New York, 1969).

89. R. E. Glasscock, "Land and People, c. 1300," in *A New History*, 2:226.

90. Mac Niocaill cites an instance of annual rent on twenty-four milk cows; it included: one cow, three calves, a pig, a sheep, cream and butter, a flitch of salt pork, lard, suet, and three handfuls of candles (*Ireland Before the Vikings*, p. 64). P. W. Joyce noted a later record which showed the tenant paying an annual rent of one animal for every seven (*Social History of Ancient Ireland*, 1:188–9).

91. MacNeill, *Celtic Ireland*, p. 169.

92. "In Anglo-Norman society ... all land was held of someone, of the king in chief, or of someone on a ladder leading to the king." (The major exception – Church land – was to disappear under Henry VIII.) The settlers "had no interest in the theoretical basis of Irish land-tenure, and were fully aware of having overthrown the Irish order." The quotations are from Mac Niocaill, *Irish Jurist*, new series, 1:293 (1966).

93. MacNeill, *Celtic Ireland*, p. 170.

94. See Hughes, pp. 4–14.

95. Speaking of warring by cattle raids, O'Grady writes, "ownership of land divested of cattle or other exchangeable property meant subjugation; permanent military occupation of such territory was not necessary" (O'Grady, p. 300). So it remained three centuries later, and these wars involved "rent and tribute ... [but] little interference in the internal affairs of the tributary" (O'Domhnaill, "Warfare in Sixteenth-century *Ireland*," *Irish Historical Studies*, 5 [1946–47]: 29–54, p. 29). See also Mac Niocaill, pp. 53, 54. MacNeill, *Celtic Ireland*, p. 122.

96. Mac Niocaill, p.54.

97. Early Brehon Law provided that orphan brotherless "daughters should obtain all the land with obligation to perform service of attack and defence, or the half of it, without obligation to perform service of attack and defence; and there is a power over them to compel them to restore the land after their time" (Alexander George Richey, ed., *Ancient Laws of Ireland*, vol . IV, *Brehon Law Tracts* [Dublin, 1879], p. 41). Under this law, the woman

would seem to have had no heirs, so that, upon her death, her land "fell back into the common fund of land out of which it had been taken" (Richey's Introduction, p. cxix). Mac Niocaill, referring to a later period (the latter half of the seventh century), suggests that this return to the common fund was made by way of the woman's son or sons, if she had any, or otherwise the "nearest male member" of the kinship group (*Ireland Before the Vikings*, p. 52).

98. Ibid., p. 58.

99. D. A. Binchy, *Crith Gablach* (Dublin, 1941), pp. 80–81. Noting that when women married they "passed to their husband's *fine* for the duration of the marriage," Mac Niocaill adds parenthetically, "some marriages were merely temporary arrangements" (*Ireland Before the Vikings*, p. 51).

100. Ibid., pp. 55, 58.

101. For this characterization of English family custom, I have relied on Lawrence Stone, *The Crisis of the Aristocracy, 1556–1641* (London, 1967), pp. 594–605. See also John P. Prendergast, *The Cromwellian Settlement of Ireland* (New York, 1868), pp. 17–18.

102. Mac Niocaill, pp. 58–9. Etymological note: "gossipred" is derived from "god-sib," god-child.

103. The practice of the stronger party demanding and holding hostages of the weaker one was regular in these times, Ireland being no exception. See O'Grady, "The Last Kings of Ireland," pp. 292, 294, 297, 301. Ordinary captives were a source of wealth, according to O'Grady, "for war captives were then [in the 12th century] sold into slavery" (p. 302).

104. G. J. Hand, *English Law in Ireland, 1290–1324* (Cambridge, 1967), p. 202.

105. Sir John Davies, *A Discovery of the True Causes why Ireland was never entirely Subdued, nor brought under Obedience of the Crowne of England, Untill the Beginning of his Majesties happie Raigne* (London, 1612).

Despite his anti-Irish bias, Davies brought to his task experience as a lawmaker and colonial administrator, a good literary style, a legal concern for precision, and a reverence for history. This work of some three hundred pages ranks in these respects with Francis Bacon's *History of the Reign of King Henry VII.*

106. *Discovery of the True Causes ...*, p. 167.

107. Ibid., pp. 167–8.

108. Ibid., p. 169.

109. Ibid., pp. 170–73.

110. Ibid., p. 182.

111. Ibid., pp. 174, 179.

112. F. X. Martin, "Diarmait Macmurchada," pp. 57–9.

113. F. X. Martin, "Overlord Becomes Feudal Lord, 1172–85," in *A New History*, 2:111; F.X. Martin, "John, Lord of Ireland, 1185–1216", in *A New History*, 2:128.

114. Martin, "Diurmait Macmurchada," pp. 64, 65; Martin, "Overlord," p. 117.

115. Otway-Ruthven, *History of Medieval Ireland*, p. 102. As is often noted, the chronicle of Giraldus Cambrensis (Gerald of Wales – who accompanied King John to Ireland in 1185) both recorded and concurred with the supercilious and disdainful Anglo-Norman references to

the Irish and their way of life. But that cannot explain the English resort to racial oppression in Ireland; sooner or later, the same chauvinistic attitude was directed by the English at the Welsh and the Scots, in whose countries a fundamentally different system of English domination was instituted.

116. Davies, p. 116.

117. See Martin, "John, Lord of Ireland," pp. 147, 150–53.

118. Immanuel Wallerstein, *The Modern World-System: Capitalist Agriculture and the Origins of the European World-Economy in the Sixteenth Century* (New York, 1974), pp. 68–9.

119. Martin, "John, Lord of Ireland," pp. 150–51.

120. Ibid., p. 153.

121. In insisting on the relevance of the parallel between incidents so widely separated in time, I appeal to the example of the Irish historian James C. Beckett. Speaking of the resentment felt by the Anglo-Irish toward English "newcomers," Beckett argues: "This parallel between the fourteenth century and the eighteenth is not merely adventitious. It indicates a real continuity of tradition.... The constitutional programme of the Anglo-Irish patriots in the reign of George III was consciously derived from precedents set by the 'English in Ireland' three or four hundred years earlier" (J. C. Beckett, *The Anglo-Irish Tradition* [Ithaca, 1976], p. 25).

122. See Introduction, n. 16.

123. Hand, p. 194.

124. Ibid., p. 188.

125. Phillips, *Life and Labor in the Old South*, p. 162.

126. John P. Prendergast, *The Cromwellian Settlement of Ireland*, second, enlarged edition (Dublin, 1875), p. 21, n. 2.

127. 4 Hening 132–3 (1723).

128. Hand, pp. 201–2.

129. "Remonstrance of the Irish Princes to Pope John XXII," 1317, p. 43.

130. *Neale v. Farmer* in *Reports of Cases in Law and Equity Argued and Determined in the Supreme Court of the State of Georgia from August 1850–May 1851*, Thomas R. Cobb, reporter, Vol. IX (Athens, Georgia, 1851), pp. 555–84. The court, far from considering this fact a loophole in the law, held it an indispensable principle because, "If [the Common Law] protects the life of the slave, why not his liberty? and if it protects his liberty, then it breaks down at once the *status* of the slave" (p. 579). The same principle had been written into law in colonial Virginia in 1723 (4 Hening 133).

131. Prendergast, p. 2, n. 1, citing Sir John Davies, *Discovery of the True Causes ...*

132. Washburn, *The American Indian and the United States*, pp. 2669–70, 2676. The Dred Scott decision rendered by the United States Supreme Court in 1857 held that Negroes were not citizens of the United States, and in the words of Chief Justice Roger B. Taney, had "no rights which a white man is bound to respect" (Richard D. Heffner, *A Documentary History of the United States, An Expanded Edition* [New York, 1956], p. 131).

133. 4 Hening 326–7 (1732).

134. J. C. Beckett, *A Short History of Ireland* (New York, 1968), p. 22; Orpen, *Ireland Under the Normans*, 4:259–60;

Otway-Ruthven, "Native Irish and English Law," p. 3; Otway-Ruthven, "Anglo-Irish Shire Government in the Thirteenth Century," *Irish Historical Studies*, 5:1–7 (1946).

135. Otway-Ruthven, "Native Irish and English Law," p. 6.

136. Douglas Hall, "Jamaica," in Cohen and Greene, eds, *Neither Slave Nor Free*, p. 201; Charles Edward Chapman, *Colonial Hispanic America*, pp. 118–19.

137. Hand, p. 207. Compare Otway-Ruthven, "Native Irish and English Law," pp. 6–7.

138. The eclipse of English power in Ireland in the fourteenth and fifteenth centuries, touched only in passing in this chapter, is dealt with in Chapter 2.

139. *Hansard Parliamentary Debates*, 2d series, vol. 72 (1844), 1172. The subject was "The State of Ireland."

140. Sean O'Domhnaill, "Warfare in Sixteenth-century Ireland," p. 46.

141. Ibid., p. 30.

142. Sigerson, *History of Land Tenures*, pp. 24–5.

143. Aidan Clarke, "The Irish Economy, 1600–60," in *A New History*, 3:169–70. The word "plantation," as found in this work, has two meanings, derived from two kinds of "planting": the planting of colonies of settlers, and the planting of agricultural crops. The British Board of Trade was for a time called, in the first sense, the "Lords of Trade and Plantations." In the Anglo-American context the term acquired its second meaning. There, at first, the term "plantation colonies" had the same colonial connotation as it did with regard to the plantation of Ulster. In time, the terms "plantation" and "plantation system" came to refer to a system of agricultural operations producing staple crops on large tracts of privately owned land.

144. J. C. Beckett, *The Anglo-Irish Tradition*, p. 131.

145. The "Act for the Settling of Ireland," commonly called the Act of Settlement, was passed on 12 August 1652 (*Statutes and Ordinances of the Interregnum, 1642–1660*, collected and edited by C. H. Firth and R. S. Raitt, 2 vols [London, 1911], 2:598–603).

The full title of the Act of Satisfaction is informative: "An Act for the speedy and effectual Satisfaction of the Adventurers [London merchants and other capitalists backers of the English war effort] for Lands in Ireland, and of the [English] Soldiers there, and of other Publique Debts, and for the Encouragement of Protestants to plant and inhabit Ireland" (ibid., 2:722).

146. Vincent Gookin, *The Great Case of Transplantation in Ireland Discussed; or Certain Considerations, wherein the many great inconveniences in the transplanting the Natives of Ireland generally out of the three provinces of Leinster, Ulster, and Munster, into the Province of Connaught, are shewn* (London, 1655), p. 26.

147. Richard Lawrence, *The Interest of England in the Irish Transplantation, Stated ... Being chiefly intended as An Answer to a scandalous seditious Pamphlet, intituled, The great case of Transplantation, discussed* (Dublin, 1655), p. 12.

148. Ibid., p. 25.

149. According to William Petty, the native Irish population of about 850,000 was reduced to around 700,000 in

the course of the war. Gardiner estimates that some 180,000 were males twenty-five years of age or older. According to Petty, 35,000–40,000 Irish soldiers, that is, approximately one-sixth of the adult male population, were sold abroad to serve in the armies of Spain, France, Flanders, etcetera (William Petty, *The Political Anatomy of Ireland* [1672] in Charles Henry Hull, ed., *The Economic Writings of Sir William Petty*, 2 vols [1899; New York, 1963], p. 150; Samuel Rawson Gardiner, "The Transplantation to Connaught," *English Historical Review*, 14:700–734 [October 1899], p. 703; Gookin, *The Great Case of Transplantation*, p. 22). Spain was probably the chief first destination of these transported men under conduct of their officers. Many were abandoned there among a hostile population. Of those enrolled in actual Spanish units, thousands deserted to France because of neglect and ill-treatment suffered under the Spanish. Some were shipped to be sold as plantation bond-laborers in Barbados, St Christopher and elsewhere, possibly Virginia in Anglo-America (Richard Bagwell, *Ireland under the Stuarts and during the Interregnum* 3 vols, [London, 1909], pp. 2:303–4, 2:310; A. E. Smith, *Colonists in Bondage: White Servitude and Convict Labor in America, 1607–1776* [Chapel Hill, 1947; New York, 1971], pp. 163–5; *The Petty Papers: Some Unpublished Writings of Sir William Petty*, edited from the Bowood Papers by the Marquis of Lansdowne, 2 vols in 1 [London, 1927; New York, 1967], p. 2:229; Philip Alexander Bruce, *Economic History of Virginia in the Seventeenth Century, An Inquiry into the Material Conditions of the People based upon Original and Contemporaneous Records*, 2 vols [New York, 1895; reprinted 1935], pp. 1:608–9).

Rather than be the primary financier of the process, the Parliamentary government worked through intermediaries, former Irish officers, English officers willing to invest in it as a business proposition, or enterprising Spanish officers, but with the King of Spain as the main ultimate payer (Robert Dunlop, ed., *Ireland under the Commonwealth, Being a Selection of Documents Relating to the Government of Ireland from 1651 to 1659* [Manchester, 1913], 2 vols; 1:177, 1:238, 2:310, 2:430; Bagwell, 2:303; Day's Proceedings, Council of State, 10 December 1652 and 9 April 1653, Great Britain Public Record Office, *Calendar of State Papers, Domestic, 1652–53*). So eager was the English government to dispose of these Irish fighters that when the Spanish Crown, or some other customer or merchant, failed to make prompt payment, the government would underwrite the process to keep it moving (Dunlop, 2:310, 2:370). During the war launched by Cromwell against Spain for the West Indies in 1655, no Irish could be sent to Spain, but, by that time the process had been completed to the general satisfaction of the English government. In August 1657, Oliver Cromwell himself, writing to the Lord Deputy and Council in Ireland, appears to be concerned only with seeing to it that proper financial settlements be made with those shippers and contractors who were unpaid as a result of the war "between us and the Spaniard" (ibid., 2:669–70). The following year, after Oliver's death, his son and

successor Richard Cromwell, in the course of discussing the same subject of unresolved debts, speaks of the advantage that had been gained by "transporting into Spain very great numbers of Irish soldiers, pestering our good people of Ireland and endangering the peace of that nation" (Richard Cromwell to the Lord Deputy and Council [in Ireland], 9 November 1658, ibid., 2:689–90).

150. Gookin, pp. 22, 26.

151. Prendergast, *Cromwellian Settlement of Ireland*, p. 98. "The object was to de-grade the evicted upper-tenant or landlord to a lower condition ... of cultivators" (Sigerson, *History of Land Tenures*, p. 80).

152. Aidan Clarke, *The Old English in Ireland, 1625–1642* (London, 1966), pp. 26, 236; Aidan Clarke, "Irish Economy, 1600–60," p. 169; Karl S. Bottigheimer, *English Money and Irish Land: The "Adventurers" in the Cromwellian Settlement of Ireland* (Oxford, 1971), p. 5, n. 1.

153. For the provisions of the Act of Settlement, see Firth and Raitt; and Gardiner, "Transplantation to Connaught."

154. W. F. T. Butler, *Confiscation in Irish History* (London, 1918), pp. 132, 156. Butler (p. 156) says that in 1641 Catholic landowners numbered at least eight thousand, or even twelve thousand. Clarke, on the other hand, says that the total of all "proprietors" could not have been more than six thousand, of whom about four thousand were Old English or Irish, presumably Catholics (Clarke, "Irish Economy, 1600–60," p. 170). A possible clue to the discrepancy may be supplied by Butler (p. 198, n. 59). Speaking of two thousand Catholics who were assigned Connaught land, he said that, "possibly many of these had only been tenants or leaseholders in 1641." Perhaps Clarke's "freeholders" do not include tenants. While in England and in Ireland most English were "freeholders" having hereditary leases, Catholic tenants generally did not have hereditary leases; they were tenants, but not freeholders. Perhaps the Butler and the Clarke figures can be reconciled on this basis. I have chosen to use Butler's in this instance, but a picture of mass expropriation is indicated in either case, and is corroborated by all historians of the period. J. G. Simms's criticisms of Butler's estimates, whatever their validity, do not impair the argument being made here as to the significance of the massive expropriation of Catholic lands (J. G. Simms, "Land Owned by Catholics in Ireland in 1688," *Irish Historical Studies*, 7:180–90 [1950–51]).

155. As a further concession to their religio-racial status, Protestants were later allowed to pay money fines instead of forfeiting lands. But they combined to spurn even that condition, and in the end the English government simply left them alone (Dunlop, 1:cxlix–cl.)

156. Dunlop, 1:cxlvi. The history of the continuous transplantation of the American Indians by the United States government, which began with the Indian Removal Act of 1832, was in many respects a virtual re-enactment of the transplantation to Connaught.

157. Butler, pp. 157–8. "The number of transplantees who finally held land west of the Shannon ... [was] above 580" (ibid., pp. 198–9).

158. The data for Catholic-held land presented in this paragraph are drawn from Butler, especially p. 162; and Simms, especially pp. 180, 182, 189–90. Of the total land, about seven out of every ten acres (71 per cent) were profitable (Simms, p. 180, citing William Petty). About five out of every eight acres of profitable land belonged to Catholics in 1641 (Butler, p. 162; Simms, pp. 180, 189).

159. Simms, pp. 182, 189.

160. The Irish historian and revolutionary martyr of 1916 James Connolly declared that Ireland lost this struggle because the Irish leaders refused "to raise the standard of the Irish nation instead of an English faction" (James Connolly, *Labour in Irish History* [New York, 1919], pp. 20–21).

161. Simms, pp. 189–90. After losing 615,000 (Irish) acres in the Williamite confiscations, the Catholics owned 1,086,000 acres. Simms says the Penal Law toll amounted to as much as the Williamite confiscations, indicating that by the middle of the eighteenth century only 471,000 of some 7.5 million acres of profitable land was still Catholic-owned. Butler, *Confiscation in Irish History*, says that the Williamite confiscations had already reduced the Catholic share to no more than one out of every twenty acres (p. 237). It is commonly accepted that Catholics owned only 5 per cent of the land at the close of the eighteenth century. Catholics made up four-fifths of the population of Ireland at the beginning of the eighteenth century (see p. 77).

162. Speech in the Irish Parliament in 1789. By this reminder, Fitzgibbon was warning his independence-minded fellow members of the Irish Parliament to reflect on the possible consequences of withdrawing from British authority (Quoted in E. M. Johnston, *Ireland in the Eighteenth Century* [Dublin, 1974], p. 161).

163. Prendergast, *Cromwellian Settlement*, pp. 180–81.

164. John Locke (1632–1704), son of a Cromwellian soldier, member of the Board of Trade and Plantations, and philosophic patron saint of the American and French Revolutions, endorsed the rationale of this anti-Catholic persecution. In the first of four famous *Letters on Toleration*, he excluded Roman Catholics from the right of toleration on the ground that they "deliver themselves up to the protection of a foreign prince … and [are] soldiers against the government."

165. Butler, p. 237.

36

The Science and Politics of Racial Research

WILLIAM H. TUCKER

The authors of 'objective'studies showing racial and genetic differences to justify social and economic differences between blacks and whites have sometimes been accused of perpetuating racist ideas. Certain studies presented as objective by some of the most prestigious intellectuals and educators in US society over many decades, have been utilized specifically for political purposes according to William H. Tucker. The author contends that sponsors and scholars participating in these studies may have been racists or civil libertarians and social liberals. Studies purporting to show how genetic difference is the basis for social status (and therefore racism is secondary or insignificant) have only served the political aims of those interests in power seeking to maintain a social and economic status quo. As the author claims, 'The truth is that though waged with scientific weapons, the goal in this controversy has always been political; indeed, the debate has no strictly scientific purpose or value' (p. 5). Furthermore, studies aimed at proving the intellectual or genetic inferiority of groups have only been used for 'oppressive and antisocial proposals'.

Introduction: To Make Nature an Accomplice

In 1947 Henry E. Garrett, full professor and chair of the Psychology Department at Columbia University, president at various times of the American Psychological Association, the Eastern Psychological Association, and the Psychometric Society, fellow of the American Association for the Advancement of Science, member of the National Research Council, and for ten years editor of the American Psychology Series, authored an article in the scholarly publication *Scientific Monthly* entitled "Negro-White Differences in Mental Ability in the United States." In support of his sharp disagreement with those who desired to explain away race differences as "somehow reprehensible and socially undesirable," Garrett cited a study of the comparative abilities of sixty-eight white and sixty black babies from two to eleven months old. Each baby had been given a series of mental tests constructed for use during the first two years of life from which a "developmental quotient"—essentially an infant IQ score—had been calculated. The average DQ for the white babies was 105, for the blacks, 92; the average DQ for the whites was higher than for the blacks at every age level, with the degree of superiority ranging from two to twenty-five points and averaging thirteen. From these results Garrett concluded that the blacks' consistently lower performance could not possibly be explained by a difference in environmental opportunities. In addition, he noted, the comparison of American whites with blacks, who frequently had some degree of mixed ancestry, did not represent "true racial differences." Garrett consequently expected an even greater disparity between the performance of African blacks and European whites.[1]

Perhaps mindful of the importance of finding these "true racial differences," some years later Hans J. Eysenck, world-renowned social scientist, founder and head of the Psychological Department and Laboratory at the Institute of Psychiatry of the University of London, and author of more than fifty books and hundreds of articles in professional journals, compared the performance of black African babies with white norms on measures of development. The African children showed a consistent precocity until age three, after which they fell behind white children. Like Garrett, Eysenck found it "implausible" that such an "astonishing difference" at the early ages could have been produced by "socio-economic differences or other extrinsic variables." The fact that these differences were opposite from those considered by Garrett did not prevent Eysenck from arriving at the same conclusion concerning blacks' innate inferiority. Eysenck found the superior performance of the black infants consistent with a little-known "general law in biology according to which the more prolonged the infancy, the greater in general are the cognitive or intellectual abilities of the species."[2]

In the United States we have come to take for granted the widespread manipulation that characterizes public media-centered culture. Every time we turn on television or look through a magazine, someone is trying to persuade us to buy a product, vote for a candidate, or adopt a point of view. But we also cherish the notion that there are safe, protected areas, oases of reason, effectively insulated from attempts to sell consumer goods or political ideologies. Here, where the atmosphere is less hysterical, calmer, more serious and reflective, scientific inquiries, disinterested in political agendas and influenced only by objective evidence, can transcend ideology in the pursuit of truth. Indeed, it is exactly on the basis of such disinterest that scientists stake their claim to public trust and respect.

There are, however, critics within the scientific community who maintain that much social research is somewhat less than a model of objective inquiry. George Albee, a professor of psychology at the University of Vermont, offered the following opinion in his address to an American Psychological Association conference as a recipient of the Award for Distinguished Contribution to Community Psychology:

I have come to believe that I have had the whole "scientific" process reversed. Instead of facts being useful as the objective building blocks of theories, rather it is more accurate to say that people, and especially social scientists, select theories that are consistent with their personal values, attitudes, and prejudices and then go out into the world or into the laboratory, to seek the facts that validate their beliefs about the world and about human nature, neglecting or denying observations that contradict their personal prejudices.[3]

These are strong words, but it is difficult to account in any other way for the identical conclusions of black inferiority Garrett and Eysenck derived from antithetical evidence.

Such consensus in the face of contradictory data is not an isolated occurrence in research on racial differences. When one scientist found at the turn of the century that blacks generally performed better than whites on tests of memory, he explained that their superior mnemonic ability was "naturally expected" since "in both races ... the memory is in decadence from primitive conditions, but ... the blacks are much nearer those conditions."[4] A decade later a famous English researcher found that on tests of memory the sons of the rich displayed "complete superiority" over the sons of the working class, a result that led him to the obvious conclusion that a disciplined memory was characteristic of greater intelligence.[5] Yet when a well-known contemporary psychologist found that poor and black children with low IQ scores had excellent memories, he concluded that memory should not properly be considered a component of "intelligence."[6]

Early demonstrations that blacks had a quicker reaction time than whites were also offered as proof that "the negro is, in the truest sense, a race inferior to that of the white" since faster reflexes were claimed to be a characteristic of lower intelligence. "Men, in proportion to their intellectuality," wrote a scientist who had found whites to react slower than both Indians and blacks, "should tend less and less to quickness of response in the automatic sphere."[7] But when research many years later showed faster reaction times for whites, this too became evidence for white intellectual superiority. Speed of reaction was now offered as an indication of "brain activity," and a leading social scientist even claimed (incorrectly) that Muhammad Ali had "a very average" reaction time.[8]

Though blacks have almost always performed lower than whites on paper-and-pencil tests, even the rare occasion on which they have scored higher has somehow also confirmed their inferiority. When two researchers found that blacks did better than whites on simple arithmetic problems, they explained that "the more complicated a brain, the more numerous its 'association fibers,' the less satisfactorily it performs the simple numerical problems which a calculating machine does so quickly and accurately."[9]

Differing evolutionary theories have also been able to produce identical conclusions about black inferiority. Many scientists in the 1920s claimed that blacks were the evolutionary predecessors of whites and that "Negroid stock," having evolved long before whites, was thus not only older but closer to its anthropoid ancestors, both physically and mentally; blacks were intellectually inferior to whites because they had evolved earlier.[10] A few decades later a distinguished anthropologist proposed that blacks had crossed the evolutionary threshold into homo sapiens long after other races and thus had had less time to develop; blacks were intellectually inferior because they had evolved later.[11]

Some studies of group differences have not violated the rules of logic as much as they have strained the bounds of credibility. In 1913 the famous psychologist Henry H. Goddard administered mental tests to a sample of newly arrived immigrants at Ellis Island, which had been carefully selected to omit both the "obviously feeble-minded" and the very few of "obviously high grade intelligence." In the group thus remaining—what Goddard called "the great mass of 'average immigrants,'"—he reported that 83 percent of Jews, 80 percent of Hungarians, 79 percent of Italians, and 87 percent of Russians were "feeble-minded." Probably anticipating the appropriate term for these results, Goddard informed his readers that "many a scientific discovery has seemed at first glance absurd." Nevertheless, he insisted, "it is never wise to discard a scientific result because of apparent absurdity," especially when it had come from a "fair and conscientious" analysis of the data.[12]

It appears Albee has not exaggerated. Although some of these examples might be dismissed as "cheap shots," egregious exceptions noteworthy by their contrast with more sober, restrained investigations that are the norm, many of them are not so much counterexamples to the mainstream as they are organic extensions of it. For over a century there have been scientists obsessed with proving that minorities, poor people, foreigners, and women are innately inferior to upper-class white males of northern European extraction.

Though some of these researchers have been overt racists, civil libertarians and social liberals have also been responsible for many foolish claims. Edward M. East, for example, a Harvard geneticist in the 1920s, "could see no reasonable excuse for oppression and discrimination on a colour-line basis … [and had] no sympathy with a regimen of repression on the part of the whites." He was positively outraged over someone "who is denied a seat in a Pullman car, a restaurant, a theatre, or a room in a college dormitory" due to the "gaucheries of a provincial people, on a par with the guffaws of a troop of yokels." Nevertheless, as a scientist, he concluded that blacks were physically as well as mentally inferior and had little of value to contribute to the higher white race. "Gene packets of African origin are not valuable supplements to the gene packets of European origin," wrote East; "it is the white germ plasm that counts."[13]

The scientific conflict over genetic differences between groups is now well into its second century. Unlike other, more traditional scientific controversies, in which the argument diminishes as new discoveries are made or as scientists with opposing views retire or die away,[14] the bitter dispute over race has arisen anew in each generation, to be debated all over again in almost exactly the same terms but with a fervor that seems more theological than scientific. Nor has the argument confined itself to academic journals and scientific conferences; the subject of racial differences has been debated in barrooms and cocktail parties and, for a scientific issue, has received unprecedented coverage in the popular press. Despite the length and intensity of the debate, however, there has been no significant advance in scientific knowledge. Although the techniques of data analysis have become increasingly sophisticated, the arguments on both sides have changed very little. Contemporary scientists often sound indistinguishable from their predecessors of thirty, sixty, or ninety years ago. More than a century of research has produced a lot of heat but virtually no light.

'NO POLITICAL, NO RELIGIOUS, AND NO SOCIAL PREJUDICES'

The truth is that though waged with scientific weapons, the goal in this controversy has always been political; indeed, the debate has no strictly scientific purpose or value. The question of genetic differences between races has arisen not out of purely scientific curiosity or the desire to find some important scientific truth or to solve some significant scientific problem but only because of the belief, explicit or unstated, that the answer has political consequences. The claim that one group is genetically less desirable or capable than another has invariably been part of what Marquis de Condorcet called an attempt "to make nature herself an accomplice of political inequality."[15] Rather than an injustice that needs to be rectified, social and political oppression thus becomes the rational—indeed, the unavoidable—reflection of natural differences.

The first suggestion that inequality should be based on nature occurred over two thousand years ago when Aristotle observed that "there are species in which a distinction is already marked, immediately at birth, between those of its members who are intended for being ruled and those who are intended to rule."[16] Applying an idiosyncratic technique for the measurement of individual differences—though one not all that different from the method used twenty-two hundred years later by the famous English scientist Sir Francis Galton— Aristotle distinguished those to be ruled as differing from others in power of reason "as the body differs from the soul, or an animal from a man," and he concluded that "it is thus clear that, just as some are by nature free, so others are by nature slaves, and for these latter the condition of slavery is both just and beneficial." [17]

Although Aristotle's reference to innate, empirically observable distinctions suggested a quasi-scientific justification for slavery—in Thomas Hobbes's words, "as if master and servant were not introduced by consent of men but by difference of wit" [18]—it was not until the nineteenth century that the linkage between science and politics was made explicit. At that time U.S. doctors and anthropologists began to assess intelligence through various anatomical and physiognomic characteristics in scientific attempts at a linear evaluation of racial and ethnic groups, and in England Galton began to study the dichotomization of nature and nurture that eventually led to the psychometric tradition. As these two lines of investigation merged at the turn of the century, a movement arose that attempted to derive moral and behavioral guidelines from what were claimed to be scientific-physicalist laws. Questions of human rights and freedoms—who should vote, who should be educated, who should have children, who should be allowed into the country—were transferred from their appropriate place in the domain of political discourse to the domain of science. In particular, an understanding of racial differences was claimed to be the key to social progress; public education, social harmony, national welfare, indeed the future of the species were all said to depend on it. What began as the study of hereditary characteristics thus quickly burgeoned into a presumptuous field marked by immodest pronouncements on the limits of democracy, the necessity of racial segregation, the futility of education, the biological inevitability of vast socioeconomic disparities, and the necessity for controlling the birthrate of certain groups.

The belief that the operation of science was synonymous with the termination of politics made appeals to scientific authority a powerful strategy for influencing public policy. Critics of the obsession with racial differences could easily be dismissed as emotional and unscientific, preferring sentimentality, idealism, and wishful thinking to the perhaps unpleasant but nonetheless undeniable truths that emerged from impartial data; the researchers had scientific objectivity and rigor on their side. As Karl Pearson, one of the greatest contributors to contemporary statistics, wrote in the introduction to a 1925 article on Jewish immigration to Great Britain, "We have no axes to grind, we have no governing body to propitiate by well advertised discoveries; we are paid by nobody to reach results of a given bias. We have no electors, no subscribers to encounter in the market place. We firmly believe that we have no political, no religious and no social prejudices.... We rejoice in numbers and figures for their own sake." [19] Thus unencumbered by bias of any kind or by political or economic pressure, Pearson was led, by the numbers and figures, to conclude that Jewish immigrants were mentally and physically inferior to the native English population, that the newcomers would develop into a "parasitic race," and that there was "no evidence that a lessening of the aliens' poverty, an improvement in their food, or an advance in their cleanliness will substantially alter their average grade of intelligence, and with it their outlook on life." Naturally, Pearson concluded, "there should be no place" in society for such a demonstrably inferior group, an opinion that was soon to be shared by the leaders of another European country. [20]

As a consequence of this viewpoint, for more than a century nature has been played as a trump card in political arguments on the side of repression. Sometimes scientists have only hinted at significant, and ominous, implications. The psychologist Lewis Terman, an early developer of the IQ test, insisted, for example, that a "less naive definition of ... democracy ... will have to square with the demonstrable facts of biological and psychological science." [21] More often, specific proposals have been offered, most of which are intolerable in a free society. When a medical journal reported the latest scientific finding in 1907—that the brain of blacks was "more animal in type and incapable of producing those thoughts which have built up civilization"—the editors found it "dreadful that we did not know these anatomical facts when we placed a vote in the possession of this brain which cannot comprehend its use" and hoped that it was not too late to deprive blacks of the franchise. [22] A popular 1933 scientific textbook opposed efforts to eradicate discrimination against blacks because these efforts ignored "biological and social facts." [23] A group of scientists in the late 1950s and 1960s attempted to overturn the unanimous Supreme Court verdict that struck down school segregation on the grounds that blacks were intellectually inferior to whites. The logic underlying all these proposals viewed political inequality as the natural consequence of biological inferiority; science should demonstrate the latter so society might have appropriate justification to implement the former. As one writer who opposed equality for blacks early in the century frankly admitted, unless blacks were "racially inferior," the "denial of ... equality appears as a colossal injustice, an immeasurable wrong." [24] The role of science was to confirm that no such injustice was taking take place.

Since the mid-1960s, in a social atmosphere much less tolerant of blatant deprivations of civil rights, the science of racial differences has encouraged more subtle political implications. For example, poverty among blacks was explained by some scientists as the economic consequence of natural inequality. Blacks' claims of continuing racial prejudice could thus be dismissed as "social para-. noia" since the real problem lay in their genes. As one well-known psychologist noted, "Failure to succeed is less apt to be perceived as personal failure if one identifies with a group which is claimed, justifiably or not, to be discriminated against. Having the status of an unprivileged caste, real or imagined, makes personal failure more tolerable."[25]

Some scientists also insisted that government programs of assistance to the poor, which had originated with Lyndon Johnson's War on Poverty, could be justified only if there were no genetic differences in ability between races. Thus, they argued, their "proof" that such differences did exist made these programs scientifically unsound.

Finally, even when the results of research have not been intended as justification for policies of repression and discrimination, they turn out to be made to order for the proponents of such policies. Whenever scientists have concluded some group to be genetically inferior, some of the investigators have wound up in either organizational or informal alliance with right-wing political groups, often fascists or racists who have been more than pleased to use scientific authority as a source of prestige for their own doctrines. The use of science for this purpose has generally been accomplished with the cooperation of, or at the very least without protest from, the scientists. That is, although it has usually been the ideologues in these coalitions who have fired the shots, the scientists have furnished the ammunition with no reservations over its use.

Though it might be argued that the political exploitation of scientific results is a *mis*use of science, the following chapters demonstrate that the effort to prove the innate intellectual inferiority of some groups has led *only* to oppressive and antisocial proposals; it has had no *other* use. Indeed, there is no "legitimate" application for such a finding. Even if there were convincing proof of genetic differences between races, as opposed to the flawed evidence that has been offered in the past, it would serve no purpose other than to satisfy curiosity about the matter. While the desire for knowledge, whether or not it has practical value, is not to be denigrated, a judicious use of our scientific resources would seem inconsistent with the pursuit of a goal that is probably scientifically chimerical and certainly lends itself to socially pernicious ends.

NOTES

1. H. E. Garrett, "Negro-White Differences in Mental Ability in the United States," *Scientific Monthly* 65 (1947): 329-33.

2. H. J. Eysenck, *The IQ Argument* (New York: Library Press, 1971), 79.

3. G. W. Albee, "The Politics of Nature and Nurture," *American Journal of Community Psychology* 65 (1982): 5.

4. G. R. Stetson, "Some Memory Tests of Whites and Blacks," *Psychological Review* 4 (1897): 288.

5. C. Burt, "Experimental Tests of General Intelligence," *British Journal of Psychology* 3 (1909): 143-44

6. A. R. Jensen, "What Is the Question? What Is the Evidence?" in *The Psychologists*, vol. 2, ed. T. S. Krawiec (New York: Oxford University Press, 1974), 222-25.

7. R. M. Bache, "Reaction Time with Reference to Race," *Psychological Reveiw* 2 (1895): 481, 479.

8. A. R. Jensen, "Techniques for Chronometric Study of Mental Abilities," in *Methodological and Statistical Advances in the Study of Individual Differences*, ed. C. R. Reynolds and V. L. Willson (New York: Plenum, 1985), 55.

9. C. B. Davenport and M. Steggerda, *Race Crossing in Jamaica* (Washington, D.C.: Carnegie Institute, 1929), 469.

10. See, for example, R. B. Bean, *The Races of Man* (New York: University Society, 1932), 30-37; and H. F. Osborn, "The Evolution of Human Races," *Natural History* 26 (January-February 1926): 5.

11. C. S. Coon, *The Origin of Races* (New York: Alfred A. Knopf, 1962).

12. H. H. Goddard, "Mental Tests and the Immigrant," *Journal of Delinquency* 2 (1917): 244, 266; the percentages appear in a table on 252.

13. E. M. East, *Heredity and Human Affairs* (New York: Charles Scribner's Sons, 1929), 200, 181, 199.

14. See T. S. Kuhn, *The Structure of Scientific Revolutions* (Chicago: University of Chicago Press, 1962).

15. A. N. de Condorcet, *Sketch for a Historical Picture of the Progress of the Human Mind*, trans. J. Barraclough (London: Weidenfeld and Nicolson, 1955 [1795]), 83.

16. E. Barker, *The Politics of Aristotle* (London: Oxford University Press, 1950), 14.

17. Ibid., 16, 17.

18. T. Hobbes, *Leviathan* (New York: Bobbs-Merrill, 1958 [1651]), 127.

19. K. Pearson and M. Moul, "The Problem of Alien Immigration into Great Britain Illustrated by an Examination of Russian and Polish Jewish Children," *Annals of Eugenics* 1 (1925): 8.

20. Ibid., 124, 125.

21. L. M. Terman, "The Psychological Determinist; or Democracy and the IQ," *Journal of Educational Research* 6 (1922): 62.

22. Unsigned editorial, *American Medicine* (April 1907): 197.

23. P. Popenoe and R. H. Johnson, *Applied Eugenics* (New York: Macmillan, 1933), 302.

24. W. B. Smith, *The Color Line* (New York: Negro Universities Press, 1969 [1905]), 71.

25. A. R. Jensen, "The Price of Inequality," *Oxford Review of Education* 1 (1975): 61.

37

The Racist Mind: Portraits
of American Neo-Nazis and Klansmen

RAPHAEL S. EZEKIEL

As the title of his book suggests, Ezekiel was interested in what goes on inside the head of members of racist organizations. Dubious about the value of formal theories of racism, Ezekiel set out to investigate empirically the experiences of people who subscribed to neo-Nazi beliefs in the mid-1990s. 'Racism is a way of perceiving the world and a way of thinking,' was how Ezekiel described his starting point. His account is informed by the view that it is impossible to exist in a culture in which racism is prevalent without being affected by it: 'It is important to discover the subtle ways our culture's racism has affected our thinking.'

His method was akin to an undercover investigator infiltrating the mob; though Ezekiel did not deceive his respondents. Over a decade, the researcher attended rallies and meetings and interviewed members of the Klan and other movements. He declared to them that he was Jewish and 'a leftist opposed to racism'. From this unpromising start, Ezekiel, in his words, 'tried to understand the life and thinking of the people I have met'. His results are quite different from those of, for example, Blaunder or Wellman, both of whom essayed similar aims: to make racism more comprehensible as a 'living' phenomenon – something that gives meaning to experience. Ezekiel's subjects were right at the fringe. His findings supply further proof that it is a mistake to assume that racism is a coherent belief system or that neo-Nazis constitute a homogeneous group.

Raymond

There was a mindlessness to Raymond's racism. He really didn't know who he was or why. Violence mattered, but so did foolish games, one-upmanship. He had the deep ignorance of the self-educated who think they know something.

The most important image he ever drew for me came as we talked about the group mission and the future as he saw it.

"When the race war breaks out ..." he began. "You run into this average middle-class American on the street, he's seen all these years of TV or he's had an uncle who fought in World War II or something, and they'll hand you back the leaflet and say,

'Oh, I don't want this.' When I meet someone like that, I reflect into the future. When the race riot breaks out—there's a date, it's already been predicted by some of the prophets of the white Christian churches, that it's going to come down in the near future. Okay, if I was in the city and say like the guy handed me back a piece of paper, my leaflet, I'd say that would make me feel bad. Because I know he'd know who I was when the race riot broke out, and I had my .22 or whatever and I'm trying to survive, and that same person that handed me back and said, 'I don't want to have anything to do with you, you people disgust me'—that same person will be expecting me to bite a bullet for him when the race war breaks out.

"And it makes me feel bad. Because as much as I hate to see a white brother die, I'm not going to bite the bullet for somebody like that."

It depressed him, he claimed smugly. Blacks were proud and unified, whereas whites had no pride, were "practically turned against their race by the propaganda they see on TV and in the media." But the race war would come, the ultimate race war. And the white masses simply wouldn't even think about it.

"They're so worried about their color TV and their new Cadillac or their new suit, that if it ever comes down to the war, when the electricity goes out and the power plants are blown up or whatever and their color TV goes off, they'll sit there in their living room and they'll kick back in their easy chair and wait for their TV to come back on.

"And when a race war breaks out, the first thing the masses are going to do, they're going to loot the big arsenal on Eight Mile Road, the first thing the masses are going to do, there's going to be mass looting. And if any of the black mobs ever get into one of those arsenals, get ahold of those M-16s and the grenades and whatever else they keep in there, you know, there's not going to be—he'll say 'Oh, there's a riot, but the National Guard will handle it.' The police could be dead! The National Guard will probably be dead if they're crazy enough to come into the neighborhoods!

"Because the population—they can make all the gun laws they want, the gun laws will stop an honest man from getting a gun. But the criminals and the *degenerate* elements of society will always be able to find firearms.

"That same white person that sat up and said, 'Oh, you people are full of shit. The race war will never happen. I don't believe anything you have to say.' *I think about what that man's face is going to look like when he turns around and looks out his window* and he sees a black nationalist standing there, and the *last thing* he sees is the flash on the M-16, when it rips his guts out and sprays them all over the back wall!"

This fantasy wraps it together: the white who won't listen, the violent black who acts, the speaker himself who is vindicated as the white sees his guts splash across the wall.

Violence in real life delighted him in memory. I was asking about happiest and saddest moments. "One of the happiest moments," he said, "was when I cranked up the first unit I'd ever cranked up. *My first street activity!* Cabaton, Missouri [not the real name]. You heard of Greensboro where five communists were killed? *We* nearly took out a Red at Cabaton. Just outside St. Louis. Our group and Storm Troopers from Chicago."

He was crowing with pride in his story. "This Red was on top of a Storm Trooper and he caught a steel helmet four times in the back of the head. They didn't think he was going to make it, but he pulled—you know, damn it to hell, he pulled through.

"We could have got rid of a Red—*first rally I ever went out on, we nearly take out a Red!*"

An important occasion. "*I fired up my first unit!* And I had my address published in the old paper—before it was the *New Order*, it was the *N.S. Report*. And I've got the first copy I was ever published in. The first envelope.

"I went to the post office box, I took out the first envelope I ever received in an *N.S. Report* post office box. And it was from, I think, [a top leader]. 'Congratulations, Comrade!'

"And he sent me a few leaflets, said, 'Here's some master copies. Give it hell!'"

"You were getting congratulations for having formed a unit?" I asked.

"I had a blond-haired, blue-eyed friend of mine," he said, "that was about the same size, he was younger, but he was as big as I was. And we just got—me and him built the whole thing, we got about six or seven good people."

Raymond's happy thoughts about hurting people came up again later in that interview. He was talking about a fight that allegedly had taken place in Chicago. "There was eight Storm Troopers who went to Daley Plaza. And there's three Jews who ran up and grabbed the first Storm Trooper off the truck, and they were going to beat him up. And they didn't know how many more was in the truck. And the other eight come piling out.

"Two of the Jews managed to run off, but the first one that got up there and grabbed that Storm Trooper, the Storm Trooper grabbed him, too, and managed to hang on to him.

"That was back before they had the ban on poles in the street, and they had these big poles [on which signs were mounted]. And they worked his head over.

"He's got a steel plate now, and he's sitting in some little private hospital somewhere, playing with his toes."

This way of speaking pleased Raymond; he figured it made him sound knowing.

Raymond spoke a lot about what he called "race mixing." "You see some ugly white girls hanging out with these black bucks. The white men won't have anything to do with them. This black guy will have her because she's a white woman, but a white man wouldn't have her because if she walked up to a mirror she'd be so ugly she'd break it. But the nigger wants her so he can brag about 'Oh, I have a white woman.'"

I spoke of an interracial married couple who were friends of mine. The woman, I said, was both white and quite beautiful.

He was taken aback. "I'd be surprised," he said weakly. "What she's doing disgusts me." That came out stronger. Then he began to recover himself. He didn't believe in it, he said. She might be beautiful on the outside, he said, but on the inside she had no racial pride. He moved into the usual rhetoric: The babies, if she had any, would be half black and half white. More than that, "in the dog world, everybody wants a Doberman. Everybody wants a purebred German shepherd or a purebred collie. Nobody wants the mutts. They gas them at the pound because nobody wants them."

The reference to gassing the undesirables came to him readily.

He wanted to explain white sexual involvement with black folk. "Maybe it's a deviation. I think it may be a form of sexual deviation because you get out and you see these white women here in Detroit who like to sleep with blacks. I'd have to categorize them with the homosexual, someone who'd be into bestiality or something like that. They get maybe into some kind of a weird sex trip. She wants to picture herself as some kind of a slave to the—she's on some kind of white guilt trip because her ancestors owned slaves and she thinks she's making up for it by sleeping with the big black buck.

"There's no way I could ever see myself going to bed with a black woman, you know. If I, if I ever reach that point, that I, if I ever lose my racial pride and I reach that point that I'm that insane that you catch me in the bed with a black woman, I hope that one of my movement brothers is considerate enough and cares enough about me to give me a bullet in my brain.

"I don't hate black people, but the thought of having sex with a black woman, it disgusts me. It's just something that's not, if there is a God, like I say, people say it's against God. I believe there is some Supreme Being and I don't believe—you know, that's, that's like homosexuality. God created Adam and Eve, he didn't create Adam and Steve. It's just, it's not right."

He was working to build a world, he said, in which his unborn child would never have to come home from school and say, "Daddy, some black kid beat me up and took my lunch money away at school." That would not work, he said; he would be in prison. He would go find out who the kid was, look up the kid's father, and say, "Hey, you know what your kid did to my kid? Better put a leash on the monkey."

The Strike Group, if it gained power, would rid the country of nonwhites. "We believe in repatriation," he said. "If we got political power, the black man would go back to Africa. The Jewish people would be sent to Israel. America would be for the white people who founded it and built it."

I asked what would happen with communists.

"Communists would be charged with treason against their race. If it was a white communist. If they were guilty of doing things which were against their race and against their country, they'd pay the penalty for treason."

"What," I asked, "is the crime of treason against the white race?"

"Having sex with a non-Aryan."

I looked at him. "And they should be killed for that?"

"Yes. Death penalty. I believe in some of the old principles. If a white woman slept with a black man, like I say, the black man, I'd repatriate him back to Africa. I wouldn't shoot him. The black man would automatically be on a boat. The woman who slept with him, she'd get a bullet in the brain.

"She'd still get a trial," he added.

This fantasy came out easily and forcefully. I thought I had better bring him back to earth. I pointed out that I had been talking about a real person, in fact a sweet and fine woman. He began to back down. He made up an escape clause for himself—maybe he would want to say that she was not worth the bother of a bullet. Then it would be okay to let her go back on the boat with her husband, join him on the trip to Africa.

I wasn't ready to leave it at this. I pointed out that on one level "we're just having a bullshit conversation, okay? On the other level, if we think about the real world, real people involved—I guess my question is, Raymond, what leads you to feel it's your business that these two people live together?"

"I told you my wife [that is, his woman friend] was pregnant with that baby?" he answered. "I don't want him to even see an interracial couple walking down the street."

"Why not?" I asked.

"I don't want him to see that."

Again: "Why not?"

"If he ever sees something like that, I want it to be in a history book. 'Great Degenerates of the Past.'

"The fact—what she's doing disgusts me. If she had any racial pride, interracial marriage is wrong. That's treason. It's wrong in the eyes of God, it just wasn't meant to be. It destroys two races. Like I say, I don't believe in killing off all of the black people—"

I interrupted: "Wait, wait. For a moment I don't want to hear that level of statement. I want to hear in terms of your own feelings."

"My own feelings?" he asked.

"Your own feeling is …" I prompted.

"Disgust," he said flatly. "It makes me want to, it just makes me want to throw them both in the gas chamber. That's my first impulse."

Again, the gas chamber.

"But I try and put myself in the position like, you remember Klaus Barbie, who was the Gestapo officer in charge of Lyons, France? He probably had to do some things he didn't like to do, but if I was in a position like that of leadership I'd try and do good things, I'd try and concentrate on doing good things for people. But in trying to clean the society and trying to remove the degenerate elements and the bad elements, you'd have to do some things you wouldn't want to do. You have to do some—when you're changing something so drastically as we're changing it, you may have to do—Like I say, we're going to have to, the repatriation of the black people and the nonwhites to their own country. But there's also going to be a lot of bad white people. When we get into political power—Like I say, if I was in a position of leadership, I'd probably have to do some things I wouldn't really care for."

This childish man, remember, is twenty-five, not eleven. This is not talk on a playground. These images of power, these fantasies that one is responsible for making social program, have been nurtured in seven years of movement work. Nothing in his life in the movement stops him, nothing demands realism.

The movement encourages this fantasy of power—here are the powerless drifting off into daydreams of power, as you and I drift, pressed by monthly bills, into daydreams of winning the lottery. But not so innocent. Note that the Klaus Barbie image wraps together virtue and violence. Note the martyrdom of the justice-seeker who must do things that are unpleasant—and who, in the case of Barbie, eventually was cornered by the unsympathetic world. Again and again, my respondents in interviews have pictured themselves as victims. Note particularly that Raymond's fantasies pair sexuality, or at least interracial sexuality, with murder: "a bullet in the brain."

Raymond had a heavy anti-Jewish agenda. Telling me about grave health issues that he had in his teens, he talked about having been saved by a Jewish doctor, but he drew no lessons from that. I pointed out to him one night that the movement literature he and I had been looking at was deeply anti-Semitic, but that in my contact with Strike Group members I mostly heard about black people, not about Jews. He agreed, saying that most of the group members had grown up in the inner city with blacks and had had little to do with Jews. They hadn't known much about Jews, he said, until they came into contact with the Nazi group. "So I guess you could say we're responsible; you could say, if we could make a reference to the Garden of Eden,

we gave these young people the apple. We gave them the knowledge."

He himself, he said, was "more anti-Jewish than I am anti-black." He could more easily accept blacks, he said, if he had to choose; blacks were typically poor and uneducated, were less dangerous. "I don't feel that they pose as much of a threat to the National Socialist movement or to the cause and goals we're fighting for.

"But you ask where I learned this, and I say my grandfather. I told you he was a States Righter back in the sixties, when the Freedom Riders were coming through the South. He was with Fields' and Stoner's National States Righters. And he spoke to me often about the Jews. He spoke often about them.

"When I'd arrive at his house and I'd sit there and I'd go through his stack of papers, *Thunderbolts*, and read his literature, I'd ask him questions. And he didn't care for the black people. He was very bigoted towards the blacks. But I have to say he was equally if not more prejudiced against the Jews. And he was vocal about it. He would speak his mind and tell people what he thought."

I asked what sort of things his grandfather had told him. Raymond replied that when he had asked about the Holocaust, his grandfather had told him that he didn't believe it happened—but that "if it did, Hitler made one mistake: He didn't get rid of every Jew in existence. So that pretty well sums up his feelings in one sentence."

I asked what else the old man had told him.

"Well, the usual part about the international banks, finance, the control of political power, control of the media, control of the money.

"He tried to impress upon me that you were all crooks. You know all the stories that are supposed to go along with the Jewish people. I think I've heard ninety-nine percent of them."

"What are some of the things you really do believe about Jews that he taught you," I asked, "that are important?"

Raymond said he believed that the media were controlled by the Jewish people and that the Jews controlled communism.

"What else I believe about the Jewish people?" he went on. "Well, I know you don't come out from under mushrooms; that's one of the old children's tales that used to be told."

I happily told him that this was the one thing he had been told that was true. "We do, Raymond. We come right out from under mushrooms." Then I again asked what he believed that seemed important.

He had to think for quite a while. Then he said, "I believe the Jews are dangerous. Anything they want to do, they have the people in political power. They have the media and they have the finance."

They were better educated, he said. He had noticed that kids in Jewish families were constantly told to study. But basically, he said, they were a political force. This turned out to mean that Jews were much to blame for the fact that the white racist movement had not gotten any further politically in the country than it had. Here he particularly laid the blame on "all the movies that have come out of Hollywood, about the evil, killing Germans, and all of the anti-National Socialist and anti-white propaganda. You look at the producers' names: Silverman. Goldberg. I watch a lot—not a *lot* of television, but I watch probably quite a few hours of TV a week, and I read the subtitles at the end of the movies. Check out who the producers and directors are."

What else did he believe? He spoke of the Holocaust as having been a hoax. Then there was a pause. He had been taught, he said, about ritual murder. "Jewish ritual murder. I didn't get to read up on it as much as I wanted, but part of the Jewish ceremony, the book said that they kidnapped children. Drained their blood for use in the ceremonies."

I asked which ceremonies.

"God only knows," he replied, "but I can show you some cartoons that—"

I interrupted that citation of "evidence" and asked whether he believed it.

"I *wonder* sometimes," he said, with a nasty tone of implication. I struck him, he said, as a fairly nice person, but he had "seen some of those rabbis in their long black coats with the hat, and, *you know.*"

Did he think, I asked, that they might kidnap children?

"Devious-looking characters," he replied.

"You halfway believe that may be the truth?" I pressed.

"I halfway believe it," he said.

I asked what else he halfway believed.

"This isn't halfway believe: I believe Israel would like to rule the world. If they can get financial power in enough countries. There are French Jews, German Jews, Polish Jews, Russian Jews. A lot of the stuff that's happening, I believe it comes from—just like it was planned—*The Protocols of the Learned Elders of Zion*. And I believe that to be an authentic document. I just believe the only reason that the *Protocols* weren't fulfilled is because World War II kind of put a damper on the plans."

One of the most powerful images arose a few moments later. I asked him to look at his statement that Jews had gotten so much education in America. Did he suppose, I asked, that Jews were smarter than the Aryans genetically?

"No," he said, "I believe they're better organized. If the Aryan families would push their young people and do the same thing the Jews were doing, there's no way the Jewish plan would make it. But like I say, we're going to have to—"

Now he interrupted himself. I guess he was about to say they were going to have to impose some sort of restriction. In any case, the thought led him to this:

"That's why the laws in Germany were passed about Jewish doctors could treat only Jews, because so many of the older German people were disgusted. They'd see some pretty little blond German girl, twelve or fourteen years old, going into the Jewish doctor, and you know what went through their minds."

"No," I said. "What went through their minds? I *don't* know."

"The usual … nightmares. They saw the little German girls being deflowered and felt and poked and felt out and—"

I interrupted his blossoming fantasy. "Why would a Jewish doctor do that any more than a Christian doctor?"

"That's one of the old cartoons I've seen," he said. "I'm not stating that that happened in all cases."

Somehow that didn't quite cover it. "Why would it happen *ever*," I asked, "any more from one than the other? Are Jews by nature more lecherous than Christians?"

He didn't know the word. "You mean 'sleepier'?"

"No," I explained. "'Lustful.'"

There was a pause. It would depend, he figured, upon the individual Jew. "But I've noticed that the pornography business, the sex business, you see all those shops around?" He went on in an insinuating tone: "Wonder *who* makes all of those pornographic movies?"

He presumed the answer was obvious. "Jews. The right wing is giving the credit to the Jewish people. I halfway believe it. Nobody's proved it to me on paper, just on instinct, I halfway believe it."

Note this example of logic. Jewish doctors had to be restricted because of fears they violated Christian German girls. Why should they have been feared? Because Jews are pornographers. How do we know that? Nobody has proved it, but we can know it's true just on instinct. This set of thoughts has at its center a powerful nugget of emotion: the scene of the Jewish doctor and the little flaxen-haired girl. Remember that Raymond's source for this image is "one of the old cartoons I've seen."

Raymond had another image for me. "I know one rumor that I heard. The Jewish rabbi who performs a little operation. That all the male members of the Jewish faith are supposed to have, the circumcision? We heard a story about how they do this surgery. After they cut the skin, something about kissing, or the blood, or something. A drop of the blood, they have to kiss it." He snickered. "Or basically give the kid some head, you know."

Later that same evening, Raymond and Rosandra were discussing their coming baby. I pointed out that they kept assuming it would be a boy, but that it could equally be a girl. That would be fine, they said, they would get it pink dresses and a stroller and it would still grow up with a National Socialist education.

I said I hoped the baby would get over it.

"She might marry the next Führer, who knows?" Raymond said.

"She might marry a Jew, too," I suggested.

"I don't think so," he said, "when we're done with her. If she does, if she marries a Jew, there's a rope in her future. I'm dead serious. If she ever comes home to me and said, 'Daddy, I met a nice Jewish boy today,' I'd ask her one question: 'Do you have a death wish?'"

"Wait a minute, Raymond," I said. "You think I'm a nice guy, right?"

"True."

Okay, I said, what if she met one of my grandchildren?

She wouldn't have the opportunity, Raymond pointed out. "We're not planning on you guys being around twenty years from now."

I laughed at him. Look here, I suggested, suppose she's on a tour in twenty years to Greenland and runs into the place where we Jews settle when the boat drifts the wrong way and she falls in love with one of my grandchildren? "I mean," I raved on, "if you think I'm nice, you ought to know my kids, because they're super nice. And my grandchildren will be out of this world!

"And she's going to fall in love with this really nice, really nice guy named Abraham Ezekiel out there in Greenland. Come back home and say, 'I met this beautiful man, Daddy. Loves music, sings all the time. Really funny, really intelligent. Down there in the lost Jewish colony in Greenland. And we're going to settle in England where nobody cares one way or the other.' What are you going to say then?" I asked.

Raymond was quick. "You're under arrest!"

We both laughed. Then he went on seriously, "She would definitely have to go to one of the re-education centers. But I doubt seriously that would ever happen. The way we educate our daughters—"

Rosandra interjected: "Or our sons."

"Or our sons. If he were to meet one of your grandchildren in the future … hmmmm. He'd probably speak and be courteous. But, I don't know. He'd probably be dreaming of a little oven somewhere in back of his head."

I was jolted. Raymond was conjuring an image of his unborn child burning my not-yet-conceived grandchildren. I demanded and received an apology.

What do you say after this tour through Raymond's mind? Why had Raymond ever concerned himself with Jews? Probably the answer is his education at the hands of his beloved grandfather, who had served under old-line racist stalwarts such as Fields and Stoner. But what is even more strange is his language—he speaks as though the Third Reich still existed and he held a position in its forces.

What's in it for him? It reminds me of kids much younger falling into roles in Dungeons and Dragons. He doesn't distinguish reality and fantasy well.

In Idaho, at the Aryan Nations compound, a picture of Adolf Hitler rests in a place of honor on the wall. The artist's rendering shows deep, intense eyes in a sensitive face, a face that is strong but suffering.

Raymond, like Paul, kept a picture of Hitler's face in his room. It had fallen down one day as we spoke; Raymond said it had come unglued. I suggested that Hitler had come unglued long before. Hurt flickered across Raymond's face, but he kept silent. Later in that interview, he expressed his adoration of the Führer.

"I almost consider Adolf Hitler to be a god. When you said that—I don't think you want to know some of the ideas I—I had some thoughts about you that would've probably scared you.

"That's my hero. One of my heroes. Hitler. One of the greatest leaders who ever walked the face of the earth.

"They said Christ came to preach salvation and save the world. It's not just me, there's many people who feel the way I do, many of the old Germans, like the ones who came and shook hands with us when we went up to the German festival at Frankenmuth, looked upon Hitler as—you know, there's a lot of people who they say Jesus Christ was a Savior. The Messiah, the prophet, come with the message.

"I know some German people who if they heard you—being a Death's-Head man, I didn't like the words, but like I said, I'm not going to, as much as I wanted to—I wanted to feed you your words, was my first impression. But I know some of the older German people who if they heard you say what you said about Hitler, would do their, would probably do their utmost to try and blow your candle out for you. They feel that strongly. You know, in their heart, just like in my heart, he will always be the Führer."

I pointed out that Raymond was the first in the group I had heard become passionate about Hitler.

"You mean almost idolize him as a God?" he said. "The SS runes and the Death's-Head aren't just on my shirt." He thumped his chest. "They are in *here*. My heart. If I were taken—if the communists came into power and they took me out and shot me tomorrow, the last two words out of my mouth would be, 'Heil Hitler!' He will always be the ultimate leader to me."

I suggested that others in the group did not have this intense attachment; he claimed not to know, not to have discussed it with them. He allowed that they probably weren't as involved. "Close as we are as brothers, you know, I'm not a mind reader. I do believe that they admire the Führer, but I still look upon him as the ultimate leader.

"If we were to come into political power, I would build a statue of Adolf Hitler five hundred foot—I'd build a statue of Hitler larger than the Statue of Liberty.

"I doubt whether any of the other brothers, that they feel the admiration for the Führer that I've felt. If he were to come back today, I would be the first person to salute him and say, 'God bless you, my Führer!'

"Like I said, he gave an ideal for our people. He gave us the pattern to follow. And I'm just trying, I'm keeping, his goals and his ideals are alive, you know, and his ideal will have a chance of coming back again. And you talk about I'm unemployed and the position I'm in? I don't even consider myself good enough to shine that man's shoes. He was the ultimate, you know. Like I say, I almost consider Hitler to be a god."

I spent a long time trying to find the roots of Raymond's attachment to Hitler. First I asked how old he had been when the feeling had become real for him.

"Believe it or not," he said, "before any of the members of my family educated me. I was sitting and I was watching the speeches on TV, the old Hitler speeches, and I was just a kid. I knew there was something about that man I liked. It was just the personality and the forcefulness. It was almost—you know the power Hitler had over the German people, it was almost a hypnotizing effect. Forty years after his death, thirty years after his death, watching the old tapes, you could still—the dynamic personality, you know. It's like the book says, when you can make an accomplishment sometime and get people to unite to do something sometimes, you're a leader; when you can do it every single day, you're a great leader. He did it every single day."

I asked again how old he had been during these experiences.

"When I was six and seven, five, six, seven years old. My grandfather spoke to me a little bit. But I'd sit in front of the TV and watch the German troops marching by. I got to see some of the old movies of the rallies. And I sat there and clapped my hands: Yeah! Yeah!

"It's nothing I could put my finger on, but I knew there was something I liked. And then when I got old enough where I could understand, I found out what he stood for and what he really stood for. And I got my first copy of *Mein Kampf*, and I got to read the thoughts. The thoughts of my Führer down on paper and see what he really felt. Then I could say, hey, this is it, this man has got the plan.

"But that was one of the proudest days of my life, when I got my first copy of *Mein Kampf*, when I actually got to sit down and read the words of the Führer. You know. It's almost like even though I never got to speak to him, when I read the words, I, in my mind, pictured the Führer saying this. And

I said, okay, even though the Führer in his body may be physically dead now, his ideals are still alive. This is the message he left for me, right here.

"I was a reader when I was a kid. I don't read as much as I did when I was a kid. I loved history, all types of history, particularly the Second World War, though. There's always been something about the National Socialist movement. At one time I got off on a kick on prehistory, and I studied the pre-historic forms of man and the genetics. And I saw what man evolved into. But then when I came to the books on Hitler and I started reading about Hitler—this is one of the ultimate human beings, I said, this is as close as we're going to get to God walking this earth right here. This is one of the ultimate human beings we're going to get."

What does Raymond's attachment mean? As with so much else, it suggests someone at a younger age, an eleven- or twelve-year-old, who feels alone, perhaps abandoned, and shaky about his own worth, who focuses on a distant figure that can be loved, a safely unavailable figure, one that overcame odds to achieve great acceptance and power. With a certain amount of self-abasement that affords some relief, the eleven-year-old can safely acknowledge the love object and merge with it, trading adoration for (often imagined) approval.

As I pressed Raymond about his involvement with Hitler, his grandfather, who had died two or three years before, became more and more our subject.

"Well, one thing, my grandfather had a lot to do with it. When I seen the Führer speaking on TV, I knew that I liked the way he spoke. And the dynamic—the personality itself and the way he conducted himself. I just always looked up to him, almost like a father figure. And then, I knew I always admired my grandfather. My grandfather, back in the forties and fifties, my grandfather always wore a Hitler mustache. He did up until about a year and half before he died, when he had the cancer and he wasn't able to take care of him-self. Then we had to take care of him.

"He wore a Hitler mustache when it wasn't pop-ular. And my grandfather always spoke highly of Adolf Hitler. He said the only mistake Hitler made was not getting rid—my grandfather hated Jewish people—he said the only thing Hitler didn't do right was not getting rid of *all* the Jewish people. But he always spoke highly of the Führer. My grand-father's the one who told me, read *Mein Kampf*. 'You really want to know what Hitler was about, the man wrote a book. Read it.'"

Raymond's father had not minded him receiving these thoughts from his grandfather. Raymond said his father "was racist, even though he was nonvio-lent and he believed in live and let live." He said his father had taught him as a kid that "we were better than the black people, taught me the same white supremacy." But his father "wasn't as much up on the Jews."

Raymond's father was a veteran of World War II. "He fought in Belgium with the American field artillery. He was decorated, so you could say my dad was an American war hero." His father's side of the family was German, and his father had told Raymond, "Be proud of your German bloodlines. The war happened. It was a terrible thing. But don't let these people make you ashamed of your German bloodline because of it." His father had taught him that the Germans were a great people, "and were descended from the Viking warriors."

Raymond had asked his father about the war, and his father had said that he didn't hate the German people or Hitler, but that he was born an American citizen, that his country drafted him and ordered him to fight. He was loyal to the country. As Raymond saw it, his father "doesn't really agree with everything that Hitler believed in. But he didn't disagree with all those things, either."

Raymond had spoken, I suggested, as though strong bonds joined him and his grandfather. He agreed with passion. I asked how one fit his father into that picture. He had to think about that a moment. Then he said that he was close to both of them. He looked up to his dad, he said, respected him and loved him, and they were fairly close—"but I'm going to say I was just as close to my grandfather as I was with my dad."

There hadn't been as many activities with his father; they would do something every once in a while, "but every time you turned around, I was fishing with Granddad or walking along beside him when he worked his garden with his little garden tractor."

This grandfather was Raymond's mother's father. The family originally had lived some 140 miles from the man but would see him once or twice a month, and in the summer Raymond's mother would leave him there for months at a time.

Raymond had been given a little white hat like the one his grandfather wore as an electrician. Raymond tried to do everything just like his grandfather. "Tried to copy him to a T. I'd even sit around and roll—if he wanted a cigarette, I'd say, 'Let me roll you one.' He rolled Bugler. And I'd roll him cigarettes. I'd say, 'C'mere, let me do that for you.' And I got to where I could roll a mean cigarette. I wanted to be just like Grandpa."

Raymond told me then of his grandfather's death. "When we finally moved near him, he was dying of cancer. He worked—he had government clearance—he worked on some of the bomb projects. He worked on the bomb project at Hanford, Washington, and was exposed to the radioactivity. He had cancer in every vital organ of his body. And I had to carry him around like a little baby. And

eventually I had to—I had to sit and watch him get ate up with cancer. He didn't believe in drugs, so he wouldn't take any; you had to just about slip him the pain medicine.

"We moved when I was twenty-one, when they found out he had cancer. He died when I was about twenty-three. He lived for two [more] years. I watched him go through two surgeries. And carried him around like a baby.

"I fed him. I sat besides his bed and I read to him from some of the old newspapers. He got to where during the last days he didn't even recognize us. All he knew was—the electricians used, you know, the old expression, 'What do you know, Joe?' And I'd come in and I'd look at him, 'What do you know, Joe?' And he'd look up at me—I'm not going to say his name, but anyway that wasn't his name. And he'd look up at me and smile and he'd say, 'Just hanging around.' He'd smile because he remembered that.

"He got to where he didn't even know us. But anyway, I'd sit and read to him, and I'd go to the store and get him treats. He lost his appetite, but he'd eat better for me than he would for anybody else. I'd fix him a bourbon and Coke, and I'd take a plate in, even if he was in one of his moods where he wouldn't eat. I'd say, 'If you'll eat this, I'll give you this.' And I'd get him to eat.

"And anyway, one day I took my father's truck and I went to the store to buy him some doughnuts. I went to a doughnut shop. And I got him three chocolate glazed doughnuts and three regular. And I got back to his house and I looked in. Nobody was there. And the house was empty. His bed had been stripped. I figured, well, they must've took him up to our house. I went up to the house and they weren't there. I had the feeling when I seen it. I called the hospital and I said, is my grandfather there? And they said yes, he had a heart—the cancer had weakened him down to where he had a heart attack.

"I said, 'Well, he's all right, isn't he?' I said, 'Tell me that my mother and grandmother are bringing him home.' And she said, 'I'm sorry, but your grandfather is dead.' And I said, 'Don't lie to me, bitch,' I said. And she starts, 'Sir, sir, I'm sorry, I'm sorry.' And I hung up on her.

"And—hmmmm. That was a bad day. I kind of—that was the day, I kind of come unhinged that day. I took my Ruger 10/22 and I went out in the backyard and chopped up some hills. I went out and started beating on trees."

"You took your what?"

"I took a carbine and I went out in the backyard—I didn't think—when my grandfather died, I—hmmmm. I didn't think it would be true. I wanted to believe it was a lie. And I was actually crying. That was—my grandfather was one of the people my world circulated around. There's very few people I'm going to say I've ever been really super close to, but my grandfather had to be one of them. I idolized him.

"And—I got mad. I said she lied to me, and I said I got to get out of this house, I'm going to go—I got my carbine. I said, I'm going to go out and shoot. I said, you know, I went out and started chopping up the hills in the back of the yard. And I mean, I went out, I walked on out into the forest. I threw the gun down, I started beating my fists against the trees. And then I fell down against the tree, and I just sat there. And I wanted to, I was just wishing the whole world would go ahead and blow up and I could go, too. And I finally got myself pulled together and I came back to the house, and my mother and grandmother finally got back, and I pretty well devoted the rest of my attention to my grandmother that day. Anything she wants is good enough for me.

"I carry three pictures in my wallet," he said, beginning to choke up, "aside from my young lady friends, who are back at the back. See the first picture: That's my mother. That's his oldest, my grandfather's oldest daughter. My mother is his oldest girl. That second is a picture of my father. And that third, I don't think I have to tell you who that man is."

There was a pause.

"That picture . . ."

He couldn't talk. He began to weep.

After a few moments, he breathed deeply and resumed in a shaky voice, "That picture . . . will be in there . . . till the day I die.

"That was—hmmmm—that was a knife in my heart, the day he died.

"My world definitely rotated around Grandpa, he was number one. So. Hmmmm. Anyway.

"What else can I say about that? The man took me flying. I loved, I've always loved airplanes. That was a man, the first man to take me up in an airplane. Say, 'Here, boy, take the controls and hold her steady.' Hey, who else will grow a beautiful garden and pick you vegetables and then peel them and . . . you ask a lot about my political beliefs and the way I feel. You know what he taught me, and now you know how I felt about my grandfather. That's probably about three fourths of my political beliefs right there. But like I say, there's still the one fourth on my own. I still always looked up to the Führer and the white racist cause. My grandfather was a States Righter. He always—the one thing he always taught me: Do what's right."

As he recovered himself, Raymond spoke a good deal more about the old fellow—how healthy he had been, how he had been a boxer as a youth, had owned a pool hall, could work hard physically even in his later years, and how drastic the physical effects of the cancer had been. "We watched him go from a hundred and seventy-five pounds to, when he died, I doubt he weighed a hundred pounds. It was just skin stretched over bone. Looking at his face, it was just a skull with some skin stretched over it, and the eyes were sunk back in deep. And the cancer was causing him great pain, so as much as I hated to lose him, the heart attack he had, in a way, it was almost a relief.

"Anyway. I watched him go down to a skeleton. What really hurt me, even, like about four months before he died, he would still have his moments when we would be there and I could sit and I could read to him, and he would be receptive to it. And he would listen and he'd say, 'Yeah, I like that, I wish I could do that,' or something like that."

We are left, then, with this strange confounding of Hitler and Raymond's grandfather, and Raymond's real attachment to his grandfather. I could learn almost nothing from Raymond about his father and mother, other than his mother's rough ability to handle Raymond's teenage behavior. Little was said to suggest attachment to either parent. Hitler and Granddad were playing in an uncrowded field.

Rosandra's mother, who lived in a small town in northern Michigan, was heavily involved with the Klan, which wanted her to organize a chapter up there. Rosandra had met Raymond when she and her mother attended one of the periodic gatherings at Bob Miles's farm. I was teasing Rosandra and Raymond one evening and asked why Rosandra's mother hadn't kept a better eye on her, not to let her wander off and run into Raymond. Rosandra said that her mom "didn't have much to say in it," and Raymond said, "That's the only type of person her mother would even let her associate with, Klan or NS [National Socialist]." Rosandra agreed, and pulled out a photo from the gathering showing herself in what she called a Klan shirt, with thunderbolts on the collar and little flags.

Raymond said that Rosandra had picked him out from the group—that he had been, along with Paul, one of the only older members present, and that Rosandra's mother had been impressed because he, Raymond, happened to be the flag bearer that day and the banner they had chosen to bring was their "Führer's standard, Adolf Hitler's standard," and that Rosandra's mother had a great admiration for Adolf Hitler.

After Raymond told me how to distinguish a "Führer's Standard" from other Nazi flags, I said, "Oh, okay. So there you were with the Standard, and Rosandra's mother saw that and said, 'Go, daughter, that man's got a pretty flag!'"

"No," Raymond said, "I broke the ice. She was sitting at a table with her mother, and my armband had come unpinned. The safety pin came open. I pulled it off and tightened it back up. That was my excuse, anyway.

"I said, 'Could you assist me with this?' We took a walk. We held hands. We wound up giving each other a smooch or two. We started looking deep into each other's eyes.

"And I didn't have to take and teach her things about the movement," Raymond continued. "Starr, my girlfriend of two years [the young woman of the motorcycle photo], was anti-black. She was very anti-black, but she didn't know a thing about a Jew. I had to teach her what little bit I knew about Jews. But I didn't have to educate Rosandra. Her mother—"

I interrupted to ask Rosandra what her mother had told her. She was reluctant to answer—"It's kind of hard to explain"—but finally quoted what her mother had said: "Don't go out with them. You bring one home, you got a shotgun!"

Raymond added, "If she brought a Jew home, her mother is anti-Semitic to the point where if you went up there with us to that area, you would very probably leave the property on the end of an assault rifle."

I asked whether the mother had taught Rosandra about blacks as well. She said yes. And what had she been taught?

"'Don't hang around with them.' It's like when I was in high school, I had this colored girlfriend. And me and her would walk back and forth, but if my mom ever seen us, she'd tell us to get in the car or get in the house."

I said I was surprised that there had been a black girl up in those northern woods.

"Not there," Rosandra said. "We were in Indiana, a town next to Hammond." She had spent her life there, and there had been many blacks, "lots of them."

Had her mother told her to watch out for them?

"Yeah. When I was going to school, I had a nigger pulled a knife on me. And the school system would not do a damn thing about it. So my mom just said, 'Go get your papers, you're quitting school.' And I said, 'Oh, good.'"

This had been the ninth grade, and that was the last she had seen of school.

Her father, who worked in a die-cast factory, had left the family when Rosandra was seven; he lived now in South Carolina and was remarried. According to Rosandra, her father "really didn't care who I hung around with."

Her mother lived now from Social Security she was collecting for Rosandra and her little brother, Rosandra said, and mostly stayed home. The Social Security came because of Rosandra's acute nearsightedness—her glasses were extraordinarily thick, she could not drive a car—and because of a finger that was crippled from birth. The finger, with a tendon that was too short, could not be straightened out. "I had an operation on it," she said. "They said all my cords and veins up here to my elbow are all tangled up together. It come out to a twenty-thousand-dollar hospital bill, just the operation." Rosandra claimed not to be bothered by the hand.

I asked what she had done after dropping out of school—had she taken a job or stayed at home?

"I was staying at home. Sleeping till noon, getting up and watching my soaps. All I did every day."

"What were your favorites?" I asked.

"*All My Children, One Life to Live*, and *General Hospital*." She was still keeping up with them "once in a while."

She also did a lot of reading. "Usually, I'm reading romance."

Rosandra was usually in the apartment when I came to interview Raymond, but she would stay in their bedroom reading, with very occasional forays out into the living room. She would offer coffee and sit and smoke a minute, but soon go back to her reading. She was eighteen years old and very shy. It pained me, as I have said, to watch her hold the dishes to her face to see them when she was cleaning up after their supper.

I doubted that she was eating well enough, and I was worried about her pregnancy. One night she interrupted us an hour after midnight because she was having cramps; she needed to get to a doctor. I drove them to the hospital and waited for quite a long time with Raymond. Raymond had talked a lot about this pregnancy and his pride in it; nevertheless, he was insensitive and self-absorbed throughout this incident. Fortunately, the trip was a false alarm, not a miscarriage.

Rosandra was quiet and easily cowed. She was glad to get out from under her mother's domination. She seemed dazed by the pregnancy; life had changed a lot more than she had expected.

Several days after the trip to the hospital, I went away for a few weeks. When I returned, I began receiving phone calls from Raymond, who had gone back to Arkansas. He desperately asked what the group members were saying about him; he believed that they were trying to incite Klan assassins to get him.

I asked Paul what had been going on. It turned out that Rosandra had needed to get away from Raymond because he had been beating her. Nolan, a group member, had helped to spirit Rosandra away from the apartment; she had stayed with Nolan's mother briefly and then gone north to her own mother. Raymond had left town shortly after Rosandra's escape. On the way out of town, Raymond phoned the Secret Service, Paul said, and reported to them that Nolan and others whom he named were secret Nazis who were plotting to assassinate the president.

According to Paul, Raymond had been cut off welfare a month before he left town; he had refused to report for the eight days a month of work that Michigan required.

Contact with Raymond and Rosandra ended there. Raymond was working at a motorcycle repair shop in Arkansas; Rosandra had gone north to have her baby.

Raymond will find some new uniform for some new play-acting; Rosandra will be bent over the sink at her mother's house, washing dishes and listening to the cries of her child. And the child?

38

The Recovery of Race in America

AARON DAVID GRESSON

Aaron Gresson believed that, by the mid-1990s, racism was a nearly defunct *topos*. Racist behavior still persisted, but the meaning of the behavior was, to use his term, 'negotiable'. The power to negotiate is crucial for Gresson, who argued that, since the watershed period of the 1960s, a process of loss and recovery has taken place, or, more accurately, *still is* taking place.

'I consider these basic questions,' Gresson stated at the outset of his book. 'How does a powerful group regain or recover the moral right to dominate other groups when the reigning cultural myths negate the direct use of supremacist ideologies?' Whites' moral hegemony was undermined in the 1960s and the concept of a racial hierarchy with whites perched obdurately at the top was not only questioned but shown to be undesirable.

Gresson continued: 'How does the most visible and vocal oppressed group renegotiate its relationship to itself and the dominant group when the liberation struggle has run its course without achieving its liberation goals?' The problem for African Americans was an exhaustion of strategies to conquer racism. By the 1990s, racism was universally condemned. The African American critique (if we may homogenize the challenge of the 1960s) was accepted. Yet the progress made had left a substantial majority of African Americans unaffected, leaving a quandary: 'How do contemporary African Americans manage the rhetorical task of Self-Other liberation in a postmodern society?' Gresson's third question follows from this: 'What myths, discourse, and rhetorical strategies are employed in the tasks of white and black recovery?'

In the extract presented here, Gresson analyzes how racism has not so much assumed new forms, but turned away from itself, or, as he put it, 'the oppressor is now the oppressed, and the victim is now the villain'. It is a heady passage to begin a powerful argument about the obliquities of contemporary racism.

White Recovery of Moral and Heroic Voice: How to Say 'Yo' Momma!' When You're Already 'the Man'

Dialectical irony implies a bondedness in which the ironist realizes her freedom only through unmasking the pretensions of her "victim," but in which the victim regains his subjectivity only through being ironized. To see someone as the victim of irony is to see that person, relative to oneself, as submerged in unreflective absolutism.

— Richard Brown (1987)

Postmodern society generates folly. It is folly to claim that by hitting men as often as men hit women, women can be "batterers" in the same sense as men are. It is folly to claim that the Soviet Union's demise means that capitalism is good and that God is on capitalism's and not communism's side. It is also folly to cry "reverse racism" and claim that Blacks, Hispanics, poor white ethnics, and other disenfranchised groups have turned the tide of oppression and now oppress privileged white men in some wholesale fashion. Yet folly reigns. And an ironic twist has occurred in race relations and related areas involving historically oppressed collectivities: the oppressor is now the oppressed, and the victim is now the villain.

In chapter 1, I described the deconstruction of oppression. This chapter returns to that theme but enlarges and examines it using the theory presented in chapter 7. More specifically, this chapter employs the idea of "rhetorical reversal" to indicate how the symbolic and substantive dimensions of racial re-empowerment seem to be occurring; it also discusses the particular rhetorical strategies employed. We can begin with the symbolic and conclude with the substantive arenas; but these two domains exist in a state of mutuality, each instructing and imitating the other. To illustrate the symbolic domain, the world of contemporary pop music presents us with the meteoric rise of a white male as the reigning "King of Rap." To illustrate the substantive domain, we can adduce both the Supreme Court and the media's management of racial incidents. Before taking up Vanilla Ice, however, I will review and briefly illustrate the dimensions of rhetorical reversal.

A MODEL OF RACIAL RECOVERY RHETORIC

Rhetorical Reversal: A Postmodern Rhetorical Strategy

Harold Isaacs opens his volume *Idols of the Tribe* with a story of a young Italian politician from Newark, New Jersey, trying to recover from the recent election of a Black mayor by the city's Black majority:

> This young ward politician has come to see that brandishing arms and threatening violence—as some of his political elders were doing—would not work in streets the whites no longer ruled. He was casting about instead for ways of negotiating a modus vivendi with the new kings of the jungle. He told about an encounter he'd had on a television panel show with a prominent Black militant leader. Without other preamble, the Black stabbed a finger at the Italian-American and said, "You're a racist son of a bitch." Without blinking, the Italian-American replied, "You're damned right, and so are you, you racist son of a bitch." (Isaacs 1977)

This passage illustrates rhetorical reversal—that is, the neutralization of a historical or factually based trope by the misuse of its moral power in relation to self. In the case Isaacs presents, it is used by an Italian-American who neutralizes the term by essentially saying to the Black man, "Yo' Momma!" "Signifying" has borne many meanings, but psychologically, they all relate to a need to handle matters with *irony*—to renegotiate the terms of endearment and the conditions for relatedness.

In the scenario described by Isaacs, we get two important insights: (1) part of the personal power of the storyteller derives from finding another with whom to share the story; and (2) collective power evolves when the other takes the story and carries it forth. I will return to this idea later when I discuss the famous Earl Butz racial slur incident. The key idea here is that whites still retain the power to negotiate around "voice" and "voicelessness." The liberation movements of the 1960s and 1970s revealed important changes in the way men of power would continue their domination of the weak.

The Italian-American politician revealed deep anxiety toward such change, and he attempted to control it. He thereby reminded us, as well, that few surrender their perceived privileges without a fight. This is no singular revelation. History repeatedly shows it. Recall that at first Esau plotted Jacob's death after his loss of power. The message of Genesis is that a change of heart is vital to the persistence of the species. It is why Esau forgives Jacob's treachery. But few of us live in mythic fairy tales. Our struggle must continue, and short of major global reconstruction, we have little evidence that the more powerful will willingly show compassion and justice for the disenfranchised.

Thus, what we seek to find in the narrative of the Italian-American from Newark is not a change of heart but a change of tactic. He might be willing to change his attitudes and values. He might be only trying to defend himself from a perceived, unmotivated attack. Both of these possibilities address the essential tension: the once-powerful must find a way of relating without the old "cultural weapons"; and this necessity introduces a rhetorical crisis of recovery. How the actor ultimately comes to relate is essential to the initial structure of the crisis he faces. Thus, the immediate need is for a change of tactic for maintaining control, and this is the source of the rhetorical dimension of recovery of racial hegemony.

The discourse of white recovery suggests the following sequence:

(1) Power shifts along racial lines (such as those that have characterized the 1960s in America and the 1990s in South Africa) create anxiety, confusion, rage (turned inward), and anger (turned outward).

(2) The incumbent leaders are perceived as traitors by members of the once-dominant group. This discourse is one of loss of entitled privileges. (The soothing of these passions during such periods becomes a major task. We saw this task underway recently with Nelson Mandela's repeated insistence that Black South Africans will not overwhelm and destroy white South Africans under democratic governance.)

(3) When a renormalization process occurs like the one that took place in the United States over the last decade, the discourse of loss persists but gradually gives way to a discourse of recovery.

(4) This discourse of recovery takes on several ironic rhetorical elements identified and conceptually interrelated in a way that helps to explain more dramatically and pragmatically certain perplexing language features and logics.

(5) These features include the following dimensions and dynamics:

  a. public (collective) efforts to recover the pragmatic and moral losses;

  b. private renegotiations of the original hierarchical arrangements in daily life;

  c. a convergence of the public and private actions and analyses;

  d. their dual justification and legitimation by various factions within the society through negation of the previous reigning rhetorical situation; and

  e. the gradual emergence of a reconciliative, inclusive formative image, purged of the negativity of the lost moral context. We see this reconciliation in the "Rainbow Coalition" metaphor, with its emphasis on unity of differences.

These elements taken together constitute "rhetorical," a process that takes place on two interrelated though distinct levels. Through the operation of these elements, white Americans have gone a long way toward recovering two myths—social messianism and manifest destiny—compromised by the conscience and imagination of the 1960s.

Rhetorical Reversal: Its Dimensions

These events provide the backdrop for the self-induced and Other-sustained sense of "righteous indignation," or "moral outrage," under-pinning rhetorical reversal. Three distinct though inter-related dimensions appear with this process.

1. *The Violation: Negative Stereotyping.* Here we have a charge that the Other has refused to accept one's actions at face value or allow for the possibility of acquiescence. This charge often resembles "the privatization of morality," where an individual is seen as the primal site of good and bad deeds. For example, a white gang member claims that an attack on a Black in a predominantly white neighborhood was over territoriality, not race. In another case, a young man writes to the editor of a local paper that an incident in which a group of Black women were harassed by a group of white males was "sexism" not "racism." The violation occurs because of an implied intentionality rooted in a collusive bond: the white person, for instance, is aroused by the Other's—a Black's—act of defining the situation.

2. *The Assertion: "Blaming the Victim."* This aspect of the reversal is characterized by an outrageous charge that the real perpetrator of hostilities is the historical victim, not the historical villain.[1] Rhetorically, however, it is merely regaining a control of meaning, making and invoking a topoi of "innocent of all guilt" for historical crimes—especially when accused by a "historical victim." This argument is reinforced by a postmodernist inversion of "innocent until proven guilty" since now the jury resides within, and is at one with, the accused.

3. *The Recovery: Disavowal of Moral Complicity through Historic Privilege.* Here we have a refusal to associate one's current privileged place in society with historic inequities that persist in current individuals and institutions. Thus, we see a refusal to acknowledge that white American wealth rests upon exploitation, especially of other races, classes, and genders, and that it continues to reproduce essentially the same patterns as existed under, say, slavery. Such a disavower has no shame nor sense of blame—hence, no moral obligation—around the plight of the oppressed: "they" are "individuals" just like oneself, capable of making it or failing just like oneself. This stance, of course, allows one to trivialize the Other's historic and structural differences.

Frederick Douglass, the slave turned abolitionist, observed that power concedes nothing not demanded of it. He seems most accurate: we find little evidence that parents, teachers, priests, or dictators give up their relative power without an argument. We might elaborate upon Douglass by observing that what has been lost will often be recovered "by whatever means necessary." Earlier we saw in Ronald Reagan's inaugural speech something to this very effect: "It is right to dream large dreams." What ought one to do to retain power, especially when history tells a story of greater kingdoms than ours falling with time? How does one defy aging, history, death?

Vampirism is one answer to this question, and the actual answer is, in fact, a variant of vampirism: taking the moral integrity and thus the root *topos* of the victim. This is hardly a new idea; it is the essential meaning of cannibalism.[2] Nor is this cannibalism absent from the more mundane and commonplace events of daily life. We can see a special case of vampirism through the prism of the rhetorical reversal technique.

RECOVERY AS SYMBOLIC REVERSAL: THE CASE OF VANILLA ICE

Here is how a recent article on contemporary developments in the world of so-called rap music ended:

> Though he embodies the macho swagger of most rappers, his is a sanitized, nonthreatening rap, a suburban version presented with crisp diction and Disneyesque dazzle. Purists don't like it and some older rap fans find it too slick, but the screaming white girls who make up his core audience certainly respond. At a time when rappers like Public Enemy and KRS-One struggle to reach mass audiences with earnest and powerful raps about poverty, self-reliance and the need to overcome societal roadblocks, it's almost perverse that the most popular rapper is a sexy white man whose lyrics rarely stray from good-time concerns. (Moon 1991)

This article focused on a rap star called Vanilla Ice. But who is this man, and why is he so important to the country and to the pursuit of an enlarged understanding of white recovery activity? The reviewer, Tom Moon of the Knight-Ridder newspapers, invests a great deal of detail in his discussion of Vanilla Ice, a twenty-two-year-old from a middle-class, white Texas town who had, within a few months, sold seven million copies of a rap album. Moreover, despite the scandal associated with his rise to fame, he has continued to gain fans among young whites, particularly but not exclusively female. By placing his recent activities within the rhetorical reversal framework, we can see the recovery message in Vanilla Ice. We can begin with the violation: his felt loss and his move to recover it.

1. *The Violation.* Most rap stars are Black or poor inner-city youth from Hispanic backgrounds. However, we are told about Vanilla Ice that

> he went to great lengths to obscure his suburban Dallas upbringing. He and manager Tommy Quon—who discovered Ice at a talent contest at his Dallas club, City Lights—created an anti-hero's life story that left many scratching their heads.
>
> In his initial bio—which was revised last month after press accounts refuted many of its claims—this rapper said he grew up near a Miami housing project, went to

the same high school 2 Live Crew's Luther Campbell attended, was seriously wounded at least once, and won hundreds of trophies in motocross racing....

> But in a *Rolling Stone* article last month, his mother seemed confused by her son's gang references. Certainly, she said, she "wasn't aware" of the stabbing that Ice said "drained half of the blood from my body." (Moon 1991)

2. *The Assertion.* The previous extract also strongly implies that Vanilla Ice sees himself as the real victim, that the Other is essentially a fraud rather than victim. But it is most evident in Vanilla Ice's own description of himself and the Others (read as Black):

> During an October interview, he elaborated grandly on these points, and explained that true rap fans could tell that he was from the streets: "The reason you don't see as many white people in (rap) is because rap comes from the streets. When I'm on stage I feel the same way as Black people feel, I can tell by the way they're moving. I grew up with mostly Black kids from the neighborhood, got into the same trouble they did, listened to the same music they did. (Moon 1991)

These are powerful and telling lines ... and lies. Vanilla Ice asserts (1) that he need only say that he has a particular plight to convince others to treat him in the same way as they treat the Black person as victim; (2) that the real differences between his and Blacks' life histories and life chances are irrelevant; and (3) that the differences between him and the Other are collapsible by personal fiat. He knows that he feels as Blacks do; therefore, he is free to fabricate a self and negate the reality of the Other as a separate and different type of self. This is precisely what the Italian-American politician, confronted by a Black militant accuser, did: exercised a right to collapse the real differences between their respective forms of racism.

To be sure, this "bio-embellishment" is largely "show-biz hype" with its own long-standing history. But when whites portrayed Blacks in the entertainment of yesteryear, that portrayal said something about the values and norms of the period. The same is true in the present case. Vanilla Ice is more than an idiosyncratic idol of the white female teenager: he is symptomatic. Indeed, several successful movies of the past decade have returned to the "Black face" to make the point that for a white to break back into the game, he must be "Black."

This portrayal of white as Black suggests that "Blackness" is arbitrary and negotiable. It also provides the ultimate rationale for why and how Blacks and whites can come together under the banner of "non-racial self" or "racelessness." (The painful irony is that "Blackness" has always been negotiable. Thus, the double bind: one really ought to let "Blackness" go, and one really ought to "be ashamed" to give it up so readily after all that

"Blacks" have given to make the folly and lie a palatable reality. This is the ultimate sham and shamefulness of oppression: one will be "politically incorrect" whatever decision one ultimately makes.)

To be "freed" of "race" after so many hundreds of years of persecution solely because of this quality is a great relief, then, for Blacks. But there is more: it gives whites even greater relief and release to hear "race" and "racism" are dead. To be given reprieve from guilt and responsibility without surrender is every postmodernist's birthright. Vanilla Ice pursues his birthright by claiming another's, and we will always have our Jacobs.

But the key dynamic propelling Vanilla Ice's self-consciously assertive recovery of his rights is a racial recovery motive rather similar to what we once called "racism." It is similar, for example, to that spirit of opportunism that inspired the imaginative white male in Boston in 1990 to kill his pregnant wife in a Black neighborhood, accuse a Black male, and *induce* the mayor, police force, and city to fall in frenzy upon the Black community. Nor is this use of stereotyping to "retribalize" the races restricted to isolated incidents. Before getting to the third reversal feature of Vanilla Ice, it will be helpful, then, to take a quick detour through film, which supplies an excellent clue to the pervasiveness of the "retribalization" process.

The movie *Rocky* presents the saga of a working-class Italian from Philadelphia who wants the glory of being a champion of the boxing ring. We all can identify with his story. But if we consider it from a recovery perspective by examining the images the movie emphasizes, the story takes on new meaning. In five *Rocky* sequels, Rocky progresses from being the loser's hero to becoming first a racial hero, then a national hero, then an international hero: in the first movie, Rocky gains the respect of the boastful Black champion, Apollo Creed, by fighting him to a draw. In the sequel, he defeats Creed. In the third movie, he wins Creed's affection, loyalty, and assistance as he battles another Black, Mr. T. In the fourth installment of the saga, Rocky returns to the ring to defeat a Russian demigod after the Russian kills Apollo Creed, always the American loyalist, in the ring. (Note that Rocky won the Russian heart well before the 1990s.) In the fifth, and presumably final, installment, Rocky does his intergenerational generative bit: he guides a young white prodigy, a young man who just happens to be, in real life, the only serious white male contender for the heavyweight championship since Black men began dominating the ring in the 1960s.

Rocky, like *The Godfather,* is mostly just good entertainment. But there is an important though subtle and understated recovery mission and message in this particular saga. Some other films have been less subtle in the recovery message.

For example, in the movie *Soul Man,* a white male refused entrance to Harvard "paints himself Black," buys an Afro wig and some gold for his neck, and goes off to Harvard, courtesy of affirmative action. He is so persuasive that he becomes a hero and even wins a beautiful Black woman, who cannot, of course, tell he "ain't the real McCoy."

Though a comedy, *Soul Man* is reminiscent of *The Stepford Wives,* a drama about white New England husbands who kill their feminist wives. The newest member of the group, a Black man, arrives at the very end of the movie, after the white wives have been destroyed and replaced by automatonic replicas. Presumably, the Black wife will get her "treatment' too.

These two movies pursue the idea that the white man, denied his birthright, must recover it. Nicer than skinheads and more polished than the Klan, the presumed audience for such movies as these is being told a story: loss can be recovered. But does Vanilla Ice really relate to this fictionalized violence toward Blacks and women? And how does his behavior symbolize a collective rather than private recovery?

Vanilla Ice symbolizes White Power, the Italian-American who takes on the Black militant in Harold Isaacs's story. He is the Rocky who defeats the loud-mouthed, Black heavyweight champion (an apparent composite of Muhammad Ali and George Foreman) before he goes on to defeat the Russian hero, with the Black champion and his trainer back in their proper place as his seconds.

Moreover, it is precisely the "inability to know he's faking" that makes Vanilla Ice a race hero. He explodes the myth of Black musical superiority and its companion myth, that "Black suffering" is related to "soul." We have even more direct evidence that Vanilla Ice is a central (and sexual) symbol of the white recovery project: he has already been described as Elvis Presley's replacement.[3] But Elvis did not have to remove a "Black champion"; Vanilla Ice did.[4]

As table 3 shows, a developmental and dialectical sequence operates here. To understand this aspect more fully, however, we need once more to return to the article on Vanilla Ice, this time focusing on the third reversal feature, the refusal.

3. *The Refusal.* Here is what Tom Moon tells us:

Ice's music is derivative in the M. C. Hammer tradition. It depends on simple, repetitive beats and uses vintage pop hits for melody and structure. Lyrically, Ice's raps are nothing special. The best ones offer an update of the "girls and cars and fun" theme that the Beach Boys made their trademark. ...Tellingly, what Ice omits from his rap is perhaps its most important element, its advocacy, its relevance to modern life. Even the most lurid and violent raps by Black artists address specific audiences and real-life conditions. That shred of truth gives them their strength and resonance. And the pop raps of

Table 3   An Illustration of the Recovery of White Voice: The Case of Male Music Idols

	Recovery Climate		
	1950s	1970s	1990s
Culture Hero	Elvis Presley	Michael Jackson	Vanilla Ice
Cultural Base	Rhythm & Blues	Rhythm & Blues	Rap/R&B
Dominant Voice	White	Minority	Nonracial[*]

[*]White voice and nonracial voice are effectively the same in a white-dominated society.
"Color" is an obsession only for the "colored" and "the white gatekeepers"; others are free to disregard color or race, to believe in the factitiousness of the ideology of subjective equality and universal suffrage.

DJ Jazzy Jeff and the Fresh Prince make sly social commentary. (Moon 1991)

Moon exposes, in these lines, the irony: Vanilla Ice does indeed address a specific audience—white men who believe that Blacks, women, gays, Jews, and others have stolen their birthright. Those millions of white women who swoon over Vanilla Ice convey merely a part of the message. From a recovery perspective, they are only an incidental audience; they are the "spoils of the victor." Nor is it stretching a point to make the comparison to Elvis.

That Vanilla Ice resembles Elvis Presley is clear to all who recall that "The King" was a white man whose "gift"—his body movement—was similar to, yet different from, those of the Black entertainers he imitated. But more can be gleaned from the association with Elvis: (1) the unquestionable dominance of the white voice in the 1950s and early 1960s meant that only a white man could be a culture hero. Few have ever questioned that Elvis (or Larry Bird after him) was a great artist. But he was only one star among so very many. Yet he was the white star in a world of Black stars. Like Tarzan in the jungle, he had to be "king." By the late 1970s, however, a Black man could hold this role, provided he could capture the white imagination and be Black but more. Michael Jackson did this.

A gifted Black child star, Michael Jackson, like Donny Osmond before him, belonged to a family of talented people. (At one point, the Osmonds and Jacksons had competing television shows.) But Michael emerged as culture hero, or "king," over other mortals. Some saw him as Peter Pan, others as the Pied Piper. For most, however, he had become a sort of "racial eunuch": deprived of the features that suggest Black manhood, Michael Jackson qualified as a hero for millions of screaming young white females. (He could even appear on the cover of the tabloids as a mate for Brooke Shields and father of her child.)

Clearly, to achieve this status, Michael had to sacrifice. His loss symbolized the preparedness of some Blacks to trivialize their "old Black selves" by rejecting aspects of self traditionally associated with "Blackness." Jackson's loss also prepared the stage for the recovery of a white male as the reigning "king of music."

Vanilla Ice embodies this recovery. Elvis Presley, by contrast, symbolically allowed whites to continue their reign. But Vanilla Ice is helping them recover a crown that involves much more than music. Blacks dominate popular music in much the same way as they dominate basketball and football. Though white men largely own these sports as professional activities, a white man must fight to participate on the court and field. Vanilla Ice fought for his place in the entertainment sun, his "piece of the action." But to own "a piece of the action," a man must "pass"—he must possess something that allows him into the game. The fabricated Vanilla Ice biography is, of course, a stereotype, but we can ask rhetorically (with Tom Moon), "But really, what does it matter? Despite—or maybe because of—the allegations, Ice's popularity has skyrocketed."

Vanilla Ice's behavior is important because it provides a means for achieving the convergence of personal and collective recovery as racial hegemony. Upon this exposure, the rhetoric of recovery appeared in his apology. His imitation of a stereotypic biography of "Black genius" both affirms and negates the moral ground previously underpinning the Black voice: racial suffering has heightened the Black man's passions and encourages his spontaneity and musical giftedness to find expression without the inhibitions accompanying white civility. That is to say, Blacks have *soul*.

By feigning the history of poverty and wretchedness of urban, minority life, Vanilla Ice imitated the larger societal drama: *white male as racial victim*. This imitation implies Blacks have substantial power and magic; that Blacks are worthy models for whites. But this imitator also negates the alleged basis for Black achievement in music and similar areas of entertainment by appearing to succeed merely by creating fictitious history of social oppression and struggle for survival—and "proving" that even a white male can be a great "rapper."

Vanilla Ice's cheerful willingness to affect the wretchedness of "Blackness" to achieve the glory of "rap star" represents a break with the past that saw Blacks as valueless and symbols of weakness. In his rejection of the ancient stereotypes he claims a "Black bio," thereby puzzling his mother and those others who may continue to prefer white to

Black. Still Vanilla Ice effects no solid break with the larger social order; rather, he becomes the white male who believes that minorities get all the breaks and that one must be like Blacks and other minorities to get so much as an even chance. Through imitation, Vanilla Ice regains a certain racial hegemony. The white man's rise to the top (in this case, of the rap world) recapitulates the rise of the Black rap star. The white star is thus at once purged and victorious. This is the heroic recovery of racial hegemony.

Vanilla Ice's career reflects a reversal of meaning that informs the logic behind the various white recovery rhetorics. Recent developments in academia and the Supreme Court enlarge the scope of this analysis and further suggest how white recovery of voice has significantly (re)silenced the Black voice. Consider for a moment white recovery in the political and social rather than cultural arena. It is, after all, the convergence of symbolic with substantive power that makes the white man awesome—and differentiates him from the Black, brown, red, or yellow man in the contemporary world.

RECOVERY DISCOURSE AS RHETORICAL
CONDITION

Practical men and women understand that "getting in the first word" beats "getting a word in edgewise." In the realm of communication, Asante and Atwater (1986) called these built-in advantages "rhetorical condition." Reminiscent of Marshall McLuhan's reflections on the mass media as the message, Asante and Atwater wrote, "What we are saying is that structure constitutes a parallel message indicating the idea of a rhetoric of form about the rhetoric of words." This notion pertains to hierarchies and inequities and helps describe the rhetorical context within which race rhetoric as recovery rhetoric has evolved. The critical point in Asante and Atwater for this discussion is an allusion to the ideological aspect of hierarchical discourse: "[H]ierarchical discourse which seeks to maintain its hierarchical position is supported by ideology. Without the ideological context, the discourse is vacuous, empty, a hollow form without power" (Asante and Atwater 1986, 170).

The individual seeking to recover or retain a sense of hegemony requires more than just privatized validation. Privatized reality is alienated discourse. It reflects the absence of communion and thus the absence of power. It is precisely when one finds through ideology a connection to others that one can move toward justification, righteous indignation, and political (re)empowerment. But individual incidents, while important, do not adequately address larger societal needs regarding the loss and recovery of hegemony in discourse. After all,

"while the condition may be negotiated by the communicators, different rhetorical situations produce different conditions because the inherent power relationships change from situation to situation' (Asante and Atwater 1986, 171). How does one learn that one's individual negotiation has "collective merit"? That is, how is one able to join one's own feelings and emotions to the collective level? What is the transformational code?

Humor as Rhetorical Condition

We have been viewing narrative as the preferred vehicle for persuasion. But other vehicles—satire and humor, for example—also serve to persuade. From this viewpoint, satire and humor are rhetorical conditions, and humor is particularly important in this regard. Humor has considerable cultural significance: it encodes many subtle, sacred, and shared meanings for a group. Humor has, moreover, a decidedly aggressive feature, as such various scholars as Henri Bergson, Sigmund Freud, and Theodore Reik have observed. It is also true that African-Americans have held for centuries a unique place in American humor. In fact, a special drama evolved out of the sharing of a racist joke during the post-radical 1970s.

In 1975, the secretary of agriculture, Earl L. Butz, was exposed as having told a racist joke involving the "prime and solitary pleasures and pursuits of Negroes"—namely, food, leisure, and sex. Butz later said that he had heard the joke from a midwestern colleague and merely shared it with his white colleagues on a private plane ride back to Washington, D.C. When Butz was forced to resign, many critics and supporters lined up to have their say. Perceiving the reactionary nature of the white American response to an incipient move toward eliminating racism, Klumpp and Hollihan observed:

> Ritual is not only the essential process of reaffirming a piety, but also the process of a rebirth through which ideology may be changed. Whether an event precipitates a conservative ritual reaffirming an old ideology or a new ideology depends on the rhetoric surrounding it. Earl Butz argued that he was simply repeating a joke heard earlier from a midwestern politician. The rationalization is believable, and of course that is the point— Earl Butz's sin was the failure to stifle his innate cultural bias. (Klumpp and Hollihan 1979, 19)

Butz suffered a failure to conceal, but his was also an expression of the way in which humor promotes the recovery of voice. Butz probably told the truth. But the deeper and more profound truth is that humor provides a vehicle for reestablishing racial hegemony without having to be identified directly with the act of aggression; after all, it's just a joke. The rhetorical power of humor inheres in its seeming neutrality. In this case, it allowed the speaker to redefine a racist act as a joke, a simple social sharing of an acknowledged "nonfactual" but "funny" bit of information. This is the hegemonic dimension of humor, and this particular use of humor reveals the hegemonic status of race relations in America: one may commit a racist act and deny it as such because the aggression is concealed in a chameleonic communication.[5]

This ability to act racist without bearing the racist label is the equivalent of recovering racial hegemony. Klumpp and Hollihan's analysis of the Butz controversy supports this argument. In particular, they point to this instance of the recovery process: Butz repeated what he had heard fully intending to establish and extend identification through the sharing and covalidation of an old value. As Klumpp and Hollihan point out, one may not consider the exposure of the racial slur or the subsequent debates and forced resignation as changing the overall situation since the social structure underpinning such thinking remains in place. Additionally, Klumpp and Hollihan maintain that this split of private and public racism permits personal racist acts to persist because no one demands sincere change.

Moreover, another, more critical form of collusion operates here. This more critical collusion is the shared stance that no continuity exists between the public and personal behavioral domains. Yet it is precisely this shared stance of nonrelationship that sustains both objective (public) and subjective (private) actions of racism. Only on certain occasions can the collusive bond be exposed and understood as such. Humor exposes subjective and objective racism. This form of collusion is precisely what gives the professional wrestling match its symbolic value and persuasive power. A brief examination of the essential drama of the pageant known as professional wrestling helps illustrate the collusive communication I have been describing.

The Wrestling Match as Rhetorical Condition

Professional wrestling has a basic form: good versus evil in a world where the odds favor evil. Most wrestlers, therefore, are cast as either good or evil. (In their carnival world, the wrestlers themselves call the good guy a "face" and the bad guy a "heel.") In professional wrestling, the referee is the judge; he (women seldom serve as judges in professional wrestling) stands for justice. But justice can be conveniently blind, and the referee often sides with the "evil" wrestlers. This unholy alliance is, in fact, what stacks the odds in favor of evil. By managing, routinely, to miss blatant "illegal acts"—actions perfectly evident to the audience—the referee induces the audience to identify with the "face." Presumably, the members of the audience associate these acts of unfairness and judicial

complicity with events in their own lives. Roland Barthes has described "the world of wrestling":

> But what wrestling is above all meant to portray is a purely moral concept: that of justice. Justice is the embodiment of a possible transgression.
>
> It is therefore easy to understand why out of five wrestling matches, only about one is fair. One must realize, let it be repeated, that "fairness" here is a role or a genre, as in the theater: the rules do not at all constitute a real constraint: they are the conventional appearances of fairness. So that in actual fact a fair fight is nothing but an exaggeratedly polite one. One must understand, of course, here, that all these polite actions are brought to the notice of the public by the most conventional gestures of fairness: shaking hands, raising the arms, ostensibly avoiding a fruitless hold which would detract from the perfection of the contest. (Barthes 1972, 21–22)

Barthes's description comes remarkably close to the paradigm Klumpp and Hollihan depicted wherein the president asks for the resignation of Earl Butz. This technique, moreover, is routinely employed. For instance, CBS once suspended its popular humorist Andy Rooney for repeating Butz's error; and ABC Sports forced "Jimmy the Greek" into early retirement for the same reason. In each of these cases the public took sides precisely as they had in the Earl Butz case, and the central claim in each instance was a denial that racism had been the intent.

In wrestling, such responses by the actors are significant because they ultimately echo the official stance. Thus, in the wrestling match, a "heel" uses some foreign substance—say, salt or ring resin—to disable his opponent. The referee claims not to have seen this ruse despite the cries of the spectators and the disabled "face." The "heel" denies wrongdoing, and the referee supports him. In the real world, we see an excellent illustration of a wrestling referee in recent Supreme Court actions.

At the conclusion of a recent *reversal* of an earlier landmark case, Justice Thurgood Marshall accused several of his peers of "selective amnesia" and of insulating "an especially invidious form of racial discrimination from the scrutiny of the Sixth Amendment." Marshall, a Black justice and member of the body voting on the earlier landmark case, declared the spirit of the previous decision violated. Like Chief Justice Earl Warren, Justice Marshall belonged to the "Old America" where racism was official policy; thus, he knows that the presence and effects of racism have not essentially changed over the past four decades. In an earlier time, this condition would have been clearly accepted as the case. But times change.

Earlier, we adduced the popularity of Vanilla Ice as evidence that times change and whites no longer accept the notion of racism as a given. We also saw

Table 4 *Rhetorical Reversal and the Supreme Court: A 'Case' of Recovery*

| | Rhetorical Situation | |
	1954	1990
Rhetor	Chief Justice Warren	Justice Scalia
Rhetorical	[Segregation] generates a	Justice Marshall's dissent
Reversal	feeling of inferiority in	rolls out the ultimate
	their [Blacks'] hearts and	weapon, the accusation
	minds in a way unlikely	of insensitivity to racial
	ever to be undone.	discrimination—which loses its intimidating
		effect if it continues to be fired so randomly.

that Vanilla Ice trivialized the historical meaning of racial protest embodied in reggae and rap music by creating a fictitious biography to support his imitation of Black rap stars and that Vanilla Ice's rhetoric is paralleled by official recovery actions and rhetoric. Observe these comments of Justice Antonin Scalia, who voted with the majority in the case Justice Marshall criticized as encouraging racism:

> Justice Marshall's dissent rolls out the ultimate weapon, the accusation of insensitivity to racial discrimination—which will lose its intimidating effect if it continues to be fired so randomly. (*New York Times*, January 23, 1990)

Table 4 clarifies Scalia's response as reclamation or recovery of rhetorical hegemony.[6] Unlike Chief Justice Earl Warren, who is of another era, Justice Scalia conveys a resistance to the idea of white aggression and dominance as "racism." Previous generations of whites may have resisted any characterization of their racism as inhumane destructiveness, but they at least knew what racism was and that they condoned and committed racist acts. Scalia's stance implies (as have several recent Supreme Court reversals of the Warren Court) that racism has become rare, existing in the actions of a few whites and the minds and random racist rhetoric of rather more Blacks.

Negotiation of Meaning and the Erosion of Moral Responsibility

Like the wrestling referee, Justice Scalia is an actor in and icon of an unjust institutional structure.[7] He reaffirmed not only a popular belief that many actions by whites that harm Blacks are not necessarily "racist" but also the refusal of whites to feel fear or guilt for behavior they do not consider racist.

When labeled as racist, such behavior is now posited as idiosyncratic, and the incidents are isolated. This sentiment has given rise to a new form of rhetoric, the rhetoric of the self. It draws its justification, righteousness, and efficacy from the presumed privacy of personal experience and privatized meaning. Its emotional fuel is (1) a historical sense

of betrayal by society and (2) an existential sense of violation by the *negative stereotyping* and moral indictment inherent in traditional racist rhetoric. As humor provides an opportunity for private but shared sentiments to find expression, so a stance like Justice Scalia's offers an opportunity for imitation and illustration of the thesis.

Vanilla Ice's recovery behavior is symbolic. The Supreme Court's recovery actions are binding and substantive. Together, the symbolic and substantive are destructive. Nowhere is this more evident than in the recent reloss of the Black voice.

The Press and the Loss of the Black Voice

A large state university newspaper provided the following account: a group of white males had a confrontation with two Black males. One of the white males was cited for "criminal mischief." He denied the incident was racially motivated, adding with presumed sarcasm, "Anything between a Black guy and a white guy is considered racially motivated." A Black person who was attacked said, "They called us niggers a couple of times. I guess I really can't say what they were thinking about. It might have been racial. I don't know" (*Daily Collegian* [Pennsylvania State University], February 13, 1990). The critical factor here is the uncertainty characterizing this exchange. It is now possible to portray interaction—even physical conflict—between persons of different race without "race" being a collectively recognized factor. The Black male *becomes* uncertain of the meaning of events. This is much as it was historically: whites control the "definition of the situation." The difference is that now power is exercised unofficially. White law enforcement officers, university officials, and the news media are the power brokers in this drama; they can and they do deny the relevance of race in an altercation. Their silence, to recall Malcolm X and Mary Daly, is the reversal.

These events parallel Justice Scalia's ruling; and a shared message is offered; racism is essentially dead, and Black persons are as likely as white persons to receive fair treatment from a random sample of jurors or find themselves in a "friendly fight." The destructive power of the denials involved in this drama parallels the wrestling match where the spectators and the "face" know the truth but cannot gain a favorable ruling from the referee. This is the meaning and experience of loss of racial voice for African-Americans at the close of the twentieth century.

Meanwhile, the recovery of the white voice occurs as only an aspect, albeit an important aspect, of a larger recovery process. The African-American shares in this larger recovery as American, but loses voice as a member of an oppressed social group. Before we take up the precise nature of the recovery and loss for African-Americans, consider one final illustration of the contextual features of this recovery of meaning-making that characterizes the American imagination of today.

A recent issue of the *Centre Daily Times* (State College, Pa.) reported that during a campaign speech a white, female gubernatorial candidate called the state governor "a redneck Irishman from Scranton." Her spokesman responded on her behalf with the following rationale: "She said it. I do not characterize it, as it is being characterized, as an ethnic slur. I don't consider it one [and] I'm Irish from Scranton" (*Centre Daily Times*, February 13, 1990).

The candidate's refusal to acknowledge the pejorative ethnic meaning in her comment reflects a privatized stance. But the appearance of someone who supports this privatized meaning is the real concern, for that person is helping the candidate to escape from a frame of historical guilt and personal responsibility to a "nothing means nothing" stance. This kind of support is a problematic, but nonetheless meaningful, feature of discourse in postmodern society: words and meanings are now negotiable. Thus, one is responsible ultimately to a privatized lexicon validated by significant Others singled out for their capacity to share this vision: the individual's right to say and do as he or she pleases and redefine (renegotiate) meaning because of the loss of collective language and meaning.

POSTMODERNISM AS PRIVILEGED RECOVERY

The condition created by the death of "official racism" is the need to define the meaning of various persistent instances of "racist behavior." Since the mere fact that one taunts or hurts a "nigger" no longer constitutes individual and collective acts of racism, one needs a validational context. This validational context has to meet two interrelated requirements with respect to human activity: (1) racist actions on the part of a public figure must be seen as private actions that may or may not reflect personal racism; and (2) racist actions on the part of private citizens must be renegotiable as episodic and free of a collective underpinning. Together, these two requirements pertain to the symbolic level of voice recovery—that is, the legitimation of the persistence of private beliefs regarding the "true nature" of things and the dramatic renegotiation of this belief.

The media constructed their coverage of Jesse Jackson's "Rainbow Coalition" campaign for the Democratic presidential nomination so as to maintain the idea of Blacks versus whites (Gresson 1987). The *New York Times, Los Angeles Times*, and *Washington Post* all reported on the "birth and death of the Rainbow Coalition" in a way that invalidated it as a basis for coalescing. In several instances, the leads of the articles reporting campaign events were misleading; in other cases, the headlines were inflammatory. Most important, however, was an evident determination to dismiss the coalition as a racial fantasy, to polarize the coalition along racial lines, and, ultimately, to reduce it to nothing more than symbolic "Black pride."[8] These events strongly suggest that a major white recovery strategy has been to deindividuate the African-American.

"Deindividuation" means to make "undifferent." For example, the military, parochial schools, and hospitals make, respectively, all their recruits, students, and patients dress alike. They make individuals look as much alike as possible in their clothes, hairstyles, the possessions permitted in the sleeping area, and so on. This is deindividuation, and its serves to "play down" that which, like wealth and family origin, makes one different from another. Both rich and poor wear white gowns in the hospital; both rich and poor wear uniforms in the military and in parochial school. And yet some differences remain. We know that a poor white or Black is more liable to be an infantry person than the child of a billionaire; we know that students who attend "City Catholic High School" are liable to be poorer than those who attend Loyola or Notre Dame High.

But why is *deindividuation* an important concept? It helps us, in the present instance, understand how Blacks and whites in the twentieth century have found a common identity yet remain different. It helps us, for example, understand how both Blacks and whites may wear Jordache jeans or Reebok tennis shoes despite the fact that Blacks earn on average less than half of what whites earn in this country and that Black families' collective net worth is a mere fraction of white wealth. It also helps us start to see how this move toward "nondifference" invites one to forget differences in both the past and the present, and probably in the future.

NOTES

1. Thus, we see, for example, the argument that women batter men as much as men batter women, and that men

are wronged by a system that favors women's rights over those of the male. Then there is the racial parallel: Blacks on predominantly white campuses are the causes of the hostilities white students express toward them. This argument is, of course, a variant of the one used by Ivy League schools to rationalize the quotas they placed on American Jews in the 1920s. We will remember that Jews had gained an undesirable quantitative presence in the elite professions, and non-Jewish whites wanted *to recover their perceived losses*. (Something very much like this is taking place today at certain universities in California and New England where Asian-Americans enter these schools in ratios beyond their representation in the general population.)

2. The anthropological understanding of cannibalism is that it was a ritual aimed at gaining the strength (spirit) of the vanquished enemy, thereby enhancing one's own spirit. Some psychoanalytic scholars have seen it too as a means of resolving the difference between self and Other: by taking you into myself, you become a part of me, and I do not have to deal with you as a separate and possibly disagreeable entity. Of course, the connection with the current discussion is that the cannibalist, like the narrator, wants to tell a story for both self and Other. For a cogent study of cannibalism from this perspective, see Eli Sagan (1974).

3. The issue of sex between Blacks and whites has been discussed widely and requires little elaboration here. Interested readers may want to refer to Joel Kovel (1970). The more significant link I want to make here is that the use of sexual energy of affect to explore larger social matters is an important rhetorical breakthrough. For a major discussion of this dynamic in the cinema, see Thomas W. Benson (1980).

4. In this regard, too, Vanilla Ice is more like a warrior. Recall that "the Great White Hope" was to come forth and defeat the Black man, Jack Johnson, who had taken the heavyweight title, married a white woman, and taunted his white victims in the ring. After Johnson was destroyed, it would not be until Muhammad Ali that a Black man would again raise his voice in the ring: Joe Louis, Floyd Patterson, and Sugar Ray Robinson were all voiceless in this regard.

5. Allow me a personal story here. Recently at a neighborhood bar a young white male struck up conversation with me. As the conversation progressed and he become more and more familiar, he began telling "Polack jokes," declaring himself part Polish. Eventually, he said, "I want to tell you this Black joke—over 95 percent of my buddies are nig—, uh, Blacks. I want to tell you this joke. This cop stopped three Blacks in a car. He hit one over the head, and the Black guy asked, 'What did you do that for?' He proceeded to the second Black guy and bopped him over the head with the nightstick as he asked to see the vehicle's registration. Again, the second Black asked, 'What did you hit me for?' but got no answer. Then the cop hit the third Black, and when he asked 'Why?' he was informed, 'Because I was fulfilling your fantasy to be hit in the head.'" The young man's companion, an older white male, was growing more visibly anxious as the story progressed, but he seemed equally interested to see my reaction. When I commented that I had heard that one before, the tension dissipated and the conversation went back to this young man's Polish heritage. Perhaps because of his drinking and background this young man did not see that this joke was an aggressive story and that it was intended to be shared with other whites, not Blacks.

6. Justice Scalia belongs to the group of three new justices selected by conservative Republican presidents. While the battles in Congress regarding the partisan orientation each of these people represented mimic "fairness" (like the wrestling match), this is largely form: *it is understood that the justices will decide the legal tenor of the country for the duration of their lives—and they are chosen to represent the interests of the controlling president and party*. The choice of the three recent justices constitutes a recovery of white voice, a recovery of the concessions made during a radical period of the country's history. In this, the current series of events only replicates the Second Reconstruction of the late nineteenth century when Black progress was halted and the infamous Jim Crow laws were enacted to ensure that Blacks could not seriously challenge—through integration—the structural arrangement encoded in the Constitution and only partially offset by its amendments.

7. L. Althusser's "repressive state apparatus" is suggestive here. The idea he conveys is that various institutions play a coordinating role with regard to the perpetuation of certain role types and relational tensions. Of course, this is a pivotal theme of political communication study. On this, see Althusser (1970; 1971). For an application of Althusser's ideas to narrative in organizations, see Dennis K. Mumby (1988).

8. Several studies have shown a parallel tendency in the media. Specifically, these studies emphasize the media's ability to cue the reader to a particular view by the items they choose to report on and the extent and duration of their coverage. These include the important work of D. A. Graber (1976; 1984).

A notable recent instance of such cueing is described in a study by J. Gregory Payne (1989). His study of the *Los Angeles Times*'s handling of the 1984 gubernatorial campaign in California revealed a proclivity to highlight Mayor Bradley's race in campaign news stories. Furthermore, analysis of press coverage revealed both polls and voter interest focusing on race in a manner otherwise consistent with campaign coverage.

A related study was reported by C. Husband (1979). Husband studied press coverage of race relations in Britain during the 1960s and found that the press, in alliance with the politicians, operated with certain preconceptions that must he followed through in order for the reports to be intelligible to the masses. He also found that such formations of the news are biased toward the elite. This was achieved partially by permitting certain politicians to dominate news coverage. It was also facilitated by reporting certain kinds of images of the "power elite" and the people it protected. For example, the British are felt to have a self-image as ultra-civilized and "fair," forever seeking to promote justice and harmonious relations.

Husband concluded "that the potentially autonomous psychological dynamic of identity maintenance can no longer be left out of any mass media functioning within situations of intergroup contact" (p. 191).

Implicit in these studies is a collusive bond between the press and the established power. Together they seek to influence opinion through appealing to the already established values and emotions.

Conclusion

Explaining the origins of racism is not a problem. Western philosophy and science since antiquity have sought to unravel the mysteries of descent, generation, inheritance and diversity by reference to a single, encapsulating framework. Race has proved an extraordinarily convenient instrument in this service. Complex human arrangements have been reduced to relatively simple terms and inequality rendered a matter of destiny.

A much harder task is explaining the persistence of racism for so long after it has been discredited. Discoveries in the biological sciences and disclosures in the social sciences have challenged perspectives based on race as an organizing concept. As Ivan Hannaford writes in his *Race: The History of an Idea in the West*, 'Above all else, these scientific works seriously call into question the definitions and presuppositions of race propounded with such certainty in the eighteenth and nineteenth centuries and upon which the tottering superstructure of modern intellectual investigation rests' (1996: 7).

Other initially persuasive ideas, such as phlogiston, germ-plasm or, *entelechy* (life-giving force), have been consigned to their place in history as ingenious though flawed attempts to advance understanding. Their retreat, or banishment has led to newer, improved and often liberating forms of knowledge. No one continues to believe in a mysterious internal vital force which directs the biological processes of an organism toward specific goals. And, if they did, they would be received in much the same way as flat-earthers: harmless cranks. But, those who cling to beliefs based on the notion of race are anything but harmless: in fact, they are malificient. As such, they debase rather than enrich culture. While it is important to ask why people accepted racism in the first place, it is now more exigent to ask why they carry on doing so.

One simple answer is that *de jure* racism is still very fresh in the minds of whites in the USA and Britain. Until the 1954 *Brown* decision, the 'separate but equal' doctrine that owed so much to nineteenth-century biological and political theory, was a legitimate part of the American constitution. (The *Plessy* ruling of 1896 ensured this, of course.) In Britain, a racialized discourse, as some writers put it, influenced thoughts about difference, color and inherited inequalities based on race. Legal attempts to eradicate racialism the practice have failed to make too much indentation on beliefs that turn on the concept of race. In both contexts, racist ideas circulate, albeit in new forms and affect social relations in a way that could have been designed to encourage their persistence.

In the nineteenth and early parts of the twentieth century, the self-fulfilling element of racism was clear enough. Identifying groups as Others and claiming to have special knowledge about their natural inferiority permitted, indeed legitimated, creating conditions under which those Others were denied education, means of worship and other staples customarily associated with a healthy way of life. Growing up with a status no better than that of cattle and living in environments that befitted cattle encouraged pitifully uneducated and impoverished creatures who resembled the Others who were once only a figment of the racists' imagination. Thus, racism fed its own perpetuation.

Some early writers, many of whose work appears in this book, analyzed the functional importance of maintaining an ideology in which racism held sway. Cox, in particular, saw racism as a highly effective adjunct to Western capitalist economies that thrived on cheap, exploitable labor. Myrdal, who bore the brunt of much of Cox's critique, sensed a certain accommodation of racism in the American creed; though he also identified an inherent tension. Later writers, especially in the 1960s, stamped out the message that racism fitted wonderfully well with an entire system founded on the control, despotism and continued disempowerment of black people.

But some contemporary writers believe that any vestigial function racism performed had disappeared by the 1990s. Joe Feagin and Hernán Vera, in their *White Racism*, insist that Americans (and presumably all who live in racist cultures) should see racism for what it actually is: 'A tremendously wasteful set of practices, legitimated by deeply embedded myths, that deprives its victims, its perpetrators, and U.S. society as a whole of much valuable human talent and energy and many social, economic, and political resources' (1995: 9).

Yet, who are the 'perpetrators' of this profligacy? In the 1950s and 1960s, they were easily identified. They were the ones that appeared on our television screens shouting about the free speech that was their natural right and the way of life they wanted to pre-serve. They were the ones that blockaded school gates to prevent African American children entering; who battered civil rights marchers and set fire to churches. And, of course, they were the ones who sometimes hid under white robes and rampaged across the south, terrorizing black people in their futile efforts to maintain the *ancien régime* of old America. That was then. Where are they now?

Nobody is owning up to being a racist today. The passing of the Reagan–Bush era has allowed a new liberalism to flower. Liberals are opposed to any kind of bigotry, racism included; they know what is best for others. Like racists of old, they assert the right to free speech, though, for the most part, it is limited to exactly that: free speech with no necessary action. This is not a condemnation of liberalism. Yet, there are occasional examples of its problems, one coming from Britain.

In 1997, a British research team published a report which detailed a new form of racist bigotry which they called 'Islamophobia'. This was a form of hatred or even resentment directed specifically against Muslims. The report's publication brought forth a welter of liberal indignation. Islam is a rapidly growing, heterogeneous faith. People the world over choose to adhere to this faith. In Britain, there are over one million Muslims. They have shown separatist tendencies, setting up their own denominational schools, their own mosques, their own businesses and other facilities. The report argued that this separatist movement has led to a specific form of phobia, whites either fearing or loathing all things Islamic. As the overwhelming majority of Muslims were of South Asian origin or descent, Islamophobia may have been a persecution based on religion (as the report suggested) or just another instance of racism.

Today, racists come in many guises. Liberals who extol the virtues of multicultural-ism are guided by the spirit of relativism. No one culture is better than another. No matter how exotic or even repulsive their habits may be, other cultures deserve regard, if not approval. But, in fleeing from any taint of racism of one kind, it is rather too easy to succumb to countless other types of coercion, exploitation and downright persecution.

Racism might be understood as a form of refusal: an attempted fight against the changes catalyzed by civil rights and the expansion of equal opportunities. It appeals to an age when whites seemed safe in their positions of dominance and when they asserted some control over a world that now seems beyond their grasp. The extract by Adorno et al. depicts the kind of world yearned for by many racists. They strike against what must seem at times like a liberal conspiracy, a suspicion that has been lent substance by the assassinations of John F. Kennedy and Martin Luther King. Both deaths have, of course, been interpreted as the result of recondite right-wing machinations. Movies like Oliver Stone's *JFK* assist thinking along these lines.

The conclusion we must reach is that racism is mutable. For many racists, the biggest shock is that society seems to change by itself; equal opportunity, anti-racism and black empowerment have gathered their own momentum (witness the Million Man and Million Woman Marches in 1995 and 1997 respectively). Culturally, racism and the equal opportunity it opposes are perfectly compatible solutions. Culture tells us to be good liberals and remain steadfast in our adherence to American values – to be good 'Americans'. This introduces contradictory demands: to be a good American implicates us in a robust defence and perhaps belligerent defense of a nation which has origins in racial oppression, bondage, and subjugation. The boundaries of this nation are constantly being reinforced and good Americans are encouraged to feel proud of this.

Myrdal's American dilemma, as we have seen in his extract, may once have seemed exactly that. But, from the vantage point of today, racism was not part of the dilemma at all, but a perverse solution to it. Someone can applaud the kinds of changes that have worked to amend some of the more glaring injustices that affect ethnic minorities yet cling to their boast of being a good American.

During the late 1980s and 1990s, many African American groups became more vocal in the demands for some form of compensation for the atrocities of slavery, an institution once described by Jesse as 'a hole on America's soul'. It is possible that, had a formal act of catharsis been conducted in the aftermath of the Civil War, when southern slaves were granted their freedom, racism might not linger as it does as the USA's most enduring problem. Of course, this may be a simplisitic piece of historical whimsy.

What distinguishes black people in the USA from their counterparts in Britain and other parts of Europe or South Africa is the longevity of slavery, or, to be exact, its effects on the material conditions and consciousness of blacks and whites alike. Carmichael, Myrdal and many of the others writers featured in this volume were acutely aware of this.

In nearly every case, the first black people to migrate to Britain, primarily from the colonial Caribbean, did so of their own free will. Needless to say, the 'push' and 'pull' factors that factor into any mass migration were at work (in this case in the postwar period), but the movement was a voluntary one. Early studies indicated that, with very few exceptions, migrants in the 1950s confidently expected that they would return to their island homes, preferably after a profitable spell working in what they had come to regard as the 'Mother Country'.

For all the inhuman exploitation, savagery and oppression they suffered under apartheid, black people in South Africa managed to hang on to their language, their religions, their culture. It is perhaps one of the unintended consequences of a system that rigidly separated groups and permitted the continuation of cultural traditions.

The African American experience is different. Blacks were alone in that they were the only people in what is, after all, a society of immigrants who did not originally come to America out of choice. The term *du jour* 'colored people' serves to emphasize the driven rootlessness of the African American experience, failing as it does to distinguish between the multitude of languages and cultures of the continent of Africa, and instead issuing a homogeneous label that may well be politically expedient, but also carries with it memories of the post-emancipation era when the term 'colored' was a polite way of describing a black person.

Let us be plain: black Americans have not capitalized on the American dream because of the obstacles that have been set before them. It is misleading to point – as did Ronald Reagan – to the entrepreneurial zeal of Koreans, or the pluck and determination of other minority groups, many from parts of Europe. Black people's forebears travelled to America not in search of riches or to escape persecution, but because they were enslaved. Unlike the others, they do not possess in their collective memory that sense of optimism or rebirth that is in some way part of the experience of other Americans of migrant origins. Racism affects black people with a sharpness and virulence not felt by other ethnic minorities. If only for this reason alone, we should reconceive its consequences and ways of ameliorating them. For too long, we have satisfied ourselves that the transition to a mature, multiethnic society would bring with it a dissolution of racism and the institutional discriminations it has fostered. This pluralistic policy now looks naive.

Peter McLaren argues that it is time to move beyond a celebration of 'liberal pluralism – because such a pluralism has an ideological center of gravity that rarely ever gets defined for what it is' (1997: 214). He means that liberal pluralists, who encourage the promotion of ethnic diversity, remain part of a society that condones paying workers 'little more than slave wages', that calls for the privatization of education and looks on while the public sphere is allowed to disintegrate.

McLaren's alternative is what he calls, in the title of his book on the subject, *Revolutionary Multiculturalism*, and this involves not only 'analyzing our cultural and social present and decolonizing the Euro-American mind but … effectively organizing our responses to and encounters with the changing economic and cultural world' (1997: 214). In an earlier work ('White terror and oppositional agency'), McLaren (1994) has referred to 'critical multiculturalism' and warns: 'Diversity must be affirmed within a politics of cultural criticism and a commitment to social justice', adding that 'We need to refocus on "structural" oppression in the forms of patriarchy, capitalism, and white supremacy'.

Cultures that espouse white supremacy are easy targets. But, what are we to do about cultures that uphold the virtues of patriarchy or capitalism? There is a coercive edge about any strategy that purports to affirm the rightness of its own moral position at the cost of others. Intuitively, we know that the kinds of subjugation and tyranny opposed in McLaren's critical multiculturalism are wrong. Yet, we still need to recognize that the reasons we 'know' they are wrong are because we are products of a particular kind of radicalized discourse which promotes its own values over those of others. McLaren wants a politically resistant, oppositional approach not only to racism, but to all forms of oppression that he finds intolerable.

This seems a laudable stance and one which will find favor with all those committed to opposing racism; but it is simply not multicultural in any meaningful sense. True, it offers an unwavering hostility toward racism and several other kinds of -isms. Yet, in terms of values, it surrenders nothing to cultures that differ from that of the critic.

One of the tendencies that is evident in recent years is found in many of the extracts selected from the mid-1960s. The term 'institutional racism' was, as we have seen, introduced by Hamilton and Carmichael. It was an effulgent concept, lighting up a completely new way of understanding and analyzing the manifold effects of racism. The term has been refined in several ways, many of them by authors appearing in this volume. There is no doubting that, in the late 1990s, its purpose was in turning our attentions away from racism as an individual phenomenon – as a property of individuals or as having consequences for individuals – and toward a more abstract formulation; in other words, as a characteristic of entire organizations or even cultures. The problem with conceiving of racism in this way has now become evident: it lessens the responsibility of individuals by offloading the blame onto entire discourses.

Institutional racism's service has been in its stimulation of debate. How can we discover it? How can we establish culpability? How can we convert it into a research instrument? How can we change social policies designed for individuals into ones that can affect entire institutions? There is no doubting that the term has reoriented thinking and had a bracing effect on all those concerned with racism, whether at a practical or a scholarly level (though, of course, those two levels are not mutually exclusive). But, by the mid-1990s, talk was no longer of institutional racism and how we might search and destroy it. Neoconservative writers, such as Thomas Sowell and Shelby Steele, and former and contemporary liberals came to constitute a chorus. All, in their own way, raised doubts, not so much about the existence of race, but about its impact. In Steele's colorful terms, racism, while once a monstrous threat to black people, had diminished to the stature of a irritating insect – which needed to be swatted. As long as ethnic minorities in general and African Americans in particular continued to labor in the role of perennial victims and squander their energies on fighting the insect-like irritant, they would not 'progress' as individuals.

The developing consensus on the insignificance of racism complemented the postmodern turn that was influencing the academies of North America and Europe. New, personalized visions of personal liberation tended to supplant older solidarity-based coalitions, themselves geared toward the condemnation of grand racial narratives. 'Big' concepts like racism lost some of their purchase, so that, by the late 1990s, efforts were redirected from emphasizing the unity, sharedness and coherence of ethnic minorities toward a celebration of uniqueness, fragmentation and diffusion of the black experience. By default or design, one of the effects of this was to undermine the potency of racism as an explanatory tool, not to mention as a rallying cry.

In his *The Recovery of Race in America*, Aaron Gresson suggests that racism is nearly defunct: by this he does not mean that forms of thought and behavior once described as racist have disappeared, but that the meaning of such thought and behavior has become negotiable. The import of Gresson's argument is that thoughts and deeds that were, until the recent past, thought to be unambiguous instances of racism (indeed, we should add, *were* instances of racism) are now not so clear-cut. "Traditionalists" will want to retain the moral force of racism and continue to use the language and imagery to effect. These include ethnic minorities and whites. Yet, there are others, again from all ethnic origins, who will confront traditionalists as 'violators of the individuality of the person'. This heterogeneous group 'disavow the traditional in favor of a private vision rooted in the experience of problematic but personally satisfying choices' (1995: 21).

On this account, there is a new, seductively plausible 'white racial story'. Many whites have reconstructed the aged racist theory that African Americans and other ethnic minorities are inferior. In the new version, they are privileged. Images of black success abound, not only from sports and entertainment, but, increasingly, from politics and high-profile professions. Compared to the likes of multimillionare superstars, many whites may be impoverished and, according to Gresson, 'they believe white men have had to pay for Black success'. In this scenario, the white male is the victim. This in itself is intimidating enough, but its iniquity expands when it begins to be examined, debated and even heeded by a variegated black population which grows in complexity, plurality and heterogeneity by the day. Hence we have what Gresson takes to be 'one of the most powerful threats to belief in the traditional racial narrative'.

If even part of this vision is to be accepted, we need to recognize not only that a new status may be being (or possibly has been) conferred on the concept of racism, but that many divergent statuses may be under discussion. But, while racism in the popular imagi-nation is under scrutiny, the basic inequalities remain and each new piece of empirical evidence supports the view that efforts to remove them have not had the impact many liberals had hoped for.

There is a line in Bryan Singer's 1995 movie *The Usual Suspects* in which one of the characters compares the mysteriously elusive arch-criminal Kaiser Soze to the devil: 'The devil's biggest trick is in persuading the world that he doesn't really exist.' We may yet look back at the final decade of the twentieth century and realize that racism's most malfeasant perpetration was not unlike the devil's.

REFERENCES

Feagin, Joe and Vera, Hernán (1995) *White Racism: The Basics*. New York: Routledge.
Gresson, Aaron D. (1995) *The Recovery of Race in America*. Minneapolis, MN: University of Minnesota Press.
Hannaford, Ivan (1996) *Race: The History of an Idea in the West*. Baltimore, MD: Johns Hopkins University Press.
McLaren, Peter (1994) 'White terror and oppositional agency', in David T. Goldberg (ed.), *Multiculturalism: A Critical Reader*. Oxford: Blackwell.
McLaren, Peter (1997) *Revolutionary Multiculturalism: Pedagogies of Dissent for the New Millennium*. Boulder, CO: Westview Press.

Index